NEW GREAT AMERICAN
BRAND NAME RECIPES COOKBOOK

PUBLICATIONS INTERNATIONAL, LTD.

ISBN: 0-7853-1006-1

Library of Congress Catalog Card Number: 92-61133

Pictured on the front cover: *Top row, left:* Country Herbed Chicken *(page 173), Center:* Chocolate Strawberry Shortcake *(page 332), Right:* Butter Crusted Pan Pizza *(page 231). Bottom row, left:* Rio Grande Quesadillas *(page 134), Center:* Pastry Chef Tarts *(page 302), Right:* Sweet & Sour Meatballs *(page 104).*

Pictured on the back cover: *Top row, left:* Antipasto with Cold Marinated Mushrooms *(page 16), Center:* Heavenly Delight Cheesecake *(page 345), Right:* Cajun Shrimp *(page 163). Bottom row, left:* Choco-Caramel Delights *(page 272), Center:* Pasta & Vegetable Toss *(page 192), Right:* Sock-It-To-Me Cake *(page 263).*

8 7 6 5 4 3 2 1

Manufactured in U.S.A.

Microwave ovens vary in wattage and power output; cooking times given with microwave directions in this book may need to be adjusted. Consult manufacturer's instructions for suitable microwave-safe cooking dishes.

CONTENTS

Your Guide to Great Cooking

The kitchen, once again, is becoming the heart of the home—a place to gather with family and friends for fabulous meals. With this trend comes the desire for the wholesome goodness of home-cooked meals. But with busy life-styles, cooks today want easy-to-follow recipes suitable for everyday or for entertaining. The NEW GREAT AMERICAN BRAND NAME RECIPES COOKBOOK will bring fresh ideas into your kitchen with little effort.

With the busy cook in mind, we've selected recipes that you can count on. Every recipe has been tested by expert home economists to assure delicious, successful results with an added bonus—the convenience of your favorite brand-name products. As you page through the book you'll see a wide variety of recipes for every occasion. We've included appetizers, beverages, soups, salads, entrées and breads. We've also devoted five chapters to exquisite desserts.

For starters, you'll find tantalizing appetizers and thirst-quenching beverages including flavorful finger foods, creamy dips and spreads, sensational snacks and fruit-filled punches. We've selected exceptional soups— from elegant bisques to hearty stews—and refreshing salads—from crispy vegetable to magnificent pasta—for first courses or substantial suppers.

Not only are your favorite recipes for meat, poultry and seafood entrées included, but you'll find special chapters on quick and easy one-dish meals and popular pasta with rich sauces. To begin your day on the right foot, look to our Eggs, Cheese and Brunch Dishes or Breads, Muffins and Coffeecakes sections for inventive morning meals. Or turn to the Pizza and Sandwiches chapter for simple lunches and midnight snacks.

And for grand finales, you won't be able to resist the incredible assortment of decadent desserts. Whole chapters are devoted to scrumptious cookies and candies, unbeatable homemade pies and pastries, and delectable cakes and cheesecakes. You'll find ways to satisfy even the sweetest sweet tooth.

Just by looking at the hundreds of full-color photographs throughout the book, meal planning will be a snap. And with a collection of recipes this comprehensive, you'll always have creative ideas for all your culinary needs. So grab your apron and start cooking—and savoring—the extraordinary results!

APPETIZERS

Start every celebration off right with a wide array of tempting appetizers. You'll find creamy dips and spreads to welcome impromptu guests, fantastic finger foods for a dazzling buffet, fast-fixin' snacks for a carefree bash and impressive first-course starters for an elegant gathering. Discover dozens of ways to make any occasion a smashing success.

Layered Taco Dip

1 pound lean ground beef
1 (4-ounce) can chopped green chilies, undrained
2 teaspoons WYLER'S® or STEERO® Beef-Flavor Instant Bouillon
1 (15- or 16-ounce) can refried beans
1 (16-ounce) container BORDEN® or MEADOW GOLD® Sour Cream
1 (1.7-ounce) package taco seasoning mix
Guacamole
Garnishes: Shredded Cheddar or Monterey Jack cheese, chopped tomatoes, sliced green onions and sliced ripe olives
LAFAMOUS® Tortilla Chips

In large skillet, brown beef; pour off fat. Add chilies and bouillon; cook and stir until bouillon dissolves. Cool. Stir in refried beans. In small bowl, combine sour cream and taco seasoning; set aside. In 7- or 8-inch springform pan or on large plate, spread beef mixture. Top with sour cream mixture and guacamole. Cover; chill several hours. Just before serving, remove side of springform pan. Garnish with cheese, tomatoes, green onions and olives. Serve with tortilla chips. Refrigerate leftovers.
Makes 12 to 15 servings

GUACAMOLE: In small bowl, mash 3 ripe avocados, pitted and peeled. Add ¾ cup chopped fresh tomato, 2 tablespoons REALIME® Lime Juice from Concentrate or REALEMON® Lemon Juice from Concentrate, ½ teaspoon seasoned salt and ⅛ teaspoon garlic salt; mix well.

Spicy Dijon Dip

1 (8-ounce) package cream cheese, softened
¼ cup GREY POUPON® Dijon or Country Dijon Mustard
¼ cup dairy sour cream
1 tablespoon finely chopped scallions
1 (4¼-ounce) can tiny shrimp, drained, or ½ cup cooked shrimp, chopped
Sliced scallions, for garnish
Assorted cut-up vegetables

In small bowl, with electric mixer at medium speed, blend cream cheese, mustard, sour cream and chopped scallions; stir in shrimp. Cover; chill at least 2 hours. Garnish with sliced scallions; serve as a dip with vegetables. *Makes 1½ cups*

Guacamole Dip

½ cup MIRACLE WHIP® Salad Dressing
1 large ripe avocado, peeled, mashed
1 tomato, seeded, chopped
2 tablespoons each: chopped onion, chopped green chilies
1 teaspoon lemon or lime juice

• Mix ingredients until well blended; refrigerate. Serve with tortilla chips. *Makes 2 cups*

Prep time: 15 minutes plus refrigerating

Spicy Dijon Dip

Left to right: Spinach Dip, Cucumber Dill Dip and French Onion Dip

French Onion Dip

2 cups sour cream
½ cup HELLMANN'S® or
   BEST FOODS® Real,
   Light or Cholesterol Free
   Reduced Calorie
   Mayonnaise
1 package (1.9 ounces)
   KNORR® French Onion
   Soup and Recipe Mix

In medium bowl combine sour cream, mayonnaise and soup mix. Cover; chill. Serve with fresh vegetables or potato chips. Garnish as desired.
Makes about 2½ cups

Spinach Dip in Bread Bowl

1 cup MIRACLE WHIP® Salad
   Dressing
1 cup sour cream
1 package (1.4 ounces)
   GOOD SEASONS® Ranch
   Salad Dressing Mix
1 package (10 ounces)
   BIRDS EYE® Chopped
   Spinach, thawed, well
   drained
1 can (8 ounces) water
   chestnuts, drained,
   chopped
½ cup chopped red bell
   pepper
1 loaf (1½ pounds) round
   sourdough bread

• Mix salad dressing, sour cream and salad dressing mix until well blended. Add spinach, water chestnuts and pepper; mix well. Refrigerate.

• Cut slice from top of bread loaf; remove center leaving 1-inch-thick shell. Cut removed bread into bite-size pieces.

• Spoon spinach dip into bread loaf just before serving. Serve with bread pieces.
Makes 3¼ cups

Prep time: 15 minutes plus refrigerating

Spinach Dip

1 package (10 ounces) frozen
   chopped spinach, thawed
   and drained
1½ cups sour cream
1 cup HELLMANN'S® or
   BEST FOODS® Real,
   Light or Cholesterol Free
   Reduced Calorie
   Mayonnaise
1 package (1.4 ounces)
   KNORR® Vegetable Soup
   and Recipe Mix
1 can (8 ounces) water
   chestnuts, drained and
   chopped (optional)
3 green onions, chopped

In medium bowl combine spinach, sour cream, mayonnaise, soup mix, water chestnuts and green onions. Cover; chill. Serve with fresh vegetables, crackers or chips. Garnish as desired.
Makes about 3 cups

Cucumber Dill Dip

1 package (8 ounces) light
   cream cheese, softened
1 cup HELLMANN'S® or
   BEST FOODS® Real,
   Light or Cholesterol Free
   Reduced Calorie
   Mayonnaise
2 medium cucumbers,
   peeled, seeded and
   chopped
2 tablespoons sliced green
   onions
1 tablespoon lemon juice
2 teaspoons snipped fresh
   dill *or* ½ teaspoon
   dried dill weed
½ teaspoon hot pepper sauce

In medium bowl beat cream cheese until smooth. Stir in mayonnaise, cucumbers, green onions, lemon juice, dill and hot pepper sauce. Cover; chill. Serve with fresh vegetables, crackers or chips. Garnish as desired.
Makes about 2½ cups

Moroccan Tomato Dip

- 1 cup (8-ounce can) CONTADINA® Tomato Sauce
- ¾ cup low-sodium garbanzo beans, rinsed and drained
- ½ cup (4 ounces) nonfat plain yogurt
- 2 tablespoons minced green onion
- 1 tablespoon finely chopped parsley
- 1½ teaspoons garlic powder
- 1 teaspoon prepared horseradish
- 1 teaspoon ground cumin
- 1 teaspoon curry powder
- ½ teaspoon paprika
  Pita Chips (recipe follows)

In blender container, process tomato sauce, garbanzo beans, and yogurt until smooth and creamy. Pour into small bowl. Stir in onion, parsley, garlic powder, horseradish, cumin, curry powder, and paprika. Cover and refrigerate 8 to 24 hours to allow flavors to blend. Serve with Pita Chips or crisp vegetable dippers.

Makes 2 cups

PITA CHIPS: Cut pita bread into wedges; separate each wedge into 2 pieces. Place on cookie sheet and brush with fresh lemon juice. Sprinkle with salt-free herb mixture of your choice. Bake in preheated 375°F oven for 7 to 9 minutes or until crisp.

Creamy Slaw Dip

- 1½ cups BORDEN® or MEADOW GOLD® Sour Cream
- 1 cup finely shredded cabbage
- 1 (8-ounce) can water chestnuts, drained and finely chopped
- ⅓ cup prepared slaw dressing
- ¼ cup sliced green onions
- 2 teaspoons WYLER'S® or STEERO® Beef-Flavor Instant Bouillon
- ¼ teaspoon garlic powder

In medium bowl, combine ingredients; mix well. Cover; chill to blend flavors. Garnish as desired. Serve with Krunchers!® Potato Chips or assorted fresh vegetables if desired. Refrigerate leftovers.

Makes about 1½ cups

Taco Dip

Taco Dip

- 12 ounces cream cheese, softened
- ½ cup dairy sour cream
- 2 teaspoons chili powder
- 1½ teaspoons ground cumin
- ⅛ teaspoon ground red pepper
- ½ cup salsa
- 2 cups shredded lettuce or lettuce leaves
- 1 cup (4 ounces) shredded Wisconsin Cheddar cheese
- 1 cup (4 ounces) shredded Wisconsin Monterey Jack cheese
- ½ cup diced plum tomatoes
- ⅓ cup sliced green onions
- ¼ cup sliced ripe olives
- ¼ cup pimiento-stuffed green olives
  Tortilla and blue corn chips

Combine cream cheese, sour cream, chili powder, cumin and red pepper in large bowl; mix until well blended. Stir in salsa. Spread onto 10-inch serving platter lined with lettuce. Top with cheeses, tomatoes, green onions and olives. Serve with chips.

Makes 10 appetizer servings

*Favorite recipe from **Wisconsin Milk Marketing Board** © 1992*

Moroccan Tomato Dip

Velveeta® Salsa Dip

**1 pound VELVEETA®
  Pasteurized Process
  Cheese Spread, cubed**
1 jar (8 ounces) salsa
**2 tablespoons chopped
  cilantro**

• In saucepan, stir VELVEETA®
Pasteurized Process Cheese
Spread and salsa over low heat
until VELVEETA® Pasteurized
Process Cheese Spread is melted.
Stir in cilantro.

• Serve hot with tortilla chips or
broiled green, red or yellow bell
pepper wedges, if desired.
Makes 3 cups

Prep time: 10 minutes
Cooking time: 10 minutes
Microwave cooking time:
  5 minutes

Microwave: • Microwave
process cheese spread and salsa
in 1½-quart microwave-safe
bowl on HIGH 5 minutes or until
VELVEETA® Pasteurized
Process Cheese Spread is melted,
stirring after 3 minutes. Stir in
cilantro. • Serve as directed.

Variations: Substitute 1 can
(14½ ounces) tomatoes, chopped,
drained, for salsa.

Substitute 1 can (10 ounces)
tomatoes and green chilies,
chopped, drained, for salsa.

Substitute VELVEETA®
Mexican Pasteurized Process
Cheese Spread with Jalapeño
Pepper, cubed, for VELVEETA®
Pasteurized Process Cheese
Spread.

Lawry's® Fiesta Dip

**1 package (1.25 ounces)
  LAWRY'S® Taco Spices &
  Seasonings**
**1 pint (16 ounces) dairy sour
  cream**

In medium bowl, combine
ingredients. Blend well.
Refrigerate until ready to serve.
Serve in medium-size bowls with
tortilla chips and fresh cut
vegetables such as carrots,
broccoli, cauliflower or zucchini
sticks.   *Makes 2 cups*

Salsa Pronto

**1 can (14½ ounces)
  DEL MONTE® Mexican
  Style Stewed Tomatoes**
¼ cup finely chopped onion
**2 tablespoons chopped fresh
  cilantro**
2 teaspoons lemon juice
1 small clove garlic, minced
**⅛ teaspoon hot pepper
  sauce***
Tortilla chips

Place tomatoes in blender
container. Cover and process on
low 2 seconds to chop tomatoes.
Combine with onion, cilantro,
lemon juice, garlic and pepper
sauce. Add additional pepper
sauce, if desired. Serve with
tortilla chips.   *Makes 2 cups*

*Substitute minced jalapeño to
taste for hot pepper sauce.

Zesty Shrimp Dip

**¼ cup mayonnaise or salad
  dressing**
**1 (8-ounce) container
  BORDEN® or MEADOW
  GOLD® Sour Cream**
**¼ cup BENNETT'S® Cocktail
  Sauce**
**1 (4¼-ounce) can ORLEANS®
  Shrimp, drained and
  soaked as label directs**
**2 tablespoons sliced green
  onion**
**1 teaspoon REALEMON®
  Lemon Juice from
  Concentrate**

In small bowl, combine
ingredients; mix well. Chill.
Serve with assorted fresh
vegetables or potato chips.
Refrigerate leftovers.
Makes about 2 cups dip

Velveeta® Salsa Dip

Clockwise from top left: Zesty Shrimp Dip, Layered Crab Spread (page 14) and Deviled Clam Mushrooms (page 26)

Black Bean Dip

1 can (15 ounces) black beans, rinsed, drained
½ cup MIRACLE WHIP® FREE® Dressing
½ cup reduced calorie sour cream
1 can (4 ounces) chopped green chilies, drained
2 tablespoons chopped cilantro
1 teaspoon chili powder
½ teaspoon garlic powder
Few drops of hot pepper sauce

• Mash beans with fork. Stir in remaining ingredients until well blended; refrigerate. Serve with tortilla chips.

Makes 2¼ cups

Prep time: 10 minutes plus refrigerating

Dijon Pesto & Cheese

½ cup chopped parsley
⅓ cup GREY POUPON® Dijon or Country Dijon Mustard
¼ cup walnuts, chopped
¼ cup grated Parmesan cheese
2 teaspoons dried basil leaves
2 cloves garlic, crushed
3 (3-ounce) packages cream cheese, well chilled
Assorted NABISCO® Crackers
Roasted red peppers and basil leaves, for garnish

In electric blender container, blend parsley, mustard, walnuts, Parmesan cheese, basil and garlic; set aside.

Roll each square of cream cheese between 2 sheets of waxed paper to an 8×4-inch rectangle. Place 1 cheese rectangle in plastic wrap-lined 8½×4½×2½-inch loaf pan; top with half the parsley mixture. Repeat layers, ending with remaining cheese rectangle. Chill at least 2 hours. Remove from pan; slice and serve on crackers garnished with peppers and basil if desired.

Makes 32 servings

Cheddar Swiss Fondue

1 tablespoon margarine or butter
½ cup chopped onion
1 clove garlic, minced
1 can (11 ounces) CAMPBELL'S® condensed Cheddar Cheese Soup
¼ cup Chablis or other dry white wine
1 teaspoon caraway seed
2 cups shredded Swiss cheese (8 ounces)

1. In 2-quart saucepan over medium heat, in hot margarine, cook onion and garlic 10 minutes, stirring often.

2. Stir in soup, wine and caraway seed. Gradually add cheese, stirring until smooth after each addition.

3. Pour cheese mixture into heated serving dish or fondue pot. Serve with *pumpernickel* or *French bread cubes* for dipping.

Makes about 2⅓ cups

Horseradish Sauce

½ cup MIRACLE WHIP® Salad Dressing
2 tablespoons chili sauce
1 tablespoon KRAFT® Prepared Horseradish

• Mix ingredients until well blended; refrigerate. Serve with chilled cooked shrimp.

Makes ¾ cup

Prep time: 5 minutes plus refrigerating

Horseradish Sauce

Bacon and Two Onion Cheesecake (left) and Savory Pepper-Herb Cheesecake (right)

Bacon and Two Onion Cheesecake

6 slices bacon, diced
1 large sweet onion, chopped
1 clove garlic, minced
1 container (15 oz.) SARGENTO® Light Ricotta Cheese
½ cup half-and-half
2 tablespoons flour
½ teaspoon salt
¼ teaspoon cayenne pepper
2 eggs
½ cup thinly sliced green onions

In 10-inch skillet, cook bacon until crisp; remove to paper towels with slotted spoon. Cook chopped onion and garlic in drippings until tender, about 6 minutes. Drain in strainer; discard bacon drippings. In bowl of electric mixer, combine ricotta cheese, half-and-half, flour, salt and pepper; blend until smooth. Add eggs, one at a time; blend until smooth. Reserve 3 tablespoons of the bacon for garnish. Stir remaining bacon, cooked onion mixture and green onions into ricotta mixture. Lightly grease side of 8- or 9-inch springform pan; pour batter into pan. Bake at 350°F 40 minutes or until center is just set. Remove to wire cooling rack; cool to room temperature. Garnish with reserved bacon; serve with assorted crackers.

Makes 10 appetizer servings

Savory Pepper-Herb Cheesecake

Crust:
1¼ cups fresh dark rye or pumpernickel breadcrumbs (about 2 slices, processed in blender or food processor)
3 tablespoons melted margarine

Filling:
1 container (15 oz.) SARGENTO® Light Ricotta Cheese
½ cup half-and-half
2 tablespoons flour
2 eggs
⅓ cup chopped mixed fresh herbs (such as parsley, basil, mint, tarragon, rosemary, thyme and oregano)
¼ cup chopped fresh chives or green onion tops
1½ teaspoons finely grated lemon peel
½ teaspoon cracked black pepper
¾ teaspoon salt

Lightly grease side of 8- or 9-inch springform pan. Combine crust ingredients; press evenly onto bottom of pan. Chill while preparing filling. In bowl of electric mixer, combine ricotta cheese, half-and-half and flour; blend until smooth. Add eggs, one at a time; blend until smooth. Blend in fresh herbs, chives, lemon peel, pepper and salt. Pour into crust; bake at 350°F 30 to 35 minutes or until center is just set. Remove to wire cooling rack; cool to room temperature.

Makes 10 appetizer servings

Salmon Cucumber Mousse

2 envelopes unflavored gelatin
1 cup cold water
2 tablespoons lemon juice
2 containers (8 ounces each) PHILADELPHIA BRAND® Soft Cream Cheese with Smoked Salmon
1 small cucumber, peeled, finely chopped

• Soften gelatin in water; stir over low heat until dissolved. Stir in lemon juice.

• Stir cream cheese, gelatin mixture and cucumber in small bowl until well blended. Pour into 1-quart mold.

• Refrigerate until firm. Unmold onto serving platter. Serve with melba toast rounds.

Makes 3 cups

Prep time: 15 minutes plus refrigerating

Salmon Cucumber Mousse

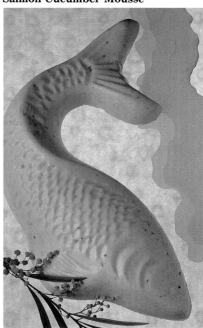

Baked Brie Wrapped in Pastry

- **¾ cup all-purpose flour**
- **¼ cup LAND O LAKES® Butter, softened**
- **1 package (3 ounces) cream cheese, softened**
- **1 round (8 ounces) Brie cheese (4¼-inch diameter)**
- **1 egg**
- **1 teaspoon water**
- **Apple slices**
- **Crackers**

In large mixer bowl combine flour, butter and cream cheese. Beat at low speed, scraping bowl often, until mixture forms a dough, 2 to 3 minutes; shape into ball. Wrap tightly in plastic wrap; refrigerate, 30 to 60 minutes.

Heat oven to 400°. Divide pastry in half. On lightly floured surface, roll out *each* half of dough to ⅛-inch thickness. Cut a 7-inch circle from *each* half. Place one circle on cookie sheet. Place Brie cheese on center of pastry circle and top with other pastry circle. Pinch edges of pastry to seal. Flute edges as desired. Decorate top with small pastry cut-outs. In small bowl beat egg with water; brush over top and sides of pastry. Bake for 15 to 20 minutes or until golden brown. Remove from cookie sheet immediately. Let stand 30 minutes to allow cheese to set. Cut into small wedges and serve with apple slices and crackers.

Makes 8 servings

Baked Brie Wrapped in Pastry

Herbed Cheese Spread

- 1 container (8 ounces) PHILADELPHIA BRAND® Light Pasteurized Process Cream Cheese Product
- ½ cup MIRACLE WHIP® FREE® Dressing
- 2 tablespoons each: chopped fresh parsley, finely chopped green onion
- 1 tablespoon each: chopped fresh oregano, chopped fresh basil and chopped fresh chives
- 1 garlic clove, minced
- 1 teaspoon anchovy paste (optional)
- ¼ teaspoon pepper

• Mix ingredients until well blended. Pipe mixture with pastry tube fitted with star tip into Belgian endive leaves, hollowed out cherry tomatoes and hollowed out summer squash slices. *Makes 1¼ cups*

Variation: Substitute 1 teaspoon dried oregano leaves, crushed, and 1 teaspoon dried basil leaves, crushed, for 2 tablespoons fresh oregano and basil.

Prep time: 20 minutes

Swiss Cheese Spread

- 2 cups (8 ounces) SARGENTO® Fancy Supreme™ Shredded Swiss Cheese
- 3 tablespoons sour cream
- 2 tablespoons minced onion
- 4 slices crisply cooked bacon, crumbled
- ½ teaspoon salt
- ½ teaspoon garlic powder

Combine all ingredients; beat until smooth and of a spreading consistency. Chill.

Makes about 2 cups

Hot Artichoke Spread

- 1 cup MIRACLE WHIP® Salad Dressing
- 1 cup (4 ounces) KRAFT® 100% Grated Parmesan Cheese
- 1 can (14 ounces) artichoke hearts, drained, chopped
- 1 can (4 ounces) chopped green chilies, drained
- 1 garlic clove, minced
- 2 tablespoons sliced green onions
- 2 tablespoons seeded, chopped tomato

• Heat oven to 350°F.
• Mix all ingredients except onions and tomatoes until well blended.
• Spoon into shallow ovenproof dish or 9-inch pie plate.
• Bake 20 to 25 minutes or until lightly browned. Sprinkle with onions and tomatoes. Serve with toasted bread cutouts.

Makes 2 cups

Prep time: 10 minutes
Cooking time: 25 minutes

Microwave: • Mix all ingredients except onions and tomatoes until well blended.
• Spoon into 9-inch pie plate. • Microwave at MEDIUM (50%) 7 to 9 minutes or until mixture is warm, stirring every 4 minutes. Stir before serving. Sprinkle with onions and tomatoes. Serve with toasted bread cutouts.

Layered Crab Spread

- 2 (8-ounce) packages cream cheese, softened
- 2 tablespoons REALEMON® Lemon Juice from Concentrate
- 1 teaspoon Worcestershire sauce
- ¼ teaspoon garlic powder
- 2 tablespoons finely chopped green onion
- ¾ cup BENNETT'S® Chili Sauce
- 1 (16-ounce) can HARRIS® or ORLEANS® Crab Meat, drained

In large mixer bowl, beat cheese, ReaLemon® brand, Worcestershire and garlic powder until fluffy; stir in onion. On serving plate, spread cheese mixture into 6-inch circle. Top with chili sauce then crabmeat. Cover; chill. Serve with crackers. Refrigerate leftovers.

Makes 12 appetizer servings

Hot Artichoke Spread

Seafood Ravioli with Fresh Tomato Sauce

**1 container (8 ounces)
PHILADELPHIA BRAND®
Soft Cream Cheese with
Herb & Garlic
¾ cup chopped LOUIS KEMP®
CRAB DELIGHTS
Chunks, rinsed
36 wonton wrappers
Cold water
Fresh Tomato Sauce**

• Stir cream cheese and crab flavored surimi seafood in medium bowl until well blended.

• For each ravioli, place 1 tablespoonful cream cheese mixture in center of one wonton wrapper. Brush edges with water. Place second wonton wrapper on top. Press edges together to seal, taking care to press out air. Repeat with remaining cream cheese mixture and wonton wrappers.

• For square-shaped ravioli, cut edges of wonton wrappers with pastry trimmer to form square. For round-shaped ravioli, place 3-inch round biscuit cutter on ravioli, making sure center of each cutter contains filling. Press down firmly, cutting through both wrappers, to trim edges. Repeat with remaining ravioli.

• Bring 1½ quarts water to boil in large saucepan. Cook ravioli, a few at a time, 2 to 3 minutes or until they rise to surface. Remove with slotted spoon. Serve hot with Fresh Tomato Sauce. *Makes 18*

Prep time: 25 minutes
Cooking time: 3 minutes per batch

Seafood Ravioli with Fresh Tomato Sauce

Fresh Tomato Sauce

**2 garlic cloves, minced
2 tablespoons olive oil
6 plum tomatoes, diced
1 tablespoon red wine
vinegar
1 tablespoon chopped
parsley**

• Cook and stir garlic in oil in medium saucepan 1 minute. Add remaining ingredients.

• Cook over low heat 2 to 3 minutes or until thoroughly heated, stirring occasionally. Cool to room temperature.

Variation: For triangle-shaped ravioli, place 2 teaspoonfuls cream cheese mixture in center of each wonton wrapper; brush edges with water. Fold in half to form triangle. Press edges together to seal, taking care to press out air. Trim edges of wonton wrapper with pastry trimmer, if desired.

Makes 36

Antipasto

- ½ **recipe Cold Marinated Mushrooms (recipe follows)**
- 4 **ounces provolone** or **mozzarella cheese, cubed**
- ¼ **cup olive** or **vegetable oil**
- 1 **teaspoon dried oregano leaves, crushed**
  Generous dash crushed red pepper
- 4 **ounces Italian sharp** or **fontinella cheese**
- 4 **ounces thinly sliced prosciutto** or **fully cooked ham**
  Lettuce leaves
- 1 **jar (10 ounces) pepperoncini, drained**
- 1 **jar (7 ounces) roasted sweet red peppers, drained**
- 1 **jar (6 ounces) marinated artichoke hearts, drained**
- 4 **ounces thinly sliced salami**

1. Prepare Cold Marinated Mushrooms. Cover and refrigerate.

2. In small bowl, combine provolone, oil, oregano and crushed red pepper. Cover and refrigerate at least 2 hours to blend flavors. Cut *half* of the Italian sharp cheese into 3-inch sticks; wrap with prosciutto slices. Cut remaining Italian sharp cheese in bite-size wedges.

3. Line a serving platter with lettuce. Drain provolone cubes, reserving marinade. Arrange provolone cubes, mushrooms, prosciutto-cheese sticks, cheese wedges and remaining ingredients on lettuce. Drizzle with reserved marinade. Cover; refrigerate.

Makes 8 to 10 appetizer servings

Prep Time: 30 minutes
Chill Time: 2 hours

Cold Marinated Mushrooms

- 1 **pound medium whole fresh mushrooms**
- ¾ **cup PREGO® Regular Spaghetti Sauce** or **PREGO® EXTRA CHUNKY Tomato, Onion and Garlic Spaghetti Sauce**
- 1 **tablespoon red wine vinegar**
  Chopped fresh parsley for garnish

Half-fill a 3-quart saucepan with water. Over high heat, heat water to boiling. Add mushrooms. Simmer 2 minutes. Drain. In bowl, combine mushrooms, spaghetti sauce and vinegar. Cover; refrigerate at least 2 hours. Stir before serving. Serve with decorative wooden toothpicks and garnish with parsley, if desired.

Makes about 3 cups or 12 appetizer servings

Prep Time: 15 minutes
Chill Time: 2 hours

Salmon Asiago Canapés

- **Margarine** or **butter**
- 1 **loaf (16 ounces)** *very thinly sliced* **white bread**
- 1 **egg**
- ¼ **pound (4 ounces) smoked salmon, skinned, boned and flaked**
- 2 **cups shredded STELLA® Asiago Cheese (8 ounces)**
- ½ **cup chopped green onions**
- 2 **tablespoons lemon juice**
- 1 **teaspoon grated fresh gingerroot**
  Pear wedges and fresh dill for garnish

1. Preheat oven to 375°F. Generously grease 24 (2½-inch) muffin cups with margarine.

2. Using 3-inch round, star or fluted cookie cutter, cut bread into desired shapes. (Save crust and scraps to make bread crumbs, if desired.) Gently press bread shapes into prepared muffin cups. Bake 5 minutes or until lightly browned.

3. In medium bowl, beat egg slightly. Stir in salmon, cheese, green onions, lemon juice and gingerroot. Fill *each* bread cup with *1 heaping tablespoon* of salmon mixture. (Canapés may be frozen at this point.)

4. Bake canapés 10 minutes (frozen canapés 12 minutes) or until cheese melts and begins to bubble. Serve immediately. Garnish with pear wedges and dill, if desired.

Makes 24 canapés or 8 appetizer servings

Cucumber Canapés

- 1 **cup cooked rice, cooled to room temperature**
- 1 **large fresh tomato, peeled and diced**
- ½ **cup chopped fresh parsley**
- ⅓ **cup sliced green onions**
- ¼ **cup chopped fresh mint**
- 2 **cloves garlic, minced**
- 3 **tablespoons plain nonfat yogurt***
- 1 **tablespoon lemon juice**
- 1 **tablespoon olive oil**
- ¼ **teaspoon ground white pepper**
- 2 **to 3 large cucumbers, peeled**

Combine rice, tomato, parsley, onions, mint, garlic, yogurt, lemon juice, oil, and pepper in large bowl. Cover and chill. Cut each cucumber crosswise into ½-inch slices; hollow out center of each slice, leaving bottom intact. Fill each cucumber slice with scant tablespoon rice mixture.

Makes about 3 dozen canapés

*Substitute low-fat sour cream for yogurt, if desired.

Favorite recipe from **USA Rice Council**

Antipasto with Cold Marinated Mushrooms

Mussels Marinara

Mussels Marinara

3 pounds fresh mussels*
    (about 5 to 6 dozen)
2 tablespoons olive *or*
    vegetable oil
¼ cup chopped onion
1 clove garlic, minced
1½ cups PREGO® Regular
    Spaghetti Sauce *or*
    PREGO® EXTRA
    CHUNKY Tomato, Onion
    and Garlic Spaghetti
    Sauce
⅓ cup Chablis *or* other dry
    white wine
    Sliced Italian bread
    Lemon slices and fresh
    marjoram sprigs for
    garnish

1. Discard any mussels that
remain open when tapped with
fingers. Scrub mussels; trim
"beards" with kitchen shears, if
necessary, and discard.

2. In 4-quart saucepan over
medium heat, in hot oil, cook
onion and garlic until tender.
Stir in spaghetti sauce and wine;
heat to boiling.

3. Reduce heat to low; add
mussels. Cover; simmer 10
minutes or until mussel shells
open, stirring occasionally.
(Discard any mussels that
remain closed.) Serve with slices
of Italian bread to soak up the
flavorful juices. Garnish with
lemon slices and marjoram
sprigs, if desired.
Makes 8 appetizers servings

Prep Time: 20 minutes
Cook Time: 10 minutes

*To make sure fresh mussels are
safe to eat, tap on any open
shells. If the mussel closes its
shell, it will be safe to eat after
cooking. Discard those that
remain open. After cooking,
discard any mussel with a closed
shell, because it was not alive
before cooking and is not safe
to eat.

Sweet and Sour Meatballs

1½ pounds lean ground beef
1 cup fresh bread crumbs
    (2 slices)
1 egg, slightly beaten
4 teaspoons WYLER'S® or
    STEERO® Beef-Flavor
    Instant Bouillon
1⅓ cups BAMA® Apricot
    Preserves
2 tablespoons REALEMON®
    Lemon Juice from
    Concentrate

In large bowl, combine beef,
crumbs, egg and *2 teaspoons*
bouillon; mix well. Shape into
1¼-inch balls. In large skillet,
brown meatballs. Remove from
pan; pour off fat. In same skillet,
combine preserves, ReaLemon®
brand and remaining *2 teaspoons*
bouillon. Over low heat, cook and
stir 10 minutes. Add meatballs;
simmer uncovered 10 minutes.
Garnish with parsley if desired.
Refrigerate leftovers.
Makes about 4 dozen

South-of-the-Border Meatballs

1¼ pounds ground beef
1 package (1.25 ounces)
    LAWRY'S® Taco Spices &
    Seasonings
¼ cup unseasoned dry bread
    crumbs
¼ cup finely chopped onion
¼ cup finely chopped green
    bell pepper
1 egg, beaten
1½ cups chunky salsa

In large bowl, combine all
ingredients except salsa; blend
well. Form into 1-inch balls. In
large skillet, brown meatballs on
all sides; drain fat. Add salsa to
skillet. Bring to a boil; reduce
heat and simmer, uncovered, 10
minutes.   *Makes 6 servings*

Presentation: Serve with your
favorite Mexican beer or sangria.

New England Maple Ribs

**2 pounds spareribs,
    pre-cooked
¾ cup CARY'S®, MAPLE
    ORCHARDS® or
    MACDONALD'S™ Pure
    Maple Syrup
¼ cup BENNETT'S® Chili
    Sauce
¼ cup chopped onion
1 tablespoon *each* vinegar
    and Worcestershire
    sauce
1 teaspoon dry mustard
1 clove garlic, finely chopped**

Combine all ingredients except ribs; pour over ribs. Refrigerate at least 4 hours, turning occasionally. Grill or broil ribs as desired, basting frequently with sauce. Refrigerate leftovers.
Makes 4 servings

Mexican Sausage Pie

**½ pound chorizo sausage
1 loaf (1 pound) frozen
    whole-wheat bread
    dough, thawed
1 package (10 ounces)
    BIRDS EYE® Chopped
    Broccoli, thawed, well
    drained
1 cup BIRDS EYE® Sweet
    Corn, thawed, well
    drained
½ pound VELVEETA® Mexican
    Pasteurized Process
    Cheese Spread with
    Jalapeño Pepper, sliced
1 egg yolk
1 teaspoon cold water
1 tablespoon cornmeal**

• Heat oven to 375°F.

• Remove sausage from casing. Brown sausage; drain. Cool.

• Roll two thirds of dough to 11-inch circle on lightly floured surface. Press onto bottom and sides of greased 9-inch springform pan.

• Layer broccoli, corn, sausage and VELVEETA® Mexican Pasteurized Process Cheese Spread with Jalapeño Pepper over dough in pan.

• Roll remaining dough to 10-inch circle; cut into 8 wedges. Place over filling, overlapping edges and sealing ends to bottom crust. Brush with combined egg yolk and water. Sprinkle with cornmeal.

• Bake 35 to 40 minutes or until deep golden brown. Let stand 10 minutes.   *Makes 10 servings*

Prep time: 20 minutes
Cooking time: 40 minutes plus standing time

Beef with Walnuts and Kiwi

**4 ounces sliced rare roast
    beef, cut into 12 uniform
    pieces
¼ cup finely chopped
    walnuts, toasted
1 tablespoon *each* fresh
    lemon juice, olive oil,
    wine vinegar and
    snipped dill
1 small clove garlic, crushed
¼ teaspoon freshly ground
    black pepper
    Dash salt
12 slices French bread, ¼ inch
    thick
2 kiwi, peeled, cut into
    12 slices
    Pimiento**

Place roast beef slices in glass dish; sprinkle with walnuts. Combine lemon juice, oil, vinegar, dill, garlic, pepper and salt. Pour over beef and walnuts, lifting meat to coat. Cover and marinate 30 minutes. Drain marinade. To assemble, arrange one piece beef with walnuts onto each bread round. Top with kiwi slice; garnish with pimiento.
Makes 12 appetizer servings

Preparation/Marinating time:
    40 minutes
Assembling time: 10 minutes

*Favorite recipe from **National Live Stock & Meat Board***

Miniature Teriyaki Pork Kabobs

**1 pound boneless pork loin,
    cut into 4×1×½-inch
    strips
1 (11-ounce) can mandarin
    oranges, drained
1 small green pepper, cut
    into 1×¼×¼-inch strips
¼ cup teriyaki sauce
1 tablespoon honey
1 tablespoon vinegar
⅛ teaspoon garlic powder**

Soak 24 bamboo skewers in cold water 20 to 30 minutes. Thread pork strips, accordion-style, with mandarin oranges onto skewers. Add green pepper strip to ends of each skewer.

For sauce, in small bowl combine teriyaki sauce, honey, vinegar and garlic powder; mix well. Brush sauce over kabobs. Broil 6 inches from heat source 5 to 6 minutes, turning and brushing with sauce occasionally until pork is cooked through.
Makes 24 servings

Preparation Time: 10 minutes
Cooking Time: 5 minutes

*Favorite recipe from **National Pork Producers Council***

Beef with Walnuts and Kiwi

Skewered Pork

Skewered Pork

½ cup unsweetened
   pineapple juice
3 tablespoons HEINZ®
   Worcestershire Sauce
1 teaspoon ground coriander
1 teaspoon minced garlic
¼ teaspoon crushed red
   pepper
⅛ teaspoon black pepper
1 pound boneless pork loin,
   cut into ⅛-inch slices

For marinade, in small bowl, combine pineapple juice, Worcestershire sauce, coriander, garlic, red pepper and black pepper. Place pork in deep bowl; pour marinade over pork. Cover; marinate in refrigerator about 1 hour. Meanwhile, soak thin bamboo skewers in water. Weave skewers through pork strips so meat lies flat. Broil, 4 to 5 inches from heat source, 2 minutes; turn. Brush with marinade; broil an additional 2 minutes or until pork is just cooked.

Makes 20 to 22 appetizers

Antipasto-on-a-Stick

8 slices cooked lean beef
   (about 12 ounces), cut
   into 1-inch strips
16 pitted ripe olives
8 small cherry tomatoes
8 cubes provolone cheese
   (¾ inch)
8 marinated artichoke heart
   quarters, drained
½ cup Italian salad dressing
2 cups torn Bibb or Romaine
   lettuce (optional)

Roll up beef strips pinwheel fashion. Alternately arrange beef pinwheels, olives, cherry tomatoes, cheese cubes and artichoke hearts on eight 9-inch skewers. Place kabobs in shallow container; pour dressing over kabobs. Refrigerate several hours or overnight. To serve, arrange skewers on top of lettuce, if desired. Pour remaining dressing over all.

Makes 8 appetizers

Preparation Time: 10 minutes

*Favorite recipe from **National Live Stock & Meat Board***

Prosciutto Fruit Bundles in Endive

2 tablespoons rice or white
   wine vinegar
1 tablespoon vegetable oil
1 tablespoon light soy sauce
1 green onion, sliced
1 (4-inch) rib celery, sliced
½ teaspoon sugar
½ teaspoon grated lime rind
¼ teaspoon ground ginger
4 slices (3×½ inch) *each:*
   cantaloupe, pineapple,
   honeydew melon
8 julienne strips (2×¼ inch)
   each: celery, green and
   red bell pepper
3 ounces thinly sliced
   domestic prosciutto ham
24 Belgian endive leaves

For dressing, combine first 8 ingredients in blender or food processor; cover and blend until fairly smooth. Place fruits and vegetables in plastic bag. Add dressing; turn to coat. Close bag securely and marinate in refrigerator 30 minutes. Meanwhile, trim excess fat from ham and discard; cut ham lengthwise into ½-inch-wide strips. Remove fruits and vegetables from dressing. Wrap ham strips around following combinations: cantaloupe/2 strips celery; pineapple/2 strips green pepper; honeydew melon/2 strips red pepper. Place each bundle on endive leaf. Cover with plastic wrap and refrigerate until serving.

Makes 24 appetizers

*Favorite recipe from **National Live Stock & Meat Board***

Chili Go Rounds

1 cup finely chopped fully-
   cooked smoked sausage
2 tablespoons HEINZ® Chili
   Sauce
1 tablespoon grated
   Parmesan cheese
¼ teaspoon ground cinnamon
¼ teaspoon dried thyme
   leaves, crushed
1 package (8 ounces)
   refrigerated crescent
   dinner rolls

In small bowl, combine sausage, chili sauce, Parmesan cheese, cinnamon and thyme. Remove half of dough from container; unroll. Place dough between 2 pieces of waxed paper and roll into 13×5×⅛-inch rectangle. Spread ½ of sausage mixture over dough. Roll, jelly-roll fashion, starting at longest side. Cut into ½-inch slices with sharp knife; place cut-side down on baking sheet. Repeat with remaining dough and sausage mixture. Bake in preheated 375°F oven, 12 to 14 minutes or until golden brown.

Makes about 4 dozen appetizers

Country Style Paté in French Bread

- **1 loaf (12 inches) French bread**
- **1 package (8 ounces) OSCAR MAYER® Braunschweiger Liver Sausage**
- **½ cup MIRACLE WHIP® Salad Dressing**
- **⅓ cup finely chopped pistachio nuts or walnuts**
- **1 tablespoon <u>each</u>: chopped onion, chopped fresh parsley**
- **½ teaspoon dry mustard**

• Slice off both ends of bread loaf. Cut loaf into fourths. Remove bread from inside of each fourth leaving ½-inch shell. Tear removed bread into small pieces.

• Mix torn bread with remaining ingredients until well blended.

• Lightly pack about ⅓ cup sausage mixture into each bread piece.

• Wrap securely in plastic wrap; refrigerate several hours or overnight. To serve, cut into ½-inch slices.

Makes 4 to 6 servings

Prep time: 25 minutes plus refrigerating

Chorizo Cheese Tarts

- **2 packages KEEBLER® Graham Cracker Ready-Crust® Tarts (12 tarts)**
- **2 egg yolks, beaten**
- **1 (12-ounce) package Mexican chorizo sausage**
- **¼ cup minced onion**
- **1 (16-ounce) jar or can chunky salsa**
- **2 eggs, beaten**
- **¾ cup (6 ounces) Mexican chihuahua or Monterey Jack cheese, grated**
- **¼ teaspoon dried oregano**

Heat oven to 350°. Brush tarts with a small amount of beaten egg yolks and bake 3 minutes. Remove from oven and prepare the filling.

Remove sausage from casing. Brown in skillet. Add onion and saute until onion is soft and sausage is well done. Mix salsa with remaining egg yolks and eggs. Spoon sausage and onion mixture into tart shells. Pour salsa-egg mixture over sausage; top with grated cheese. Sprinkle with oregano. Bake at 350° for 20 to 25 minutes or until filling is set and cheese is melted.

Makes 12 servings

Reuben Rolls

Reuben Rolls

- **⅓ cup HELLMANN'S® or BEST FOODS® Real, Light or Cholesterol Free Reduced Calorie Mayonnaise**
- **1 tablespoon Dijon-style mustard**
- **½ teaspoon caraway seeds**
- **1 cup (4 ounces) cooked corned beef, finely chopped**
- **1 cup (4 ounces) shredded Swiss cheese**
- **1 cup sauerkraut, rinsed, drained and patted dry with paper towels**
- **1 package (10 ounces) refrigerated pizza crust dough**

In medium bowl combine mayonnaise, mustard and caraway seeds. Add corned beef, cheese and sauerkraut; toss to blend well. Unroll dough onto large ungreased cookie sheet. Gently stretch to 14×12-inch rectangle. Cut dough lengthwise in half. Spoon half of the filling onto each piece, spreading to within 1 inch of edges. From long side, roll each jelly-roll style; pinch to seal edges. Arrange rolls, seam-side down, 3 inches apart. Bake in 425°F oven 10 minutes or until golden brown. Let stand 5 minutes. Cut into 1-inch slices.

Makes about 30 appetizers

Country Style Paté in French Bread

Garlic Spinach Turnovers

Pastry
- 1½ cups all-purpose flour
- ¼ teaspoon salt
- ½ cup LAND O LAKES® Butter
- 1 egg, slightly beaten
- 3 tablespoons milk

Filling
- 1 tablespoon LAND O LAKES® Butter
- ½ teaspoon minced fresh garlic
- 2 cups torn fresh spinach leaves
- 1 cup fresh mushroom slices (¼ inch)
- ½ cup coarsely chopped red pepper (1 medium)
- ½ cup coarsely chopped onion (1 medium)
- 2 tablespoons freshly grated Parmesan cheese
- ¼ teaspoon coarsely ground pepper
- ⅛ teaspoon salt
  Dash ground red pepper
- 1 egg, slightly beaten
- 1 tablespoon milk

For pastry, in medium bowl combine flour and ¼ teaspoon salt; cut in ½ cup butter until crumbly. In small bowl stir together 1 egg and 3 tablespoons milk. Add egg mixture to flour mixture; stir until dough leaves side of bowl. Shape into ball. Wrap in plastic wrap; refrigerate while preparing filling.

For filling, in 10-inch skillet cook 1 tablespoon butter until sizzling; stir in garlic. Cook over medium heat, stirring occasionally, until garlic is tender, 1 to 2 minutes. Add spinach leaves, mushrooms, chopped red pepper and onion. Continue cooking, stirring occasionally, until vegetables are tender crisp, 3 to 4 minutes. Stir in Parmesan cheese, pepper, ⅛ teaspoon salt and ground red pepper. Set aside. Cut pastry dough in half.

Heat oven to 400°. On lightly floured surface, roll out half of dough to 12×9-inch rectangle. Cut *each* rectangle into 12 (3-inch) squares. Place *about 1 teaspoon* filling on one half of *each* square; fold other half over, forming triangle. Press edges with fork to seal. Place on ungreased cookie sheets; with knife cut 2 diagonal slits in *each* turnover. Repeat with remaining pastry dough and filling. In small bowl stir together 1 egg and 1 tablespoon milk; brush over turnovers. Bake for 8 to 12 minutes or until lightly browned.
Makes 2 dozen turnovers

Bacon Appetizer Crescents

- 1 package (8 ounces) PHILADELPHIA BRAND® Cream Cheese, softened
- 8 slices OSCAR MAYER® Bacon, crisply cooked, crumbled
- ⅓ cup (1½ ounces) KRAFT® 100% Grated Parmesan Cheese
- ¼ cup finely chopped onion
- 2 tablespoons chopped fresh parsley
- 1 tablespoon milk
- 2 cans (8 ounces each) refrigerated crescent dinner rolls
- 1 egg, beaten
- 1 teaspoon cold water

• Heat oven to 375°F.

• Beat cream cheese, bacon, Parmesan cheese, onion, parsley and milk in small mixing bowl at medium speed with electric mixer until well blended.

• Separate dough into eight rectangles; firmly press perforations together to seal. Spread each rectangle with 2 rounded measuring tablespoonfuls cream cheese mixture.

• Cut each rectangle in half diagonally; repeat with opposite corners. Cut in half crosswise to form six triangles. Roll up triangles, starting at short ends.

• Place on greased cookie sheet; brush with combined egg and water. Sprinkle with poppy seed, if desired.

• Bake 12 to 15 minutes or until golden brown. Serve immediately.
Makes about 4 dozen

Prep time: 30 minutes
Cooking time: 15 minutes

Bacon Appetizer Crescents

Polenta Strips with Creamy Salsa Spread

Polenta Strips with Creamy Salsa Spread

1 package (8 ounces) cream cheese, softened
2 tablespoons chili sauce
2 tablespoons dairy sour cream
1 tablespoon diced green chiles
½ teaspoon LAWRY'S® Seasoned Pepper
3 cups water
1 teaspoon LAWRY'S® Seasoned Salt
¾ cup instant polenta, uncooked
¼ cup chopped fresh cilantro
¼ cup grated Parmesan cheese
½ cup vegetable oil

For Creamy Salsa Spread, in small bowl, blend together cream cheese, chili sauce, sour cream, green chiles and Seasoned Pepper; chill. In medium saucepan, bring water and Seasoned Salt to a boil. Add polenta in a slow stream, stirring constantly. Reduce heat; simmer, uncovered, 20 minutes or until mixture pulls away from side of pan. Stir in cilantro. Pour mixture into lightly greased 8×4×3-inch loaf pan. Let cool at least 30 minutes to set. Remove from pan. Cut loaf into very thin slices; sprinkle both sides with cheese. Broil 3 inches from heat 5 minutes or until slightly golden brown. In large skillet, heat oil and fry slices until brown and crisp. Place on paper towels to drain. Serve with Creamy Salsa Spread.

Makes 3 dozen strips

Presentation: Great with grilled beef, pork or chicken entrées.

Hint: To prepare in advance, prepare recipe up to loaf stage, then refrigerate (up to 2 weeks) until ready to fry.

Spinach-Cheese Boreks

1 container (8 ounces) PHILADELPHIA BRAND® Soft Cream Cheese with Chives & Onion
1 package (10 ounces) BIRDS EYE® Chopped Spinach, thawed, well drained
⅓ cup chopped roasted red bell peppers, drained
⅛ teaspoon pepper
9 frozen phyllo sheets, thawed
6 tablespoons PARKAY® Margarine, melted

• Heat oven to 375°F.

• Stir cream cheese, spinach, red bell peppers and pepper in medium bowl until well blended.

• Lay one sheet phyllo dough on flat surface. Brush with margarine; cut lengthwise into four 18×3⅓-inch strips.

• For each appetizer, spoon about 1 tablespoon filling about 1 inch from one end of each strip. Fold the end over filling at 45-degree angle. Continue folding as you would a flag to form a triangle that encloses filling.

• Repeat with remaining phyllo and filling.

• Place triangles on cookie sheet. Brush with margarine.

• Bake 12 to 15 minutes or until golden brown. *Makes 36*

Prep time: 30 minutes
Cooking time: 15 minutes

Notes: Thaw phyllo sheets in refrigerator 8 to 12 hours before using. Because phyllo sheets dry out very quickly, have filling prepared before removing sheets from refrigerator. For best results, work quickly and keep phyllo sheets covered with damp cloth to prevent sheets from drying out.

Before making final folds of triangle, place small herb sprig on phyllo. Fold dough over herb (herb will be on top of appetizer). Bake as directed.

Spinach-Cheese Boreks

Mini Quiches

- **1 package (15 ounces) refrigerated pie crusts (2 crusts)**
- **½ cup (2 ounces) KRAFT® Natural Gourmet Shredded Swiss Cheese**
- **⅓ cup MIRACLE WHIP® Salad Dressing**
- **2 tablespoons half and half**
- **2 eggs, beaten**
- **2 tablespoons chopped green onion**
- **½ teaspoon dry mustard**
- **¼ cup chopped OSCAR MAYER® Ham**

• Heat oven to 425°F.

• On lightly floured surface, roll each pie crust to 12-inch circle. Cut each pie crust into twelve circles using 2½-inch biscuit cutter; place in lightly greased cups of miniature muffin pans. Prick bottoms and sides with fork.

• Bake 10 minutes. Remove from oven. Reduce oven temperature to 350°F.

• Mix all remaining ingredients except ham until well blended. Spoon 1 tablespoon cheese mixture into each pastry-lined muffin cup; top evenly with ham.

• Bake 25 to 30 minutes or until golden brown. Immediately remove from pan.   *Makes 24*

Prep time: 20 minutes
Cooking time: 30 minutes

Cocktail Party Tray

- **1 pound large raw shrimp, peeled and deveined**
- **1 pound chicken wing drumettes**
- **1 pound skinned boneless chicken breasts, cut into strips**
- **1½ cups BENNETT'S® Chili or Hot Seafood Sauce**
- **1 (12-ounce) jar BENNETT'S® Cocktail Sauce**

In 3 separate plastic bags, combine shrimp, chicken wings and chicken strips each with *½ cup* chili or hot seafood sauce. Marinate in refrigerator a few hours or overnight. Remove from sauce. Broil or grill until done, turning frequently. Serve with cocktail sauce. Refrigerate leftovers.   *Makes 12 servings*

Tip: Shrimp can be arranged on skewers with water chestnuts or tomatillo wedges before broiling.

Southwestern Potato Skins

- **6 large russet potatoes**
- **¾ pound ground beef**
- **1 package (1.25 ounces) LAWRY'S® Taco Spices & Seasonings**
- **¾ cup water**
- **¾ cup sliced green onions**
- **1 medium tomato, chopped**
- **1 can (2¼ ounces) sliced ripe olives, drained**
- **1 cup (4 ounces) grated Cheddar cheese**
- **1 recipe Lawry's® Fiesta Dip (page 10)**

Pierce potatoes with fork. Microwave on HIGH 30 minutes; let cool. Cut in half and scoop out potatoes leaving ¼-inch shell. In medium skillet, brown ground beef until crumbly; drain fat. Stir in Taco Spices & Seasonings and water. Bring to a boil; reduce heat and simmer, uncovered, 15 minutes. Stir in green onions. Spoon meat mixture into potato shells. Top with tomato, olives and cheese. Place on baking sheet and heat under broiler to melt cheese. Spoon dollops of Lawry's® Fiesta Dip on each shell.

Makes 1 dozen appetizers

Presentation: Sprinkle with additional sliced green onions. Serve with salsa.

Deluxe Fajita Nachos

- **2½ cups shredded, cooked chicken**
- **1 package (1.27 ounces) LAWRY'S® Spices & Seasonings for Fajitas**
- **⅓ cup water**
- **8 ounces tortilla chips**
- **1¼ cups (5 ounces) grated Cheddar cheese**
- **1 cup (4 ounces) grated Monterey Jack cheese**
- **1 large tomato, chopped**
- **1 can (2¼ ounces) sliced ripe olives, drained**
- **¼ cup sliced green onions Salsa**

In medium skillet, combine chicken, Spices & Seasonings for Fajitas and water; blend well. Bring to a boil; reduce heat and simmer 3 minutes. In large shallow ovenproof platter, arrange chips. Top with chicken and cheeses. Place under broiler to melt cheese. Top with tomato, olives, green onions and desired amount of salsa.

Makes 4 appetizer or 2 main-dish servings

Presentation: Serve with guacamole and sour cream.

Substitution: 1¼ pounds cooked ground beef can be used in place of shredded chicken.

Hint: For a spicier version, add sliced jalapeños.

Deviled Deviled Eggs

- **6 hard-cooked eggs**
- **⅓ cup MIRACLE WHIP® Salad Dressing**
- **2 tablespoons finely chopped green onion**
- **1 teaspoon KRAFT® Pure Prepared Mustard**
- **½ teaspoon hot pepper sauce**
- **⅛ teaspoon salt**

• Cut eggs in half. Remove yolks; mash. Blend in remaining ingredients. Refill whites.   *Makes 12*

Prep time: 25 minutes

Deluxe Fajita Nachos

Scandinavian Smörgåsbord

Scandinavian Smörgåsbord

- 36 slices party bread, crackers or flat bread
  Reduced-calorie mayonnaise or salad dressing
  Mustard
- 36 small lettuce leaves or Belgian endive leaves
- 1 can (9¼ ounces) STARKIST® Tuna, drained and flaked or broken into chunks
- 2 hard-cooked eggs, sliced
- ¼ pound frozen cooked bay shrimp, thawed
- ½ medium cucumber, thinly sliced
- 36 pieces steamed asparagus tips or pea pods
  Capers, plain yogurt, dill sprigs, pimento strips, red or black caviar, sliced green onion for garnish

Arrange party bread on a tray; spread each with 1 teaspoon mayonnaise and/or mustard. Top with a small lettuce leaf. Top with tuna, egg slices, shrimp, cucumber or steamed vegetables. Garnish as desired.

Makes 36 appetizers

Appetizer Crab Balls

- ½ pound crab meat, cartilage removed
- 1½ cups soft bread crumbs
- 1 egg, slightly beaten
- 2 tablespoons HEINZ® Seafood Cocktail Sauce
- 2 tablespoons mayonnaise or salad dressing
- 2 tablespoons minced green onion
- 1 tablespoon chopped fresh parsley
- ½ teaspoon dry mustard
  Dash ground red pepper
  Dash black pepper
- 1 cup crushed potato chips
  HEINZ® Seafood Cocktail Sauce

In large bowl, combine crab meat, bread crumbs, egg, cocktail sauce, mayonnaise, green onion, parsley, mustard, red pepper and black pepper. Cover; chill at least 1 hour. Form mixture into 36 balls, using a rounded teaspoon for each. Roll in crushed chips; place on baking sheet. Bake in preheated 425°F oven, 10 to 12 minutes or until hot and golden brown. Serve with additional cocktail sauce for dipping.

Makes 36 appetizers

Deviled Clam Mushrooms

- 12 large mushrooms
  Melted margarine or butter
- 1 clove garlic, minced
- 2 tablespoons margarine or butter
- 1 tablespoon flour
- 1 (6½-ounce) can SNOW'S® or DOXSEE® Minced Clams, drained, reserving 2 tablespoons liquid
- 1 cup fresh bread crumbs (2 slices)
- 1 tablespoon chopped parsley
- 2 teaspoons Worcestershire sauce
- ½ teaspoon dry mustard

Preheat oven to 400°. Remove and finely chop mushroom stems; set aside. Brush caps with melted margarine. In medium skillet, cook garlic in *2 tablespoons* margarine until tender. Stir in flour. Add chopped mushroom stems and remaining ingredients except mushroom caps; mix well. Mound into mushroom caps; place in shallow baking pan. Bake 8 to 10 minutes or until hot. Refrigerate leftovers.

Makes 12 appetizers

Microwave: Prepare mushrooms as directed above. In 1-quart glass measure with handle, combine garlic and margarine. Cook on 100% power (high) 1 to 1½ minutes or until garlic is tender. Stir in flour then chopped mushroom stems and remaining ingredients except mushroom caps; mix well. Mound into mushroom caps; arrange on microwave-safe plate. Cook on 100% power (high) 5 to 6 minutes, rotating plate once.

Homemade Shrimp Butter

**½ cup LAND O LAKES®
     Butter, softened
¼ cup mayonnaise
1 package (8 ounces) cream
     cheese, softened
3 tablespoons finely chopped
     onion
1 can (4¼ ounces) broken
     shrimp, rinsed, drained
1 tablespoon lemon juice
     Assorted crackers**

In small mixer bowl combine butter, mayonnaise and cream cheese. Beat at medium speed, scraping bowl often, until light and fluffy, 2 to 3 minutes. Add onion, shrimp and lemon juice; continue beating until well mixed, 1 to 2 minutes. Serve with crackers. Store refrigerated.

Makes 2 cups

Scallops in Hot Sauce

**¼ cup olive or vegetable oil
5 cloves garlic, coarsely
     chopped
1 pound bay scallops
¾ cup slivered red bell
     peppers
¾ cup slivered green bell
     pepper
½ cup chopped onion
½ teaspoon TABASCO®
     pepper sauce
¼ teaspoon salt
2 tablespoons drained
     capers**

In large skillet heat oil; sauté garlic until golden. Add scallops, peppers, onion, Tabasco® sauce and salt. Cook, stirring constantly, until scallops turn opaque and vegetables are crisp-tender. Stir in capers. Serve hot.

Makes about 4 cups

Dipper's Chicken Nuggets

**2 whole chicken breasts,
     split, skinned and boned
     Vegetable oil
1 egg
⅓ cup water
⅓ cup all-purpose flour
2 teaspoons sesame seeds
1½ teaspoons salt
     Dipping Sauces
     (recipes follow)
     Red onion rings, for
     garnish**

Cut chicken into 1-inch pieces. Heat 3 inches oil in large heavy saucepan over medium-high heat until oil reaches 375°F; adjust heat to maintain temperature. Meanwhile, beat egg and water in large bowl until well mixed. Add flour, sesame seeds and salt, stirring to form smooth batter. Dip chicken pieces into batter, draining off excess. Fry chicken, a few pieces at a time, in hot oil about 4 minutes or until golden brown. Drain on paper towels. Serve with Dipping Sauces; garnish with onion rings.

Makes 8 servings

Dipping Sauces

NIPPY PINEAPPLE SAUCE: Mix 1 jar (12 ounces) pineapple preserves, ¼ cup prepared mustard and ¼ cup prepared horseradish in small saucepan. Cook and stir over low heat 5 minutes.

DILL SAUCE: Combine ½ cup sour cream, ½ cup mayonnaise, 2 tablespoons finely chopped dill pickle and 1 teaspoon dill weed in small bowl. Cover; refrigerate 1 hour.

ROYALTY SAUCE: Combine 1 cup catsup, 6 tablespoons butter or margarine, 2 tablespoons vinegar, 1 tablespoon brown sugar and ½ teaspoon dry mustard in small saucepan. Cook and stir over low heat 5 minutes.

*Favorite recipe from **National Broiler Council***

Dipper's Chicken Nuggets

Nutty Chicken Wings

18 broiler-fryer chicken wings, disjointed, tips discarded
2 eggs
1 tablespoon vegetable oil
1 teaspoon salt
¼ teaspoon pepper
1 cup fine, dry bread crumbs
1 cup finely chopped walnuts
Honey Mustard Dip (recipe follows)

In shallow bowl, beat together eggs, oil, salt and pepper. In second shallow container, place bread crumbs and nuts; mix well. Dip wing pieces in egg mixture, then in crumb mixture, 2 or 3 at a time, turning to coat on all sides. Place wings in greased shallow baking pan. Bake in 400°F oven 30 minutes or until brown and fork tender.

Makes 36 appetizers

HONEY MUSTARD DIP: In small bowl, mix together 1 cup mayonnaise, 2 tablespoons honey, 1 tablespoon prepared mustard, ½ teaspoon coriander and ⅛ teaspoon ground red pepper.

*Favorite recipe from **Delmarva Poultry Industry***

Hot 'n' Honeyed Chicken Wings

3 pounds chicken wings
¾ cup PACE® Picante Sauce
⅔ cup honey
⅓ cup soy sauce
¼ cup Dijon-style mustard
3 tablespoons vegetable oil
2 tablespoons grated fresh ginger
½ teaspoon grated orange peel
Additional PACE® Picante Sauce

Cut off and discard wing tips; cut each wing in half at joint. Place in 13×9-inch baking dish. Combine ¾ cup picante sauce, honey, soy sauce, mustard, oil, ginger and orange peel in small bowl; mix well. Pour over chicken wings. Cover and refrigerate at least 6 hours or overnight.

Preheat oven to 400°F. Place chicken wings and sauce in single layer on foil-lined 15×10-inch jelly-roll pan. Bake 40 to 45 minutes or until brown. Serve warm with additional picante sauce. Garnish as desired.

Makes about 34 appetizers

Deep-Fried Eggplant Sticks

3 tablespoons Chef Paul Prudhomme's VEGETABLE MAGIC®
1 large eggplant, peeled and cut into sticks measuring about 3 inches×½ inch
1½ cups all-purpose flour
1 large egg
1 cup evaporated milk
3½ cups vegetable oil
3 cups unseasoned bread crumbs
Powdered sugar

Evenly sprinkle 1 tablespoon Vegetable Magic over eggplant sticks. Set aside.

Add remaining 2 tablespoons Vegetable Magic to flour and mix well. Set aside.

Beat egg with evaporated milk. Set aside.

Pour oil into 12-inch heavy skillet. Heat over high heat until oil reaches 350°. When oil reaches 250°, dredge eggplant sticks through seasoned flour and drop into egg-milk mixture. Then dredge through bread crumbs, making sure the pieces are separate and well coated. Fry in 350° oil, one batch at a time, 2 to 3 minutes or until golden brown and crisp. (Make sure to turn the pieces early in the cooking process so they cook evenly.) Drain on paper towels, and, while still warm, dust with powdered sugar.

Makes 10 servings

Fried Mozzarella Sticks

1 package (16 ounces) mozzarella cheese
½ cup all-purpose flour
⅛ teaspoon ground red pepper
2 eggs
1 tablespoon water
½ cup Italian-seasoned fine dry bread crumbs
Vegetable oil for frying
1 cup PREGO® Regular Spaghetti Sauce *or* PREGO® Tomato and Basil Spaghetti Sauce

1. Cut cheese into 1¾- by 1- by ½-inch sticks (32 sticks). On waxed paper, combine flour and pepper. In small bowl, beat together eggs and water. Dip cheese sticks in flour mixture, coating well; then dip in egg mixture and roll in bread crumbs.

2. In 10-inch skillet, heat ½ inch oil to 375°F. Meanwhile, in 1-quart saucepan over medium heat, heat spaghetti sauce until hot.

3. Fry cheese sticks in single layer, a few at a time, until golden brown and just until cheese begins to melt, turning once. Drain on paper towels; keep warm. Repeat with remaining cheese sticks. Serve cheese sticks with hot spaghetti sauce for dipping.

Makes 32 appetizers or 8 appetizer servings

Prep Time: 20 minutes
Cook Time: 20 minutes

Hot 'n' Honeyed Chicken Wings

Broiled Cheese Triangles

> **4 pocket pita breads (5- to 6-inch diameter)**
> **Melted butter or margarine**
> **1½ cups shredded process American cheese**
> **¼ cup HEINZ® Tomato Ketchup**
> **2 tablespoons finely chopped green bell pepper**
> **2 tablespoons finely chopped ripe olives**
> **2 tablespoons mayonnaise or salad dressing**

Split each pita in half horizontally; brush split sides with butter. Cut each pita half into 6 triangles. Place on baking sheet; bake in preheated 350°F oven, 6 to 8 minutes or until crisp and golden brown. Meanwhile, in medium bowl, combine cheese, ketchup, green pepper, olives and mayonnaise. Spread cheese mixture on pita triangles; place on baking sheet. Broil, 5 to 6 inches from heat source, 2 to 3 minutes or until cheese is melted.

Makes 48 appetizers

Note: Pita toast may be prepared in advance. Cool and store in airtight container for up to 7 days.

Crispy Tortellini Bites

> **⅓ cup grated Parmesan cheese**
> **1 teaspoon dried basil, crushed**
> **½ teaspoon LAWRY'S® Seasoned Pepper**
> **⅛ teaspoon cayenne pepper**
> **1 package (8 or 9 ounces) cheese tortellini**
> **⅓ cup vegetable oil**
> **1 cup dairy sour cream**
> **¾ to 1 teaspoon LAWRY'S® Garlic Powder with Parsley**

In medium bowl, combine cheese, basil, Seasoned Pepper and cayenne; set aside. Cook tortellini according to package directions, omitting salt. Run cold water over tortellini; drain. In large skillet, heat oil. Fry cooled tortellini in oil until golden-crisp; drain. Toss cooked tortellini in cheese-spice mixture. In small bowl, blend sour cream and Garlic Powder with Parsley. Serve tortellini with sour cream mixture for dipping.   *Makes 6 servings*

Presentation: Serve with frill toothpicks or mini-skewers.

Hint: Can also be served with prepared LAWRY'S® Extra Rich & Thick Spaghetti Sauce.

Candied Walnuts

> **2 cups sugar**
> **½ cup water**
> **1 teaspoon vanilla**
> **4 cups walnut halves and pieces**

Bring sugar and water to a rolling boil. Boil 1 minute. Stir in vanilla and walnuts; stir until coating sets. Spread on cookie sheet to cool.   *Makes 1 pound*

Orange Candied Walnuts: Use ½ cup orange juice in place of water and 1 teaspoon orange extract in place of vanilla. Cook as directed.

Spiced Walnuts: Add 1 teaspoon *each* ground cinnamon and nutmeg to sugar mixture. Cook as directed.

Sour Cream Walnuts: Substitute ½ cup sour cream or plain yogurt for water. Cook as directed.

*Favorite recipe from **Walnut Marketing Board***

Taco Snack Mix

> **4 cups SPOON SIZE® Shredded Wheat**
> **4 cups pretzel sticks**
> **4 cups tortilla chips**
> **1 (1¼-ounce) package ORTEGA® Taco Seasoning Mix**
> **¼ cup BLUE BONNET® Margarine, melted**

In large bowl, combine cereal, pretzels, tortilla chips and taco seasoning mix. Drizzle with margarine, tossing to coat well. Store in airtight container.

Makes 12 cups

Taco Snack Mix

Cheesy Sun Crisps

2 cups (8 ounces) shredded Cheddar cheese
½ cup grated Parmesan cheese
½ cup sunflower oil margarine, softened
3 tablespoons water
1 cup all-purpose flour
¼ teaspoon salt (optional)
1 cup uncooked quick oats
⅔ cup roasted, salted sunflower kernels

Beat cheeses, margarine and water in large bowl until well blended. Add flour and salt; mix well. Stir in oats and sunflower kernels; mix until well combined. Shape dough into 12-inch long roll; wrap securely. Refrigerate about 4 hours (dough may be stored up to 1 week in refrigerator).

Preheat oven to 400°F. Lightly grease cookie sheets. Cut roll into ⅛- to ¼-inch slices; flatten each slice slightly. Place on prepared cookie sheets. Bake 8 to 10 minutes until edges are light golden brown. Remove immediately; cool on wire rack.

Makes 4 to 5 dozen crackers

*Favorite recipe from the **National Sunflower Association***

Holiday Trail Mix

1 box (8 ounces) DOLE® Whole or Chopped Dates
1 cup DOLE® Whole Almonds, toasted
1 cup DOLE® Raisins
1 cup dried banana chips
1 cup dried apricots
½ cup sunflower seed nuts

• Combine all ingredients in large bowl. Holiday Trail Mix will keep up to 2 weeks in a closed container in the refrigerator.

Makes 11 servings

Preparation Time: 5 minutes

Zesty Snack Mix

Crispy Bagel Chips

1 envelope LIPTON® Golden Onion Recipe Soup Mix
½ cup butter or margarine, melted
1 teaspoon basil leaves
½ teaspoon oregano leaves
¼ teaspoon garlic powder
4 to 5 plain bagels, cut into ⅛-inch slices

Preheat oven to 250°F. In small bowl, thoroughly blend all ingredients except bagels; generously brush on both sides of bagel slices. On two ungreased baking sheets, arrange bagel slices and bake 50 minutes or until crisp and golden. Store in airtight container up to 1 week.

Makes about 28 chips

Zesty Snack Mix

8 cups prepared popcorn
1½ cups dry roasted unsalted mixed nuts
3 tablespoons BLUE BONNET® Margarine, melted
2 tablespoons GREY POUPON® Dijon Mustard
1 (0.7-ounce) package Italian salad dressing mix
1 cup seedless raisins

In large bowl, combine popcorn and nuts; set aside. In small bowl combine margarine, mustard and salad dressing mix. Pour over popcorn mixture, tossing to coat well. Spread in 15½×10½×1-inch baking pan. Bake at 325°F for 15 minutes, stirring after 10 minutes. Remove from oven; stir in raisins. Spread on paper towels to cool. Store in airtight container.

Makes about 6 cups

Cheese Popcorn

2 quarts popped popcorn
⅓ cup butter or margarine
½ cup SARGENTO® Grated Parmesan, Parmesan and Romano or Italian-Style Cheese

Spread freshly popped popcorn in flat pan; keep hot and crisp in 200°F oven. Melt butter; add grated cheese. Pour mixture over popcorn. Stir until evenly coated with cheese mixture.

Makes 2 quarts

BEVERAGES

Quench your thirst on a hot summer day with refreshing fruity coolers. Or warm up a nippy winter night with hot cocoas and ciders. Refreshing punches, frosty milk shakes, festive party drinks and comforting hot toddies make celebrations—whether large or small—extra special.

Sparkling White Sangria

- **1 cup KARO® Light Corn Syrup**
- **1 orange, sliced**
- **1 lemon, sliced**
- **1 lime, sliced**
- **½ cup orange-flavored liqueur**
- **1 bottle (750 ml) dry white wine**
- **2 tablespoons lemon juice**
- **1 bottle (12 ounces) club soda or seltzer, chilled**
- **Additional fresh fruit (optional)**

In large pitcher combine corn syrup, orange, lemon and lime slices and liqueur. Let stand 20 to 30 minutes, stirring occasionally. Stir in wine and lemon juice. Refrigerate. Just before serving, add soda and ice cubes. If desired, garnish with additional fruit.
Makes about 6 (8-ounce) servings

Preparation Time: 15 minutes, plus standing and chilling

Sangria

- **¾ cup sugar**
- **¾ cup orange juice**
- **⅓ cup REALEMON® Lemon Juice from Concentrate**
- **⅓ cup REALIME® Lime Juice from Concentrate**
- **2 (750 ml) bottles medium-dry red wine, chilled**
- **Orange, peach or plum slices**
- **Ice**

In pitcher, combine sugar and juices; stir until sugar dissolves. Cover; chill. Just before serving, add wine and fruit. Serve over ice.   *Makes about 2 quarts*

Sangria Slush: Omit fruit and ice. Combine sugar, juices and wine; pour into freezer-proof container. Cover; freeze 8 hours or overnight.

Sangria Blush

- **1 cup orange juice**
- **½ cup sugar**
- **1 bottle (1.5 liters) white Zinfandel wine**
- **¼ cup lime or lemon juice**
- **1 orange, thinly sliced and seeded**
- **1 lime, thinly sliced and seeded**
- **16 to 20 ice cubes**

Combine orange juice and sugar in small pan. Cook over medium heat, stirring occasionally, until sugar is dissolved. Pour into 2-quart container with tight-fitting lid. Add wine, lime juice and sliced fruits. Cover; refrigerate 2 hours for flavors to blend. Place ice cubes in small punch bowl or large pitcher. Pour wine mixture over ice.   *Makes 8 servings*

Sparkling White Sangria

Sangrita

Bloody Mary Mix

**1 quart vegetable juice
     cocktail**
**2 tablespoons HEINZ®
     Worcestershire Sauce**
**1 tablespoon fresh lime or
     lemon juice**
¼ teaspoon granulated sugar
¼ teaspoon pepper
¼ teaspoon hot pepper sauce
⅛ teaspoon garlic powder

In pitcher, thoroughly combine
vegetable juice, Worcestershire
sauce, lime juice, sugar, pepper,
hot pepper sauce and garlic
powder; cover and chill. Serve
over ice. Garnish with celery
stalks and lime wedges, if
desired.   *Makes 1 quart*

Note: To prepare Bloody Mary
Cocktail, add 3 or 4 parts Bloody
Mary Mix to 1 part vodka.

Purple Passion

**1 (6-ounce) can frozen grape
     juice concentrate, thawed**
3 juice cans cold water
1 juice can vodka
**½ cup REALEMON® Lemon
     Juice from Concentrate**
¼ cup sugar
     Ice
     **Purple grapes and mint
     leaves, optional**

In pitcher, combine all
ingredients except ice, grapes
and mint; stir until sugar
dissolves. Cover; chill. Serve over
ice; garnish with grapes and
mint if desired.
        Makes about 1 quart

Sugar-Peach Champagne Cocktail

**2 fresh California peaches,
     sliced**
¼ cup sugar
**1 bottle (750 ml) pink
     Champagne**

Roll peach slices in sugar and
place 2 or 3 slices in each of 4
glasses. Fill with Champagne.
        Makes 4 servings

Tip: Turn this into a fruit starter
for Sunday brunch by filling a
Champagne glass with fruit
slices. Top with Champagne.

*Favorite recipe from **California Tree
Fruit Agreement***

Pacific Sunset

**1 can (6 ounces) or ¾ cup
     DOLE® Pineapple Juice,
     chilled**
**⅓ cup orange juice, chilled
     Ice cubes**
**1 tablespoon grenadine
     syrup
     Lime wedge for garnish**

• Combine juices in tall glass.
Add ice. Slowly add grenadine.
Garnish with lime wedge.
        Makes 1 serving

Sangrita

**1 can (12 ounces) tomato
     juice**
1½ cups orange juice
¼ cup lime or lemon juice
**1 tablespoon finely minced
     onion**
⅛ teaspoon salt
**¼ teaspoon hot pepper sauce
     Ice cubes**
**4 small celery stalks with
     leafy tops**

Combine juices, onion, salt and
hot pepper sauce in 1-quart
container with tight-fitting lid.
Cover; refrigerate 2 hours for
flavors to blend. Pour into ice-
filled tumblers. Add celery stalk
to each glass for stirrer.
        Makes 4 servings

Wahiawa Refresher

**1 bottle (40 ounces) DOLE®
     Pure & Light Mandarin
     Tangerine Juice, chilled**
**5 cups DOLE® Pineapple
     Juice, chilled**
**1 bottle (25.4 ounces)
     sparkling cider, chilled**
**1 can (15 ounces) real cream
     of coconut**
**1 DOLE® Orange, thinly
     sliced for garnish
     DOLE® Fresh or frozen
     Strawberries for garnish**

• Combine all ingredients in
punch bowl.
        Makes 20 servings

Kokomo Quencher

**2 bottles (32 ounces each)
lemon-lime soda, chilled
1 bottle (40 ounces) DOLE®
Pure & Light Orchard
Peach Juice, chilled
5 cups DOLE® Pineapple
Juice, chilled
2 cups fresh or frozen
blackberries
1 can (15 ounces) real cream
of coconut
1 lime, thinly sliced for
garnish**

• Combine all ingredients in
large punch bowl.

Makes 28 servings

Sunlight Sipper

**1½ cups DOLE® Pine-Passion-
Banana Juice, chilled
1 tablespoon peach
schnapps
1 tablespoon light rum
1 tablespoon orange liqueur
Cracked ice**

• Pour juice, schnapps, rum and
orange liqueur in 2 glasses. Add
ice. Garnish as desired

Makes 2 servings

**Clockwise from top: Raspberry
Mint Cooler, Kokomo Quencher
and Sunlight Sipper**

Raspberry Mint Cooler

**1 to 2 cups fresh mint leaves
5 cups DOLE® Pineapple
Juice, chilled
2 cups DOLE® Fresh or
frozen Raspberries
1 can (6 ounces) frozen
limeade concentrate,
thawed
1 bottle (32 ounces) lemon-
lime soda, chilled
1 lime, thinly sliced for
garnish, optional**

• Rub mint leaves around sides
of punch bowl, then drop the
bruised leaves in bottom of bowl.

• Combine remaining ingredients
in punch bowl.

Makes 15 servings

ReaLemonade

**½ cup sugar
½ cup REALEMON® Lemon
Juice from Concentrate
3¼ cups cold water
Ice**

In pitcher, dissolve sugar in
ReaLemon® brand; add water.
Cover; chill. Serve over ice.

Makes about 1 quart

Variations

ReaLimeade: Substitute
REALIME® Lime Juice from
Concentrate for ReaLemon®
brand.

Sparkling: Substitute club soda
for cold water.

Slushy: Reduce water to ½ cup.
In blender container, combine
sugar, ReaLemon® brand and ½
cup water. Gradually add 4 cups
ice cubes, blending until smooth.
Serve immediately.

Pink: Stir in 1 to 2 teaspoons
grenadine syrup *or* 1 to 2 drops
red food coloring.

Minted: Stir in 2 to 3 drops
peppermint extract.

Low Calorie: Omit sugar. Add 4
to 8 envelopes sugar substitute
or 1½ teaspoons liquid sugar
substitute.

Southern Sunshine

Southern Sunshine

**2 cups orange juice
½ cup REALEMON® Lemon
Juice from Concentrate
¼ cup sugar
1 (32-ounce) bottle lemon-
lime carbonated
beverage, chilled
¾ cup Southern Comfort®
liqueur,* optional
Ice**

In pitcher, combine juices and
sugar; stir until sugar dissolves.
Cover; chill. Just before serving,
add carbonated beverage and
liqueur if desired. Serve over ice.

Makes about 7 cups

Tip: Recipe can be doubled.

*Southern Comfort is a registered trademark of
the Southern Comfort Corporation.

Brewed Iced Tea

2 quarts cold water
6 individual tea bags

In large saucepan, bring water to a boil. Pour into heat-proof pitcher or bowl; add tea bags. Cover; steep 4 minutes. Remove tea bags. Cool. Serve over Lemon Ice Cubes if desired.

Makes about 2 quarts

Lemon Ice Cubes

1 quart cold water
½ cup REALEMON® Lemon Juice from Concentrate
Mint leaves or fruit pieces, optional

Combine water and ReaLemon® brand. Pour into ice cube trays. Place mint leaf or fruit piece in each cube if desired; freeze. Serve with iced tea, lemonade or carbonated beverages.

Makes about 2 dozen

Lemony Light Cooler

3 cups white grape juice *or* 1 (750 ml) bottle dry white wine, chilled
½ to ¾ cup sugar
½ cup REALEMON® Lemon Juice from Concentrate
1 (32-ounce) bottle club soda, chilled
Strawberries, plum, peach or orange slices or other fresh fruit
Ice

In pitcher, combine grape juice, sugar and ReaLemon® brand; stir until sugar dissolves. Cover; chill. Just before serving, add club soda and fruit. Serve over ice.　　*Makes about 7 cups*

Tip: Recipe can be doubled.

Kahlúa® Toasted Almond

8 ounces (1 cup) KAHLÚA®
4 ounces (½ cup) amaretto liqueur
Cream or milk

For each serving, pour 1 ounce Kahlúa® and ½ ounce amaretto liqueur over ice in tall glass. Fill with cream; stir.

Makes 8 servings

Apple Cinnamon Cream Liqueur

1 (14-ounce) can EAGLE® Brand Sweetened Condensed Milk (NOT evaporated milk)
1 cup apple schnapps
2 cups (1 pint) BORDEN® or MEADOW GOLD® Whipping Cream *or* Half-and-Half
½ teaspoon ground cinnamon
Ice

In blender container, combine all ingredients except ice; blend until smooth. Serve over ice.

Brewed Iced Tea

Store tightly covered in refrigerator. Stir before serving.
Makes about 1 quart

FUZZY NAVEL CREAM LIQUEUR: Omit apple schnapps and cinnamon. Add 1 cup peach schnapps and ¼ cup frozen orange juice concentrate, thawed. Proceed as above.

Peppermint Stick Punch

1½ cups sugar
1½ cups REALIME® Lime Juice from Concentrate
1 cup vodka or water
2 tablespoons white creme de menthe *or* ⅛ teaspoon peppermint extract
2 (32-ounce) bottles club soda, chilled
Candy canes

In punch bowl, combine all ingredients except club soda and candy canes; stir until sugar dissolves. Just before serving, add club soda. Hang candy canes on edge of punch bowl or place in each punch cup for stirrer.

Makes about 2½ quarts

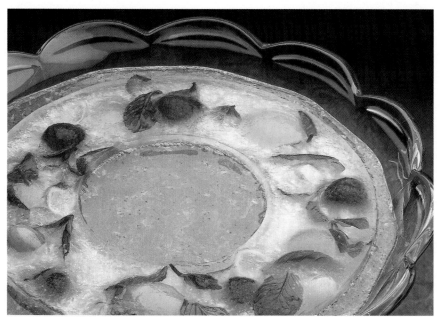

Fruit Medley Punch

DELLA ROBBIA ICE RING:
Combine 2 (12-ounce) cans ginger ale (1½ cups) and ½ cup ReaLemon® brand. Pour 2½ cups mixture into 1-quart ring mold; freeze. Arrange apricot halves, green grapes, strawberries, orange peel strips or other fruits and mint on top of ice. Slowly pour remaining ReaLemon® brand mixture over fruit; freeze.

Zesty Punch Sipper

> **2 bottles (32 ounces each) ginger ale, chilled**
> **6 cups DOLE® Pineapple Orange Juice, chilled**
> **1 can (6 ounces) frozen lemonade concentrate, thawed**
> **1 DOLE® Orange, thinly sliced for garnish, optional**
> **1 lime, thinly sliced for garnish, optional**

• Combine all ingredients in large punch bowl or two large pitchers.   *Makes 20 servings*

Pineapple Raspberry Punch

> **5 cups DOLE® Pineapple Juice**
> **1 quart raspberry cranberry drink**
> **1 pint fresh raspberries or frozen raspberries**
> **1 lemon, thinly sliced Ice**

Chill ingredients. Combine in punch bowl.
Makes 12 servings

Chi Chi Punch

> **6 cups DOLE® Pineapple Orange Juice, chilled**
> **1 can (15 ounces) cream of coconut**
> **3 cups vodka**
> **1 quart lemon-lime soda Cracked ice**
> **1 orange, thinly sliced Mint sprigs**

• Blend 1 cup pineapple orange juice and cream of coconut in blender. Add to punch bowl with remaining pineapple orange juice. Stir in vodka.

• Just before serving, add lemon-lime soda and ice. Garnish with orange slices and mint sprigs.
Makes 30 (4-ounce) servings

Preparation Time: 10 minutes

Fruit Medley Punch

> **Della Robbia Ice Ring or ice**
> **2 (10-ounce) packages frozen strawberries in syrup, thawed**
> **3 cups apricot nectar, chilled**
> **3 cups cold water**
> **1 cup REALEMON® Lemon Juice from Concentrate**
> **1 cup sugar**
> **1 (6-ounce) can frozen orange juice concentrate, thawed**
> **3 (12-ounce) cans ginger ale, chilled**

Prepare ice ring in advance if desired. In blender container, purée strawberries. In large punch bowl, combine puréed strawberries and remaining ingredients except ginger ale and ice ring; stir until sugar dissolves. Just before serving, add ginger ale and ice ring.
Makes about 3½ quarts

Zesty Punch Sipper

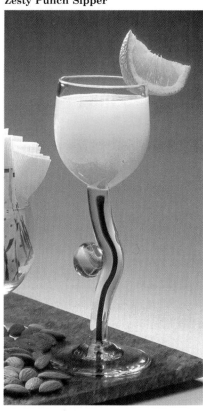

Clockwise from left: Cherry Punch, Meridian Cooler and
Piña Colada Mocktail

Piña Colada Mocktail

**1½ cups DOLE® Pineapple
Juice, chilled
⅓ cup canned real cream of
coconut
1½ teaspoons rum extract
Crushed ice**

• Place all ingredients in
blender. Process until smooth.
Makes 4 servings

Piña Colada Smoothie

**½ cup Piña Colada Smoothie
Base (recipe follows)
1 small ripe banana
1 cup pineapple juice
4 cups ice cubes
¾ cup rum (optional)
Fresh fruit (optional)**

Prepare Piña Colada Smoothie
Base. In blender combine ½ cup
Smoothie Base with banana and
pineapple juice; process until
smooth. With blender running,
add ice cubes, several at a time,
then rum. Process until thick
and smooth. If desired, garnish
with fresh fruit.
*Makes about 6
(6-ounce) servings*

Piña Colada Smoothie Base

**1 cup KARO® Light Corn
Syrup
1 can (8 ounces) crushed
pineapple in
unsweetened juice,
undrained
1 can (15 ounces) cream of
coconut
¼ cup lime juice**

In blender combine ingredients;
process until smooth. Store
covered in refrigerator up to 1
week.   *Makes 3½ cups base*

Preparation Time: 10 minutes

Meridian Cooler

**5 cups DOLE® Pine-Orange-
Guava Juice, chilled
1 bottle (25.4 ounces)
sparkling cider, chilled
2 cups DOLE® Fresh or
frozen Raspberries
1 DOLE® Orange, thinly
sliced for garnish**

• Combine all ingredients in
large punch bowl.
Makes 10 to 12 servings

Cherry Punch

**1 can (6 ounces) frozen
lemonade concentrate
5 cups DOLE® Pure & Light
Mountain Cherry Juice,
chilled
1 bottle (28 ounces) mineral
water, chilled
DOLE® Lemon slices for
garnish
Mint sprigs for garnish**

• Thaw and reconstitute
lemonade in large punch bowl
according to label directions.
Add remaining ingredients.
Makes 16 servings

Daiquiri in Paradise

**2 ripe, medium DOLE®
Bananas, peeled
2 cups crushed ice
⅔ cup frozen DOLE® Pine-
Passion-Banana Juice
concentrate, thawed
½ cup water
¼ cup dark or light rum
¼ cup orange liqueur**

• Combine all ingredients in
blender; puree until slushy.
Serve in stemmed glasses.
Garnish as desired.
Makes 6 servings

Mai Tai Slush

**1½ cups DOLE® Pineapple
Juice
1 pint lemon or lime sherbet
1 cup crushed ice
¼ cup rum
2 tablespoons orange liqueur
Lime slices**

• Combine all ingredients, except
lime slices, in blender. Process
until well blended. Pour into
glasses. Garnish with lime slices.
Makes 4 to 6 servings

Frozen Margaritas

½ cup tequila
⅓ cup REALIME® Lime Juice
   from Concentrate
¼ cup triple sec or other
   orange-flavored liqueur
1 cup confectioners' sugar
4 cups ice cubes

In blender container, combine all ingredients except ice; blend well. Gradually add ice, blending until smooth. Serve immediately.
Makes about 1 quart

Strawberry Margaritas

1 (10-ounce) package frozen
   strawberries in syrup,
   partially thawed
¼ cup REALIME® Lime Juice
   from Concentrate
¼ cup tequila
¼ cup confectioners' sugar
2 tablespoons triple sec or
   other orange-flavored
   liqueur
3 cups ice cubes

In blender container, combine all ingredients except ice; blend well. Gradually add ice, blending until smooth. Serve immediately.
Makes about 1 quart

**Strawberry Margarita (top) and
Frozen Margarita (bottom)**

Banana Shake

2 ripe bananas, cut up (about
   2 cups)
1 (14-ounce) can EAGLE®
   Brand Sweetened
   Condensed Milk
   (NOT evaporated milk)
1 cup cold water
⅓ cup REALEMON® Lemon
   Juice from Concentrate
2 cups ice cubes

In blender container, combine all ingredients except ice; blend well. Gradually add ice, blending until smooth. Garnish as desired. Refrigerate leftovers. (Mixture stays thick and creamy in refrigerator.)
Makes about 5 cups

Variations

Strawberry-Banana: Reduce bananas to ½ cup; add 1½ cups fresh strawberries, cleaned and hulled *or* 1 cup frozen unsweetened strawberries, partially thawed. Proceed as above.

Mixer Method: Omit ice cubes. In large mixer bowl, mash fruit; gradually beat in ReaLemon® brand, sweetened condensed milk and 2½ cups cold water. Chill before serving.

Santa's Special Malted Cocoa

2½ cups chocolate ice cream
1½ cups milk
6 tablespoons sugar
3 tablespoons NESTLÉ®
   Cocoa
3 tablespoons CARNATION®
   Original Malted Milk
   Powder

In blender container, place all ingredients. Cover; blend until smooth. Serve immediately.
Makes about 4 cups

Easy Pudding Milk Shake

Easy Pudding Milk Shakes

3 cups cold milk
1 package (4-serving size)
   JELL-O® Instant Pudding
   and Pie Filling, any flavor
1½ cups ice cream, any flavor

POUR milk into blender. Add pudding mix and ice cream; cover. Blend at high speed 30 seconds or until smooth. Pour into glasses. Serve immediately. (Mixture thickens as it stands. Thin with additional milk, if desired.)
*Makes about 5 cups or
4 to 6 servings*

Homemade Hot Cocoa

½ **cup sugar**
⅓ **cup NESTLÉ® Cocoa**
4 **cups milk, divided**

In large saucepan, stir sugar and cocoa until smooth. Gradually add about ⅓ cup milk, stirring constantly until smooth paste forms. Gradually stir in remaining milk. Cook over medium heat, stirring frequently, until hot. *Do not boil.* Pour into 4 heat-proof mugs.

Makes four 1-cup servings

Hot "White Chocolate"

One 6-oz. pkg. (3 foil-wrapped bars) NESTLÉ® Premier White baking bars, divided
½ **cup heavy or whipping cream**
1 **quart milk**
¼ **cup almond flavored liqueur**

Coarsely grate ½ foil-wrapped bar (1 oz.) Premier White baking bar; set aside for garnish.

In small mixer bowl, beat heavy cream until stiff peaks form; set aside. In medium saucepan, combine remaining 2½ foil-wrapped bars (5 oz.) Premier White baking bars, broken up, and milk. Cook over medium heat, stirring constantly, until Premier White baking bars are melted. Remove from heat; stir in liqueur.

Pour into five heat-proof mugs; top with whipped cream. Garnish with grated Premier White baking bar.

Makes five 1-cup servings

Mexican Coffee Olé

¾ **cup firmly packed brown sugar**
¼ **cup unsweetened cocoa**
2 **teaspoons ground cinnamon**
4 **cups freshly brewed coffee**
Whipped cream

Stir brown sugar, cocoa and cinnamon into hot coffee; blend well to dissolve. Pour into individual mugs and top with whipped cream.

Makes 4 cups

*Favorite recipe from **Lawry's**® **Foods, Inc.***

Hot Pineapple Spice Infusion

6 **cups DOLE® Pineapple Juice**
2 **DOLE® Apples, cored, sliced**
2 **cinnamon sticks**
½ **cup brown sugar, packed**
½ **cup honey**
½ **teaspoon whole cloves**
¼ **teaspoon anise seed, optional**

• Combine all ingredients in Dutch oven. Heat to a simmer.

• Steep 15 minutes. Strain to remove spices before serving.

Makes 8 servings

Hot Pineapple Spice Infusion

Wisconsin Spicy Apple Eggnog

2 beaten eggs
3 cups milk
2 cups light cream or
  half-and-half
⅓ cup sugar
½ teaspoon ground cinnamon
  Dash salt
¾ cup apple brandy
  Ground nutmeg

In a large saucepan, combine beaten eggs, milk, light cream or half-and-half, sugar, cinnamon and salt. Cook and stir over medium heat until mixture is slightly thickened and heated through, but *do not boil*. Remove from heat; stir in apple brandy. To serve, ladle mixture into 12 heat-proof glasses or cups. Sprinkle each serving with nutmeg. Serve warm.

Makes 12 (4-ounce) servings

*Favorite recipe from **Wisconsin Milk Marketing Board** © 1992*

Hot Buttered Rum

1 cup granulated sugar
1 cup firmly packed brown
  sugar
1 cup LAND O LAKES®
  Butter
2 cups vanilla ice cream,
  softened
  Rum *or* rum extract
  Boiling water
  Ground nutmeg

In 2-quart saucepan combine granulated sugar, brown sugar and butter. Cook over low heat, stirring occasionally, until butter is melted and sugar is dissolved, 6 to 8 minutes. In large mixer bowl combine cooked mixture with ice cream; beat at medium speed, scraping bowl often, until smooth, 1 to 2 minutes. Store refrigerated up to 2 weeks. For *each* serving, fill mug with ¼ *cup* mixture, *1 ounce* rum or ¼ *teaspoon* rum extract and ¾ *cup* boiling water; sprinkle with nutmeg.

Makes 16 servings (4 cups)

Hot Spiced Cider

Hot Spiced Cider

2 quarts apple cider
⅔ cup KARO® Light or Dark
  Corn Syrup
3 cinnamon sticks
½ teaspoon whole cloves
1 lemon, sliced
  Cinnamon sticks and
  lemon slices (optional)

In medium saucepan stir cider, corn syrup, cinnamon sticks, cloves and lemon slices. Bring to boil over medium-high heat. Reduce heat; simmer 15 minutes. Remove spices. If desired, garnish each serving with a cinnamon stick and lemon slice.

Makes about 10 servings

Preparation Time: 20 minutes

Hawaiian Tea

3 cups DOLE® Pineapple
  Orange Juice
1 cinnamon stick
2 tablespoons chopped
  crystallized ginger
¼ teaspoon anise seed
¼ teaspoon whole cloves
1 orange tea bag
1 peppermint tea bag
  Brown sugar, optional

• Combine juice and spices in saucepan. Bring to a boil. Reduce heat; simmer 1 minute.

• Add tea bags. Cover and steep 5 to 7 minutes. Sweeten with brown sugar, if desired.

Makes 3 servings

SOUPS

What better way to comfort yourself on a chilly day than with the wonderful aroma of soup simmering on the stove. Try a satisfying chicken noodle soup, a spicy seafood gumbo, a robust pork stew or a flavorful beef chili. From hearty vegetable soups to creamy, elegant bisques to refreshing chilled soups, you'll find soups for starters, intimate gatherings and informal lunches and suppers.

Swiss Broccoli Soup

**2 tablespoons minced onion
1 tablespoon butter
1 jar (12 ounces) HEINZ® HomeStyle Chicken Gravy
1¼ cups milk
1 package (10 ounces) frozen chopped broccoli, cooked, drained
1 cup shredded Swiss cheese
Dash salt and pepper**

In 2-quart saucepan, sauté onion in butter until tender. Stir in gravy, milk and broccoli; heat slowly, stirring occasionally. Add cheese, salt and pepper; heat until cheese is melted, stirring frequently.

Makes 4 servings (about 4 cups)

Creamy Tomato Bisque

**2 cups water
1 (14½-ounce) can whole tomatoes, undrained
½ cup chopped celery
2 tablespoons chopped onion
5 teaspoons WYLER'S® or STEERO® Chicken-Flavor Instant Bouillon *or* 5 Chicken-Flavor Bouillon Cubes
2 medium fresh tomatoes, pared and diced
¼ cup margarine or butter
3 tablespoons flour
2 cups (1 pint) BORDEN® or MEADOW GOLD® Coffee Cream *or* Half-and-Half
1 tablespoon sugar**

In large kettle or Dutch oven, combine water, canned tomatoes, celery, onion and bouillon; cover and simmer 20 minutes. In blender or food processor, purée tomato mixture. In same pan, cook fresh tomatoes in *2 tablespoons* margarine about 5 minutes; remove from pan. In same pan, melt remaining *2 tablespoons* margarine; stir in flour. Add cream; over low heat, cook and stir until thickened. Stir in bouillon mixture, tomatoes and sugar; heat through (*do not boil*). Garnish as desired. Refrigerate leftovers.

Makes about 1½ quarts

Watercress Potato Soup

**1 tablespoon margarine or butter
2 cups chopped watercress
½ cup chopped onion
1½ cups water
1 can (10¾ ounces) CAMPBELL'S® condensed Cream of Potato Soup
⅛ teaspoon ground nutmeg
Watercress for garnish**

1. In 1½-quart saucepan over medium heat, in hot margarine, cook watercress and onion until onion is tender, stirring occasionally. Add water. Heat to boiling. Reduce heat to low. Cover; cook 10 minutes. Drain mixture, reserving liquid. Set aside.

2. In covered blender or food processor, blend watercress mixture until smooth. Add soup; blend until smooth. Add reserved liquid and nutmeg; blend until almost smooth. Return to saucepan; heat through. Garnish with watercress.

Makes about 3 cups or 4 servings

Tip: This is also delicious served cold like classic vichyssoise. Just refrigerate at least 4 hours before serving.

Swiss Broccoli Soup

Dogwood Blossom Soup

½ cup (1 stick) unsalted
　　butter
4 cups minced cauliflower
　　(about 1 pound)
2 cups chopped onions
1 tablespoon Chef Paul
　　Prudhomme's
　　VEGETABLE MAGIC®
4 cups chicken broth or
　　water, in all
6 ounces cooked ham,
　　minced
2 bay leaves
¼ teaspoon ground nutmeg
4 cups heavy cream, in all
6 cups very small
　　cauliflowerets (no larger
　　than ½ inch)

In 5-quart saucepan over
medium-high heat, melt butter.
When butter comes to a hard
sizzle, stir in minced cauliflower
and onions. Reduce heat to
medium. Cook about 14 minutes,
stirring occasionally. Let
mixture stick slightly but not
brown. Stir in Vegetable Magic
and cook 13 minutes more,
stirring occasionally and more
frequently toward end of cooking
time, again taking care not to let
mixture brown. Stir in 2 cups
broth and cook about 10 minutes,
stirring occasionally. Add ham,
bay leaves and nutmeg. Stir well
and cook about 5 minutes. Add
remaining broth, stir well and
cook 7 minutes more or until
mixture comes to a rolling boil.
Whisk in 2 cups cream and cook,
whisking occasionally, about 8
minutes or until cream has
reduced and thickened
somewhat. Whisk in the
remaining cream and cook,
whisking frequently, about 12
minutes or until soup has
reduced and thickened enough to
coat a spoon. Add cauliflowerets
and cook, whisking frequently,
10 minutes or until soup comes
to a boil. Reduce heat to low and
cook, whisking occasionally, 10
minutes or until cauliflowerets
are tender yet still firm.

Let soup set 10 to 15 minutes
before serving for flavors to
blend. Remove bay leaves before
serving.

Makes about 10 cups

Corn & Red Pepper Soup

2 tablespoons butter or
　　margarine
2 cups seeded and coarsely
　　chopped red bell peppers
1 medium onion, thinly sliced
1 can (14½ ounces) ready-to-
　　serve chicken broth
1 package (10 ounces) frozen
　　whole kernel corn or
　　fresh kernels cut from
　　4 large ears
½ teaspoon ground cumin
½ cup sour cream
　　Salt
　　White pepper
　　Sunflower seeds for
　　garnish

Melt butter in 3-quart saucepan
over medium heat. Add bell
peppers and onion; cook until
tender. Add chicken broth, corn
and cumin. Bring to a boil.
Cover; reduce heat and simmer
20 minutes or until corn is
tender. Pour into blender or food
processor; process until smooth.
Pour into sieve set over bowl;
press mixture with rubber
spatula to extract all liquid.
Discard pulp. Return liquid to
pan; whisk in sour cream until
evenly blended. Add salt and
pepper to taste. Reheat but do
not boil. Serve in individual
bowls. Garnish with sunflower
seeds.　　*Makes 4 servings*

Chilly Cucumber Soup

2 tablespoons butter or
　　margarine
2 tablespoons all-purpose
　　flour
4 large cucumbers, peeled,
　　seeded and finely
　　chopped (about 3½ cups)
¼ cup finely chopped parsley
¼ cup finely chopped celery
　　leaves
1 envelope LIPTON® Golden
　　Onion Recipe Soup Mix
2 cups water
2 cups (1 pint) light cream or
　　half-and-half

Dogwood Blossom Soup

In large saucepan, melt butter and cook flour over medium heat, stirring constantly, 3 minutes. Add cucumbers, parsley and celery leaves. Reduce heat to low and cook 8 minutes or until vegetables are tender. Stir in golden onion recipe soup mix thoroughly blended with water. Bring to a boil, then simmer covered 15 minutes. Remove from heat, then cool.

In food processor or blender, puree soup mixture. Stir in cream; chill. Serve cold and garnish, if desired, with cucumber slices and lemon peel.

Makes about 6 (1-cup) servings

Chilled Avocado Soup

**3 small onion slices, each
    ¼ inch thick, divided
1 can (14½ ounces) ready-to-
    serve chicken broth
½ cup plain yogurt
1½ tablespoons lemon juice
1 large ripe avocado, halved
    and pitted
3 to 5 drops hot pepper
    sauce
    Salt
    White pepper
¼ cup finely chopped tomato
¼ cup finely chopped
    cucumber
    Cilantro sprigs for garnish
    Additional chopped
        tomatoes and cucumbers
        for garnish**

Place 1 onion slice, chicken broth, yogurt and lemon juice in blender or food processor; process until well blended. Remove pulp from avocado; spoon into blender. Process until smooth. Pour into medium container with tight-fitting lid. Add hot pepper sauce and salt and pepper to taste. Finely chop the remaining 2 onion slices; add to soup. Stir in tomato and cucumber. Cover and refrigerate 2 hours or up to 24 hours. Serve in individual bowls. Garnish with cilantro and additional chopped tomato and cucumber, if desired.

Makes 6 servings

Chilled Avocado Soup (top) and Corn & Red Pepper Soup (bottom)

Gazpacho

**1½ pounds fresh tomatoes,
    seeded and chopped
1½ cups tomato juice
1 medium cucumber, peeled,
    seeded and chopped
¼ cup finely chopped green
    bell pepper
¼ cup finely chopped onion
2 tablespoons olive or
    vegetable oil
2 tablespoons white wine
    vinegar
1½ teaspoons LAWRY'S®
    Garlic Salt
¼ teaspoon dried oregano,
    crushed
    LAWRY'S® Seasoned
    Pepper**

In large bowl, combine all ingredients except Seasoned Pepper; blend well. Refrigerate until chilled. Add a sprinkle of Seasoned Pepper to each serving.

Makes 5 to 6 servings

Presentation: Serve in individual chilled bowls.

Hint: For more spice, stir in ¼ teaspoon hot pepper sauce before chilling.

Scandinavian Raspberry Soup

Scandinavian Raspberry Soup

2 (10-ounce) packages frozen red raspberries in syrup, thawed
½ cup orange juice
¼ cup REALEMON® Lemon Juice from Concentrate
1 tablespoon cornstarch
1 tablespoon sugar, optional
¾ cup chablis or other dry white wine
Fresh orange sections
Raspberries, orange rind twists or mint leaves, optional
BORDEN® or MEADOW GOLD® Sour Cream

In blender or food processor, purée *1 package* raspberries; strain to remove seeds. In medium saucepan, combine puréed raspberries, orange juice, ReaLemon® brand, cornstarch and sugar if desired; mix well. Over medium heat, cook and stir until slightly thickened and clear; cool. Stir in remaining *1 package* raspberries and wine. Cover; chill. To serve, place several orange sections in each bowl; add soup. Garnish with raspberries, orange twists or mint leaves; serve with sour cream. Refrigerate leftovers.

Makes about 3 cups

Quick Gazpacho

1 can (10¾ ounces) CAMPBELL'S® condensed Tomato Soup
1 soup can water
1 tablespoon wine vinegar
1 teaspoon olive oil
1 clove garlic, minced
¼ teaspoon dried basil leaves, crushed
1 cup seeded and chopped cucumber
½ cup chopped sweet red or green pepper
1 tablespoon chopped onion
Fresh basil leaves for garnish

1. In medium bowl, stir soup until smooth. Stir in water, vinegar, oil, garlic and dried basil; blend well. Stir in cucumber, red pepper and onion. Cover; refrigerate until serving time, at least 6 hours.

2. Serve in chilled bowls. Garnish with fresh basil.

Makes about 3½ cups or 4 servings

Quick Gazpacho

Hearty Minestrone Gratiné

1 cup diced celery
1 cup diced zucchini
1 can (28 oz.) tomatoes with liquid, chopped
2 cups water
2 teaspoons sugar
1 teaspoon dried Italian herb seasoning
1 can (15 oz.) garbanzo beans, drained
4 (3×½-inch) slices French bread, toasted
1 cup (4 oz.) SARGENTO® Fancy Supreme™ Shredded Mozzarella Cheese
2 tablespoons SARGENTO® Fancy Supreme™ Shredded Parmesan Cheese
Freshly chopped parsley

Spray a large saucepan or Dutch oven with nonstick cooking spray. Over medium heat, sauté celery and zucchini until tender. Add tomatoes, water, sugar and herb seasoning. Simmer, uncovered, 15 to 20 minutes. Add garbanzo beans and heat an additional 10 minutes.

Meanwhile, heat broiler. Place toasted French bread on broiler pan. Divide Mozzarella on bread slices. Broil until cheese melts. Ladle soup into bowls and top with Mozzarella French bread. Sprinkle Gourmet Parm cheese over each bowl and garnish with parsley. Serve immediately.

Makes 4 servings

Garden-Style Vegetable Bisque

- **2 tablespoons margarine or butter**
- **1 small zucchini, halved lengthwise and cut into ½-inch slices**
- **2 medium carrots, cut into 2-inch matchstick-thin strips**
- **½ cup thinly sliced celery**
- **1 clove garlic, minced**
- **½ teaspoon dried oregano leaves, crushed**
- **1 can (11 ounces) CAMPBELL'S® condensed Cheddar Cheese Soup**
- **1 can (10¾ ounces) CAMPBELL'S® condensed Cream of Potato Soup**
- **1 soup can milk**
- **1 soup can water**
- **1½ cups chopped cooked chicken**
- **1 medium tomato, seeded and chopped**

1. In 3-quart saucepan over medium heat, in hot margarine, cook zucchini, carrots, celery, garlic and oregano 10 minutes or until vegetables are tender, stirring occasionally.

2. Add soups, milk and water; stir until smooth. Stir in chicken and tomato. Cover; heat through, stirring occasionally.

Makes about 7½ cups or 5 servings

Garden-Style Vegetable Bisque

Italian Vegetable Soup

- **1 pound bulk Italian sausage**
- **2 cups chopped onion**
- **2 cloves garlic, finely chopped**
- **7 cups water**
- **4 medium carrots, pared, sliced**
- **1 (28-ounce) can whole tomatoes, undrained and broken up**
- **2 tablespoons WYLER'S® or STEERO® Beef-Flavor Instant Bouillon *or* 6 Beef-Flavor Bouillon Cubes**
- **1 teaspoon Italian seasoning**
- **¼ teaspoon pepper**
- **1½ cups coarsely chopped zucchini**
- **1 (15-ounce) can garbanzos, drained**
- **1 cup uncooked CREAMETTE® Rotini or Elbow Macaroni**

In large kettle or Dutch oven, brown sausage, onion and garlic; pour off fat. Add water, carrots, tomatoes, bouillon, Italian seasoning and pepper; bring to a boil. Reduce heat; cover and simmer 30 minutes. Add zucchini, beans and rotini. Cook 15 to 20 minutes or until rotini is tender, stirring occasionally. Refrigerate leftovers.

Makes about 2½ quarts

Summer Garden Soup

1 can (10½ ounces)
  CAMPBELL'S®
  condensed Chicken
  Broth
⅔ cup water
½ cup zucchini cut in 2-inch
  matchstick-thin strips
½ cup seeded and chopped
  tomato
½ cup frozen whole kernel
  corn
⅓ cup chopped carrot
¼ cup chopped onion
1½ teaspoons chopped fresh
  basil leaves*

In 2-quart saucepan over high
heat, combine broth, water,
zucchini, tomato, corn, carrot
and onion. Heat to boiling.
Reduce heat to low. Cook 10
minutes or until vegetables are
tender, stirring occasionally. Stir
in basil.
Makes about 3 cups or 3 servings

To microwave: In 1½-quart
microwave-safe casserole,
combine all ingredients *except*
fresh basil. Cover with lid;
microwave on HIGH 12 minutes
or until vegetables are tender,
stirring twice during cooking.
Stir in basil.

*If fresh basil isn't available, use
½ teaspoon crushed dried basil—
just add it before the soup
simmers.

Summer Garden Soup

Quick Garden Cheese Soup

1 cup sliced celery
1 cup chopped onion
2 tablespoons margarine or
  butter
⅔ cup unsifted flour
4 cups water
2 tablespoons WYLER'S® or
  STEERO® Chicken-Flavor
  Instant Bouillon *or*
  6 Chicken-Flavor
  Bouillon Cubes
¼ teaspoon pepper
2 cups frozen broccoli,
  cauliflower and carrot
  combination
1 cup frozen hash browns
  potatoes
3 cups BORDEN® or
  MEADOW GOLD® Milk *or*
  Half-and-Half
2½ cups (10 ounces) shredded
  Cheddar cheese

In large kettle or Dutch oven,
cook celery and onion in
margarine until tender; stir in
flour until smooth. Gradually
add water then bouillon, pepper
and vegetables; bring to a boil.
Reduce heat; cover and simmer
15 minutes. Add milk and
cheese. Cook and stir until
cheese melts and soup is hot
(*do not boil*). Garnish as desired.
Refrigerate leftovers.
Makes about 2 quarts

Classic French Onion Soup

4 cups thinly sliced sweet
  onions
1 clove garlic, finely chopped
¼ cup margarine or butter
5½ cups water
⅓ cup dry sherry *or* white
  wine *or* water
7 teaspoons WYLER'S® or
  STEERO® Beef-Flavor
  Instant Bouillon *or*
  7 Beef-Flavor Bouillon
  Cubes
6 (¾-inch thick) slices French
  bread, buttered and
  toasted
6 (8×4-inch) slices Swiss
  cheese, cut in half
  crosswise

In large saucepan, cook onions
and garlic in margarine until
tender. Add water, sherry and
bouillon. Bring to a boil; reduce
heat. Cover and simmer 30
minutes, stirring occasionally.
Ladle into 6 ovenproof soup
bowls; top each with a bread slice
and cheese. Broil until cheese
melts. Serve immediately.
Refrigerate leftovers.
Makes 6 servings

Bean Soup Santa Fe

1¼ cups dry black beans
½ cup dry pinto beans
6 cups water
1 can (14½ ounces) beef
  broth
1 can (14½ ounces) stewed
  tomatoes, undrained
1½ cups water
1 package (1.27 ounces)
  LAWRY'S® Spices &
  Seasonings for Fajitas
2 tablespoons LAWRY'S®
  Minced Onion with Green
  Onion Flakes
1 teaspoon dry parsley
  flakes

In Dutch oven, soak black beans and pinto beans in 6 cups water for 1 hour. Bring to a boil; reduce heat, cover and simmer 1 hour. Drain beans and rinse. Return to Dutch oven; add remaining ingredients. Bring to a boil; reduce heat, cover and simmer 1 hour.   *Makes 4 servings*

Sherried Black Bean Soup

  2 cans (16 ounces each) black beans, drained
1½ cups water
  1 medium onion, chopped
  1 cup sliced celery
  1 cup diced carrots
  1 tablespoon olive oil
  2 cups chicken broth
  1 can (4 ounces) diced green chiles, drained
  ½ cup rice bran (optional)
  ¼ teaspoon ground black pepper
  1 tablespoon dry sherry
  3 cups hot cooked brown rice
  ½ cup sliced green onions for garnish
  ½ cup finely chopped tomato for garnish

Reserve 1 cup black beans. Place remaining beans and water in food processor or blender; process until smooth. Cook onion, celery, and carrots in oil in Dutch oven over medium-high heat until tender crisp. Add broth, chiles, bran, pepper, and whole and puréed beans. Reduce heat; simmer, uncovered, 10 to 15 minutes. Remove from heat; stir in sherry. Top each serving with ½ cup rice. Garnish with green onions and tomato.
Makes 6 (1⅓-cup) servings

Favorite recipe from **USA Rice Council**

Carrot-Rice Soup

Old-Fashioned Bean Soup

  6 cups water
  1 pound navy beans, washed, sorted
  8 cups water
  2 large meaty smoked ham hocks
  2 medium onions, chopped
  2 medium carrots, chopped
  2 ribs celery, chopped
  1 bay leaf
  1 teaspoon salt
  ¼ teaspoon pepper
  ½ cup HEINZ® Tomato Ketchup

In large saucepot, bring 6 cups water to a boil. Add beans; boil 2 minutes. Remove from heat; cover and let stand 1 hour. Drain beans, discarding water. In same saucepan, combine beans, 8 cups water, ham hocks, onions, carrots, celery, bay leaf, salt and pepper. Bring to a boil. Reduce heat; cover and simmer 2½ to 3 hours or until beans are tender. Discard bay leaf. Cut meat from bones; return meat to soup. Stir in ketchup; heat through.
Makes 10 servings
(about 11 cups)

Carrot-Rice Soup

  1 pound carrots, peeled and chopped
  1 medium onion, chopped
  1 tablespoon margarine
  4 cups chicken broth, divided
  ¼ teaspoon dried tarragon leaves
  ¼ teaspoon ground white pepper
2¼ cups cooked rice
  ¼ cup light sour cream
    Snipped parsley or mint for garnish

Cook carrots and onion in margarine in large saucepan or Dutch oven over medium-high heat 2 to 3 minutes or until onion is tender. Add 2 cups broth, tarragon, and pepper. Reduce heat; simmer 10 minutes. Combine vegetables and broth in food processor or blender; process until smooth. Return to saucepan. Add remaining 2 cups broth and rice; thoroughly heat. Dollop sour cream on each serving of soup. Garnish with parsley.   *Makes 6 servings*

Favorite recipe from **USA Rice Council**

Quick Beef Soup

Beef Barley Vegetable Soup

1 pound beef shanks, cracked
7 cups water
1 (14½-ounce) can stewed tomatoes
¾ cup chopped onion
2 tablespoons WYLER'S® or STEERO® Beef-Flavor Instant Bouillon *or* 6 Beef-Flavor Bouillon Cubes
½ teaspoon basil leaves
1 bay leaf
½ cup regular barley
3 medium carrots, pared and chopped
1½ cups chopped celery

In large kettle or Dutch oven, combine shanks, water, tomatoes, onion, bouillon, basil and bay leaf. Bring to a boil. Reduce heat; cover and simmer 1 hour. Remove shanks from stock; cut meat into ½-inch pieces. Skim off fat. Add meat and barley; bring to a boil. Reduce heat; cover and simmer 30 minutes. Add carrots and celery; cook 30 minutes longer. Remove bay leaf. Refrigerate leftovers.
Makes about 2½ quarts

Turkey Wild Rice Pumpkin Soup

2 tablespoons margarine or butter
½ cup chopped onions
½ cup sliced celery
4 cups chicken or turkey broth
1 can (16 ounces) solid-pack pumpkin
2 cups (10 ounces) cubed cooked BUTTERBALL® Turkey
2 cups cooked wild rice
1 cup half and half
1 teaspoon seasoned salt
½ teaspoon ground cinnamon

Quick Beef Soup

1½ pounds lean ground beef
1 cup chopped onion
2 cloves garlic, finely chopped
1 can (28 ounces) tomatoes, undrained
6 cups water
6 beef bouillon cubes
¼ teaspoon pepper
½ cup uncooked orzo
1½ cups frozen peas, carrots and corn vegetable blend
French bread (optional)

Cook beef, onion and garlic in large saucepan over medium-high heat until beef is brown, stirring to separate meat; drain fat.

Purée tomatoes with juice in covered blender or food processor. Add tomatoes, water, bouillon cubes and pepper to meat mixture. Bring to a boil; reduce heat to low. Simmer, uncovered, 20 minutes. Add orzo and vegetables. Simmer 15 minutes more. Serve with French bread.
Makes 6 servings

*Favorite recipe from **North Dakota Beef Commission***

Cook and stir margarine, onions and celery in Dutch oven over medium heat until vegetables are crisp-tender, about 5 minutes. Add broth and pumpkin. Bring to a boil; reduce heat and simmer 5 minutes. Stir in turkey, rice, half and half, salt and cinnamon. Heat to serving temperature; do not boil.

Makes 8 servings

Wild Rice Soup

  2 cups water
  ½ cup uncooked wild rice
  ½ teaspoon salt
  3 tablespoons BUTTER FLAVOR CRISCO®
  ½ cup chopped green bell pepper
  ½ cup chopped celery
  ⅓ cup chopped onion
  1 clove garlic, minced
  2 tablespoons all-purpose flour
1½ teaspoons instant chicken bouillon granules
  ½ teaspoon salt
  ⅛ teaspoon pepper
  ⅛ teaspoon bouquet garni seasoning
  ¾ cup cubed fully cooked ham
  1 medium carrot, grated
  2 tablespoons snipped fresh parsley
  2 cups milk
  2 cups half-and-half

In 2-quart saucepan combine water, wild rice and salt. Heat to boiling. Reduce heat; cover and simmer 30 minutes or until tender. Drain in colander. Set aside. In 2-quart saucepan melt Butter Flavor Crisco®. Add green pepper, celery, onion and garlic. Cook and stir over medium heat about 7 minutes or until tender. Stir in flour, bouillon granules, salt, pepper and bouquet garni. Add cooked rice, ham, carrot, parsley, milk and half-and-half. Cook over medium heat 15 to 20 minutes or until very hot, stirring occasionally. Serve hot. Refrigerate leftover soup.

Makes 4 to 6 servings

Albondigas Soup

  1 pound ground beef
  ¼ cup long-grain rice
  1 egg
  1 tablespoon chopped fresh cilantro
  1 teaspoon LAWRY'S® Seasoned Salt
  ¼ cup ice water
  2 cans (14½ ounces each) chicken broth
  1 can (14½ ounces) whole peeled tomatoes, undrained and cut up
  ¼ cup chopped onion
  1 stalk celery, diced
  1 large carrot, diced
  1 medium potato, diced
  ¼ teaspoon LAWRY'S® Garlic Powder with Parsley

In medium bowl, combine ground beef, rice, egg, cilantro, Seasoned Salt and ice water; form into small meatballs. In large saucepan, combine broth with vegetables and Garlic Powder with Parsley. Bring to a boil; add meatballs. Reduce heat, cover and simmer 30 to 40 minutes, stirring occasionally.

Makes 6 to 8 servings

Presentation: Serve with lemon wedges and warm tortillas.

Hint: For a lower salt version, use homemade chicken broth or low-sodium chicken broth.

Albondigas Soup

Hearty Meatball Soup

½ pound ground beef
½ pound bulk pork sausage
1 egg
½ teaspoon salt (optional)
⅛ teaspoon pepper (optional)
4 cups water
1 envelope (4-serving size) onion soup mix
1 can (16 ounces) stewed tomatoes
1 can (15¼ ounces) red kidney beans, drained
1 cup diced carrots
1 cup Original MINUTE® Rice
2 tablespoons chopped parsley

Mix ground beef, sausage, egg, salt and pepper thoroughly in medium bowl. Shape into tiny balls. (Brown meatballs in skillet, if desired.)

Bring water to boil in large saucepan; stir in soup mix. Reduce heat; cover and simmer 10 minutes. Add meatballs, tomatoes, kidney beans and carrots; simmer 15 minutes longer. Stir in rice. Cover; remove from heat. Let stand 5 minutes. Add parsley.

Makes 8 to 10 servings

Pepperoni Pizza Soup

1 can (26 ounces) CAMPBELL'S® condensed Tomato Soup
1 soup can water
⅔ cup sliced pepperoni
1 teaspoon dried Italian seasoning, crushed
Shredded mozzarella cheese
Croutons

In 2-quart saucepan, combine soup, water, pepperoni and Italian seasoning. Over medium heat, heat through. Serve topped with cheese and croutons.

Makes about 6 cups or 4 servings

Variation: Substitute ½ pound cooked, drained ground beef for pepperoni.

Pepperoni Pizza Soup for Two: In 1-quart saucepan, combine 1 can (10¾ ounces) Campbell's® condensed Tomato Soup, 1 soup can water, ⅓ cup sliced pepperoni and ½ teaspoon dried Italian seasoning, crushed. Proceed as directed above.

Makes about 2½ cups or 2 servings

Tomato, Chicken and Mushroom Soup

¼ pound mushrooms, sliced*
1 tablespoon margarine or butter
2 cans (13¾ ounces each) chicken broth
2 cups diced cooked chicken
1 can (14½ ounces) whole tomatoes, cut up
1 can (8 ounces) tomato sauce
1 carrot, thinly sliced
1 envelope GOOD SEASONS® Italian Salad Dressing Mix
¾ cup Original MINUTE® Rice

Cook and stir mushrooms in hot margarine in large saucepan. Add broth, chicken, tomatoes, tomato sauce, carrot and salad dressing mix; stir well. Bring to boil. Reduce heat; cover and simmer 10 minutes. Stir in rice. Cover; remove from heat. Let stand 5 minutes.

Makes 8 servings

*You may use 1 jar (4.5 ounces) drained sliced mushrooms for the fresh mushrooms.

Chicken Noodle Soup

1 (46-fluid ounce) can COLLEGE INN® Chicken Broth
½ pound skinless, boneless chicken, cut into bite-size pieces
1½ cups uncooked medium egg noodles
1 cup sliced carrots
½ cup chopped onion
⅓ cup sliced celery
1 teaspoon dried dill weed
¼ teaspoon black pepper

In large saucepan, over medium-high heat, heat chicken broth, chicken, noodles, carrots, onion, celery, dill and pepper to a boil. Reduce heat; simmer 20 minutes or until chicken and noodles are cooked. *Makes 8 servings*

Hearty Chicken and Rice Soup

10 cups chicken broth
1 medium onion, chopped
1 cup sliced celery
1 cup sliced carrots
¼ cup snipped parsley
½ teaspoon cracked black pepper
½ teaspoon dried thyme leaves
1 bay leaf
1½ cups chicken cubes (about ¾ pound)
2 cups cooked rice
2 tablespoons fresh lime juice
Lime slices for garnish

Combine broth, onion, celery, carrots, parsley, pepper, thyme, and bay leaf in Dutch oven. Bring to a boil; stir once or twice. Reduce heat; simmer, uncovered, 10 to 15 minutes. Add chicken; simmer, uncovered, 5 to 10 minutes or until chicken is cooked. Remove and discard bay leaf. Stir in rice and lime juice just before serving. Garnish with lime slices.

Makes 8 servings

Favorite recipe from **USA Rice Council**

Hearty Chicken and Rice Soup

Curried Chicken-Vegetable Chowder

1 can (10¾ ounces) CAMPBELL'S® condensed Cream of Chicken Soup
1 can (10½ ounces) CAMPBELL'S® condensed Chicken Broth
2 cups water
½ teaspoon curry powder
⅛ teaspoon dried thyme leaves, crushed
⅛ teaspoon pepper
2 cups cubed peeled potatoes (3 medium)
2 cups cubed cooked chicken
1 cup broccoli flowerets
1 cup sliced fresh mushrooms
½ cup sweet red pepper cut in strips

1. In 3-quart saucepan, stir soup until smooth. Gradually stir in broth, water, curry, thyme and pepper. Over medium heat, heat to boiling. Add potatoes. Boil 10 minutes.

2. Add chicken, broccoli, mushrooms and red pepper. Reduce heat to low. Cover; cook 5 minutes or until vegetables are tender.
Makes about 8 cups or 6 servings

Chicken Cilantro Bisque

6 ounces boneless, skinless chicken breasts, cut into chunks
2½ cups low-sodium chicken broth
½ cup cilantro leaves
½ cup sliced green onions
¼ cup sliced celery
1 large clove garlic, minced
½ teaspoon ground cumin
⅓ cup all-purpose flour
1½ cups (12-ounce can) *undiluted* CARNATION® Evaporated Skimmed Milk
Fresh ground pepper, to taste

In large saucepan, combine chicken, broth, cilantro, green onions, celery, garlic and cumin. Heat to boiling; reduce heat and boil gently, covered, for 15 minutes. Pour soup into blender container. Add flour. Cover and blend, starting at low speed, until smooth. Pour mixture back into saucepan. Cook over medium heat, stirring constantly, until mixture comes to a boil and thickens. Remove from heat. Gradually stir in milk. Reheat just to serving temperature. Do not boil. Season with pepper to taste. Garnish as desired.
Makes about 4 servings

Boston Fish Chowder

4 slices bacon
½ cup chopped celery
½ cup chopped onion
1 clove garlic, finely chopped
¼ cup unsifted flour
4 cups water
2 tablespoons WYLER'S® or STEERO® Chicken-Flavor Instant Bouillon *or* 6 Chicken-Flavor Bouillon Cubes
1½ cups pared, cubed potatoes
1 pound fish fillets, fresh or frozen, thawed, cut into bite-size pieces
2 cups (1 pint) BORDEN® or MEADOW GOLD® Coffee Cream *or* Half-and-Half
2 tablespoons chopped pimiento

In large kettle or Dutch oven, cook bacon until crisp; remove and crumble. In drippings, cook celery, onion and garlic until tender; stir in flour. Gradually add water and bouillon, stirring until smooth and well blended; bring to a boil. Add potatoes. Reduce heat and cook 10 minutes. Stir in fish; cook 15 minutes. Add cream and pimiento; heat through (*do not boil*). Garnish with bacon. Refrigerate leftovers.
Makes about 2 quarts

Curried Chicken-Vegetable Chowder

Asparagus and Surimi Seafood Soup

3 cans (10½ ounces *each*) low-sodium chicken broth (about 4 cups)
2 thin slices fresh ginger
2 cups diagonally sliced (½-inch-long) asparagus pieces (about ¾ pound)
¼ cup sliced green onions
3 tablespoons rice vinegar or white wine vinegar
¼ teaspoon crushed red pepper
8 to 12 ounces Surimi Seafood, crab flavored, chunk style or leg style, cut diagonally

Bring chicken broth and ginger to a boil in a large saucepan. Add asparagus, green onions, vinegar and crushed pepper. Simmer 5 minutes or until the asparagus is crisp tender. Add Surimi Seafood and simmer 5 minutes or until seafood is hot. Remove and discard ginger. Serve hot.

Makes 4 servings

Favorite recipe from **National Fisheries Institute**

"Dearhearts" Seafood Bisque

2 tablespoons olive oil
1 onion, finely chopped
3 pounds fresh baby artichokes, outer leaves removed, leaf tips trimmed and hearts cut into quarters
2 cups chicken broth
½ cup white wine
1 pound mixed shellfish (shrimp, crab, scallops), cleaned and shells removed
1 cup heavy cream
2 tablespoons chopped parsley
1 teaspoon salt
½ teaspoon ground nutmeg
¼ teaspoon white pepper

"Dearhearts" Seafood Bisque

Heat oil in large saucepan; add onion and cook gently for 5 minutes or until softened. Add artichokes, broth and wine. Cover and simmer 20 to 30 minutes or until artichokes are tender and a leaf pulls away easily. Process mixture in food processor or blender until smooth. Return soup to saucepan. Stir in shellfish, cream, parsley, salt, nutmeg and pepper. Simmer very gently, uncovered, over low heat 5 to 10 minutes. *Do not boil* or shellfish will become tough.

Makes 6 servings

Favorite recipe from **Castroville Artichoke Festival**

Hasty Bouillabaisse

5 green onions, thinly sliced
½ cup chopped green pepper
1 clove garlic, minced
2 tablespoons minced parsley
2 tablespoons olive or vegetable oil
1 can (14½ ounces) stewed or whole tomatoes
1 cup red wine
¾ teaspoon dried thyme leaves
¼ teaspoon dried rosemary, crushed
¼ teaspoon TABASCO® sauce
1 can (16 ounces) mixed vegetables or peas and carrots or 2 cans (8 ounces each) other vegetables (beans, corn, carrots, peas, etc.)
1 can (7 ounces) tuna, drained and flaked
1 can (6 ounces) crabmeat, flaked and cartilage removed
1 can (6 ounces) minced clams, drained
1 can (4¼ ounces) shrimp, rinsed and drained

In large saucepan, cook onions, green pepper, garlic and parsley in oil over medium heat until tender. Add tomatoes, wine and seasonings. Simmer 10 minutes. Add vegetables and seafood. Simmer 10 minutes more or until heated through.

Makes 6 to 8 servings

Favorite recipe from **Canned Food Information Council**

Savory Seafood Soup

24 small littleneck clams*
1 tablespoon olive or vegetable oil
1 cup chopped onion
4 cloves garlic, minced
4 cups PREGO® Regular Spaghetti Sauce
2½ cups water
1 can (16 ounces) white kidney beans, undrained
1 can (14½ ounces) chicken broth
½ cup sliced celery
1 medium bay leaf
½ teaspoon dried thyme leaves, crushed
½ teaspoon dried basil leaves, crushed
1 package (9 ounces) frozen Italian green beans (about 1½ cups)
1½ pounds fresh or thawed, frozen orange roughy, monkfish or other fish fillets, cut into 2-inch pieces

1. Discard any clams that stay open when tapped with fingers; scrub.

2. In 6-quart Dutch oven over medium heat, in hot oil, cook onion and garlic until tender. Stir in next 8 ingredients.

3. Heat to boiling. Reduce heat to low. Cover; simmer 20 minutes, stirring occasionally. Stir in green beans. Over medium heat, heat to boiling.

4. Add clams and fish. Cover; cook 5 minutes or until fish flakes easily and clam shells open. Discard bay leaf and any clams that remain closed.

Makes about 16 cups or 8 main-dish servings

Prep Time: 25 minutes
Cook Time: 20 minutes

*To make sure fresh clams are safe to eat, tap on any open shells. If the clam closes its shell, it will be safe to eat after cooking. Discard those that remain open. After cooking, discard any clam with a closed shell, because it is not safe to eat.

Seafood Gumbo

½ cup chopped onion
½ cup chopped green pepper
½ cup (about 2 ounces) sliced fresh mushrooms
1 clove garlic, minced
2 tablespoons margarine
1 can (28 ounces) whole tomatoes, undrained
2 cups chicken broth
½ to ¾ teaspoon ground red pepper
½ teaspoon dried thyme leaves
½ teaspoon dried basil leaves
1 package (10 ounces) frozen cut okra, thawed
¾ pound white fish, cut into 1-inch pieces
½ pound peeled, deveined shrimp
3 cups hot cooked rice

Cook onion, green pepper, mushrooms, and garlic in margarine in large saucepan or Dutch oven over medium-high heat until tender crisp. Stir in tomatoes and juice, broth, red pepper, thyme, and basil. Bring to a boil. Reduce heat; simmer, uncovered, 10 to 15 minutes. Stir in okra, fish, and shrimp; simmer until fish flakes with fork, 5 to 8 minutes. Serve rice on top of gumbo.   *Makes 6 servings*

To microwave: Combine onion, green pepper, mushrooms, garlic, and margarine in deep 2- to 3-quart microproof baking dish. Cover and cook on HIGH 4 minutes; stir after 2 minutes. Stir in tomatoes and juice, broth, red pepper, thyme, and basil. Cover and cook on HIGH 10 minutes; stir. Reduce setting to MEDIUM (50% power) and cook, covered, 10 to 12 minutes. Stir in okra, fish, and shrimp; cook, covered, on HIGH 5 minutes. Let stand 5 minutes. Serve rice on top of gumbo.

Favorite recipe from **USA Rice Council**

Seafood Gumbo

Winter Lamb Stew

lamb to saucepan. Heat to boiling. Reduce heat to low. Cover; cook 25 minutes.

3. Add squash, corn and pepper. Cover; cook 15 minutes more or until lamb and vegetables are tender. Stir in parsley.

Makes 4 servings

Variation: Use beef stew meat instead of lamb if your family prefers. Just increase the cooking time about 20 minutes.

Sage and Rosemary Pork Stew

> **2 pounds boneless pork shoulder roast, cut into ¾-inch cubes**
> **1 tablespoon vegetable oil**
> **2 cans (14½ ounces each) chicken broth**
> **1 cup water**
> **½ cup sliced green onions**
> **1 tablespoon minced fresh rosemary *or* 1 teaspoon dried rosemary**
> **1 teaspoon minced fresh sage *or* ⅛ teaspoon dried sage**
> **¼ teaspoon salt**
> **⅛ teaspoon pepper**
> **2 cups cubed, unpeeled new potatoes**
> **½ pound fresh green beans, cut up**
> **⅓ cup all-purpose flour**
> **⅔ cup half-and-half**

Heat oil in Dutch oven. Brown pork cubes over medium-high heat. Stir in broth, water, onions and seasonings. Bring to a boil; reduce heat. Simmer uncovered for 20 minutes. Stir in potatoes and beans; simmer 15 to 20 minutes or until tender. Combine flour and half-and-half; mix until smooth. Gradually stir into stew. Cook and stir until thickened.

Makes 6 servings

*Favorite recipe from **National Pork Producers Council***

Pescado Viejo
(Fish Stew)

> **2 medium onions, chopped**
> **1 green bell pepper, diced**
> **1 tablespoon vegetable oil**
> **2 cans (14½ ounces each) whole peeled tomatoes, undrained and cut up**
> **1 large red potato**
> **1 can (14½ ounces) beef broth**
> **⅓ cup red wine**
> **1 bay leaf**
> **1 package (1.5 ounces) LAWRY'S® Original Style Spaghetti Sauce Spices & Seasonings**
> **¾ teaspoon LAWRY'S® Garlic Powder with Parsley**
> **½ teaspoon LAWRY'S® Seasoned Salt**
> **½ teaspoon celery seed**
> **1 pound halibut or swordfish steaks, rinsed and cubed**

In Dutch oven, sauté onions and bell pepper in oil until tender. Stir in remaining ingredients except fish. Bring to a boil; reduce heat, cover and simmer 20 minutes. Add fish. Simmer 10 to 15 minutes longer or until fish flakes easily with fork. Remove bay leaf before serving.

Makes 10 servings

Winter Lamb Stew

> **1 tablespoon vegetable oil**
> **1 pound boneless lamb shoulder roast, cut into ¾-inch pieces**
> **½ cup coarsely chopped onion**
> **1 teaspoon paprika**
> **1 can (10¾ ounces) CAMPBELL'S® condensed Beefy Mushroom Soup**
> **1 can (8 ounces) tomatoes, undrained, cut up**
> **1 soup can water**
> **1 pound butternut or acorn squash, peeled, seeded and cut into ½-inch pieces (about 2 cups)**
> **1 cup whole kernel corn**
> **⅛ teaspoon pepper**
> **2 tablespoons chopped fresh parsley**

1. In 4-quart saucepan over medium heat, in hot oil, cook lamb *half* at a time, until browned, stirring often. Remove lamb as it browns.

2. In same saucepan over medium heat, cook onion and paprika 2 minutes, stirring occasionally. Stir in soup, tomatoes and water. Return

Arizona Turkey Stew

- 5 medium carrots, cut into thick slices
- 1 large onion, cut into ½-inch pieces
- 3 tablespoons olive or vegetable oil
- 1 pound sliced turkey breast, cut into 1-inch strips
- 1 teaspoon LAWRY'S® Garlic Powder with Parsley
- 3 tablespoons all-purpose flour
- 8 small red potatoes, cut into ½-inch cubes
- 1 package (10 ounces) frozen peas, thawed
- 8 ounces sliced fresh mushrooms
- 1 package (1.62 ounces) LAWRY'S® Spices & Seasonings for Chili
- 1 cup beef broth
- 1 can (8 ounces) tomato sauce

In large skillet, sauté carrots and onion in oil until tender. Stir in turkey strips and Garlic Powder with Parsley; cook 3 minutes or until turkey is just browned. Stir in flour. Pour mixture into 3-quart casserole dish. Stir in remaining ingredients. Bake, covered, in 450°F oven 40 to 45 minutes or until potatoes are tender. Let stand 5 minutes before serving.

Makes 8 to 10 servings

Presentation: Perfect with a crisp green salad.

Hint: Spoon dollops of prepared dumpling mix on top of casserole during the last 15 minutes of baking.

Stove Top Directions: Prepare as above in Dutch oven. Bring mixture to a boil; reduce heat, cover and simmer 40 to 45 minutes or until potatoes are tender. Let stand 5 minutes before serving.

Bistro Burgundy Stew

- 1 pound sirloin beef, cut into 1½-inch pieces
- 3 tablespoons all-purpose flour
- 6 slices bacon, cut into 1-inch pieces (about ¼ pound)
- 2 cloves garlic, pressed
- 3 carrots, peeled and cut into 1-inch pieces (about 1½ cups)
- ¾ cup Burgundy or other dry red wine
- ½ cup GREY POUPON® Dijon Mustard or GREY POUPON® Country Dijon Mustard
- 12 small mushrooms
- 1½ cups scallions, cut into 1½-inch pieces

Coat beef with flour; set aside. In large skillet, over medium heat, cook bacon until just done; pour off excess fat. Add beef and garlic; cook until browned. Add carrots, wine and mustard; cover. Simmer 30 minutes or until carrots are tender, stirring occasionally. Stir in mushrooms and scallions; cook 10 minutes more, stirring occasionally. Garnish as desired.

Makes 6 servings

Santa Fe Stew Olé

- 1 tablespoon vegetable oil
- 1½ pounds beef stew meat, cut into small bite-size pieces
- 1 can (28 ounces) stewed tomatoes, undrained
- 2 medium carrots, sliced into ¼-inch pieces
- 1 medium onion, chopped
- 1 package (1.25 ounces) LAWRY'S® Taco Spices & Seasonings
- 2 tablespoons diced green chiles
- ½ teaspoon LAWRY'S® Seasoned Salt
- ¼ cup water
- 2 tablespoons all-purpose flour
- 1 can (15 ounces) pinto beans, drained

In Dutch oven, heat oil; brown stew meat. Add tomatoes, carrots, onion, Taco Spices & Seasonings, green chiles and Seasoned Salt; blend well. Bring to a boil; reduce heat, cover and simmer 40 minutes. In small bowl, combine water and flour; blend well. Add to stew mixture. Add pinto beans and simmer an additional 15 minutes.

Makes 4 servings

Santa Fe Stew Olé

Bunkhouse Chili

2 pounds lean beef for stew, cut into ½-inch cubes
2 tablespoons vegetable oil
1 medium green bell pepper, chopped
1 medium onion, chopped
1 cup chopped celery
2 cloves garlic, minced
1 can (16 ounces) whole peeled tomatoes, cut into bite-size pieces
1½ cups (12 ounces) beer
1 cup HEINZ® Thick and Rich Original Recipe or Old Fashioned Barbecue Sauce
1 to 2 tablespoons chili powder
1 teaspoon dried oregano leaves, crushed
1 teaspoon salt
¼ teaspoon pepper
2 cans (15 to 17 ounces each) red kidney or pinto beans, drained
Shredded Cheddar cheese
Sliced green onions

In Dutch oven or large saucepot, brown beef, one layer at a time, in oil. Add green pepper, onion, celery and garlic; sauté until tender-crisp. Stir in tomatoes, beer, barbecue sauce, chili powder, oregano, salt and pepper. Cover; simmer 1 hour, stirring occasionally. Add kidney beans; simmer, uncovered, 45 minutes, stirring occasionally. Sprinkle with cheese and green onions just before serving.

*Makes 6 to 8 servings
(about 8 cups)*

Italian-Style Chili

1 pound lean ground beef
¾ cup chopped onion
1 (26-ounce) jar CLASSICO® Di Napoli (Tomato & Basil) Pasta Sauce
1½ cups water
1 (14½-ounce) can whole tomatoes, undrained and broken up
1 (4-ounce) can sliced mushrooms, drained
2 ounces sliced pepperoni
1 tablespoon WYLER'S® or STEERO® Beef-Flavor Instant Bouillon *or* 3 Beef-Flavor Bouillon Cubes
1 tablespoon chili powder
2 teaspoons sugar

In large kettle or Dutch oven, brown meat with onion; pour off fat. Add remaining ingredients; bring to a boil. Reduce heat; simmer uncovered 30 minutes, stirring occasionally. Garnish as desired. Refrigerate leftovers.

Makes about 2 quarts

Tex-Mex Two Bean Chili

2 tablespoons olive oil
1 cup chopped onion
1 cup chopped green pepper
2 large garlic cloves, pressed
1 pound lean stew meat, cut into ½-inch cubes
½ pound bulk hot Italian sausage*
1¾ cups (15-ounce can) CONTADINA® Tomato Puree
1¾ cups (14.5-ounce can) beef broth
1¼ cups water
⅔ cup (6-ounce can) CONTADINA® Tomato Paste
½ cup (4-ounce can) diced green chiles
3 tablespoons chili powder
1½ teaspoons ground cumin
1 teaspoon salt
1 teaspoon sugar
1 teaspoon dried oregano leaves, crushed
⅛ teaspoon cayenne pepper (optional)
1½ cups (15-ounce can) pinto beans, rinsed and drained
1½ cups (15-ounce can) kidney beans, rinsed and drained

In 6-quart saucepan, heat oil; sauté onion, green pepper and garlic 3 to 4 minutes, or until tender. Add stew meat and sausage, stirring to crumble sausage; cook 5 to 6 minutes. Blend in tomato puree, broth, water, tomato paste, green chiles, chili powder, cumin, salt, sugar, oregano and cayenne pepper, if desired. Bring to a boil. Reduce heat; simmer uncovered 1½ hours, stirring occasionally. Mix in beans. Cover and simmer additional 30 minutes.

Makes 6 servings

Note: If link sausage is used, remove casings before sautéing.

From top to bottom: Italian-Style Chili and Quick Garden Cheese Soup (page 48)

Tex-Mex Two Bean Chili

In Dutch oven, sauté onions, green pepper and garlic in oil. Add turkey and cook until lightly browned. Add tomatoes, chili sauce, chili powder, lemon pepper, basil, thyme and hot pepper sauce. Cover; simmer 45 minutes. Add kidney beans; simmer an additional 20 minutes. Serve topped with green onions, cheese and sour cream.   *Makes 8 servings*

Hearty Meatless Chili

1 envelope LIPTON® Onion, Onion-Mushroom or Beefy Mushroom Recipe Soup Mix
4 cups water
1 can (16 ounces) chick peas or garbanzo beans, rinsed and drained
1 can (16 ounces) red kidney beans, rinsed and drained
1 can (14½ ounces) whole peeled tomatoes, drained and chopped (reserve liquid)
1 cup uncooked lentils, rinsed
1 large stalk celery, coarsely chopped
1 tablespoon chili powder
2 teaspoons ground cumin
1 medium clove garlic, finely chopped
¼ teaspoon crushed red pepper
Hot cooked brown or regular rice
Shredded Cheddar cheese

In large saucepan or stockpot, combine all ingredients except rice and cheese. Bring to a boil, then simmer covered for 20 minutes or until lentils are almost tender. Remove cover and simmer, stirring occasionally, an additional 30 minutes or until liquid is almost absorbed and lentils are tender. Serve, if desired, over rice and top with shredded cheese.
Makes 6 to 8 servings

Texas Fajita Chili

1¼ cups chopped onion
1 cup chopped green bell pepper
1 tablespoon vegetable oil
2 cans (15¼ ounces each) kidney beans, drained
1 pound shredded, cooked pork or beef
1 can (14½ ounces) whole peeled tomatoes, undrained and cut up
1 cup LAWRY'S® Fajitas Skillet Sauce
1 can (7 ounces) whole kernel corn, drained
½ cup tomato juice or beer
1½ teaspoons chili powder

In large skillet, sauté onion and bell pepper in oil 10 minutes or until tender. Stir in kidney beans, shredded meat, tomatoes, Fajitas Skillet Sauce, corn, tomato juice and chili powder. Bring mixture to a boil; reduce heat, cover and simmer 20 minutes.

Makes 6 servings

Presentation: Serve in individual bowls topped with grated Monterey Jack cheese or sour cream. If desired, serve with dash of hot pepper sauce.

Hearty Turkey Chili

1 cup chopped onions
1 cup chopped green pepper
2 cloves garlic, minced
1 tablespoon vegetable oil
2 pounds ground raw turkey
2 cans (14½ ounces each) tomatoes, cut into bite-size pieces
1 bottle (12 ounces) HEINZ® Chili Sauce
1 tablespoon chili powder
1 teaspoon lemon pepper seasoning
1 teaspoon dried basil leaves, crushed
½ teaspoon dried thyme leaves, crushed
⅛ to ¼ teaspoon hot pepper sauce
2 cans (15½ ounces each) kidney beans, drained
Sliced green onions
Shredded Cheddar cheese
Dairy sour cream or plain yogurt

SALADS

Salads are not only refreshing and healthy, but easy to prepare and delicious! Sample an unbeatable variety of crisp vegetable salads, tossed green salads, creamy salad dressings, molded gelatin salads, ever-popular pasta salads, delightful fruit salads and main-dish meat, poultry and seafood salads. Whether you're looking for a simple side dish, a light lunch or a substantial supper, you'll find it here.

Ensalada Simplese

5 cups torn lettuce (combination of romaine and iceberg)
½ cup chopped zucchini
1 can (7 ounces) whole kernel corn, drained
½ cup diced red bell pepper
¼ cup sliced green onions
⅓ cup dairy sour cream
2 tablespoons mayonnaise
1 teaspoon lemon juice
¾ teaspoon dry mustard
½ teaspoon LAWRY'S® Seasoned Salt
½ teaspoon LAWRY'S® Garlic Powder with Parsley

In large bowl, combine lettuce, zucchini, corn, bell pepper and green onions. Refrigerate. In separate small bowl, combine remaining ingredients. Refrigerate. To serve, gently toss greens and dressing.

Makes 4 to 6 servings

Hint: Adding shredded, cooked chicken or cooked shrimp turns this salad into a main dish.

Dilly Cucumber Salad

1 (8-ounce) container BORDEN® or MEADOW GOLD® Sour Cream
¼ cup REALEMON® Lemon Juice from Concentrate
2 to 3 tablespoons sugar
1 teaspoon salt
½ teaspoon dill weed
1 medium cucumber, seeded and sliced
1 medium sweet white onion, sliced and separated into rings

In medium bowl, combine sour cream, ReaLemon® brand, sugar, salt and dill weed; mix well. Add cucumber and onion. Cover; chill. Refrigerate leftovers.

Makes about 3 cups

Tip: Recipe can be doubled.

Avocado Raspberry Spice Salad

¼ cup seedless raspberry jam
3 tablespoons vegetable oil
2½ tablespoons white wine vinegar
¾ teaspoon LAWRY'S® Lemon Pepper Seasoning
¾ teaspoon LAWRY'S® Seasoned Salt
2½ cups shredded napa cabbage
1½ cups shredded red cabbage
2 medium tomatoes, cut into wedges
1 avocado, cubed
½ medium cucumber, thinly sliced
2 tablespoons chopped green onion

In container with stopper or lid, combine raspberry jam, oil, vinegar, Lemon Pepper Seasoning and Seasoned Salt; blend well. On 4 individual serving plates, arrange napa and red cabbage. Decoratively arrange tomatoes, avocado and cucumber on top. Sprinkle with green onion. Drizzle dressing over each serving.

Makes 4 servings

Presentation: Serve with a light French bread or croissants.

Ensalada Simplese

Herbed Tomato Cucumber Salad

Mustard Tarragon Marinade

> **3 tablespoons red wine vinegar**
> **1 tablespoon Dijon mustard**
> **1½ teaspoons dried tarragon**
> **2 tablespoons olive oil**

Combine first three ingredients. Slowly whisk oil into mixture until slightly thickened.

Walnut Dressing

> **½ cup walnuts**
> **¼ cup olive or vegetable oil**
> **2 tablespoons REALEMON® Lemon Juice from Concentrate**
> **½ clove garlic**

In blender or food processor, combine ingredients; blend until nuts are finely chopped. Cover; chill. Serve with fruit or green salads. Refrigerate leftovers.

Makes about ½ cup

Tip: Recipe can be doubled.

Dill Onion Vinaigrette

> **½ cup vegetable oil**
> **⅓ cup HEINZ® Apple Cider Vinegar**
> **2 tablespoons chopped green onions**
> **1 teaspoon dried dill weed**
> **½ teaspoon salt**
> **½ teaspoon dry mustard**

In jar, combine all ingredients; cover and shake vigorously. Chill to blend flavors. Shake again before serving with mixed garden salads.

Makes about 1 cup

Herbed Tomato Cucumber Salad

> **½ cup MIRACLE WHIP® FREE® Dressing**
> **1 cucumber, peeled, seeded, chopped**
> **⅓ cup each: finely chopped red onion, finely chopped fresh basil**
> **¼ teaspoon salt**
> **3 tomatoes, sliced**

• Mix all ingredients except tomatoes until well blended; refrigerate. Spoon over tomatoes.

Makes 6 servings

Prep time: 10 minutes plus refrigerating

Marinated Vegetable Spinach Salad

> **Mustard Tarragon Marinade (recipe follows)**
> **8 ounces fresh mushrooms, quartered**
> **2 slices purple onion, separated into rings**
> **16 cherry tomatoes, halved**
> **4 cups fresh spinach leaves, washed and stems removed**
> **3 slices (3 oz.) SARGENTO® Preferred Light™ Sliced Mozzarella Cheese, cut into julienne strips**
> **Fresh ground black pepper**

Prepare marinade. Place mushrooms, onion and tomatoes in bowl. Toss with marinade and let stand 15 minutes. Meanwhile, wash and dry spinach leaves. Arrange on 4 individual serving plates. Divide marinated vegetables between plates and top each salad with ¼ of the cheese. Serve with fresh ground pepper, if desired.

Makes 4 servings

Italian Herb Dressing

- **⅔ cup vegetable oil**
- **⅓ cup HEINZ® Gourmet Wine Vinegar**
- **1 clove garlic, split**
- **1 teaspoon dry mustard**
- **½ teaspoon salt**
- **½ teaspoon dried basil leaves, crushed**
- **½ teaspoon dried oregano leaves, crushed**
- **¼ teaspoon crushed red pepper**

In jar, combine all ingredients; cover and shake vigorously. Chill to blend flavors. Remove garlic; shake again before serving over tossed green salads.

Makes 1 cup

Thousand Island Dressing

- **⅔ cup PET® Light Evaporated Skimmed Milk**
- **⅔ cup bottled chili sauce**
- **⅔ cup HOLLYWOOD® Safflower Oil**
- **¼ cup sweet pickle relish**
- **1 tablespoon lemon juice**
- **1 tablespoon sugar**
- **1 teaspoon salt**
- **⅛ teaspoon ground black pepper**

Using a wire whisk combine all ingredients in a small bowl. Refrigerate until well chilled. Serve over tossed green salad.

Makes about 2 cups

Rosy Cucumber Dressing

- **½ cup HEINZ® Chili Sauce**
- **½ cup mayonnaise or salad dressing**
- **½ cup coarsely shredded unpeeled cucumber, drained**
- **1 tablespoon grated onion**

In small bowl, combine chili sauce, mayonnaise, cucumber and onion. Cover; chill several hours to blend flavors. Serve over mixed salad greens.

Makes about 1½ cups

Buttermilk Pepper Dressing

- **1 cup buttermilk**
- **½ cup MIRACLE WHIP® Salad Dressing**
- **2 tablespoons KRAFT® 100% Grated Parmesan Cheese**
- **1 teaspoon coarse grind pepper**
- **1 garlic clove, minced**

• Mix ingredients until well blended; refrigerate. Serve with mixed salad greens.

Makes 1 cup

Prep time: 5 minutes plus refrigerating

Family French Dressing

- **½ cup HEINZ® Tomato Ketchup**
- **½ cup vegetable oil**
- **¼ cup HEINZ® Apple Cider Vinegar**
- **1 tablespoon confectioners sugar**
- **1 clove garlic, split**
- **¼ teaspoon salt**
- **Dash pepper**

In jar, combine all ingredients; cover and shake vigorously. Chill to blend flavors. Remove garlic; shake again before serving over tossed green salads.

Makes 1¼ cups

Buttermilk Pepper Dressing

Yogurt Dressing

2 cups plain lowfat yogurt
4 teaspoons chopped fresh
**   mint *or* ¼ teaspoon dried**
**   dill weed**
⅛ teaspoon TABASCO®
**   pepper sauce**

In small bowl combine yogurt, mint and Tabasco® pepper sauce; mix well. Cover; refrigerate.
Makes 2 cups

Creamy Warm Bacon Dressing

4 slices OSCAR MAYER®
**   Bacon, chopped**
1 garlic clove, minced
1 cup MIRACLE WHIP® Salad
**   Dressing**
½ cup milk

• Cook bacon until crisp. Drain, reserving 1 tablespoon drippings.

• Heat reserved drippings, bacon and garlic over low heat 1 minute.

• Stir in salad dressing and milk. Continue cooking, stirring occasionally, until thoroughly heated. Serve with spinach salad.   *Makes 1½ cups*

Prep time: 10 minutes
Cooking time: 10 minutes

Celery Seed Dressing

½ cup sugar
¼ cup REALEMON® Lemon
**   Juice from Concentrate**
2 teaspoons cider vinegar
1 teaspoon dry mustard
½ teaspoon salt
½ cup vegetable oil
1 teaspoon celery seed or
**   poppy seed**

In blender or food processor, combine all ingredients except oil and celery seed; blend until smooth. On low speed, continue blending, slowly adding oil. Stir in celery seed. Cover; chill. Serve with salad of lettuce and sliced sweet onion if desired. Refrigerate leftovers.   *Makes about 1 cup*

Celery Seed Dressing

Marinated Confetti Coleslaw

5 cups coarsely shredded
**   cabbage (about 1 pound)**
1 large fresh tomato, seeded
**   and diced**
½ cup chopped green bell
**   pepper**
⅓ cup sliced green onions
½ cup REALEMON® Lemon
**   Juice from Concentrate**
⅓ cup sugar
⅓ cup vegetable oil
1 teaspoon salt
½ teaspoon dry mustard

In medium bowl, combine cabbage, tomato, green pepper and green onions. In small saucepan, combine remaining ingredients; bring to a boil. Pour over vegetables. Cover; chill 4 hours or overnight to blend flavors. Refrigerate leftovers.
Makes 6 to 8 servings

Creamy Warm Bacon Dressing

Pineapple-Chili-Cheese Slaw

1 can (20 ounces) DOLE®
   Pineapple Chunks in
   Juice
6 cups shredded DOLE®
   Green Cabbage
1 cup shredded red cabbage
1 can (15¼ ounces) dark red
   kidney beans, drained
1 can (4 ounces) diced green
   chiles
1 can (4 ounces) sliced ripe
   olives
1½ cups (6 ounces) shredded
   Cheddar cheese

Cumin-Garlic Dressing
½ cup reserved pineapple
   juice
¼ cup white vinegar
1 teaspoon ground cumin
½ teaspoon salt
1 clove garlic, pressed

• Drain pineapple; reserve ½ cup
juice for dressing.

• Combine all salad ingredients
in bowl. Pour Cumin-Garlic
Dressing over salad; toss to coat.
Makes 4 to 6 servings

Cumin-Garlic Dressing: Combine
all dressing ingredients in screw-
top jar; shake well.

Preparation Time: 20 minutes

Cashew Pea Salad

½ cup MIRACLE WHIP®
   FREE® Dressing
2 tablespoons lemon juice
½ teaspoon dill weed
1 package (10 ounces) BIRDS
   EYE® Peas, thawed,
   drained
2 cups cauliflowerets
1 can (8 ounces) sliced water
   chestnuts, drained
¼ cup chopped red onion
¼ cup cashews

Santa Fe Potato Salad

• Mix salad dressing, juice and
dill until well blended. Add all
remaining ingredients except
cashews; mix well. Refrigerate.
Sprinkle with cashews just
before serving.
Makes 6 cups

Prep time: 15 minutes plus
   refrigerating

Santa Fe Potato Salad

6 medium white potatoes
½ cup vegetable oil
½ cup red wine vinegar
1 package (1.25 ounces)
   LAWRY'S® Taco Spices &
   Seasonings
1 can (7 ounces) whole
   kernel corn, drained
⅔ cup sliced celery
⅔ cup shredded carrot
⅔ cup chopped red or green
   bell pepper
2 cans (2¼ ounces each)
   sliced ripe olives, drained
½ cup chopped red onion
2 tomatoes, wedged, halved

In large saucepan, cook potatoes
in boiling water to cover until
tender, about 40 minutes; drain.
Cool slightly; cut into cubes. In
small bowl, combine oil, vinegar
and Taco Spices & Seasonings.
Add to warm potatoes and toss
gently to coat. Cover; refrigerate
at least 1 hour. Gently fold in
remaining ingredients.
Refrigerate until thoroughly
chilled. *Makes 10 servings*

Presentation: Serve in lettuce-
lined bowl with hamburgers or
deli sandwiches.

Creamier Version: Prepare
potatoes as above. Replace the
vinegar and oil with ½ cup *each*
mayonnaise, dairy sour cream
and salsa. Mix with Taco Spices
& Seasonings and continue as
above.

Green Bean, New Potato & Ham Salad

3 pounds new potatoes, quartered
⅔ cup cold water
1 pound green beans, cut in half
¾ cup MIRACLE WHIP® FREE® Dressing
⅓ cup stone ground mustard
2 tablespoons red wine vinegar
2 cups cubed OSCAR MAYER® Ham
½ cup chopped green onions

• Place potatoes and ⅓ cup water in 3-quart microwave-safe casserole; cover.

• Microwave on HIGH 13 minutes. Stir in beans. Microwave 7 to 13 minutes or until tender; drain.

• Mix salad dressing, mustard and vinegar in large bowl until well blended. Add potatoes, beans and remaining ingredients; mix lightly. Refrigerate.   *Makes 12 cups*

Prep time: 15 minutes plus refrigerating
Microwave cooking time: 26 minutes

Bacon Ranch Potato Salad

3 pounds new potatoes, cut into ¼-inch slices
⅓ cup cold water
½ cup MIRACLE WHIP® Salad Dressing
¼ cup RANCHER'S CHOICE® Creamy Dressing
¼ teaspoon each: salt, pepper
⅛ teaspoon garlic powder
6 slices OSCAR MAYER® Bacon, crisply cooked, crumbled
½ cup each: celery slices, thin red bell pepper strips, sliced green onions

• Place potatoes and water in 3-quart microwave-safe casserole; cover.

• Microwave on HIGH 14 to 16 minutes or until tender, stirring after 8 minutes. Drain.

• Mix dressings and seasonings in large bowl until well blended. Add potatoes and remaining ingredients; mix well. Serve immediately or refrigerate.
   Makes 8 cups

Prep time: 15 minutes
Microwave cooking time: 16 minutes

Microwave Potato Salad

7 cups (2½ pounds) cubed red potatoes
⅓ cup cold water
¾ cup MIRACLE WHIP® Salad Dressing
¼ cup milk
¾ cup (3 ounces) KRAFT® Natural Shredded Cheddar Cheese
¾ cup (3 ounces) KRAFT® Natural Shredded Swiss Cheese
½ cup sliced green onions
2 hard-cooked eggs, chopped
½ teaspoon each: salt, pepper

• Place potatoes and water in 3-quart microwave-safe casserole; cover.

• Microwave on HIGH 16 to 18 minutes or until tender, stirring after 9 minutes. Drain.

• Add remaining ingredients; mix well. Refrigerate.
   Makes 7 cups

Prep time: 20 minutes plus refrigerating
Microwave cooking time: 18 minutes

Seafood Pea-Ista Salad

½ cup mayonnaise or salad dressing
¼ cup zesty Italian salad dressing
2 tablespoons grated Parmesan cheese
2 cups canned green or yellow black-eyed peas, rinsed
8 ounces corkscrew pasta, cooked, rinsed and drained
1½ cups chopped imitation crabmeat (about 8 ounces)
1 cup broccoli flowerets, partially cooked
½ cup chopped green pepper
½ cup chopped tomato
¼ cup sliced green onions

Combine mayonnaise, Italian salad dressing and cheese in large bowl; blend well. Add peas, pasta, imitation crabmeat, broccoli, pepper, tomato and onions; toss gently to mix. Cover; refrigerate at least 2 hours.
   Makes 4 to 6 servings

*Favorite recipe from the **Black-Eyed Pea Jamboree—Athens, Texas***

Lanai Pasta Salad

1 can (20 ounces) DOLE® Pineapple Chunks in Juice
3 cups cooked spiral pasta
2 cups DOLE® Sugar Peas
1 cup sliced DOLE® Carrots
1 cup sliced cucumbers
½ cup bottled reduced-calorie Italian salad dressing
¼ cup chopped cilantro or parsley

• Drain pineapple; reserve ¼ cup juice. Combine pineapple, reserved juice and remaining ingredients in large bowl; toss to coat.   *Makes 6 to 8 servings*

Preparation Time: 15 minutes

Seafood Pea-Ista Salad

Pasta Salad in Artichoke Cups

Ham Tortellini Salad

- **1 (7- to 8-ounce) package cheese-filled spinach tortellini**
- **3 cups (12 ounces) ARMOUR® Lower Salt Ham, cut into ¾-inch cubes**
- **½ cup sliced green onions**
- **10 cherry tomatoes, cut in half**
- **1 cup bottled low sodium creamy buttermilk *or* reduced calorie zesty Italian salad dressing**
- **Leaf lettuce or butterhead lettuce, washed and drained**
- **¼ cup finely chopped red pepper**

Cook tortellini according to package directions omitting salt; drain and run under cold water to cool. Combine all ingredients *except* leaf lettuce and red pepper in large bowl. Toss until well blended. Serve on lettuce-lined salad plates. Sprinkle with red pepper. Serve immediately.
Makes 6 servings

Pasta Salad in Artichoke Cups

- **5 cloves garlic**
- **½ cup white wine**
- **6 medium artichokes for cups**
- **1 lemon, cut into halves**
- **1 tablespoon *plus* 1 teaspoon olive oil, divided**
- **Chicken broth**
- **Basil Vinaigrette Dressing (recipe follows)**
- **8 ounces uncooked corkscrew pasta or pasta twists, cooked, rinsed and drained**
- **½ teaspoon dried basil leaves, crushed**
- **2 cups sliced cooked artichoke hearts (not marinated)**

Simmer garlic and wine in small saucepan 10 minutes. Meanwhile, cut bottoms of artichokes flat and remove outer leaves. Cut 1 inch from tops; snip tips from remaining leaves and rub ends with lemon. Add artichokes, wine-garlic mixture and 1 tablespoon oil to 2 inches boiling chicken broth in large saucepan. Cover; simmer 25 to 30 minutes or until leaves pull easily from base. Drain.

Prepare Basil Vinaigrette Dressing. Sprinkle pasta with remaining 1 teaspoon oil and basil.

Combine pasta, sliced artichoke hearts and 1 cup dressing in large bowl; toss gently to coat. Carefully spread outer leaves of whole artichokes; remove the small heart leaves and scoop out the fuzzy choke. Fill with pasta mixture. Cover; refrigerate until serving time. Serve with remaining dressing. Garnish as desired.   *Makes 6 servings*

BASIL VINAIGRETTE DRESSING: Combine ⅓ cup wine vinegar, 2 tablespoons Dijon mustard and 3 minced garlic cloves in blender or food processor. Cover; pulse until well mixed. Add ¾ cup coarsely cut fresh basil leaves; pulse to blend. With motor running, slowly pour in 1 cup olive oil. Add salt and pepper to taste.

*Favorite recipe from **Castroville Artichoke Festival***

Ham Tortellini Salad

Beef & Pasta Salad

3 cups CREAMETTE® Rotini, cooked as package directs and drained
1 pound boneless stir-fry beef strips
2 teaspoons WYLER'S® or STEERO® Beef-Flavor Instant Bouillon
2 tablespoons vegetable or olive oil
1 cup bottled Italian salad dressing
6 ounces Provolone cheese, cut into cubes
1 large green bell pepper, cut into strips
1 cup cherry tomato halves
½ cup sliced pitted ripe olives
Grated Parmesan cheese, optional

In large skillet, brown meat and *1 teaspoon* bouillon in oil; remove from skillet. In large bowl, combine meat, rotini, salad dressing and remaining *1 teaspoon* bouillon; let stand 15 minutes. Add remaining ingredients except Parmesan cheese; mix well. Cover; chill. Serve with Parmesan cheese if desired. Refrigerate leftovers.

Makes 4 servings

Rainbow Pasta Salad

8 ounces uncooked tricolor corkscrew pasta, cooked, rinsed, drained and cooled
2 cans (4½ ounces each) medium shrimp, drained or ½ pound cooked fresh shrimp, peeled
½ cup chopped walnuts (optional)
¼ cup French salad dressing
¼ cup mayonnaise
2 tablespoons sliced pimiento-stuffed green olives
1 teaspoon finely chopped onion
Lettuce leaves
Grape clusters (optional)
Lemon peel strips (optional)

Combine pasta, shrimp, walnuts, salad dressing, mayonnaise, olives and onion in large bowl; toss gently to coat. Cover; refrigerate at least 2 hours. Serve over lettuce. Garnish with grapes and lemon peel.

Makes 4 servings

Favorite recipe from **North Dakota Wheat Commission**

Creamy Pesto Pasta Salad

1 package (7 ounces) refrigerated prepared pesto
½ cup MIRACLE WHIP® Salad Dressing
3 cups (8 ounces) rotini, cooked, drained
½ cup pitted ripe olive slices
3 tablespoons chopped sun-dried tomatoes in oil, drained
½ teaspoon pepper

• Mix pesto and salad dressing until well blended. Add remaining ingredients; mix well. Refrigerate.   *Makes 4 cups*

Prep time: 15 minutes plus refrigerating

The Best Macaroni Salad

5 cups (16 ounces) elbow macaroni, cooked, drained
1 cup MIRACLE WHIP® Salad Dressing
1 cup each: chopped red bell pepper, chopped cucumber
1 package (8 ounces) KRAFT® Natural Cheddar Cheese, cubed
½ cup chopped green onions
½ teaspoon each: salt, coarse grind pepper

• Mix ingredients until well blended; refrigerate.
Makes 8¼ cups

Prep time: 15 minutes plus refrigerating

Rainbow Pasta Salad

Thai Chicken Fettuccine Salad

- 1 cup PACE® Picante Sauce
- ¼ cup chunky peanut butter
- 2 tablespoons honey
- 2 tablespoons orange juice
- 1 teaspoon soy sauce
- ½ teaspoon ground ginger
- 6 ounces uncooked fettuccine, hot cooked and drained
- 3 chicken breast halves (about 12 ounces), boned, skinned and cut into 1-inch pieces
- 2 tablespoons vegetable oil Lettuce or savoy cabbage leaves (optional)
- ¼ cup coarsely chopped cilantro
- ¼ cup peanut halves
- ¼ cup thin red pepper strips, cut into halves Additional PACE® Picante Sauce (optional)

Combine picante sauce, peanut butter, honey, orange juice, soy sauce and ginger in small saucepan. Cook and stir over low heat until blended and smooth. Reserve ¼ cup picante sauce mixture. Place fettuccine in large bowl. Pour remaining picante sauce mixture over fettuccine; toss gently to coat.

Cook chicken in oil in large skillet over medium-high heat until browned and cooked, about 5 minutes. Add reserved picante sauce mixture; mix well. Arrange fettuccine over lettuce-lined platter. Top with chicken mixture. Sprinkle cilantro, peanut halves and pepper strips over top. Refrigerate to cool to room temperature. Serve with additional picante sauce. Garnish as desired.

Makes 4 servings

Chicken Salad Deluxe

- 1¼ cups prepared buttermilk salad dressing
- ½ cup mayonnaise
- 3 tablespoons half-and-half
- 1¾ teaspoons Beau Monde seasoning
- 1 teaspoon salt
- ½ teaspoon pepper
- 5 whole chicken breasts (about 2 pounds), skinned, cooked and cubed
- 10 ounces uncooked 100% semolina medium shell macaroni, cooked, rinsed, drained and cooled
- 3 cups diced celery
- 2½ cups seedless green grapes, cut lengthwise into halves
- 1 package (12 ounces) slivered almonds, reserve 1 tablespoon for garnish
- 2 cans (2.25 ounces each) sliced water chestnuts, drained
- ½ cup chopped onion Lettuce leaves Parsley (optional) Sliced star fruit (optional) Cantelope slices

Combine salad dressing, mayonnaise, half-and-half, seasoning, salt and pepper in small bowl; blend well. Cover; refrigerate overnight to blend flavors.

Combine chicken, shells, celery, grapes, almonds, water chestnuts and onion in large bowl. Pour dressing over salad; toss gently to coat. Serve on lettuce. Garnish with reserved almonds, parsley and star fruit. Serve with cantelope slices.

Makes 20 servings

*Favorite recipe from **North Dakota Wheat Commission***

Thai Chicken Fettuccine Salad

Chicken Salad Deluxe

Party Pasta Salad

1 package (12 ounces)
    corkscrew pasta
1 can (20 ounces) DOLE®
    Pineapple Chunks in
    Juice
1 cup vegetable oil
½ cup distilled white vinegar
1 tablespoon Dijon mustard
1 tablespoon Worcestershire
    sauce
1 clove garlic, pressed
    Salt and pepper to taste
3 cups DOLE® Cauliflower
    florettes
3 cups DOLE® Broccoli
    florettes
1 DOLE® Red Bell Pepper,
    seeded, chunked
1 cup DOLE® Whole Natural
    Almonds, toasted

• Cook noodles according to
package directions.

• Drain pineapple; reserve 3
tablespoons juice for dressing.

• For dressing, combine reserved
juice, oil, vinegar, mustard,
Worcestershire sauce, garlic, salt
and pepper in a screw-top jar;
shake well.

• Combine noodles and
cauliflower in large bowl. Pour
dressing over salad; toss to coat.

• Cover and marinate in
refrigerator overnight.

• Add broccoli, red pepper and
almonds; toss to coat.
    Makes 12 to 15 servings

Preparation Time: 20 minutes
Cook Time: 10 minutes
Marinate Time: overnight

Black Bean and Rice Salad

2 cups cooked rice, cooled to
    room temperature
1 cup cooked black beans*
1 medium tomato, seeded
    and chopped
½ cup (2 ounces) shredded
    Cheddar cheese
    (optional)
1 tablespoon snipped parsley
¼ cup prepared light Italian
    dressing
1 tablespoon lime juice
    Lettuce leaves

Combine rice, beans, tomato,
cheese and parsley in large bowl.
Pour dressing and lime juice
over rice mixture; toss lightly.
Serve on lettuce leaves.
    Makes 4 servings

*Substitute canned black beans,
drained, for the cooked beans, if
desired.

*Favorite recipe from **USA Rice
Council***

Party Pasta Salad

Cobb Salad

• Mix salad dressing, soy sauce and ginger until well blended.

• Add chicken, pea pods, carrots, onions and sesame seeds; mix well. Refrigerate. Serve on lettuce-covered platter.

Makes 4 servings

Variation: Substitute 3 cups chopped cooked chicken for fried chicken.

Prep time: 20 minutes plus refrigerating

Cobb Salad

   4 skinless boneless chicken breast halves, cooked, cooled
   ⅔ cup vegetable oil
   ⅓ cup HEINZ® Distilled White or Apple Cider Vinegar
   1 clove garlic, minced
   2 teaspoons dried dill weed
   1½ teaspoons granulated sugar
   ½ teaspoon salt
   ¼ teaspoon pepper
   8 cups torn salad greens, chilled
   1 large tomato, diced
   1 medium green bell pepper, diced
   1 small red onion, chopped
   ¾ cup crumbled blue cheese
   6 slices bacon, cooked, crumbled
   1 hard-cooked egg, chopped

Shred chicken into bite-size pieces. For dressing, in jar, combine oil, vinegar, garlic, dill, sugar, salt and pepper; cover and shake vigorously. Pour ½ cup dressing over chicken; toss well to coat. Toss greens with remaining dressing. Line each of 4 large individual salad bowls with greens; mound chicken mixture in center. Arrange mounds of tomato, green pepper, onion, cheese, bacon and egg around chicken.

Makes 4 servings

Spicy Cajun Rice Salad

   2 cups Original MINUTE® Rice
   ½ cup prepared GOOD SEASONS® Italian or Zesty Italian Salad Dressing
   1½ teaspoons hot pepper sauce
   2 teaspoons prepared hot spicy mustard
   2 hard-cooked eggs, chopped
   ½ cup diced celery
   ½ cup toasted chopped pecans
   ¼ cup sliced scallions
   ¼ cup sliced stuffed green olives
   ¼ cup chopped parsley
   ¼ cup sweet pickle relish
   1 tablespoon diced dill pickle

Prepare rice according to package directions.

Combine salad dressing, pepper sauce and mustard in small bowl; blend well. Combine rice with remaining ingredients in large bowl. Spoon dressing mixture over salad, tossing to coat. Cover and chill.

Makes 6 servings

Chinese Chicken Salad

   ½ cup MIRACLE WHIP® Salad Dressing
   1 tablespoon soy sauce
   ½ teaspoon ground ginger
   4 large pieces carry-out fried chicken, chilled, coarsely chopped (about 3 cups)
   1 cup Chinese pea pods, sliced lengthwise
   ½ cup shredded carrot
   ¼ cup chopped green onions
   1 tablespoon sesame seeds, toasted
   3 cups shredded lettuce

Grilled Chicken Salad

- ¾ **pound boned and skinned chicken breast**
- ½ **teaspoon salt**
- ½ **teaspoon ground black pepper**
- 1½ **cups diagonally sliced small zucchini**
- 3 **cups cooked rice, cooled to room temperature**
- 1 **can (14 ounces) artichoke hearts, drained**
- ¾ **cup fresh snow peas, blanched***
- ½ **medium-sized red pepper, cut into 1-inch cubes**
- ⅓ **cup light Italian salad dressing**
- 1 **teaspoon chopped fresh basil leaves**
  Lettuce leaves

Season chicken with salt and black pepper. Grill or broil chicken breast. Add zucchini during last 5 minutes of grilling or broiling. Cover and chill chicken and zucchini; cut chicken into ¾-inch cubes. Combine rice, chicken, zucchini, artichokes, snow peas, and red pepper in large bowl. Blend dressing and basil in small bowl. Pour over salad; toss lightly. Serve on lettuce leaves.

Makes 4 servings

*Substitute frozen snow peas, thawed, for fresh snow peas, if desired.

Favorite recipe from **USA Rice Council**

Grilled Chicken Salad

California Chicken Salad

Lemon-Mustard Dressing
- ⅔ **cup olive or vegetable oil**
- ⅓ **cup lemon juice**
- 1½ **teaspoons dry mustard**
  Salt and pepper, to taste

Salad
- 1 **package (6 ounces) long-grain and wild rice blend**
- 2¾ **cups chicken broth, divided**
- 2 **whole chicken breasts, split, boned and skinned**
- 2 **stalks celery, thinly sliced**
- 1 **green bell pepper, chopped**
- ½ **cup chopped red onion**
- 16 **lettuce leaves**
- 3 **fresh California peaches, sliced**

In small bowl, combine all dressing ingredients; set aside. In medium, covered saucepan, cook rice and seasoning packet in 1¾ cups broth 30 minutes. Cool. Meanwhile, in large, covered skillet, poach chicken breasts in remaining 1 cup broth 15 to 20 minutes or until cooked through. Cool; shred chicken. Combine rice with celery, bell pepper and onion. Line serving platter or individual salad plates with lettuce leaves. Arrange ⅔ cup rice, chicken and peach slices on lettuce. Serve Lemon-Mustard Dressing separately.

Makes 4 servings

Favorite recipe from **California Tree Fruit Agreement**

Tropical Chicken Salad

4 cups cubed cooked chicken or turkey
2 large oranges, peeled, sectioned and drained
1½ cups cut-up fresh pineapple, drained
1 cup seedless green grape halves
1 cup sliced celery
¾ cup mayonnaise or salad dressing
3 to 4 tablespoons REALEMON® Lemon Juice from Concentrate
½ teaspoon ground ginger
½ teaspoon salt
½ to ¾ cup nuts

In large bowl, combine chicken, fruit and celery; mix well. Cover; chill. In small bowl, combine remaining ingredients except nuts. Cover; chill. Just before serving, combine chicken mixture, dressing and nuts. Serve in hollowed-out pineapple shells or on lettuce leaves if desired. Refrigerate leftovers.

Makes 4 to 6 servings

Oriental Chicken Salad

4 skinned boneless chicken breast halves (about 1½ pounds)
½ cup water
⅓ cup cider vinegar
3 tablespoons vegetable oil
2 tablespoons brown sugar
1 tablespoon soy sauce
2 teaspoons WYLER'S® or STEERO® Chicken-Flavor Instant Bouillon or 2 Chicken-Flavor Bouillon Cubes
Napa (Chinese cabbage)
Alfalfa sprouts, fresh mushrooms, carrot curls and pea pods

Arrange chicken in shallow baking dish. In small saucepan, combine water, vinegar, *1 tablespoon* oil, sugar, soy sauce and bouillon; cook and stir until bouillon dissolves. Cool. Reserving *½ cup* dressing, pour remainder over chicken. Cover; marinate in refrigerator 30 minutes. Remove chicken from marinade. In skillet, cook chicken in remaining *2 tablespoons* oil until tender. Cut into thin slices. Line plates with napa. Top with chicken, sprouts, mushrooms, carrots and pea pods. Serve with reserved dressing. Refrigerate leftovers.

Makes 4 servings

Mexican Chicken Salad

1 pound skinned boneless chicken breasts, cut into strips
2 tablespoons margarine or butter
½ cup water
2 teaspoons WYLER'S® or STEERO® Chicken-Flavor Instant Bouillon or 2 Chicken-Flavor Bouillon Cubes
1 teaspoon chili powder
½ teaspoon ground cumin
½ teaspoon garlic powder
1½ cups BORDEN® or MEADOW GOLD® Sour Cream, at room temperature
4 tortillas or tostada shells, fried or warmed
Shredded lettuce
Garnishes: chopped tomato, sliced green onions and pitted ripe olives

In large skillet, brown chicken in margarine. Add water, bouillon, chili powder, cumin and garlic powder. Cover; simmer 5 to 10 minutes or until chicken is tender. Stir in sour cream; heat through (*do not boil*). Top each tortilla with lettuce then chicken mixture. Garnish as desired. Refrigerate leftovers.

Makes 4 servings

Turkey Ensalada con Queso

2 cups cooked rice, cooled to room temperature
1½ cups cooked turkey breast cubes
½ cup (2 ounces) jalapeño Monterey Jack cheese, cut into ½-inch cubes
1 can (4 ounces) diced green chiles, undrained
2 tablespoons snipped parsley
¼ cup cholesterol free, reduced calorie mayonnaise
¼ cup plain nonfat yogurt
Lettuce leaves
Tomato wedges for garnish

Combine rice, turkey, cheese, chiles, and parsley in large bowl. Blend mayonnaise and yogurt; add to rice mixture and toss lightly. Serve on lettuce leaves; garnish with tomato wedges.

Makes 4 servings

Favorite recipe from **USA Rice Council**

Oriental Chicken Salad

Smoked Turkey & Artichoke Salad with Hearts of Palm

½ cup MIRACLE WHIP® Salad Dressing
⅓ cup KRAFT® House Italian Dressing
½ teaspoon coarse grind pepper
¼ teaspoon dried tarragon leaves, crushed
3 cups cubed LOUIS RICH® Hickory Smoked Breast of Turkey
1 can (14 ounces) artichoke hearts, drained, quartered
⅓ cup each: chopped green, red and yellow bell peppers
1 can (14 ounces) hearts of palm, drained
1 pint cherry tomatoes

• Mix dressings and seasonings until well blended.

• Stir in turkey, artichokes and peppers; refrigerate. Serve with hearts of palm and tomatoes.
Makes 6 cups

Prep time: 20 minutes plus refrigerating

Turkey Waldorf Salad

⅔ cups HELLMANN'S® or BEST FOODS® Real, Light or Cholesterol Free Reduced Calorie Mayonnaise
2 tablespoons lemon juice
½ teaspoon salt
¼ teaspoon freshly ground pepper
2 cups diced cooked turkey or chicken
2 red apples, cored and diced
⅔ cup sliced celery
½ cup chopped walnuts

In large bowl combine mayonnaise, lemon juice, salt and pepper. Add turkey, apples and celery; toss to coat well. Cover; chill. Just before serving, sprinkle with walnuts.
Makes about 4 to 6 servings

Tucson Turkey Salad

1 (8-ounce) container BORDEN® or MEADOW GOLD® Sour Cream
1 tablespoon REALIME® Lime Juice from Concentrate
2 teaspoons WYLER'S® or STEERO® Chicken-Flavor Instant Bouillon
½ teaspoon ground cumin
Dash hot pepper sauce
½ pound smoked cooked turkey breast, thinly sliced
½ pound Cheddar cheese, thinly sliced
1 medium apple, cored and sliced
1 cup sliced celery
½ cup thin strips pared jicama
Lettuce leaves
½ cup chopped walnuts, toasted

In medium bowl, combine sour cream, ReaLime® brand, bouillon, cumin and hot pepper sauce. Cover; chill 1 hour. Arrange turkey, cheese, apple, celery and jicama on lettuce. Top with walnuts. Serve with dressing.* Refrigerate leftovers.
Makes 4 servings

*For thinner dressing, add milk to desired consistency.

Smoked Turkey & Artichoke Salad with Hearts of Palm

Layered Turkey Salad

1½ cups salad dressing or mayonnaise
1 hard-cooked egg, pressed through a sieve or finely chopped
2 tablespoons chopped fresh parsley
2 tablespoons REALEMON® Lemon Juice from Concentrate
1 tablespoon finely chopped onion
2 teaspoons WYLER'S® or STEERO® Chicken-Flavor Instant Bouillon
8 cups torn mixed salad greens
2 cups cubed cooked turkey or chicken
2 cups shredded carrots
1 ounce alfalfa sprouts (about 2 cups)
1 (8-ounce) can sliced water chestnuts, drained
1½ cups (6 ounces) shredded Swiss cheese
4 ounces fresh pea pods *or* 1 (6-ounce) package frozen pea pods, thawed
½ cup coarsely chopped cashews

In small bowl, combine salad dressing, egg, parsley, ReaLemon® brand, onion and bouillon. Cover; chill. In large serving bowl, layer greens, turkey, carrots, sprouts, water chestnuts, cheese and pea pods. Stir dressing and pour over salad; sprinkle with cashews. Refrigerate leftovers.

Makes 8 to 10 servings

From top to bottom: Layered Turkey Salad, Tropical Chicken Salad (page 76) and Tucson Turkey Salad

Oriental Shrimp Salad with Puff Bowl

1 pound small raw shrimp, peeled, deveined and cooked
4 ounces fresh pea pods *or* 1 (6-ounce) package frozen pea pods, thawed
1 (8-ounce) can sliced water chestnuts, drained
1 cup sliced fresh mushrooms (about 4 ounces)
1 cup diagonally sliced celery
2 ounces fresh bean sprouts (about 1 cup)
¼ cup sliced green onions
¾ cup mayonnaise or salad dressing
¼ cup REALEMON® Lemon Juice from Concentrate
1 tablespoon prepared horseradish
¼ to ½ teaspoon garlic salt
Puff Bowl, optional

In large bowl, combine all ingredients except Puff Bowl; mix well. Cover; chill. Just before serving, spoon into Puff Bowl or onto lettuce. Refrigerate leftovers.

Makes 4 to 6 servings

Puff Bowl

2 eggs
½ cup unsifted flour
½ cup BORDEN® or MEADOW GOLD® Milk
¼ teaspoon salt
2 tablespoons margarine or butter, melted

Preheat oven to 425°. In small mixer bowl, beat eggs until frothy. Gradually beat in flour; beat until smooth. Add remaining ingredients; mix well. Pour into well-greased 9-inch pie plate. Bake 15 minutes. *Reduce oven temperature to 350°;* continue baking 10 to 15 minutes or until browned. Cool.

Salmon Salad Provençal

Combine hot rice and peas in large bowl; toss lightly. Add tuna, celery, onions, and capers. Combine lemon juice, oil, curry powder, and pepper sauce in small jar with lid. Pour over rice mixture; toss lightly. Cover and chill 30 minutes. Serve on shredded lettuce and garnish with tomato wedges.

Makes 6 servings

Favorite recipe from **USA Rice Council**

Paella Salad

1 can (13¾ ounces) chicken broth (1¾ cups)
⅔ cup cold water
2¼ cups MINUTE® Premium Long Grain Rice, uncooked
¼ teaspoon saffron threads, crushed
3 cups chopped cooked chicken
2 packages (6 ounces each) frozen cooked tiny shrimp, thawed
1 pound smoked sausage, sliced, halved, browned
2 cups coarsely chopped tomato
1 package (10 ounces) BIRDS EYE® Peas, thawed, drained
⅔ cup MIRACLE WHIP® Salad Dressing
¼ cup finely chopped red onion
½ teaspoon minced garlic Salt and pepper

• Bring broth and water to boil; stir in rice and saffron. Cover; remove from heat. Let stand 5 minutes or until liquid is absorbed. Cool.

• Mix remaining ingredients until well blended. Stir in rice mixture.   *Makes 8 servings*

Prep time: 25 minutes
Cooking time: 5 minutes plus standing

Salmon Salad Provençal

⅓ cup REALEMON® Lemon Juice from Concentrate
⅓ cup olive or vegetable oil
1 teaspoon sugar
½ teaspoon dry mustard
½ teaspoon salt
¼ teaspoon basil leaves
¼ teaspoon oregano leaves
1 pound fresh or frozen salmon, poached *or* 1 (15½-ounce) can salmon, drained and flaked
¾ pound small new potatoes, cooked and quartered
½ pound fresh green beans, *or* 1 (9-ounce) package frozen cut green beans, cooked and chilled
Lettuce leaves
Tomatoes, hard-cooked eggs and ripe olives

In large shallow dish, combine ReaLemon® brand, oil, sugar, mustard, salt, basil and oregano;

add salmon and potatoes. Cover; chill. Arrange salmon, potatoes and green beans on lettuce; garnish with tomatoes, eggs and olives. Spoon remaining dressing over salad. Refrigerate leftovers.

Makes 4 servings

Curried Tuna Salad

3 cups hot cooked rice
½ cup frozen peas
1 to 2 cans (6½ ounces each) tuna, packed in water, drained and flaked
¾ cup chopped celery
¼ cup sliced green onions
1 tablespoon drained capers (optional)
¼ cup lemon juice
2 tablespoons olive oil
¼ teaspoon curry powder
¼ teaspoon hot pepper sauce Shredded romaine lettuce
2 medium tomatoes, cut into wedges, for garnish

Tuna & Fresh Fruit Salad

Shrimp Antipasto

1 cup vegetable oil
**⅔ cup REALEMON® Lemon
    Juice from Concentrate**
**2 tablespoons Dijon-style
    mustard**
2 teaspoons sugar
1½ teaspoons thyme leaves
1 teaspoon salt
**1½ pounds raw medium
    shrimp, peeled, deveined
    and cooked**
**6 ounces Provolone cheese,
    cut into cubes**
**1 (6-ounce) can pitted ripe
    olives, drained**
**4 ounces Genoa salami, cut
    into cubes**
**1 large red bell pepper, cut
    into squares**

In large shallow dish or plastic
bag, combine oil, ReaLemon®
brand, mustard, sugar, thyme
and salt; add shrimp, cheese and
olives. Cover; marinate in
refrigerator 6 hours or overnight,
stirring occasionally. Add salami
and red pepper; toss. Drain;
garnish as desired. Refrigerate
leftovers.

Makes about 8 cups

Tip: Cooked scallops can be
substituted for all or part of the
shrimp.

Salsa Shrimp in Papaya

Lemon juice
**12 ounces cooked bay shrimp,
    rinsed and drained**
¾ cup chunky salsa
**½ teaspoon LAWRY'S®
    Lemon Pepper
    Seasoning**
**¼ teaspoon LAWRY'S® Garlic
    Powder with Parsley**
**3 ripe papayas, halved,
    peeled and seeds
    removed**

In medium bowl, sprinkle lemon
juice over shrimp. Add salsa,
Lemon Pepper Seasoning and
Garlic Powder with Parsley;
cover and marinate in
refrigerator 1 hour or overnight.
Fill each papaya half with
marinated shrimp.

Makes 6 servings

Presentation: Arrange papaya
halves on lettuce leaves. Garnish
each with chopped parsley and
lemon slices.

Tuna & Fresh Fruit Salad

Lettuce leaves (optional)
**1 can (12½ ounces)
    STARKIST® Tuna,
    drained and broken into
    chunks**
**4 cups slices or wedges
    fresh fruit***
**¼ cup silvered almonds
    (optional)**

Fruit Dressing
**1 container (8 ounces)
    lemon, mandarin orange
    or vanilla low-fat yogurt**
2 tablespoons orange juice
¼ teaspoon ground cinnamon

Line a large platter or 4
individual plates with lettuce
leaves, if desired. Arrange tuna
and desired fruit in a decorative
design over lettuce. Sprinkle
almonds over salad, if desired.

For Fruit Dressing: In a small
bowl stir together yogurt, orange
juice and cinnamon until well
blended. Serve dressing with
salad.   *Makes 4 servings*

*Suggested fresh fruit: Apples,
bananas, berries, citrus fruit,
kiwifruit, melon, papaya,
peaches or pears.

Salsa Shrimp in Papaya

Beef Asparagus Salad

½ cup **MIRACLE WHIP®
 FREE® Dressing**
⅓ cup <u>each</u>: finely chopped
 green, red and yellow bell
 peppers
2 tablespoons skim milk
2 tablespoons finely
 chopped fresh basil or
 2 teaspoons dried basil
 leaves, crushed
2 tablespoons chopped
 green onions
¼ teaspoon <u>each</u>: salt,
 pepper
1 pound <u>each</u>: roast beef
 slices, asparagus spears,
 cooked
3 tomatoes, sliced
1 cucumber, sliced
1 summer squash, sliced

• Mix salad dressing, bell
peppers, milk, basil, onions, salt
and pepper until well blended;
refrigerate.

• Arrange remaining ingredients
on serving platter. Serve with
salad dressing mixture.

Makes 8 servings

Prep time: 20 minutes plus
 refrigerating

Western Steak Salad

⅔ cup vegetable oil
¼ cup lime juice
2 tablespoons **HEINZ® 57
 Sauce**
2 tablespoons **HEINZ®
 Gourmet Wine Vinegar**
½ teaspoon salt
¼ cup **HEINZ® 57 Sauce**
1 tablespoon lime juice
1 tablespoon vegetable oil
½ teaspoon hot pepper sauce
1 pound boneless beef
 sirloin steak
6 cups torn romaine lettuce
8 cherry tomatoes, halved
1 small avocado, peeled, cut
 into chunks
1 small red onion, halved,
 sliced

For dressing, in jar combine
⅔ cup oil, ¼ cup lime juice, 2
tablespoons 57 Sauce, vinegar
and salt. Cover and shake
vigorously; chill to blend flavors.
In small bowl, combine ¼ cup
57 Sauce, 1 tablespoon lime
juice, 1 tablespoon oil and hot
pepper sauce. Brush on both
sides of steak; let stand 30
minutes. Broil steak, 3 to 4
inches from heat source, to
desired doneness, turning and
brushing once with marinade.
Let steak stand while preparing
salad mixture. In large bowl,
combine romaine, tomatoes,
avocado and onion; toss with ½
cup dressing and divide among 4
salad bowls. Thinly slice steak
across grain; arrange on top of
salad mixture. Serve salad with
remaining dressing, if desired.

*Makes 4 servings
(about 1¼ cups dressing)*

Beef Asparagus Salad

Sesame Pork Salad

**3 cups cooked rice
1½ cups slivered cooked pork*
¼ pound fresh snow peas, julienned
1 medium cucumber, peeled, seeded and julienned
1 medium red pepper, julienned
½ cup sliced green onions
2 tablespoons sesame seeds, toasted (optional)**

Combine all ingredients in large bowl; stir well. Pour Sesame Dressing over rice mixture; toss lightly. Serve at room temperature or slightly chilled.
Makes 6 servings

Sesame Dressing

**¼ cup chicken broth
3 tablespoons rice or white wine vinegar
3 tablespoons soy sauce
1 tablespoon peanut oil
1 teaspoon sesame oil**

Combine all ingredients in small jar with lid; shake vigorously.
Makes about ¾ cup

*Substitute 1½ cups slivered cooked chicken for pork, if desired.

*Favorite recipe from **USA Rice Council***

Stir-Fry Beef Salad

Sesame Pork Salad

Stir-Fry Beef Salad

**1 pound boneless beef sirloin steak
2 tablespoons olive oil, divided
1 tablespoon grated fresh ginger root
1 clove garlic, minced
1 small red onion, chopped
1 cup (about 4 ounces) fresh mushrooms, quartered
3 tablespoons cider vinegar
1 tablespoon soy sauce
1 tablespoon honey
3 cups hot cooked rice
½ pound fresh spinach, torn into bite-size pieces
1 medium tomato, seeded and coarsely chopped**

Partially freeze steak; slice across the grain into ⅛-inch strips. Set aside. Heat 1 tablespoon oil, ginger root, and garlic in large skillet or wok over high heat until hot. Stir-fry beef (half at a time) 1 to 2 minutes. Remove beef; keep warm. Add remaining 1 tablespoon oil; heat until hot. Add onion and mushrooms; cook 1 to 2 minutes. Stir in vinegar, soy sauce, and honey. Bring mixture to a boil. Add beef and rice; toss lightly. Serve over spinach. Top with tomato; serve immediately.
Makes 6 servings

*Favorite recipe from **USA Rice Council***

Hearty Roast Beef, Pear and Pea Pod Salad

Salad
  1 head lettuce
  10 ounces sliced rare roast beef, cut into strips
  2 carrots, peeled, cut into matchstick pieces
  3 fresh California Bartlett pears, cored and sliced
  1 small red onion, halved and thinly sliced
  10 ounces fresh Chinese pea pods (about 1¼ cups), trimmed
  ¼ cup pitted ripe or cured black olives (optional garnish)

Mustard Vinaigrette
  1 bottle (8 ounces) Italian salad dressing
  2 teaspoons Dijon-style mustard

On serving platter or individual plates, arrange lettuce leaves. Place remaining salad ingredients on top. In small bowl, combine vinaigrette ingredients and drizzle over salad.   *Makes 4 servings*

Tip: To keep fruit colors bright, dip pear slices in Mustard Vinaigrette as you cut them, or cut pears just before serving.

Favorite recipe from **California Tree Fruit Agreement**

Fandangled Fajitas Salad

  1 pound boneless, skinless chicken breasts, thinly sliced
  1 tablespoon vegetable oil
  1 package (1.27 ounces) LAWRY'S® Spices & Seasonings for Fajitas
  ¼ cup water
  4 cups shredded lettuce
  1 can (15 ounces) pinto beans, drained and rinsed
  1 medium onion, slivered
  1 medium green or red bell pepper, slivered
  1 medium tomato, thinly sliced
  1 avocado, thinly sliced
  Fandangled Dressing (recipe follows)

In large skillet, brown chicken pieces in oil; drain fat. Add Spices & Seasonings for Fajitas and water; blend well. Bring to a boil; reduce heat and simmer, uncovered, 3 to 5 minutes. On individual serving plates, arrange lettuce and layer beans, onion, bell pepper, tomato and avocado. Top with equal portions of prepared fajitas mixture. Serve Fandangled Dressing on the side.   *Makes 4 servings*

Presentation: Serve with tortilla chips.

Hint: Ground beef or steak strips can be used in place of chicken.

Fandangled Dressing

  1⅓ cups chunky salsa
  ¼ cup vegetable oil
  2 tablespoons red wine vinegar
  2 tablespoons lime juice

In container with stopper or lid, combine all ingredients; blend well.   *Makes about 1½ cups*

Aztec Chili Salad

  1 pound ground beef
  1 package (1.62 ounces) LAWRY'S® Spices & Seasonings for Chili
  ½ cup water
  1 can (15¼ ounces) kidney beans, undrained
  1 can (14½ ounces) whole peeled tomatoes, undrained and cut up
  ½ cup dairy sour cream
  3 tablespoons mayonnaise
  1 fresh medium tomato, diced
  ¼ cup chopped fresh cilantro
  ½ teaspoon LAWRY'S® Seasoned Pepper
  1 head lettuce
  1 red bell pepper, sliced
  ¼ cup sliced green onions
  1½ cups (6 ounces) grated Cheddar cheese
  ¼ cup sliced ripe olives

In large skillet, brown ground beef until crumbly; drain fat. Stir in Spices & Seasonings for Chili, water, beans and canned tomatoes; blend well. Bring to a boil; reduce heat and simmer, uncovered, 10 minutes. For dressing, in blender or food processor, blend sour cream, mayonnaise, fresh tomato, cilantro and Seasoned Pepper. Refrigerate until chilled. On 6 individual plates, layer lettuce, chili meat, bell pepper, green onions, cheese and olives. Drizzle with chilled dressing.   *Makes 6 servings*

Presentation: Serve with jicama wedges arranged around salad plates.

Hint: Ground turkey or shredded chicken can be used in place of ground beef in chili mixture.

Aztec Chili Salad

Summer Fruit Salad

Kona Ham Hawaiian

**1 can (20 ounces) DOLE®
   Pineapple Chunks in
   Syrup***
½ pound ham, cut into strips
½ cup sliced DOLE® Celery
**1 firm, medium DOLE®
   Banana, peeled, sliced**
**1 cup halved DOLE®
   Strawberries**
**½ cup cholesterol-free,
   reduced-calorie
   mayonnaise**
**¼ teaspoon dry mustard
   DOLE® Salad Greens**

• Drain pineapple; reserve 1 tablespoon syrup.

• Combine pineapple, ham, celery, banana and strawberries in bowl.

• Combine mayonnaise, mustard and reserved syrup in small bowl. Pour over salad; toss to coat.

• Serve in salad bowl lined with salad greens.

Makes 4 servings

*Use pineapple packed in juice, if desired.

Preparation Time: 20 minutes

Summer Fruit Salad

**2 cups cooked rice, cooled to
   room temperature**
½ cup quartered strawberries
½ cup grape halves
**2 kiwifruit, sliced into
   quarters**
½ cup pineapple tidbits
½ cup banana slices
¼ cup pineapple juice
**2 tablespoons plain nonfat
   yogurt**
**1 tablespoon honey
   Lettuce leaves**

Combine rice and fruit in large bowl. Blend pineapple juice, yogurt, and honey in small bowl. Pour over rice mixture; toss lightly. Serve on lettuce leaves.

Makes 4 servings

Favorite recipe from **USA Rice Council**

Jicama Orange Burst Salad

¼ cup vegetable oil
**1 tablespoon red wine
   vinegar**
1 tablespoon sugar
2 teaspoons fresh lime juice
**½ teaspoon LAWRY'S®
   Seasoned Salt**
**½ teaspoon LAWRY'S®
   Seasoned Pepper**
**¼ teaspoon dry mustard
   Lettuce**
**3 medium navel oranges,
   peeled and sectioned**
**1 small jicama, peeled and
   julienne-cut into 1-inch
   pieces**
½ cup sliced green onions
¼ cup diced red onion

In medium bowl, combine oil, vinegar, sugar, lime juice, Seasoned Salt, Seasoned Pepper and mustard; blend well. Refrigerate. On bed of lettuce, arrange orange sections, jicama and green and red onions. Drizzle dressing over salad.

Makes 1¼ cups

Poppy Seed Fruit Sauce

**½ cup MIRACLE WHIP®
   FREE® Dressing**
**1 container (8 ounces)
   lemon-flavored lowfat
   yogurt**
2 tablespoons skim milk
**1 tablespoon each: packed
   brown sugar, poppy
   seeds**

• Mix ingredients until well blended; refrigerate. Serve over fresh fruit. *Makes 1⅔ cups*

Prep Time: 5 minutes plus refrigerating

Poolside Fruit Salad Platter with Honey-Lemon Yogurt Dip

Fruit
2 kiwifruit, peeled and sliced
2 fresh plums, sliced
1 fresh California nectarine, sliced
1 fresh California peach, sliced
1 fresh California Bartlett pear, cored and sliced
⅓ cup fresh blueberries (optional)

Honey-Lemon Yogurt Dip
1 cup nonfat lemon yogurt
1 tablespoon honey
1 strip lemon peel (optional garnish)

Line serving platter with kiwifruit. Top with remaining fruit. In small bowl, combine yogurt and honey. Spoon over fruit. Garnish with lemon peel, if desired.   *Makes 6 servings*

Favorite recipe from **California Tree Fruit Agreement**

California Salad

2 cups assorted DOLE®
    Fresh Fruit
3 ounces Brie or Camembert cheese
3 ounces cooked baby shrimp
Crisp DOLE® Salad Greens

Paradise Dressing
¼ cup frozen DOLE® Pine-Orange-Guava Juice concentrate,* thawed
3 tablespoons honey
2 teaspoons lime juice
1 teaspoon lime zest

• Arrange fruit, cheese and shrimp on 2 salad plates lined with salad greens. Serve with Paradise Dressing.
    Makes 2 servings

PARADISE DRESSING: Combine all ingredients in screw-top jar; shake well. Serve over fruit.
    Makes ½ cup

*Do not reconstitute.

Preparation Time: 20 minutes

Ribbon Squares

1 package (4-serving size) JELL-O® Brand Gelatin, Lemon Flavor
1 package (4-serving size) JELL-O® Brand Gelatin, Cherry, Raspberry or Strawberry Flavor
1 package (4-serving size) JELL-O® Brand Gelatin, Lime Flavor
3 cups boiling water
1 package (8 ounces) PHILADELPHIA BRAND® Cream Cheese, softened
1 can (8¼ ounces) crushed pineapple in syrup, undrained
1 cup thawed COOL WHIP® Whipped Topping
½ cup MIRACLE WHIP® Salad Dressing
1½ cups cold water
Canned pineapple slices, drained (optional)
Celery leaves (optional)

DISSOLVE each flavor of gelatin in separate bowls, using 1 cup of the boiling water for each.

BLEND lemon gelatin into cream cheese, beating until smooth. Add pineapple with syrup. Chill until slightly thickened. Stir in whipped topping and salad dressing. Chill until thickened. Stir ¾ cup of the cold water into cherry gelatin; pour into 9-inch square pan. Chill until set but not firm. Stir remaining ¾ cup cold water into lime gelatin; chill until slightly thickened. Spoon lemon gelatin mixture over cherry gelatin layer in pan. Chill until set but not firm. Top with lime gelatin. Chill until firm, about 4 hours or overnight. Unmold; cut into squares. Garnish with pineapple slices and celery leaves, if desired.   *Makes 12 servings*

Prep time: 1 hour
Chill time: 6 hours

Poppy Seed Fruit Sauce

Under-the-Sea Salad

- **1 can (16 ounces) pear halves in syrup, undrained**
- **1 package (4-serving size) JELL-O® Brand Gelatin, Lime Flavor**
- **1 cup boiling water**
- **¼ cup cold water**
- **1 tablespoon lemon juice**
- **1 package (8 ounces) PHILADELPHIA BRAND® Cream Cheese, softened**
- **⅛ teaspoon ground ginger**
- **Salad greens (optional)**
- **Seedless red grapes (optional)**

DRAIN pears, reserving ½ cup syrup. Dice pears; set aside. Dissolve gelatin in boiling water. Add reserved syrup, cold water and lemon juice. Measure 1¼ cups gelatin into 8×4-inch loaf pan. Chill until set but not firm. Place cream cheese in blender; cover. Blend at low speed until smooth and creamy. Very slowly add remaining gelatin and ginger. Blend at low speed until smooth, about 15 seconds. Chill until thickened. Fold in pears. Spoon over gelatin in pan. Chill until firm, about 2 hours. Unmold. Garnish with crisp salad greens, additional pears and grapes, if desired.

Makes 8 servings

Light Under-the-Sea Salad:
Prepare Under-the-Sea Salad as directed, using pear halves in juice or light syrup, Jell-O® Brand Sugar Free Gelatin and Light Philadelphia Brand® Cream Cheese.

Prep time: 20 minutes
Chill time: 3 hours

Muffin Pan Snacks

Under-the-Sea Salad

Muffin Pan Snacks

- **1 package (4-serving size) JELL-O® Brand Gelatin, any flavor**
- **¾ cup boiling water**
- **½ cup cold water**
- **Ice cubes**
- **1½ cups diced fresh fruit or vegetables**

DISSOLVE gelatin in boiling water. Combine cold water and ice cubes to make 1 cup. Add to gelatin, stirring until slightly thickened. Remove any unmelted ice. Add fruit. Chill until thickened, about 10 minutes.

PLACE foil baking cups in muffin pans, or use small individual molds. Spoon gelatin mixture into cups or molds, filling each about ⅔ full. Chill until firm, about 2 hours.

PEEL away foil cups carefully or dip molds in warm water for about 5 seconds to unmold.

Makes 6 servings

Prep time: 15 minutes
Chill time: 2 hours

Spiced Cranberry-Orange Mold

1 bag (12 ounces) cranberries*
½ cup sugar*
2 packages (4-serving size each) or 1 package (8-serving size) JELL-O® Brand Gelatin, Orange or Lemon Flavor
1½ cups boiling water
1 cup cold water*
1 tablespoon lemon juice
¼ teaspoon ground cinnamon
⅛ teaspoon ground cloves
1 orange, sectioned and diced
½ cup chopped walnuts
Orange slices (optional)
White kale or curly leaf lettuce (optional)

PLACE cranberries in food processor; cover. Process until finely chopped. Mix with sugar; set aside.

DISSOLVE gelatin in boiling water. Add cold water, lemon juice and spices. Chill until thickened. Fold in cranberry mixture, oranges and walnuts. Spoon into 5-cup mold. Chill until firm, about 4 hours. Unmold. Garnish with orange slices and kale, if desired.

Makes 10 servings

*1 can (16 ounces) whole berry cranberry sauce may be substituted for fresh cranberries. Omit sugar and reduce cold water to ½ cup.

Prep time: 20 minutes
Chill time: 4 hours

Waldorf Salad

2 packages (4-serving size each) or 1 package (8-serving size) JELL-O® Brand Gelatin, Lemon Flavor
1½ cups boiling water
1 tablespoon lemon juice
1 cup cold water
Ice cubes
½ cup MIRACLE WHIP® Salad Dressing
1½ cups diced apples
¾ cup diced celery
¼ cup chopped walnuts

DISSOLVE gelatin in boiling water. Add lemon juice. Combine cold water and ice cubes to make 2 cups. Add to gelatin, stirring until slightly thickened. Remove any unmelted ice. Stir in salad dressing with wire wisk; chill until thickened.

FOLD apples, celery and walnuts into gelatin mixture. Pour into 5-cup mold. Chill until firm, about 3 hours. Unmold. Serve with crisp salad greens and additional salad dressing, if desired.   *Makes 10 servings*

Prep time: 20 minutes
Chill time: 3 hours

Strawberry Miracle Mold

2 packages (4-serving size) JELL-O® Brand Gelatin, Strawberry Flavor
1½ cups boiling water
1¾ cups cold water
½ cup MIRACLE WHIP® Salad Dressing
Assorted Fruit

• Dissolve gelatin in boiling water; add cold water. Gradually add to salad dressing, mixing until blended.

• Pour into lightly oiled 1-quart mold or glass serving bowl; chill until firm. Unmold onto serving plate; serve with fruit.
Makes 4 to 6 servings

Prep time: 10 minutes plus chilling

Strawberry Miracle Mold

MEATS

Today's meat is leaner than ever before! So serve hearty main dishes of beef, pork, veal or lamb for fast family meals or sophisticated entrées for memorable evenings. With dozens of new ideas for grilling, roasting and stir-frying, you can sample sizzling steaks and flavorful kabobs, succulent pork chops and tasty pork tenderloin plus savory international specialties such as Mexican Beef & Rice and Szechuan Shredded Pork.

Fast Beef Roast with Mushroom Sauce

- **1 boneless beef rib eye roast (about 2 pounds)**
- **2 tablespoons vegetable oil**
- **4 cups water**
- **1 can (10¾ ounces) condensed beef broth**
- **1 cup dry red wine**
- **2 cloves garlic, minced**
- **1 teaspoon dried marjoram leaves**
- **4 black peppercorns**
- **3 whole cloves**
  Mushroom Sauce (recipe follows)

Tie roast with heavy string at 2-inch intervals. Heat oil in Dutch oven over medium-high heat. Cook roast until evenly browned. Pour off drippings. Add water, broth, wine, garlic, marjoram, peppercorns and cloves; bring to boil. Reduce heat to medium-low; cover and simmer 15 minutes per pound. Check temperature with instant-read thermometer; temperature should be 130°F for rare. *Do not overcook.* Remove roast to serving platter; reserve cooking liquid. Cover roast tightly with plastic wrap or foil; allow to stand 10 minutes before carving (temperature will continue to rise to 140°F for rare). Prepare Mushroom Sauce. Remove strings from roast. Carve into thin slices and top with Mushroom Sauce. Serve with assorted vegetables, if desired.
Makes 6 to 8 servings

Note: A boneless beef rib eye roast will yield three to four 3-ounce cooked servings per pound.

Mushroom Sauce

- **1 tablespoon butter**
- **1 cup sliced fresh mushrooms**
- **1 cup beef cooking liquid, strained**
- **1½ teaspoons cornstarch**
- **¼ teaspoon salt**
- **2 dashes pepper**
- **1 tablespoon thinly sliced green onion tops**

Melt butter in medium saucepan over medium-high heat. Add mushrooms; cook and stir 5 minutes. Remove; reserve. Add liquid, cornstarch, salt and pepper to pan. Bring to a boil; cook and stir until thickened, 1 to 2 minutes. Remove from heat. Stir in mushrooms and onion.

*Favorite recipe from **National Live Stock and Meat Board***

Marinated Flank Steak

- **1 (1- to 1½-pound) flank steak**
- **½ cup REALEMON® Lemon Juice from Concentrate**
- **¼ cup vegetable oil**
- **2 teaspoons WYLER'S® or STEERO® Beef-Flavor Instant Bouillon**
- **2 cloves garlic, finely chopped**
- **1 teaspoon ground ginger**

Place meat in shallow dish or plastic bag. In small bowl, combine remaining ingredients. Pour over meat. Cover; marinate in refrigerator 4 to 6 hours, turning occasionally. Remove meat from marinade; grill or broil as desired, basting frequently with marinade. Refrigerate leftovers.
Makes 4 to 6 servings

Fast Beef Roast with Mushroom Sauce

Southwest Pot Roast

¼ **cup all-purpose flour**
2 **teaspoons garlic salt**
½ **teaspoon ground red pepper**
4 **to 5 pounds boneless beef rump roast**
1 **tablespoon vegetable oil**
1 **(13¾-ounce) can COLLEGE INN® Beef Broth**
2 **tablespoons WRIGHT'S® Natural Hickory Seasoning**
2 **cups green or red bell pepper slices**
2 **cups onion wedges**
3 **ears corn-on-the-cob, cut into 1-inch chunks**

In shallow bowl, combine flour, garlic salt and ground red pepper. Coat beef with flour mixture. In 8-quart saucepan, brown beef in oil. Add beef broth and hickory seasoning. Bring to a boil; reduce heat. Cover tightly and simmer 2 hours. Add peppers, onions and corn. Cover; simmer 45 minutes longer or until vegetables and beef are fork-tender. To serve, thinly slice beef and serve with vegetables and sauce.   *Makes 6 servings*

Beef Tenderloin en Croute

1 **beef tenderloin (3 to 4 pounds)**
1 **package (17¼ ounces) frozen ready-to-bake puff pastry sheets**
½ **pound mushrooms, finely chopped**
2 **tablespoons PARKAY® Margarine**
1 **container (8 ounces) PHILADELPHIA BRAND® Soft Cream Cheese with Herb & Garlic**
¼ **cup seasoned dry bread crumbs**
2 **tablespoons Madeira wine**
1 **tablespoon chopped fresh chives**
¼ **teaspoon salt**
1 **egg, beaten**
1 **tablespoon cold water**

• Heat oven to 425°F.

• Tie meat with string at 1-inch intervals, if necessary. Place meat on rack in baking pan.

• Roast 45 to 50 minutes or until meat thermometer registers 135°F. Remove from oven; cool 30 minutes in refrigerator. Remove string.

• Thaw puff pastry sheets according to package directions.

• Cook and stir mushrooms in margarine in large skillet 10 minutes or until liquid evaporates.

• Add cream cheese, bread crumbs, wine, chives and salt; mix well. Cool.

• On lightly floured surface, overlap pastry sheets ½ inch to form 14×12-inch rectangle; press edges firmly together to seal. Trim length of pastry 2½ inches longer than length of meat.

• Spread mushroom mixture over top and sides of meat. Place meat in center of pastry.

• Fold pastry over meat; press edges together to seal. Decorate top with pastry trimmings, if desired.

• Brush pastry with combined egg and water. Place meat in greased 15×10×1-inch jelly roll pan.

• Bake 20 to 25 minutes or until pastry is golden brown. Let stand 10 minutes before slicing.
    Makes 8 to 10 servings

Prep time: 25 minutes plus refrigerating
Cooking time: 1 hour and 15 minutes

Beef Tenderloin en Croute

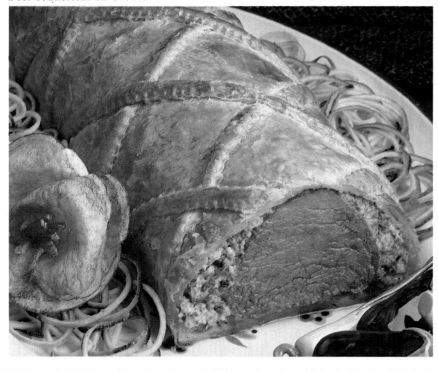

Versatile Barbecue Sauce

¼ **cup chopped onion**
1 **clove garlic, finely chopped**
2 **tablespoons margarine or butter**
1 **cup ketchup**
⅓ **cup firmly packed brown sugar**
¼ **cup REALEMON® Lemon Juice from Concentrate**
1 **tablespoon Worcestershire sauce**
2 **teaspoons WYLER'S® or STEERO® Beef- or Chicken-Flavor Instant Bouillon *or* 2 Beef- or Chicken-Flavored Bouillon Cubes**
1 **teaspoon prepared mustard**

In small saucepan, cook onion and garlic in margarine until tender. Add remaining ingredients; bring to a boil. Reduce heat; simmer uncovered 20 minutes, stirring occasionally. Use as a basting sauce for grilled beef, chicken or pork. Refrigerate leftovers.

Makes about 1½ cups

Microwave: In 1-quart glass measure with handle, melt margarine on 100% power (high) 30 to 45 seconds. Add onion and garlic; cook on 100% power (high) 1½ to 2 minutes or until tender. Add remaining ingredients. Cook loosely covered on 100% power (high) 3 to 5 minutes or until mixture boils; stir. Reduce heat to 50% power (medium); cook covered 4 to 5 minutes to blend flavors.

Soy Marinated London Broil

Herb-Marinated Chuck Steak

1 **pound boneless beef chuck shoulder steak, cut 1 inch thick**
¼ **cup chopped onion**
2 **tablespoons *each* chopped parsley and white vinegar**
1 **tablespoon vegetable oil**
2 **teaspoons Dijon-style mustard**
1 **clove garlic, minced**
½ **teaspoon dried thyme leaves**

Combine onion, parsley, vinegar, oil, mustard, garlic and thyme. Place beef chuck shoulder steak in plastic bag; add onion mixture, spreading evenly over both sides. Close bag securely; marinate in refrigerator 6 to 8 hours (or overnight, if desired), turning at least once. Pour off marinade; discard. Place steak on rack in broiler pan so surface of meat is 3 to 5 inches from heat source. Broil about 16 minutes for rare (18 minutes for medium), turning once. Carve steak diagonally across the grain into thin slices. Garnish as desired.

Makes 4 servings

*Favorite recipe from **National Live Stock and Meat Board***

Soy Marinade

½ **cup REALEMON® Lemon Juice from Concentrate**
½ **cup soy sauce**
½ **cup vegetable oil**
3 **tablespoons ketchup**
3 to 4 **cloves garlic, finely chopped**
¼ **teaspoon pepper**

In large shallow dish or plastic bag, combine ingredients; add beef, pork or chicken. Cover; marinate in refrigerator 4 hours or overnight, turning occasionally. Remove meat from marinade; grill or broil as desired, basting frequently with additional ReaLemon® brand. Refrigerate leftover meat.

Makes about 1½ cups

Holiday Beef Steaks with Vegetable Saute and Hot Mustard Sauce

Flank Steak with Pineapple Chili Sauce

> **1 can (8 ounces) DOLE®
> Crushed Pineapple in
> Juice**
> **1 beef flank steak
> (1½ pounds)**
> **Salt and pepper to taste**
> **¾ cup chili sauce**
> **¼ teaspoon garlic powder**
> **1 to 2 drops hot pepper
> sauce**

• Drain pineapple well; save juice for a beverage.

• Season steak with salt and pepper. Broil 4 inches from heat 5 to 7 minutes on each side for medium-rare.

• Combine drained pineapple, chili sauce, garlic powder and hot pepper sauce in saucepan. Cook over medium heat until heated through.

• Slice steak across the grain into thin slices. Top with chili sauce.
Makes 4 to 6 servings

Preparation Time: 10 minutes
Cook Time: 15 minutes

Holiday Beef Steaks with Vegetable Saute and Hot Mustard Sauce

> **Boneless beef top loin
> steaks, cut 1 inch thick**
> **½ cup plain yogurt**
> **1 teaspoon cornstarch**
> **¼ cup condensed beef broth**
> **2 teaspoons coarse-grained
> mustard**
> **1 teaspoon *each* prepared
> grated horseradish and
> Dijon-style mustard**
> **¼ teaspoon sugar**
> **½ teaspoon lemon pepper**
> **1 package (16 ounces) frozen
> whole green beans**
> **1 cup quartered large
> mushrooms**
> **1 tablespoon butter**
> **¼ cup water**

Place yogurt and cornstarch in medium saucepan and stir until blended. Stir in beef broth, coarse-grained mustard, horseradish, Dijon-style mustard and sugar; reserve. Press lemon pepper into surface of boneless beef top loin steaks. Place steaks on rack in broiler pan so surfaces are 3 to 4 inches from heat. Broil steaks about 15 minutes for rare (20 minutes for medium), turning once. Meanwhile cook beans and mushrooms in butter in large frying pan over medium heat 6 minutes, stirring occasionally. Add water; cover and continue cooking 6 to 8 minutes, stirring occasionally until beans are tender. Cook reserved sauce over medium-low heat 5 minutes, stirring until sauce is slightly thickened. Serve steaks and vegetables with sauce.   *Makes 6 servings*

Preparation Time: 15 minutes
Cooking Time: 15 minutes

Note: A boneless beef top loin steak will yield four 3-ounce cooked servings per pound.

*Favorite recipe from **National Live Stock and Meat Board***

Steak Mardi Gras

> **1 beef flank steak (1 pound)**
> **1 tablespoon vegetable oil**
> **1 jar (12 ounces) HEINZ®
> HomeStyle Mushroom or
> Brown Gravy**
> **1 can (8 ounces) stewed
> tomatoes**
> **3 tablespoons chopped fresh
> parsley**
> **1 teaspoon HEINZ® Gourmet
> Wine Vinegar**
> **½ teaspoon granulated sugar**
> **⅛ to ¼ teaspoon hot pepper
> sauce**

In large skillet, cook steak in oil to desired doneness, turning once; remove and keep warm. In same skillet, stir in remaining ingredients; heat until bubbly. Thinly slice steak diagonally across the grain; spoon sauce over. Serve with rice, if desired.
Makes 4 servings

Italian Pepper Steak

8 beef loin tenderloin steaks, each cut ½ inch thick (about 1½ pounds total)
¼ teaspoon salt
¼ teaspoon black pepper
1 tablespoon olive *or* vegetable oil
2 large green *or* sweet red peppers, cut into thin strips
1 large onion, cut into wedges
2 cloves garlic, minced
¼ cup Burgundy *or* other dry red wine
1 cup PREGO® Regular Spaghetti Sauce
Fresh parsley sprigs for garnish

1. Sprinkle steaks with salt and black pepper; set aside.

2. In 10-inch skillet over medium-high heat, in hot oil, cook green peppers, onion and garlic just until tender. With slotted spoon, remove vegetables to bowl.

3. In same skillet, over medium-high heat, cook *half* of steaks 2 to 3 minutes or until browned, turning once. Remove steaks to serving platter and keep warm. Repeat with remaining steaks, adding more oil, if necessary.

4. Add Burgundy to skillet, stirring to scrape up any browned bits. Add vegetable mixture and spaghetti sauce. Heat to boiling; simmer 1 minute. Spoon mixture over steaks on platter. Garnish with parsley sprigs, if desired.
Makes 4 main-dish servings

Prep Time: 15 minutes
Cook Time: 20 minutes

Italian Pepper Steak

Steak Supreme Tacos

1 pound sirloin steak or pork butt, cooked and shredded or chopped
1 package (1.25 ounces) LAWRY'S® Taco Spices & Seasonings
¾ cup water
1 can (15 ounces) pinto beans, drained
½ cup sliced green onions
½ cup chopped tomato
1 package (10 count) LAWRY'S® Taco Shells
Shredded lettuce
Avocado chunks
2 cups (8 ounces) grated Monterey Jack cheese

In large skillet, combine meat, Taco Spices & Seasonings and water. Bring to a boil; reduce heat and simmer, uncovered, 7 minutes. Stir in beans, green onions and tomato. Heat Taco Shells in 350°F oven 5 minutes. Spoon warm meat mixture into shells. Top with lettuce, avocado and cheese. *Makes 10 tacos*

Presentation: Serve with Lawry's® Fiesta Dip (page 10) or a mixture of sour cream and salsa.

Hint: Double recipe for a larger fiesta!

Carne Asada

    1 (1¼-pound) top sirloin
       steak
    2 tablespoons vegetable oil
    ½ cup LAWRY'S® Fajitas
       Skillet Sauce
    ¼ cup orange juice
    ½ teaspoon dried oregano,
       crushed
       Salsa

Pierce steak with fork on both sides and coat with oil; place in large resealable plastic bag. In measuring cup, combine Fajitas Skillet Sauce, orange juice and oregano; pour over steak. Marinate in refrigerator 1 to 2 hours, turning steak occasionally. Remove steak; reserve marinade. Broil steak 4 to 5 minutes on each side until cooked to desired doneness, basting often with reserved marinade. Serve with salsa.

Makes 4 servings

Presentation: Thinly slice steak for taco or burrito filling, or serve with refried beans and Mexican rice for a hearty meal.

Sombrero Taco Cups

    1 pound ground beef or pork
    1 package (1.25 ounces)
       LAWRY'S® Taco Spices &
       Seasonings
    ¾ cup water
    ¼ cup salsa
    2 packages (8 ounces each)
       refrigerator biscuits
    ½ cup (2 ounces) grated
       Cheddar cheese

In medium skillet, brown ground beef until crumbly; drain fat. Add Taco Spices & Seasonings and water; blend well. Bring to a boil; reduce heat and simmer, uncovered, 10 minutes. Stir in salsa. Separate biscuits and press each biscuit into an ungreased muffin cup. Spoon equal amounts of meat mixture into each muffin cup; sprinkle each with cheese. Bake, uncovered, in 350°F oven 12 minutes or until biscuit cups are browned and cheese melts.

Makes 12 pastries

Presentation: Serve as a main dish or as a snack.

Hint: For an extra treat, flatten any leftover biscuit dough into disks; sprinkle with cinnamon-sugar mixture and bake in 350°F oven 5 to 7 minutes or until golden.

Spicy Burrito Bonanza

    ½ pound ground beef
    ½ pound spicy pork sausage
    1 medium tomato, chopped
    ¼ cup thinly sliced green
       onions
    1½ teaspoons chili powder
    ½ teaspoon LAWRY'S® Garlic
       Powder with Parsley
    1 can (8¼ ounces) refried
       beans
    6 large flour tortillas, warmed
    1½ cups (6 ounces) grated
       Monterey Jack cheese
       Shredded lettuce

In large skillet, brown ground beef and sausage; drain fat. Add tomato, green onions, chili powder and Garlic Powder with Parsley; blend well. Bring to a boil; reduce heat and simmer, uncovered, 10 minutes. Add refried beans; heat 5 minutes. Spread ½ cup meat mixture on each warm tortilla. Top with a sprinkling of cheese and lettuce. Fold in sides and roll to enclose filling.   *Makes 6 servings*

Presentation: Serve topped with sour cream and avocado slices.

Beef Fajitas

    ½ cup REALEMON® Lemon
       Juice from Concentrate
       or REALIME® Lime Juice
       from Concentrate
    ¼ cup vegetable oil
    2 cloves garlic, finely
       chopped
    2 teaspoons WYLER'S® or
       STEERO® Beef-Flavor
       Instant Bouillon
    1 (1- to 1½-pound) top round
       steak
    10 (6-inch) flour tortillas,
       warmed as package
       directs
       Garnishes: Picante sauce,
       shredded lettuce,
       shredded Cheddar
       cheese and sliced green
       onions

In large shallow dish or plastic bag, combine ReaLemon® brand, oil, garlic and bouillon; add steak. Cover; marinate in refrigerator 6 hours or overnight. Remove steak from marinade; grill or broil 8 to 10 minutes on each side or until steak is cooked to desired doneness, basting frequently with marinade. Slice steak diagonally into thin strips; place on tortillas. Top with one or more garnishes; fold tortillas. Serve immediately. Refrigerate leftovers.   *Makes 10 fajitas*

Carne Asada

Mexican Beef Stir-Fry

- **1 pound beef flank steak**
- **2 tablespoons vegetable oil**
- **1 teaspoon ground cumin**
- **1 teaspoon garlic salt**
- **1 teaspoon dried oregano leaves**
- **1 red bell pepper, cut into thin strips**
- **1 medium onion, chopped**
- **1 to 2 jalapeño peppers, seeded and cut into slivers***

Cut beef flank steak diagonally across the grain into ⅛-inch-thick slices. Combine oil, cumin, garlic salt and oregano. Heat 1 tablespoon of the oil mixture in large nonstick frying pan until hot. Add red pepper, onion and jalapeño peppers; stir-fry over medium-high heat 2 to 3 minutes or until tender-crisp. Remove from pan; reserve. Stir-fry beef strips (½ at a time) in remaining oil mixture 1 to 2 minutes. Return vegetables to frying pan and heat through.

Makes 4 servings

Serving Suggestions: Mexican Beef Stir-Fry may be served on a lettuce raft, in taco shells or on tostada shells. Top with guacamole, if desired.

Preparation Time: 15 minutes
Cooking Time: 10 minutes

*Wear rubber gloves when working with jalapeño peppers and wash hands with warm soapy water. Avoid touching face or eyes.

*Favorite recipe from **National Live Stock and Meat Board***

Santa Fe Burrito Bake

Mexican Beef Stir-Fry

Santa Fe Burrito Bake

- **1½ pounds ground beef**
- **1 cup water**
- **1 can (4 ounces) chopped green chiles, undrained**
- **1 package (1.25 ounces) taco seasoning mix, dry**
- **2 cups Wheat CHEX® brand cereal, crushed to ¾ cup**
- **1 loaf frozen bread dough, thawed**
- **1 cup (4 ounces) shredded Cheddar cheese**
- **1 teaspoon margarine or butter, melted**
- **Chili powder**
- **Salsa, sour cream and shredded lettuce**

Preheat oven to 350°F. In large skillet over medium heat cook meat 5 minutes or until no longer pink; drain. Stir in water, chiles and seasoning mix. Add cereal, stirring until well combined; set aside. Roll bread dough into a 15×10-inch rectangle. Spread 2 cups reserved meat mixture in a 4-inch-wide strip lengthwise down center of bread. Top with cheese. Cover with remaining 2 cups meat mixture. Bring sides of dough up over filling. Seal top and sides well. Place seam side down on ungreased baking sheet. Brush with margarine. Sprinkle with chili powder. Bake 30 to 35 minutes or until golden brown. Slice and serve with salsa, sour cream and lettuce.

Makes 6 servings

To decorate top: Cut 1-inch-wide strip from a short side of dough; reserve. Decorate loaf with reserved dough before brushing with margarine.

Mexican Beef and Rice

1 pound ground beef
8 scallions thinly sliced*
1 can (16 ounces) tomato sauce
1 cup water
¼ cup sliced pitted ripe olives or stuffed green olives
1 tablespoon chili powder
1½ cups Original MINUTE® Rice
Tortilla chips (optional)

Brown beef with scallions in large skillet, breaking beef into small pieces. Stir in tomato sauce, water, olives and chili powder. Bring to full boil. Stir in rice. Cover; remove from heat. Let stand 5 minutes. Fluff with fork. Serve with tortilla chips.

Makes 4 servings

Microwave Directions: Combine all ingredients except tortilla chips in microwavable dish. Cover and cook on HIGH 10 minutes, stirring halfway through cooking time. Let stand 5 minutes. Fluff with fork. Serve with tortilla chips.

Makes 4 servings

*You may use 1 cup chopped onion for the scallions.

Mexican Beef and Rice

Thai Beef

1 pound ground round
1 teaspoon crushed red pepper
1 medium red onion, sliced
1 medium green bell pepper, chopped
¼ cup REALEMON® Lemon Juice from Concentrate
2 teaspoons finely chopped fresh mint leaves *or* ½ teaspoon dried mint leaves
1 teaspoon WYLER'S® or STEERO® Beef-Flavor Instant Bouillon
2 cups hot cooked rice
⅔ cup seeded, chopped cucumber
12 lettuce leaves

In large skillet, brown meat and red pepper; pour off fat. Add onion, green pepper, ReaLemon® brand, mint and bouillon; mix well. Simmer uncovered until vegetables are tender. Meanwhile, combine rice and cucumber; keep warm. Place about ¼ cup rice mixture and ⅓ cup meat mixture on each lettuce leaf; roll up. Serve immediately. Refrigerate leftovers.

Makes 4 to 6 servings

Saucy Beef and Vegetable Stir-Fry

Saucy Beef and Vegetable Stir-Fry

**1 beef flank steak (1 pound),
cut into ¼-inch strips
1 teaspoon minced fresh
gingerroot
2 tablespoons vegetable oil
1½ cups broccoli flowerets
1 cup julienne-cut zucchini
1 cup sliced fresh
mushrooms
½ cup red or green bell
pepper chunks
1 jar (12 ounces) HEINZ®
HomeStyle Brown with
Onions Gravy
2 tablespoons soy sauce
Dash pepper
Chow mein noodles or hot
cooked rice**

In preheated large skillet or
wok, stir-fry steak and
gingerroot in oil; remove. Stir-fry
broccoli, zucchini, mushrooms
and red pepper 2 to 3 minutes or
until tender-crisp, adding more
oil if necessary. Stir in gravy, soy
sauce and pepper. Return steak
to skillet; heat 1 to 2 minutes or
until hot. Serve with chow mein
noodles. Garnish with sesame
seeds, if desired.

*Makes 4 servings
(about 4½ cups)*

Mandarin Beef

**1 pound beef flank steak
3 tablespoons lite soy sauce,
divided
6 teaspoons vegetable oil,
divided
1 tablespoon cornstarch
3 teaspoons brown sugar,
divided
¼ pound green beans, cut
diagonally into 2-inch
pieces
1 package (10 ounces) frozen
asparagus,* thawed and
cut diagonally into
2-inch pieces
¼ pound mushrooms, sliced
2 tablespoons dry sherry
6 green onions, cut into
2-inch slivers
½ teaspoon Oriental dark
roasted sesame oil****

Cut beef flank steak lengthwise
in half. Cut steak across the
grain into ⅛-inch-thick strips.
Combine 1 tablespoon of the soy
sauce, 1 teaspoon of the oil, the
cornstarch and 1 teaspoon of the
brown sugar; pour over beef
strips and marinate 30 minutes.

Heat nonstick frying pan over
medium heat; add remaining 5
teaspoons oil. Stir-fry green
beans 3 to 4 minutes in oil; add
asparagus and mushrooms and
cook 2 minutes. Remove
vegetables; keep warm. Combine
sherry, remaining 2 tablespoons
soy sauce and 2 teaspoons brown
sugar; reserve. Stir-fry beef (⅓ at
a time) 2 to 3 minutes; reserve.
Return beef, vegetables and
sherry mixture to frying pan and
heat through. Stir in green
onions. Add sesame oil and stir.
Serve immediately.

Makes 4 servings

Preparation Time: 15 minutes
Marinating Time: 30 minutes
Cooking Time: 15 minutes

*Twelve ounces fresh asparagus
may be substituted. Cut into
2-inch diagonal pieces; blanch
2 minutes before stir-frying.

**Dark roasted sesame oil may
be found in the imported
(oriental) section of the
supermarket.

*Favorite recipe from **National Live
Stock and Meat Board***

Gingered Beef

Gingered Beef

- 1 pound boneless beef
  sirloin steak, cut ½ inch
  thick
- ⅓ cup diagonally sliced
  celery
- 1 small red bell pepper, cut
  into strips
- 1 to 2 teaspoons grated fresh
  gingerroot
- 2 tablespoons vegetable oil,
  divided
- 1 cup sliced fresh
  mushrooms
- 1 cup snow pea pods
- 1 jar (12 ounces) HEINZ®
  HomeStyle Brown Gravy
- ⅓ cup sliced water chestnuts
- 4 green onions, cut into
  ½-inch lengths
- 1 tablespoon soy sauce
  Hot cooked rice

Cut steak across the grain into
⅛-inch strips; set aside. In
preheated large skillet or wok,
stir-fry celery, red pepper and
gingerroot in 1 tablespoon oil
1 minute. Add mushrooms and
snow peas and stir-fry 1 to 2
minutes longer or until
vegetables are tender-crisp;
remove. Stir-fry beef in
remaining 1 tablespoon oil. Add
gravy, water chestnuts, green
onions and soy sauce. Return
vegetables to skillet; heat
through. Serve over rice.
*Makes 4 servings
(about 5 cups)*

Pineapple Beef Curry

- 1 pound ground beef
- 2 teaspoons curry powder
- 1 can (10½ ounces)
  CAMPBELL'S®
  condensed Beef Broth
- 1 can (8 ounces) tomatoes,
  drained, cut up
- 1 can (8 ounces) crushed
  pineapple in juice,
  undrained
- 3 tablespoons tomato paste
- 2 tablespoons apricot
  preserves
- 4 green onions, diagonally
  sliced
  Hot cooked rice
  Assorted condiments
  (see Tip)

1. In 10-inch skillet over
medium heat, cook beef until
browned, stirring to separate
meat. Add curry; cook 2 minutes
more.

2. Stir in broth, tomatoes,
pineapple, tomato paste and
preserves. Heat to boiling.
Reduce heat to low. Cook 10
minutes, stirring occasionally.

3. Stir in green onions; cook 5
minutes more or until tender,
stirring occasionally. Serve over
rice with assorted condiments.
*Makes about 4 cups
or 4 servings*

Tip: Be creative with the
condiments: chopped green and
sweet red peppers, sliced green
onions, canned pineapple chunks,
flaked coconut, mandarin orange
segments and peanuts.

Pineapple Beef Curry

Savory Beef Rolls

**1 medium green bell pepper,
  cut into chunks
1 medium onion, sliced
1 clove garlic, minced
1 tablespoon vegetable oil
1 cup prepared stuffing
¼ cup grated Parmesan
  cheese
4 beef cubed steaks
  (6 ounces each)
1 cup water
¾ cup HEINZ® Chili Sauce
1 teaspoon instant beef
  bouillon granules or
  1 bouillon cube**

In large skillet, sauté green
pepper, onion and garlic in oil
until tender-crisp; remove. In
small bowl, combine stuffing and
Parmesan cheese. Place ¼ cup
stuffing mixture on each steak;
roll, jelly-roll fashion, and secure
with toothpicks. In skillet, brown
steak rolls, adding more oil if
necessary. In medium bowl,
combine water, chili sauce,
bouillon and sautéed vegetables;
pour over beef rolls. Cover;
simmer 30 minutes, basting
occasionally. Remove toothpicks;
spoon sauce over rolls.

*Makes 4 servings
(about 2⅓ cups sauce)*

Fruited Beef Kabobs

**1 small green bell pepper, cut
  into 1-inch pieces
1 can (8 ounces) pineapple
  chunks in juice
¾ pound sirloin steak, cut
  into 1-inch cubes
1 can (10½ ounces) mandarin
  oranges, drained
1 onion, cut into wedges
1 package (1.27 ounces)
  LAWRY'S® Spices &
  Seasonings for Fajitas
½ cup undiluted orange juice
  concentrate
½ teaspoon freshly grated
  orange peel**

In medium microwave-safe bowl,
place bell pepper. Cover and
microwave on HIGH 3 minutes.
Let cool. Drain pineapple;
reserve juice. Alternately thread
bell pepper, beef cubes, orange
segments, pineapple and onion
on wooden skewers. Place kabobs
in 13×9×2-inch glass baking
pan. Combine Spices &
Seasonings for Fajitas, orange
juice concentrate, reserved
pineapple juice and orange peel;
pour over kabobs. Cover and
marinate in refrigerator 2 hours
or overnight. Bake, covered, in
350°F oven 15 to 20 minutes or
until beef is to desired doneness.
Uncover, baste with marinade
and place under broiler. Broil 1
to 2 minutes to brown.

Makes 6 servings

Presentation: Serve with crisp
green salad and a rice side dish.

Hint: If desired, you may omit
cooking bell pepper in microwave
oven.

Zesty Beef Stroganoff

**1 (1- to 1¼-pound) sirloin
  steak, cut into ⅛-inch
  strips
¼ cup margarine or butter
8 ounces fresh mushrooms,
  sliced (about 2 cups)
½ cup sliced onion
1 clove garlic, finely chopped
2 tablespoons flour
1 cup water
3 tablespoons REALEMON®
  Lemon Juice from
  Concentrate
3 tablespoons dry red wine
2 teaspoons WYLER'S® or
  STEERO® Beef-Flavor
  Instant Bouillon
¼ teaspoon pepper
1 (8-ounce) container
  BORDEN® or MEADOW
  GOLD® Sour Cream, at
  room temperature
  CREAMETTE® Egg
  Noodles, cooked as
  package directs
Chopped parsley**

In large skillet, over medium-
high heat, brown sirloin in
margarine; remove from pan. In
same skillet, cook and stir
mushrooms, onion and garlic
until tender; stir in flour. Add
water, ReaLemon® brand, wine,
bouillon and pepper; cook and
stir until slightly thickened. Stir
in sour cream then meat; heat
through. *Do not boil.* Serve on
noodles; garnish with parsley.
Refrigerate leftovers.

Makes 4 servings

Sherried Beef

**¾ pound beef top round steak
1 cup water
¼ cup dry sherry
3 tablespoons soy sauce
2 large carrots, cut into
  diagonal slices
1 large green pepper, cut into
  strips
1 medium onion, cut into
  chunks
2 tablespoons vegetable oil,
  divided
1 tablespoon cornstarch
2 cups hot cooked rice**

Partially freeze steak; slice
across the grain into ⅛-inch
strips. Combine water, sherry,
and soy sauce. Pour over beef in
dish; marinate 1 hour. Stir-fry
vegetables in 1 tablespoon oil in
large skillet over medium-high
heat. Remove from skillet; set
aside. Drain beef; reserve
marinade. Brown beef in
remaining 1 tablespoon oil.
Combine cornstarch with
reserved marinade in bowl. Add
vegetables and marinade to beef.
Cook, stirring, until sauce is
thickened; cook 1 minute longer.
Serve over rice.

Makes 4 servings

*Favorite recipe from **USA Rice
Council***

Sherried Beef

Meatballs in Sour Cream Sauce

- 1 pound lean ground beef
- 1 cup soft bread crumbs
- 1 egg, slightly beaten
- ¼ cup grated Parmesan cheese
- ¼ cup milk
- ½ teaspoon onion powder
- ½ teaspoon garlic salt
- ⅛ teaspoon pepper
- 1 tablespoon vegetable oil
- 1 tablespoon paprika
- 1 medium onion, halved, sliced
- 1 jar (12 ounces) HEINZ® Mushroom or Brown Gravy
- ½ cup dairy sour cream
- Hot cooked noodles

In large bowl, combine beef, bread crumbs, egg, Parmesan cheese, milk, onion powder, garlic salt and pepper. Form into 20 meatballs, using a rounded tablespoon for each. In large skillet, brown meatballs in oil; drain excess fat. Sprinkle meatballs with paprika; add onion. Cover; cook over low heat 10 minutes. In medium bowl, combine gravy and sour cream; pour over meatballs. Heat slowly, basting meatballs frequently. *Do not boil.* Serve over noodles. Garnish with chopped parsley, if desired.

Makes 4 servings

Saucy Meatballs

- 1 pound lean ground beef
- ⅔ cup grated Parmesan cheese
- ½ cup seasoned dry bread crumbs
- ½ cup milk
- 1 egg, slightly beaten
- 2 tablespoons vegetable oil
- 1 tablespoon all-purpose flour
- 1 can (28 ounces) whole peeled tomatoes, cut into bite-size pieces
- ⅓ to ½ cup HEINZ® 57 Sauce
- ½ teaspoon salt
- Hot buttered noodles

In large bowl, combine beef, Parmesan cheese, bread crumbs, milk and egg. Form into 20 meatballs using a rounded tablespoon for each. In large skillet, brown meatballs in oil; drain excess fat. Sprinkle flour over meatballs, stirring gently to coat. In medium bowl, combine tomatoes, 57 Sauce and salt; pour over meatballs. Simmer, uncovered, 25 minutes or until sauce is desired consistency, stirring occasionally. Serve meatballs and sauce over noodles.

Makes 5 servings (about 3 cups sauce)

Sweet & Sour Meatballs

- 1½ pounds lean ground beef
- 1 (8-ounce) can water chestnuts, drained and chopped
- 2 eggs, slightly beaten
- ⅓ cup plain dry bread crumbs
- 4 teaspoons WYLER'S® or STEERO® Beef-Flavor Instant Bouillon
- 1 tablespoon Worcestershire sauce
- 1 cup water
- ½ cup firmly packed light brown sugar
- ½ cup REALEMON® Lemon Juice from Concentrate
- ¼ cup ketchup
- 2 tablespoons cornstarch
- ¼ teaspoon salt
- 1 cup diced red and green bell peppers
- Hot cooked rice

In large bowl, combine meat, water chestnuts, eggs, crumbs, bouillon and Worcestershire; mix well. Shape into 1¼-inch meatballs. In large skillet, brown meatballs. Remove from pan; pour off fat. In same skillet, combine remaining ingredients except peppers and rice; mix well. Over medium heat, cook and stir until sauce thickens. Reduce heat. Add meatballs; simmer uncovered 10 minutes. Add peppers; heat through. Serve with rice. Garnish with parsley if desired. Refrigerate leftovers.

Makes 6 to 8 servings

Meatballs in Sour Cream Sauce

Saucy Veal and Vegetables

Saucy Veal and Vegetables

- **2 cups quartered fresh mushrooms**
- **1 cup julienne-cut carrots**
- **1 small zucchini, halved lengthwise, cut into ¼-inch slices**
- **4 green onions, sliced**
- **½ teaspoon dried basil leaves, crushed**
- **½ teaspoon salt**
- **¼ teaspoon pepper**
- **¼ teaspoon dried oregano leaves, crushed**
- **2 tablespoons vegetable oil, divided**
- **1 pound boneless veal cutlets, cut into thin strips**
- **2 tablespoons dry white wine**
- **1 jar (12 ounces) HEINZ® HomeStyle Chicken Gravy**
- **¼ cup dairy sour cream Hot cooked spaghetti or linguine**

In large skillet, sauté mushrooms, carrots, zucchini, green onions, basil, salt, pepper and oregano in 1 tablespoon oil; remove. Add remaining 1 tablespoon oil. Quickly brown veal in 2 batches; remove. Add wine; heat. Stir in gravy and sour cream. Return veal and vegetables to skillet; heat slowly. *Do not boil.* Serve over hot spaghetti.

Makes 4 servings (about 4 cups)

Glazed Meat Loaf

- **½ cup ketchup**
- **⅓ cup firmly packed light brown sugar**
- **¼ cup REALEMON® Lemon Juice from Concentrate**
- **1 teaspoon dry mustard**
- **1½ pounds lean ground beef**
- **1½ cups fresh bread crumbs (3 slices)**
- **¼ cup finely chopped onion**
- **1 egg, slightly beaten**
- **1 teaspoon WYLER'S® or STEERO® Beef-Flavor Instant Bouillon**

Preheat oven to 350°. In small bowl, combine ketchup, sugar, *1 tablespoon* ReaLemon® brand and mustard. In large bowl, combine remaining ingredients and ⅓ cup ketchup mixture; mix well. In shallow baking dish, shape into loaf. Bake 1 hour; pour off fat. Pour remaining ketchup mixture over loaf; bake 10 minutes longer. Garnish as desired. Refrigerate leftovers.

Makes 4 to 6 servings

Easy Cheesy Meat Loaf

- **1½ pounds lean ground beef**
- **2 cups fresh bread crumbs (4 slices)**
- **1 cup tomato juice**
- **½ cup chopped onion**
- **2 eggs, slightly beaten**
- **2 teaspoons WYLER'S® or STEERO® Beef-Flavor Instant Bouillon**
- **¼ teaspoon pepper**
- **6 slices BORDEN® Singles Process American Cheese Food**

Preheat oven to 350°. In bowl, combine all ingredients except cheese food. In shallow baking dish, shape half the mixture into loaf. Cut *4 slices* cheese food into strips; arrange on meat. Top with remaining meat; press edges together to seal. Bake for 1 hour. Top with remaining cheese food slices. Refrigerate leftovers.

Makes 4 to 6 servings

Tasty Pork Ragout

Lime-Basted Lamb Kabobs

Lime-Herb Marinade
- ¾ cup lime juice (about 6 limes)
- ¼ cup olive or vegetable oil
- ⅓ cup sugar
- 1 teaspoon dried cilantro leaves
- 1 teaspoon fresh or dried rosemary
- 1 clove garlic, minced
- ½ teaspoon black pepper

Lamb Kabobs
- 1½ to 2 pounds trimmed lamb, cut into 1¼-inch cubes
- 1 package (10 ounces) pearl onions, blanched and peeled
- 4 fresh California peaches, halved, pitted
- ½ cup nonfat plain yogurt (optional)

In large zip-top plastic bag, combine marinade ingredients. Reserve 3 tablespoons marinade. Add lamb and pearl onions; close bag securely. Refrigerate 30 minutes, turning bag every 10 minutes. Remove lamb and onions, reserving marinade for basting. Thread lamb and onions alternately onto 4 to 6 skewers.

Cook kabobs on uncovered grill over medium, direct heat, turning frequently and brushing with marinade, about 16 minutes for medium rare, 20 minutes for medium and 24 minutes for well done. Brush peaches with marinade and place directly on grill during last 8 minutes, turning after 4 minutes.

Combine reserved 3 tablespoons marinade with yogurt, if desired. Serve as a sauce with lamb and peaches.

Makes 4 to 6 servings

Tips: To blanch onions, place whole onions in boiling water. Return to a boil and simmer about 6 minutes; drain and let stand until cool enough to handle. Trim stem end and skin will slip off easily.

If using wooden skewers, soak in water 20 minutes before grilling.

Favorite recipe from **California Tree Fruit Agreement**

Greek Lamb Sauté with Mostaccioli

- ½ (1-pound) package CREAMETTE® Mostaccioli, uncooked
- 1 medium green bell pepper, chopped
- 1 medium onion, chopped
- 1 medium eggplant, peeled, seeded and cut into 1-inch cubes
- 2 cloves garlic, finely chopped
- 1 tablespoon olive or vegetable oil
- ½ pound lean boneless lamb, cut into ¾-inch cubes
- 2 fresh tomatoes, pared, seeded and chopped
- ¼ teaspoon ground nutmeg
- ¼ cup grated Parmesan cheese

Prepare mostaccioli as package directs; drain. In large skillet, cook and stir green pepper, onion, eggplant and garlic in oil until tender-crisp. Add lamb; cook until tender. Stir in tomatoes and nutmeg; heat through. Toss meat mixture with hot cooked mostaccioli and Parmesan cheese. Serve immediately. Refrigerate leftovers. *Makes 8 servings*

Tasty Pork Ragout

- ½ pound pork loin, cubed
- 1 small onion, cut into wedges
- 1 large clove garlic, pressed
- ½ teaspoon dried rosemary, crumbled
- 2 tablespoons margarine
  Salt and pepper to taste
- 1 chicken bouillon cube
- ½ cup boiling water
- 2 cups DOLE® Cauliflower florettes
- 1 cup sliced DOLE® Carrots
- 1 cup hot cooked rice

- In 10-inch skillet, sauté pork, onion, garlic and rosemary in margarine over medium-high heat until pork is browned; turn once. Sprinkle with salt and pepper to taste.

- Dissolve bouillon in water in cup; stir into pork mixture. Reduce heat. Cover; simmer 20 minutes.

- Add cauliflower and carrots. Cover; simmer 5 minutes longer or until tender-crisp. Serve over rice. *Makes 2 servings*

Preparation Time: 10 minutes
Cook Time: 30 minutes

Pork 'n' Spicy Apples

¼ **cup HEINZ® 57 Sauce**
¼ **cup apple jelly**
¼ **cup apple juice**
1 **teaspoon cornstarch**
⅛ **teaspoon ground cinnamon**
Dash ground allspice
1 **pound boneless pork loin**
¼ **cup all-purpose flour**
¼ **teaspoon salt**
⅛ **teaspoon pepper**
1 **tablespoon vegetable oil**
2 **large Granny Smith or Golden Delicious apples, peeled, quartered, sliced ½ inch thick**
1 **tablespoon butter or margarine**

In small bowl, combine 57 Sauce, jelly, apple juice, cornstarch, cinnamon and allspice; set aside. Cut pork into 4 slices; flatten each slice to ¼-inch thickness. In small bowl, combine flour, salt and pepper. Dust pork lightly with flour mixture. In large skillet, sauté pork in oil until cooked, about 3 minutes on each side; remove and keep warm. In same skillet, sauté apples in butter 2 to 3 minutes; remove. Pour 57 Sauce mixture into skillet; heat, stirring constantly, until jelly is melted and sauce is thickened. Return apples to skillet; heat through. Spoon apples and sauce over pork.
Makes 4 servings

Pork Loin Roulade

4 **boneless center pork loin slices, about 1 pound**
½ **red bell pepper, cut into strips**
½ **green bell pepper, cut into strips**
1 **teaspoon vegetable oil**
⅔ **cup orange juice**
⅔ **cup bottled barbecue sauce**
1 **tablespoon prepared Dijon-style mustard**

Place pork slices between 2 pieces of plastic wrap. Pound with mallet to about ¼-inch thickness.

Place several red and green pepper strips crosswise on each pork portion; roll up jelly-roll style. Secure rolls with wooden toothpicks.

In nonstick skillet, brown pork rolls in vegetable oil. Drain fat from pan. Combine orange juice, barbecue sauce and mustard; add to skillet. Bring mixture to boiling; reduce heat. Cover and simmer 10 to 12 minutes or until pork is tender. Remove toothpicks to serve.
Makes 4 servings

Preparation Time: 20 minutes
Cooking Time: 12 minutes

Favorite recipe from **National Pork Producers Council**

Pork Loin Roulade

Citrus & Spice Pork Loin Roast

- 1 package (1.25 ounces) LAWRY'S® Taco Spices & Seasonings
- ¾ cup orange marmalade
- ½ teaspoon LAWRY'S® Garlic Powder with Parsley
- 1 (3-pound) boneless pork loin roast

In small bowl, combine Taco Spices & Seasonings, orange marmalade and Garlic Powder with Parsley; blend well. Score pork roast with sharp knife. Place pork roast in large resealable plastic bag and cover with marmalade mixture. Marinate in refrigerator 45 minutes. Remove pork; wrap in foil and place in baking dish. Bake in 350°F oven 1 hour. Open and fold back foil; bake 30 minutes longer or until roast is glazed and internal temperature reaches 170°F on a meat thermometer. Cool 10 minutes before slicing.

Makes 6 servings

Presentation: Slice pork thinly and serve drippings that remain in foil as a flavorful gravy. Garnish with parsley and orange peel, if desired.

Honey Mustard Pork Tenderloin

- ¼ cup vegetable oil
- 2 tablespoons brown sugar
- 2 tablespoons honey
- 2 tablespoons REALEMON® Lemon Juice from Concentrate
- 1 tablespoon Dijon-style mustard
- 2 teaspoons WYLER'S® or STEERO® Beef-Flavor or Chicken-Flavor Instant Bouillon
- 1 (¾- to 1-pound) pork tenderloin

In large shallow dish or plastic bag, combine all ingredients except tenderloin. Add tenderloin. Cover; marinate in refrigerator 6 hours or overnight. Remove tenderloin from marinade. Grill or broil 30 to 35 minutes or until meat thermometer inserted in center reaches 160°, basting frequently with heated marinade. Refrigerate leftovers.

Makes 2 to 4 servings

Dilled Pork Scallopini

- 1 pound pork tenderloin All-purpose flour
- 1 egg, slightly beaten
- 1 tablespoon water
- ½ cup seasoned dry bread crumbs
- 2 tablespoons butter or margarine
- 1 medium carrot, cut into julienne strips
- 1 jar (12 ounces) HEINZ® HomeStyle Brown Gravy
- 3 tablespoons half-and-half or milk
- 1 teaspoon lemon juice
- ½ teaspoon dried dill weed
- 1 tablespoon dairy sour cream

Cut pork crosswise into 12 slices; flatten to ¼-inch thickness. Dust pork lightly with flour. In shallow dish, combine egg and water. Dip pork into egg mixture, then coat with crumbs. In large skillet, sauté pork in butter, a few pieces at a time, about 3 minutes on each side or until golden brown, adding more butter if necessary. Keep pork warm while preparing sauce. For sauce, sauté carrot in same skillet until tender-crisp, 1 to 2 minutes. Stir in gravy, half-and-half, lemon juice and dill; heat through. Stir sour cream into sauce just before serving. Spoon sauce over pork.

Makes 4 servings
(about 1¾ cups sauce)

Pork Tenderloin Waldorf

- 2 pork tenderloins (about 1½ pounds)
- ¾ cup BAMA® Apple Jelly
- ¼ cup REALEMON® Lemon Juice from Concentrate
- ¼ cup soy sauce
- ¼ cup vegetable oil
- 1 tablespoon finely chopped fresh ginger root
- 1 cup chopped apple
- 1 cup fresh bread crumbs (2 slices)
- ¼ cup finely chopped celery
- ¼ cup chopped pecans

Partially slit tenderloins lengthwise, being careful not to cut all the way through; arrange in shallow dish. In small saucepan, combine jelly, ReaLemon® brand, soy sauce, oil and ginger; cook and stir until jelly melts. Reserving *3 tablespoons* jelly mixture, pour remainder over meat. Cover; marinate in refrigerator 4 hours or overnight. Place meat in shallow baking pan. Combine apple, crumbs, celery, nuts and reserved jelly mixture. Spread slits open; fill with apple mixture. Bake 30 minutes in preheated 375° oven. Loosely cover meat, bake 10 minutes longer or until meat thermometer reaches 160°. Refrigerate leftovers.

Makes 4 to 6 servings

From top to bottom: Sweet & Sour Meatballs (page 104) and Pork Tenderloin Waldorf

Saucy Pork and Peppers

2 fresh limes
¼ cup 62%-less-sodium soy sauce
1 teaspoon oregano leaves
½ teaspoon thyme leaves
   Dash cayenne pepper
4 cloves garlic, crushed
2 to 3 fresh parsley sprigs
1 bay leaf
1 pound pork tenderloin, trimmed and cut into 1-inch cubes
1 tablespoon olive oil
1 teaspoon brown sugar
2 medium onions, each cut into 8 pieces
2 medium tomatoes, each cut into 8 pieces and seeded
1 large red bell pepper, cut into 8 pieces
1 large green bell pepper, cut into 8 pieces

Squeeze juice from limes, reserving peel. In small bowl, combine lime juice, lime peel, soy sauce, oregano, thyme, cayenne pepper, garlic, parsley and bay leaf; blend well. Place pork cubes in plastic bag or non-metal bowl. Pour lime mixture over pork,

Saucy Pork and Peppers

turning to coat. Seal bag or cover dish; marinate at least 2 hours or overnight in refrigerator, turning pork several times.

Remove lime peel, parsley sprigs and bay leaf from marinade; discard. Remove pork from marinade, reserving marinade. Drain pork well. Heat oil in large skillet over high heat. Add brown sugar; stir until sugar is dissolved. Add pork cubes; cook and stir about 5 minutes or until pork is browned. Reduce heat to low. Add onions, tomatoes, bell peppers and reserved marinade; simmer 10 to 15 minutes or until pork is tender.
Makes 4 servings

*Favorite recipe from **National Pork Producers Council***

Pork Valenciana

1½ pounds boneless pork loin, cut into ¾-inch cubes
2 tablespoons olive oil, divided
2 yellow onions, peeled and chopped
1 green pepper, seeded and chopped
2 cloves garlic, minced
1 8-ounce can whole tomatoes, undrained
½ teaspoon salt
1 bay leaf
¼ teaspoon pepper
4 cups water
2 cups uncooked rice
2 chicken bouillon cubes
½ cup sherry (optional)
⅛ teaspoon saffron threads
1 cup peas
1 small jar pimientos, drained
12 green olives

Brown pork in 1 tablespoon of the oil over medium-high heat; remove. Add onions, green pepper, garlic and remaining 1 tablespoon oil. Continue cooking until slightly brown, about 5 minutes. Return pork to pan and stir in tomatoes, salt, bay leaf and pepper. Add water, rice, bouillon and sherry. Dissolve saffron in small amount of water

and add to pan. Bring to boil; cover and simmer over low heat 15 minutes. Remove bay leaf. Garnish with peas, pimientos and olives.   *Makes 8 servings*

Preparation Time: 15 minutes
Cooking Time: 20 minutes

*Favorite recipe from **National Pork Producers Council***

Spicy-Sweet Pineapple Pork

1 pound pork loin, cut into ½-inch strips or cubes
¾ cup LAWRY'S® Fajitas Skillet Sauce
1 tablespoon finely chopped fresh ginger
2 tablespoons vegetable oil
1 green bell pepper, cut into chunks
3 green onions, diagonally sliced into 1-inch pieces
1 cup hot salsa
3 tablespoons brown sugar
2 tablespoons cornstarch
2 cans (8 ounces each) pineapple chunks in juice
½ cup whole cashews

Place pork in large resealable plastic bag. Combine Fajitas Skillet Sauce and ginger; add to pork and marinate in refrigerator 1 hour. In large skillet or wok, heat 1 tablespoon oil. Add bell pepper and green onions and stir-fry 3 minutes; remove and set aside. Add pork and remaining 1 tablespoon oil to skillet; stir-fry 5 minutes or until just browned. Return bell pepper and green onions to skillet. In small bowl, combine salsa, brown sugar, cornstarch and juice from one can pineapple. Add to skillet; cook until thickened, stirring constantly. Drain remaining can pineapple. Add all pineapple chunks and cashews; simmer 5 minutes.   *Makes 6 servings*

Presentation: Serve over hot fluffy rice.

Pork Satay

1 pound boneless stir-fry pork strips
3 tablespoons REALEMON® Lemon Juice from Concentrate
2 tablespoons peanut butter
2 tablespoons soy sauce
1 tablespoon brown sugar
1 tablespoon vegetable oil
2 cloves garlic, finely chopped
¼ teaspoon crushed red pepper
Peanut Dipping Sauce

Arrange meat in shallow dish. In small bowl, combine ReaLemon® brand, peanut butter, soy sauce, sugar, oil, garlic and red pepper; mix well. Pour over meat. Cover; marinate in refrigerator 4 hours or overnight, turning occasionally. Thread meat on skewers. Grill or broil as desired, brushing frequently with marinade. Serve with warm Peanut Dipping Sauce. Refrigerate leftovers.

Makes 4 servings

PEANUT DIPPING SAUCE: In small saucepan, combine ½ cup COCO LOPEZ® Cream of Coconut, 3 tablespoons peanut butter, 2 tablespoons ReaLemon® Lemon Juice from Concentrate, 2 tablespoons soy sauce and ¼ teaspoon crushed red pepper; mix well. Cook and stir until peanut butter melts and mixture boils. Reduce heat; simmer uncovered 5 minutes, stirring occasionally.

Makes about ¾ cup

Mu Shu-Style Fajitas

Mu Shu-Style Fajitas

1 tablespoon IMPERIAL® Margarine
2 eggs, beaten
¼ teaspoon LAWRY'S® Garlic Powder with Parsley
1 medium carrot, diagonally cut into thin slices
2 tablespoons vegetable oil
1 pound boneless pork, cut into thin strips
1 cup LAWRY'S® Fajitas Skillet Sauce
2 cups shredded cabbage
1 cup sliced fresh mushrooms
1 can (8 ounces) sliced bamboo shoots, drained
6 medium green onions, diagonally cut into 1-inch pieces
1 teaspoon lemon juice
8 medium flour tortillas, warmed

In large skillet, melt margarine and scramble eggs with Garlic Powder with Parsley; remove and set aside. In same skillet, sauté carrot in 1 tablespoon oil until crisp-tender; remove and set aside. In same skillet, brown pork in remaining 1 tablespoon oil; drain fat. Add Fajitas Skillet Sauce; blend well. Bring to a boil; reduce heat and simmer, uncovered, 3 to 5 minutes. Add eggs, carrots and remaining ingredients except tortillas; heat 2 minutes until vegetables are crisp-tender. Serve piping hot mixture wrapped in warm flour tortillas. *Makes 8 servings*

Presentation: Serve with plum sauce, if desired.

Hint: Also works well with boneless, skinless chicken breast strips.

Sesame Pork with Broccoli

1 can (14½ ounces) chicken broth
2 tablespoons cornstarch
1 tablespoon soy sauce
4 green onions and tops, finely diced
1 pound pork tenderloin, trimmed
1 tablespoon vegetable oil
1 clove garlic, minced
1½ pounds fresh broccoli, cut into bite-size pieces (about 7 cups)
2 tablespoons sliced pimiento, drained
2 tablespoons sesame seed, lightly toasted

In small bowl, combine chicken broth, cornstarch and soy sauce; blend well. Stir in green onions; set aside. Cut pork tenderloin lengthwise into quarters; cut each quarter into bite-size pieces. Heat oil in wok or heavy skillet over medium-high heat. Add pork and garlic; stir-fry 3 to 4 minutes or until pork is tender. Remove pork; keep warm. Add broccoli and broth mixture to wok. Cover and simmer over low heat 8 minutes. Add cooked pork and pimiento; cook just until mixture is hot, stirring frequently. Sprinkle with sesame seed. Serve immediately.

Makes 6 servings

*Favorite recipe from **National Pork Producers Council***

Szechuan Shredded Pork

1½ pounds pork shoulder blade steak
1 can (10¾ ounces) CAMPBELL'S® condensed Golden Mushroom Soup
½ cup water
¼ cup dry sherry
1 tablespoon soy sauce
½ teaspoon ground ginger
½ teaspoon crushed red pepper
2 tablespoons vegetable oil, divided
½ cup diagonally sliced carrot
½ medium sweet red or green pepper, cut into 2-inch matchstick-thin strips
Hot cooked rice

1. Remove bone from steak; thinly slice steak, discarding excess fat. Set aside.

2. In small bowl, combine soup, water, sherry, soy sauce, ginger and crushed red pepper.

3. In 10-inch skillet over high heat, in *1 tablespoon* hot oil, stir-fry carrot and red pepper strips until tender-crisp. Transfer to bowl.

4. In same skillet, in remaining oil, stir-fry pork *half* at a time, until pork is no longer pink. Stir in cooked vegetables and soup mixture. Heat to boiling. Serve over rice. *Makes 4 servings*

Chop Suey

¼ cup flour
2 teaspoons salt
½ pound cubed veal
½ pound cubed pork
⅓ cup CRISCO® Shortening
1 cup chopped onion
1 cup celery, cut into 1-inch pieces
1 cup beef stock or bouillon
½ cup soy sauce
2 tablespoons molasses
1 can (16 ounces) bean sprouts, drained
Hot cooked rice

Combine flour and salt in large plastic food storage bag; add meat cubes and toss lightly to coat. Brown in hot Crisco® in Dutch oven; add onion and continue browning. Stir in celery, beef stock, soy sauce and molasses. Cover and cook over low heat for 25 minutes. Add bean sprouts; cook 15 minutes more. Thicken with additional flour, if necessary. Serve over hot cooked rice. Refrigerate leftovers.

Makes 4 to 6 servings

Oriental Fried Rice

3 cups cooked brown rice, cold
½ cup slivered cooked roast pork
½ cup finely chopped celery
½ cup bean sprouts*
⅓ cup sliced green onions
1 egg, beaten
Vegetable cooking spray
¼ teaspoon black pepper
2 tablespoons soy sauce

Combine rice, pork, celery, bean sprouts, onions, and egg in large skillet coated with cooking spray. Cook, stirring, 3 minutes over high heat. Add pepper and soy sauce. Cook, stirring, 1 minute longer. *Makes 6 servings*

To microwave: Combine rice, pork, celery, bean sprouts, and onions in shallow 2-quart microproof baking dish coated with cooking spray. Cook on HIGH 2 to 3 minutes. Add egg, pepper, and soy sauce. Cook on HIGH 1 to 2 minutes or until egg is set, stirring to separate grains.

*Substitute canned bean sprouts, rinsed and drained, for the fresh bean sprouts, if desired.

Tip: When preparing fried rice always begin with cold rice. The grains separate better if cold and it's a great way to use leftover rice.

*Favorite recipe from **USA Rice Council***

Sesame Pork with Broccoli

Stuffed Pork Chops

Stuffed Pork Chops

**4 rib pork chops, cut
    1¼ inches thick, slit for
    stuffing
1½ cups prepared stuffing
1 tablespoon vegetable oil
    Salt and pepper
1 bottle (12 ounces) HEINZ®
    Chili Sauce**

Trim excess fat from chops. Place
stuffing in pockets of chops;
secure with wooden toothpicks or
string. In large skillet, brown
chops in oil; season with salt and
pepper. Place chops in 2-quart
oblong baking dish. Pour chili
sauce over chops. Cover with foil;
bake in 350°F oven, 30 minutes.
Stir sauce; turn and baste chops.
Cover; bake an additional 30 to
40 minutes or until chops are
cooked. Remove toothpicks. Skim
excess fat. Spoon sauce over
chops.   *Makes 4 servings*

California Pork Cutlets

**2 firm, medium DOLE®
    Bananas, peeled
2 tablespoons vegetable oil
4 pork cutlets, ¼ inch thick
½ teaspoon dried rosemary,
    crumbled
    Salt and pepper to taste
½ cup orange juice
½ teaspoon cornstarch
¼ cup DOLE® Raisins**

• Cut bananas in half crosswise,
then lengthwise to make 8 slices.
In 12-inch nonstick skillet, sauté
bananas in hot oil over medium-
high heat until lightly browned;
turn once. Remove bananas.

Pork Strips Florentine

**1 pound boneless pork strips
1 package (6 ounces)
    seasoned long grain and
    wild rice mix, uncooked
1⅔ cups hot water
1 can (2.8 ounces) DURKEE®
    French Fried Onions
¼ teaspoon DURKEE® Garlic
    Powder
1 package (10 ounces) frozen
    chopped spinach, thawed
    and well drained
2 tablespoons diced
    pimiento (optional)
½ cup (2 ounces) shredded
    Swiss cheese**

Preheat oven to 375°F. In 8×12-
inch baking dish, combine pork
strips, rice, contents of rice
seasoning packet, hot water,
½ can Durkee® French Fried
Onions and garlic powder. Bake,
covered, for 30 minutes. Stir
spinach and pimiento into meat
mixture. Bake, covered, 10
minutes or until pork and rice
are done. Top with cheese and
remaining onions; bake,
uncovered, 3 minutes or until
onions are golden brown.
    Makes 4 servings

• Sprinkle pork with rosemary, salt and pepper. In same skillet, sauté pork, 1 to 2 minutes on each side.

• Blend orange juice and cornstarch in cup. Stir into skillet. Add raisins. Heat to a boil. Reduce heat. Cover; simmer 5 minutes.

• Arrange bananas and 2 cutlets on 2 plates. Spoon sauce over top. *Makes 2 servings*

Preparation Time: 5 minutes
Cook Time: 10 minutes

Island Pork Chops

1 can (8 ounces) pineapple chunks
1 tablespoon cornstarch
⅔ cup HEINZ® Chili Sauce
⅓ cup raisins
1 tablespoon brown sugar
⅛ teaspoon ground cinnamon
4 boneless pork loin chops (½ inch thick, about 5 ounces each)
1 tablespoon vegetable oil
Hot cooked couscous or rice

Drain pineapple, reserving juice. In medium bowl, blend juice with cornstarch; stir in pineapple, chili sauce, raisins, sugar and cinnamon and set aside. In large skillet, lightly brown pork in oil; drain excess fat. Pour pineapple mixture over pork. Cover; simmer 10 minutes or until pork is cooked. Serve pork and sauce with couscous.

Makes 4 servings
(about 2 cups sauce)

Pork Cutlets with Garden Vegetables

1½ pounds pork cutlets
2 teaspoons vegetable oil
2½ cups peeled, chopped fresh tomatoes
1 can (8 ounces) tomato sauce
½ cup chopped onion
¼ cup chopped fresh chiles *or* 4-ounce can diced green chiles
1 clove garlic, minced
2 tablespoons fresh lime juice
½ teaspoon salt
¼ teaspoon ground cumin
1 cup julienne-cut carrots
1 cup julienne-cut zucchini
¼ cup raisins
¼ cup slivered almonds

Heat oil in nonstick frying pan. Brown pork cutlets over medium-high heat. Stir in tomatoes, tomato sauce, onion, chiles, garlic, lime juice, salt and cumin. Cover; simmer 20 minutes. Stir in carrots, zucchini and raisins. Cover; simmer 10 minutes longer or until vegetables are tender. Stir in almonds. *Makes 6 servings*

Preparation Time: 15 minutes
Cooking Time: 30 minutes

*Favorite recipe from **National Pork Producers Council***

Island Pork Chops

Pineapple Sweet-Sour Spareribs

**1 can (8¼ ounces) DOLE®
  Pineapple Chunks in
  Syrup***
¼ cup soy sauce, divided
3 tablespoons cornstarch
3 to 4 pounds lean spareribs
**2 to 3 tablespoons
  vegetable oil**
1 cup cider vinegar
¾ cup brown sugar, packed
⅓ cup water
2 cloves garlic, pressed
**1 piece (2 inches) ginger
  root, peeled, minced**

• Drain pineapple; reserve syrup.

• Combine 2 tablespoons soy sauce and cornstarch in small bowl. Rub soy sauce mixture onto ribs.

• In 12-inch skillet, sauté ribs, in batches, in oil over medium-high heat until browned.

• Combine reserved syrup, remaining 2 tablespoons soy sauce, vinegar, brown sugar, water, garlic and ginger root in Dutch oven. Add ribs. Heat to a boil. Reduce heat. Cover; simmer 1 hour, stirring occasionally.

• Spoon off fat. Stir in pineapple; heat through.

Makes 3 to 4 servings

*Use pineapple packed in juice, if desired.

Preparation Time: 5 minutes
Cook Time: 1 hour 15 minutes

Oven Barbecued Spareribs

**3 to 4 pounds pork spareribs
  HEINZ® Thick and Rich
  Hickory Smoke or Old
  Fashioned Barbecue
  Sauce***

Cut spareribs into sections of 2 ribs each. Arrange ribs, rounded side down, on rack in shallow baking pan or on broiler pan. Bake in 350°F oven, 30 minutes. Turn; bake an additional 30 minutes. Drain excess fat, if necessary. Turn ribs; brush generously with barbecue sauce. Bake 10 minutes. Turn; brush generously with barbecue sauce. Bake an additional 10 minutes.

Makes 3 to 4 servings

***For Honey 'n' Spice Oven
Barbecued Ribs,** substitute mixture of ½ cup Heinz® 57 Sauce and ¼ cup honey for barbecue sauce. Brush on ribs as directed above.

Bavarian Kielbasa with Noodles

**6 ounces uncooked egg
  noodles**
**¾ pound smoked kielbasa,
  cut up**
1 medium onion, sliced
**1 can (10¾ ounces)
  CAMPBELL'S®
  condensed Cream of
  Mushroom Soup**
1 soup can milk
**1½ cups frozen cut green
  beans**
**⅛ teaspoon pepper
  Spicy brown mustard**

1. Cook noodles according to package directions; drain. Meanwhile, in 10-inch skillet over medium heat, cook kielbasa and onion until browned, stirring often. Spoon off fat.

2. Add soup; stir until smooth. Gradually stir in milk. Add beans and pepper. Heat to boiling. Reduce heat to low. Cover; cook 5 minutes or until beans are tender, stirring occasionally.

3. Stir cooked noodles into skillet. Heat 2 minutes, stirring often. Serve with mustard.

*Makes about 6 cups
or 4 servings*

Ham with Fruited Mustard Sauce

Honey Glazed Ham

Ham with Fruited Mustard Sauce

**1 fully cooked ham slice
(1 to 1¼ pounds), cut
½ inch thick***
**1 tablespoon butter or
margarine**
**1 can (8 ounces) pineapple
slices**
¼ cup HEINZ® 57 Sauce
2 tablespoons honey
**1 tablespoon prepared
mustard**
**1½ teaspoons cornstarch
Dash ground allspice**

Cut ham into 4 serving portions. In large skillet, sauté ham in butter about 3 to 4 minutes on each side or until heated through. Meanwhile, drain pineapple, reserving juice. In small bowl, combine juice, 57 Sauce, honey, mustard, cornstarch and allspice. Remove ham from skillet; keep warm.

Pour 57 Sauce mixture into skillet and cook until thickened. Return ham to skillet. Top each ham portion with pineapple slice and spoon sauce over; heat through.   *Makes 4 servings
(about ⅔ cup sauce)*

*A 1-pound piece of Canadian bacon, cut into 4 slices, may be substituted.

Honey Glazed Ham

**¼ cup MAPLE ORCHARDS®
Pure Honey**
**3 tablespoons light brown
sugar**
**2 teaspoons prepared
mustard**

Combine ingredients. Use to baste ham frequently during last hour of baking.
*Makes enough to glaze
a 4-pound ham*

Ham Glaze

**1 cup KARO® Light or Dark
Corn Syrup**
½ cup packed brown sugar
**3 tablespoons prepared
mustard**
**½ teaspoon ground ginger
Dash ground cloves**

In medium saucepan combine corn syrup, brown sugar, mustard, ginger and cloves. Bring to boil over medium heat; boil 5 minutes, stirring constantly. Brush on ham frequently during last 30 minutes of baking.
Makes about 1 cup

Preparation Time: 10 minutes

Microwave Directions: In 1½-quart microwavable bowl combine all ingredients. Microwave on HIGH (100%), 6 minutes. Glaze ham as above.

POULTRY

Looking for new ways to prepare economical, low-fat poultry? From classics such as Chicken Fricassee and Chicken Cordon Bleu to foreign fare such as Polynesian Chicken and Rio Grande Quesadillas, you won't need to look any further. Discover how versatile and easy poultry can be with new ideas for baking, stir-frying and grilling. And with ground turkey and turkey cutlets so readily available, this bird is no longer just for the holidays.

Chicken Cordon Bleu

4 large skinless boneless chicken breast halves (about 1¼ pounds)
4 slices lean baked ham
4 ounces Swiss cheese, cut into 4 sticks
2 tablespoons butter or margarine
1 cup sliced fresh mushrooms
¼ teaspoon dried thyme leaves, crushed
⅛ teaspoon ground nutmeg
⅛ teaspoon pepper
2 tablespoons dry white wine
1 jar (12 ounces) HEINZ® HomeStyle Chicken Gravy

Place chicken between waxed paper or plastic wrap and flatten to ¼-inch thickness. Place 1 ham slice and 1 cheese stick on each breast half. Roll chicken, jelly-roll fashion, tucking ends in; secure with wooden toothpicks. In large skillet, brown chicken on all sides in butter; remove. In same skillet, sauté mushrooms, thyme, nutmeg and pepper until mushrooms are tender. Stir in wine, then add gravy. Return chicken to skillet. Cook over low heat, covered, 10 minutes or until chicken is cooked, turning once. Remove toothpicks before serving. *Makes 4 servings (about 1⅔ cups sauce)*

Special Lemony Chicken

¼ cup unsifted flour
1 teaspoon salt
¼ teaspoon pepper
6 skinned boneless chicken breast halves (about 1½ pounds)
¼ cup margarine or butter
¼ cup REALEMON® Lemon Juice from Concentrate
8 ounces fresh mushrooms, sliced (about 2 cups)
Hot cooked rice

In plastic bag, combine flour, salt and pepper. Add chicken, a few pieces at a time; shake to coat. In large skillet, brown chicken in margarine. Add ReaLemon® brand and mushrooms. Reduce heat; cover and simmer 15 minutes or until mushrooms are tender and chicken is cooked through. Serve with rice; garnish with parsley if desired. Refrigerate leftovers. *Makes 6 servings*

Easy Peach Glaze

1 (10-ounce) jar BAMA® Peach or Apricot Preserves (1 cup)
2 tablespoons REALEMON® Lemon Juice from Concentrate
1 tablespoon margarine or butter

In small saucepan, combine ingredients; bring to a boil. Reduce heat; simmer uncovered 10 to 15 minutes. Use to glaze chicken, ham loaf, ham, pork, carrots or sweet potatoes. *Makes about 1 cup*

Chicken Cordon Bleu

Sierra Chicken Bundles

Classic Savory Chicken Divan

¾ pound boneless skinless chicken breasts, cut into strips
2 teaspoons oil
1 cup water
1 tablespoon dry sherry
1 package (10 ounces) BIRDS EYE® Broccoli Spears or Deluxe Broccoli Florets, thawed
1 can (10¾ ounces) condensed cream of chicken soup
1½ cups Original MINUTE® Rice
½ cup shredded Cheddar cheese

Cook and stir chicken in hot oil in large skillet until lightly browned. Add water, sherry, broccoli and soup. Bring to full boil, separating broccoli spears. Stir in rice. Cover; remove from heat. Let stand 5 minutes. Fluff with fork. Arrange on platter. Sprinkle with cheese.

Makes 4 servings

Microwave Directions: Place chicken and oil in 2-quart microwavable dish. Cook at HIGH 3 minutes, stirring once. Add water, sherry, broccoli, soup and rice. Cover and cook at HIGH 6 minutes longer. Let stand 5 minutes. Arrange on platter. Sprinkle with cheese.

Makes 4 servings

Sierra Chicken Bundles

2 cups prepared Mexican or Spanish-style rice mix
¼ cup thinly sliced green onions
½ teaspoon LAWRY'S® Seasoned Pepper
4 whole boneless, skinless chicken breasts
½ cup unseasoned dry bread crumbs
¼ cup grated Parmesan cheese
½ teaspoon chili powder
½ teaspoon LAWRY'S® Garlic Salt
¼ teaspoon ground cumin
¼ cup IMPERIAL® Margarine, melted

In medium bowl, combine prepared rice, green onions and Seasoned Pepper. Pound chicken breasts between 2 sheets of waxed paper to ¼-inch thickness. Place about ⅓ cup rice mixture in center of each chicken breast; roll and tuck ends under and secure with wooden skewers. In pie plate, combine remaining ingredients except margarine; blend well. Roll chicken bundles in margarine, then in crumb mixture. Place seam-side down in 12×8×2-inch baking dish. Bake, uncovered, in 400°F oven 15 to 20 minutes or until chicken is cooked through. Remove skewers before serving.

Makes 4 servings

Presentation: Serve with assorted steamed vegetables and corn bread.

Lemon-Broccoli Chicken

- 1 lemon
- 1 tablespoon vegetable oil
- 4 skinless, boneless chicken breast halves (about 1 pound)
- 1 can (10¾ ounces) CAMPBELL'S® condensed Cream of Broccoli *or* Cream of Mushroom Soup
- ¼ cup milk
- ⅛ teaspoon pepper
  Fresh marjoram sprigs *and* carrot curls for garnish

1. Cut 4 thin slices from lemon; set aside. Squeeze *2 teaspoons* juice from remaining lemon; set aside.

2. In 10-inch skillet over medium-high heat, in hot oil, cook chicken 10 minutes or until browned on both sides. Spoon off fat.

3. In bowl, combine soup and milk. Stir in reserved lemon juice and pepper; pour over chicken. Top chicken with lemon slices.

4. Reduce heat to low. Cover; cook 5 minutes or until chicken is no longer pink, stirring occasionally. Garnish with marjoram and carrot curls, if desired.
   Makes 4 main-dish servings

Lemon-Broccoli Turkey: Prepare Lemon-Broccoli Chicken as directed above, *except* substitute *4 raw turkey cutlets* (about 1 pound) for the chicken. In step 2, cook turkey about 8 minutes until turkey is browned and no longer pink. Continue as directed above in step 3.

Stuffed Chicken Breasts

- 4 skinless, boneless chicken breast halves (about 1 pound), pounded to ¼-inch thickness
- ½ teaspoon ground black pepper, divided
- ¼ teaspoon salt
- 1 cup cooked brown rice (cooked in chicken broth)
- ¼ cup minced tomato
- ¼ cup (about 1 ounce) finely shredded mozzarella cheese
- 3 tablespoons toasted rice bran* (optional)
- 1 tablespoon chopped fresh basil
  Vegetable cooking spray

Season insides of chicken breasts with ¼ teaspoon pepper and salt. Combine rice, tomato, cheese, bran, basil, and remaining ¼ teaspoon pepper. Spoon rice mixture on top of pounded chicken breasts; fold over and secure sides with wooden toothpicks soaked in water. Wipe off outsides of chicken breasts with paper towel. Coat a large skillet with cooking spray and place over medium-high heat until hot. Cook stuffed chicken breasts 1 minute on each side or just until golden brown. Transfer chicken to shallow baking pan. Bake at 350°F. for 8 to 10 minutes.   *Makes 4 servings*

*To toast rice bran, spread on baking sheet and bake at 325°F. for 7 to 8 minutes.

Favorite recipe from **USA Rice Council**

Stuffed Chicken Breasts

Easy Basil Chicken with Rice

- **1 can (10½ ounces) CAMPBELL'S® condensed Chicken Broth**
- **1 can (16 ounces) stewed tomatoes**
- **2 cloves garlic, minced**
- **1 teaspoon dried basil leaves, crushed**
- **2 cups cubed cooked chicken**
- **1½ cups quick-cooking rice, uncooked**
- **1 cup frozen peas**
- **¼ teaspoon hot pepper sauce**

1. In 3-quart saucepan over high heat, heat broth, tomatoes, garlic and basil to boiling. Add chicken, rice, peas and hot pepper sauce. Return to boiling. Remove from heat.

2. Cover; let stand 5 minutes or until most of the liquid is absorbed. Fluff rice with fork before serving.

Makes about 5 cups or 4 servings

Chicken with Peach-Champagne Sauce

Chicken
- **1 whole chicken breast, split, boned and skinned**
- **2 teaspoons lemon juice Pepper, to taste**
- **1 fresh California peach, sliced**

Peach-Champagne Sauce
- **1 tablespoon margarine or butter**
- **1 tablespoon minced red onion**
- **1 tablespoon all-purpose flour**
- **¼ cup Champagne or white wine**

- **Spinach noodles, cooked (optional)**

For Chicken, in small microwave-safe baking dish, arrange chicken with thicker parts to the outside. Sprinkle with lemon juice and pepper. Cover with waxed paper and microwave on HIGH 5 minutes or until no longer pink and cooked through. Add peach slices to chicken and cook on HIGH 1 to 2 minutes longer; reserve cooking liquid.

For Sauce, in 4-cup glass measure, combine margarine and onion. Cook on HIGH 1 minute. Stir in flour and 3 tablespoons cooking liquid. Stir in Champagne. Cook on HIGH 3 minutes until thickened, stirring after 1½ minutes. Serve chicken and peaches on noodles. Spoon sauce over chicken.

Makes 2 servings

*Favorite recipe from **California Tree Fruit Agreement***

Chicken with Peach-Champagne Sauce

Creamy Chicken and Mushrooms

    1 cup chicken broth
    ⅓ cup HEINZ® 57 Sauce
    1 tablespoon cornstarch
    1 teaspoon lemon juice
    ⅛ teaspoon pepper
    1 pound skinless boneless
        chicken breasts, cut into
        1-inch pieces
    2 tablespoons vegetable oil,
        divided
    1 cup sliced fresh
        mushrooms
    1 medium onion, sliced
    ⅓ cup dairy sour cream
    ½ cup coarsely chopped
        unsalted peanuts
        (optional)
    Hot cooked noodles
    Chopped fresh parsley

For sauce, in medium bowl, combine broth, 57 Sauce, cornstarch, lemon juice and pepper; set aside. In large skillet, sauté chicken in 1 tablespoon oil until cooked, about 5 minutes; remove. Sauté mushrooms and onion in same skillet in remaining 1 tablespoon oil until onion is tender. Stir in sauce mixture; cook until thickened. Gradually stir in sour cream. Return chicken to skillet; heat slowly. *Do not boil.* Stir in peanuts. Serve chicken over noodles; garnish with parsley.

Makes 4 servings (about 4 cups)

Dressed Chicken Breasts with Angel Hair Pasta

Dressed Chicken Breasts with Angel Hair Pasta

    1 cup prepared HIDDEN
        VALLEY RANCH®
        Original Ranch® Salad
        Dressing
    ⅓ cup Dijon-style mustard
    4 whole chicken breasts,
        halved, skinned, boned
        and pounded thin
    ½ cup butter or margarine
    ⅓ cup dry white wine
    10 ounces angel hair pasta,
        cooked and drained
    Chopped parsley

In small bowl, whisk together salad dressing and mustard; set aside. In medium skillet, saute chicken in butter until browned; transfer to dish. Keep warm. Pour wine into skillet; cook over medium-high heat, scraping up any browned bits from bottom of skillet, about 5 minutes. Whisk in dressing mixture; blend well. Serve chicken with sauce over pasta; sprinkle with parsley.

Makes 8 servings

Chicken Parisian

- **¼ cup unsifted flour**
- **¼ teaspoon paprika**
- **¼ teaspoon pepper**
- **6 skinned boneless chicken breast halves (about 2 pounds)**
- **3 tablespoons margarine or butter**
- **8 ounces fresh mushrooms, sliced (about 2 cups)**
- **½ cup water**
- **¼ cup dry white wine**
- **2 teaspoons WYLER'S® or STEERO® Chicken-Flavor Instant Bouillon _or_ 2 Chicken-Flavor Bouillon Cubes**
- **2 teaspoons chopped parsley**
- **¼ teaspoon thyme leaves**

In plastic bag, combine flour, paprika and pepper. Add chicken, a few pieces at a time; shake to coat. In skillet, brown chicken in margarine; remove from pan. In same skillet, add remaining ingredients; simmer 3 minutes. Add chicken; simmer covered 20 minutes or until tender. Refrigerate leftovers.

Makes 6 servings

Chicken l'Orange

- **4 skinless boneless chicken breast halves (about 1 pound)**
- **2 tablespoons butter or margarine**
- **Salt and pepper**
- **2 teaspoons cornstarch**
- **⅔ cup orange juice**
- **⅓ cup HEINZ® 57 Sauce**
- **¼ cup orange marmalade**
- **Toasted slivered almonds***

*To toast almonds, spread almonds in shallow baking pan; bake in preheated 350°F oven, 8 to 10 minutes or until lightly browned.

Lightly flatten chicken breasts. In large skillet, sauté chicken in butter until cooked, about 8 to 10 minutes; season with salt and pepper. Remove chicken; set aside. In small bowl, dissolve cornstarch in orange juice; stir in 57 Sauce and marmalade. Pour into skillet. Heat, stirring constantly, until mixture is hot and thickened. Return chicken to skillet; heat through. Spoon sauce over chicken; garnish with almonds.   _Makes 4 servings (about 1 cup sauce)_

Chicken Fricassee

- **¼ cup all-purpose flour**
- **½ teaspoon salt**
- **½ teaspoon paprika**
- **⅛ teaspoon pepper**
- **2½ to 3 pounds broiler-fryer chicken pieces**
- **2 tablespoons vegetable oil**
- **1 jar (12 ounces) HEINZ® HomeStyle Chicken or Turkey Gravy**
- **¼ teaspoon ground nutmeg**

In small bowl, combine flour, salt, paprika and pepper. Coat chicken with flour mixture. In large skillet, brown chicken in oil; drain excess fat. In medium bowl, combine gravy and nutmeg with any remaining flour mixture; pour over chicken. Cover; simmer 50 to 60 minutes or until chicken is tender, basting occasionally.

Makes 5 to 6 servings (about 1½ cups gravy)

Chicken with Vegetables

- **1 can (10¾ ounces) CAMPBELL'S® condensed Creamy Chicken Mushroom Soup**
- **¼ cup milk**
- **¼ teaspoon dried thyme leaves, crushed**
- **4 skinless, boneless chicken breast halves (about 1 pound)**
- **2 cups carrots cut in 2-inch matchstick-thin strips**
- **2 cups zucchini cut in 2-inch matchstick-thin strips**
- **Fresh thyme leaves for garnish**

1. In 10-inch skillet, combine soup, milk and dried thyme. Over medium heat, heat to boiling. Add chicken and carrots. Reduce heat to low. Cover; cook 10 minutes, stirring occasionally.

2. Add zucchini. Cover; cook 5 minutes or until chicken is no longer pink. Garnish with fresh thyme.   _Makes 4 servings_

Tip: Look for packaged spinach noodle nests at your supermarket. Or make your own by twirling pasta with fork before serving.

Chicken with Vegetables

Quick Chicken Cacciatore

Quick Chicken Cacciatore

4 skinned boneless chicken breast halves (about 1 pound), lightly seasoned with salt and pepper
Flour
2 cloves garlic, finely chopped
4 tablespoons olive oil
1 (26-ounce) jar CLASSICO® Di Napoli (Tomato & Basil) or Di Sicila (Ripe Olives & Mushrooms) Pasta Sauce
1 small green bell pepper, cut into strips
1 small red bell pepper, cut into strips
2 slices Provolone cheese, cut in half
1 (7-ounce) package of 2 cups uncooked CREAMETTES® Elbow Macaroni, cooked as package directs and drained
Chopped parsley

Coat chicken with flour. In large skillet, brown chicken and garlic in *3 tablespoons* oil; remove chicken from pan. Add pasta sauce then chicken. Bring to a boil; reduce heat. Cover and simmer 20 minutes, adding peppers during last 5 minutes. Uncover; top each chicken breast with half cheese slice. Toss hot cooked macaroni with remaining *1 tablespoon* oil and parsley. Serve with chicken and sauce. Refrigerate leftovers.

Makes 4 servings

Chicken Florentine

¾ pound boneless skinless chicken breasts, cut into strips
1 small onion, chopped
2 tablespoons margarine or butter
1 garlic clove, minced
1 package (10 ounces) BIRDS EYE® Chopped Spinach, thawed
1 cup chicken broth
½ cup water
1 cup Original MINUTE® Rice
⅓ cup grated Parmesan cheese

Cook and stir chicken and onion in hot margarine in large skillet until chicken is lightly browned. Add garlic and cook 30 seconds. Add spinach, broth and water. Bring to boil. Reduce heat; simmer 3 minutes. Stir in rice and cheese. Cover; remove from heat. Let stand 5 minutes. Fluff with fork.   *Makes 3 servings*

Microwave Directions: Thaw and drain spinach, reduce broth to ¾ cup and omit margarine. Mix together chicken, onion and garlic in microwavable dish. Cover and cook at HIGH 3 minutes. Stir in spinach, broth, water and rice. Cover and cook at HIGH 6 minutes longer. Stir in cheese.   *Makes 3 servings*

Cheesy Chicken Tetrazzini

2 whole skinless boneless chicken breasts, cut into 1-inch pieces (about 1½ pounds)
2 tablespoons butter or margarine
1½ cups sliced mushrooms
1 small red pepper, cut into julienne strips
½ cup sliced green onions
¼ cup all-purpose flour
1¾ cups chicken broth
1 cup light cream or half-and-half
2 tablespoons dry sherry
½ teaspoon salt
¼ teaspoon pepper
¼ teaspoon dried thyme, crushed
1 package (8 ounces) tri-color rotelle pasta, cooked until just tender and drained
¼ cup grated Parmesan cheese
2 tablespoons chopped parsley
1 cup shredded NOKKELOST® Jarlsberg or Jarlsberg Lite Cheese

In skillet, brown chicken in butter. Add mushrooms; cook until brown. Add pepper and green onions; cook several minutes, stirring occasionally. Stir in flour and cook several minutes until blended. Gradually blend in chicken broth, cream and sherry. Cook, stirring, until thickened and smooth. Add salt, pepper and thyme. Toss with pasta, Parmesan cheese and parsley. Spoon into 1½-quart lightly greased baking dish. Bake at 350°F 30 minutes. Top with Jarlsberg cheese. Bake until cheese is melted.

Makes 6 servings

Apple Curry Chicken

Apple Curry Chicken

2 whole chicken breasts, split, skinned and boned
1 cup apple juice, divided
¼ teaspoon salt
Dash of pepper
1½ cups plain croutons
1 medium-size apple, chopped
½ cup finely chopped onion
¼ cup raisins
2 teaspoons brown sugar
1 teaspoon curry powder
¾ teaspoon poultry seasoning
⅛ teaspoon garlic powder

Preheat oven to 350°F. Lightly grease shallow baking dish. Arrange chicken breasts in a single layer in prepared pan. Combine ¼ cup apple juice, salt and pepper in small bowl. Brush all of mixture over chicken. Combine croutons, apple, onion, raisins, sugar, curry powder, poultry seasoning and garlic powder in large bowl. Stir in remaining ¾ cup apple juice; spread over chicken. Cover; bake about 45 minutes or until chicken is tender. Garnish as desired. *Makes 4 servings*

Favorite recipe from **Delmarva Poultry Industry, Inc.**

Chicken Apple Sauté

4 skinned boneless chicken breast halves (about 1½ pounds)
1 tablespoon margarine or butter
1 medium all-purpose apple, cored and sliced
1 cup apple juice
1 tablespoon brown sugar, optional
1 tablespoon cornstarch
2 teaspoons WYLER'S® or STEERO® Chicken-Flavor Instant Bouillon
⅛ teaspoon *each* ground cinnamon and nutmeg
½ cup chopped walnuts, toasted

Preheat oven to 350°. In large skillet, brown chicken in margarine; pour off fat. Add apple slices. Combine apple juice, sugar, cornstarch, bouillon and spices. Pour over chicken and apple slices; bring to a boil. Reduce heat; cover and simmer 10 minutes. Cook uncovered 5 minutes or until tender. Garnish with walnuts. Refrigerate leftovers.

Makes 4 servings

Kung Pao Chicken

- **5 teaspoons soy sauce, divided**
- **5 teaspoons dry sherry, divided**
- **3½ teaspoons cornstarch, divided**
- **¼ teaspoon salt**
- **3 skinless boneless chicken breast halves, cut into bite-size pieces**
- **2 tablespoons chicken broth or water**
- **1 tablespoon red wine vinegar**
- **1½ teaspoons sugar**
- **3 tablespoons vegetable oil, divided**
- **⅓ cup salted peanuts**
- **6 to 8 small dried hot chili peppers**
- **1½ teaspoons minced fresh ginger**
- **2 green onions, cut into 1½-inch pieces**

For marinade, combine 2 teaspoons soy sauce, 2 teaspoons sherry, 2 teaspoons cornstarch and salt in large bowl; mix well. Add chicken; stir to coat well. Let stand 30 minutes. Combine remaining 3 teaspoons soy sauce, 3 teaspoons sherry, chicken broth, vinegar, sugar and remaining 1½ teaspoons cornstarch in small bowl; mix well and set aside. Heat 1 tablespoon oil in wok or large skillet over medium heat. Add peanuts and cook until golden. Remove peanuts and set aside. Heat remaining 2 tablespoons oil in wok over medium heat. Add chili peppers and stir-fry until peppers just begin to darken, about 1 minute. Increase heat to high. Add chicken and stir-fry 2 minutes. Add ginger; stir-fry until chicken is cooked through, about 1 minute more. Add onions and peanuts to wok. Stir cornstarch mixture and add to pan; cook and stir until sauce boils and thickens.

Makes 3 servings

Kung Pao Chicken

Crispy Chicken Stir-Fry

- **1 DOLE® Fresh Pineapple**
- **Vegetable oil**
- **½ cup peanuts**
- **1 egg**
- **Cornstarch**
- **Soy sauce**
- **1 pound boneless, skinless chicken breasts, chunked**
- **1 onion, sliced**
- **2 large cloves garlic, pressed**
- **1 tablespoon chopped ginger root**
- **1 cup water**
- **¼ cup pale dry sherry**
- **¼ teaspoon ground cloves**
- **¼ teaspoon ground cinnamon**
- **1 bunch DOLE® Broccoli, cut into florettes**
- **1 DOLE® Red Bell Pepper, seeded, chunked**

• Twist crown from pineapple. Cut pineapple in half lengthwise, then cut pineapple in half again. Cut fruit from shells with knife. Trim off core and cut fruit into bite-size chunks. Measure 2 cups pineapple; refrigerate remainder for another use.

• In 10-inch skillet, heat about ½ inch oil over medium-high heat. Brown peanuts. Remove with slotted spoon to paper towels.

• Combine egg, ⅓ cup cornstarch and 2 teaspoons soy sauce in shallow dish. Coat chicken with batter. In same skillet, sauté chicken in hot oil over medium-high heat until browned. Remove with slotted spoon; drain on paper towels.

• Drain oil, reserving 2 tablespoons in skillet. Stir-fry onion, garlic and ginger root 1 minute. Combine water, ¼ cup soy sauce, 2 teaspoons cornstarch, sherry and spices in small bowl. Stir into skillet; add broccoli and pepper.

• Reduce heat. Cover; simmer 1 to 2 minutes until broccoli is tender-crisp and sauce boils and thickens. Stir in pineapple, peanuts and chicken; heat through.   *Makes 4 servings*

Preparation Time: 15 minutes
Cook Time: 15 minutes

Chicken Cashew

1½ pounds skinned boneless
    chicken breasts, cut into
    bite-size pieces
2 teaspoons WYLER'S® or
    STEERO® Chicken-Flavor
    Instant Bouillon *or*
    2 Chicken-Flavor
    Bouillon Cubes
1¼ cups boiling water
2 tablespoons soy sauce
1 tablespoon cornstarch
2 teaspoons brown sugar
½ teaspoon ground ginger
2 tablespoons vegetable oil
8 ounces fresh mushrooms,
    sliced (about 2 cups)
½ cup sliced green onions
1 small green bell pepper,
    sliced
1 (8-ounce) can sliced water
    chestnuts, drained
½ cup cashews
    Hot cooked rice

In small saucepan, dissolve
bouillon in water. Combine soy
sauce, cornstarch, sugar and
ginger; stir into bouillon
mixture. In large skillet, brown
chicken in oil. Add bouillon
mixture; cook and stir until
slightly thickened. Add
mushrooms, onions, green pepper
and water chestnuts; simmer
uncovered 5 to 8 minutes,
stirring occasionally. Remove
from heat; add ¼ *cup* cashews.
Serve with rice. Garnish with
remaining ¼ *cup* cashews.
Refrigerate leftovers.
Makes 4 servings

Chicken Cashew

Ginger-Spiced Chicken

1 pound boneless skinless
    chicken breasts, cut into
    strips
2 tablespoons oil
1 medium red pepper, cut
    into thin strips
1 medium green pepper, cut
    into thin strips
1 cup sliced mushrooms
1 cup chicken broth
3 tablespoons soy sauce
4 teaspoons cornstarch
1 teaspoon garlic powder
1 teaspoon ground ginger
    Original MINUTE® Rice
⅓ cup cashews or peanuts
    (optional)

Stir-fry chicken in hot oil in
large skillet until browned. Add
peppers and mushrooms; stir-fry
until peppers are crisp-tender.

Mix broth, soy sauce, cornstarch,
garlic powder and ginger; add to
skillet. Bring to boil; boil 1
minute.

Meanwhile, prepare 4 servings
rice as directed on package,
omitting margarine and salt.
Serve chicken and vegetables
over rice. Sprinkle with cashews.
Makes 4 servings

Sweet Sour Chicken Sauté

1 can (8 ounces) pineapple chunks
1 tablespoon cornstarch
⅓ cup HEINZ® Apple Cider Vinegar
¼ cup firmly packed brown sugar
⅛ teaspoon black pepper
Vegetable cooking spray
1 small red bell pepper, cut into thin strips
1 small green bell pepper, cut into thin strips
1 medium onion, thinly sliced
1 pound skinless boneless chicken breasts, cut into ½-inch strips

Drain pineapple; reserve juice. Combine juice with cornstarch, vinegar, sugar and black pepper; set aside. Spray large skillet with cooking spray. Sauté bell peppers and onion until tender-crisp; remove. Spray skillet again; sauté chicken 2 to 3 minutes or until chicken changes color. Stir in reserved vinegar mixture; cook 2 to 3 minutes or until chicken is cooked and sauce is thickened. Add vegetables and pineapple; heat, stirring occasionally. Serve with rice if desired. *Makes 4 servings*

Polynesian Chicken

2½ pounds frying chicken pieces
½ cup seasoned all-purpose flour
¼ cup margarine or butter
1 can (8¼ ounces) pineapple chunks in syrup
2 tablespoons brown sugar
1 tablespoon vinegar
1¼ cups water
½ teaspoon salt
1½ cups Original MINUTE® Rice
1 scallion, sliced

Coat chicken with seasoned flour. Brown chicken well in hot margarine in large skillet. Drain pineapple, reserving ¼ cup syrup. Combine reserved syrup, brown sugar and vinegar in small bowl; pour over chicken. Turn chicken, skin side down. Reduce heat; cover and simmer until fork tender, about 20 minutes or until heated through. Move chicken to side of skillet.

Add pineapple, water and salt. Bring to full boil. Stir in rice. Cover; remove from heat. Let stand 5 minutes. Fluff with fork. Garnish with scallion.
Makes 4 servings

Note: Flour may be seasoned with ¼ teaspoon each pepper and ground nutmeg, or ½ teaspoon paprika and ¼ teaspoon ground ginger.

Chicken-Rice Amandine

¾ pound boneless skinless chicken breasts, cut into strips
1 tablespoon oil
2 cups water
1 tablespoon cornstarch
2 cups (½ package) BIRDS EYE® FARM FRESH Broccoli, Green Beans, Pearl Onions and Red Peppers
¼ teaspoon salt
¼ teaspoon pepper
¼ teaspoon dried tarragon
1 chicken bouillon cube
1½ cups Original MINUTE® Rice
3 tablespoons sliced almonds

Cook and stir chicken in hot oil in large skillet until lightly browned. Mix water and cornstarch in bowl; stir into chicken. Add vegetables, seasonings and bouillon cube. Cook and stir until mixture thickens and comes to full boil. Stir in rice. Cover; remove from heat. Let stand 5 minutes. Fluff with fork and sprinkle with almonds. *Makes 4 servings*

Microwave Directions: Omit oil. Combine all ingredients except almonds in microwavable dish. Cover and cook at HIGH 6 minutes. Stir, cover and cook 6 to 7 minutes longer, or until heated through. Let stand 5 minutes. Fluff with fork and sprinkle with almonds.
Makes 4 servings

Chicken Broccoli Stir-Fry

1 pound skinned boneless chicken breasts, cut into bite-size pieces
1 egg white, beaten
5 teaspoons soy sauce
2 teaspoons cornstarch
¼ cup vegetable oil
8 ounces fresh mushrooms, sliced (about 2 cups)
3 cups broccoli flowerets, steamed
2 tablespoons REALEMON® Lemon Juice from Concentrate
2 tablespoons dry sherry, optional
1 tablespoon chopped pimiento, optional
Hot cooked rice

In medium bowl, combine egg white, *3 teaspoons* soy sauce and cornstarch; add chicken. Cover; refrigerate 1 hour. In large skillet, over high heat, brown chicken in oil; remove. Add mushrooms; cook and stir until tender-crisp. Add chicken and remaining ingredients except rice; heat through. Serve with rice. Refrigerate leftovers.
Makes 4 servings

Polynesian Chicken

Chicken with Pineapple Salsa

Chicken with Pineapple Salsa

- **1 can (20 ounces) DOLE® Crushed Pineapple in Juice**
- **4 boneless, skinless chicken breast halves**
- **1 large clove garlic, pressed**
- **1 teaspoon ground cumin Salt and pepper to taste**
- **1 tablespoon vegetable oil**
- **½ cup minced DOLE® Red Bell Pepper**
- **¼ cup minced DOLE® Green Bell Pepper**
- **1 tablespoon minced DOLE® Green Onion**
- **2 teaspoons minced cilantro**
- **2 teaspoons minced fresh or canned jalapeño chiles**
- **1 teaspoon lime zest**

• Drain pineapple; reserve juice.

• Rub chicken with garlic; sprinkle with cumin, salt and pepper. In 12-inch skillet, sauté chicken in hot oil over medium-high heat until browned; turn once. Add ½ cup pineapple juice to chicken. Reduce heat. Cover; simmer 7 to 10 minutes.

• For salsa, combine pineapple, remaining reserved juice and remaining ingredients in bowl.

• Cut each breast into slices. Serve chicken with pineapple salsa.   *Makes 4 servings*

Preparation Time: 5 minutes
Cook Time: 15 minutes

Sautéed Pineapple Chicken Amandine

- **1 DOLE® Fresh Pineapple**
- **2 boneless, skinless chicken breast halves**
- **½ teaspoon dried thyme, crumbled**
- **¼ teaspoon rubbed sage**
- **⅛ teaspoon ground red pepper**
- **1 clove garlic, pressed**
- **1 egg white, lightly beaten**
- **3 tablespoons DOLE® Chopped Almonds**
- **2 teaspoons vegetable oil, divided**
- **Zest from 1 DOLE® Orange**

• Twist crown from pineapple. Cut pineapple in half lengthwise. Refrigerate half for later use, such as a snack. Cut fruit from shell with knife. Cut fruit crosswise into thin slices.

• Pound chicken to ½-inch thickness. Combine thyme, sage and red pepper in cup.

• Rub chicken with garlic; sprinkle with herb mixture. Dip chicken in egg white, then coat with almonds.

• In 8-inch nonstick skillet, sauté pineapple in 1 teaspoon hot oil over medium-high heat. Remove from skillet.

• Add remaining 1 teaspoon oil to skillet. In covered skillet, sauté chicken over medium-high heat until browned; turn once. Sprinkle orange zest over pineapple. Serve chicken with pineapple.

Makes 2 servings

Preparation Time: 15 minutes
Cook Time: 15 minutes

Caribbean Pineapple Chicken

- **1 DOLE® Fresh Pineapple**
- **1 tablespoon vegetable oil**
- **2 boneless, skinless chicken breast halves**
- **1 clove garlic, pressed**
- **2 teaspoons all-purpose flour**
- **¼ cup water**
- **2 to 3 tablespoons honey**
- **1 to 2 tablespoons soy sauce Zest and juice from 1 lime**
- **¼ teaspoon coconut extract Pinch ground red pepper**
- **1 tablespoon flaked coconut, optional**
- **1 to 2 teaspoons minced cilantro, optional**

• Twist crown from pineapple. Cut pineapple in half lengthwise. Refrigerate half for another use. Cut fruit from shell with knife. Cut fruit crosswise into 6 slices.

• In 8-inch nonstick skillet, sauté pineapple in oil over medium-high heat until slightly browned. Remove to plates.

• Rub chicken with garlic; sprinkle with flour. In same skillet, sauté chicken, covered, in pan juices over medium-high heat until browned; turn once.

• Mix water, honey, soy sauce, lime juice, coconut extract and red pepper in cup; pour into skillet. Cover; simmer 12 to 15 minutes. Remove chicken to serving plates.

• Arrange chicken on plates. Spoon sauce over top. Sprinkle with coconut, lime zest and cilantro.   *Makes 2 servings*

Preparation Time: 10 minutes
Cook Time: 20 minutes

Chicken with Pineapple Mustard Glaze

**1 can (20 ounces) DOLE®
    Pineapple Chunks in
    Syrup***
**2 chickens (2 pounds each),
    split in half**
4 large cloves garlic
¼ cup margarine, melted
¼ cup chopped parsley
**1 teaspoon dried thyme,
    crumbled**
⅓ cup honey
¼ cup Dijon mustard
1 tablespoon cornstarch

• Drain pineapple; reserve syrup. Arrange chicken, skin side up, on rack in roasting pan. Split each garlic clove lengthwise into 3 or 4 pieces and insert under skin of chicken.

• Combine margarine, parsley and thyme in a cup. Brush generously over chicken. Roast in 400°F oven 30 minutes.

• Combine honey, mustard, ¼ cup reserved pineapple syrup and any remaining margarine mixture in small bowl. Mix well. Brush generously onto chicken. Roast 10 minutes longer.

• Combine pineapple, remaining reserved pineapple syrup and cornstarch with honey sauce in saucepan. Cook, stirring, until sauce boils and thickens. Serve over chicken.

Makes 4 servings

*Use pineapple packed in juice, if desired.

Preparation Time: 10 minutes
Cook Time: 40 minutes

Chicken Sensation

**1 green-tip DOLE® Banana,
    peeled**
1 tablespoon olive oil
**2 boneless, skinless chicken
    breast halves**
2 cloves garlic, pressed
**1 teaspoon dried rosemary,
    crumbled**
Salt and pepper to taste
½ cup pitted ripe olives
½ cup cooked pearl onions*
**Zest and juice from
    1 DOLE® Orange**
½ cup DOLE® Chopped Dates
**1 teaspoon DOLE® Lemon
    zest**
½ teaspoon cornstarch

• Cut banana in half crosswise, then lengthwise to make 4 pieces.

• In 8-inch nonstick skillet, sauté banana in oil over medium-high heat until slightly browned.

Chicken Sensation

• Rub chicken with garlic and rosemary; sprinkle with salt and pepper. In same skillet, sauté chicken, covered, over medium-high heat until browned; turn once. Add olives and onions.

• Blend orange zest, orange juice, dates, lemon zest and cornstarch in small bowl. Stir into skillet. Cook, stirring, until sauce boils and thickens, 1 to 2 minutes.

Makes 2 servings

*Use cocktail or canned boiled pearl onions, if desired.

Preparation Time: 5 minutes
Cook Time: 15 minutes

Rio Grande Quesadillas

- **2 cups shredded, cooked chicken**
- **1 package (1.25 ounces) LAWRY'S® Taco Spices & Seasonings**
- **¾ cup water**
- **1 can (16 ounces) refried beans**
- **6 large flour tortillas**
- **1½ cups (6 ounces) grated Monterey Jack cheese**
- **¼ cup chopped pimiento**
- **¼ cup chopped green onions**
- **¼ cup chopped fresh cilantro Vegetable oil**

In medium skillet, combine chicken, Taco Spices & Seasonings and water. Bring to a boil; reduce heat and simmer, uncovered, 15 minutes. Stir in refried beans. On ½ side of each tortilla, spread approximately ⅓ cup of chicken-bean mixture. Layer cheese, pimiento, green onions and cilantro on top of each tortilla. Fold each in half. In large skillet, heat a small amount of oil and quickly fry folded tortilla on each side until slightly crisp. Repeat with each folded tortilla.

Makes 6 servings

Presentation: Cut each quesadilla in quarters and serve with chunky salsa and guacamole.

Rio Grande Quesadillas

Green Chile Chicken

- **1 pound skinless boneless chicken breasts, cut into thin strips**
- **1 medium onion, sliced**
- **1 clove garlic, pressed**
- **2 tablespoons vegetable oil**
- **1 (12-ounce) jar ORTEGA® Mild Thick and Chunky Salsa**
- **1 (4-ounce) can ORTEGA® Diced Green Chiles**
- **½ teaspoon dried oregano leaves**
  Hot cooked rice or flour tortillas
  Dairy sour cream, optional

In medium skillet, over medium-high heat, cook chicken, onion and garlic in oil until chicken is no longer pink. Add salsa, chiles and oregano. Simmer, uncovered, 10 minutes. Serve over rice or in tortillas. Top with sour cream, if desired. *Makes 6 servings*

Tortilla Stack Tampico

- **1¼ cups shredded, cooked chicken**
- **1 package (1.25 ounces) LAWRY'S® Taco Spices & Seasonings**
- **1 cup water**
- **1 can (8 ounces) tomato sauce**
- **8 medium corn tortillas**
- **2 cups (8 ounces) grated Monterey Jack or Cheddar cheese**
- **1 can (4 ounces) whole green chiles, rinsed and seeds removed**
- **1 can (4¼ ounces) chopped ripe olives**
- **½ cup salsa**
  Sliced green onions

In large skillet, combine chicken, Taco Spices & Seasonings, water and tomato sauce. Bring to a boil; reduce heat and simmer, uncovered, 10 minutes. Lightly grease 12×8×2-inch baking dish. Dip tortillas in chicken mixture. Place 2 tortillas in bottom of baking dish. Top with ½ of chicken mixture. Sprinkle with ⅔ cup cheese and top with 2 more tortillas. Layer chiles on top of tortillas. Sprinkle with ½ of olives, reserving half, about 2 tablespoons for garnish. Sprinkle ⅔ cup cheese over olives. Top with 2 more tortillas and remaining chicken mixture. Top with remaining 2 tortillas. Pour salsa over tortillas. Garnish with remaining ⅔ cup cheese, reserved 2 tablespoons olives and green onions. Bake, uncovered, in 350°F oven 15 to 20 minutes or until heated through and cheese melts. Cut each stack into quarters to serve.

Makes 8 servings

Presentation: Serve with dollops of sour cream and wedges of fresh pineapple and watermelon, if desired.

Hints: If made in advance, cover tightly with foil or plastic wrap to prevent tortillas from drying out. One can (4 ounces) diced green chiles can be used in place of whole chiles.

Arroz con Pollo Burritos

Arroz con Pollo Burritos

2½ cups shredded, cooked chicken
1 package (1.25 ounces) LAWRY'S® Taco Spices & Seasonings
3¼ cups water
2 tablespoons vegetable oil
1 cup long-grain rice
1 can (8 ounces) tomato sauce
1 teaspoon LAWRY'S® Lemon Pepper Seasoning
1 large tomato, chopped
¼ cup chopped green onions
8 medium flour tortillas, warmed
Grated Cheddar cheese

In large deep skillet, combine chicken, Taco Spices & Seasonings and ¾ cup water. Bring to a boil; reduce heat and simmer, uncovered, 10 minutes. Remove and set aside. In same skillet, heat oil. Add rice; sauté until golden. Add remaining 2½ cups water, tomato sauce and Lemon Pepper Seasoning. Bring to a boil; reduce heat, cover and simmer 20 minutes. Stir in chicken mixture, tomato and green onions; blend well. Heat 5 minutes. Place a heaping ½ cup filling on each tortilla. Fold in sides and roll to enclose filling. Place filled burritos seam-side down on baking sheet. Sprinkle with cheese. Heat in 350°F oven 5 minutes to melt cheese.

Makes 8 servings

Presentation: Garnish with salsa and guacamole.

Cancun Chicken

1 DOLE® Fresh Pineapple
2 boneless, skinless chicken
   breast halves
   Salt and pepper to taste
½ teaspoon ground cumin
¼ teaspoon dried oregano,
   crumbled
⅛ teaspoon ground cloves
1 tablespoon olive oil
¾ cup DOLE® Pineapple
   Juice
1 tablespoon lime juice
1 teaspoon cornstarch
1 teaspoon minced cilantro

• Twist crown from pineapple. Cut pineapple in half lengthwise. Refrigerate half for another use, such as pasta salad. Cut fruit from shell with a knife. Cut fruit crosswise into 6 slices.

• Pound chicken to ½-inch thickness. Sprinkle with salt and pepper. Combine cumin, oregano and cloves in cup. Sprinkle over chicken.

• In 8-inch skillet, sauté pineapple in hot oil over medium-high heat about 1 minute. Remove from skillet.

• In same skillet, sauté chicken in pan juices. Reduce heat. Cover; simmer 1 to 2 minutes. Remove to plate.

• Blend pineapple juice, lime juice and cornstarch in cup. Pour into skillet. Cook, stirring, until sauce boils and thickens. Stir in cilantro. Serve sauce over chicken and pineapple.

Makes 2 servings

Preparation Time: 15 minutes
Cook Time: 10 minutes

Skewered Chicken with Hawaiian Relish

1 medium DOLE® Fresh
   Pineapple
1 cup papaya or DOLE®
   Orange chunks
½ cup minced DOLE® Red
   Bell Pepper or pimento
2 tablespoons diced green
   chiles
1 teaspoon minced cilantro
   Zest and juice from 1 lime
3 boneless, skinless chicken
   breast halves
1 tablespoon honey

• Soak 4 bamboo skewers in water 5 minutes.

• Twist crown from pineapple. Cut pineapple in half lengthwise. Refrigerate half for another use, such as fruit salad. Cut fruit from shell with knife. Cut fruit into tidbits.

• Combine pineapple, papaya, bell pepper, chiles and cilantro in bowl.

• Sprinkle half of lime juice over relish; set aside.

• Cut each chicken breast into 6 to 8 chunks; skewer on bamboo skewers. Combine remaining half of lime juice and honey in small bowl. Spoon 1 tablespoon honey mixture over chicken.

• Place skewers on broiler rack or pan. Broil 6 inches from heat 4 minutes; turn over. Spoon remaining sauce over chicken. Broil 4 to 5 minutes longer.

• Remove to plate. Cover for 1 minute to complete cooking, if necessary. Serve with relish. Garnish with lime zest.

Makes 2 servings

Preparation Time: 20 minutes
Cook Time: 10 minutes

Cancun Chicken

Honey 'n' Spice Chicken Kabobs

Honey 'n' Spice Chicken Kabobs

- **1 medium green bell pepper, cut into 1-inch squares**
- **4 skinless boneless chicken breast halves (about 1 pound)**
- **1 can (8 ounces) pineapple chunks, drained**
- **½ cup HEINZ® 57 Sauce**
- **¼ cup honey**
  Melted butter or margarine

In small saucepan, blanch green pepper in boiling water 1 minute; drain. Cut each chicken breast half into 4 pieces. Alternately thread chicken, green pepper and pineapple onto skewers. In small bowl, combine 57 Sauce and honey. Brush kabobs with butter, then 57 Sauce mixture. Broil, about 6 inches from heat source, 12 to 14 minutes or until chicken is cooked, turning and brushing with 57 Sauce mixture once.
Makes 4 servings

Herb Marinated Chicken Kabobs

- **4 skinless boneless chicken breast halves (about 1 pound)**
- **2 small zucchini, cut into ½-inch slices**
- **1 large red bell pepper, cut into 1-inch squares**
- **½ cup HEINZ® Gourmet Wine Vinegar**
- **½ cup tomato juice**
- **2 tablespoons vegetable oil**
- **1 tablespoon chopped onion**
- **1 tablespoon brown sugar**
- **2 cloves garlic, minced**
- **½ teaspoon dried oregano leaves, crushed**
- **½ teaspoon pepper**

Lightly flatten chicken breasts; cut each breast lengthwise into 3 strips. In large bowl, combine chicken, zucchini and red pepper. For marinade, in jar, combine remaining ingredients; cover and shake vigorously. Pour marinade over chicken and vegetables. Cover; marinate in refrigerator about 1 hour. Drain chicken and vegetables, reserving marinade. Alternately thread chicken and vegetables onto skewers; brush with marinade. Broil, 3 to 5 inches from heat source, 8 to 10 minutes or until chicken is cooked, turning and brushing occasionally with marinade.
Makes 4 servings

Grilled Chicken Fajitas

- **1 cup MIRACLE WHIP® Salad Dressing**
- **¼ cup lime juice**
- **3 garlic cloves, minced**
- **1 teaspoon each: dried oregano leaves, crushed, ground cumin**
- **4 boneless skinless chicken breast halves (about 1¼ pounds)**
- **1 each: green, red and yellow bell pepper, quartered**
- **1 onion, cut into 6 wedges**
- **4 flour tortillas (8 inch), warmed**
  Sour cream
  Salsa

• Mix salad dressing, juice, garlic and seasonings until well blended. Pour over chicken. Marinate in refrigerator at least 20 minutes; drain.

• Place chicken on grill over medium-hot coals (coals will have slight glow) or rack of broiler pan. Grill, covered, **or** broil 10 minutes.

• Place vegetables on grill or broiler pan. Continue cooking chicken and vegetables 10 minutes or until tender, turning chicken and vegetables occasionally.

• Slice chicken and bell peppers into strips. Fill tortillas with chicken and vegetables. Top with sour cream and salsa; roll up.

Makes 6 servings

Prep time: 15 minutes plus marinating
Grilling time: 20 minutes

Grilled Greek Chicken

- **1 cup MIRACLE WHIP® Salad Dressing**
- **½ cup chopped fresh parsley**
- **¼ cup dry white wine or chicken broth**
- **1 lemon, sliced, cut in half**
- **2 tablespoons dried oregano leaves, crushed**
- **1 tablespoon each: garlic powder, pepper**
- **2 broiler-fryer chickens, cut up (2½ to 3 pounds each)**

• Mix all ingredients except chicken until well blended. Pour over chicken. Marinate in refrigerator at least 20 minutes; drain.

• Place chicken on grill over medium-hot coals (coals will have slight glow). Grill, covered, 20 to 25 minutes on each side or until tender.

Makes 8 servings

Prep time: 10 minutes plus marinating
Grilling time: 50 minutes

Mediterranean Marinade

- **⅓ cup olive or vegetable oil**
- **¼ cup REALEMON® Lemon Juice from Concentrate**
- **3 tablespoons dry sherry or water**
- **2 teaspoons rosemary leaves, crushed**
- **2 cloves garlic, finely chopped**
- **1½ teaspoons WYLER'S® or STEERO® Chicken- or Beef-Flavor Instant Bouillon**

In large shallow dish or plastic bag, combine ingredients; add chicken, beef or pork. Cover; marinate in refrigerator 4 hours or overnight, turning occasionally. Remove meat from marinade; grill or broil as desired, basting frequently with heated marinade. Refrigerate leftover meat.

Makes about 1 cup

Spicy Microwave Grilled Chicken

- **1 cup MIRACLE WHIP® Salad Dressing**
- **1 package (1.25 ounces) taco seasoning mix**
- **2 broiler-fryer chickens, cut up (2½ to 3 pounds each)**

• Mix salad dressing and taco seasoning mix until well blended.

• Arrange chicken in 13×9-inch microwave-safe baking dish. Brush with salad dressing mixture. Cover with plastic wrap; vent.

• Microwave on HIGH 15 minutes, turning dish after 8 minutes.

• Place chicken on grill over medium-hot coals (coals will have slight glow). Grill, covered, 5 to 10 minutes on each side or until tender and browned.

Makes 6 to 8 servings

Prep time: 5 minutes
Cooking time: 20 minutes
Microwave cooking time:
  15 minutes

Spicy Microwave Grilled Chicken

Chicken Breasts with Chunky Salsa

Chicken Breasts with Chunky Salsa

- ½ cup **MIRACLE WHIP**® Salad Dressing
- ½ cup **RANCHER'S CHOICE**® Creamy Dressing
- ½ teaspoon ground red pepper
- 4 boneless skinless chicken breast halves (about 1¼ pounds) **Chunky Salsa**

• Mix dressings and red pepper until well blended.

• Place chicken on grill over medium-hot coals (coals will have slight glow) or rack of broiler pan. Grill, covered, **or** broil 8 to 10 minutes on each side or until tender, brushing frequently with dressing mixture. Serve with Chunky Salsa.   *Makes 4 servings*

Note: For more flavor, marinate chicken in dressing mixture 20 minutes or more before cooking.

Chunky Salsa

- 1 cup prepared salsa
- ½ cup finely chopped tomato
- ¼ cup finely chopped green bell pepper
- 2 tablespoons chopped cilantro

• Stir ingredients until well blended.

Prep time: 15 minutes
Cooking time: 20 minutes

Southern Barbecued Chicken

- ⅔ cup **HEINZ**® Tomato Ketchup
- 1 tablespoon honey
- 2 teaspoons lemon juice Dash hot pepper sauce
- 2 to 2½ pounds broiler-fryer chicken pieces

In small bowl, combine all ingredients except chicken. Broil or grill chicken 25 to 30 minutes, turning once. Brush ketchup mixture on chicken; cook an additional 5 to 10 minutes or until chicken is tender, turning and brushing with ketchup mixture.

Makes 4 to 5 servings
(about ¾ cup sauce)

Herb-Marinated Chicken Breasts

- ¾ cup **MIRACLE WHIP**® Salad Dressing
- ¼ cup dry white wine
- 2 cloves garlic, minced
- 2 tablespoons finely chopped green onion
- 2 teaspoons dried basil leaves, crushed
- 1 teaspoon dried thyme leaves, crushed
- 6 boneless skinless chicken breast halves (about 1¾ pounds)

Mix dressing, wine, garlic, onion and seasonings until well blended. Pour dressing mixture over chicken. Cover; marinate in refrigerator several hours or overnight. Drain. Place chicken on greased rack of broiler pan. Broil 4 to 6 minutes on each side or until tender.

Makes 6 servings

Variation: For outdoor grilling: Place chicken on greased grill over low coals (coals will be ash gray). Grill, uncovered, 4 to 6 minutes on each side or until tender.

Southern Fried Chicken Strips

- ¾ cup **BORDEN**® or **MEADOW GOLD**® Buttermilk
- 1 tablespoon **WYLER'S**® or **STEERO**® Chicken-Flavor Instant Bouillon
- ½ teaspoon oregano leaves
- 1 pound skinned boneless chicken breasts, cut into strips
- 1¼ cups unsifted flour
- 1 to 2 teaspoons paprika Vegetable oil Peach Dipping Sauce

In large bowl, combine buttermilk, bouillon and oregano; let stand 10 minutes. Stir in chicken. Let stand 30 minutes to blend flavors. In plastic bag, combine flour and paprika. Add chicken, a few pieces at a time; shake to coat. Dip in buttermilk mixture again; coat with flour again. In large skillet, fry chicken strips in hot oil until golden on both sides. Drain on paper towels. Serve with Peach Dipping Sauce. Refrigerate leftovers.

Makes 4 servings

PEACH DIPPING SAUCE: In blender container, combine 1 (16-ounce) jar BAMA® Peach or Apricot Preserves (1½ cups), ¼ cup Dijon-style mustard and 2 tablespoons REALEMON® Lemon Juice from Concentrate; blend until smooth.

Makes about 2 cups

Versatile Chicken

¾ cup BORDEN® or MEADOW GOLD® Buttermilk
1 tablespoon WYLER'S® or STEERO® Chicken-Flavor Instant Bouillon
½ teaspoon oregano leaves, optional
3 pounds chicken pieces
1 cup unsifted flour
1 teaspoon paprika
¼ cup margarine or butter, melted

In large bowl, combine buttermilk, bouillon and oregano if desired; let stand 10 minutes. Add chicken, stirring to coat. Let stand 30 minutes to blend flavors. In plastic bag, combine flour and paprika. Add chicken, a few pieces at a time; shake to coat. Arrange chicken in 13×9-inch baking dish. Drizzle with margarine. Bake at 350° for 1 hour or until golden. Refrigerate leftovers.

Makes 4 to 6 servings

Tip: To fry chicken, omit melted margarine; fry in vegetable oil.

Oven Barbecued Chicken

1 cup unsifted flour
1 teaspoon salt
3 pounds chicken pieces
¼ cup plus 2 tablespoons margarine or butter, melted
¼ cup chopped onion
1 clove garlic, finely chopped
1 cup ketchup
¼ cup firmly packed brown sugar
¼ cup REALEMON® Lemon Juice from Concentrate
¼ cup water
2 tablespoons Worcestershire sauce

Preheat oven to 350°. In plastic bag, combine flour and salt. Add chicken, a few pieces at a time; shake to coat. Place in greased 13×9-inch baking dish; drizzle with ¼ cup margarine. Bake uncovered 30 minutes. Meanwhile, in small saucepan, cook onion and garlic in remaining *2 tablespoons* margarine until tender. Add remaining ingredients; simmer uncovered 10 minutes. Pour over chicken; bake uncovered 30 minutes longer or until tender. Refrigerate leftovers.

Makes 4 to 6 servings

Versatile Chicken

Forty-Clove Chicken Filice

    1 (3-pound) frying chicken,
        cut into serving pieces
    40 cloves fresh garlic, peeled
        and left whole
    ½ cup dry white wine
    ¼ cup dry vermouth
    ¼ cup olive oil
    4 ribs celery, thickly sliced
    2 tablespoons finely chopped
        parsley
    2 teaspoons dried basil
    1 teaspoon dried oregano
        Pinch of crushed red
        pepper
    1 lemon
        Salt and black pepper to
        taste

Preheat oven to 375°F. Place chicken pieces, skin-side up, in a single layer in shallow baking pan. Combine garlic, wine, vermouth, oil, celery, parsley, basil, oregano and red pepper in medium-sized bowl; mix thoroughly. Sprinkle garlic mixture over chicken pieces. Remove peel from lemon in thin strips; place peel throughout pan. Squeeze juice from lemon and pour over the top. Season with salt and black pepper. Cover pan with aluminum foil. Bake 40 minutes. Remove foil and bake another 15 minutes. Garnish as desired.

Makes 4 to 6 servings

Favorite recipe from **The Fresh Garlic Association**

Forty-Clove Chicken Filice

Broiled Lemon Chicken

    4 skinless boneless chicken
        breast halves
        (about 1 pound)
    ¼ cup HEINZ® Worcestershire
        Sauce
    2 tablespoons lemon juice
    1 teaspoon minced garlic
    ½ teaspoon pepper
    ½ teaspoon grated lemon
        peel
        Vegetable oil

Lightly flatten chicken breasts to uniform thickness. For marinade, in small bowl, combine Worcestershire sauce, lemon juice, garlic, pepper and lemon peel. Place chicken in shallow dish; pour marinade over chicken. Cover; chill 30 minutes, turning once. Place chicken on broiler pan; brush with oil. Broil, 4 to 5 inches from heat source, 3 to 4 minutes; turn. Brush with marinade, then with oil; broil an additional 3 to 4 minutes or until cooked.

Makes 4 servings

Crispy Chicken Parmesan

    2 broiler-fryer chickens,
        cut up, skinned
        (2½ to 3 pounds each)
    1¼ cups MIRACLE WHIP®
        Salad Dressing
    2 cups corn flake crumbs
    1 cup (4 ounces) KRAFT®
        100% Grated Parmesan
        Cheese
    ¼ teaspoon pepper

• Heat oven to 350°F.

• Brush chicken with salad dressing.

• Mix crumbs, cheese and pepper; coat chicken. Place on rack of broiler pan.

• Bake 1 hour or until tender.

Makes 6 to 8 servings

Prep time: 15 minutes
Cooking time: 1 hour

Baked Chicken Reuben

Lemon Herb Cornish Hens

**2 (1½-pound) Rock Cornish hens, split in half lengthwise or
3 pounds chicken pieces
Salt and pepper
2 tablespoons finely chopped onion
1 clove garlic, finely chopped
¼ cup vegetable oil
¼ cup REALEMON® Lemon Juice from Concentrate
2 teaspoons WYLER'S® or STEERO® Chicken-Flavor Instant Bouillon or
2 Chicken-Flavor Bouillon Cubes
1 teaspoon chopped parsley
1 teaspoon rosemary leaves, crushed**

Season hens lightly with salt and pepper. In small saucepan, cook onion and garlic in oil until tender. Add remaining ingredients except hens; simmer uncovered 10 minutes. Grill hens about 1 hour or until tender and crisp, turning and basting frequently with sauce. Refrigerate leftovers.

Makes 4 servings

Oven Method: Place hens on rack in roasting pan. Bake at 375° for 1 hour and 15 minutes, basting frequently.

Baked Chicken Reuben

**4 whole chicken breasts, split, skinned and boned
¼ teaspoon salt
⅛ teaspoon pepper
1 can (16 ounces) sauerkraut, well drained
4 (6×4-inch) slices Swiss cheese
1¼ cups Thousand Island salad dressing**

Preheat oven to 325°F. Place chicken in a single layer in greased baking pan. Sprinkle with salt and pepper. Press excess liquid from sauerkraut; spoon over chicken. Arrange cheese slices over sauerkraut. Pour dressing evenly over the top. Cover pan with aluminum foil. Bake about 1½ hours or until chicken is tender.

Makes 6 to 8 servings

*Favorite recipe from **National Broiler Council***

Turkey a la King

- ⅓ cup BUTTER FLAVOR CRISCO®
- ⅓ cup chopped green pepper
- 2 tablespoons chopped green onion
- 5 tablespoons all-purpose flour
- 1 teaspoon seasoned salt
- ⅛ teaspoon pepper
- 1½ cups milk
- ¾ cup water
- 1 teaspoon instant chicken bouillon granules
- 2 cups cubed cooked turkey or chicken
- 1 can (8 ounces) mushroom stems and pieces, drained
- 1 cup frozen peas
- 1 jar (2 ounces) sliced pimiento, drained
-   Toast points or patty shells
- ¼ cup sliced or slivered almonds, optional

In 3-quart saucepan melt Butter Flavor Crisco®. Add green pepper and onion. Cook and stir over medium heat until tender. Stir in flour, seasoned salt and pepper. Blend in milk, water and bouillon granules. Cook and stir over medium heat for about 10 minutes, or until mixture thickens and bubbles. Stir in turkey, mushrooms, peas and pimiento. Continue cooking for about 5 minutes, or until hot and peas are tender. Serve over toast points or in patty shells. Top with almonds, if desired. Refrigerate leftovers.

Makes 4 to 6 servings

Country-Style Turkey

- 1 pound boneless skinless turkey or chicken, cut into strips
- 1 small onion, chopped
- 2 tablespoons margarine or butter
- 2 cups milk
- 1 package (10 ounces) BIRDS EYE® Mixed Vegetables
- 1 teaspoon salt
- ¾ teaspoon poultry seasoning
- 1½ cups Original MINUTE® Rice

Cook and stir turkey and onion in hot margarine in large skillet until lightly browned. Add milk, vegetables, salt and poultry seasoning. Bring to full boil. Stir in rice. Cover; remove from heat. Let stand 5 minutes. Fluff with fork.   *Makes 4 servings*

Microwave Directions: Omit margarine and reduce milk to 1¾ cups. Mix turkey and onion in 2½-quart microwavable dish. Cover and cook at HIGH 3 minutes. Add remaining ingredients. Cover and cook at HIGH 7 minutes. Stir, cover and cook at HIGH 5 minutes longer or until liquid is absorbed. Fluff with fork.   *Makes 4 servings*

Turkey Mushroom Piccata

- ½ cup unsifted flour
- ½ teaspoon basil leaves
- ½ teaspoon paprika
- 1 pound fresh turkey breast slices
- ¼ cup plus 2 tablespoons REALEMON® Lemon Juice from Concentrate
- ¼ cup margarine or butter
- 1 cup sliced fresh mushrooms
- ½ cup water
- 1 teaspoon WYLER'S® or STEERO® Chicken-Flavor Instant Bouillon

Combine flour, basil and paprika. Dip turkey slices in ¼ cup ReaLemon® brand, then flour mixture. In large skillet, brown turkey in margarine 2 minutes on each side or until no longer pink. Remove from skillet; keep warm. Add mushrooms, water, bouillon and remaining *2 tablespoons* ReaLemon® brand; cook until mushrooms are tender. Pour over turkey slices. Garnish with parsley. Refrigerate leftovers.

Makes 4 servings

Turkey Vegetable Roll-Ups

- ½ cup *each* thin strips carrots, red bell pepper, summer squash and zucchini
- 1 pound fresh turkey breast slices
- ¼ cup unsifted flour
- ¼ teaspoon paprika
- 2 tablespoons vegetable oil
- ⅓ cup water
- ¼ cup REALEMON® Lemon Juice from Concentrate
- 2 tablespoons dry sherry, optional
- 1 tablespoons WYLER'S® or STEERO® Chicken-Flavor Instant Bouillon
- ½ teaspoon thyme leaves

Place equal amounts of vegetables on center of turkey slices; roll up from narrow edge. Combine flour and paprika; coat roll-ups. In large skillet, brown in oil. Add remaining ingredients; cover and simmer 10 minutes or until turkey is no longer pink. Refrigerate leftovers.

Makes 4 to 6 servings

Top to bottom: Turkey Vegetable Roll-Ups and Chicken Parisian (page 124)

Turkey Vegetable Medley

Turkey Vegetable Medley

**4 fresh turkey breast slices
   or 4 skinned boneless
   chicken breast halves
1 tablespoon vegetable oil
½ cup water
2 teaspoons WYLER'S® or
   STEERO® Chicken-Flavor
   Instant Bouillon or
   2 Chicken-Flavor
   Bouillon Cubes
½ teaspoon thyme leaves or
   tarragon
¼ teaspoon onion powder
1 cup thin strips carrots
1 cup each thin strips red
   and green bell peppers**

In large skillet, brown turkey in oil. Add water, bouillon, thyme, onion powder and carrots. Cover; simmer 10 minutes. Add peppers; cover and cook 5 minutes longer or until tender. Refrigerate leftovers.   *Makes 4 servings*

Poached Turkey Tenderloins with Tarragon Sauce

**1 to 1½ pounds turkey
   tenderloins
¾ cup white wine
½ cup chopped celery
¼ cup sliced green onions
3 tablespoons chopped fresh
   tarragon or 1 teaspoon
   dry crushed tarragon
½ teaspoon salt
¼ teaspoon white pepper
   Water
   Steamed spinach
   Tarragon Sauce
   (recipe follows)**

In a large skillet, arrange tenderloins in a single layer. Add wine, celery, onions, tarragon, salt, pepper and enough water to cover tenderloins. Cover skillet and poach over low heat about 40 minutes or until no longer pink in center. Remove tenderloins, reserving poaching liquid for Tarragon Sauce.* Slice tenderloins into ½-inch medallions. To serve, arrange medallions on steamed spinach. Drizzle with Tarragon Sauce. Garnish with strips of lemon peel, if desired.
     Makes 4 servings

*Note: Recipe may be prepared to this point, cooled, covered and refrigerated for up to two days.

Tarragon Sauce

**Reserved poaching liquid
3 tablespoons cold water
2 tablespoons cornstarch
2 tablespoons chopped fresh
   tarragon or ½ teaspoon
   dry crushed tarragon
½ cup plain low-fat yogurt
1 tablespoon chopped
   parsley
1 tablespoon lemon juice**

In a saucepan over high heat, bring reserved poaching liquid to boil for 5 to 10 minutes to reduce liquid; strain. Measure 2 cups liquid and return to saucepan. Bring to boil. Combine cold water and cornstarch. Stir into boiling liquid. Reduce heat and add tarragon. Over low heat, cook sauce until slightly thickened. Stir in yogurt, parsley and lemon juice.

*Favorite recipe from **National Turkey Federation***

Apple & Herb Stuffing

**2 cups sliced celery
1½ cups chopped onion
½ cup margarine or butter
1¾ cups hot water
1 tablespoon WYLER'S® or
   STEERO® Chicken-Flavor
   Instant Bouillon or
   3 Chicken-Flavor
   Bouillon Cubes
12 cups dry bread cubes
   (about 16 slices bread)
3 cups coarsely chopped
   apple
1 cup toasted slivered
   almonds
1 tablespoon chopped
   parsley
2 teaspoons poultry
   seasoning
¼ teaspoon rubbed sage
   Rich Turkey Gravy**

In large skillet, cook celery and onion in margarine until tender. Add water and bouillon; cook until bouillon dissolves. In large bowl, combine remaining ingredients except Rich Turkey Gravy; add bouillon mixture. Mix well. Loosely stuff turkey just before roasting. Place remaining stuffing in greased baking dish. Bake at 350° for 30 minutes or until hot. Serve with Rich Turkey Gravy, if desired. Refrigerate leftovers.
     Makes about 2½ quarts

RICH TURKEY GRAVY: In medium skillet, stir ¼ to ⅓ cup flour into ¼ cup pan drippings; cook and stir until dark brown. Stir in 2 cups hot water and 2 teaspoons Wyler's® or Steero® Chicken-Flavor Instant Bouillon *or* 2 Chicken-Flavor Bouillon Cubes; cook and stir until thickened and bouillon is dissolved. Refrigerate leftovers.

Makes about 1½ cups

Turkey Breast with Southwestern Corn Bread Dressing

5 cups corn bread, coarsely crumbled
4 English muffins, coarsely crumbled
3 mild green chilies, roasted, peeled, seeded and chopped
1 red bell pepper, roasted, peeled, seeded and chopped
¾ cup pine nuts, toasted
1 tablespoon fresh cilantro, chopped
1 tablespoon fresh parsley, chopped
1½ teaspoons *each* fresh basil, thyme and oregano, chopped, *or* 1 teaspoon *each* dried basil, thyme and oregano
1 pound bulk turkey sausage
3 cups chopped celery
1 cup chopped onions
2 to 4 tablespoons turkey broth or water
1 bone-in turkey breast (5 to 6 pounds)
2 tablespoons chopped garlic
½ cup fresh cilantro, chopped

1. Preheat oven to 325°F.

2. In large bowl combine corn bread, muffins, chilies, red pepper, pine nuts, 1 tablespoon cilantro, parsley, basil, thyme and oregano.

3. In large skillet, over medium-high heat, sauté sausage, celery and onions 8 to 10 minutes or until sausage is no longer pink and vegetables are tender. Combine with corn bread mixture. Add broth if mixture is dry. Set aside.

4. Loosen skin on both sides of turkey breast, being careful not to tear skin and leaving it connected at breast bone. Spread 1 tablespoon garlic under loosened skin over each breast half. Repeat procedure with ¼ cup cilantro on each side.

5. In lightly greased 13×9×2-inch roasting pan, place turkey breast. Spoon half of stuffing mixture under breast cavity. Spoon remaining stuffing into a lightly greased 2-quart casserole; refrigerate. Roast turkey breast, uncovered, 2 to 2½ hours or until meat thermometer registers 170°F in deepest portion of breast. Bake remaining stuffing, uncovered, along with turkey breast during last 45 minutes.

Makes 12 servings

*Favorite recipe from **National Turkey Federation***

Turkey Breast with Southwestern Corn Bread Dressing

Turkey Fajitas

⅓ cup **REALEMON® Lemon Juice from Concentrate** *or* **REALIME® Lime Juice from Concentrate**
2 tablespoons **vegetable oil**
1 tablespoon **WYLER'S® or STEERO® Chicken-Flavor Instant Bouillon**
3 cloves **garlic, finely chopped**
2 (½-pound) **fresh turkey breast tenderloins, pierced with fork**
8 (8-inch) **flour tortillas, warmed as package directs**
   Garnishes: Shredded lettuce and cheese, sliced ripe olives and green onions, salsa, guacamole and sour cream

In large shallow dish or plastic bag, combine ReaLemon® brand, oil, bouillon and garlic; add turkey. Cover; marinate in refrigerator 4 hours or overnight, turning occasionally. Remove turkey from marinade. Grill or broil 10 minutes on each side or until no longer pink, basting frequently with additional ReaLemon® brand. Let stand 10 minutes. Cut turkey into thin slices; place on tortillas. Top with one or more garnishes; fold tortillas. Serve immediately. Refrigerate leftovers.   *Makes 4 servings*

Turkey Fajitas

Spicy Pineapple-Cranberry Sauce & Turkey

1 can (20 ounces) **DOLE® Pineapple Tidbits in Juice**
1 can (16 ounces) **jellied cranberry sauce**
½ cup **frozen orange juice concentrate, thawed***
¼ teaspoon **ground allspice Zest from 1 DOLE® Orange**
6 fresh **turkey breast slices (1½ pounds)**
1 teaspoon **garlic salt**
¼ teaspoon **pepper**
¼ cup **all-purpose flour**
1 teaspoon **rubbed sage**
2 tablespoons **margarine**

• Drain pineapple; save juice for beverage.

• Combine cranberry sauce and orange juice concentrate in saucepan. Heat over medium heat until blended. Add pineapple, allspice and orange zest.

• Sprinkle turkey with garlic salt and pepper. Combine flour and sage in shallow dish. Coat turkey with flour mixture.

• In 12-inch skillet, sauté turkey in margarine over medium-high heat 2 to 2½ minutes on each side. Serve with sauce.
      Makes 6 servings

*Do not reconstitute.

Preparation Time: 15 minutes
Cook Time: 10 minutes

Sweet & Sour Meatballs with Vegetables

1 pound ground turkey
2 cups Multi-Bran CHEX® brand cereal, crushed to ¾ cup
¼ cup chopped onion
¼ cup cholesterol-free egg product *or* 1 egg, beaten
2 tablespoons chopped fresh parsley
1 clove garlic, minced
1 teaspoon lite soy sauce
¼ teaspoon ground ginger
¼ cup water
16 ounces frozen Oriental *or* mixed vegetables, prepared according to package directions, drained
1 cup prepared sweet and sour sauce
Hot cooked rice (optional)

In medium bowl combine turkey, cereal, onion, egg, parsley, garlic, soy sauce and ginger. Mix well. Using 1 rounded tablespoon meat mixture for each, shape into 2-inch balls. Brown meatballs in lightly greased skillet over medium heat, turning often. Add water; cover and cook over low heat 8 to 10 minutes or until no longer pink, stirring occasionally. Drain. Add vegetables and sweet and sour sauce; cook over low heat, stirring gently until meatballs are coated and sauce and vegetables are warm. Serve over rice, if desired.

Makes 6 servings

Toluca Taters

Toluca Taters

1 package (1.62 ounces) LAWRY'S® Spices & Seasonings for Chili
1 pound ground turkey
1 can (15¼ ounces) kidney beans, undrained
1 can (14½ ounces) whole peeled tomatoes, undrained and cut up
½ cup water
8 medium russet potatoes, washed and pierced with fork
1 cup (4 ounces) grated Cheddar cheese
½ cup thinly sliced green onions

In large glass bowl, prepare Spices & Seasonings for Chili with ground turkey, kidney beans, tomatoes and water according to package microwave directions; keep warm. Microwave potatoes on HIGH 25 minutes, turning over after 12 minutes. Slit potatoes lengthwise and pull back skin. Fluff with fork. Top each potato with ½ to ¾ cup prepared chili, 2 tablespoons cheese and 1 tablespoon green onions.

Makes 8 servings

Honey Mustard Turkey Loaf

1½ pounds ground fresh turkey
1 cup fresh bread crumbs (2 slices)
½ cup BORDEN® or MEADOW GOLD® Milk
¼ cup chopped onion
1 egg, beaten
2 teaspoons WYLER'S® or STEERO® Chicken-Flavor Instant Bouillon
2½ teaspoons prepared mustard
1 teaspoon poultry seasoning
2 tablespoons honey
1 tablespoon brown sugar

Preheat oven to 350°. Combine turkey, crumbs, milk, onion, egg, bouillon, *1 teaspoon* mustard and poultry seasoning; mix well. In shallow baking dish, shape into loaf. Bake 40 minutes. Combine remaining *1½ teaspoons* mustard, honey and brown sugar. Spoon over loaf; bake 10 minutes longer or until no longer pink. Refrigerate leftovers.

Makes 4 to 6 servings

SEAFOOD

Seafood is finding its way onto more dinner tables than ever before—and for good reason. It's delicious, nutritious and cooks quickly. Serve salmon with a creamy chive sauce, red snapper with a mushroom-rice stuffing or a seafood stir-fry sure to impress friends and family. From spicy Cajun Shrimp to succulent Scallop Kabobs, you'll discover innovative ways to add fish and shellfish to your menus.

Lemon Broiled Fish

½ cup margarine or butter, melted
¼ cup REALEMON® Lemon Juice from Concentrate
2 cups fresh bread crumbs (4 slices)
1 tablespoon chopped parsley
½ teaspoon paprika
1 pound fish fillets, fresh or frozen, thawed

In small bowl, combine margarine and ReaLemon® brand. In medium bowl, combine crumbs, parsley and ¼ cup margarine mixture. Add paprika to remaining margarine mixture; dip fish into mixture. Broil until fish flakes with fork; top with crumb mixture. Return to broiler; heat through. Refrigerate leftovers.
Makes 4 servings

Tangy Cocktail Sauce

¾ cup BENETT'S® Chili Sauce
3 tablespoons REALEMON® Lemon Juice from Concentrate
½ teaspoon prepared horseradish
½ teaspoon Worcestershire sauce

In small bowl, combine all ingredients. Cover; chill. Serve with fish or seafood. Refrigerate leftovers. *Makes about 1 cup*

Quick Tartar Sauce

¾ cup mayonnaise or salad dressing
2 tablespoons pickle relish, drained
1 tablespoon chopped green onion
1 tablespoon REALEMON® Lemon Juice from Concentrate

In small bowl, combine all ingredients. Cover; chill. Serve with fish or seafood. Refrigerate leftovers. *Makes about 1 cup*

Lemon Butter Sauce

½ cup margarine or butter
3 tablespoons REALEMON® Lemon Juice from Concentrate
⅛ teaspoon salt, optional

In small saucepan, melt margarine; stir in ReaLemon® brand and salt if desired. Serve with fish, seafood or vegetables. Refrigerate leftovers.
Makes about ⅔ cup

Parsley Lemon: Add 1 tablespoon chopped parsley.

Herb Lemon: Add 1 teaspoon oregano leaves or dill weed.

Almond Lemon: Add ¼ cup sliced toasted almonds.

Clockwise from top: Lemon Broiled Fish, Lemon Butter Sauce, Tangy Cocktail Sauce and Quick Tartar Sauce

Almondine Fish

• Arrange fish fillets in 12×8-inch microwave dish with thickest parts to outside edges of dish. Drizzle with margarine, then sprinkle with bread crumbs and paprika. Cover with waxed paper. Microwave on HIGH 5 to 9 minutes, rotating dish after 3 minutes. Fish is done when thin areas flake easily with a fork and thick areas are fork tender. Let fish stand 2 to 3 minutes; serve with pineapple sauce.

Makes 4 servings

Preparation Time: 10 minutes
Cook Time: 20 minutes

Almondine Fish

½ cup margarine or butter, melted
3 tablespoons REALEMON® Lemon Juice from Concentrate
3 tablespoons sliced almonds, toasted
1 pound fish fillets, fresh or frozen, thawed

Combine margarine and ReaLemon® brand; reserve ¼ cup. Add almonds to remaining margarine mixture; set aside. Broil or grill fish as desired, basting frequently with reserved ¼ cup margarine mixture. Serve with almond sauce. Refrigerate leftovers.   *Makes 4 servings*

Herb Fish: Omit almonds. Add 1 teaspoon dill weed.

Garlic Fish: Omit almonds. Add ½ teaspoon garlic powder.

Saucy Fish Fillets

1 can (8 ounces) DOLE® Pineapple Tidbits in Juice
1 tablespoon sugar
1 tablespoon cider vinegar
1½ teaspoons cornstarch
½ teaspoon instant chicken bouillon granules
¼ teaspoon ground ginger
Pinch ground red pepper
¼ cup sliced DOLE® Green Onions
¼ cup sliced water chestnuts
4 white fish fillets, ½ inch thick
2 tablespoons margarine, melted
½ cup bread crumbs
Paprika

• **To microwave:** Drain pineapple; reserve juice. For sauce, add enough water to juice to make ⅔ cup liquid. In microwave bowl, whisk together juice mixture, sugar, vinegar, cornstarch, bouillon, ginger and red pepper. Microwave on HIGH 4 to 5 minutes, until sauce boils and thickens, whisking after 2 minutes to prevent lumps. Stir in green onions, water chestnuts and pineapple; set aside.

Crispy Oven Fish

2½ cups finely crushed KRUNCHERS!® Potato Chips
½ cup grated Parmesan cheese
2 tablespoons chopped parsley
½ cup mayonnaise or salad dressing
¼ cup REALEMON® Lemon Juice from Concentrate
1 pound fish fillets, fresh or frozen, thawed

Preheat oven to 400°. Combine chips, cheese and parsley. In small bowl, combine mayonnaise and 2 *tablespoons* ReaLemon® brand. Dip fish in remaining 2 *tablespoons* ReaLemon® brand, then mayonnaise mixture, then chip mixture. Arrange in greased baking dish. Bake 5 to 10 minutes or until fish flakes with fork. Refrigerate leftovers.

Makes 4 servings

Baja Fish and Rice Bake

3 tablespoons vegetable oil
¾ cup chopped onion
½ cup chopped celery
1 clove garlic, minced
½ cup rice
3½ cups (two 14.5-ounce cans) CONTADINA® Stewed Tomatoes, cut-up
1 teaspoon lemon pepper
½ teaspoon salt
⅛ teaspoon cayenne pepper
1 pound fish fillets (any firm, white fish)
¼ cup finely chopped fresh parsley
Lemon slices (optional)

Preheat oven to 400°F. In large skillet, heat oil; sauté onion, celery and garlic. Stir in rice; sauté about 5 minutes, or until rice browns slightly. Add tomatoes with juice, lemon pepper, salt and cayenne pepper. Place fish in 12×7½×2-inch baking dish. Spoon rice mixture over fish. Cover with foil; bake 45 to 50 minutes or until rice is tender. Allow to stand 5 minutes before serving. Sprinkle with parsley. Garnish with lemon slices, if desired.
Makes 6 servings

Baja Fish and Rice Bake

Crispy Oven Fish

Lemon Fish Roll-Ups

1 cup cooked rice
1 (10-ounce) package frozen chopped broccoli, thawed and well drained
1 cup (4 ounces) shredded Cheddar cheese
⅓ cup margarine or butter, melted
⅓ cup REALEMON® Lemon Juice from Concentrate
½ teaspoon salt
¼ teaspoon pepper
8 fish fillets, fresh or frozen, thawed (about 2 pounds)

Preheat oven to 375°. In medium bowl, combine rice, broccoli and cheese. In small bowl, combine margarine, ReaLemon® brand, salt and pepper; add *¼ cup* to broccoli mixture. Place equal amounts of broccoli mixture on fillets; roll up. Place seam-side down in shallow baking dish; pour remaining margarine mixture over roll-ups. Bake 20 minutes or until fish flakes with fork. Garnish with paprika if desired. Refrigerate leftovers.
Makes 8 servings

Microwave: Prepare fish as above. Arrange in shallow baking dish. Cook tightly covered on 100% power (high) 10 to 12 minutes or until fish flakes with fork, rotating dish once. Serve as above.

Fish Rolls Primavera

1 cup shredded carrots
1 cup shredded zucchini
2 tablespoons finely chopped onion
½ cup fresh bread crumbs (1 slice)
⅛ teaspoon thyme leaves
¼ cup margarine or butter, melted
¼ cup REALEMON® Lemon Juice from Concentrate
4 fish fillets, fresh or frozen, thawed (about 1 pound)

Preheat oven to 375°. In medium bowl, combine vegetables, crumbs and thyme. In small bowl, combine margarine and ReaLemon® brand; add ¼ cup to vegetable mixture. Place equal amounts of vegetable mixture on fillets; roll up. Place seam-side down in shallow baking dish; pour remaining margarine mixture over fish rolls. Bake 15 minutes or until fish flakes with fork. Refrigerate leftovers.

Makes 4 servings

Rice-Stuffed Fish Fillets with Mushroom Sauce

3 cups cooked rice
¼ cup diced pimientos
2 tablespoons snipped parsley
1 teaspoon grated lemon peel
¼ teaspoon salt
¼ teaspoon ground white pepper
1 pound white fish fillets*
Vegetable cooking spray
2 teaspoons margarine, melted
½ teaspoon seasoned salt
¼ teaspoon paprika
Mushroom Sauce (recipe follows)
Lemon slices for garnish

Combine rice, pimientos, parsley, lemon peel, salt, and pepper in large bowl. Place fillets in shallow baking dish coated with cooking spray. Spoon rice mixture on lower portion of each fillet. Fold over to enclose rice mixture; fasten with wooden toothpicks soaked in water. Brush fillets with margarine; sprinkle with seasoned salt and paprika. Bake at 400°F. for 10 to 15 minutes or until fish flakes easily with fork. Prepare Mushroom Sauce while fillets are baking. Transfer fillets to serving platter; garnish platter with lemon slices. Serve fillets with Mushroom Sauce.

Makes 4 servings

*Haddock, orange roughy, sole, or turbot may be used.

Mushroom Sauce

2 cups (about 8 ounces) sliced fresh mushrooms
½ cup sliced green onions
1 teaspoon margarine
½ cup water
⅓ cup white wine
1 tablespoon white wine Worcestershire sauce
½ cup cholesterol free, reduced calorie mayonnaise

Cook mushrooms and onions in margarine in large skillet until tender. Add water, wine, and Worcestershire sauce; bring to a boil. Reduce sauce slightly. Stir in mayonnaise; keep warm.

*Favorite recipe from **USA Rice Council***

Spicy Island Fish Sauté

2 white fish fillets (orange roughy or sole), ½ pound
Juice from 1 lime
1 clove garlic, pressed
2 teaspoons minced ginger root
1 teaspoon minced cilantro
⅛ to ¼ teaspoon ground red pepper
2 firm, medium DOLE® Bananas, peeled
2 tablespoons margarine

Fish Rolls Primavera

- Arrange fish in shallow glass casserole dish.

- Combine lime juice, garlic, ginger, cilantro and red pepper in small bowl. Pour over fish. Cover and marinate in refrigerator 15 minutes or overnight.

- Cut bananas in half crosswise, then lengthwise to make 8 pieces.

- In 12-inch nonstick skillet, sauté bananas in margarine over medium-high heat until lightly browned. Remove bananas to plate.

- Remove fish from marinade. In same skillet, cook fish, covered, over medium-high heat 7 to 10 minutes or until fish flakes easy when tested with a fork, turning fish once.

- Remove fish to plate. Arrange bananas on plate with fish.

Makes 2 servings

Preparation Time: 5 minutes
Marinate Time: 15 minutes or overnight
Cook Time: 15 minutes

Lemon Rice Stuffed Sole

Vegetable cooking spray
½ **cup thinly sliced celery**
¼ **cup chopped onion**
3 **cups cooked brown rice**
2 **teaspoons grated lemon peel**
¼ **teaspoon salt**
¼ **teaspoon dried thyme leaves**
⅛ **teaspoon ground black pepper**
2 **tablespoons lemon juice**
1 **pound fresh or frozen sole fillets***
2 **teaspoons margarine, melted**
1 **tablespoon snipped parsley**
¼ **teaspoon seasoned salt**

*Substitute any white-fleshed fish such as haddock, turbot, or white fish for the sole, if desired.

Coat large skillet with cooking spray and place over medium-high heat until hot. Add celery and onion; cook 2 to 3 minutes or until tender. Stir in rice, lemon peel, salt, thyme, pepper, and lemon juice. Spoon rice mixture on lower portion of each fillet. Fold over to enclose rice mixture; fasten with wooden toothpicks soaked in water. Place remaining rice mixture in bottom of shallow baking dish coated with cooking spray. Place fillets on top of rice. Brush fish with margarine. Sprinkle with parsley and seasoned salt. Bake, uncovered, at 400°F. for 10 to 15 minutes or until fish flakes easily with fork.

Makes 4 servings

Favorite recipe from **USA Rice Council**

Orange Roughy with Cucumber Relish

Orange Roughy with Cucumber Relish

1 **can (11 ounces) mandarin orange segments, drained**
1 **small cucumber, peeled, seeded, finely chopped**
⅓ **cup HEINZ® Distilled White Vinegar**
1 **green onion, minced**
1 **tablespoon snipped fresh dill***
Nonstick cooking spray
4 **orange roughy fillets (about 5 ounces each)**
Dill sprigs (optional)

Reserve 8 orange segments for garnish; coarsely chop remaining segments. In medium bowl, combine chopped oranges, cucumber, vinegar, green onion and dill. Spray broiler pan with cooking spray; place fish on pan. Spoon 1 tablespoon liquid from cucumber mixture over each fillet. Broil, 3 to 4 inches from heat source, 8 to 10 minutes or until fish turns opaque and just flakes when tested with fork. To serve, spoon cucumber relish on top of fish. Garnish with reserved orange segments and dill sprigs. *Makes 4 servings*

*1 teaspoon dried dill weed may be substituted.

Baked Stuffed Snapper

Clean and butterfly fish. Combine rice, mushrooms, water chestnuts, onions, pimiento, parsley, lemon peel, salt, and pepper; toss lightly. Fill cavity of fish with rice mixture; enclose filling with wooden toothpicks soaked in water. Place fish in 13×9×2-inch baking dish coated with cooking spray; brush fish with margarine. Bake fish at 400°F. for 18 to 20 minutes or until fish flakes easily with fork. Wrap remaining rice in foil and bake in oven with fish.

Makes 4 servings

Tip: One lemon will yield about 1 tablespoon grated lemon peel.

Favorite recipe from **USA Rice Council**

Pescado Borracho
(Drunken Fish)

    1½ pounds red snapper fillets
        All-purpose flour
    4 tablespoons vegetable oil
    1 small onion, chopped
    1 can (14½ ounces) whole
        peeled tomatoes,
        undrained and cut up
    1 package (1.25 ounces)
        LAWRY'S® Taco Spices &
        Seasonings
    2 tablespoons diced green
        chiles
    ½ cup dry red wine

Dip fish in flour to coat. In large skillet, brown fish in 2 tablespoons oil. In 2-quart oblong baking dish, place browned fish; set aside. Add remaining 2 tablespoons oil and onion to skillet; sauté onion about 5 minutes or until soft. Add remaining ingredients except wine. Bring to a boil, stirring constantly; add wine and blend well. Pour tomato mixture over fish. Bake, uncovered, in 400°F oven 15 to 20 minutes or until fish flakes easily with fork.

Makes 4 to 6 servings

Presentation: Serve each fillet with sauce; garnish with parsley.

Saucy Topped Flounder

    1 pound flounder fillets
        Butter or margarine
        Salt and pepper
    ½ cup HEINZ® Tartar Sauce
        Paprika

Divide fish into 4 portions; arrange in 2-quart oblong baking dish. Dot fish with about 1 teaspoon butter; season with salt and pepper. Bake in preheated 375°F oven, 10 to 12 minutes or until fish is almost cooked. Remove from oven; carefully spoon off liquid. Spread tartar sauce on each portion of fish; sprinkle with paprika. Return to oven; bake 5 minutes or until fish just turns opaque and just flakes when tested with fork.

Makes 4 servings

Baked Stuffed Snapper

    1 red snapper (1½ pounds)
    2 cups hot cooked rice
    1 can (4 ounces) sliced
        mushrooms, drained
    ½ cup diced water chestnuts
    ¼ cup thinly sliced green
        onions
    ¼ cup diced pimiento
    2 tablespoons chopped
        parsley
    1 tablespoon grated lemon
        peel
    ½ teaspoon salt
    ⅛ teaspoon ground black
        pepper
        Vegetable cooking spray
    1 tablespoon margarine,
        melted

Spanish-Style Baked Catfish

1½ **pounds catfish fillets**
½ **cup yellow cornmeal**
  Paprika
1 **medium onion, chopped**
1 **tablespoon olive or**
  vegetable oil
1 **cup chunky salsa**
¼ **cup sliced ripe olives**
1 **teaspoon LAWRY'S® Garlic**
  Salt
1 **teaspoon freshly grated**
  lemon peel
  Chopped fresh parsley

Rinse and cut catfish into serving pieces; dip in cornmeal to coat. Place in lightly greased 12×8×2-inch baking dish. Sprinkle with paprika. Bake in 425°F oven 20 to 25 minutes or until fish flakes easily with fork. In medium skillet, sauté onion in oil 3 minutes or until tender. Stir in salsa, olives, Garlic Salt and lemon peel; heat through. Serve over baked fish. Sprinkle with parsley.   *Makes 6 servings*

Presentation: Serve with lemon wedges.

Hint: Seasoned dry bread crumbs can be used in place of cornmeal.

Salmon with Chive Sauce

½ **cup MIRACLE WHIP® Salad**
  Dressing
¼ **cup finely chopped fresh**
  chives
2 **tablespoons finely chopped**
  fresh thyme leaves or
  2 **teaspoons dried thyme**
  leaves, crushed
2 **tablespoons finely**
  chopped fresh dill or
  2 **teaspoons dill weed**
¼ **teaspoon salt**
⅛ **teaspoon pepper**
¼ **cup dry white wine or**
  chicken broth
2 **salmon steaks**
  (about ¾ pound)

• Mix salad dressing, herbs, salt and pepper until well blended. Reserve ⅓ cup salad dressing mixture to serve later with cooked salmon. Stir wine into remaining salad dressing mixture; brush on salmon.

• Place salmon on grill over hot coals (coals will be glowing) or rack of broiler pan. Grill, covered, **or** broil 5 to 8 minutes on each side or until fish flakes easily with fork. Serve with reserved salad dressing mixture.
Makes 2 servings

Prep time: 10 minutes
Grilling time: 16 minutes

Salmon with Chive Sauce

Dilly Salmon Loaf

- 1 (15½-ounce) can salmon, drained and flaked
- 2 cups fresh bread crumbs (4 slices)
- 2 eggs, beaten
- ¼ cup finely chopped onion
- 3 tablespoons margarine or butter, melted
- 2 tablespoons REALEMON® Lemon Juice from Concentrate
- ½ teaspoon salt
- ¼ teaspoon dill weed
  Lemony Dill Sauce

Preheat oven to 350°. In large bowl, combine all ingredients except Lemony Dill Sauce; mix well. Shape into loaf; place in greased shallow baking dish. Bake 35 to 40 minutes. Let stand 5 minutes before serving. Serve with Lemony Dill Sauce; garnish as desired. Refrigerate leftovers.

Makes 4 to 6 servings

LEMONY DILL SAUCE: In small saucepan, melt ⅓ cup margarine or butter. Add ¾ cup mayonnaise, 1 egg, ¼ cup ReaLemon® brand, 2 tablespoons water, 1 tablespoon sugar, 1 teaspoon WYLER'S® or STEERO® Chicken-Flavor Instant Bouillon and ¼ teaspoon dill weed; mix well. Over low heat, cook and stir until thickened (*do not boil*). Refrigerate leftovers.

Makes about 1½ cups

Microwave: For Salmon Loaf, combine ingredients as above. Shape into loaf; place in greased 8-inch baking dish. Cook on 70% power (medium-high) 10 to 11 minutes or until center of loaf is firm, rotating ¼ turn after 5 minutes. Cover with foil; let stand 5 minutes. Serve as above.

For Lemony Dill Sauce, in 1-quart glass measure with handle, melt margarine on 100% power (high) 45 seconds to 1 minute. Add remaining ingredients; mix well. Cook on 70% power (medium-high) 2 to 2½ minutes or until thickened, stirring after 1 minute (*do not boil*).

Salmon with Mustard Dill Sauce

- ¼ cup mayonnaise or salad dressing
- ¼ cup BORDEN® or MEADOW GOLD® Sour Cream
- 1 tablespoon sliced green onion
- 1 teaspoon Dijon-style mustard
- ⅓ cup plus 1 teaspoon REALEMON® Lemon Juice from Concentrate
- 1½ teaspoons dill weed
- 4 (1-inch-thick) salmon steaks (about 1½ pounds)

In small bowl, combine mayonnaise, sour cream, green onion, mustard, *1 teaspoon* ReaLemon® brand and *½ teaspoon* dill weed. Cover; chill. In large shallow dish or plastic bag, combine remaining *⅓ cup* ReaLemon® brand and *1 teaspoon* dill weed; add salmon. Cover; marinate in refrigerator 1 hour. Grill, broil or bake until fish flakes with fork. Serve with dill sauce. Refrigerate leftovers.

Makes 4 servings

Seafood Royale

- 4 tablespoons butter or margarine, divided
- 2 tablespoons all-purpose flour
- ½ teaspoon dried dill weed
- ¼ teaspoon seasoned salt
- 1½ cups (12-ounce can) undiluted CARNATION® Evaporated Milk
- ½ cup dry white wine
- ½ cup shredded Swiss cheese
- 1½ cups sliced mushrooms
- ½ cup finely sliced green onions
- 1 pound salmon, cooked, bones and skin removed
- 6 rolls or puff pastry shells

In medium saucepan, melt *2 tablespoons* butter. Whisk in flour, dill and salt; heat until bubbling. Add evaporated milk; stir constantly over medium heat until well thickened. Add wine and cheese; stir until blended. Keep warm. In small skillet, sauté mushrooms and green onions in *remaining 2 tablespoons* butter. Combine sauce, mushrooms, onions and salmon over low heat; stir gently. Serve in hollowed out rolls or puff pastry shells.

Makes 6 servings

Baja Fruited Salmon

- 1 large navel orange, peeled and diced
- 1 small grapefruit, peeled and diced
- 1 medium tomato, seeded and diced
- ¼ cup diced red onion
- 1 small jalapeño, seeded and finely chopped
- 2 tablespoons snipped fresh cilantro
- 2 tablespoons red wine vinegar
- 1 tablespoon vegetable oil
- ½ teaspoon LAWRY'S® Seasoned Salt
- ¼ teaspoon LAWRY'S® Garlic Powder with Parsley
- 4 (5 ounces each) salmon steaks
  Lemon juice

In medium bowl, combine all ingredients except salmon and lemon juice; refrigerate. Brush salmon steaks with lemon juice. Grill or broil 5 inches from heat source 5 to 7 minutes on each side or until fish flakes easily with fork. Spoon chilled fruit salsa over salmon.

Makes 4 servings

Presentation: Serve with pan-fried potatoes. Garnish with parsley and lemon slices.

Baja Fruited Salmon

Tuna Veronique

- **2 leeks or green onions**
- **½ cup thin carrot strips**
- **1 stalk celery, cut diagonally into slices**
- **1 tablespoon vegetable oil**
- **1¾ cups *or* 1 can (14½ ounces) chicken broth**
- **2 tablespoons cornstarch**
- **⅓ cup dry white wine**
- **1¼ cups seedless red and green grapes, cut into halves**
- **1 can (12½ ounces) STARKIST® Tuna, drained and broken into chunks**
- **1 tablespoon chopped chives**
- **¼ teaspoon white or black pepper**
- **4 to 5 slices bread, toasted and cut into quarters *or* 8 to 10 slices toasted French bread**

If using leeks, wash thoroughly between leaves. Cut off white portion; trim and slice ¼ inch thick. Discard green portion. For green onions, trim and slice ¼ inch thick. In a large nonstick skillet sauté leeks, carrot and celery in oil for 3 minutes. In a small bowl stir together chicken broth and cornstarch until smooth; stir into vegetables. Cook and stir until mixture thickens and bubbles. Stir in wine; simmer for 2 minutes. Stir in grapes, tuna, chives and pepper. Cook for 2 minutes more to heat through. To serve, ladle sauce over toast points.

Makes 4 to 5 servings

Preparation time: 20 minutes

Tuna in Red Pepper Sauce

- **2 cups chopped red bell peppers (about 2 peppers)**
- **½ cup chopped onion**
- **1 clove garlic, minced**
- **2 tablespoons vegetable oil**
- **¼ cup dry red or white wine**
- **¼ cup chicken broth**
- **2 teaspoons sugar**
- **¼ teaspoon black pepper**
- **1 red bell pepper, slivered and cut into ½-inch pieces**
- **1 yellow or green bell pepper, slivered and cut into ½-inch pieces**
- **½ cup julienne-strip carrots**
- **1 can (9¼ ounces) STARKIST® Tuna, drained and broken into chunks**
- **Hot cooked pasta or rice**

In skillet sauté 2 cups chopped bell peppers, onion and garlic in oil for 5 minutes, or until vegetables are very tender. In blender or food processor container place vegetable mixture; cover and process until puréed. Return to pan; stir in wine, chicken broth, sugar and black pepper. Keep warm. In 2-quart saucepan steam bell pepper pieces and carrots over simmering water for 5 minutes. Stir steamed vegetables into sauce with tuna; cook for 2 minutes, or until heated through. Serve tuna mixture over pasta or rice. *Makes 4 to 5 servings*

Preparation time: 20 minutes

Tuna Veronique

Tuna in Red Pepper Sauce

Rainbow Trout Santa Fe

2 tablespoons olive oil
4 CLEAR SPRINGS® Brand Idaho Rainbow Trout fillets (4 ounces *each*)
2 teaspoons butter
2 cloves garlic, minced
¼ cup chopped green onion
1 small tomato, peeled, seeded and diced
½ cup fresh or frozen whole corn kernels
½ cup snow peas, cut in half diagonally
2 tablespoons chopped cilantro or parsley
1 to 1½ teaspoons finely chopped jalapeño pepper*
1 teaspoon fresh lemon juice
¼ teaspoon salt
Dash white pepper
¼ cup heavy cream
Flour or corn tortilla chips

*Wear rubber gloves when working with jalapeño peppers and wash hands with warm soapy water. Avoid touching face or eyes.

Heat oil over medium-high heat in large skillet. Sauté trout 1 to 2 minutes on each side or until fish flakes easily; set aside. Melt butter over medium heat. Sauté garlic and green onion, about 1 minute. Add tomato, corn, snow peas, cilantro, jalapeño, lemon juice, salt and pepper. Simmer about 2 to 3 minutes. Stir in cream; gently simmer about 1 minute more. Top trout with sauce. Serve immediately with tortilla chips.

Makes 4 servings

Broiled Rainbow Trout with Herb Mayonnaise

6 tablespoons regular or light mayonnaise
1 clove garlic, minced
1 tablespoon lemon juice
Herbs to taste
Dash of pepper
4 CLEAR SPRINGS® Brand Idaho Rainbow Trout fillets (4 ounces *each*)

Combine mayonnaise, garlic, lemon juice, herbs and pepper in bowl; mix well. Cover flesh side of each trout fillet with ¼ of mayonnaise mixture. Broil 4 inches from heat source for about 3 to 5 minutes, or until fish flakes with a fork and topping is bubbly.

Makes 2 to 4 servings

"Crab" Cakes

2 eggs, beaten
½ cup plain dry bread crumbs
¼ cup REALEMON® Lemon Juice from Concentrate
¼ cup sliced green onions
½ teaspoon dry mustard
½ pound imitation crab blend, flaked
Additional dry bread crumbs
Vegetable oil

In medium bowl, combine eggs, ½ cup crumbs, ReaLemon® brand, green onions and mustard. Fold in crab blend. Shape into 8 cakes; coat with additional crumbs. In large skillet, brown in hot oil until golden on both sides. Refrigerate leftovers. *Makes 4 servings*

"Crab" Cakes

Oriental Seafood Stir-Fry

With slotted spoon, remove shrimp from marinade; stir-fry 2 to 3 minutes, or until shrimp turn pink. Add mushrooms; stir-fry 2 to 3 minutes, adding 1 tablespoon water if necessary to prevent sticking. Stir cornstarch and 6 tablespoons water into marinade; add to skillet and cook about 30 seconds, until thickened. Add celery and remaining ingredients and stir-fry 3 to 4 minutes, until bean sprouts are soft, but still crisp. Serve over hot brown rice, if desired. *Makes 4 servings*

Oriental Seafood Stir-Fry

½ cup water
3 tablespoons REALEMON®
   Lemon Juice from
   Concentrate
3 tablespoons soy sauce
1 tablespoon brown sugar
1 tablespoon cornstarch
2 ounces fresh pea pods
¾ cup sliced fresh
   mushrooms
¾ cup diced red bell pepper
1 medium onion, cut into
   wedges
1 tablespoon vegetable oil
½ pound imitation crab blend,
   flaked
   Shredded napa (Chinese
   cabbage), angel hair
   pasta or rice noodles

In small bowl, combine water, ReaLemon® brand, soy sauce, sugar and cornstarch. In large skillet or wok, over medium-high heat, cook and stir vegetables in oil until tender-crisp; remove. Add soy mixture; over medium heat, cook and stir until slightly thickened. Add vegetables and crab blend; heat through. Serve with napa, pasta or noodles. Refrigerate leftovers.
Makes 4 servings

Oriental Almond Stir-Fry

2 tablespoons dry sherry
1 tablespoon soy sauce
½ teaspoon sugar
¼ teaspoon ground ginger
1 clove garlic, minced
¾ pound shrimp, peeled and
   deveined
1 tablespoon vegetable oil,
   divided
2 cups diagonally sliced
   celery (¼ inch thick)
2 cups fresh mushrooms,
   sliced
1 tablespoon cornstarch
6 tablespoons water
1 package (10 ounces) frozen
   peas (about 2 cups)
1½ cups bean sprouts
¼ cup BLUE DIAMOND®
   Blanched Whole
   Almonds

Make marinade by combining first five ingredients in a medium bowl. Add shrimp and let stand at least 10 minutes, stirring occasionally. Using heavy non-stick skillet or wok, heat 1½ teaspoons oil over medium-high heat. Add celery and stir-fry 1 minute. Remove from pan and set aside. Heat remaining 1½ teaspoons oil.

Sonora Shrimp

2 tablespoons IMPERIAL®
   Margarine
1 medium green bell pepper,
   coarsely chopped
½ cup chopped onion
½ cup chopped celery
1 can (14½ ounces) whole
   peeled tomatoes,
   undrained and cut up
½ cup dry white wine
½ teaspoon LAWRY'S®
   Seasoned Salt
½ teaspoon LAWRY'S®
   Seasoned Pepper
¼ teaspoon LAWRY'S® Garlic
   Powder with Parsley
¼ teaspoon dried thyme,
   crushed
1 pound medium shrimp,
   peeled and deveined
1 can (2¼ ounces) sliced ripe
   olives, drained

In large skillet, melt margarine and sauté bell pepper, onion and celery. Add remaining ingredients except shrimp and olives; blend well. Bring to a boil; reduce heat and simmer, uncovered, 15 minutes, stirring occasionally. Add shrimp and olives; cook 10 minutes or until shrimp turn pink.
Makes 4 to 6 servings

Presentation: Serve over hot fluffy rice.

Sweet & Sour Shrimp

Sweet & Sour Shrimp

  1 (20-ounce) can juice-pack
      pineapple chunks,
      drained, reserving juice
  ¾ cup cold water
  ⅓ cup REALEMON® Lemon
      Juice from Concentrate
  ⅓ cup firmly packed light
      brown sugar
  3 tablespoons cornstarch
  3 tablespoons soy sauce
  ⅛ teaspoon ground ginger
  1 pound medium raw shrimp,
      peeled and deveined
  1 (8-ounce) can sliced water
      chestnuts, drained
  1 green bell pepper, cut into
      chunks
      Hot cooked rice

In large skillet, combine reserved pineapple juice, water, ReaLemon® brand, sugar, cornstarch, soy sauce and ginger. Over medium heat, cook and stir until thick and clear. Add shrimp; cook 3 minutes. Add remaining ingredients except rice; heat through. Serve with rice. Refrigerate leftovers.

Makes 4 servings

Cajun Shrimp

  1 cup sliced fresh
      mushrooms
  6 green onions, sliced
  2 tablespoons butter or
      margarine
  1 medium tomato, chopped
  ½ cup HEINZ® Thick and Rich
      Cajun Style Barbecue
      Sauce
  1 tablespoon lemon juice
  ¼ teaspoon salt
  1 pound raw medium-size
      shrimp, shelled, deveined
      Hot cooked rice

In large skillet, sauté mushrooms and green onions in butter 1 to 2 minutes. Add tomato, barbecue sauce, lemon juice and salt; heat to boiling. Stir in shrimp. Simmer, uncovered, 4 to 5 minutes or until shrimp turn pink, stirring frequently. Serve over rice.

Makes 4 servings (about 3 cups)

Cajun Shrimp

Seafood Cacciatore

- **1 pound shrimp, cleaned**
- **1 small onion, chopped**
- **2 garlic cloves, minced**
- **2 tablespoons oil**
- **1 can (14½ ounces) whole tomatoes in juice**
- **1 can (8 ounces) tomato sauce**
- **1½ cups water**
- **1 medium green pepper, cut into thin strips**
- **¾ teaspoon dried basil**
- **½ teaspoon dried oregano**
- **½ teaspoon salt**
- **⅛ teaspoon ground red pepper**
- **1 chicken bouillon cube**
- **1½ cups Original MINUTE® Rice**
- **8 clams, well scrubbed**

Cook and stir shrimp with onion and garlic in hot oil in large skillet until shrimp turn pink. Stir in tomatoes with juice, tomato sauce, water, green pepper, seasonings and bouillon cube. Bring to full boil, breaking up tomatoes with spoon. Stir in rice. Cover; remove from heat. Let stand 5 minutes.

Meanwhile, place clams on rack in pan with water below rack. Bring to boil. Cover and steam 5 to 10 minutes or until clams open. Discard any unopened clams. Fluff rice mixture with fork and serve topped with clams.   *Makes 4 servings*

Shrimp in Pastry Puffs

- **6 frozen patty shells**
- **2 tablespoons margarine or butter**
- **2 cups sliced fresh mushrooms**
- **1 can (10¾ ounces) CAMPBELL'S® condensed Cream of Celery Soup**
- **¼ cup Chablis or other dry white wine**
- **½ cup frozen peas**
- **1½ pounds small shrimp, shelled and deveined**

1. Preheat oven and bake patty shells according to package directions; keep warm.

2. Meanwhile, in 10-inch skillet over medium heat, in hot margarine, cook mushrooms until tender and liquid is evaporated, stirring occasionally.

3. Stir in soup, wine and peas. Reduce heat to low. Heat until boiling. Stir in shrimp; cook until shrimp turn pink and opaque. Spoon shrimp mixture over patty shells.
Makes about 5 cups or 6 servings

Tip: For a special touch, sprinkle with a little snipped fresh parsley, chives or watercress.

Baked Shrimp Feast

- **½ cup margarine, melted**
- **1 clove garlic, pressed**
- **1 tablespoon Italian seasonings**
- **¼ teaspoon black pepper**
- **2 pounds jumbo shrimp (21 to 26 per pound)**
- **1 pound French bread, sliced or torn into bite-size pieces**

• Preheat oven to 350°F. Combine margarine, garlic, seasonings and pepper in shallow 3-quart casserole dish. Add shrimp; toss to coat shrimp. Cover with foil; bake 25 minutes.

• Pour juices from shrimp into serving bowl to use as a dipping herb sauce for French bread.

• To eat, slip shell from shrimp with one pull, holding tail. Dunk bread in dipping herb sauce.
Makes 6 to 8 servings

Preparation Time: 5 minutes
Cook Time: 25 minutes

Favorite recipe from **Dole Food Company, Inc.**

Tex-Mex Stir-Fry

- **2 tablespoons vegetable oil**
- **1½ cups broccoli flowerettes**
- **2 carrots, thinly sliced diagonally**
- **1 red or green bell pepper, thinly sliced**
- **½ cup thinly sliced celery**
- **1 pound medium shrimp, peeled and deveined**
- **⅓ cup LAWRY'S® Fajitas Skillet Sauce**
- **2 tablespoons brown sugar**
- **1 teaspoon ground ginger**
- **1 teaspoon dry mustard**
- **3 cups chilled, cooked rice Sliced almonds, lightly toasted (optional)**

In large skillet or wok, heat 1 tablespoon oil; add broccoli, carrots, bell pepper and celery. Stir-fry 3 minutes. Remove; set aside. Add remaining 1 tablespoon oil and shrimp to same *hot* skillet; stir-fry 3 minutes. Return vegetables to skillet. Pour in Fajitas Skillet Sauce, brown sugar, ginger and mustard. Cook 2 minutes longer, tossing gently to blend. Cover and set aside. In *hot* medium skillet, place chilled rice. Stir-fry over high heat 3 to 5 minutes or until slightly crisp and browned. Serve shrimp and vegetables over rice. Sprinkle with almonds, if desired.   *Makes 6 servings*

Presentation: Accompany with almond or fortune cookies.

Hint: One pound thinly sliced boneless chicken or pork can be used in place of shrimp. Add 2 teaspoons chopped cilantro for extra flavor.

Tex-Mex Stir-Fry

Shrimp Scampi

- 1½ cups Original MINUTE® Rice
- 1 small onion, chopped
- 1 tablespoon oil
- ¾ pound medium shrimp, cleaned
- 2 to 3 garlic cloves, minced
- 1 bottle (8 ounces) clam juice
- 1 tablespoon cornstarch
- 1 tablespoon chopped parsley
- 1 tablespoon lemon juice
  Dash pepper
- 1 red pepper, diced

Prepare rice as directed on package; keep warm.

Cook and stir onion in hot oil in large skillet until tender but not browned. Add shrimp and garlic; cook and stir until shrimp are pink.

Meanwhile, mix clam juice, cornstarch, parsley, lemon juice and pepper. Add to skillet with red pepper. Bring to boil 1 minute. Serve shrimp mixture over rice.   *Makes 4 servings*

Barbecued Shrimp with Spicy Rice

- 1 pound large shrimp, peeled and deveined
- 4 wooden* or metal skewers
  Vegetable cooking spray
- ⅓ cup prepared barbecue sauce
  Spicy Rice (recipe follows)

Thread shrimp on skewers. To broil in oven, place on broiler rack coated with cooking spray. Broil 4 to 5 inches from heat 4 minutes. Brush with barbecue sauce. Turn and brush with remaining barbecue sauce. Broil 2 to 4 minutes longer or until shrimp are done. To cook on outdoor grill, cook skewered shrimp over hot coals 4 minutes. Brush with barbecue sauce. Turn and brush with remaining barbecue sauce. Grill 4 to 5 minutes longer or until shrimp are done. Serve with Spicy Rice.
    Makes 4 servings

*Soak wooden skewers in water before using to prevent burning.

Spicy Rice

- ½ cup sliced green onions
- ½ cup minced carrots
- ½ cup minced red pepper
- 1 jalapeño or serrano pepper, minced
- 1 tablespoon vegetable oil
- 2 cups cooked rice (cooked in chicken broth)
- 2 tablespoons snipped fresh cilantro
- 1 tablespoon lime juice
- 1 teaspoon soy sauce
  Hot pepper sauce to taste

Barbecued Shrimp with Spicy Rice

Spicy Southern Shrimp Kabobs

Cook onions, carrots, red pepper, and jalapeño pepper in oil in large skillet over medium-high heat until tender crisp. Stir in rice, cilantro, lime juice, soy sauce, and pepper sauce; cook until thoroughly heated. Serve with Barbecued Shrimp.

To microwave: Combine onions, carrots, red pepper, jalapeño pepper, and oil in 2-quart microproof baking dish. Cook on HIGH 2 to 3 minutes or until vegetables are tender crisp. Add rice, cilantro, lime juice, soy sauce, and pepper sauce. Cook on HIGH 3 to 4 minutes, stirring after 2 minutes, or until thoroughly heated. Serve with Barbecued Shrimp.

Favorite recipe from **USA Rice Council**

Spicy Southern Shrimp Kabobs

- **1 DOLE® Fresh Pineapple**
- **1 pound jumbo shrimp (24 to 26 per pound), peeled, deveined**
- **6 spicy Italian sausages, cut into 1-inch pieces**
- **½ medium DOLE® Red Bell Pepper, seeded, chunked**
- **½ medium DOLE® Green Bell Pepper, seeded, chunked**
- **¼ cup margarine, melted**
- **¾ teaspoon dried oregano, crumbled**
- **¾ teaspoon dried thyme, crumbled**
- **½ teaspoon salt**
- **¼ teaspoon ground red pepper**
- **¼ teaspoon black pepper**

• Twist crown from pineapple. Cut pineapple in half lengthwise. Cut fruit from shell with knife. Cut fruit into chunks.

• For each kabob, arrange 2 pineapple chunks, 2 shrimp, 2 sausage chunks and 2 red or green bell pepper chunks on skewers. Or, arrange as desired to increase the number for appetizer portions. Arrange skewers on rack in broiler pan coated with cooking spray or oil. Combine margarine and seasonings in cup; brush over kabobs.

• Broil 6 inches from heat 8 to 10 minutes, basting and turning occasionally, or until shrimp are opaque. Cool slightly before serving. *Makes 12 kabobs*

Preparation Time: 20 minutes
Cook Time: 10 minutes

Scallop Kabobs

Tropical Kabobs with Peanut Sauce

    1 can (20 ounces) DOLE®
        Pineapple Chunks in
        Juice
    1 pound large shrimp,
        peeled, deveined
    ½ cup canned real cream of
        coconut
    1 tablespoon vegetable oil
    2 teaspoons soy sauce
    2 cloves garlic, minced
    ¼ teaspoon crushed red
        pepper flakes
    2 small DOLE® Red or Green
        Bell Peppers, seeded,
        chunked

Peanut Sauce
    ½ cup canned real cream of
        coconut
    ¼ cup smooth peanut butter
    2 tablespoons soy sauce
    1 tablespoon lemon juice
    ¼ teaspoon crushed red
        pepper flakes

• Drain pineapple; reserve juice.

• Place shrimp in shallow dish. Combine reserved juice, cream of coconut, oil, soy sauce, garlic and pepper flakes in small bowl. Pour over shrimp. Cover and marinate in refrigerator 15 minutes or overnight.

• On skewers, arrange shrimp, pineapple chunks and bell peppers.

• Grill or broil 6 inches from heat 7 minutes on each side or until shrimp turn opaque. Baste frequently with marinade. Serve with Peanut Sauce. Refrigerate leftovers.

Makes 4 to 6 servings

PEANUT SAUCE: Combine all ingredients in small saucepan. Cook, stirring, until peanut butter melts and mixture begins to boil. Reduce heat. Simmer, uncovered, 10 minutes, stirring occasionally. Serve at room temperature.

Preparation Time: 25 minutes
Marinate Time: 15 minutes or
    overnight
Cook Time: 20 minutes

Scallop Kabobs

    ¼ cup REALEMON® Lemon
        Juice from Concentrate
    2 tablespoons vegetable oil
    1 teaspoon oregano leaves
    ½ teaspoon basil leaves
    1 clove garlic, finely chopped
    ⅛ teaspoon salt
    1 pound sea scallops
    8 ounces fresh mushrooms
    2 small zucchini, cut into
        chunks
    2 small onions, cut into
        wedges
    ½ red, yellow or green bell
        pepper, cut into bite-size
        pieces

In shallow dish, combine ReaLemon® brand, oil and seasonings; add scallops. Cover; marinate in refrigerator 2 hours, stirring occasionally. Skewer scallops alternately with vegetables. Grill or broil as desired, basting frequently with additional ReaLemon® brand. Refrigerate leftovers.

Makes 4 servings

Curried Scallops in Rice Ring

        Vegetable cooking spray
    1½ pounds bay scallops
    1 tablespoon margarine
    1 medium onion, chopped
    1 teaspoon all-purpose flour
    ½ teaspoon salt
    1 bottle (8 ounces) clam juice
    1 cup evaporated skim milk
    1 red apple, cored and
        chopped
    ½ teaspoon curry powder
    6 cups hot cooked rice
    1 tablespoon snipped
        parsley
    1 tablespoon diced pimiento
        Chutney, chopped peanuts,
        grated coconut, and
        raisins for condiments
        (optional)

Coat large skillet with cooking spray and place over medium heat until hot. Add scallops; cook until scallops are almost done, 2 to 3 minutes. Remove scallops from skillet; keep warm. Melt margarine in skillet; add onion and cook 1 to 2 minutes or until tender. Stir in flour and salt; cook, stirring, 2 minutes over medium-high heat. Gradually add clam juice and milk, stirring constantly until thickened. Stir in scallops, apple, and curry powder. Keep warm. Combine rice, parsley, and pimiento; pack into 2-quart ring mold coated with cooking spray. Unmold onto serving platter and fill center of ring with curried scallops. Serve with chutney, chopped peanuts, grated coconut, and raisins.

Makes 6 servings

Favorite recipe from **USA Rice Council**

Scallops Primavera

Scallops Primavera

- **1 pound scallops**
- **¼ cup REALEMON® Lemon Juice from Concentrate**
- **1 cup thinly sliced carrots**
- **3 cloves garlic, finely chopped**
- **⅓ cup margarine or butter**
- **8 ounces fresh mushrooms, sliced (about 2 cups)**
- **¾ teaspoon thyme leaves**
- **2 teaspoons cornstarch**
- **½ teaspoon salt**
- **¼ cup diagonally sliced green onions**
- **4 ounces fresh pea pods *or* 1 (6-ounce) package frozen pea pods, thawed**
- **2 tablespoons dry sherry**
- **Hot cooked rice**

In shallow baking dish, combine scallops and ReaLemon® brand. Cover; marinate in refrigerator 30 minutes, stirring occasionally. In large skillet, over high heat, cook and stir carrots and garlic in margarine until tender-crisp, about 3 minutes. Add mushrooms and thyme; cook and stir about 5 minutes. Stir cornstarch and salt into scallop mixture; add to skillet. Cook and stir until scallops are opaque, about 4 minutes. Add onions, pea pods and sherry; heat through. Serve with rice. Refrigerate leftovers. *Makes 4 servings*

Spiced Broiled Lobster

- **4 Maine lobsters (1 to 1½ pounds *each*)**
- **Boiling water**
- **½ cup WISH-BONE® Lite Italian Dressing**
- **½ small onion, halved**
- **1 tablespoon ketchup**
- **1 tablespoon snipped dill***
- **2 teaspoons Dijon-style mustard**
- **⅛ teaspoon hot pepper sauce**

Place each lobster on its stomach. With tip of sharp knife, make 2 deep criss-cross cuts in each lobster head. Immediately plunge into boiling water and boil 30 seconds or until lobster turns red. Remove from water; let cool slightly. Place each lobster on its back, then make lengthwise cut down each lobsters tail; set aside. In food processor or blender, process remaining ingredients; set aside.

In large shallow aluminum-foil-lined baking pan or on broiler rack, arrange prepared lobsters stomach side up, then brush tails with ⅓ of the dressing mixture. Broil on lower rack 20 minutes or until lobster meat turns opaque. (If lobsters brown too quickly, loosely cover with aluminum foil.) Serve with remaining dressing mixture for dipping. *Makes 4 servings*

*Substitution: Use 1 teaspoon dried dill weed.

ONE-DISH MEALS

Having a busy day? Try Quick and Easy Tamale Pie or One Skillet Spicy Chicken 'n Rice. Casseroles, skillet dinners and pot pies not only make great comfort food but save time for the busy cook. Whether you're entertaining a crowd or bringing a dish to a potluck dinner, these one-dish meals are easy to serve and make ahead.

Dairyland Confetti Chicken

Casserole
 1 cup diced carrots
 ¾ cup chopped onion
 ½ cup diced celery
 ¼ cup chicken broth
 1 can (10½ ounces) cream of chicken soup
 1 cup dairy sour cream
 3 cups cubed cooked chicken
 ½ cup (4 ounces) sliced mushrooms
 1 teaspoon Worcestershire sauce
 1 teaspoon salt
 ⅛ teaspoon pepper

Confetti Topping
 1 cup sifted all-purpose flour
 2 teaspoons baking powder
 ½ teaspoon salt
 2 eggs, slightly beaten
 ½ cup milk
 1 tablespoon chopped green pepper
 1 tablespoon chopped pimiento
 1¼ cups (5 ounces) shredded Wisconsin Cheddar cheese, divided

For casserole: In saucepan, combine carrots, onion, celery and chicken broth. Simmer 20 minutes. In 3-quart casserole, mix soup, sour cream, chicken cubes, mushrooms, Worcestershire sauce, salt and pepper. Add simmered vegetables and liquid; mix well.

For confetti topping: In mixing bowl, combine flour, baking powder and salt. Add eggs, milk, green pepper, pimiento and 1 cup of the cheese. Mix just until well blended. Drop tablespoons of topping onto casserole and bake in 350°F oven for 40 to 45 minutes or until golden brown. Sprinkle with remaining ¼ cup cheese and return to oven until melted. Garnish as desired.
Makes 6 to 8 servings

Favorite recipe from **Wisconsin Milk Marketing Board** © 1992

Ranch-Style Chicken Casserole

 1 envelope LIPTON® Onion Recipe Soup Mix
 1½ cups buttermilk
 1 tablespoon all-purpose flour
 2 cloves garlic, finely chopped
 1 pound boneless skinless chicken breasts
 2 cups frozen mixed vegetables
 ¼ cup dry bread crumbs
 1 tablespoon butter or margarine, melted
 Paprika (optional)

Preheat oven to 350°F.

In small bowl, thoroughly combine onion recipe soup mix, buttermilk, flour and garlic; set aside.

In lightly greased 2-quart shallow casserole, arrange chicken breasts and vegetables; add soup mixture. Bake, covered, 20 minutes. Remove cover and top with bread crumbs combined with butter. Continue baking, uncovered, 25 minutes. Sprinkle, if desired, with paprika.
Makes 4 servings

Dairyland Confetti Chicken

One Skillet Spicy Chicken 'n Rice

Chicken Enchilada Casserole

1 medium onion, chopped
2 tablespoons vegetable oil
4 cups shredded, cooked chicken or turkey
1 can (15 ounces) tomato sauce
1 can (14½ ounces) whole peeled tomatoes, undrained and cut up
1 package (1.25 ounces) LAWRY'S® Taco Spices & Seasonings
½ teaspoon LAWRY'S® Garlic Powder with Parsley
1 dozen medium corn tortillas
2 cans (2¼ ounces each) sliced ripe olives, drained
3 cups (12 ounces) grated Monterey Jack cheese

In large skillet, sauté onion in oil. Add chicken, tomato sauce, tomatoes, Taco Spices & Seasonings and Garlic Powder with Parsley; blend well. Bring to a boil; reduce heat and simmer, uncovered, 15 minutes. In 13×9×2-inch glass baking dish, place 4 corn tortillas. Pour ⅓ of chicken mixture on tortillas, spreading evenly. Layer with ⅓ of olives and ⅓ of cheese. Repeat layers 2 times, ending with cheese. Bake, uncovered, in 350°F oven 30 to 40 minutes or until heated through and cheese melts.

Makes 8 to 10 servings

Presentation: Serve with prepared Mexican rice and a green salad.

Hint: For a crowd-pleasing entrée, simply double the recipe.

One Skillet Spicy Chicken 'n Rice

¼ cup all-purpose flour
1 teaspoon LAWRY'S® Seasoned Salt
6 to 8 chicken pieces, skinned
2 tablespoons vegetable oil
2 cans (14½ ounces each) whole peeled tomatoes, undrained and cut up
1 package (1.25 ounces) LAWRY'S® Taco Spices & Seasonings
1 cup thinly sliced celery
1 cup long-grain rice
½ cup chopped onion

In plastic bag, combine flour and Seasoned Salt. Add chicken; shake to coat well. In large skillet, brown chicken in oil; continue cooking, uncovered, over low heat 15 minutes. Add remaining ingredients; blend well. Bring to a boil; reduce heat, cover and simmer 20 minutes or until liquid is absorbed and chicken is cooked through.

Makes 4 to 6 servings

Presentation: Sprinkle with chopped parsley.

Brown Rice Chicken Bake

3 cups cooked brown rice
1 package (10 ounces) frozen green peas
2 cups cooked chicken breast cubes
½ cup cholesterol free, reduced calorie mayonnaise
⅓ cup slivered almonds, toasted (optional)
2 teaspoons soy sauce
¼ teaspoon ground black pepper
¼ teaspoon garlic powder
¼ teaspoon dried tarragon leaves
Vegetable cooking spray

Combine rice, peas, chicken, mayonnaise, almonds, soy sauce, and seasonings in bowl. Transfer to 3-quart baking dish coated with cooking spray. Cover and bake at 350°F. for 15 to 20 minutes. *Makes 6 servings*

Favorite recipe from **USA Rice Council**

Chicken Broccoli Bake

2 cups chopped cooked broccoli
2 cups cubed cooked chicken or turkey
2 cups soft bread cubes
2 cups shredded process sharp American cheese
1 jar (12 ounces) HEINZ® HomeStyle Chicken or Turkey Gravy
½ cup undiluted evaporated milk
Dash pepper

In buttered 9-inch square baking dish, layer broccoli, chicken, bread cubes and cheese. In medium bowl, combine gravy, milk and pepper; pour over chicken-broccoli mixture. Bake in 375°F oven, 40 minutes. Let stand 5 minutes.
Makes 6 servings

Country Herbed Chicken

2 tablespoons vegetable oil
2½- to 3-pound broiler-fryer chicken, cut up
2 cans (10¾ ounces *each*) CAMPBELL'S® condensed Creamy Chicken Mushroom Soup
½ cup Chablis or other dry white wine
2 tablespoons chopped fresh parsley
½ teaspoon dried thyme leaves, crushed
¼ teaspoon dried rosemary leaves, crushed
½ pound whole baby carrots*
8 small whole white onions*
Hot cooked small red potatoes (optional)

1. In 5-quart Dutch oven over medium-high heat, in hot oil, cook chicken 10 minutes or until browned on all sides. Remove chicken; set aside. Spoon off fat.

2. Add soup, wine, parsley, thyme and rosemary; stir until smooth. Return chicken to Dutch oven. Heat to boiling. Reduce heat to low. Cover; cook 15 minutes. Add carrots and onions. Simmer 20 minutes or until chicken is no longer pink and juices run clear. Serve with steamed red potatoes, if desired.
Makes 4 servings

*Substitute sliced carrots and quartered cooking onions for the same delicious results.

Country Herbed Chicken

Chicken Broccoli Rice Skillet

2 tablespoons margarine or butter
1 pound skinless, boneless chicken breasts, cut into thin strips
2 cups frozen broccoli cuts
¾ cup sliced carrots
1 can (10¾ ounces) CAMPBELL'S® condensed Cream of Broccoli Soup
1 cup milk
⅛ teaspoon pepper
1¼ cups *uncooked* quick-cooking rice

1. In 10-inch skillet over medium-high heat, in hot margarine, cook *half* of chicken until browned. Remove; set aside. Repeat with remaining chicken.

2. Add broccoli and carrots. Cook until tender-crisp, stirring occasionally.

3. Stir in soup, milk and pepper. Return chicken to skillet. Heat to boiling. Reduce heat to low. Cover; cook 10 minutes or until chicken is no longer pink, stirring occasionally.

4. Stir in rice. Cover; remove from heat. Let stand 5 minutes. Fluff mixture with fork before serving.

Makes about 5½ cups or 4 main-dish servings

Chicken and Rice Paprikash

3 teaspoons paprika, divided
¾ teaspoon salt
¼ teaspoon pepper
6 medium chicken thighs
1 can (14½ or 16 ounces) whole tomatoes
1 small onion, sliced and separated into rings
1 teaspoon chicken bouillon granules
2 cloves garlic, minced
1 cup UNCLE BEN'S® CONVERTED® Brand Rice, uncooked
1 large green pepper, cut into thin strips
Light sour cream or plain yogurt (optional)

Combine 1½ teaspoons of the paprika, salt and pepper. Rub seasonings onto chicken thighs, coating all surfaces with mixture; set aside. Drain tomatoes, reserving juice. Chop tomatoes; set aside. Add enough water to juice to equal 2 cups. Combine tomato liquid, onion, bouillon granules, garlic and remaining 1½ teaspoons paprika in 12-inch skillet. Bring to a boil. Stir in rice and tomatoes. Arrange chicken thighs on top of rice mixture. Cover tightly and simmer 20

minutes. Add green pepper. Remove from heat. Let stand covered until all liquid is absorbed, about 5 minutes. Serve with light sour cream or plain yogurt, if desired.

Makes 6 servings

Fancy Chicken Puff Pie

4 tablespoons butter or margarine
¼ cup chopped shallots
¼ cup all-purpose flour
1 cup chicken stock or broth
¼ cup sherry
Salt to taste
⅛ teaspoon white pepper
Pinch ground nutmeg
¼ pound ham, cut into 2×¼-inch strips
3 cups cooked PERDUE® chicken, cut into 2×¼-inch strips
1½ cups fresh asparagus pieces *or* 1 (10-ounce) package frozen asparagus pieces
1 cup (½ pint) heavy cream
Chilled pie crust for a 1-crust pie *or* 1 sheet frozen puff pastry
1 egg, beaten

In medium saucepan, over medium-high heat, melt butter; sauté shallots lightly. Stir in flour; cook 3 minutes. Add broth and sherry. Heat to boiling, stirring constantly; season to taste with salt, pepper and nutmeg. Reduce heat to low and simmer 5 minutes. Stir in ham, chicken, asparagus and cream. Pour chicken mixture into ungreased 9-inch pie plate.

Preheat oven to 425°F. Cut 8-inch circle from crust. Cut hearts from extra dough with cookie cutter, if desired. Place circle on cookie sheet moistened with cold water. Pierce with fork, brush with egg and decorate with hearts; brush hearts with egg.

Fancy Chicken Puff Pie

Bake crust and filled pie plate 10 minutes; reduce heat to 350°F and bake additional 10 to 15 minutes, or until pastry is golden brown and filling is hot and set. With a spatula, place pastry over hot filling and serve immediately.

Makes 4 servings

Chicken Cheese Puff

- **1 can (20 ounces) DOLE® Crushed Pineapple in Juice**
- **8 eggs, lightly beaten**
- **3 cups shredded Monterey Jack cheese**
- **2 cups small curd cottage cheese**
- **2 cups diced, cooked chicken***
- **1 can (4 ounces) chopped green chiles**
- **½ cup all-purpose flour**
- **1 teaspoon baking powder**
- **½ teaspoon salt**
- **2 tablespoons margarine, melted**
- **⅓ cup grated Parmesan cheese**

• Drain pineapple; save juice for a beverage.

• Blend pineapple, eggs, Monterey Jack cheese, cottage cheese, chicken, chiles, flour, baking powder and salt in medium bowl.

• Coat bottom of 13×9-inch baking pan with margarine. Pour chicken mixture into pan. Sprinkle with Parmesan cheese.

• Bake in 350°F oven 40 to 45 minutes or until toothpick inserted near center comes out clean.   *Makes 8 servings*

*Or use roasted chicken from the deli.

Preparation Time: 10 minutes
Bake Time: 45 minutes

Turkey-Vegetable Pot Pie

Turkey-Vegetable Pot Pie

- **1 package (16 ounces) frozen mixed vegetables (broccoli, cauliflower and carrots)**
- **2 tablespoons margarine or butter**
- **½ cup chopped onion**
- **½ cup sliced celery**
- **½ teaspoon dried thyme leaves, crushed**
- **1 can (10¾ ounces) CAMPBELL'S® condensed Cream of Broccoli Soup**
- **1 can (10¾ ounces) CAMPBELL'S® condensed Cream of Chicken Soup**
- **1 cup milk**
- **3 cups diced cooked turkey or chicken**
- **¼ teaspoon pepper**
- **1 package (8 ounces) refrigerated crescent rolls**

1. Preheat oven to 375°F. Cook vegetables according to package directions; drain.

2. Meanwhile, in 2-quart saucepan over medium heat, in hot margarine, cook onion, celery and thyme until onion is tender, stirring occasionally. Add soups and milk; stir until smooth.

3. In 12- by 8-inch baking dish, combine turkey, cooked vegetables and pepper. Add soup mixture, stirring gently to mix.

4. Unroll crescent rolls without separating pieces. Firmly press perforations to seal. Cut dough lengthwise into 8 strips, about ¾ inch wide. Arrange dough strips over chicken mixture to form a lattice, cutting strips as necessary to fit. Press ends of strips to baking dish.

5. Bake 30 minutes or until golden brown. Cover edges with foil after 20 minutes of baking if pastry browns too quickly.

Makes 6 servings

Turkey 'n Stuffing Bake

¼ cup (½ stick) butter or
   margarine
1¼ cups boiling water
3½ cups seasoned stuffing
   crumbs*
1 can (2.8 ounces) DURKEE®
   French Fried Onions
1 can (10¾ ounces)
   condensed cream of
   celery soup
¾ cup milk
1½ cups (7 ounces) cubed,
   cooked turkey
1 package (10 ounces) frozen
   peas, thawed

Combine butter and water; stir
until butter melts. Pour over
seasoned stuffing crumbs; toss
lightly. Stir in ½ can Durkee®
French Fried Onions. Spoon
stuffing mixture into 9-inch
shallow baking dish. Press
stuffing across bottom and up
sides of dish to form a shell.
Combine soup, milk, turkey and
peas; pour into stuffing shell.
Bake, covered, at 350°F for 30
minutes. Top with remaining
onions and bake, uncovered, 5
minutes longer.
   Makes 4 to 6 servings

*Three cups leftover stuffing
may be substituted for butter,
water and stuffing crumbs. If
stuffing is dry, stir in water, 1
tablespoon at a time, until moist
but not wet.

Turkey and Wild Rice Bake

1 package (6 ounces) wild
   and white rice mix,
   uncooked
2⅓ cups water
2 cups cooked turkey, cubed
1 can (4 ounces)
   mushrooms, drained
1 can (14 ounces) whole
   artichoke hearts, drained
   and quartered
1 jar (2 ounces) chopped
   pimiento, drained
1 cup shredded Swiss
   cheese

Preheat oven to 350°F. In 2-quart
lightly greased casserole combine
rice with seasoning packet,
water, turkey, mushrooms,
artichokes and pimiento. Cover
and bake 1 hour and 15 minutes
or until liquid is absorbed.

Top casserole with cheese.
Return to oven and bake,
uncovered, 5 to 10 minutes or
until cheese is melted and golden
brown.   *Makes 6 servings*

*Favorite recipe from **National Turkey Federation***

Classy Cassoulet

6 slices bacon
¼ cup seasoned dry bread
   crumbs
1 pound hot or sweet Italian
   sausage, cut into 1-inch-
   thick slices
1 medium onion, cut into 6
   wedges
3 cloves garlic, finely
   chopped
1 can (16 ounces) sliced
   carrots, drained
1 can (16 ounces) zucchini,
   drained
1 can (8 ounces) stewed
   tomatoes
½ cup chopped celery
1 teaspoon beef-flavored
   instant bouillon granules
1½ teaspoons dried parsley
   flakes
1 bay leaf
2 cans (15 ounces each)
   butter beans, 1 can
   drained, 1 can undrained

Sauté bacon in large skillet,
turning until crisp and browned,
about 8 minutes. Remove with
slotted spoon to paper towels to
drain. Set aside skillet with
bacon drippings. Combine 2
tablespoons of the bacon
drippings with bread crumbs in
small bowl. Set aside.

Sauté sausage, onion and garlic
in skillet with bacon drippings
until sausage is no longer pink,
12 to 15 minutes. Drain off fat,
leaving sausage mixture in
skillet. Stir carrots, zucchini,

tomatoes, celery, bouillon,
parsley, bay leaf and 1 can
drained butter beans into skillet
with sausage. Add can of
undrained butter beans. Bring to
a boil; lower heat and simmer,
uncovered, for 10 minutes or
until mixture is heated through
and celery is tender. Remove bay
leaf.

Place sausage mixture into one
2-quart or 6 individual broiler-
proof casseroles. Crumble bacon
over top; sprinkle with bread
crumb mixture. Broil 5 inches
from heat 1 minute or until
crumbs are golden; be careful not
to burn crumbs. Serve hot with
garnish of sliced, canned
cranberry sauce.
   Makes 6 servings

*Favorite recipe from **Canned Food Information Council***

Pork Skillet Normandy

2 large all-purpose apples,
   cored, pared and sliced
¼ cup REALEMON® Lemon
   Juice from Concentrate
1 (¾- to 1-pound) pork
   tenderloin, cut into
   ¼-inch slices
½ cup unsifted flour
¼ cup margarine or butter
½ cup apple cider or juice
1 cup (½ pint) BORDEN® or
   MEADOW GOLD®
   Whipping Cream,
   unwhipped
1 teaspoon WYLER'S® or
   STEERO® Chicken-Flavor
   Instant Bouillon

In medium bowl, combine apples
and ReaLemon® brand. Coat
meat with flour. In large skillet,
brown meat in margarine;
remove from skillet. Stir in apple
mixture and cider, scraping
bottom of skillet. Cook and stir 3
minutes or until apples are
tender-crisp. Slowly add cream
and bouillon, stirring constantly.
Add meat; simmer uncovered 5
to 10 minutes or until tender.
Refrigerate leftovers.
   Makes 4 servings

Classy Cassoulet

Sausage Skillet Dinner

Red Beans and Rice

Vegetable cooking spray
½ **cup chopped onion**
½ **cup chopped celery**
½ **cup chopped green pepper**
2 **cloves garlic, minced**
2 **cans (15 ounces each) red beans,* drained**
½ **pound fully-cooked low-fat turkey sausage, cut into ¼-inch slices**
1 **can (8 ounces) tomato sauce**
1 **teaspoon Worcestershire sauce**
¼ **teaspoon ground red pepper**
¼ **teaspoon hot pepper sauce**
3 **cups hot cooked rice Hot pepper sauce (optional)**

Coat Dutch oven with cooking spray and place over medium-high heat until hot. Add onion, celery, green pepper, and garlic. Cook 2 to 3 minutes. Add beans, sausage, tomato sauce, Worcestershire sauce, red pepper, and ¼ teaspoon pepper sauce. Reduce heat; cover and simmer 15 minutes. Serve beans with rice and additional pepper sauce.

Makes 6 servings

*Substitute your favorite bean for the red beans, if desired.

Favorite recipe from **USA Rice Council**

Sausage Skillet Dinner

12 **ounces fully cooked smoked pork link sausage, cut diagonally into 1-inch pieces**
2 **tablespoons water**
1 **medium onion**
2 **small red cooking apples**
2 **tablespoons butter, divided**
12 **ounces natural frozen potato wedges**
¼ **cup cider vinegar**
3 **tablespoons sugar**
½ **teaspoon caraway seed**
2 **tablespoons chopped parsley**

Place sausage and water in large nonstick frying pan; cover tightly and cook over medium heat 8 minutes, stirring occasionally. Meanwhile cut onion into 12 wedges; core and cut each apple into 8 wedges. Remove sausage to warm platter. Pour off drippings. Cook and stir onion and apples in 1 tablespoon of the butter in same frying pan 4 minutes or until apples are just tender. Remove to sausage platter. Heat remaining 1 tablespoon butter; add potatoes and cook, covered, over medium-high heat 5 minutes or until potatoes are tender and golden brown, stirring occasionally. Combine vinegar, sugar and caraway seed. Reduce heat; return sausage, apple mixture and vinegar mixture to frying pan and cook 1 minute, or until heated through, stirring gently. Sprinkle with parsley.

Makes 4 servings

Preparation time: 5 minutes
Cooking time: 18 minutes

Favorite recipe from **National Live Stock and Meat Board**

Red Beans and Rice

German-Style Potato Supper

- 1 pound link smoked sausage, cut into 1-inch slices
- 4 cups frozen potatoes O'Brien
- 1 cup water
- 2 teaspoons WYLER'S® or STEERO® Beef-Flavor Instant Bouillon
- ¼ cup REALEMON® Lemon Juice from Concentrate
- 2 tablespoons sugar
- 2 teaspoons cornstarch
- ½ teaspoon dry mustard

In large skillet, brown sausage. Stir in potatoes, *¾ cup* water and bouillon; bring to a boil. Cover and simmer 10 minutes. In small bowl, combine remaining ingredients; mix well. Pour over meat mixture; simmer uncovered 5 minutes or until thick and bubbly. Serve immediately. Refrigerate leftovers.

Makes 4 servings

Polish Reuben Casserole

- 2 cans (10¾ ounces each) condensed cream of mushroom soup
- 1⅓ cups milk
- ½ cup chopped onion
- 1 tablespoon prepared mustard
- 2 cans (16 ounces each) sauerkraut, rinsed and drained
- 1 package (8 ounces) uncooked medium-width noodles
- 1½ pounds Polish sausage, cut into ½-inch pieces
- 2 cups (8 ounces) shredded Swiss cheese
- ¾ cup whole wheat bread crumbs
- 2 tablespoons butter, melted

Combine soup, milk, onion and mustard in medium bowl; blend well. Spread sauerkraut in greased 13×9-inch pan. Top with uncooked noodles. Spoon soup

Polish Reuben Casserole

mixture evenly over top. Top with sausage, then cheese. Combine crumbs and butter in small bowl; sprinkle over top. Cover pan tightly with foil. Bake in preheated 350°F. oven 1 hour or until noodles are tender. Garnish as desired.

Makes 8 to 10 servings

Favorite recipe from **North Dakota Wheat Comission**

Swissed Ham and Noodles Casserole

- 2 tablespoons butter
- ½ cup chopped onion
- ½ cup chopped green pepper
- 1 can (10½ ounces) condensed cream of mushroom soup
- 1 cup dairy sour cream
- 1 package (8 ounces) medium noodles, cooked and drained
- 2 cups (8 ounces) shredded Wisconsin Swiss cheese
- 2 cups cubed cooked ham (about ¾ pound)

In 1-quart saucepan melt butter; sauté onion and green pepper. Remove from heat; stir in soup and sour cream. In buttered 2-quart casserole layer ⅓ of the noodles, ⅓ of the Swiss cheese, ⅓ of the ham and ½ soup mixture. Repeat layers, ending with final ⅓ layer of noodles, cheese and ham. Bake in preheated 350°F oven 30 to 45 minutes or until heated through.

Makes 6 to 8 servings

Favorite recipe from **Wisconsin Milk Marketing Board © 1992**

Deli-in-a-Skillet

Patchwork Casserole

- 2 pounds ground beef
- 2 cups chopped green bell pepper
- 1 cup chopped onion
- 2 pounds frozen Southern-style hash-brown potatoes, thawed
- 2 cans (8 ounces each) tomato sauce
- 1 cup water
- 1 can (6 ounces) tomato paste
- 1 teaspoon salt
- ½ teaspoon dried basil, crumbled
- ¼ teaspoon ground black pepper
- 1 pound pasteurized process American cheese, thinly sliced

Cook and stir beef in large skillet over medium heat until crumbled and brown, about 10 minutes; drain off fat.

Add green pepper and onion; sauté until tender, about 4 minutes. Stir in all remaining ingredients except cheese.

Spoon ½ of the meat mixture into 13×9×2-inch baking pan or 3-quart baking dish; top with ½ of the cheese. Spoon remaining meat mixture evenly on top of cheese.

Cover pan with aluminum foil. Bake in preheated 350°F oven 45 minutes.

Cut remaining cheese into decorative shapes; place on top of casserole. Let stand, loosely covered, until cheese melts, about 5 minutes.

Makes 8 to 10 servings

Beef 'n' Tater Bake

- 1½ pounds lean ground beef
- 1 cup soft bread crumbs
- 1 egg, slightly beaten
- ½ cup chopped onion
- ⅓ cup HEINZ® Tomato Ketchup
- ½ teaspoon salt
- ⅛ teaspoon pepper
- 1 cup shredded process sharp American cheese, divided
- 3 cups seasoned hot mashed potatoes

Deli-in-a-Skillet

- ½ pound corned beef, cooked and cut into pieces*
- 1 can (14 ounces) sauerkraut
- 1½ cups water
- 1½ cups Original MINUTE® Rice
- ½ cup prepared thousand island dressing
- 3 ounces Swiss cheese, cut into strips

Mix corned beef, sauerkraut and water in large skillet. Bring to full boil. Stir in rice. Pour dressing over rice and top with cheese. Cover; remove from heat. Let stand 5 minutes.

Makes 4 servings

*You may use knockwurst or other luncheon meat cut into pieces in place of the corned beef.

Patchwork Casserole

In large bowl, combine beef, bread crumbs, egg, onion, ketchup, salt and pepper. Pat meat mixture firmly into 8-inch square baking dish. Bake in 350°F oven, 30 minutes. Remove from oven; drain excess fat. In large bowl, combine ¾ cup cheese with potatoes. Spread potatoes evenly over meat; sprinkle with remaining ¼ cup cheese. Return to oven; bake an additional 20 minutes or until meat is cooked through and potatoes are hot.

Makes 6 servings

Santa Fe Casserole Bake

- **1 pound lean ground beef**
- **1 package (1.25 ounces) LAWRY'S® Taco Spices & Seasonings**
- **2 cups chicken broth**
- **¼ cup all-purpose flour**
- **1 cup dairy sour cream**
- **1 can (7 ounces) diced green chiles**
- **1 package (11 ounces) corn or tortilla chips**
- **2 cups (8 ounces) grated Monterey Jack or Cheddar cheese**
- **½ cup sliced green onions with tops**

Santa Fe Casserole Bake

In medium skillet, brown meat and stir until crumbly; drain fat. Add Taco Spices & Seasonings; blend well. In small bowl, combine broth and flour. Add to meat mixture; bring to a boil to slightly thicken liquid. Stir in sour cream and chiles; blend well. In 13×9×2-inch lightly greased glass baking dish, place ½ of chips. Top with ½ of beef mixture, ½ of sauce, ½ of cheese and ½ of green onions. Layer again with remaining ingredients ending with green onions. Bake, uncovered, in 375°F oven for 20 minutes. Let stand 5 minutes before cutting.

Makes 6 servings

Beef Ziti Casserole

- **8 ounces uncooked ziti or mostaccioli macaroni**
- **2 cups frozen mixed vegetables (zucchini, green beans and carrots)**
- **1 pound ground beef**
- **2 cans (10¾ ounces *each*) CAMPBELL'S® condensed Golden Mushroom Soup**
- **1 can (8 ounces) tomatoes, undrained, cut up**
- **1 teaspoon dried basil leaves, crushed**
- **¼ teaspoon pepper**
- **⅛ teaspoon garlic powder**
- **1 cup shredded sharp American process cheese (4 ounces)**

1. Preheat oven to 400°F. Cook ziti and mixed vegetables according to package directions for *each*; drain. Return cooked ziti and vegetables to cooking pot used to cook ziti.

2. Meanwhile, in 10-inch skillet over medium heat, cook beef until browned, stirring to separate meat. Spoon off fat.

3. Stir in soup, tomatoes, basil, pepper and garlic. Heat through. Add soup mixture to ziti mixture; mix well. Spoon into greased 12- by 8-inch baking dish. Cover with foil; bake 15 minutes.

4. Uncover; sprinkle with cheese. Bake 5 minutes more or until cheese melts.

Makes about 7½ cups or 6 servings

Easy Kids' Taco-Mac

1 pound ground turkey
1 package (1.25 ounces)
    LAWRY'S® Taco Spices &
    Seasonings
1 can (14½ ounces) whole
    peeled tomatoes,
    undrained and cut up
1 cup water
8 ounces dry macaroni or
    small spiral pasta
½ cup sliced celery
1 package (8½ ounces) corn
    muffin mix
1 egg
⅓ cup milk

In medium skillet, brown ground turkey until crumbly. Blend in Taco Spices & Seasonings, tomatoes, water, pasta and celery. Bring to a boil; reduce heat, cover and simmer 20 minutes. In medium bowl, combine corn muffin mix, egg and milk; stir with fork just to mix. Place meat mixture in 2½-quart casserole dish. Spoon dollops of corn muffin mix on top. Bake in 400°F oven 15 to 20 minutes or until golden.

Makes 6 to 8 servings

Presentation: Sprinkle with grated cheese.

Saucy Beef and Zucchini Skillet

1 medium onion, sliced
2 tablespoons butter or
    margarine
4 cups sliced zucchini
    (¼ inch thick)
1 pound lean ground beef
1 cup HEINZ® Tomato
    Ketchup
¼ cup grated Parmesan
    cheese
2 teaspoons lemon juice
¼ teaspoon dried thyme
    leaves, crushed
¼ teaspoon dried oregano
    leaves, crushed
¼ teaspoon pepper
1 medium tomato, coarsely
    chopped

In large skillet, sauté onion in butter until onion is tender. Add zucchini and sauté 1 minute; remove and set aside. In same skillet, brown beef; drain excess fat. Stir in ketchup, Parmesan cheese, lemon juice, thyme, oregano and pepper. Add reserved zucchini and onion; stir in tomato. Simmer, covered, 10 minutes, stirring occasionally.

Makes 4 servings
(about 5½ cups)

Skillet Sauerbraten

¾ pound boneless beef
    sirloin steak
⅔ cup crushed gingersnaps
    (about 10 cookies)
½ teaspoon salt
1 tablespoon vegetable oil
1 medium onion, sliced into
    rings
3 ribs celery, sliced
2 carrots, thinly sliced
1½ cups beef broth
⅓ cup cider vinegar
2 tablespoons cornstarch
2 tablespoons water
3 cups hot cooked brown
    rice

Partially freeze steak; slice diagonally across grain into ⅛-inch strips. Combine gingersnap crumbs and salt in medium bowl. Dredge steak slices into crumb mixture; set aside. Heat oil in large skillet over medium-high heat until hot. Add half of steak slices, stirring to brown both sides. Cook for 2 minutes or until done. Reserve and keep warm. Repeat with remaining steak slices. Add onion, celery, and carrots to hot skillet; cook for 5 minutes or until tender crisp. Add broth and vinegar; reduce heat and simmer 5 minutes. Combine cornstarch with water. Add to skillet, stirring constantly, until thickened; cook 1 minute longer. Add reserved steak slices; pour mixture over rice.

Makes 6 servings

*Favorite recipe from **USA Rice Council***

Quick and Easy Tamale Pie

½ pound ground beef
¼ cup sliced green onions
2 envelopes LIPTON® Tomato
    Cup-A-Soup Instant Soup
½ cup water
1 can (7 ounces) whole
    kernel corn, drained
2 tablespoons chopped
    pitted ripe olives
    (optional)
¼ teaspoon chili powder
3 slices (¾ ounce each)
    American cheese, halved
2 corn muffins, cut into
    ½-inch cubes

In medium skillet, brown ground beef with green onions. Stir in instant tomato soup mix, water, corn, olives and chili powder until well blended. Place in 1-quart casserole. Top with cheese, then evenly spread muffin cubes over cheese. Bake at 350°F for 5 to 10 minutes or until cheese is melted.   *Makes 2 servings*

Microwave Directions: In shallow microwave-safe 1-quart casserole, microwave ground beef with green onions at HIGH (Full Power) 2½ minutes or until beef is no longer pink, stirring once. Stir in instant tomato soup mix, water, corn, olives and chili powder until well blended. Top with cheese, then evenly spread muffin cubes over cheese. Microwave at HIGH 5 minutes or until heated through and cheese is melted, turning casserole once.

Quick and Easy Tamale Pie

Spanish Rice and Meatballs

**6 slices bacon
1 pound lean ground beef
½ cup soft bread crumbs
1 egg, slightly beaten
½ teaspoon salt
⅛ teaspoon pepper
½ cup chopped onion
½ cup sliced celery
⅔ cup uncooked white rice
1½ cups water
1 can (16 ounces) whole peeled tomatoes, cut into bite-size pieces
⅓ cup HEINZ® 57 Sauce
¼ teaspoon pepper
⅛ teaspoon hot pepper sauce
1 green bell pepper, cut into ¾-inch chunks**

In large skillet, cook bacon until crisp; remove, coarsely crumble and set aside. Drain drippings, reserving 1 tablespoon. In large bowl, combine beef, bread crumbs, egg, salt and ⅛ teaspoon pepper. Form into 20 meatballs, using a rounded tablespoon for each. In same skillet, brown meatballs in reserved drippings; remove. In same skillet, sauté onion and celery until tender-crisp; drain excess fat. Add rice, water, tomatoes, 57 Sauce, ¼ teaspoon pepper and hot pepper sauce. Cover; simmer 20 minutes. Stir in bacon, meatballs and green pepper. Cover; simmer an additional 10 minutes or until rice is tender and liquid is absorbed, stirring occasionally.

*Makes 4 servings
(4 cups rice mixture)*

Spanish Rice and Meatballs

Cheeseburger Pie

**1 (9-inch) unbaked pastry shell, pricked
8 slices BORDEN® Singles Process American Cheese Food
1 pound lean ground beef
½ cup tomato sauce
⅓ cup chopped green bell pepper
⅓ cup chopped onion
1 teaspoon WYLER'S® or STEERO® Beef-Flavor Instant Bouillon *or*
1 Beef-Flavor Bouillon Cube
3 eggs, well beaten
2 tablespoons flour**

Preheat oven to 450°. Bake pastry shell 8 minutes; remove from oven. *Reduce oven temperature to 350°.* Cut *6 slices* cheese food into pieces. In large skillet, brown meat; pour off fat. Add tomato sauce, green pepper, onion and bouillon; cook and stir until bouillon dissolves. Remove from heat; stir in eggs, flour and cheese food pieces. Turn into prepared pastry shell. Bake 20 to 25 minutes or until hot. Arrange remaining *2 slices* cheese food on top. Bake 3 to 5 minutes longer or until cheese food begins to melt. Refrigerate leftovers.

Makes one 9-inch pie

Fiesta Beef Pot Pie

**Crust
1⅔ cups all-purpose flour
⅓ cup yellow cornmeal
2 tablespoons toasted wheat germ
1 teaspoon salt
⅓ cup finely shredded Cheddar cheese
¾ cup CRISCO® Shortening
5 to 7 tablespoons cold water**

**Filling
1 pound lean boneless beef chuck, cut into ¼- to ½-inch chunks
1 tablespoon CRISCO® Shortening
½ cup chopped green pepper*
½ cup chopped onion*
1 can (14½ ounces) Mexican-style stewed tomatoes,* *undrained*
1 can (8½ ounces) whole kernel corn, drained
1 can (4 ounces) sliced mushrooms, drained
½ cup water
⅓ cup tomato paste
2 teaspoons sugar
1 teaspoon chili powder
½ teaspoon ground cumin
¼ teaspoon salt
⅛ teaspoon crushed red pepper (optional)
⅓ cup sliced black olives**

**Glaze and Topping
1 egg, beaten
¼ teaspoon salt
⅓ cup shredded Cheddar cheese**

1. **For crust,** combine flour, cornmeal, wheat germ and 1 teaspoon salt in large bowl. Cut in ⅓ cup cheese and ¾ cup

*If Mexican-style tomatoes are unavailable, use plain stewed tomatoes. Increase green pepper and onion to ⅔ cup each. Add 1 tablespoon diced jalapeno pepper and ¼ teaspoon garlic powder.

Crisco® with pastry blender (or 2 knives) until flour is just blended to form pea-sized chunks. Sprinkle with water, 1 tablespoon at a time. Toss lightly with fork until dough forms a ball. Divide dough in half. Press each half to form 5- to 6-inch "pancake." Roll bottom crust into circle; transfer to 9-inch pie plate. Trim edge even with pie plate.

2. **For filling**, brown beef in 1 tablespoon Crisco® in large skillet. Remove beef with slotted spoon. Add green pepper and onion to skillet and cook until tender. Add beef, undrained tomatoes, corn, mushrooms, water, tomato paste, sugar, chili powder, cumin, ¼ teaspoon salt and red pepper, if desired. Cover. Bring to a boil. Reduce heat and simmer 30 minutes, stirring occasionally. Remove from heat. Stir in olives. Spoon hot filling into unbaked pie crust. Moisten pastry edge with water.

3. Heat oven to 425°F. Roll top crust same as bottom; lift top crust onto filled pie. Trim ½ inch beyond edge of pie plate. Fold top edge under bottom crust. Flute. Cut slits in top crust to allow steam to escape.

4. **For glaze and topping**, combine egg and ¼ teaspoon salt. Brush lightly over top crust. Bake at 425°F for 30 to 40 minutes or until crust is golden brown. Sprinkle with ⅓ cup cheese. Serve hot or warm. Refrigerate leftover pie.
One 9-inch Pie

Meat and Potato Pie

Filling
- ¼ cup CRISCO® Shortening
- 1 pound sirloin steak, trimmed and cut into ½-inch cubes
- ½ cup ½-inch diced onion
- ½ cup ½-inch diced carrots
- ¼ cup tomato paste
- ½ teaspoon dried basil leaves
- ½ teaspoon dried thyme leaves
- ½ teaspoon garlic powder
- 1 can (10½ ounces) condensed double strength beef broth
- 4½ cups peeled, ¾-inch cubed Idaho (russet) potatoes
- 1 tablespoon cornstarch
- 2 tablespoons cold water
- ½ cup frozen green peas, thawed

Crust
- 9-inch Classic Crisco® Double Crust (see page 303)

1. **For filling**, melt Crisco® in large saucepan. Add steak. Brown on medium-high heat. Add onion and carrots. Cook until onion starts to brown, stirring often. Add tomato paste, basil, thyme and garlic powder. Cook 2 or 3 minutes, stirring constantly. Add broth and potatoes. Reduce heat to low; cover and simmer until potatoes are cooked through but still firm.

2. Dissolve cornstarch in water. Add to saucepan. Cook and stir until thickened. Remove from heat. Stir in peas. Cool to room temperature.

3. **For crust**, heat oven to 375°F. Prepare recipe and press bottom crust into 9-inch deep-dish pie plate or casserole. Spoon in filling. Moisten pastry edge with water. Cover pie with top crust. Cut slits in top crust to allow steam to escape. Bake at 375°F for 30 to 35 minutes or until browned. Serve hot. Refrigerate leftover pie.   *One 9-inch Pie*

Meat and Potato Pie

Spring Lamb Skillet

2 teaspoons olive oil
1 pound boneless lamb, cut into 1-inch cubes
2 cups thinly sliced yellow squash
2 cups (about 8 ounces) sliced fresh mushrooms
2 medium tomatoes, seeded and chopped
½ cup sliced green onions
3 cups cooked brown rice
½ teaspoon dried rosemary leaves
½ teaspoon salt
½ teaspoon cracked black pepper

Heat oil in large skillet over medium heat until hot. Add lamb and cook 3 to 5 minutes or until lamb is browned. Remove from skillet; reserve. Add squash, mushrooms, tomatoes, and onions; cook 2 to 3 minutes or until vegetables are tender. Stir in rice, rosemary, salt, pepper, and reserved lamb. Cook until thoroughly heated.
Makes 6 servings

*Favorite recipe from **USA Rice Council***

Shrimp La Louisiana

1 tablespoon margarine
1½ cups uncooked rice*
1 medium onion, chopped
1 green pepper, chopped
2¾ cups beef broth
¼ teaspoon salt
¼ teaspoon ground black pepper
¼ teaspoon hot pepper sauce
1 pound medium shrimp, peeled and deveined
1 can (4 ounces) sliced mushrooms, drained
3 tablespoons snipped parsley
¼ cup sliced green onions for garnish (optional)

*Recipe based on regular-milled long grain white rice.

Melt margarine in 3-quart saucepan. Add rice, onion, and green pepper. Cook 2 to 3 minutes. Add broth, salt, black pepper, and pepper sauce; bring to a boil. Cover and simmer 15 minutes. Add shrimp, mushrooms, and parsley. Cook 5 minutes longer or until shrimp turn pink. Garnish with green onions.
Makes 8 servings

*Favorite recipe from **USA Rice Council***

Paella

1 tablespoon olive oil
½ pound chicken breast chunks
1 cup uncooked rice*
1 medium onion, chopped
1 clove garlic, minced
1½ cups chicken broth*
1 can (8 ounces) stewed tomatoes, chopped, reserving liquid
½ teaspoon paprika
⅛ to ¼ teaspoon ground red pepper
⅛ teaspoon ground saffron
½ pound medium shrimp, peeled and deveined
1 small red pepper cut into strips
1 small green pepper cut into strips
½ cup frozen green peas

Heat oil in Dutch oven over medium-high heat until hot. Add chicken and stir until browned. Add rice, onion, and garlic. Cook, stirring, until onion is tender and rice is lightly browned. Add broth, tomatoes, tomato liquid, paprika, ground red pepper, and saffron. Bring to a boil; stir. Reduce heat; cover and simmer 10 minutes. Add shrimp, pepper strips, and peas. Cover and simmer 10 minutes or until rice is tender and liquid is absorbed.
Makes 6 servings

*If using medium grain rice, use 1¼ cups of broth; for parboiled rice, use 1¾ cups of broth.

*Favorite recipe from **USA Rice Council***

Cajun Catfish Skillet

2 cups water
1 cup uncooked rice*
¼ teaspoon salt
¼ teaspoon ground red pepper
¼ teaspoon ground white pepper
¼ teaspoon ground black pepper
½ cup minced green onions
½ cup minced green pepper
½ cup minced celery
2 cloves garlic, minced
1 tablespoon margarine
1 pound catfish nuggets or other firm flesh white fish**
1 can (15½ ounces) tomato sauce
1 teaspoon dried oregano leaves

Combine water, rice, salt, red pepper, white pepper, and black pepper in 3-quart saucepan. Bring to a boil; stir. Reduce heat; cover and simmer 15 minutes or until rice is tender and liquid is absorbed. Cook onions, green pepper, celery, and garlic in margarine in large skillet over medium-high heat until tender. Stir vegetable mixture, catfish nuggets, tomato sauce, and oregano into hot rice. Cover and cook over medium heat 7 to 8 minutes or until catfish flakes with fork. *Makes 4 servings*

*Recipe based on regular-milled long grain white rice.

**Substitute 1 pound chicken nuggets for fish, if desired.

*Favorite recipe from **USA Rice Council***

Paella

Bayou Jambalaya

- **1 medium onion, sliced**
- **½ cup chopped green bell pepper**
- **1 clove garlic, minced**
- **1 cup uncooked white rice**
- **2 tablespoons butter or margarine**
- **1 cup HEINZ® Tomato Ketchup**
- **2¼ cups water**
- **1 tablespoon HEINZ® Vinegar**
- **⅛ teaspoon black pepper**
- **⅛ teaspoon ground red pepper**
- **1 medium tomato, coarsely chopped**
- **1 cup cubed cooked ham**
- **½ pound deveined shelled raw medium-size shrimp**

In large skillet, sauté onion, green pepper, garlic and rice in butter until onion is tender. Stir in ketchup, water, vinegar, black pepper, red pepper, tomato and ham. Cover; simmer 20 to 25 minutes or until rice is tender. Add shrimp; simmer, uncovered, 3 to 5 minutes or until shrimp turn pink, stirring occasionally.

Makes 4 to 6 servings (about 6 cups)

Microwave Directions: Place onion, green pepper, garlic and butter in 3-quart microwave-safe casserole. Cover dish with lid or vented plastic wrap; microwave at HIGH (100%) 3 to 4 minutes, stirring once. Stir in rice, ketchup, water, vinegar, black pepper, red pepper, tomato and ham. Cover and microwave at HIGH 10 to 12 minutes or until mixture comes to a boil. Microwave at MEDIUM (50%) 18 to 20 minutes until rice is cooked, stirring once. Stir in shrimp; cover and microwave at HIGH 2 to 3 minutes or until shrimp turn pink. Let stand, covered, 5 minutes before serving.

Bayou Jambalaya

Old-Fashioned Tuna Noodle Casserole

- **¼ cup plain dry bread crumbs**
- **3 tablespoons butter or margarine, melted and divided**
- **1 tablespoon finely chopped parsley**
- **½ cup chopped onion**
- **½ cup chopped celery**
- **1 cup water**
- **1 cup milk**
- **1 package LIPTON® Noodles & Sauce—Butter**
- **2 cans (6½ ounces each) tuna, drained and flaked**

In small bowl, thoroughly combine bread crumbs, 1 tablespoon of the butter and the parsley; set aside.

In medium saucepan, melt remaining 2 tablespoons butter and cook onion with celery over medium heat, stirring occasionally, 2 minutes or until onion is tender. Add water and milk; bring to a boil. Stir in noodles & butter sauce. Continue boiling over medium heat, stirring occasionally, 8 minutes or until noodles are tender. Stir in tuna. Turn into greased 1-quart casserole, then top with bread crumb mixture. Broil until bread crumbs are golden.

Makes about 4 servings

Quick and Easy Tuna Rice with Peas

- **1 package (10 ounces) BIRDS EYE® Green Peas**
- **1¼ cups water**
- **1 can (11 ounces) condensed Cheddar cheese soup**
- **1 can (12½ ounces) tuna, drained and flaked**
- **1 chicken bouillon cube**
- **¼ teaspoon pepper**
- **1½ cups Original MINUTE® Rice**

Bring peas, water, soup, tuna, bouillon cube and pepper to full boil in large saucepan. Stir in rice. Cover; remove from heat. Let stand 5 minutes. Fluff with fork. *Makes 4 servings*

Cheesy Tuna and Twists

- 8 ounces uncooked corkscrew macaroni
- 2 tablespoons margarine or butter
- 1 package (10 ounces) frozen mixed vegetables, thawed
- 1 clove garlic, minced
- 1 can (10¾ ounces) CAMPBELL'S® condensed Cream of Mushroom Soup
- ¾ cup milk
- 1½ cups shredded mozzarella cheese (6 ounces)
- ⅛ teaspoon pepper Generous dash ground nutmeg
- 1 can (6½ ounces) tuna, drained Chopped pimento for garnish

1. Cook macaroni according to package directions; drain.

2. Meanwhile, in 10-inch skillet over medium heat, in hot margarine, cook mixed vegetables and garlic 2 minutes, stirring often.

3. Add soup to skillet; stir until smooth. Gradually stir in milk. Add cheese, pepper and nutmeg; heat until cheese melts, stirring occasionally.

4. Stir in tuna and cooked macaroni. Heat through. Garnish with pimento.

Makes about 6 cups or 4 servings

Tip: For a heartier cheese flavor, use sharp Cheddar instead of mozzarella.

Crab and Rice Primavera

Crab and Rice Primavera

- 1½ cups BIRDS EYE® FARM FRESH Broccoli, Green Beans, Pearl Onions and Red Peppers
- ¼ cup water
- 1⅓ cups milk
- ¾ pound imitation crabmeat or crabmeat
- 2 tablespoons margarine or butter
- 1 teaspoon garlic powder
- ¾ teaspoon dried basil
- 1½ cups Original MINUTE® Rice
- ½ cup grated Parmesan cheese

Bring vegetables and water to boil in medium saucepan, stirring occasionally. Reduce heat; cover and simmer 3 minutes.

Add milk, imitation crabmeat, margarine, garlic powder and basil. Bring to full boil. Stir in rice and cheese. Cover; remove from heat. Let stand 5 minutes. Fluff with fork.

Makes 4 servings

PASTA

Perk up your meals with popular pasta and make any meal a spectacular occasion. Create luscious lasagnas, magnificent manicottis, savory sauces, fabulous fettuccines and much more. Serve Pasta & Vegetable Toss, Rigatoni with Sausage or Seafood Primavera and grace your home with the ambience of Italy. Or try other ethnic flavors with Beef Oriental and Tacos in Pasta Shells.

Tortellini Primavera

- 1 cup sliced mushrooms
- ½ cup chopped onion
- 1 garlic clove, minced
- 2 tablespoons PARKAY® Margarine
- 1 package (10 ounces) BIRDS EYE® Chopped Spinach, thawed, well drained
- 1 container (8 ounces) PHILADELPHIA BRAND® Soft Cream Cheese
- 1 medium tomato, chopped
- ¼ cup milk
- ¼ cup (1 ounce) KRAFT® 100% Grated Parmesan Cheese
- 1 teaspoon Italian seasoning
- ¼ teaspoon salt
- ¼ teaspoon pepper
- 8 to 9 ounces fresh or frozen cheese-filled tortellini, cooked, drained

Cook and stir mushrooms, onion and garlic in margarine in large skillet. Add all remaining ingredients except tortellini; mix well. Cook until mixture just begins to boil, stirring occasionally. Stir in tortellini; cook until thoroughly heated.

Makes 4 servings

Prep time: 10 minutes
Cooking time: 10 minutes

Pasta Primavera

- 1 medium onion, finely chopped
- 1 large clove garlic, minced
- 2 tablespoons butter or margarine
- ¾ pound asparagus, cut diagonally into 1½-inch pieces
- ½ pound mushrooms, sliced
- 1 medium zucchini, sliced
- 1 carrot, sliced
- 1 cup half-and-half or light cream
- ½ cup chicken broth
- 1 tablespoon flour
- 2 teaspoons dried basil
- 1 pound fettucine, uncooked
- ¾ cup (3 ounces) SARGENTO® Fancy Supreme™ Shredded Parmesan & Romano Cheese

In large skillet, cook onion and garlic in butter over medium heat until onion is tender. Add asparagus, mushrooms, zucchini and carrot; cook, stirring constantly, 2 minutes. Increase heat to high. Combine half-and-half, broth, flour and basil; add to skillet. Allow mixture to boil, stirring occasionally, until thickened. Meanwhile, cook fettucine according to package directions; drain. In serving bowl, combine cooked fettucine with sauce and Parmesan & Romano cheese.

Makes 8 servings

Tortellini Primavera

Pasta & Vegetable Toss

½ cup chopped onion
1 clove garlic, finely chopped
1 teaspoon Italian seasoning
1 tablespoon olive oil
¼ cup water
2 teaspoons WYLER'S® or STEERO® Beef-Flavor Instant Bouillon
2 cups broccoli flowerets
2 cups sliced zucchini
8 ounces fresh mushrooms, sliced (about 2 cups)
1 medium red bell pepper, cut into thin strips
½ (1-pound) package CREAMETTE® Fettuccini, cooked as package directs and drained

In large skillet, cook onion, garlic and Italian seasoning in oil until tender. Add water, bouillon and vegetables. Cover and simmer 5 to 7 minutes until vegetables are tender-crisp. Toss with hot fettuccini. Serve immediately. Refrigerate leftovers.   *Makes 4 servings*

Fresh Tomato Pasta Andrew

1 pound fresh tomatoes, cut into wedges
1 cup packed fresh basil leaves
2 cloves garlic, chopped
2 tablespoons olive oil
8 ounces Camenzola cheese *or* 6 ounces ripe Brie plus 2 ounces Stilton cheese, each cut into small pieces
Salt and white pepper to taste
4 ounces uncooked angel hair pasta, vermicelli or other thin pasta, hot cooked and drained
Grated Parmesan cheese

Place tomatoes, basil, garlic and oil in covered food processor or blender; pulse on and off until ingredients are coarsely chopped but not puréed. Combine tomato mixture and Camenzola cheese in large bowl. Season to taste with salt and white pepper. Add pasta; toss gently until cheese melts. Serve with Parmesan cheese. Garnish as desired.
*Makes 2 main-dish or
4 appetizer servings*

Pasta Delight

Pasta Delight

1 medium zucchini, sliced
1 tablespoon olive oil
2 tablespoons chopped shallots
2 cloves garlic, chopped
1 medium tomato, diced
2 tablespoons chopped fresh basil *or* ½ teaspoon dried basil, crushed
2 tablespoons grated Parmesan cheese
12 ounces uncooked penne pasta, hot cooked and drained

Cook and stir zucchini in hot oil in large skillet over medium-high heat. Reduce heat to medium. Add shallots and garlic; cook 1 minute. Add tomato; cook and stir 45 seconds. Add basil and cheese. Pour vegetable mixture over penne in large bowl; toss gently to mix.
Makes 4 to 6 servings

*Favorite recipe from **National Pasta Association***

Pasta & Vegetable Toss

Penne with Artichokes

- **1 package (10 ounces) frozen artichokes**
- **1¼ cups water**
- **2 tablespoons lemon juice**
- **5 cloves garlic, minced**
- **2 tablespoons olive oil, divided**
- **2 ounces sun-dried tomatoes in oil, drained**
- **2 small dried hot red peppers, crushed**
- **2 tablespoons chopped parsley**
- **¼ teaspoon salt**
- **¼ teaspoon pepper**
- **¾ cup fresh bread crumbs**
- **1 tablespoon chopped garlic**
- **12 ounces uncooked penne, hot cooked and drained**
- **1 tablespoon grated Romano cheese**

Cook artichokes in water and lemon juice in medium saucepan over medium heat until tender. Cool artichokes, then cut into quarters. Reserve artichoke liquid.

Cook and stir the 5 minced cloves garlic in 1½ tablespoons oil in large skillet over medium-high heat until golden. Reduce heat to low. Add artichokes and tomatoes; simmer 1 minute. Stir in artichoke liquid, red peppers, parsley, salt and pepper. Simmer 5 minutes.

Meanwhile, cook and stir bread crumbs and 1 tablespoon chopped garlic in remaining ½ tablespoon oil. Pour artichoke sauce over penne in large bowl; toss gently to coat. Sprinkle with bread crumb mixture and cheese.

Makes 4 to 6 servings

*Favorite recipe from **National Pasta Association***

Fusilli Pizzaiolo

Fusilli Pizzaiolo

- **8 ounces mushrooms, sliced**
- **1 large red pepper, diced**
- **1 large green pepper, diced**
- **1 large yellow pepper, diced**
- **10 green onions, chopped**
- **1 large onion, diced**
- **8 cloves garlic, coarsely chopped**
- **3 large shallots, chopped**
- **½ cup chopped fresh basil *or* 2 teaspoons dried basil leaves, crushed**
- **2 tablespoons chopped fresh oregano *or* 1 teaspoon dried oregano, crushed**
- **Dash crushed red pepper**
- **¼ cup olive oil**
- **4 cups canned tomatoes, chopped**
- **Salt and pepper to taste**
- **1 package (16 ounces) uncooked fusilli or spaghetti, hot cooked and drained**
- **2 tablespoons chopped parsley (optional)**

Cook and stir mushrooms, peppers, onions, garlic, shallots, basil, oregano and crushed red pepper in hot oil in large skillet until lightly browned. Add tomatoes with juice; bring to a boil. Reduce heat to low; simmer 20 minutes. Season to taste with salt and pepper. Place fusilli on plates. Spoon sauce over fusilli. Garnish with parsley.

Makes 6 to 8 servings

*Favorite recipe from **National Pasta Association***

Luscious Vegetarian Lasagna

Luscious Vegetarian Lasagna

1 can (14½ ounces) tomatoes, undrained
1 can (12 ounces) tomato sauce
1 teaspoon dried oregano leaves, crushed
1 teaspoon dried basil leaves, crushed
Dash black pepper
1 large onion, chopped
1½ teaspoons minced garlic
2 tablespoons olive oil
2 small zucchini, chopped
8 ounces mushrooms, sliced
1 large carrot, chopped
1 green pepper, chopped
1 cup (4 ounces) shredded mozzarella cheese
2 cups 1% milkfat cottage cheese
1 cup grated Parmesan or Romano cheese
8 ounces uncooked lasagna noodles, cooked, rinsed and drained
Parsley sprigs (optional)

Simmer tomatoes with juice, tomato sauce, oregano, basil and black pepper in medium saucepan over low heat. Cook and stir onion and garlic in hot oil in large skillet over medium-high heat until onion is golden. Add zucchini, mushrooms, carrot and green pepper. Cook and stir until vegetables are tender, 5 to 10 minutes. Stir vegetables into tomato mixture; simmer 15 minutes. Combine mozzarella, cottage and Parmesan cheeses in large bowl; blend well.

Spoon about 1 cup sauce in bottom of 12×8-inch pan. Place a layer of noodles over sauce, then ½ of the cheese mixture and ½ of the remaining sauce. Repeat layers of noodles, cheese mixture and sauce. Bake in preheated 350°F. oven 30 to 45 minutes or until bubbly. Let stand 10 minutes. Garnish with parsley.
Makes 6 to 8 servings

Substitution: Other vegetables may be added or substituted for the ones listed above.

*Favorite recipe from **North Dakota Dairy Promotion Commission***

Spinach Pesto

1 bunch fresh spinach, washed, dried and chopped
1 cup fresh parsley leaves
⅔ cup grated Parmesan cheese
½ cup walnut pieces
6 cloves fresh garlic, crushed
4 flat anchovy filets
1 tablespoon dried tarragon leaves, crushed
1 teaspoon dried basil leaves, crushed
1 teaspoon salt
½ teaspoon pepper
¼ teaspoon anise or fennel seed
1 cup olive oil
Hot cooked pasta twists, spaghetti or shells
Mixed salad (optional)

Place all ingredients except oil, pasta and salad in covered food processor. Process until mixture is smooth. With motor running, add oil in thin stream. Adjust seasonings, if desired. Pour desired amount over pasta; toss gently to coat. Serve with salad. Garnish as desired.
Makes 2 cups sauce

Note: Sauce will keep about 1 week in a covered container in the refrigerator.

*Favorite recipe from **The Fresh Garlic Association***

Spinach Pesto

Spinach-Garlic Pasta with Garlic-Onion Sauce

Spinach-Garlic Pasta
1½ cups all-purpose flour, divided
2 eggs *plus* 4 yolks
1 tablespoon olive oil
½ pound fresh spinach, blanched, squeezed dry and finely chopped
6 large cloves fresh garlic, crushed and finely chopped
½ teaspoon salt

Garlic-Onion Sauce
½ cup butter
1 tablespoon olive oil
1 pound Vidalia or other sweet onions, sliced
⅓ cup chopped fresh garlic (about 12 large cloves)
1 tablespoon honey (optional)
¼ cup Marsala wine
Grated Parmesan cheese (optional)

For pasta, place 1 cup flour in large bowl. Make well in center; place eggs, yolks and olive oil in well. Add spinach, garlic and salt. Mix, working in more flour as needed. Knead until dough is smooth. Cover with plastic wrap. Let rest 15 to 30 minutes. Roll dough to desired thickness with pasta machine. Cut into desired width. Cook in boiling water about 2 minutes; drain.

For sauce, heat butter and oil in large skillet over medium heat. Add onions and garlic; cover and cook until soft. Add honey; reduce heat to low. Cook, uncovered, 30 minutes, stirring occasionally. Add wine; cook 5 to 10 minutes more. Pour sauce over pasta; toss gently to coat. Serve with cheese. Garnish as desired.

Makes 2 to 4 servings

Favorite recipe from **The Fresh Garlic Association**

Spinach Stuffed Manicotti

1 teaspoon dried rosemary leaves, crushed
1 teaspoon dried sage leaves, crushed
1 teaspoon dried oregano leaves, crushed
1 teaspoon dried thyme leaves, crushed
1 teaspoon chopped fresh garlic
1½ teaspoons olive oil
1½ cups canned or fresh tomatoes, chopped
1 package (10 ounces) frozen spinach, cooked, drained and squeezed dry
4 ounces ricotta cheese
1 slice whole wheat bread, torn into coarse crumbs
2 egg whites, lightly beaten
8 uncooked manicotti shells, cooked, rinsed and drained
Yellow pepper rings (optional)
Sage sprig (optional)

Cook and stir rosemary, sage, oregano, thyme and garlic in oil in small saucepan over medium heat about 1 minute; do not let herbs turn brown. Add tomatoes; reduce heat to low. Simmer 10 minutes, stirring occasionally.

Combine spinach, cheese and bread crumbs in medium bowl. Fold in egg whites. Stuff manicotti with spinach mixture. Place ⅓ of the tomato mixture on bottom of 13×9-inch pan. Arrange manicotti in pan. Pour remaining tomato mixture over manicotti. Cover with foil. Bake in preheated 350°F. oven 30 minutes or until bubbly. Garnish with yellow pepper rings and sage sprig.

Makes 4 servings

Favorite recipe from **National Pasta Association**

Spinach Stuffed Manicotti

Three-Cheese Manicotti

- 1 container (15 ounces) ricotta cheese
- ¾ cup grated Parmesan cheese (3 ounces)
- 1 cup shredded mozzarella cheese (4 ounces), divided
- 2 tablespoons fresh chopped parsley
- ¼ teaspoon salt
- ¼ teaspoon pepper
- ⅛ teaspoon garlic powder Generous dash ground nutmeg
- 8 manicotti shells, cooked and drained
- 1½ cups PREGO® Regular Spaghetti Sauce *or* PREGO® EXTRA CHUNKY Mushroom and Onion Spaghetti Sauce, divided

1. In medium bowl, combine ricotta, Parmesan, ½ cup of mozzarella, parsley, salt, pepper, garlic powder and nutmeg. Stuff *each* shell using *about ¼ cup* of filling.

2. Spoon ½ cup of spaghetti sauce onto bottom of 10- by 6-inch baking dish. Place stuffed shells in single layer over sauce. Spoon remaining 1 cup spaghetti sauce over shells; cover with foil.

3. Bake at 350°F. for 35 minutes; uncover. Sprinkle with remaining ½ cup mozzarella; bake 5 minutes more or until cheese melts.
   Makes 4 main-dish servings

Prep Time: 20 minutes
Cook Time: 40 minutes

Rigatoni with Four Cheeses

- 3 cups milk
- 1 tablespoon chopped carrot
- 1 tablespoon chopped celery
- 1 tablespoon chopped onion
- 1 tablespoon parsley sprigs
- ½ bay leaf
- ¼ teaspoon black peppercorns
- ¼ teaspoon hot pepper sauce Dash ground nutmeg
- ¼ cup butter
- ¼ cup all-purpose flour
- ½ cup grated Wisconsin Parmesan cheese
- ¼ cup grated Wisconsin Romano cheese
- 12 ounces uncooked rigatoni, cooked and drained
- 1½ cups (6 ounces) shredded Wisconsin Cheddar cheese
- 1½ cups (6 ounces) shredded Wisconsin mozzarella cheese
- ¼ teaspoon chili powder

Combine milk, carrot, celery, onion, parsley, bay leaf, peppercorns, hot pepper sauce and nutmeg in medium saucepan. Bring to a boil. Reduce heat to low; simmer 10 minutes. Strain; reserve milk.

Melt butter in another medium saucepan over medium heat. Stir in flour. Gradually stir in reserved milk. Cook, stirring constantly, until thickened. Remove from heat. Add Parmesan and Romano cheeses, stirring until blended. Combine pasta and sauce in large bowl; toss gently to coat. Combine Cheddar and mozzarella cheeses in medium bowl. Place ½ of the pasta mixture in buttered 2-quart casserole. Sprinkle cheese mixture over top; place remaining pasta mixture on top. Sprinkle with chili powder. Bake in preheated 350°F. oven 25 minutes or until bubbly. Garnish as desired.   *Makes 6 servings*

Favorite recipe from **Wisconsin Milk Marketing Board** © 1992

Rigatoni with Four Cheeses

Spicy Ravioli and Cheese

- 1 medium red bell pepper, thinly sliced
- 1 medium green bell pepper, thinly sliced
- 1 medium yellow bell pepper, thinly sliced
- 1 tablespoon olive or vegetable oil
- ½ teaspoon LAWRY'S® Seasoned Salt
- ¼ teaspoon LAWRY'S® Garlic Powder with Parsley
- ¼ teaspoon sugar
- 1 package (8 or 9 ounces) fresh or frozen ravioli
- 1½ cups chunky salsa
- 4 ounces mozzarella cheese, thinly sliced
- 2 green onions, sliced

Spicy Ravioli and Cheese

Place bell peppers in baking dish; sprinkle with oil, Seasoned Salt, Garlic Powder with Parsley and sugar. Broil 15 minutes or until tender and browned, turning once. Prepare ravioli according to package directions. Pour ½ of salsa in bottom of 8-inch square baking dish. Alternate layers of bell peppers, ravioli, cheese and green onions. Pour remaining salsa over layers. Cover with foil; bake in 350°F oven 15 to 20 minutes or until heated through and cheese melts.   *Makes 4 to 6 servings*

Presentation: Serve as either a side dish or as a main dish.

Hint: You may also prepare this recipe in individual casseroles.

Creamy Fettuccini Toss

- ¼ cup margarine or butter
- 1 tablespoon flour
- 2 teaspoons WYLER'S® or STEERO® Chicken-Flavor Instant Bouillon
- ¾ teaspoon basil leaves
- ¼ teaspoon garlic powder
- ⅛ teaspoon pepper
- 1 cup (½ pint) BORDEN® or MEADOW GOLD® Coffee Cream *or* Half-and-Half
- 1 cup BORDEN® or MEADOW GOLD® Milk
- ½ (1-pound) package CREAMETTE® Fettuccini
- ¼ cup grated Parmesan cheese

In medium saucepan, melt margarine; stir in flour, bouillon, basil, garlic powder and pepper. Gradually add cream and milk. Cook and stir until bouillon dissolves and sauce thickens slightly, about 15 minutes. Meanwhile, cook fettuccini as package directs; drain. Remove sauce from heat; add cheese. In large bowl, pour sauce over *hot* fettuccini; stir to coat. Garnish with parsley, walnuts and bacon if desired. Serve immediately. Refrigerate leftovers.
Makes 6 to 8 servings

Pasta and Broccoli

- 1 bunch broccoli, steamed
- 1 clove garlic, finely chopped
- 2 tablespoons olive oil
- ¾ cup (3 ounces) shredded American or mozzarella cheese
- ½ cup grated Parmesan cheese
- ¼ cup butter
- ¼ cup chicken broth
- 3 tablespoons white wine
- 1 package (16 ounces) uncooked ziti macaroni, hot cooked and drained

Chop broccoli; set aside. Cook and stir garlic in hot oil in large skillet over medium-high heat until lightly browned. Add broccoli; cook and stir 3 to 4 minutes. Add American cheese, Parmesan cheese, butter, broth and wine; stir. Simmer until cheese melts.

Pour sauce over ziti in large bowl; toss gently to coat. Garnish as desired.
Makes 6 to 8 servings

Favorite recipe from **National Pasta Association**

Ham & Vegetable Primavera

½ **pound lean cooked ham, cut into strips**
1 **medium red bell pepper, cut into strips**
3 **ounces fresh pea pods (1½ cups)**
1 **cup sliced fresh mushrooms**
⅓ **cup sliced green onions**
1½ **teaspoons Italian seasoning**
1 **clove garlic, finely chopped**
2 **tablespoons olive or vegetable oil**
1 **tablespoon flour**
½ **cup water**
3 **tablespoons REALEMON® Lemon Juice from Concentrate**
1 **teaspoon WYLER'S® or STEERO® Chicken-Flavor Instant Bouillon**
½ **(1-pound) package CREAMETTE® Spaghetti, cooked as package directs and drained**
2 **tablespoons grated Parmesan cheese**

In large skillet, cook red pepper, pea pods, mushrooms, onions, Italian seasoning and garlic in oil until tender-crisp. Stir in flour then water, ReaLemon® brand and bouillon. Add ham; cook and stir until thickened and bubbly. Toss with hot spaghetti and cheese. Refrigerate leftovers.
Makes 4 servings

Lazy Lasagna

1 **pound ground beef**
1 **jar (32 ounces) spaghetti sauce**
1 **pound cottage cheese**
8 **ounces dairy sour cream**
8 **uncooked lasagna noodles**
3 **packages (6 ounces each) sliced mozzarella cheese (12 slices)**
½ **cup grated Parmesan cheese**
1 **cup water**

Cook beef in large skillet over medium-high heat until meat is brown, stirring to separate meat; drain fat. Add spaghetti sauce. Reduce heat to low. Heat through, stirring occasionally; set aside. Combine cottage cheese and sour cream in medium bowl; blend well.

Spoon 1½ cups of the meat sauce in bottom of 13×9-inch pan. Place ½ of the uncooked noodles over sauce, then ½ of the cottage cheese mixture, 4 slices of the mozzarella, ½ of the remaining meat sauce and ¼ cup of the Parmesan cheese. Repeat layers starting with the noodles. Top with remaining 4 slices of mozzarella cheese. Pour water around the sides of the pan. Cover tightly with foil. Bake in preheated 350°F. oven 1 hour. Uncover; bake 20 minutes more or until bubbly. Let stand 15 to 20 minutes. Garnish as desired.
Makes 8 to 10 servings

*Favorite recipe from **North Dakota Dairy Promotion Commission***

Tacos in Pasta Shells

1¼ **pounds ground beef**
1 **package (3 ounces) cream cheese with chives, cubed and softened**
1 **teaspoon salt**
1 **teaspoon chili powder**
18 **uncooked jumbo pasta shells, cooked, rinsed and drained**
2 **tablespoons butter, melted**
1 **cup prepared taco sauce**
1 **cup (4 ounces) shredded Cheddar cheese**
1 **cup (4 ounces) shredded Monterey Jack cheese**
1½ **cups crushed tortilla chips**
1 **cup dairy sour cream**
3 **green onions, chopped**
Leaf lettuce (optional)
Small pitted ripe olives (optional)
Cherry tomatoes (optional)

Cook beef in large skillet over medium-high heat until brown, stirring to separate meat; drain fat. Reduce heat to medium-low. Add cream cheese, salt and chili powder; simmer 5 minutes.

Toss shells with butter; fill with beef mixture. Arrange shells in buttered 13×9-inch pan. Pour taco sauce over each shell. Cover with foil. Bake in preheated 350°F. oven 15 minutes. Uncover; top with Cheddar cheese, Monterey Jack cheese and chips. Bake 15 minutes more or until bubbly. Top with sour cream and onions. Garnish with lettuce, olives and tomatoes.
Makes 4 to 6 servings

*Favorite recipe from **Southeast United Dairy Industry Association, Inc.***

Tacos in Pasta Shells

Sunday Super Stuffed Shells

Combine spinach, parsley, bread crumbs, eggs, minced garlic and Parmesan in large bowl; blend well. Season to taste with salt. Add cooled meat mixture; blend well. Fill shells with stuffing.

Spread about 1 cup of the spaghetti sauce over bottom of greased 12×8-inch pan. Arrange shells in pan. Pour remaining sauce over shells. Cover with foil. Bake in preheated 375°F. oven 35 to 45 minutes or until bubbly. Serve with zucchini. Garnish as desired.

Makes 9 to 12 servings

Favorite recipe from **The Fresh Garlic Association**

Sunday Super Stuffed Shells

    3 cloves fresh garlic
    2 tablespoons olive oil
    ¾ pound ground veal
    ¾ pound ground pork
    1 package (10 ounces) frozen
        chopped spinach,
        cooked, drained and
        squeezed dry
    1 cup parsley, finely chopped
    1 cup bread crumbs
    2 eggs, beaten
    3 cloves fresh garlic, minced
    3 tablespoons grated
        Parmesan cheese
    Salt to taste
    1 package (12 ounces)
        uncooked jumbo pasta
        shells, cooked, rinsed
        and drained
    3 cups spaghetti sauce
        Sautéed zucchini slices
        (optional)

Cook and stir the 3 whole garlic cloves in hot oil in large skillet over medium heat until garlic is browned. Discard garlic. Add veal and pork; cook until lightly browned, stirring to separate meat; drain fat. Set aside.

Beef Oriental

    1 pound ground beef
    7 green onions, diagonally
        sliced into 2-inch pieces
    3 tablespoons soy sauce
    ¼ teaspoon ground ginger
    2 to 3 ribs celery, diagonally
        sliced into 1-inch pieces
    8 mushrooms, sliced
    1 package (20 ounces) frozen
        pea pods, rinsed under
        hot water and drained
    1 can (8 ounces) tomato
        sauce
    3 cups uncooked corkscrew
        pasta, cooked and
        drained
    3 fresh tomatoes, cut into
        wedges
    1 cup (4 ounces) shredded
        Cheddar cheese, divided
    1 green pepper, cut into thin
        slices

Beef Oriental

Cook beef, onions, soy sauce and ginger in wok over medium-high heat until meat is brown, stirring to separate meat. Push mixture up the side of the wok. Add celery and mushrooms; stir-fry 2 minutes. Push up the side. Add pea pods and tomato sauce; cook 4 to 5 minutes, stirring every minute. Add pasta, tomatoes and ¾ cup of the cheese. Stir gently to combine all ingredients. Cook 1 minute. Add green pepper; sprinkle remaining cheese over top. Reduce heat to low; cook until heated through.

Makes 4 servings

Favorite recipe from **North Dakota Beef Commission**

Spinach Lasagna

Spinach Lasagna

- **1 pound lean ground beef**
- **2 jars (15½ ounces each) spaghetti sauce**
- **1 can (6 ounces) tomato paste**
- **1 can (4 ounces) mushroom stems and pieces, drained**
- **¼ cup chopped onion**
- **½ teaspoon parsley flakes**
- **½ teaspoon dried oregano leaves, crushed**
- **½ teaspoon dried basil leaves, crushed**
- **¼ teaspoon garlic powder Seasoned salt and pepper to taste**
- **1 pound dry curd cottage cheese**
- **3 cups (12 ounces) shredded mozzarella cheese, divided**
- **3 ounces grated Romano cheese**
- **1 egg, lightly beaten**
- **1 package (10 ounces) frozen chopped spinach, thawed and squeezed dry**
- **8 ounces uncooked lasagna noodles, cooked, rinsed and drained**
- **3 ounces sliced pepperoni (optional)**
- **½ cup grated Parmesan cheese**

Cook beef in large skillet over medium-high heat until brown, stirring to separate meat; drain fat. Add spaghetti sauce, tomato paste, mushrooms, onion and seasonings. Bring to a boil, stirring constantly; set aside.

Combine cottage cheese, 1 cup of the mozzarella cheese, Romano cheese, egg and spinach in medium bowl. Spoon 1½ cups meat sauce in bottom of 13×9-inch pan. Place a layer of noodles over sauce, then ½ of the cheese mixture and pepperoni. Sprinkle with Parmesan cheese. Repeat layers of sauce, noodles and cheese mixture. Sprinkle with remaining mozzarella. Bake in preheated 350°F. oven 30 to 45 minutes or until bubbly. Broil for a few minutes to brown cheese, if desired. Let stand 10 minutes.

Makes 8 to 10 servings

Favorite recipe from **North Dakota Wheat Commission**

Zesty Meatballs and Macaroni

- **½ pound ground beef**
- **½ pound sweet (mild) Italian sausage, casing removed**
- **⅓ cup Italian-seasoned fine dry bread crumbs**
- **1 egg, beaten**
- **¼ cup chopped onion**
- **2 tablespoons grated Parmesan *or* Romano cheese**
- **⅛ teaspoon pepper**
- **4½ cups PREGO® Regular Spaghetti Sauce *or* PREGO® EXTRA CHUNKY Mushroom and Green Pepper Spaghetti Sauce**
- **3 cups dry corkscrew macaroni, cooked and drained (5 cups cooked)**
- **Grated Parmesan *or* Romano cheese for garnish**

1. In large bowl, combine beef, sausage, bread crumbs, egg, onion, 2 tablespoons cheese and pepper until well mixed. Shape into 2-inch meatballs (about 16). Arrange in 15- by 10-inch jelly-roll pan.

2. Broil meatballs 5 inches from heat, 8 minutes or until browned, turning once during cooking. Drain on paper towels.

3. Place meatballs in 4-quart saucepan. Add spaghetti sauce. Heat to boiling. Reduce heat to low. Cover; simmer 20 minutes or until meatballs are thoroughly cooked and no longer pink inside, stirring occasionally.

4. To serve: Toss sauce with hot macaroni. Serve with additional cheese, if desired.

Makes about 5 cups or 4 main-dish servings

Prep Time: 30 minutes
Cook Time: 30 minutes

Spaghetti & Meatballs

- **1 pound lean ground beef**
- **½ cup finely chopped onion**
- **¾ cup grated Parmesan cheese**
- **½ cup fresh bread crumbs (1 slice)**
- **1 (26-ounce) jar CLASSICO® Pasta Sauce, any flavor**
- **1 egg**
- **2 teaspoons WYLER'S® or STEERO® Beef-Flavor Instant Bouillon**
- **1 teaspoon Italian seasoning**
- **8 ounces fresh mushrooms, sliced (about 2 cups)**
- **1 (1-pound) package CREAMETTE® Spaghetti, cooked as package directs and drained**

In large bowl, combine meat, onion, cheese, crumbs, *½ cup* pasta sauce, egg, bouillon and Italian seasoning; mix well. Shape into meatballs. In large kettle or Dutch oven, brown meatballs; pour off fat. Stir in remaining pasta sauce and mushrooms; simmer uncovered 15 minutes or until hot. Serve over hot cooked spaghetti. Refrigerate leftovers.

Makes 6 to 8 servings

Skillet Pasta Roma

- **½ pound Italian sausage, sliced or crumbled**
- **1 large onion, coarsely chopped**
- **1 large clove garlic, minced**
- **2 cans (14½ ounces each) DEL MONTE® Chunky Pasta Style Stewed Tomatoes**
- **1 can (8 ounces) DEL MONTE® Tomato Sauce**
- **1 cup water**
- **8 ounces uncooked rigatoni or spiral pasta**
- **8 mushrooms, sliced (optional)**
- **Grated Parmesan cheese and parsley (optional)**

In large skillet, brown sausage. Add onion and garlic. Cook until onion is soft; drain. Stir in stewed tomatoes, tomato sauce, water and pasta. Cover and bring to a boil; reduce heat. Simmer, covered, 25 to 30 minutes or until pasta is tender, stirring occasionally. Stir in mushrooms; simmer 5 minutes. Serve in skillet garnished with cheese and parsley, if desired.

Makes 4 servings

Prep time: 15 minutes
Cook time: 30 minutes

Rigatoni with Sausage

- **1 pound sweet (mild) Italian sausage, casing removed**
- **2 cups PREGO® Regular Spaghetti Sauce**
- **¼ cup Burgundy *or* other dry red wine *or* water**
- **¼ cup sliced pepperoncini**
- **1 clove garlic, minced**
- **½ cup pitted ripe olives, quartered**
- **½ cup shredded Asiago cheese (2 ounces)**
- **3½ cups dry rigatoni, cooked and drained (4 cups cooked)**

1. In 10-inch skillet over medium heat, cook sausage until thoroughly cooked and no pink remains, stirring to separate meat. Spoon off fat.

2. Stir in spaghetti sauce, wine, pepperoncini and garlic. Heat to boiling. Reduce heat to low; simmer 5 minutes, stirring occasionally. Add olives, cheese and hot rigatoni; toss to coat.

Makes about 6 cups or 4 main-dish servings

Prep Time: 5 minutes
Cook Time: 20 minutes

To Microwave: *Reduce wine or water to 2 tablespoons.* In 2½-quart microwave-safe casserole, crumble sausage. Cover with paper towel. Microwave on HIGH 5 to 7 minutes or until sausage is thoroughly cooked and no pink remains, stirring once during cooking. Spoon off fat. Stir in spaghetti sauce, 2 tablespoons wine, pepperoncini and garlic. Cover with lid; microwave on HIGH 5 minutes or until hot and bubbly, stirring once during cooking. Continue as directed above in step 2.

Fettuccine with Duckling and Roasted Red Peppers

Fettuccine with Duckling and Roasted Red Peppers

1 frozen duckling (4½ to 5½ pounds), thawed and quartered
Garlic powder
Onion salt
2 tablespoons butter or margarine, melted
1½ tablespoons all-purpose flour
1¼ cups heavy cream
2 tablespoons grated Parmesan cheese
1 pound uncooked fettuccine, hot cooked and drained
½ cup prepared roasted red peppers, drained
¼ cup chopped walnuts
¼ cup sliced pitted ripe olives

Place duckling, skin-side up, on rack in shallow pan. Sprinkle with garlic powder and onion salt. Cook in 350°F. oven about 1½ hours or until internal temperature registers 185°F. when tested with a meat thermometer. Cool; remove bones and skin. Cut duckling into bite-sized pieces; set aside.

Combine butter and flour in medium saucepan; blend well. Cook 1 minute over medium heat. Gradually stir in cream. Stir in cheese. Cook until sauce thickens, stirring constantly.

Place fettuccine in large bowl. Add duckling, peppers, walnuts and olives. Pour sauce over fettuccine; toss gently to coat. Garnish as desired.

Makes 4 main-dish or 8 appetizer servings

Sweet Garlic with Chicken Pasta

Sweet Garlic with Chicken Pasta

8 ounces garlic, minced
5½ tablespoons olive oil
1½ pounds shiitake mushrooms, sliced
2 cups fresh plum tomatoes, diced
1 cup chopped green onions
1 teaspoon crushed red pepper
2 cups chicken broth
1½ pounds chicken breasts, grilled, skinned, boned and diced
1 package (16 ounces) uncooked bow tie noodles, cooked, rinsed and drained
4 ounces cilantro, chopped and divided

Cook and stir garlic in hot oil in large skillet over medium-high heat until lightly browned. Add mushrooms, tomatoes, green onions and crushed red pepper. Cook and stir 2 minutes more. Add broth; simmer mixture to reduce slightly. Add chicken, noodles and ½ of the cilantro; heat through. Garnish with remaining cilantro.

Makes 6 to 8 servings

*Favorite recipe from **National Pasta Association***

Turkey Orzo Italiano

¼ pound sliced mushrooms
½ cup sliced green onions
2 tablespoons margarine
2 cups turkey broth or reduced-sodium chicken bouillon
1 cup orzo pasta, uncooked
½ teaspoon Italian seasoning
½ teaspoon salt
⅛ teaspoon white pepper
2 cups cooked cubed turkey

In large skillet, over medium-high heat, sauté mushrooms and onions in margarine for 1 minute. Add turkey broth and bring to a boil.

Stir in orzo, Italian seasoning, salt and pepper; bring to a boil. Reduce heat and simmer, covered, 15 minutes or until orzo is tender and liquid has been absorbed. Stir in turkey and heat through. *Makes 4 servings*

*Favorite recipe from **National Turkey Federation***

An Early Spring Pasta

1 cup Oriental Dressing
(recipe follows)
8 ounces cooked turkey
breast, cut into julienne
strips
4 ounces carrots, cut into
julienne strips
4 ounces asparagus,
diagonally sliced into
1-inch pieces
4 ounces spinach, chopped
12 ounces uncooked linguine,
hot cooked and drained

Heat Oriental Dressing in large saucepan over high heat to a boil. Add turkey, carrots, asparagus and spinach; reduce heat to medium. Cook 2 to 3 minutes. Pour sauce over linguini in large bowl; toss gently to coat.

Makes 4 to 6 servings

Oriental Dressing

1 large onion, sliced
1 cup water
¼ cup *each* soy sauce and
rice vinegar
1 tablespoon *each* garlic and
ginger root, minced
1 tablespoon *each* sesame
oil and lemon juice
1½ teaspoons *each* sugar and
pepper
1½ teaspoons hot pepper
sauce
2 tablespoons cornstarch
¼ cup water

Spread onion on large baking pan. Heat in preheated 400°F. oven until edges are dark brown, about 15 minutes. Purée onion in covered food processor. Place onion and remaining ingredients except cornstarch and ¼ cup water in medium saucepan. Bring to a boil. Combine cornstarch and ¼ cup water in cup until smooth. Gradually stir into dressing mixture. Heat until mixture boils, stirring constantly. Reduce heat to low; simmer 2 to 3 minutes.

*Favorite recipe from **National Pasta Association***

Seafood Primavera

1 medium onion, chopped
4 green onions, chopped
⅓ cup olive oil
3 carrots, cut into strips
1 zucchini, cut into strips
1 *each* small red and yellow
pepper, cut into strips
3 ounces snow peas
⅓ cup sliced mushrooms
3 cloves garlic, minced
½ pound *each* scallops and
shrimp, peeled and
deveined
⅔ cup clam juice
⅓ cup dry white wine
1 cup heavy cream
½ cup freshly grated
Parmesan cheese
⅔ cup flaked crabmeat
2 tablespoons *each* lemon
juice and chopped
parsley
¼ teaspoon *each* dried basil
leaves and dried oregano
leaves, crushed
Freshly ground black
pepper to taste
1 package (8 ounces)
uncooked linguine, hot
cooked and drained

Cook and stir onions in hot oil in large skillet over medium-high heat until soft. Add vegetables and garlic; reduce heat to low. Cover; simmer until vegetables are tender. Remove; set aside. Cover and cook scallops and shrimp in same skillet over medium-low heat until opaque. Remove; reserve liquid in pan. Add clam juice; bring to a boil. Add wine; cook over medium-high heat 3 minutes, stirring constantly. Reduce heat to low; add cream, stirring constantly. Add cheese; stir until smooth. Cook until thickened.

Add vegetables, shrimp, scallops and crabmeat to sauce. Heat through. Add remaining ingredients except linguine. Pour over linguine in large bowl; toss gently to coat. Serve with additional grated Parmesan cheese, if desired.

Makes 6 servings

Seafood Lasagna

1 large onion, chopped
2 tablespoons butter or
margarine
1½ cups cream-style cottage
cheese
1 package (8 ounces) cream
cheese, cubed, softened
2 teaspoons dried basil
leaves, crushed
½ teaspoon salt
⅛ teaspoon pepper
1 egg, lightly beaten
2 cans (10¾ ounces each)
cream of mushroom
soup
⅓ cup milk
1 clove garlic, minced
½ cup dry white wine
½ pound bay scallops
½ pound flounder fillets,
cubed
½ pound medium shrimp,
peeled and deveined
1 package (16 ounces)
lasagna, cooked, rinsed
and drained
1 cup (4 ounces) shredded
mozzarella cheese
2 tablespoons grated
Parmesan cheese

Cook onion in hot butter in medium skillet over medium heat until tender, stirring frequently. Stir in cottage cheese, cream cheese, basil, salt and pepper; mix well. Stir in egg; set aside.

Combine soup, milk and garlic in large bowl until well blended. Stir in wine, scallops, flounder and shrimp.

Place a layer of overlapping noodles in greased 13×9-inch pan. Spread ½ of the cheese mixture over noodles. Place a layer of noodles over cheese mixture and top with ½ of the seafood mixture. Repeat layers. Sprinkle with mozzarella and Parmesan cheeses. Bake in preheated 350°F. oven 45 minutes or until bubbly. Let stand 10 minutes.

Makes 8 to 10 servings

*Favorite recipe from **New Jersey Department of Agriculture***

Seafood Primavera

Shrimp Noodle Supreme

Shrimp Noodle Supreme

- 1 package (8 ounces) uncooked spinach noodles, hot cooked and drained
- 1 package (3 ounces) cream cheese, cubed and softened
- 1½ pounds medium shrimp, peeled and deveined
- ½ cup butter, softened
  Salt and pepper to taste
- 1 can (10¾ ounces) condensed cream of mushroom soup
- 1 cup dairy sour cream
- ½ cup half-and-half
- ½ cup mayonnaise
- 1 tablespoon chopped chives
- 1 tablespoon chopped parsley
- ½ teaspoon Dijon mustard
- ¾ cup (6 ounces) shredded sharp Cheddar cheese
  Tomato wedges (optional)
  Parsley sprigs (optional)
  Lemon slices (optional)
  Paprika (optional)

Combine noodles and cream cheese in medium bowl. Spread noodle mixture in bottom of greased 13×9-inch glass casserole. Cook shrimp in butter in large skillet over medium-high heat until pink and tender, about 5 minutes. Season to taste with salt and pepper. Spread shrimp over noodles.

Combine soup, sour cream, half-and-half, mayonnaise, chives, chopped parsley and mustard in another medium bowl. Spread over shrimp. Sprinkle Cheddar cheese over top. Bake in preheated 325°F. oven 25 minutes or until hot and cheese melts. Garnish with tomato, parsley sprigs, lemon slices and paprika.   *Makes 6 servings*

*Favorite recipe from **Southeast United Dairy Industry Association, Inc.***

Extra-Easy Seafood and Pasta

- 1¾ cups PREGO® Regular Spaghetti Sauce
- 1 pound desired fresh fish and shellfish*
- ½ cup light cream
- 8 ounces dry thin spaghetti, cooked and drained (3½ cups cooked)
- 1 lemon, cut into wedges

In 2-quart saucepan over medium heat, combine spaghetti sauce and seafood; heat to boiling. Reduce heat to low; simmer 7 minutes or until the seafood is thoroughly cooked, stirring occasionally. Stir in cream. Heat through; *do not boil.* Serve over hot spaghetti along with lemon wedges.

    Makes about 4 cups or 4 main-dish servings

Prep Time: 10 minutes
Cook Time: 10 minutes

*Use any combination of the following: firm white fish fillets, cut into 1-inch pieces (such as orange roughy or monkfish); medium shrimp, peeled and deveined; or bay scallops.

Garlic Shrimp with Noodles

- 4 tablespoons butter, divided
- ¼ cup finely chopped onion
- 2 cups water
- 1 package LIPTON® Noodles & Sauce — Butter & Herb
- 2 tablespoons olive oil
- 1 tablespoon finely chopped garlic
- 1 pound raw medium shrimp, cleaned
- 1 can (14 ounces) artichoke hearts, drained and halved
- ¼ cup finely chopped parsley
- Pepper to taste

In medium saucepan, melt 2 tablespoons of the butter; add onion and cook until tender. Add water and bring to a boil. Stir in noodles & butter & herb sauce; continue boiling over medium heat, stirring occasionally, 8 minutes or until noodles are tender.

Meanwhile, in large skillet, heat remaining 2 tablespoons butter with olive oil; cook garlic over medium-high heat 30 seconds. Add shrimp and artichokes; cook, stirring occasionally, 3 minutes or until shrimp turn pink. Stir in parsley and pepper. To serve, combine shrimp mixture with hot noodles. Garnish, if desired, with watercress.

Makes about 4 servings

Shrimp in Angel Hair Pasta Casserole

- 1 tablespoon butter
- 2 eggs
- 1 cup half-and-half
- 1 cup plain yogurt
- ½ cup (4 ounces) shredded Swiss cheese
- ⅓ cup crumbled feta cheese
- ⅓ cup chopped parsley
- ¼ cup chopped fresh basil *or* 1 teaspoon dried basil leaves, crushed
- 1 teaspoon dried oregano leaves, crushed
- 1 package (9 ounces) uncooked fresh angel hair pasta
- 1 jar (16 ounces) mild, thick and chunky salsa
- 1 pound medium shrimp, peeled and deveined
- ½ cup (4 ounces) shredded Monterey Jack cheese
- Snow peas (optional)
- Plum tomatoes stuffed with cottage cheese (optional)

With 1 tablespoon butter, grease 12×8-inch pan. Combine eggs, half-and-half, yogurt, Swiss cheese, feta cheese, parsley, basil and oregano in medium bowl; mix well. Spread ½ of the pasta on bottom of prepared pan. Cover with salsa. Add ½ of the shrimp. Cover with remaining pasta. Spread egg mixture over pasta and top with remaining shrimp. Sprinkle Monterey Jack cheese over top. Bake in preheated 350°F. oven 30 minutes or until bubbly. Let stand 10 minutes. Garnish with snow peas and stuffed plum tomatoes.

Makes 6 servings

Favorite recipe from **Southeast United Dairy Industry Association, Inc.**

Shrimp in Angel Hair Pasta Casserole

Scallops with Vermicelli

- 1 pound bay scallops
- 2 tablespoons fresh lemon juice
- 2 tablespoons chopped parsley
- 1 onion, chopped
- 1 clove garlic, minced
- 2 tablespoons olive oil
- 2 tablespoons butter, divided
- 1½ cups canned Italian tomatoes, undrained and cut up
- 2 tablespoons chopped fresh basil *or* ½ teaspoon dried basil, crushed
- ¼ teaspoon dried oregano leaves, crushed
- ¼ teaspoon dried thyme leaves, crushed
- 2 tablespoons heavy cream Dash ground nutmeg
- 12 ounces uncooked vermicelli, hot cooked and drained

Rinse scallops. Combine scallops, lemon juice and parsley in glass dish. Cover; marinate in refrigerator while preparing sauce.

Cook and stir onion and garlic in oil and 1 tablespoon of the butter in large skillet over medium-high heat until onion is tender. Add tomatoes with juice, basil, oregano and thyme. Reduce heat to low. Cover; simmer 30 minutes, stirring occasionally.

Drain scallops. Cook and stir scallops in remaining 1 tablespoon butter in another large skillet over medium heat until scallops are opaque, about 2 minutes. Add cream, nutmeg and tomato mixture.

Pour sauce over vermicelli in large bowl; toss gently to coat. Garnish as desired.

Makes 4 servings

Favorite recipe from **New Jersey Department of Agriculture**

Linguine with Lemon Clam Sauce

- ¼ cup chopped onion
- 1 clove garlic, finely chopped
- 2 tablespoons margarine or butter
- 2 tablespoons olive or vegetable oil
- 2 (6½-ounce) cans SNOW'S® or DOXSEE® Chopped Clams, drained, reserving ⅔ cup liquid
- 2 tablespoons REALEMON® Lemon Juice from Concentrate
- ½ teaspoon cracked black pepper
- 1 bay leaf
- 1 tablespoon chopped parsley
- ¼ to ½ pound CREAMETTE® Linguine, cooked as package directs and drained
  Grated Parmesan cheese

In medium skillet, cook onion and garlic in margarine and oil until golden. Add reserved clam liquid, ReaLemon® brand, pepper and bay leaf. Bring to a boil; simmer uncovered 5 minutes. Stir in clams and parsley; heat through. Remove bay leaf; serve with hot linguine, cheese and additional pepper. Refrigerate leftovers.

Makes 2 to 3 servings

Scallops with Vermicelli

Tortellini with Three-Cheese Tuna Sauce

- 1 pound cheese-filled spinach and egg tortellini
- 2 green onions, thinly sliced
- 1 clove garlic, minced
- 1 tablespoon butter or margarine
- 1 cup low-fat ricotta cheese
- ½ cup low-fat milk
- 1 can (9¼ ounces) STARKIST® Tuna, drained and broken into chunks
- ½ cup shredded low-fat mozzarella cheese
- ¼ cup grated Parmesan or Romano cheese
- 2 tablespoons chopped fresh basil *or* 2 teaspoons dried basil, crushed
- 1 teaspoon grated lemon peel
  Fresh tomato wedges for garnish (optional)

Tortellini with Three-Cheese Tuna Sauce

Cook tortellini in boiling salted water according to package directions. When tortellini is nearly done, in another saucepan sauté onions and garlic in butter for 2 minutes. Remove from heat. Whisk in ricotta cheese and milk. Add tuna, cheeses, basil and lemon peel. Cook over medium-low heat until mixture is heated and cheeses are melted.

Drain pasta; add to sauce. Toss well to coat; garnish with tomato wedges if desired. Serve immediately.

Makes 4 to 5 servings

Preparation time: 25 minutes

Crabmeat with Herbs and Pasta

- 1 small onion, minced
- 1 carrot, shredded
- 1 clove garlic, minced
- ⅓ cup olive oil
- 3 tablespoons butter or margarine
- 6 ounces flaked crabmeat
- ¼ cup chopped fresh basil *or* 1 teaspoon dried basil leaves, crushed
- 2 tablespoons chopped parsley
- 1 tablespoon lemon juice
- ½ cup chopped pine nuts (optional)
- ½ teaspoon salt
- ½ package (8 ounces) vermicelli, hot cooked and drained

Cook and stir onion, carrot and garlic in hot oil and butter in large skillet over medium-high heat until vegetables are tender, but not brown. Reduce heat to medium. Stir in crabmeat, basil, parsley and lemon juice. Cook 4 minutes, stirring constantly. Stir in pine nuts and salt. Pour sauce over vermicelli in large bowl; toss gently to coat. Garnish as desired. *Makes 4 servings*

*Favorite recipe from **New Jersey Department of Agriculture***

SIDE DISHES

Discover sensational side dishes that will steal the show. Accompany your next meal with crisp vegetables, perfect potatoes and irresistible rice dishes such as Cheddar Sesame Garden Vegetables, Skewered Grilled Potatoes and Spanish Rice au Gratin. You'll find a stuffing for Cornish hens, a mideastern pilaf for kabobs, a colorful vegetable mix to liven up any meat dish, plus much more to enhance all kinds of meals.

Curry-Sauced Cauliflower

**4 cups cauliflowerets
1 can (10¾ ounces) CAMPBELL'S® condensed Cream of Celery Soup
½ cup milk
½ cup shredded Cheddar cheese (2 ounces)
½ teaspoon curry powder Generous dash pepper
1 cup frozen peas, thawed
½ cup diced sweet red pepper Toasted sliced almonds for garnish**

1. In covered 10-inch skillet over medium heat, in ½ inch boiling water, cook cauliflower 5 minutes or until tender-crisp. Drain in colander.

2. In same skillet, combine soup, milk, cheese, curry and pepper. Add cooked cauliflower, peas and red pepper. Over medium heat, cook 5 minutes or until vegetables are tender, stirring often. Garnish with almonds.

Makes about 5 cups or 10 servings

To microwave: In 2-quart microwave-safe casserole, place cauliflower in ½ inch water. Cover with lid; microwave on HIGH 10 minutes or until tender-crisp. Drain in colander. In same casserole, stir soup, milk, cheese, curry and pepper until smooth. Add cooked cauliflower, peas and red pepper. Cover; microwave on HIGH 3 minutes or until vegetables are tender and cheese melts, stirring once during cooking. Garnish as directed in step 2.

Colorful Cauliflower Bake

**1 cup KELLOGG'S® ALL-BRAN® cereal
2 tablespoons margarine, melted
¼ teaspoon garlic salt
¼ cup flour
½ teaspoon salt
⅛ teaspoon white pepper
1⅓ cups skim milk
1 chicken bouillon cube
1 package (16 ounces) frozen, cut cauliflower, thawed, well drained
½ cup sliced green onions
2 tablespoons drained, chopped pimento**

1. Combine Kellogg's® All-Bran® cereal, margarine and garlic salt; set aside.

2. In 3-quart saucepan, combine flour, salt and pepper. Gradually add milk, mixing until smooth, using a wire whip if necessary. Add bouillon cube. Cook, stirring constantly, over medium heat until bubbly and thickened. Remove from heat.

3. Add cauliflower, onions and pimento, mixing until combined. Spread evenly in 1½-quart serving dish. Sprinkle with cereal mixture.

4. Bake at 350° about 20 minutes or until thoroughly heated and sauce is bubbly.

Makes 6 servings

Note: 3½ cups fresh cauliflower flowerets, cooked crisp-tender, may be substituted for frozen cauliflower.

Curry-Sauced Cauliflower

Lemon Vegetable Sauté

1 cup DOLE® Broccoli florettes
1 cup DOLE® Cauliflower florettes
2 tablespoons margarine, divided
1 tablespoon water
2 tablespoons sugar
1 small DOLE® Lemon, thinly sliced

• In 10-inch skillet, sauté vegetables in 1 tablespoon margarine over medium-high heat. Reduce heat to medium-low. Cover; cook 3 to 4 minutes or until tender-crisp.

• Add remaining 1 tablespoon margarine, water and sugar. Mix until blended and glazed. Stir in lemon until well mixed and heated. Serve with baked pork chops, ham steaks or deli-roasted chicken, if desired.

Makes 2 servings

Preparation Time: 10 minutes
Cook Time: 10 minutes

Peas and Carrots in Thyme Sauce

Lemon-Herb Broccoli

1 bunch DOLE® Broccoli, cut into florettes
2 tablespoons margarine
3 to 4 tablespoons lemon juice
1 tablespoon Dijon mustard
½ teaspoon dried marjoram, crumbled

• Steam broccoli over boiling water in saucepan 3 to 4 minutes until tender-crisp.

• Melt margarine in another saucepan over medium heat. Blend in lemon juice, mustard and marjoram. Spoon over broccoli. Serve with grilled chicken breast or fish steaks, if desired.

Makes 2 to 3 servings

Preparation Time: 5 minutes
Cook Time: 10 minutes

Broccoli Bake

1 can (10¾ ounces) CAMPBELL'S® condensed Cream of Broccoli Soup
½ cup milk
1 teaspoon soy sauce Dash pepper
1 package (20 ounces) frozen broccoli cuts, cooked and drained
1 can (2.8 ounces) French fried onions, divided

1. In 10- by 6-inch baking dish, combine soup, milk, soy sauce and pepper. Stir in broccoli and ½ can of onions.

2. Bake, uncovered, at 350°F. for 25 minutes. Top with remaining onions. Bake 5 minutes more.

Makes about 4½ cups or 6 side-dish servings

To microwave: In 10- by 6-inch microwave-safe baking dish, combine soup, milk, soy sauce and pepper. Stir in broccoli and ½ *can* of onions. Cover with waxed paper; microwave on HIGH 8 minutes, rotating dish halfway through cooking. Top with remaining onions. Microwave, uncovered, on HIGH 1 minute more.

Tip: You can substitute 1 bunch (about 1½ pounds) fresh broccoli, cut up, cooked and drained *or* 2 packages (10 ounces *each*) frozen broccoli spears, cooked and drained, for the broccoli cuts.

Green Bean Bake: Prepare Broccoli Bake as directed above *except* substitute 1 can (10¾ ounces) CAMPBELL'S® condensed *Cream of Mushroom Soup* for the cream of broccoli soup and substitute 4 cups cooked and drained *green beans* for the broccoli.

Peas and Carrots in Thyme Sauce

1 tablespoon margarine or butter
1 small onion, chopped
¼ teaspoon dried thyme leaves, crushed
1 can (10¾ ounces) CAMPBELL'S® condensed Cream of Celery Soup
⅓ cup milk
Generous dash pepper
1 bag (16 ounces) frozen peas
1 cup carrots, cut into 2-inch matchstick-thin strips

1. In 2-quart saucepan over medium heat, in hot margarine, cook onion and thyme until onion is tender, stirring occasionally.

2. Stir in soup, milk and pepper. Add peas and carrots. Heat to boiling. Reduce heat to low. Cover; cook 8 minutes or until vegetables are tender, stirring occasionally.

Makes about 3½ cups or 4 servings

Honey Glazed Carrots

3 tablespoons margarine
2 tablespoons brown sugar
1 tablespoon honey
3 cups diagonally sliced DOLE® Carrots, cooked

• Melt margarine in skillet over medium heat. Blend in sugar and honey.

• Add cooked carrots. Stir and coat until well glazed. Serve with sautéed pork chops or chicken cutlets, if desired.

Makes 2 to 3 servings

Preparation Time: 3 minutes
Cook Time: 5 minutes

Confetti Corn

6 medium tomatoes
2 tablespoons IMPERIAL® Margarine
⅓ cup chopped green onions
⅓ cup chopped red bell pepper
1 package (10 ounces) frozen corn, thawed
2 tablespoons vinegar
2 tablespoons chopped fresh cilantro
1 teaspoon LAWRY'S® Garlic Salt

Cut ¼ inch off top of tomatoes. Hollow out, reserving pulp. Chop pulp into chunks; set aside. In medium skillet, melt margarine and sauté green onions and bell pepper. Add corn, vinegar, tomato pulp, cilantro and Garlic Salt; blend well. Heat 5 minutes or until flavors are blended. Place tomato shells on baking dish and heat in 350°F oven 5 minutes. Spoon tomato-corn mixture into shells.

Makes 6 servings

Presentation: Serve on a lettuce-lined platter as a side dish with grilled chicken, fish or beef entrées.

Home-Style Creamed Corn Casserole

2 cans (17 ounces each) cream-style corn
1 cup Original MINUTE® Rice
1 egg, slightly beaten
½ teaspoon salt
⅛ teaspoon pepper
⅛ teaspoon ground nutmeg (optional)

Combine all ingredients in large bowl; mix well. Pour into greased 9-inch square baking dish. Bake at 375° for 25 minutes or until liquid is absorbed. Garnish as desired.   *Makes 6 servings*

Microwave Directions:
Combine all ingredients in large bowl; mix well. Pour into greased 9-inch square microwavable dish. Cover and cook at HIGH 15 minutes or until liquid is absorbed. Garnish as desired.

Makes 6 servings

Confetti Corn

Tomato-Bread Casserole

- **½ pound-loaf French bread, sliced**
- **3 tablespoons IMPERIAL® Margarine, softened**
- **1 can (14½ ounces) whole peeled tomatoes, cut up**
- **1½ pounds fresh tomatoes, thinly sliced**
- **1 cup lowfat cottage or ricotta cheese**
- **¼ cup olive or vegetable oil**
- **¾ teaspoon LAWRY'S® Seasoned Salt**
- **½ teaspoon dried oregano, crushed**
- **½ teaspoon LAWRY'S® Garlic Powder with Parsley**
- **½ cup Parmesan cheese**

Spread bread slices with margarine; cut into large cubes. Arrange on jelly-roll pan. Toast in 350°F oven about 7 minutes. Place ½ of cubes in greased 13×9×2-inch baking dish. Drain canned tomatoes, reserving liquid. Top bread cubes with ½ of fresh tomato slices, ½ reserved tomato liquid, ½ of cottage cheese, ½ of oil, ½ of canned tomatoes, ½ of Seasoned Salt, ½ of oregano and ½ of Garlic Powder with Parsley. Repeat layers. Sprinkle with Parmesan cheese. Bake, covered, in 350°F oven 40 minutes. Uncover and bake 5 minutes longer to brown top.

Makes 8 to 10 servings

Presentation: Sprinkle with parsley. Serve with any grilled or baked meat, fish or poultry entrée.

Simply Green Beans

- **1 pound fresh green beans, ends removed and cut in half crosswise**
- **1 tablespoon IMPERIAL® Margarine, melted**
- **3 tablespoons coarsely grated Romano cheese**
- **¼ to ½ teaspoon LAWRY'S® Seasoned Pepper**
- **¼ teaspoon LAWRY'S® Garlic Powder with Parsley**

In large saucepan, bring 2 quarts of water to a boil; add beans. After water has returned to a boil, cook beans 4 minutes. Drain; run under cold water. In medium skillet, melt margarine; sauté green beans 3 minutes or until tender. Add remaining ingredients; toss well. Serve hot.

Makes 4 servings

Hint: Great accompaniment to roast chicken or fresh fish fillets.

Microwave Directions: In microwave-safe shallow dish, place green beans and ¼ cup water. Cover with plastic wrap, venting one corner. Microwave on HIGH 14 to 16 minutes, stirring after 7 minutes; drain. Add margarine, Seasoned Pepper and Garlic Powder with Parsley. Stir; let stand covered 1 minute. Sprinkle with cheese.

Cheddar Sesame Garden Vegetables

- **½ cup *undiluted* CARNATION® Evaporated Skimmed Milk**
- **1 tablespoon plus 2 teaspoons all-purpose flour**
- **¼ cup water**
- **1 teaspoon country Dijon-style mustard**
- **½ cup (2 ounces) shredded reduced-fat Cheddar cheese**
- **3 to 4 cups cooked fresh vegetables,* drained**
- **1 tablespoons toasted sesame seeds**

In small saucepan, whisk small amount of milk into flour. Stir in remaining milk with water and mustard. Cook over medium heat, stirring constantly, until mixture comes to a boil and thickens. Add cheese; stir until melted. Serve over vegetables. Sprinkle with sesame seeds.

Makes 2 servings

*Your choice of carrots, summer squash, broccoli, cauliflower or asparagus.

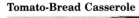

Tomato-Bread Casserole

Saltillo Zucchini

Ratatouille

**2 cloves garlic, finely
 chopped**
¼ cup vegetable oil
**1 medium eggplant, pared
 and cut into cubes
 (about 4 to 6 cups)**
**2 small zucchini, cut into
 ½-inch slices
 (about 2 cups)**
**1 large sweet onion, thinly
 sliced**
**1 medium green bell pepper,
 cut into ¼-inch strips**
**1 (8-ounce) can stewed
 tomatoes**
**2 tablespoons chopped fresh
 parsley**
**4 teaspoons WYLER'S® or
 STEERO® Beef-Flavor
 Instant Bouillon or
 4 Beef-Flavor Bouillon
 Cubes**
1 tablespoon flour
1 teaspoon basil leaves
1 teaspoon oregano leaves

In large saucepan or Dutch oven,
cook garlic in oil until lightly
browned. Add remaining
ingredients; cover and simmer 15
minutes. Uncover and stir; cook
10 minutes longer or until
vegetables are tender.
Refrigerate leftovers.
Makes 6 servings

Squash Olé

6 medium zucchini
**1 can (12 ounces) whole
 kernel corn, drained**
2 eggs, beaten
¼ cup chopped chives
**2 teaspoons LAWRY'S®
 Seasoned Salt**
**½ cup (2 ounces) grated
 sharp Cheddar cheese
 Paprika**

In large saucepan, cook zucchini
in boiling water to cover 5
minutes. Cut in half lengthwise;
remove pulp. Chop pulp into
small pieces, then combine with
corn, eggs, chives and Seasoned
Salt. Pour mixture into zucchini
shells. Place in 2-quart oblong
baking dish. Sprinkle with
cheese and paprika. Bake,
uncovered, in 350°F oven 30
minutes or until cheese melts.
Makes 6 servings

Presentation: Serve with grilled
chicken or fish entrées.

Saltillo Zucchini

½ cup chopped onion
¼ cup sliced celery
2 tablespoons vegetable oil
3½ cups cubed zucchini
1 medium tomato, chopped
**¾ teaspoon LAWRY'S® Garlic
 Salt**
**½ teaspoon LAWRY'S®
 Seasoned Pepper**
**¼ teaspoon dried oregano,
 crushed**

In medium skillet, sauté onion
and celery in oil 5 minutes. Add
remaining ingredients. Bring to
a boil; reduce heat and simmer,
covered, 10 minutes.
Makes 4 servings

Presentation: Serve with any
entrée and fresh bread.

Ratatouille

Skewered Grilled Potatoes

Crispened New Potatoes

1½ lbs. very small, scrubbed new potatoes (about 12)
½ cup QUAKER® Oat Bran™ hot cereal, uncooked
2 tablespoons grated Parmesan cheese
1 tablespoon snipped fresh parsley *or* 1 teaspoon dried parsley flakes
½ teaspoon snipped fresh dill *or* ½ teaspoon dried dill weed
½ teaspoon paprika
¼ cup skim milk
1 egg white, slightly beaten
1 tablespoon margarine, melted

Heat oven to 400°F. Lightly spray 11×7-inch dish with no-stick cooking spray or oil lightly. Cook whole potatoes in boiling water 15 minutes. Drain; rinse in cold water.

In shallow dish, combine oat bran, cheese, parsley, dill and paprika. In another shallow dish, combine milk and egg white. Coat each potato in oat bran mixture; shake off excess. Dip into egg mixture, then coat again with oat bran mixture. Place into prepared dish; drizzle with margarine. Cover; bake 10 minutes. Uncover; bake an additional 10 minutes or until potatoes are tender.

Makes 4 servings

Skewered Grilled Potatoes

2 pounds red potatoes, quartered
⅓ cup cold water
½ cup MIRACLE WHIP® Salad Dressing
¼ cup dry white wine or chicken broth
2 teaspoons dried rosemary leaves, crushed
1 teaspoon garlic powder

• Place potatoes and water in 2-quart microwave-safe casserole; cover.

• Microwave on HIGH 12 to 15 minutes or until tender, stirring after 8 minutes. Drain.

• Mix remaining ingredients until well blended. Stir in potatoes. Refrigerate 1 hour. Drain, reserving marinade.

• Arrange potatoes on skewers. Place on grill over hot coals (coals will be glowing). Grill, covered, 6 to 8 minutes or until potatoes are tender and golden brown, brushing occasionally with reserved marinade and turning after 4 minutes.

Makes 8 servings

Prep time: 20 minutes plus refrigerating
Grilling time: 8 minutes
Microwave cooking time: 15 minutes

Monterey Potatoes

4 cups peeled and sliced russet potatoes
¾ cup sliced red bell pepper
¼ cup chopped shallots
1 tablespoon all-purpose flour
1 teaspoon LAWRY'S® Garlic Salt
½ teaspoon dried basil, crushed
¼ teaspoon dry mustard
½ cup milk
1 cup (4 ounces) grated Monterey Jack cheese

In lightly greased 8-inch square microwave-safe baking dish, combine potatoes, bell pepper and shallots. Cover with plastic wrap, venting one corner. Microwave on HIGH 10 to 12 minutes, stirring every 4 minutes. Set aside and keep covered. In 2-cup glass measure, combine flour, Garlic Salt, basil and mustard; blend well. Gradually stir in milk. Microwave on HIGH 3 minutes, stirring after 1½ minutes. Add cheese; stir until cheese melts. Pour over potato mixture and toss to coat.

Makes 4 servings

Presentation: Serve as a side dish for most entrées.

Spicy Potatoes Olé

- **1 package (24 ounces) frozen diced potatoes (5 cups)**
- **2 tablespoons margarine or butter**
- **1 cup diced zucchini**
- **½ teaspoon chili powder**
- **1 can (11 ounces) CAMPBELL'S® condensed Nacho Cheese Soup**
- **1 can (8 ounces) whole kernel corn, drained**
- **½ cup shredded Monterey Jack cheese (2 ounces)**

1. In 3-quart saucepan over high heat, heat 1 quart salted water to boiling. Add potatoes. Return to boiling. Cook 2 minutes or until potatoes are tender. Drain in colander, reserving *½ cup* of the cooking liquid; set aside.

2. In same saucepan over medium heat, in hot margarine, cook zucchini and chili powder 2 minutes, stirring often.

3. Stir in soup, corn, cheese, cooked potatoes and reserved *½ cup* liquid. Cook 5 minutes or until heated through, stirring often. Serve with *sour cream*, if desired.   *Makes about 6 cups or 8 servings*

To microwave: In 2-quart microwave-safe casserole, combine potatoes and margarine. Cover with lid; microwave on HIGH 6 minutes or until potatoes are tender, stirring once during heating. Stir in zucchini, chili powder, soup and corn. Cover; microwave on HIGH 5 minutes or until vegetables are tender. Sprinkle with cheese. Let stand, uncovered, 2 minutes. Serve as directed above in step 3.

Savory Grilled Potatoes in Foil

- **½ cup MIRACLE WHIP® Salad Dressing**
- **3 garlic cloves, minced**
- **½ teaspoon paprika**
- **¼ teaspoon each: salt, pepper**
- **3 baking potatoes, cut into ¼-inch slices**
- **1 large onion, sliced**

• Mix salad dressing and seasonings in large bowl until well blended. Stir in potatoes and onions to coat.

• Divide potato mixture evenly among six 12-inch square pieces of heavy-duty foil. Seal each to form packet.

• Place foil packets on grill over medium-hot coals (coals will have slight glow). Grill, covered, 25 to 30 minutes or until potatoes are tender.
    Makes 6 servings

Prep time: 15 minutes
Grilling time: 30 minutes

Dole® Hawaiian Baked Potatoes

- **1 can (8 ounces) DOLE® Crushed Pineapple in Juice**
- **2 baking potatoes, baked***
- **½ cup pasteurized process cheese spread or canned cheese soup, heated**
- **½ cup chopped ham or 2 slices cooked, chopped bacon**
- **2 tablespoons chopped DOLE® Green Bell Pepper**
- **2 tablespoons chopped DOLE® Green Onion**

• Drain pineapple; save juice for a beverage.

• Split and open baked potatoes.

• Combine remaining ingredients in small bowl. Spoon over potatoes.   *Makes 2 servings*

*Prick potatoes with fork. Microwave on HIGH 10 to 15 minutes until fork inserts easily.

Preparation Time: 5 minutes
Cook Time: 15 minutes

Savory Grilled Potatoes in Foil

Kahlúa® Candied Yams

**4 medium-sized yams,
cooked* _or_ 1 can
(1 lb. 3 oz.) yams**
¼ cup butter
**⅓ cup firmly packed brown
sugar**
¼ cup KAHLÚA®

Cut yams in serving size pieces.
In heavy skillet, melt butter with
sugar. Add Kahlúa®; cook 1
minute. Add yams; turn until
brown on all sides. Cover. Reduce
heat; cook about 15 minutes.
Turn yams once more before
serving.
Makes 4 to 6 servings

*In large saucepan, boil yams
until tender but still firm.
Remove from pan; let cool
slightly. Peel.

Maple Glazed Sweet Potatoes

**1½ pounds sweet potatoes or
yams, cooked, peeled
and quartered**
**½ cup CARY'S®, MAPLE
ORCHARDS® or
MACDONALD'S™ Pure
Maple Syrup**
½ cup orange juice
**3 tablespoons margarine or
butter, melted**
1 tablespoon cornstarch
**1 teaspoon grated orange
peel**

Preheat oven to 350°F. Arrange
sweet potatoes in 1½-quart
shallow baking dish. Combine
remaining ingredients; pour over
potatoes. Bake 40 minutes or
until hot and sauce is thickened,
basting frequently. Refrigerate
leftovers.
Makes 6 to 8 servings

Vegetable Couscous

**1 can (10½ ounces)
CAMPBELL'S®
condensed Chicken
Broth**
1½ cups couscous, uncooked
2 tablespoons vegetable oil
**1 cup sliced fresh
mushrooms**
1 cup chopped onions
1 cup shredded carrots
**1 teaspoon grated fresh
ginger**
2 cloves garlic, minced
1 tablespoon soy sauce
1 tablespoon lemon juice

1. In 2-quart saucepan over high
heat, heat broth to boiling.
Remove from heat. Stir in
couscous. Cover; let stand 5
minutes.

2. Meanwhile, in 10-inch skillet
over medium heat, in hot oil,
cook mushrooms, onions, carrots,
ginger and garlic until
vegetables are tender-crisp,
stirring often. Stir in soy sauce
and lemon juice.

3. Add couscous. Heat through.
_Makes about 5 cups
or 10 servings_

Tip: Reheat leftover Vegetable
Couscous in your microwave
oven. Stir in 1 or 2 tablespoons
water, if needed.

Quick Vegetable Rice: Prepare
Vegetable Couscous as directed
above, _except_ substitute 1⅓ cups
uncooked _quick-cooking rice_ for
the couscous.

Easy Mideastern Pilaf

1½ cups beef broth
1 medium onion, chopped
¼ cup raisins
**2 tablespoons margarine or
butter**
**1½ cups Original MINUTE®
Rice**
½ cup sliced almonds
**2 tablespoon chopped
parsley**

Combine broth, onion, raisins
and margarine in medium
saucepan. Bring to full boil. Stir
in rice. Cover; remove from heat.
Let stand 5 minutes. Stir in
almonds and parsley. Serve with
kabobs or your favorite main
dish. _Makes 4 servings_

Oriental Rice Pilaf

½ cup chopped onion
1 clove garlic, minced
1 tablespoon sesame oil
1¾ cups beef broth
1 cup uncooked rice*
**1 tablespoon reduced-
sodium soy sauce**
**⅛ to ¼ teaspoon red pepper
flakes**
**⅓ cup thinly sliced green
onions**
⅓ cup diced red pepper
**2 tablespoons sesame seeds,
toasted**

Cook onion and garlic in oil in
2- to 3-quart saucepan over
medium heat until onion is
tender. Add broth, rice, soy
sauce, and pepper flakes. Bring
to a boil; stir once or twice.
Reduce heat; cover and simmer
15 minutes or until rice is tender
and liquid is absorbed. Stir
remaining ingredients into
cooked rice; cover and let stand 5
minutes. Fluff with fork.
Makes 6 servings

To microwave: Combine onion,
garlic, and oil in deep 2- to
3-quart microproof baking dish.
Cover and cook on HIGH 2
minutes. Add broth, rice, soy
sauce, and pepper flakes; stir.
Cover and cook on HIGH 5
minutes. Reduce setting to
MEDIUM (50% power) and cook,
covered, 15 minutes or until rice
is tender and liquid is absorbed.
Stir remaining ingredients into
cooked rice; cover and let stand 5
minutes. Fluff with fork.

*Recipe based on regular-milled
long grain white rice.

Favorite recipe from **USA Rice
Council**

Oriental Rice Pilaf

Bacon Pilaf

- 2 tablespoons unsalted margarine or butter
- 2 medium tomatoes, coarsely chopped
- ¼ cup sliced green onions
- 8 slices ARMOUR® Lower Salt Bacon, cooked crisp and crumbled
- 1 cup uncooked rice
- 1 teaspoon no salt added chicken-flavor instant bouillon

Melt margarine in large skillet or saucepan over medium heat. Add tomatoes and green onions; sauté for 2 minutes. Stir in 2 cups water and remaining ingredients. Heat to boiling; reduce heat and cover. Simmer about 20 to 25 minutes, or until liquid is absorbed. Fluff rice with fork before serving. Garnish with parsley, if desired.

Makes 4 to 6 servings

Spicy Monterey Rice

- 2 cups water
- 1 cup uncooked long grain rice
- 1 tablespoon WYLER'S® or STEERO® Chicken-Flavor Instant Bouillon *or* 3 Chicken-Flavor Bouillon Cubes
- 1 (16-ounce) container BORDEN® or MEADOW GOLD® Sour Cream, at room temperature
- 1½ cups (6 ounces) shredded Colby cheese
- 1 cup (4 ounces) shredded Monterey Jack cheese
- 1 (4-ounce) can chopped green chilies, undrained
- ½ cup chopped red bell pepper
- ⅛ teaspoon pepper

Preheat oven to 350°. In medium saucepan, combine water, rice and bouillon; bring to a boil. Reduce heat; cover and simmer 15 minutes or until rice is tender. In large bowl, combine all ingredients except ½ cup Colby cheese; mix well. Turn into buttered 1½-quart baking dish. Bake 20 to 25 minutes. Top with remaining ½ cup cheese; bake 3 minutes longer or until cheese melts. Let stand 5 minutes. Refrigerate leftovers. Garnish as desired. *Makes 6 servings*

Spicy Thai Rice

- 2 cups water
- 1 cup uncooked rice*
- ¼ cup chopped green onions
- 2 fresh red chiles, seeded and chopped
- 1 tablespoon snipped cilantro
- 1 tablespoon margarine
- 1 teaspoon minced fresh ginger root
- ¾ teaspoon salt
- ⅛ teaspoon ground turmeric
- 1 to 2 teaspoons lime juice
  Chopped roasted peanuts for garnish (optional)
  Red pepper flakes for garnish (optional)

Combine water, rice, onions, chiles, cilantro, margarine, ginger root, salt, and turmeric in 2- to 3-quart saucepan. Bring to a boil; stir once or twice. Reduce heat; cover and simmer 15 minutes or until rice is tender and liquid is absorbed. Stir in lime juice; fluff with fork. Garnish with peanuts and pepper flakes.

Makes 6 servings

*Recipe based on regular-milled long grain rice. For medium grain rice, use 1½ cups water. For brown rice, cook 45 minutes.

*Favorite recipe from **USA Rice Council***

Spicy Thai Rice

Arroz Blanco

1 tablespoon margarine
½ cup chopped onion
2 cloves garlic, minced
1 cup uncooked rice*
2 cups chicken broth

Melt margarine in 2- to 3-quart saucepan over medium heat. Add onion and garlic; cook until onion is tender. Add rice and broth. Bring to a boil; stir. Reduce heat; cover and simmer 15 minutes or until rice is tender and liquid is absorbed. Fluff with fork.   *Makes 6 servings*

To microwave: Combine margarine, onion, and garlic in deep 2- to 3-quart microproof baking dish. Cover and cook on HIGH 2 minutes. Stir in rice and broth; cover and cook on HIGH 5 minutes. Reduce setting to MEDIUM (50% power) and cook 15 minutes or until rice is tender and liquid is absorbed. Let stand 5 minutes. Fluff with fork.

*Recipe based on regular-milled long grain white rice.

Tip: Prepare a double batch of Arroz Blanco to have one batch ready for Rice with Tomato and Chiles or Green Rice (recipes follow) later in the week.

*Favorite recipe from **USA Rice Council***

Rice with Tomato and Chiles

1 green pepper, diced
½ cup chopped onion
1 jalapeño pepper, chopped
1 tablespoon olive oil
1 recipe Arroz Blanco
1 can (14½ ounces) whole tomatoes, drained and chopped
⅛ teaspoon dried oregano leaves
2 tablespoons snipped cilantro for garnish

Clockwise from top: Arroz Blanco, Green Rice and Rice with Tomato and Chiles

Cook green pepper, onion, and jalapeño pepper in oil in large skillet over medium-high heat until tender crisp. Stir in rice mixture, tomatoes, and oregano; cook 5 minutes longer. Garnish with cilantro.

Makes 6 servings

To microwave: Combine green pepper, onion, jalapeño pepper, and oil in 2- to 3-quart microproof baking dish. Cook on HIGH 3 to 4 minutes. Add rice mixture, tomatoes, and oregano; cover with waxed paper and cook on HIGH 3 to 4 minutes, stirring after 2 minutes. Garnish with cilantro.

Tip: To reduce the heat level of jalapeño peppers, scrape and discard the seeds and membranes before chopping.

*Favorite recipe from **USA Rice Council***

Green Rice

2 Anaheim chiles
1 jalapeño pepper
1 tablespoon margarine or olive oil
¼ cup sliced green onions
¼ cup snipped cilantro
1 recipe Arroz Blanco
¼ teaspoon dried oregano leaves

Chop chiles and pepper in food processor or blender until minced but not liquid. Melt margarine in large skillet over low heat. Add chile mixture and cook 1 minute over medium heat. Stir in onions and cilantro; cook 15 to 30 seconds. Add rice mixture and oregano; heat through.
Makes 6 servings

*Favorite recipe from **USA Rice Council***

Pepper Rice

Antipasto Rice

1½ cups water
½ cup tomato juice
1 cup uncooked rice*
1 teaspoon dried basil leaves
1 teaspoon dried oregano
  leaves
½ teaspoon salt (optional)
1 can (14 ounces) artichoke
  hearts, drained and
  quartered
1 jar (7 ounces) roasted red
  peppers, drained and
  chopped
1 can (2¼ ounces) sliced ripe
  olives, drained
2 tablespoons snipped
  parsley
2 tablespoons lemon juice
½ teaspoon ground black
  pepper
2 tablespoons grated
  Parmesan cheese

Combine water, tomato juice, rice, basil, oregano, and salt in 2- to 3-quart saucepan. Bring to a boil; stir once or twice. Reduce heat; cover and simmer 15 minutes or until rice is tender and liquid is absorbed. Stir in artichokes, red peppers, olives, parsley, lemon juice, and black pepper. Cook 5 minutes longer or until thoroughly heated. Sprinkle with cheese.

Makes 8 servings

*Recipe based on regular-milled long grain rice. For medium grain rice, use 1¼ cups water and cook for 15 minutes. For parboiled rice, use 1¾ cups water and cook for 20 to 25 minutes. For brown rice, use 1¾ cups water and cook for 45 to 50 minutes.

*Favorite recipe from **USA Rice Council***

Pepper Rice

2 teaspoons vegetable oil
1 teaspoon hot chili oil
½ cup diced red pepper
½ cup diced yellow pepper
½ cup diced green pepper
2 to 3 cloves fresh garlic,
  minced
3 cups cooked rice
½ teaspoon seasoned salt

Heat oils in large skillet; add peppers and garlic. Cook until tender. Stir in rice and salt. Cook 3 minutes, stirring constantly, until thoroughly heated.

Makes 6 servings

To microwave: Combine oils, peppers, and garlic in 2-quart microproof baking dish. Cook on HIGH 2 to 3 minutes. Add rice and salt; cook on HIGH 2 to 3 minutes or until rice is thoroughly heated.

Tip: Use lemon juice or toothpaste to remove garlic odor from hands after mincing.

*Favorite recipe from **USA Rice Council***

Spanish Rice au Gratin

Vegetable cooking spray
½ cup chopped onion
½ cup chopped celery
⅓ cup chopped green pepper
1 can (16 ounces) whole
  tomatoes, drained and
  chopped
1 teaspoon chili powder
½ teaspoon Worcestershire
  sauce
2 cups cooked brown rice
½ cup (2 ounces) shredded
  Cheddar cheese

Coat large skillet with cooking spray and place over medium-high heat until hot. Add onion, celery, and green pepper; cook until tender crisp. Add tomatoes, chili powder, and Worcestershire sauce. Stir in rice. Reduce heat; simmer about 5 minutes to blend flavors. Remove from heat. Top with cheese; cover and allow cheese to melt, about 3 minutes.

Makes 4 servings

Tip: Add your favorite canned beans, cooked ground beef, or chicken for a main-dish version.

*Favorite recipe from **USA Rice Council***

Antipasto Rice

Spinach Feta Rice

1 cup uncooked rice*
1 cup chicken broth
1 cup water
1 medium onion, chopped
1 cup (about 4 ounces) sliced fresh mushrooms
2 cloves garlic, minced
  Vegetable cooking spray
1 tablespoon lemon juice
½ teaspoon dried oregano leaves
6 cups shredded fresh spinach leaves (about ¼ pound)
4 ounces feta cheese, crumbled
  Freshly ground black pepper
  Chopped pimiento for garnish (optional)

Combine rice, broth, and water in medium saucepan. Bring to a boil; stir once or twice. Reduce heat; cover and simmer 15 minutes or until rice is tender and liquid is absorbed. Cook onion, mushrooms, and garlic in large skillet coated with cooking spray until onion is tender. Stir in lemon juice and oregano. Add spinach, cheese, mushroom mixture, and pepper to rice; toss lightly until spinach is wilted. Garnish with pimiento.

Makes 6 servings

*Recipe based on regular-milled long grain rice.

Favorite recipe from **USA Rice Council**

Pesto Rice and Vegetables

1½ cups packed basil, arugula, watercress, or spinach leaves
1 clove garlic
⅓ cup grated Parmesan cheese
1 tablespoon olive oil
  Vegetable cooking spray
1½ cups broccoli flowerets
1 cup sliced carrots
3 cups cooked brown or white rice

Finely mince basil and garlic in food processor. Add cheese and oil; pulse until well combined, scraping bowl as necessary. Coat large skillet with cooking spray and place over medium-high heat until hot. Cook broccoli and carrots until tender crisp. Stir in rice and basil mixture. Serve immediately.

Makes 6 servings

Favorite recipe from **USA Rice Council**

Saucy Peas and Rice

1 cup sliced mushrooms
1 tablespoon margarine or butter
1 package (10 ounces) BIRDS EYE® Green Peas
1 can (10¾ ounces) condensed cream of mushroom soup
1 cup milk
  Dash of pepper
1½ cups Original MINUTE® Rice

Cook and stir mushrooms in hot margarine in large skillet until lightly browned. Add peas, soup, milk and pepper. Bring to boil; reduce heat, cover and simmer 2 minutes. Stir in rice. Cover; remove from heat. Let stand 5 minutes. Fluff with fork.

Makes 4 servings

Microwave Directions: Mix ingredients in microwavable dish. Cover and cook at HIGH 3 minutes. Stir; cover and cook at HIGH 6 minutes longer. Fluff with fork.   *Makes 4 servings*

Saucy Peas and Rice

Quick Risotto

2¼ cups chicken broth, divided
1 cup uncooked rice*
Vegetable cooking spray
½ cup thinly sliced carrots
½ cup thinly sliced yellow squash
½ cup thinly sliced zucchini
¼ cup dry white wine
½ cup grated Parmesan cheese
¼ teaspoon ground white pepper

Combine 1¾ cups broth and rice in 3-quart saucepan. Bring to a boil; stir once or twice. Reduce heat; cover and simmer 15 minutes or until rice is tender and liquid is absorbed. Coat large skillet with cooking spray and place over medium-high heat until hot. Cook carrots, squash, and zucchini 2 to 3 minutes or until tender crisp. Add wine; cook 2 minutes longer. Set aside and keep warm. Add remaining ½ cup broth to hot rice; stir over medium-high heat until broth is absorbed. Stir in cheese, pepper, and reserved vegetables. Serve immediately.

Makes 6 servings

To microwave: Combine rice and 2 cups broth in 2-quart baking dish. Cover and cook on HIGH 5 minutes, then on MEDIUM (50% power) for 15 minutes. Cook carrots, squash, and zucchini in microproof dish coated with cooking spray on HIGH 3 to 4 minutes or until tender crisp; stir after 2 minutes. Combine with remaining ingredients and add to rice. Cook on HIGH 1 to 2 minutes, stirring after 1 minute.

*Recipe based on regular-milled medium grain rice.

Tip: Medium grain rice will yield the best consistency for risottos, but long grain rice can be used.

Favorite recipe from **USA Rice Council**

Carrots in Orange Rice

1½ cups sliced carrots
⅓ cup orange juice
⅓ cup raisins (optional)
1 cup Original MINUTE® Rice
½ teaspoon grated orange rind

Cook carrots in medium saucepan with water to cover until tender, about 10 minutes. Drain, reserving ¾ cup cooking liquid. Combine measured liquid, orange juice and raisins in medium saucepan. Bring to boil. Stir in rice and orange rind. Cover; remove from heat. Let stand 5 minutes. Stir in carrots.

Makes 4 servings

Lemon Rice

1 cup uncooked rice*
1 teaspoon margarine (optional)
1 clove garlic, minced
1 teaspoon grated lemon peel
⅛ to ¼ teaspoon ground black pepper
2 cups chicken broth
2 tablespoons snipped fresh parsley

Combine rice, margarine, garlic, lemon peel, pepper, and broth in 2- to 3-quart saucepan. Bring to a boil; stir once or twice. Reduce heat; cover and simmer 15 minutes or until rice is tender and liquid is absorbed. Stir in parsley.

Makes 6 servings

To microwave: Combine rice, margarine, garlic, lemon peel, pepper, and broth in deep 2- to 3-quart microproof baking dish. Cover and cook on HIGH 5 minutes. Reduce setting to MEDIUM (50% power) and cook 15 minutes or until rice is tender and liquid is absorbed. Stir in parsley.

*Recipe based on regular-milled long grain white rice.

Favorite recipe from **USA Rice Council**

Sherried Mushroom Rice

1 garlic clove, minced
1½ tablespoons margarine or butter
2 cups sliced mushrooms
¼ cup chopped red pepper
1 cup chicken broth
¼ cup water
¼ cup dry sherry or chicken broth
2 teaspoons dried minced onion
½ teaspoon salt
1½ cups Original MINUTE® Rice
2 tablespoons grated Parmesan cheese
1 tablespoon chopped parsley

Cook and stir garlic in hot margarine in large skillet 1 minute. Add mushrooms and red pepper; cook, stirring occasionally, 2 minutes.

Add broth, water, sherry, onion flakes and salt. Bring to boil. Stir in rice. Cover; remove from heat. Let stand 5 minutes. Fluff with fork and sprinkle with grated cheese and parsley. Serve with steak or your favorite main dish. Garnish as desired.

Makes 4 servings

Microwave Directions: Cut margarine into pieces. Cook garlic, margarine and mushrooms in microwavable dish at HIGH 2 to 3 minutes. Stir in remaining ingredients except Parmesan cheese and parsley. Cover and cook at HIGH 4 minutes. Fluff with fork and sprinkle with parmesan cheese and parsley. Serve with steak or your favorite main dish.

Makes 4 servings

Lemon Rice

Wild Rice Sauté

½ **cup sliced, fresh**
   mushrooms
¼ **cup chopped green onions**
1 **clove garlic, minced**
2 **tablespoons HOLLYWOOD®**
   Safflower Oil
3 **cups cooked wild rice**
¼ **teaspoon salt**
¼ **teaspoon ground black**
   pepper
¼ **teaspoon dried rosemary**
   sprigs
2 **tablespoons peach**
   schnapps liqueur

In a large skillet, sauté
mushrooms, onions and garlic in
hot oil for 1½ minutes. Add rice,
seasonings and peach schnapps;
cook 1½ minutes longer, stirring
frequently.   *Makes 6 servings*

Almond Brown Rice Stuffing

⅓ **cup slivered almonds**
2 **teaspoons margarine**
2 **medium tart red apples,**
   cored and diced
½ **cup chopped onion**
½ **cup chopped celery**
½ **teaspoon poultry**
   seasoning
¼ **teaspoon dried thyme**
   leaves
¼ **teaspoon ground white**
   pepper
3 **cups cooked brown rice**
   (cooked in chicken broth)

Cook almonds in margarine in
large skillet over medium-high
heat until golden brown. Add
apples, onion, celery, poultry
seasoning, thyme, and pepper;
cook until vegetables are tender

crisp. Stir in rice; cook until
thoroughly heated. Serve or use
as stuffing for poultry or pork
roast. Stuffing may be baked in
covered baking dish at 375°F. for
15 to 20 minutes.
     Makes 6 servings

Variations: For Mushroom
Stuffing, add 2 cups (about 8
ounces) sliced mushrooms; cook
with apples, onion, celery, and
seasonings.

For Raisin Stuffing, add ½ cup
raisins; cook with apples, onion,
celery, and seasonings.

Favorite recipe from **USA Rice
Council**

Apricot and Walnut Brown Rice Stuffing

½ **cup chopped onion**
½ **cup chopped celery**
1 **teaspoon margarine**
3 **cups cooked brown rice**
⅔ **cup coarsely chopped**
   dried apricots
¼ **cup coarsely chopped**
   walnuts
¼ **cup raisins, plumped***
2 **tablespoons snipped**
   parsley
½ **teaspoon dried thyme**
   leaves
¼ **teaspoon salt**
¼ **teaspoon rubbed sage**
¼ **teaspoon ground black**
   pepper
½ **cup chicken broth**

Cook onion and celery in
margarine in large skillet over
medium-high heat until tender
crisp. Add rice, apricots, walnuts,
raisins, parsley, thyme, salt,
sage, pepper, and broth; transfer
to 2-quart baking dish. Bake in
covered baking dish at 375°F. for
15 to 20 minutes. (Stuffing may
be baked inside poultry.)
     Makes 6 servings

*To plump raisins, cover with 1
cup boiling water. Let stand 1 to
2 minutes; drain.

Favorite recipe from **USA Rice
Council**

Almond Brown Rice Stuffing

Brown Rice Royal

**2 cups (about 8 ounces)
    sliced fresh mushrooms**
**½ cup thinly sliced green
    onions**
1 tablespoon vegetable oil
**3 cups cooked brown rice
    (cooked in beef broth)**

Cook mushrooms and onions in
oil in large skillet over medium-
high heat until tender. Add rice.
Stir until thoroughly heated.
Makes 6 servings

To microwave: Combine
mushrooms, onions, and oil in
2-quart microproof baking dish.
Cook on HIGH 2 to 3 minutes.
Add rice; continue to cook on
HIGH 3 to 4 minutes, stirring
after 2 minutes, or until
thoroughly heated.

*Favorite recipe from **USA Rice
Council***

Brown Rice Royal

Parmesan Gnocchi

1 cup milk
½ cup margarine *or* butter
½ teaspoon salt
1 cup all-purpose flour
4 eggs
**⅔ cup grated STELLA®
    Parmesan Cheese (about
    3 ounces), divided**
**2 tablespoons margarine *or*
    butter, melted**

1. In 5-quart Dutch oven, over
medium heat, heat 3 quarts
salted water to boiling. Reduce
heat so water maintains a
simmer.

2. Meanwhile, in 2-quart
saucepan over medium heat,
heat milk, ½ cup margarine and
salt to boiling. Boil until
margarine melts, stirring
occasionally. Remove from heat.
Quickly stir in flour all at once
until mixture forms a ball and
dough leaves side of pan.

3. Beat in eggs, one at a time,
until dough is shiny and smooth.
Beat in ⅓ *cup* of cheese.

4. Drop dough by teaspoonfuls
(about 1-inch pieces), 10 at a
time, into the simmering water.
Cook 4 minutes or until gnocchi
float to surface.

5. Remove gnocchi with slotted
spoon to colander; drain well.
Repeat with remaining dough.

6. Place gnocchi in greased 1½-
quart baking dish. Drizzle with 2
tablespoons melted margarine;
sprinkle with remaining ⅓ cup
cheese. Serve immediately or
bake in preheated 425°F. oven 10
minutes or until golden.
Makes 6 side-dish servings

Prep Time: 25 minutes
Cook Time: 25 minutes

Lemon Garlic Pasta Toss

**3 cloves garlic, finely
    chopped**
¼ cup olive or vegetable oil
**3 tablespoons REALEMON®
    Lemon Juice from
    Concentrate**
**2 teaspoons WYLER'S® or
    STEERO® Chicken-Flavor
    Instant Bouillon**
⅛ teaspoon pepper
**½ (1-pound) package
    CREAMETTE® Spaghetti,
    cooked as package
    directs and drained**
**¼ cup grated Parmesan
    cheese**
¼ cup chopped fresh parsley

In small skillet, cook garlic in oil
until golden. Add ReaLemon®
brand, bouillon and pepper; cook
and stir until bouillon dissolves.
In large bowl, toss hot pasta with
garlic mixture, cheese and
parsley; serve immediately.
Refrigerate leftovers.

Makes 4 servings

PIZZA & SANDWICHES

Pizza—one of America's favorite foods—is as much fun to make as it is to eat since you add your favorite tempting toppings. And with increasing popularity comes an array of innovative ingredients from pesto and shrimp to artichokes and pineapple. And sandwiches are not just for lunch boxes anymore. From grilled sizzling chicken sandwiches to pita pockets filled with spectacular salads to gourmet burgers, sandwiches are also perfect for outdoor dining or casual suppers.

Create-Your-Own Pizza

2 tablespoons olive *or* vegetable oil
2 cloves garlic, minced
1 package (16 ounces) hot roll mix
⅔ cup grated Parmesan cheese (about 2 ounces)

1. Preheat oven to 425°F. Grease 2 large cookie sheets. In small bowl, combine oil and garlic; set aside.

2. Prepare hot roll mix according to package directions for pizza crust. Divide dough in half; cover and let rest 5 minutes.

3. On lightly floured surface, roll 1 dough piece into a 12-inch round; place on prepared cookie sheet. Gently fold and roll edge of dough round to make 10-inch circle. Repeat with remaining dough piece. Brush *each* circle with oil mixture; sprinkle with cheese.

4. Bake prepared dough circles on 2 racks in oven 12 minutes or until golden brown, rotating cookie sheets halfway through baking for more even browning, if necessary. (Dough puffs up and spreads as it bakes.) Cool; wrap and freeze, if desired.
Makes 2 (12-inch) crusts

TO MAKE A PIZZA: Preheat oven to 425°F. Place fresh baked or frozen crust on cookie sheet. Spread crust with *⅔ cup PREGO® Regular Spaghetti Sauce, if desired. Top with 1½ cups desired Toppings (see below). Sprinkle with 1 cup shredded mozzarella cheese.* Bake 10 minutes or until hot and bubbly. Let stand 5 minutes. Cut into wedges.

Prep Time for Crusts: 35 minutes
Prep Time for Pizza: 10 minutes
Cook Time: 10 minutes

Toppings

Cooked Meats and Cooked Seafood: sweet (mild) or hot Italian sausage; ground beef, chicken, pork or turkey; fully cooked ham; sliced pepperoni or salami; drained flaked canned tuna, salmon or crabmeat; drained canned anchovy fillets, clams or shrimp.

Vegetables: thinly sliced green, sweet red or yellow peppers; sliced fresh or drained canned mushrooms; thinly sliced or shredded zucchini or yellow squash; small cooked broccoli flowerettes; drained canned artichoke hearts, cut up; cooked asparagus spears, cut up; sliced tomatoes or snipped sun-dried tomatoes; sliced or chopped onion or green onions; sliced, pitted ripe or green olives.

Create-Your-Own Pizza

Shrimp and Artichoke Pizzas

1 piece (2 ounces) Parmesan cheese
1 jar (6 ounces) marinated artichoke hearts
½ pound medium shrimp, shelled, deveined and *each* halved lengthwise
1 clove garlic, minced
1 loaf (16 ounces) frozen white bread dough, thawed
1 cup PREGO® Regular Spaghetti Sauce, divided
½ cup diagonally sliced green onions
1 tablespoon drained capers, optional

1. Preheat oven to 425°F. Lightly grease 2 cookie sheets. Using a very fine shredder, shred cheese into long, thin strips; set aside.

2. Drain artichoke hearts, reserving *2 tablespoons* of marinade. Cut *each* artichoke in quarters. In small bowl, combine shrimp with reserved marinade and garlic; toss to coat well.

3. In 8-inch skillet over high heat, cook shrimp and garlic, stirring frequently, 2 minutes or until shrimp are pink and opaque; set aside.

4. Divide thawed dough into 4 equal parts. On prepared cookie sheets, pat *each* piece of dough into an 8-inch round. Spread *each* round with ¼ cup of spaghetti sauce. Top with shrimp, artichoke hearts, green onions, capers and cheese.

5. Bake on 2 racks in oven 10 minutes or until crusts are lightly browned, rotating cookie sheets halfway through baking for more even browning, if necessary. Let stand 5 minutes. Cut into wedges.
Makes 4 main-dish servings

Prep Time: 25 minutes
Cook Time: 10 minutes

Tip: To thaw frozen bread dough, remove the dough from the package and place it in a rectangular baking dish. Thaw, covered, in the refrigerator overnight or at room temperature for about 5 hours.

Shrimp and Artichoke Pizzas

Spinach Pesto Pizza

1 package (10 ounces) frozen chopped spinach, thawed and well drained
½ cup grated Romano cheese (2 ounces)
¼ cup olive *or* vegetable oil
1 teaspoon dried basil leaves, crushed
1 clove garlic
1 loaf (16 ounces) frozen white bread dough, thawed*
1 cup PREGO® Regular Spaghetti Sauce *or* PREGO® EXTRA CHUNKY Tomato, Onion and Garlic Spaghetti Sauce
1 cup shredded fontinella cheese (4 ounces)
½ cup sliced large pitted ripe olives

1. Preheat oven to 400°F. Lightly grease 14-inch pizza pan or 15- by 10-inch jelly-roll pan.

2. In covered blender or food processor, combine spinach, Romano, oil, basil and garlic. Blend until smooth.

3. Pat dough into prepared pan. Spread spinach mixture to within 1 inch of edge. Spread spaghetti sauce over spinach mixture.

4. Bake 20 minutes; sprinkle with fontinella and olives. Bake 5 minutes more or until crust is lightly browned and cheese melts. Let stand 5 minutes. Cut into wedges or squares.
Makes 8 side-dish servings

Prep Time: 20 minutes
Cook Time: 25 minutes

*Thaw frozen bread dough overnight in the refrigerator or let stand, covered, at room temperature 5 hours.

Butter Crusted Pan Pizza

Butter Crusted Pan Pizza

Pizza Dough
1 package (¼ ounce) active dry yeast
½ cup warm water (105° to 115°F)
½ cup LAND O LAKES® Butter, melted, cooled (105° to 115°F)
3 to 3½ cups all-purpose flour
¼ cup freshly grated Parmesan cheese
2 teaspoons salt
3 eggs

Topping
¼ cup LAND O LAKES® Butter
3 cups (3 medium) thinly sliced onions
1 teaspoon minced fresh garlic
8 medium Roma (Italian) tomatoes, sliced ⅛ inch thick
1 teaspoon dried basil leaves
½ teaspoon coarsely ground pepper
½ cup freshly grated Parmesan cheese

For pizza dough, in large mixer bowl dissolve yeast in warm water. Add ½ cup cooled butter, *2 cups* flour, ¼ cup Parmesan cheese, salt and eggs. Beat at medium speed, scraping bowl often, until smooth, 1 to 2 minutes. By hand, stir in enough remaining flour to make dough easy to handle. Turn dough onto lightly floured surface; knead until smooth and elastic, 3 to 5 minutes. Place in greased bowl; turn greased side up. Cover; let rise in warm place until double in size, about 1 hour. Dough is ready if indentation remains when touched. Punch down dough; divide in half. Let stand 10 minutes.

Heat oven to 400°. For topping, in 10-inch skillet melt ¼ cup butter until sizzling. Add onions and garlic; cook over medium heat, stirring occasionally, until onions are tender, 6 to 8 minutes. Set aside. Pat one half of dough on bottom of greased 12-inch pizza pan. Repeat for second pizza. Divide sautéed onions between pizzas. On *each* pizza arrange half of tomato slices; sprinkle *each* with ½ *teaspoon* basil leaves and ¼ *teaspoon* coarsely ground pepper. Sprinkle *each* with ¼ *cup* Parmesan cheese. If desired, arrange additional suggested topping ingredients on pizzas. Bake for 16 to 22 minutes or until golden brown.
Makes 2 (12-inch) pizzas

Tip: Additional suggested toppings: sautéed red, yellow *or* green peppers; tiny cooked shrimp; chopped marinated artichokes; sliced green *or* ripe olives; etc.

Hawaiian Pineapple Pizza

1 long loaf (1 pound) French bread
1½ cups pizza sauce
4 ounces Canadian bacon, slivered
1 small DOLE® Green Bell Pepper, sliced
1 can (20 ounces) DOLE® Pineapple Tidbits in Juice, drained
2 cups shredded mozzarella cheese

• Cut bread lengthwise. Spread with pizza sauce.

• Top with remaining ingredients. Broil 4 inches from heat until cheese melts.
Makes 6 to 8 servings

Preparation Time: 15 minutes
Cook Time: 10 minutes

Popover Pizza

1 pound ground beef
1 large onion, chopped
2 cups PREGO® Regular Spaghetti Sauce
⅓ cup Chablis *or* other dry white wine
2 eggs
1 cup milk
1 tablespoon olive *or* vegetable oil
1 cup all-purpose flour
2 cups shredded mozzarella cheese (8 ounces)
½ cup grated Parmesan cheese (2 ounces)

1. Preheat oven to 400°F. In 10-inch skillet over medium heat, cook beef and onion until beef is thoroughly cooked and no pink remains, stirring to separate meat. Spoon off fat.

2. Add spaghetti sauce and wine; heat to boiling. Reduce heat to low. Simmer 10 minutes, stirring occasionally.

3. Meanwhile, in large bowl with wire whisk or fork, beat eggs, milk and oil. Add flour; beat until smooth.

4. Spoon hot meat sauce mixture into 13- by 9-inch baking dish. Sprinkle with mozzarella. Pour batter evenly over mixture. Sprinkle with Parmesan. Bake 30 minutes or until topping is puffed and golden brown. Cut into squares; *serve immediately.*
Makes 6 main-dish servings

Prep Time: 25 minutes
Cook Time: 30 minutes

Flip-Over Garden Pizza

Flip-Over Garden Pizza

⅓ cup olive *or* vegetable oil
1 medium eggplant, peeled and cubed (about 3 cups)
1 large green *or* sweet red pepper, cut into thin strips
1 medium onion, sliced
1 small zucchini, sliced
2 cloves garlic, minced
1 cup PREGO® Regular Spaghetti Sauce
¼ cup grated Parmesan cheese (1 ounce)
1 package (10 ounces) refrigerated pizza crust dough
1 cup shredded mozzarella cheese (4 ounces)

1. Preheat oven to 425°F.

2. In 10-inch ovenproof skillet over medium heat, in hot oil, cook eggplant, pepper, onion, zucchini and garlic until pepper is tender-crisp, stirring occasionally. Stir in spaghetti sauce and Parmesan; set aside.

3. Unroll and gently stretch pizza crust dough over vegetable mixture in skillet. Gently tuck edge of dough between vegetables and side of skillet. Bake 20 minutes or until crust is golden brown.

4. To serve: Carefully invert onto serving platter. Sprinkle with mozzarella. Let stand 5 minutes. Cut into wedges.
   Makes 8 side-dish servings

Prep Time: 20 minutes
Cook Time: 20 minutes

Mexicali Pizza

    Vegetable oil
 2 large flour tortillas *or* 4 small flour tortillas
 1 pound ground beef
 1 package (1.25 ounces) LAWRY'S® Taco Spices & Seasonings
 ¾ cup water
 1½ cups (6 ounces) grated Monterey Jack or Cheddar cheese
 3 tablespoons diced green chiles
 2 medium tomatoes, sliced
 1 can (2¼ ounces) sliced ripe olives, drained
 ½ cup salsa

In large skillet, pour in oil to ¼ inch depth; heat. (For small tortillas, use small skillet.) Fry each flour tortilla about 5 seconds. While still pliable, turn tortilla over. Fry until golden brown. (Edges of tortilla should turn up about ½ inch.) Drain well on paper towels. In medium skillet, brown ground beef until crumbly; drain fat. Add Taco Spices & Seasonings and water; blend well. Bring to a boil; reduce heat and simmer, uncovered, 5 minutes. Place fried tortillas on pizza pan. Layer taco meat, ½ of cheese, chiles, tomatoes, remaining ½ of cheese, olives and salsa on each fried tortilla. Bake, uncovered, in 425°F oven 15 minutes for large pizzas or 7 to 8 minutes for small pizzas.   *Makes 4 servings*

Presentation: For large pizza, cut into wedges for serving. Small pizzas may be cut in half or left whole.

Hint: One pound ground turkey or 1½ cups shredded, cooked chicken can be used in place of beef.

Vegetable Rice Pizza

Vegetable Rice Pizza

3 cups cooked rice
1 egg, beaten
1 cup (4 ounces) shredded mozzarella cheese, divided
Vegetable cooking spray
⅔ cup tomato sauce
2 teaspoons Italian seasoning
¼ teaspoon garlic powder
¼ teaspoon ground black pepper
1 tablespoon grated Parmesan cheese (optional)
1 cup (about 4 ounces) sliced fresh mushrooms
¾ cup thinly sliced zucchini
¼ cup sliced ripe olives
¼ cup diced red pepper
1 tablespoon snipped parsley

Combine rice, egg, and ⅓ cup mozzarella cheese in large bowl. Press into 12-inch pizza pan or 10-inch pie pan coated with cooking spray. Bake at 400°F. for 5 minutes. Combine tomato sauce, Italian seasoning, garlic powder, and black pepper in small bowl; spread over rice crust. Sprinkle with Parmesan cheese. Layer ⅓ cup mozzarella cheese, mushrooms, zucchini, olives, and red pepper. Top with remaining ⅓ cup mozzarella cheese and parsley. Bake at 400°F. for 8 to 10 minutes.

Makes 4 servings

Favorite recipe from **USA Rice Council**

Turkey and Cheese Calzones

1 package (16 ounces) hot roll mix
1 pound ground raw turkey
1 cup chopped onion
¾ cup PREGO® Regular Spaghetti Sauce
⅓ cup sliced pitted ripe olives
¼ cup chopped roasted sweet red pepper
1 cup shredded fontinella cheese (4 ounces)
1 cup diced provolone cheese (6 ounces)

1. Preheat oven to 425°F. Grease 2 large cookie sheets.

2. Prepare hot roll mix for pizza crust according to package directions. Divide dough into 6 pieces. Cover; let rest 5 minutes.

3. Meanwhile, in 10-inch skillet over medium heat, cook turkey and onion until turkey is thoroughly cooked and no pink remains, stirring to separate meat. Remove from heat.

4. Stir in spaghetti sauce, olives and roasted peppers, then fontinella and provolone; set aside.

5. On lightly floured surface roll *each* dough piece into 9-inch round. Spoon *about ½ cup* of turkey mixture on *half* of each round. Fold each circle over to form half round. Roll edges and crimp well to seal. Place on prepared cookie sheets.

6. Bake on 2 racks in oven 15 minutes or until crust is golden brown, rotating cookie sheets halfway through baking for more even browning, if necessary. Let stand 5 minutes.

Makes 6 sandwiches

Prep Time: 25 minutes
Cook Time: 15 minutes

Mini Broccoli Pizzas

2 cups small broccoli flowerets
½ cup sweet red pepper cut in strips
1 can (10¾ ounces) CAMPBELL'S® condensed Cream of Broccoli Soup
¼ teaspoon garlic powder
¼ teaspoon dried Italian seasoning, crushed
6 English muffins, split and toasted
2 cups shredded mozzarella cheese (8 ounces)

1. Preheat oven to 375°F.

2. Meanwhile, in small saucepan over high heat, in boiling water, cook broccoli and red pepper 3 minutes. Drain well; set aside.

3. In small bowl, combine soup, garlic and Italian seasoning. Spread soup mixture evenly over 12 muffin halves; place on cookie sheets. Top each with cooked broccoli and red pepper. Sprinkle with cheese. Bake 10 minutes or until cheese melts. Serve immediately.

Makes 12 mini pizzas

Tip: Choose from a variety of toppers such as: sliced pepperoni, chopped artichoke hearts, cooked shrimp, sliced green onions and sliced olives.

Mini Broccoli Pizzas

Tasty Turkey Burgers

1 pound ground fresh turkey
½ cup BENNETT'S® Chili Sauce
½ cup plain dry bread crumbs
1 egg, slightly beaten
¼ cup chopped green onions
1 teaspoon WYLER'S® or STEERO® Chicken-Flavor Instant Bouillon
Hamburger buns, split

In medium bowl, combine all ingredients except buns. Shape into 4 to 6 patties. Grill, broil or pan-fry as desired. Serve on buns with additional Bennett's® Chili Sauce. Garnish as desired. Refrigerate leftovers.

Makes 4 to 6 sandwiches

Burger Toppers

"Secret Recipe" Sauce

¾ cup MIRACLE WHIP® FREE® Dressing
3 tablespoons dill pickle relish
3 tablespoons catsup

• Mix ingredients until well blended; refrigerate.

Makes ¾ cup

Prep time: 5 minutes plus refrigerating

Zippy Mustard Sauce

¾ cup MIRACLE WHIP® FREE® Dressing
2 tablespoons KRAFT® Pure Prepared Mustard
2½ teaspoons Worcestershire sauce

• Mix ingredients until well blended; refrigerate.

Makes ¾ cup

Prep time: 5 minutes plus refrigerating

Cucumber Onion Sauce

½ cup MIRACLE WHIP® FREE® Dressing
¼ cup seeded chopped cucumber
1 tablespoon chopped onion

• Mix ingredients until well blended; refrigerate.

Makes ¾ cup

Prep time: 5 minutes plus refrigerating

All-American Cheeseburgers

1 pound lean ground beef
1 tablespoon WYLER'S® or STEERO® Beef-Flavor Instant Bouillon
¼ cup chopped onion
4 slices BORDEN® Singles Process American Cheese Food
4 hamburger buns, split, buttered and toasted
Lettuce
4 slices tomato

In medium bowl, combine beef, bouillon and onion; mix well. Shape into 4 patties. Grill or broil to desired doneness. Top with cheese food slices; heat until cheese food begins to melt. Top bottom halves of buns with lettuce, tomato and meat patties. Serve open-face or with bun tops. Refrigerate leftovers.

Makes 4 servings

Variations

Santa Fe Burgers: Add 3 tablespoons salsa or taco sauce to ground beef. On a warm tortilla, spread refried beans; top with shredded lettuce, cooked burger, cheese food slice, salsa and sour cream.

Kansas City Burgers: Add ½ cup thawed frozen hash browns and 2 tablespoons barbecue sauce to ground beef. Place each cooked burger on bun; top with cheese food slice, cooked, crumbled bacon and sliced green onion.

Seasoned Burgers

1 pound lean ground beef
1 teaspoon WYLER'S® or STEERO® Beef-Flavor Instant Bouillon

Combine ingredients; shape into patties. Grill or broil 5 to 7 minutes on each side or to desired doneness. Serve as desired.

Makes 4 servings

Variations

Italian Burgers: Combine beef mixture with 2 tablespoons grated Parmesan cheese and 1 teaspoon Italian seasoning. Prepare as above. Serve with pizza sauce. Garnish as desired.

Oriental Burgers: Combine beef mixture with 1 (8-ounce) can water chestnuts, drained and chopped, and ¼ cup sliced green onions. Prepare as above. Top with pineapple slice; serve with sweet and sour sauce.

Mexican Burgers: Combine beef mixture with 1 (4-ounce) can chopped green chilies, drained, and ¼ cup chopped onion. Prepare as above. Serve with sour cream and salsa.

Garden Burgers: Combine beef mixture with 1 tablespoon chopped green bell pepper and 2 tablespoons Thousand Island salad dressing. Prepare as above. Serve with coleslaw and chopped tomato.

Mid-West Burgers: Combine beef mixture with ½ cup frozen hash browns potatoes, thawed, and 2 tablespoons barbecue sauce. Prepare as above. Serve with barbecue sauce.

German Burgers: Combine beef mixture with 2 tablespoons chopped dill pickle and 1 teaspoon caraway seed. Prepare as above. Serve with sauerkraut if desired.

Clockwise from top left: Mexican Burger, Oriental Burger, Garden Burger and Italian Burger

Gourmet Olé Burgers

- 1½ pounds ground beef
- 1 package (1.25 ounces) LAWRY'S® Taco Spices & Seasonings
- ¼ cup ketchup
- Monterey Jack cheese slices
- Salsa

In medium bowl, combine ground beef, Taco Spices & Seasonings and ketchup; blend well. Shape into patties. Grill or broil burgers 5 to 7 minutes on each side or to desired doneness. Top each burger with a slice of cheese. Return to grill or broiler until cheese melts. Top with a dollop of salsa.

Makes 6 to 8 servings

Presentation: Serve on lettuce-lined hamburger buns. Garnish with avocado slices, if desired.

Hint: Cut cheese with cookie cutters for interesting shapes.

Gourmet Olé Burger

Barbecue Ham Sandwiches

- 1 cup ketchup
- 3 tablespoons REALEMON® Lemon Juice from Concentrate
- ¼ cup chopped onion
- ¼ cup firmly packed brown sugar
- 2 tablespoons Worcestershire sauce
- 1 teaspoon prepared mustard
- 1 pound thinly sliced cooked ham
- Buns or hard rolls, split

In medium saucepan, combine all ingredients except ham and buns. Simmer uncovered 5 minutes. Add ham; heat through. Serve on buns. Refrigerate leftovers.

Makes 6 to 8 sandwiches

Sloppy Joes

- 1 pound lean ground beef
- 1 (12-ounce) bottle BENNETT'S® Chili Sauce
- 1 teaspoon prepared mustard
- 1 teaspoon vinegar
- 1 teaspoon WYLER'S® or STEERO® Beef-Flavor Instant Bouillon
- 6 hamburger buns, split and toasted

In large skillet, brown meat; pour off fat. Add chili sauce, mustard, vinegar and bouillon; bring to a boil. Reduce heat; cover and simmer 15 minutes. Serve on buns. Refrigerate leftovers.

Makes 6 sandwiches

Sizzling Chicken Sandwiches

- 4 boneless, skinless chicken breast halves
- 1 package (1.27 ounces) LAWRY'S® Spices & Seasonings for Fajitas
- 1 cup chunky salsa
- ¼ cup water
- Lettuce
- 4 large sandwich buns, split
- 4 slices Monterey Jack cheese
- Red onion slices
- Avocado slices
- Chunky salsa

Place chicken in large resealable plastic bag. In small bowl, combine Spices & Seasonings for Fajitas, 1 cup salsa and water; pour over chicken. Marinate in refrigerator 2 hours. Remove chicken; reserve marinade. Grill or broil 5 to 7 minutes on each side, basting frequently with marinade, until chicken is cooked through. Place on lettuce-lined sandwich buns. Top with cheese, onion, avocado and salsa.

Makes 4 servings

Hint: Do not baste chicken with marinade during last 5 minutes of cooking.

Party Hero

¾ pound creamy coleslaw
⅓ cup bottled salad dressing
    (Thousand Island,
    creamy Italian or creamy
    blue cheese)
1 (8-inch) round loaf of bread
    (French, Italian, rye or
    sourdough), about
    1½ pounds
    Leaf lettuce
½ pound cooked turkey,
    thinly sliced
½ pound cooked ham, thinly
    sliced
¼ pound Cheddar, Muenster
    or Swiss cheese, sliced

Drain excess liquid from coleslaw; add *2 tablespoons* bottled dressing to coleslaw, mixing well. Cut a thin slice from top of bread; spread cut surface of slice with some of the bottled dressing. Hollow out bread, leaving about ½-inch-thick bread shell. Line bread shell with lettuce; brush with remaining bottled dressing. Press turkey onto bottom; cover with half of coleslaw mixture. Repeat with ham, remaining coleslaw mixture and cheese. Garnish with lettuce; cover with top bread slice. Place 6 to 8 long wooden picks into sandwich to secure. Chill no longer than 4 to 6 hours before serving. To serve, cut between picks to form 6 to 8 wedge-shaped sandwiches.

Makes 6 to 8 sandwiches

Favorite recipe from M&M/Mars

Party Hero

Marinated French Dip

2 cups water
⅓ cup REALEMON® Lemon
    Juice from Concentrate
⅓ cup soy sauce
1 medium onion, thinly sliced
2 teaspoons WYLER'S® or
    STEERO® Beef-Flavor
    Instant Bouillon *or*
    2 Beef-Flavor Bouillon
    Cubes
1 teaspoon thyme leaves
2 cloves garlic, finely
    chopped
1 (2-pound) beef brisket,
    pierced
6 French bread rolls, cut in
    half

In large shallow baking dish, combine all ingredients except brisket and bread; add brisket. Cover; marinate in refrigerator 6 hours or overnight, turning occasionally. Cover; roast at 325° for 2 to 2½ hours or until tender, turning after 45 minutes. Remove meat from baking dish; reserve cooking juices. Cut brisket into thin slices; serve on rolls with juices for dipping. Refrigerate leftovers.

Makes 6 to 8 servings

Tuna Cobb Salad Pockets

⅓ cup vegetable oil
¼ cup REALEMON® Lemon
    Juice from Concentrate
2 teaspoons red wine
    vinegar, optional
1 teaspoon sugar
½ teaspoon Worcestershire
    sauce
⅛ teaspoon garlic powder
1 (6½-ounce) can tuna,
    drained and flaked
2 cups shredded lettuce
½ cup diced avocado
½ cup diced tomato
1 hard-cooked egg, chopped
2 tablespoons cooked,
    crumbled bacon
2 tablespoons crumbled blue
    cheese
4 Pita bread rounds, cut in
    half

In medium bowl, combine oil, ReaLemon® brand, vinegar, sugar, Worcestershire and garlic powder; pour over tuna. Cover; marinate in refrigerator 1 hour. Stir in remaining ingredients except Pita bread. Serve in Pita bread. Refrigerate leftovers.

Makes 4 sandwiches

Sesame Chicken in Pitas

Sesame Chicken in Pitas

**½ cup MIRACLE WHIP®
   FREE® Dressing**
**1 tablespoon <u>each</u>: soy
   sauce, toasted sesame
   seeds**
**1 teaspoon sesame oil
   (optional)**
⅛ teaspoon ground ginger
**1 cup chopped cooked
   chicken**
**½ cup <u>each</u>: chopped
   Chinese pea pods,
   chopped red bell pepper**
¼ cup cashews
**2 whole wheat pita breads,
   cut in half**

• Mix dressing, soy sauce, sesame seeds, oil and ginger until well blended.

• Add chicken, vegetables and cashews; mix well. Spoon into pita pockets.

Makes 2 servings

Prep time: 15 minutes

Apple and Cheese Pitas

½ cup mayonnaise
1 tablespoon honey
**2 teaspoons Dijon-style
   mustard**
**2 whole wheat pita
   bread rounds
   (6 inches diameter)**
4 leaf lettuce leaves
**8 slices STELLA® Provolone
   Cheese**
**1 large apple, cored and
   thinly sliced**
**½ cup alfalfa sprouts
   Fresh strawberries,
   seedless green grapes,
   carrot sticks and fresh
   celery leaves for garnish**

1. In small bowl, combine mayonnaise, honey and mustard; set aside.

2. Cut *each* pita bread round in half, forming 4 pockets total. Spread *each* pocket with some mayonnaise mixture. Tuck a lettuce leaf, 2 cheese slices and ¼ of apple slices into *each* pocket. Top *each* sandwich with some sprouts. Garnish with strawberries, grapes, carrot sticks and celery leaves, if desired.

Makes 4 sandwich halves

Prep Time: 15 minutes

Amigo Pita Pocket Sandwiches

1 pound ground turkey
**1 package (1.25 ounces)
   LAWRY'S® Taco Spices &
   Seasonings**
**1 can (6 ounces) tomato
   paste**
½ cup water
**½ cup chopped green bell
   pepper**
**1 can (7 ounces) whole
   kernel corn, drained**
**8 pita breads
   Curly lettuce leaves
   Grated Cheddar cheese**

In large skillet, brown turkey; drain fat. Add remaining ingredients except pita bread, lettuce and cheese; blend well. Bring to a boil; reduce heat and simmer, uncovered, 15 minutes. Cut off top ¼ of pita breads. Open pita breads to form pockets. Line each with lettuce leaves. Spoon ½ cup filling into each pita bread and top with cheese.   *Makes 8 servings*

Presentation: Serve with vegetable sticks and fresh fruit.

Amigo Pita Pocket Sandwiches

Tuna Sandwich Melts

½ cup MIRACLE WHIP® Salad Dressing
1 can (6½ ounces) tuna in water, drained
½ cup chopped celery
½ cup (¼ pound) cubed VELVEETA® Pasteurized Process Cheese Spread
¼ cup chopped onion
4 hamburger buns, split

• Mix all ingredients except buns until well blended. Fill each bun with ½ cup tuna mixture. Place two sandwiches on paper towel.

• Microwave on HIGH 1 minute or until thoroughly heated. Repeat with remaining sandwiches.

Makes 4 sandwiches

Prep time: 15 minutes
Microwave cooking time: 2 minutes

Croissant Sandwich

1 beef flank steak (1¼ to 1½ pounds)
HEINZ® Worcestershire Sauce
1 package (3 ounces) cream cheese, softened
2 tablespoons minced green onions
1 tablespoon HEINZ® Worcestershire Sauce
Generous dash pepper
4 to 6 croissants, split, heated
Spinach, romaine or lettuce leaves

Generously sprinkle both sides of steak with Worcestershire sauce; broil steak 3 inches from heat source, 5 to 6 minutes per side. Cover; chill. In small bowl, combine cream cheese, green onions, 1 tablespoon Worcestershire sauce and pepper. Thinly slice meat diagonally across grain. Spread half of each croissant with cream cheese mixture; arrange one portion of meat on top. Cover meat with spinach; top with remaining croissant half.

Makes 4 to 6 servings
(½ cup cheese mixture)

Curried Turkey and Ham Croissants

1 pound fresh asparagus *or* 1 (10-ounce) package frozen asparagus spears, cooked and drained
12 ounces thinly sliced cooked ham
12 ounces thinly sliced cooked turkey breast
6 ounces sliced Swiss cheese
8 croissants, split
Curry Sauce

Preheat oven to 350°. Arrange equal amounts of asparagus, ham, turkey and cheese on bottom half of each croissant. Place top halves of croissants on cheese. Bake 10 to 15 minutes or until hot. Meanwhile, make Curry Sauce; spoon over croissants. Garnish with paprika if desired. Refrigerate leftovers.

Makes 8 servings

CURRY SAUCE: In small saucepan, melt ¼ cup margarine or butter; stir in 2 tablespoons flour, ½ teaspoon curry powder and ¼ teaspoon salt. Gradually add 1½ cups BORDEN® or MEADOW GOLD® Coffee Cream *or* Half-and-Half; over medium heat, cook and stir until thickened, about 5 minutes. Remove from heat; slowly stir in ¼ cup REALEMON® Lemon Juice from Concentrate.

Makes about 1½ cups

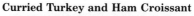

Curried Turkey and Ham Croissant

EGGS, CHEESE & BRUNCH DISHES

Rise and shine! You'll look forward to your wake-up call with this collection of glorious brunch recipes. Dazzle guests with a breathtaking buffet of frittatas, quiches and pancakes. From Brunch Potato Cassoulet to Scandinavian Salmon-Cheddar Pie, these enticing dishes are great morning, noon and night.

Saucy Mediterranean Frittata

Sauce

- **1 can (8 ounces) tomato sauce**
- **1 teaspoon dried minced onion**
- **¼ teaspoon dried basil leaves, crushed**
- **¼ teaspoon dried oregano leaves, crushed**
- **⅛ teaspoon minced dried garlic**
- **⅛ teaspoon pepper**

Frittata

- **⅓ cup chopped onion**
- **1 tablespoon olive oil**
- **1 medium tomato, chopped**
- **1 tablespoon finely chopped fresh basil *or* 1 teaspoon dried basil leaves, crushed**
- **¼ teaspoon dried oregano leaves, crushed**
- **⅓ cup cooked orzo**
- **⅓ cup chopped pitted ripe olives**
- **8 eggs**
- **½ teaspoon salt**
- **⅛ teaspoon pepper**
- **2 tablespoons butter**
- **½ cup (2 ounces) shredded mozzarella cheese**

For sauce, combine all sauce ingredients in small saucepan. Simmer over medium-low heat 5 minutes, stirring often. Set aside; keep warm.

For frittata, cook and stir onion in hot oil in *ovenproof* 10-inch skillet until tender. Add tomato, basil and oregano; cook and stir 3 minutes. Stir in orzo and olives; set aside. Beat eggs, salt and pepper in medium bowl. Stir in tomato mixture; set aside. Melt butter in same skillet. Add egg mixture; sprinkle with cheese. Cook over low heat 8 to 10 minutes until bottom and most of middle is set. Broil 1 to 2 minutes or until top is browned. Serve with sauce. Garnish as desired. Cut into wedges to serve.   *Makes 4 to 6 servings*

*Favorite recipe from **Kansas Poultry Association***

Italian Baked Frittata

- **1 cup broccoli flowerets**
- **½ cup sliced mushrooms**
- **½ red pepper, cut into rings**
- **2 green onions, sliced into 1-inch pieces**
- **1 tablespoon BLUE BONNET® Margarine**
- **8 eggs**
- **¼ cup GREY POUPON® Dijon Mustard or GREY POUPON® Country Dijon Mustard**
- **¼ cup water**
- **½ teaspoon Italian seasoning**
- **1 cup shredded Swiss cheese (4 ounces)**

In 10-inch ovenproof skillet, over medium-high heat, cook broccoli, mushrooms, red pepper and onions in margarine until tender-crisp, about 5 minutes. Remove from heat.

In small bowl, with electric mixer at medium speed, beat eggs, mustard, water and Italian seasoning until foamy; stir in cheese. Pour mixture into skillet over vegetables. Bake at 375°F for 20 to 25 minutes or until set. Serve immediately.

Makes 4 servings

Italian Baked Frittata

Italian Frittata

2 tablespoons margarine *or* butter
½ cup chopped onion
8 eggs
1 cup shredded fontinella cheese (4 ounces)
½ cup seeded and chopped tomato
2 tablespoons chopped fresh parsley
⅛ teaspoon pepper
2 tablespoons grated Parmesan cheese
1 cup PREGO® Regular Spaghetti Sauce
Sliced cherry tomatoes and fresh celery leaves for garnish

1. In 10-inch *oven-safe* skillet or omelet pan over medium heat, in hot margarine, cook onion until tender.

2. Meanwhile, in large bowl, beat eggs. Stir in fontinella, tomato, parsley and pepper. Pour over onion. Reduce heat to low.

3. Cook 6 minutes or until eggs are set 1 inch from edge. *Do not stir.* Remove from heat.

4. Sprinkle Parmesan over top. Broil 6 inches from heat 5 minutes or until golden brown.

5. Meanwhile, in 1-quart saucepan over medium heat, heat spaghetti sauce until hot.

6. To serve: Cut into wedges; top with spoonfuls of hot spaghetti sauce. Garnish with sliced cherry tomatoes and celery leaves, if desired.

Makes 4 main-dish servings

Prep Time: 15 minutes
Cook Time: 15 minutes

Cheesy Mushroom Frittata

Mushroom Frittata

1 teaspoon butter or margarine
1 medium zucchini, shredded
1 medium tomato, chopped
1 can (4 ounces) sliced mushrooms, drained
6 eggs, beaten
¼ cup milk
2 teaspoons Dijon mustard
½ teaspoon LAWRY'S® Seasoned Salt
½ teaspoon LAWRY'S® Seasoned Pepper
2 cups (8 ounces) grated Swiss cheese

In large, ovenproof skillet, melt butter and sauté zucchini, tomato and mushrooms 1 minute. In large bowl, combine remaining ingredients; blend well. Pour egg mixture into skillet; cook 10 minutes over low heat. To brown top, place skillet under broiler 2 to 3 minutes.

Makes 4 servings

Presentation: Serve directly from skillet or remove frittata to serving dish. Serve with additional Swiss cheese and fresh fruit.

Hint: Try serving frittata with prepared Lawry's® Spaghetti Sauce Seasoning Blend with Imported Mushrooms.

Italian Frittata

Cheesy Mushroom Frittata

1 can (10¾ ounces)
     CAMPBELL'S®
     condensed Cream of
     Mushroom Soup
6 eggs, slightly beaten
1½ cups shredded mozzarella
     cheese (6 ounces),
     divided
¼ teaspoon dried basil
     leaves, crushed
⅛ teaspoon pepper
2 tablespoons margarine or
     butter
1 cup sliced fresh
     mushrooms
1 medium onion, chopped
     Chopped fresh parsley for
     garnish
     Tomato wedges for garnish
     Fresh basil leaves for
     garnish

1. In medium bowl with wire whisk, beat soup until smooth. Gradually blend in eggs, *1 cup* of the cheese, the basil and pepper.

2. In 10-inch *oven-safe* omelet pan or skillet over medium heat, in hot margarine, cook mushrooms and onion until mushrooms are tender and liquid is evaporated, stirring occasionally.

3. Pour mixture into skillet. Reduce heat to low. Cook 6 minutes or until eggs are set 1 inch from edge. *Do not stir.* Remove from heat.

4. Broil 6 inches from heat 5 minutes or until frittata is puffy and lightly browned. Top with remaining cheese. Cover; let stand 2 minutes or until cheese melts. Garnish with parsley, tomato wedges and fresh basil.

Makes 5 servings

Turkey and Rice Quiche

3 cups cooked rice, cooled to
     room temperature
1½ cups chopped cooked
     turkey
1 medium tomato, seeded
     and finely diced
¼ cup sliced green onions
¼ cup finely diced green
     pepper
1 tablespoon chopped fresh
     basil *or* 1 teaspoon
     dried basil
½ teaspoon seasoned salt
⅛ to ¼ teaspoon ground red
     pepper
½ cup skim milk
3 eggs, beaten
     Vegetable cooking spray
½ cup (2 ounces) shredded
     Cheddar cheese
½ cup (2 ounces) shredded
     mozzarella cheese

Combine rice, turkey, tomato, onions, green pepper, basil, salt, red pepper, milk, and eggs in 13×9×2-inch pan coated with cooking spray. Top with cheeses. Bake at 375°F. for 20 minutes or until knife inserted near center comes out clean. To serve, cut quiche into 8 squares; cut each square diagonally into 2 triangles.   *Makes 8 servings (2 triangles each)*

Favorite recipe from **USA Rice Council**

Turkey and Rice Quiche

Wisconsin Swiss Linguine Tart

Wisconsin Swiss Linguine Tart

½ cup butter, divided
2 cloves garlic, minced
30 thin French bread slices
3 tablespoons all-purpose flour
1 teaspoon salt
¼ teaspoon white pepper
Dash ground nutmeg
2½ cups milk
¼ cup grated Wisconsin Parmesan cheese
2 eggs, beaten
8 ounces fresh linguine, cooked and drained
2 cups (8 ounces) shredded Wisconsin Swiss cheese, divided
⅓ cup sliced green onions
2 tablespoons minced fresh basil *or* 1 teaspoon dried basil leaves, crushed
2 plum tomatoes, each cut lengthwise into eighths

Melt ¼ cup butter in small saucepan over medium heat. Add garlic; cook 1 minute. Brush 10-inch pie plate with butter mixture. Line bottom and side of pie plate with bread, allowing 1-inch overhang. Brush bread with remaining butter mixture. Bake in preheated 400°F. oven 5 minutes or until lightly browned.

Melt remaining ¼ cup butter in medium saucepan over low heat. Stir in flour and seasonings. Gradually stir in milk; cook, stirring constantly, until thickened. Add Parmesan cheese. Stir some of the sauce into eggs; stir back into sauce. Set aside. Combine linguine, 1¼ cups Swiss cheese, onions and basil in large bowl. Pour sauce over linguine mixture; toss to coat. Pour into crust. Arrange tomatoes on top; sprinkle with remaining ¾ cup Swiss cheese. Bake in preheated 350°F. oven 25 minutes or until warm; let stand 5 minutes. Garnish as desired.
Makes 8 servings

Favorite recipe from **Wisconsin Milk Marketing Board** © *1992*

Double Onion Quiche

3 cups thinly sliced yellow onions
3 tablespoons butter or margarine
1 cup thinly sliced green onions
3 eggs
1 cup heavy cream
½ cup grated Parmesan cheese
¼ teaspoon hot pepper sauce
1 package (1 ounce) HIDDEN VALLEY RANCH® Milk Recipe Original Ranch® Salad Dressing Mix
1 9-inch deep-dish pastry shell, baked and cooled
Sprig fresh oregano

Preheat oven to 350°F. In medium skillet, sauté yellow onions in butter, stirring occasionally, about 10 minutes. Add green onions and cook 5 minutes longer. Remove from heat and let cool.

In large bowl, whisk eggs until frothy. Whisk in cream, cheese, pepper sauce and salad dressing mix. Stir in onion mixture. Pour egg and onion mixture into baked and cooled pastry shell. Bake until top is browned and knife inserted in center comes out clean, 35 to 40 minutes. Cool on wire rack 10 minutes before slicing. Garnish with oregano.
Makes 8 servings

Vegetable-Ricotta Pie

2 tablespoons vegetable oil
1 cup shredded carrots
1 cup sliced fresh mushrooms
½ cup finely chopped onion
2 garlic cloves, minced (optional)
¾ cup fresh or thawed and drained frozen chopped spinach
3 eggs
1 container (15 ounces) POLLY-O® Ricotta Cheese
¾ teaspoon salt
¼ teaspoon ground nutmeg
1 unbaked 9-inch quiche or pie shell

Preheat oven to 425°F. In medium skillet over medium heat, heat oil. In hot oil, sauté carrots, mushrooms, onion and garlic, 3 to 5 minutes until tender-crisp. Stir in spinach and cook 1 minute longer; remove from heat.

In medium bowl, beat eggs. Stir in ricotta, salt and nutmeg until well blended. Stir in vegetable mixture; mix well.

Pour mixture into pie shell. Bake 10 minutes. *Reduce oven temperature to 375°F.* Bake 35 minutes longer or until filling is set and crust is golden brown. Serve hot or refrigerate to serve cold or at room temperature.

Makes 6 servings

Preparation time: 20 minutes
Baking time: 45 minutes

Vegetable & Cheese Pot Pie

2 tablespoons butter or margarine
½ cup sliced green onions
1¾ cups water
1 package LIPTON® Noodles & Sauce—Chicken Flavor
1 package (16 ounces) frozen mixed vegetables, partially thawed
1 cup shredded mozzarella cheese (4 ounces)
1 teaspoon prepared mustard
½ cup milk
1 tablespoon all-purpose flour
Salt and pepper to taste
Pastry for 9-inch single-crust pie
1 egg yolk
1 tablespoon water

Preheat oven to 425°F. In large saucepan, melt butter and cook green onions over medium heat 3 minutes or until tender. Add 1¾ cups water and bring to a boil. Stir in noodles & chicken flavor sauce and vegetables, then continue boiling over medium heat, stirring occasionally, 7 minutes or until noodles are almost tender. Stir in cheese, mustard and milk blended with flour. Cook over medium heat, stirring frequently, 2 minutes or until thickened. Add salt and pepper.

Turn into greased 1-quart round casserole or soufflé dish, then top with pastry. Press pastry around edge of casserole to seal; trim excess pastry, then flute edges. (Use extra pastry to make decorative shapes.) Brush pastry with egg yolk beaten with 1 tablespoon water. With tip of knife, make small slits in pastry. Bake 12 minutes or until crust is golden brown.

Makes 4 servings

Vegetable-Ricotta Pie

Scandinavian Salmon-Cheddar Pie

    3 large eggs
    ¼ cup milk
    3 tablespoons chopped
       parsley, divided
    2 tablespoons butter, melted
    2 tablespoons minced green
       onion
    1 tablespoon plus 1 teaspoon
       lemon juice
    1 teaspoon Worcestershire
       sauce
    ½ teaspoon dry mustard
    2 cups (8 ounces) shredded
       Wisconsin Cheddar
       cheese
    ½ pound fresh cooked, flaked
       salmon *or* 1 can
       (6½ ounces) salmon,
       drained, deboned and
       flaked
    1 (9-inch) pie shell, baked
       and cooled
    ¾ cup dairy sour cream
    ¾ cup finely chopped
       cucumber
    1 teaspoon dill weed
    ⅛ teaspoon ground white
       pepper

Heat oven to 425°F. Beat eggs in large bowl; add milk, 2 tablespoons of the parsley, the butter, green onion, 1 tablespoon lemon juice, Worcestershire sauce and mustard; mix well. Fold in cheese and salmon; pour into cooled pie shell. Bake 20 to 25 minutes or until just set and crust is golden brown. Let stand 10 minutes before serving. Combine sour cream, cucumber, remaining 1 tablespoon parsley, dill, remaining 1 teaspoon lemon juice and pepper; mix well. Dollop each serving with sour cream mixture.

Makes 6 servings

Favorite recipe from **Wisconsin Milk Marketing Board** © **1992**

Rice Bran Granola Cereal

    2 cups uncooked old-
       fashioned rolled oats
    1 cup crisp rice cereal
    ¾ cup rice bran
    ¾ cup raisins
    ⅓ cup slivered almonds
    1 tablespoon ground
       cinnamon
    ⅓ cup honey
    1 tablespoon margarine,
       melted
    Vegetable cooking spray

Combine oats, cereal, bran, raisins, almonds, and cinnamon in large bowl; stir in honey and margarine. Spread mixture on baking sheet coated with cooking spray. Bake in preheated 350°F. oven for 8 to 10 minutes. Let cool. Serve as a topping for yogurt and/or fresh fruit. Store in a tightly covered container.

Makes 10 (½-cup) servings

Tip: Can be served as a cereal (with milk) or as a snack.

Favorite recipe from **USA Rice Council**

Scandinavian Salmon-Cheddar Pie

Praline Pancakes

    1½ cups skim milk
    2 tablespoons margarine,
       melted
    2 teaspoons brandy
    1 teaspoon vanilla extract
    1 cup all-purpose flour
    2 tablespoons sugar
    1 teaspoon baking powder
    ¼ teaspoon salt
    ⅛ teaspoon ground cinnamon
    1 cup cooked rice, cooled
    ⅓ cup pecans, coarsely
       chopped
    4 egg whites, stiffly beaten
    Vegetable cooking spray
    Reduced-calorie syrup
       (optional)

Combine milk, margarine, brandy, vanilla, flour, sugar, baking powder, salt, and cinnamon in large bowl; stir until smooth. Stir in rice and pecans. Fold in beaten egg whites. Pour scant ¼ cup batter onto hot griddle coated with cooking spray. Cook over medium heat until bubbles form on top and underside is lightly browned. Turn to brown other side. Serve warm drizzled with syrup.   *Makes 6 servings*

Favorite recipe from **USA Rice Council**

Rice Bran Buttermilk Pancakes

> **1 cup rice flour or**
> **all-purpose flour**
> **¾ cup rice bran**
> **1 tablespoon sugar**
> **1 teaspoon baking powder**
> **½ teaspoon baking soda**
> **1¼ cups low-fat buttermilk**
> **3 egg whites, beaten**
> **Vegetable cooking spray**
> **Fresh fruit or reduced-**
> **calorie syrup (optional)**

Sift together flour, bran, sugar, baking powder, and baking soda into large bowl. Combine buttermilk and egg whites in small bowl; add to flour mixture. Stir until smooth. Pour ¼ cup batter onto hot griddle coated with cooking spray. Cook over medium heat until bubbles form on top and underside is lightly browned. Turn to brown other side. Serve with fresh fruit or syrup.   *Makes about 10 (4-inch) pancakes*

Variation: For Cinnamon Pancakes, add 1 teaspoon ground cinnamon to dry ingredients.

Favorite recipe from **USA Rice Council**

Rice Bran Buttermilk Pancakes

Brunch Rice

Brown Rice, Mushroom, and Ham Hash

- 1 tablespoon olive oil
- 2 cups (about 8 ounces) sliced fresh mushrooms
- 1 small onion, minced
- 1 clove garlic, minced
- 3 cups cooked brown rice
- 1 cup (6 ounces) diced turkey ham
- ½ cup chopped walnuts (optional)
- ¼ cup snipped parsley
- 1 tablespoon white wine vinegar
- 1 tablespoon Dijon mustard
- ¼ teaspoon ground black pepper

Heat oil in Dutch oven or large saucepan over medium-low heat until hot. Add mushrooms, onion, and garlic; cook until tender. Stir in rice, ham, walnuts, parsley, vinegar, mustard, and pepper; cook, stirring until thoroughly heated.
Makes 8 servings

Favorite recipe from **USA Rice Council**

Brunch Rice

- 1 teaspoon margarine
- ¾ cup shredded carrots
- ¾ cup diced green pepper
- ¾ cup (about 3 ounces) sliced fresh mushrooms
- 6 egg whites, beaten
- 2 eggs, beaten
- ½ cup skim milk
- ½ teaspoon salt
- ¼ teaspoon black pepper
- 3 cups cooked brown rice
- ½ cup (2 ounces) shredded Cheddar cheese
- 6 corn tortillas, warmed (optional)

Heat margarine in large skillet over medium-high heat until hot. Add carrots, green pepper, and mushrooms; cook 2 minutes. Combine egg whites, eggs, milk, salt, and black pepper in small bowl. Reduce heat to medium and pour egg mixture over vegetables. Continue stirring 1½ to 2 minutes. Add rice and cheese; stir gently to separate grains. Heat 2 minutes. Serve immediately or spoon mixture into warmed corn tortillas.
Makes 6 servings

Favorite recipe from **USA Rice Council**

Breakfast in a Cup

- 3 cups cooked rice
- 1 cup (4 ounces) shredded Cheddar cheese, divided
- 1 can (4 ounces) diced green chiles
- 1 jar (2 ounces) diced pimientos, drained
- ⅓ cup skim milk
- 2 eggs, beaten
- ½ teaspoon ground cumin
- ½ teaspoon salt
- ½ teaspoon ground black pepper
  Vegetable cooking spray

Combine rice, ½ cup cheese, chiles, pimientos, milk, eggs, cumin, salt, and pepper in large bowl. Evenly divide mixture into 12 muffin cups coated with cooking spray. Sprinkle with remaining ½ cup cheese. Bake at 400°F. for 15 minutes or until set. *Makes 12 servings*

Tip: Breakfast cups may be stored in the freezer in tightly sealed container or freezer bag. To reheat frozen breakfast cups, microwave each cup on HIGH 1 minute.

Favorite recipe from **USA Rice Council**

Brunch Potato Cassoulet

Brunch Potato Cassoulet

- **2 tablespoons unsalted margarine or butter**
- **2 cups (8 ounces) ARMOUR® Lower Salt Ham, cut into ½-inch cubes**
- **2 cups frozen natural potato wedges**
- **1 cup sliced mushrooms**
- **½ cup chopped red onion**
- **½ cup chopped green bell pepper**
- **1 cup frozen speckled butter beans, cooked according to package directions, omitting salt, drained Lower salt cheese (optional)**

Preheat oven to 350°F. Melt margarine in large skillet over medium heat. Add ham, potatoes, mushrooms, onion and green bell pepper; cook over medium heat about 5 to 6 minutes, or until onion is soft. Stir in cooked beans. Transfer to medium earthenware pot or ovenproof Dutch oven. Bake, covered, about 10 to 12 minutes, or until heated through. If desired, sprinkle with lower salt cheese and broil 4 to 6 inches from heat source about 2 to 3 minutes or until cheese is melted and slightly browned.

Makes 4 to 6 servings

Ham Breakfast Sandwich

- **1 ounce Neufchatel or light cream cheese, softened**
- **2 teaspoons apricot spreadable fruit**
- **2 teaspoons plain nonfat yogurt**
- **6 slices raisin bread Lettuce leaves**
- **1 package (6 ounces) ECKRICH® Lite Lower Salt Ham**
- **3 Granny Smith apple rings**

Combine cheese, spreadable fruit and yogurt in small bowl. Spread on bread slices. To make each sandwich: Place lettuce on 1 slice bread. Top with 2 slices ham, 1 apple ring and another slice of bread.   *Makes 3 sandwiches*

Egg Foo Yong

- **2 cups water**
- **1 tablespoon soy sauce**
- **4 teaspoons WYLER'S® or STEERO® Chicken-Flavor Instant Bouillon**
- **2 tablespoons cornstarch**
- **3 eggs, well beaten**
- **1 (16-ounce) can fancy mixed Chinese-style vegetables, well drained**
- **1 (4¼-ounce) can ORLEANS® Shrimp, drained and soaked as label directs**
- **½ cup chopped green onions Vegetable oil Hot cooked rice**

In medium saucepan, combine *1½ cups* water, soy sauce and *2 teaspoons* bouillon. Cook and stir until bouillon dissolves. Mix cornstarch and remaining *½ cup* water; stir into bouillon mixture. Cook until thickened; set aside. In medium bowl, combine remaining ingredients except oil and rice. Let stand 10 minutes; stir. In large skillet, heat small amount of oil. Pour about ¼ cup egg mixture into pan to form each patty. Fry, a few at a time, until golden on both sides. Serve hot with sauce and rice. Refrigerate leftovers.

Makes 4 to 6 servings

Ham Breakfast Sandwich

BREADS, MUFFINS & COFFEECAKES

Fill your kitchen with the tantalizing aromas of homemade bread fresh from the oven! From quick-to-make muffins to slow-rising yeast breads, you'll create new family favorites. Make breakfast extra special with a heartwarming buttery coffeecake. Enhance a lunch-time salad with aromatic herb popovers. Or round off a hearty meal with wholesome wheat bread.

Apricot Date Mini-Loaves

1 package DUNCAN HINES® Bakery Style Cinnamon Swirl Muffin Mix
½ teaspoon baking powder
2 egg whites
⅔ cup water
½ cup chopped dried apricots
½ cup chopped dates

1. Preheat oven to 350°F. Grease four 5⅜×2⅝×1⅞-inch mini-loaf pans.

2. Combine muffin mix and baking powder in large bowl. Break up any lumps. Add egg whites, water, apricots and dates. Stir until well blended, about 50 strokes.

3. Knead swirl packet from Mix for 10 seconds before opening. Cut off one end of swirl packet. Squeeze contents onto batter. Swirl into batter with knife or spatula, folding from bottom of bowl to get an even swirl. Do not completely mix into batter. Divide evenly into pans. Sprinkle with contents of topping packet from Mix.

4. Bake at 350°F for 30 to 35 minutes or until toothpick inserted in center comes out clean. Cool 15 minutes. Loosen loaves from pans. Lift out with knife. Cool completely. Garnish as desired.   *4 Mini-Loaves*

Tip: This recipe may also be baked in greased 8½×4½×2½-inch loaf pan at 350°F for 55 to 60 minutes or until toothpick inserted in center comes out clean. Cool 10 minutes before removing loaf from pan.

Chocolate Chunk Banana Bread

2 eggs, lightly beaten
1 cup mashed ripe bananas (about 3 medium bananas)
⅓ cup vegetable oil
¼ cup milk
2 cups all-purpose flour
1 cup sugar
2 teaspoons CALUMET® Baking Powder
¼ teaspoon salt
1 package (4 ounces) BAKER'S® GERMAN'S® Sweet Chocolate, coarsely chopped
½ cup chopped nuts

HEAT oven to 350°F.

STIR eggs, bananas, oil and milk until well blended. Add flour, sugar, baking powder and salt; stir until just moistened. Stir in chocolate and nuts. Pour into greased 9×5-inch loaf pan.

BAKE for 55 minutes or until toothpick inserted in center comes out clean. Cool in pan 10 minutes. Remove from pan to cool on wire rack.

Makes 1 loaf

Prep time: 20 minutes
Baking time: 55 minutes

Apricot Date Mini-Loaves

Banana Macadamia Nut Bread

Banana Bran Loaf

> **1 cup mashed ripe bananas**
>   **(about 2 large)**
> **½ cup sugar**
> **⅓ cup liquid vegetable oil**
>   **margarine**
> **2 egg whites**
> **⅓ cup skim milk**
> **1¼ cups all-purpose flour**
>   **1 cup QUAKER® Oat Bran™**
>   **hot cereal, uncooked**
> **2 teaspoons baking powder**
> **½ teaspoon baking soda**

Heat oven to 350°F. Lightly spray 8×4-inch or 9×5-inch loaf pan with no stick cooking spray or oil lightly. Combine bananas, sugar, margarine, egg whites and milk; mix well. Add combined flour, oat bran, baking powder and baking soda, mixing just until moistened. Pour into prepared pan. Bake 55 to 60 minutes or until wooden pick inserted in center comes out clean. Cool 10 minutes in pan; remove to wire rack. Cool completely.

Makes 16 servings

Tips:

To freeze bread slices: Layer waxed paper between each slice of bread. Wrap securely in foil or place in freezer bag. Seal, label and freeze.

To reheat bread slices: Unwrap frozen bread slices; wrap in paper towel. Microwave at HIGH about 30 seconds for each slice, or until warm.

Corn Bread

> **¼ cup CRISCO® Shortening**
> **¼ cup sugar**
> **2 egg whites**
> **1 cup all-purpose flour**
> **1 cup yellow cornmeal**
> **4 teaspoons baking powder**
> **½ teaspoon salt (optional)**
> **1¼ cups skim milk**

Banana Macadamia Nut Bread

> **2 cups all-purpose flour**
> **¾ cup sugar**
> **½ cup LAND O LAKES®**
>   **Butter, softened**
> **2 eggs**
> **1 teaspoon baking soda**
> **½ teaspoon salt**
> **1 tablespoon grated orange**
>   **peel**
> **1 teaspoon vanilla**
> **1 cup mashed ripe bananas**
>   **(2 medium)**
> **¼ cup orange juice**
> **1 cup flaked coconut**
> **1 jar (3½ ounces) coarsely**
>   **chopped macadamia**
>   **nuts *or* walnuts (¾ cup)**

Heat oven to 350°. In large mixer bowl combine flour, sugar, butter, eggs, baking soda, salt, orange peel and vanilla. Beat at low speed, scraping bowl often, until well mixed, 2 to 3 minutes. Add bananas and orange juice. Continue beating, scraping bowl often, until well mixed, 1 minute. By hand, stir in coconut and nuts. (Batter will be thick.) Spread into 1 greased 9×5-inch loaf pan or 3 greased 5½×3-inch mini-loaf pans.

Bake 9×5-inch loaf for 60 to 65 minutes or mini loaves for 35 to 45 minutes, or until wooden pick inserted in center comes out clean. Cool 10 minutes; remove from pan.

Makes 1 (9×5-inch) loaf
or 3 mini loaves

1. Heat oven to 425°F. Grease 9-inch square pan.

2. Cream Crisco® and sugar with fork in medium bowl until blended. Add egg whites. Beat until fairly smooth.

3. Combine flour, cornmeal, baking powder and salt (if used) in separate bowl. Add to shortening mixture alternately with milk. Stir until dry ingredients are just moistened. Pour into pan.

4. Bake at 425°F for 20 minutes or until light golden brown around edges. Cut in squares. Serve warm.

Makes 9 servings

Pear Nut Bread with Citrus Cream Cheese

Pear Nut Bread
> **1 package (14 ounces) nut bread mix**
> **⅛ teaspoon ground nutmeg**
> **1 fresh California Bartlett pear, cored and finely chopped (about 1¼ cups)**

Citrus Cream Cheese
> **1 package (8 ounces) light cream cheese (Neufchatel), softened**
> **1 tablespoon finely grated orange peel**

Grease and flour 8×4×3-inch loaf pan. Prepare bread mix according to package directions, adding nutmeg and *substituting pear for ½ the liquid required.* Bake according to package directions. In small bowl, combine cream cheese and orange peel. Spread Citrus Cream Cheese on Pear Nut Bread.   *Makes 1 loaf*

*Favorite recipe from **California Tree Fruit Agreement***

Lemon Blueberry Poppy Seed Bread

Bread
> **1 package DUNCAN HINES® Bakery Style Blueberry Muffin Mix**
> **2 tablespoons poppy seed**
> **1 egg**
> **¾ cup water**
> **1 tablespoon grated lemon peel**

Drizzle
> **½ cup confectioners sugar**
> **1 tablespoon lemon juice**

1. Preheat oven to 350°F. Grease and flour 8½×4½×2½-inch loaf pan.

2. Rinse blueberries from Mix with cold water and drain.

3. **For bread,** combine muffin mix and poppy seed in medium bowl. Break up any lumps. Add egg and water. Stir until moistened, about 50 strokes. Fold in blueberries and lemon peel. Pour into pan. Sprinkle with contents of topping packet from Mix. Bake at 350°F for 1 hour or until toothpick inserted in center comes out clean. Cool in pan 10 minutes. Loosen loaf from pan. Invert onto cooling rack. Turn right-side up. Cool completely.

4. **For drizzle,** combine confectioners sugar and lemon juice in small bowl. Stir until smooth. Drizzle over loaf.

1 Loaf (12 Slices)

Tip: To help keep topping intact when removing loaf from pan, place aluminum foil over top.

Lemon Blueberry Poppy Seed Bread

Apple-Cranberry Muffins

1¾ cup *plus* 2 tablespoons
    all-purpose flour
½ cup sugar, divided
1½ teaspoons baking powder
½ teaspoon baking soda
½ teaspoon salt
1 egg
¾ cup milk
¾ cup sweetened applesauce
¼ cup butter or margarine,
    melted
1 cup fresh cranberries,
    coarsely chopped
½ teaspoon ground cinnamon

In medium bowl, combine 1¾ cups flour, ¼ cup sugar, baking powder, baking soda and salt. In small bowl, combine egg, milk, applesauce and butter; mix well. Add egg mixture to flour mixture; stir just until moistened. Batter will be lumpy; do not overmix. In small bowl, toss cranberries with remaining 2 tablespoons flour; fold into batter. Spoon batter evenly into 12 greased 2¾-inch muffin cups. In measuring cup, combine remaining ¼ cup sugar and cinnamon. Sprinkle over tops of muffins. Bake in preheated 400°F oven 20 to 25 minutes or until golden brown. Remove to wire rack to cool.
Makes 1 dozen muffins

*Favorite recipe from **Western New York Apple Growers Association, Inc.***

Apple-Walnut Muffins

2 cups all-purpose flour
⅔ cup sugar
2¼ teaspoons baking powder
¾ teaspoon salt
¼ teaspoon ground cinnamon
1 egg
⅔ cup milk
3 tablespoons vegetable oil
1 teaspoon grated lemon
    peel
¾ teaspoon vanilla
1 cup chopped DIAMOND®
    Walnuts
¾ cup coarsely grated pared
    apple

In medium bowl, sift flour with sugar, baking powder, salt and cinnamon. In small bowl, beat egg; add milk, oil, lemon peel and vanilla. Stir into dry ingredients, mixing just until flour is moistened. Fold in walnuts and apple. Spoon batter into 12 greased 2½-inch muffin cups. Bake in preheated 400°F oven 20 to 25 minutes or until golden brown and wooden pick inserted in center comes out clean.   *Makes 12 muffins*

Banana Blueberry Muffins

2 extra-ripe, medium DOLE®
    Bananas, peeled
2 eggs
1 cup firmly packed brown
    sugar
½ cup butter or margarine,
    melted
1 cup blueberries
1 teaspoon vanilla
2¼ cups all-purpose flour
2 teaspoons baking powder
½ teaspoon ground cinnamon
½ teaspoon salt

Purée bananas in blender. In medium bowl, combine 1 cup puréed bananas, eggs, sugar and butter until well blended. Stir in blueberries and vanilla. In large bowl, combine flour, baking powder, cinnamon and salt. Stir banana mixture into flour mixture until evenly moistened. Spoon batter into well greased 2½-inch muffin cups. Bake in 350°F oven 25 to 30 minutes or until wooden pick inserted in center comes out clean. Serve warm.   *Makes 12 muffins*

Pecan Peach Muffins

Topping (recipe follows)
1½ cups all-purpose flour
½ cup granulated sugar
2 teaspoons baking powder
1 teaspoon ground cinnamon
¼ teaspoon salt
½ cup butter or margarine,
    melted
¼ cup milk
1 egg
2 medium peaches, peeled,
    diced (about 1 cup)

Preheat oven to 400°F. Paper-line 12 (2½-inch) muffin cups. Prepare Topping; set aside.

In large bowl, combine flour, granulated sugar, baking powder, cinnamon and salt. In small bowl, combine butter, milk and egg until blended. Pour into flour mixture, stirring just until moistened. Fold in peaches. Spoon into muffin cups. Sprinkle Topping over batter. Bake 20 to 25 minutes or until wooden pick inserted in center comes out clean. Remove from pan.
Makes 12 muffins

TOPPING: In small bowl, combine ½ cup chopped pecans, ⅓ cup packed brown sugar, ¼ cup all-purpose flour and 1 teaspoon ground cinnamon. Add 2 tablespoons melted butter or margarine, stirring until mixture is crumbly.

**Clockwise from top right: Apple-Cranberry Muffins, Wholesome Wheat Bread (page 266) and
Nut-Filled Christmas Wreath (page 264)**

Chocolate Chunk Sour Cream Muffins

1½ **cups all-purpose flour**
½ **cup sugar**
1½ **teaspoons CALUMET®**
   Baking Powder
½ **teaspoon cinnamon**
¼ **teaspoon salt**
2 **eggs, lightly beaten**
½ **cup milk**
½ **cup sour cream or plain**
   yogurt
¼ **cup (½ stick) margarine,**
   melted
1 **teaspoon vanilla**
1 **package (4 ounces)**
   BAKER'S® GERMAN'S®
   Sweet Chocolate,
   chopped

HEAT oven to 375°F.

MIX flour, sugar, baking powder, cinnamon and salt; set aside. Stir eggs, milk, sour cream, margarine and vanilla in large bowl until well blended. Add flour mixture; stir just until moistened. Stir in chocolate.

FILL 12 paper- or foil-lined muffin cups ⅔ full with batter.

BAKE for 30 minutes or until toothpick inserted in center comes out clean. Remove from pan to cool on wire rack.

Makes 12 muffins

Prep time: 15 minutes
Baking time: 30 minutes

Streusel Raspberry Muffins

Pecan Streusel Topping
   (recipe follows)
1½ **cups all-purpose flour**
½ **cup sugar**
2 **teaspoons baking powder**
½ **cup milk**
½ **cup butter or margarine,**
   melted
1 **egg, beaten**
1 **cup fresh or individually**
   frozen whole unsugared
   raspberries

Preheat oven to 375°F. Grease or paper-line 12 (2½-inch) muffin cups. Prepare Pecan Streusel Topping; set aside.

In large bowl, combine flour, sugar and baking powder. In small bowl, combine milk, butter and egg until blended. Stir into flour mixture just until moistened. Spoon ½ of the batter into muffin cups. Divide raspberries among cups, then top with remaining batter. Sprinkle Pecan Streusel Topping over tops. Bake 25 to 30 minutes or until golden and wooden pick inserted in center comes out clean. Remove from pan.

Makes 12 muffins

PECAN STREUSEL TOPPING: In small bowl, combine ¼ cup *each* chopped pecans, firmly packed brown sugar and all-purpose flour. Stir in 2 tablespoons melted butter or margarine until mixture resembles moist crumbs.

Lemon Glazed Zucchini Muffins

2 **cups all-purpose flour**
⅔ **cup granulated sugar**
1 **tablespoon baking powder**
1 **teaspoon salt**
½ **teaspoon ground nutmeg**
2 **teaspoons grated lemon**
   peel
¾ **cup chopped walnuts,**
   pecans or hazelnuts
½ **cup dried fruit bits or**
   golden raisins
½ **cup milk**
⅓ **cup vegetable oil**
2 **eggs**
1 **cup zucchini, shredded,**
   packed into cup, not
   drained
½ **cup powdered sugar**
2 to 3 **teaspoons lemon juice**

Preheat oven to 400°F. Grease well or paper-line 12 (2½-inch) muffin cups. In large bowl, combine flour, granulated sugar, baking powder, salt, nutmeg and lemon peel. Stir in nuts and fruit. In small bowl, combine

Left to right: Chocolate Chunk Sour Cream Muffins and Chocolate Chunk Banana Bread (page 250)

milk, oil and eggs until blended. Pour into flour mixture; add zucchini, stirring just until moistened. Spoon into muffin cups. Bake 20 to 25 minutes or until wooden pick inserted in center comes out clean. Remove from pan. Meanwhile, in small bowl, combine powdered sugar and lemon juice until smooth. Drizzle over warm muffins.

Makes 12 muffins

Cinnamon Spiced Microwave Muffins

> 1½ cups all-purpose flour
> ½ cup sugar
> 2 teaspoons baking powder
> ½ teaspoon salt
> ½ teaspoon ground nutmeg
> ½ teaspoon ground coriander
> ½ teaspoon ground allspice
> ½ cup milk
> ⅓ cup butter or margarine, melted
> 1 egg
> ¼ cup sugar
> 1 teaspoon ground cinnamon
> ¼ cup butter or margarine, melted

In large bowl, combine flour, ½ cup sugar, baking powder, salt, nutmeg, coriander and allspice. In small bowl, combine milk, ⅓ cup melted butter and egg. Stir into flour mixture just until moistened.

Line 6 microwavable muffin-pan cups with double paper liners. Spoon batter into each cup, filling ½ full. Microwave at HIGH (100%) 2½ to 4½ minutes or until wooden pick inserted in center comes out clean. Rotate dish ½ turn halfway through cooking. Let stand 5 minutes. Remove from pan. Repeat procedure with remaining batter.

Meanwhile, combine remaining ¼ cup sugar and cinnamon in a shallow dish. Roll warm muffins in remaining ¼ cup melted butter, then sugar-cinnamon mixture. Serve warm.

Makes about 12 muffins

Chocolate Cherry Cordial Muffins

Chocolate Cherry Cordial Muffins

> 2 cups all-purpose flour
> ¼ cup granulated sugar
> ¼ cup firmly packed brown sugar
> 2 teaspoons baking powder
> ½ teaspoon baking soda
> ½ teaspoon salt
> One 11½-oz. pkg. (2 cups) NESTLÉ® Toll House® Milk Chocolate Morsels, divided
> ½ cup candied cherries, chopped, or raisins
> ¾ cup milk
> ⅓ cup vegetable oil
> 1 egg

Preheat oven to 375°F. Grease twelve muffin cups or line with cupcake liners. In large bowl, combine flour, granulated sugar, brown sugar, baking powder, baking soda and salt. Stir in 1¾ cups milk chocolate morsels and cherries; set aside.

In small bowl, combine milk, oil and egg. Stir into flour mixture just until moistened. Spoon into prepared muffin cups (muffin cups will be full). Sprinkle with remaining ¼ cup milk chocolate morsels.

Bake 18 to 21 minutes until golden. Cool 5 minutes; remove from pan. *Makes 1 dozen*

Mini Morsel Tea Biscuits

Preheat oven to 400°F. Grease two large cookie sheets. In large bowl, combine flour, sugar, baking powder and salt. With pastry blender or two knives, cut in butter until mixture resembles coarse crumbs. Stir in mini morsels; set aside. In small bowl, beat three eggs with evaporated milk and vanilla extract. Stir into dry ingredients just until soft dough forms.

Turn dough onto well-floured surface. Knead briefly. Pat dough to ¾-inch thickness. Cut with 2½-inch fluted round biscuit cutter. Place on prepared cookie sheets. Beat remaining egg with milk; brush over dough.

Bake 15 to 17 minutes until golden brown. Serve warm.

Makes about 1½ dozen

Peanut Orange Breakfast Puffs

        2 cups sifted all-purpose
            flour
        1 tablespoon baking powder
        1 teaspoon salt
     ¼ cup sugar
        1 egg, beaten
        1 cup milk
     ¼ cup peanut oil
     ½ cup chopped salted
            peanuts

Topping
     ¼ cup sugar
        1 teaspoon grated orange
            peel
     ¼ cup butter or margarine,
            melted

In large bowl, sift together flour, baking powder, salt and ¼ cup sugar. In small bowl, combine egg, milk and peanut oil. Add liquid all at once to flour mixture, stirring only until moistened. Fold in chopped peanuts. Fill greased 2½-inch muffin cups ⅔ full. Bake in preheated 425°F oven 15 to 20 minutes or until tops are lightly browned. Meanwhile, in small bowl, blend ¼ cup sugar and orange peel until crumbly. When muffins are baked, remove from muffin cups and immediately dip tops in melted butter, then in orange-sugar mixture. Serve warm.

Makes 12 muffins

Favorite recipe from **Oklahoma Peanut Commission**

Mini Morsel Tea Biscuits

        4 cups all-purpose flour
     ⅓ cup sugar
        2 tablespoons baking powder
     ½ teaspoon salt
     ½ cup (1 stick) butter or
            margarine
        1 cup (half of 12-oz. pkg.)
            NESTLÉ® Toll House®
            Semi-Sweet Chocolate
            Mini Morsels
        4 eggs, divided
        1 cup CARNATION®
            Evaporated Milk
     1½ teaspoons vanilla extract
        2 tablespoons milk

Southern Biscuit Muffins

     2½ cups all-purpose flour
     ¼ cup sugar
     1½ tablespoons baking powder
     ¾ cup cold butter or
            margarine
        1 cup cold milk

Preheat oven to 400°F. Grease 12 (2½-inch) muffin cups. (These muffins brown better on the sides and bottom when baked without paper liners.) In large bowl, combine flour, sugar and baking powder. Cut in butter until mixture resembles coarse crumbs. Stir in milk just until flour mixture is moistened. Spoon into muffin cups. Bake 20 minutes or until golden. Remove from pan. Cool on wire rack. Serve with jelly, jam or honey.

Makes 12 muffins

Southern Biscuit Muffin

Bacon Cheese Muffins

½ pound bacon
  (10 to 12 slices)
  Vegetable oil
1 egg, beaten
¾ cup milk
1¾ cups all-purpose flour
¼ cup sugar
1 tablespoon baking powder
1 cup (4 ounces) shredded
  Wisconsin Cheddar
  cheese
½ cup crunchy nutlike cereal
  nuggets

Preheat oven to 400°F. In large skillet, cook bacon over medium-high heat until crisp. Drain, reserve drippings. If necessary, add oil to drippings to measure ⅓ cup. In small bowl, combine ⅓ cup drippings, egg and milk; set aside. Crumble bacon; set aside.

In large bowl, combine flour, sugar and baking powder. Make well in center. Add drippings-egg mixture all at once to flour mixture, stirring just until moistened. Batter should be lumpy. Fold in bacon, cheese and cereal. Spoon into buttered or paper-lined 2½-inch muffin cups, filling about ¾ full. Bake 15 to 20 minutes or until golden. Remove from pan. Cool on wire rack.   *Makes 12 muffins*

*Favorite recipe from **Wisconsin Milk Marketing Board** © 1992*

Calico Bell Pepper Muffins

¼ cup *each* finely chopped
  red, yellow and green
  bell pepper
¼ cup butter or margarine
2 cups all-purpose flour
2 tablespoons sugar
1 tablespoon baking powder
¾ teaspoon salt
½ teaspoon dried basil leaves
1 cup milk
2 eggs

Preheat oven to 400°F. Grease or paper-line 12 (2½-inch) muffin cups. In small skillet, over medium-high heat, cook peppers in butter until color is bright and peppers are tender crisp about 3 minutes. Set aside.

In large bowl, combine flour, sugar, baking powder, salt and basil. In small bowl, combine milk and eggs until blended. Add milk mixture and peppers and any liquid in skillet to flour mixture. Stir just until moistened. Spoon into muffin cups. Bake 15 minutes or until golden and wooden pick inserted in center comes out clean. Remove from pan. Serve warm.
          Makes 12 muffins

Calico Bell Pepper Muffins

Fresh Sage & Pepper Popovers

Popovers
> **3 eggs, room temperature**
> **1¼ cups milk, room temperature**
> **1¼ cups all-purpose flour**
> **1½ teaspoons fresh sage leaves,* rubbed**
> **¼ teaspoon coarsely ground pepper**
> **¼ teaspoon salt**

Sage Butter
> **½ cup LAND O LAKES® Butter, softened**
> **1½ teaspoons fresh sage leaves,* rubbed**
> **¼ teaspoon coarsely ground pepper**

Heat oven to 450°. For popovers, in small mixer bowl beat eggs at medium speed, scraping bowl often, until light yellow, 1 to 2 minutes. Add milk; continue beating for 1 minute to incorporate air. By hand, stir in all remaining popover ingredients. Pour batter into greased 6-cup popover pan or 6 custard cups. Bake for 15 minutes; *reduce temperature to 350°. Do not open oven.* Continue baking for 25 to 30 minutes or until golden brown.

For Sage Butter, in small mixer bowl beat all Sage Butter ingredients at low speed, scraping bowl often, until light and fluffy, 1 to 2 minutes; set aside.

Insert knife in popovers to allow steam to escape. Serve immediately with sage butter.
Makes 6 popovers

Tip: Eggs and milk should be at room temperature (72°F) to help ensure successful popovers.

*You may substitute ½ teaspoon dried sage leaves, crumbled, for the 1½ teaspoons fresh sage leaves, rubbed.

Italian Parmesan Twists

> **1 cup grated Parmesan cheese**
> **1½ teaspoons Italian herb seasoning***
> **1 loaf frozen bread dough, thawed**
> **⅓ cup LAND O LAKES® Butter, melted**
> **Pizza sauce, warmed**

Heat oven to 450°. In 9-inch pie pan combine Parmesan cheese and Italian seasoning. Divide dough into 8 sections; divide *each* section into 4 pieces. (There should be 32 pieces of dough.) Roll *each* piece into 4-inch rope. Dip *each* rope in melted butter; roll in Parmesan mixture. Twist rope 3 times. Place on greased cookie sheets. Bake for 7 to 9 minutes or until golden brown. Serve warm with pizza sauce.
Makes 32 twists

*You may substitute ¼ teaspoon *each* dried oregano leaves, dried marjoram leaves and dried basil leaves and ⅛ teaspoon rubbed sage for the 1½ teaspoons Italian herb seasoning.

Broiled Herb Baguettes

> **¼ cup MIRACLE WHIP® Salad Dressing**
> **½ teaspoon each: garlic salt, Italian seasoning**
> **4 drops hot pepper sauce**
> **2 tablespoons KRAFT® 100% Grated Parmesan Cheese**
> **4 French bread rolls, split**

• Mix all ingredients except bread until well blended.

• Evenly spread salad dressing mixture onto bread halves. Broil 3 to 4 minutes or until golden brown. *Makes 4 servings*

Prep time: 5 minutes
Cooking time: 4 minutes

Quicky Sticky Buns

> **3 tablespoons packed brown sugar, divided**
> **¼ cup KARO® Light or Dark Corn Syrup**
> **¼ cup coarsely chopped pecans**
> **2 tablespoons softened MAZOLA® Margarine, divided**
> **1 can (8 ounces) refrigerated crescent dinner rolls**
> **1 teaspoon cinnamon**

Preheat oven to 350°F. In small bowl combine 2 tablespoons of the brown sugar, the corn syrup, pecans and 1 tablespoon of the margarine. Spoon about 2 teaspoons mixture into each of 9 (2½-inch) muffin pan cups. Unroll entire crescent roll dough; pinch seams together to form 1 rectangle. Combine remaining 1 tablespoon brown sugar and the cinnamon. Spread dough with remaining 1 tablespoon margarine; sprinkle with cinnamon mixture. Roll up from short end. Cut into 9 slices. Place one slice in each prepared muffin pan cup. Bake 25 minutes or until golden brown. Immediately invert pan onto cookie sheet or tray; cool 10 minutes.
Makes 9 buns

Preparation Time: 15 minutes
Bake Time: 25 minutes, plus cooling

Quicky Sticky Buns

Hot Cross Buns

Buns:
    2 pkgs. active dry yeast
    ½ cup warm water
        (105° to 115°F)
    1 cup warm milk
        (105° to 115°F)
    ½ cup (1 stick) butter,
        softened
    ½ cup granulated sugar
    3 eggs
    ½ teaspoon salt
    ½ teaspoon vanilla extract
    5 to 5½ cups all-purpose
        flour, divided
    1 cup raisins
    ½ teaspoon cinnamon
One 12-oz.pkg. (2 cups)
        NESTLÉ® Toll House®
        Semi-Sweet Chocolate
        Morsels

Glaze:
    1 cup confectioners' sugar
    2 tablespoons milk

Buns: Grease two 13×9-inch baking pans. In small bowl, dissolve yeast in warm water; let stand 10 minutes. In large bowl, combine warm milk, butter, granulated sugar, eggs, salt and vanilla extract. Add yeast mixture. Stir in 2 cups flour, raisins and cinnamon. Gradually stir in enough remaining flour to make a soft dough. Turn dough onto lightly floured surface. Knead 2 minutes. Knead in semi-sweet chocolate morsels; continue kneading 3 minutes or until dough is smooth and elastic.

Place dough in lightly greased bowl; turn over to grease surface. Cover with cloth towel; let rise in warm place (70° to 75°F) until double in bulk, about 1 hour. Punch down dough; cover and let rise 30 minutes longer.

Punch down dough; divide into 24 pieces. Shape each piece into a smooth ball. Place 12 balls in each prepared pan. Cover; let rise in warm place until double in bulk, about 45 minutes.

Preheat oven to 350°F. Bake 20 to 25 minutes until golden brown. Cool 15 minutes.

Glaze: In small bowl, combine confectioners' sugar and milk, stirring until smooth. Drizzle glaze over buns, forming a cross on each. Serve warm or cool completely. *Makes 24 buns*

Almond Butter Loaves

Crust
    ½ cup firmly packed brown
        sugar
    ⅓ cup butter or margarine,
        softened
    1 cup toasted almonds, finely
        chopped (see Tip)
    ½ cup all-purpose flour

Cake
    1 package DUNCAN HINES®
        Moist Deluxe Butter
        Recipe Golden Cake Mix
    3 eggs
    ⅔ cup water
    ½ cup butter or margarine,
        softened

Glaze
    1 cup confectioners sugar
    1 to 2 tablespoons water
    ¼ teaspoon almond extract
    3 tablespoons sliced
        almonds, for garnish

1. Preheat oven to 350°F. Grease and flour two 9×5×3-inch loaf pans.

2. **For crust,** combine brown sugar and ⅓ cup butter in large bowl. Beat at medium speed with electric mixer until light and fluffy. Stir in toasted almonds and flour. Blend well. Divide and press evenly into pans.

3. **For cake,** combine cake mix, eggs, ⅔ cup water and ½ cup butter in large bowl. Beat at medium speed with electric mixer for 4 minutes. Pour into pans. Bake at 350°F for 45 to 50 minutes or until toothpick inserted in center comes out clean. Cool in pans 10 minutes. Invert onto cooling racks, crust-side up. Cool completely.

4. **For glaze,** combine confectioners sugar, 1 tablespoon water and almond extract in small bowl. Stir until smooth. Add water, 1 teaspoon at a time, until glaze is desired consistency. Spoon over cooled loaves. Sprinkle sliced almonds over top. *2 Loaves (16 Slices)*

Note: For ease in slicing loaves, use a serrated knife.

Tip: To toast almonds, spread in a single layer on baking sheet. Bake at 325°F for 6 to 8 minutes or until fragrant and light golden brown. Cool before chopping.

Almond Butter Loaf

Cranberry Streusel Coffee Cake

Cake Batter
1½ cups flour
1½ teaspoons baking powder
½ teaspoon salt
6 tablespoons (¾ stick) unsalted butter, softened
¾ cup granulated sugar
2 teaspoons grated orange peel
2 eggs
½ cup milk

Streusel
½ cup light brown sugar
¼ cup flour
½ teaspoon cinnamon
2 tablespoons butter, softened
½ cup chopped walnuts

Cranberry Filling
1½ cups OCEAN SPRAY® fresh or frozen Cranberries
¼ cup granulated sugar
2 tablespoons orange juice

1. Preheat oven to 350°F. Grease and flour 8-inch square cake pan. Stir together flour, baking powder and salt on piece of waxed paper until well mixed.

2. Cream together 6 tablespoons butter, ¾ cup granulated sugar and orange peel in large bowl. Add eggs, one at a time, beating well after each addition. Stir in flour mixture alternately with milk, beginning and ending with flour. Set batter aside.

3. For streusel, combine all streusel ingredients in small bowl. Mix together with fork until crumbly; set aside.

4. For cranberry filling, place filling ingredients in a small saucepan. Cook over medium heat, stirring constantly, until berries start to pop. Remove from heat; cool to room temperature.

5. Spread half of the cake batter over bottom of prepared pan. Sprinkle with half of the streusel; spoon on half of the cranberry filling. Cover with remaining batter; top with remaining filling and streusel.

Sock-It-To-Me Cake

6. Bake 50 to 60 minutes until toothpick inserted in center comes out clean. Cool on wire rack. Serve warm or cool slightly.

Makes about 9 servings

Sock-It-To-Me Cake

Streusel Filling
1 package DUNCAN HINES® Moist Deluxe Butter Recipe Golden Cake Mix, divided
2 tablespoons brown sugar
2 teaspoons ground cinnamon
1 cup finely chopped pecans

Cake
4 eggs
1 cup dairy sour cream
⅓ cup CRISCO® Oil or CRISCO® PURITAN® Oil
¼ cup water
¼ cup granulated sugar

Glaze
1 cup confectioners sugar
1 tablespoon milk

1. Preheat oven to 375°F. Grease and flour 10-inch tube pan.

2. **For streusel filling**, combine 2 tablespoons cake mix, brown sugar and cinnamon in medium bowl. Stir in pecans. Set aside.

3. **For cake**, combine remaining cake mix, eggs, sour cream, oil, water and granulated sugar in large bowl. Beat at medium speed with electric mixer for 2 minutes. Pour two-thirds of batter into pan. Sprinkle with streusel filling. Spoon remaining batter evenly over filling. Bake at 375°F for 45 to 55 minutes or until toothpick inserted in center comes out clean. Cool in pan 25 minutes. Invert onto serving plate. Cool completely.

4. **For glaze,** combine confectioners sugar and milk in small bowl. Stir until smooth. Add more milk to thin glaze as needed. Drizzle over cake.

12 to 16 Servings

Tip: For a quick glaze, heat ½ cup Duncan Hines® Vanilla Frosting in small saucepan over medium heat, stirring constantly, until thin.

Breakfast Raisin Ring

Breakfast Raisin Ring

- 1 package (8 ounces) **PHILADELPHIA BRAND®** Cream Cheese, cubed
- 1 cup cold water
- 1 package (16 ounces) hot roll mix
- 1 egg
- 1 teaspoon vanilla
- ½ cup packed brown sugar
- ⅓ cup **PARKAY®** Margarine
- ¼ cup granulated sugar
- 1½ teaspoons ground cinnamon
- 1½ teaspoons vanilla
- ½ cup golden raisins Vanilla Drizzle

• Blend 6 ounces cream cheese and water in small saucepan. Cook over low heat until mixture reaches 115° to 120°F, stirring occasionally.

• Stir hot roll mix and yeast packet in large bowl. Add cream cheese mixture, egg and 1 teaspoon vanilla, mixing until dough pulls away from sides of bowl.

• Knead dough on lightly floured surface 5 minutes or until smooth and elastic. Cover; let rise in warm place 20 minutes.

• Beat remaining cream cheese, brown sugar, margarine, granulated sugar, cinnamon and

1½ teaspoons vanilla in small mixing bowl at medium speed with electric mixer until well blended.

• Roll out dough to 20×12-inch rectangle; spread cream cheese mixture over dough to within 1½ inches from outer edges of dough. Sprinkle with raisins.

• Roll up from long end, sealing edges. Place, seam-side down, on greased cookie sheet; shape into ring, pressing ends together to seal. Make 1 inch cuts through ring from outer edge at 2-inch intervals. Cover; let rise in warm place 30 minutes.

• Heat oven to 350°F.

• Bake 30 to 40 minutes or until golden brown. Cool slightly. Drizzle with Vanilla Drizzle.

Makes 8 to 10 servings

Prep time: 30 minutes plus rising
Cooking time: 40 minutes

Vanilla Drizzle

- 1 cup powdered sugar
- 1 to 2 tablespoons milk
- 1 teaspoon vanilla
- ½ teaspoon ground cinnamon (optional)

• Mix ingredients in small bowl until smooth.

Nut-Filled Christmas Wreath

- 2 tablespoons warm water (105° to 115°F)
- 1 package active dry yeast
- 3 tablespoons sugar, divided
- 2 eggs
- ¼ cup butter or margarine, melted, cooled
- 3 tablespoons milk
- ¾ teaspoon salt
- ½ teaspoon ground cardamom
- 2½ to 3 cups all-purpose flour Cherry-Nut Filling (recipe follows) Almond Icing (recipe follows)

In large bowl, combine water, yeast and 1 tablespoon sugar; stir to dissolve yeast. Let stand until bubbly, about 5 minutes. Add remaining 2 tablespoons sugar, eggs, butter, milk, salt and cardamom; mix well. Stir in 1½ cups flour until smooth. Stir in enough remaining flour to make dough easy to handle. Turn out onto lightly floured surface. Knead 10 minutes or until dough is smooth and elastic, adding as much remaining flour as needed to prevent sticking. Shape dough into ball. Place in large, lightly greased bowl; turn dough once to grease surface. Cover with waxed paper; let rise in warm place (85°F) until doubled, about 1 hour. Meanwhile, prepare Cherry-Nut Filling.

Punch dough down. Roll out dough on floured surface into 24×9-inch rectangle. Sprinkle Cherry-Nut Filling over dough to within 1 inch from edges. Roll up dough, jelly-roll style, beginning on 24-inch side; pinch seam to seal. Using sharp knife; cut roll in half lengthwise; turn each half cut-side up. Carefully twist halves together, keeping cut sides up to expose filling. Place dough on greased cookie sheet; shape into a ring. Pinch ends together to seal. Cover; let stand in warm place until almost doubled, about 45 minutes. Bake in preheated 375°F oven 20 minutes or until evenly browned. Remove bread from cookie sheet to wire rack; cool slightly. Prepare Almond Icing; drizzle over warm bread. Serve warm or at room temperature.

Makes 1 coffee cake

CHERRY-NUT FILLING: In medium bowl, combine ¾ cup chopped nuts (hazelnuts, almonds, walnuts or pecans), ¼ cup *each* all-purpose flour, chopped candied red cherries, chopped candied green cherries, and softened butter or margarine, 2 tablespoons brown sugar and ½ teaspoon almond extract; mix well.

ALMOND ICING: In small bowl, combine 1 cup sifted powdered sugar, 1 to 2 tablespoons milk and ¼ teaspoon almond extract; blend until smooth.

Apricot Cardamom Wreath

Apricot Cardamom Wreath

Bread
- **1 cup granulated sugar**
- **1 teaspoon ground cardamom**
- **½ cup LAND O LAKES® Butter**
- **1 can (12 ounces) evaporated milk**
- **2 teaspoons salt**
- **2 packages (¼ ounce *each*) active dry yeast**
- **¼ cup warm water (105° to 115°F)**
- **½ cup dairy sour cream**
- **3 eggs**
- **6 to 7 cups all-purpose flour**

Filling
- **2 to 2½ cups water**
- **¼ cup brandy *or* water**
- **1 package (6 ounces) dried apricots (2 cups)**
- **1 egg, slightly beaten**
- **2 tablespoons milk**
- **Large crystal sugar**

For bread, in 2-quart saucepan stir together granulated sugar and cardamom; add butter, evaporated milk and salt. Cook over medium heat, stirring occasionally, until butter is melted, 5 to 8 minutes. Cool to warm (105° to 115°F). In large mixer bowl dissolve yeast in ¼ cup warm water; stir in warm milk mixture, sour cream, 3 eggs and *3 cups* flour. Beat at medium speed, scraping bowl often, until smooth, 1 to 2 minutes. By hand, stir in enough remaining flour to make dough easy to handle. Turn dough onto lightly floured surface; knead until smooth and elastic, about 5 minutes. Place in greased bowl; turn greased side up. Cover; let rise in warm place until double in size, about 1 to 1½ hours. Dough is ready if indentation remains when touched.

For filling, in 2-quart saucepan combine *2 cups* water, brandy and apricots. Cook over low heat, stirring occasionally and adding small amounts of additional water, if necessary, until apricots are tender and mixture is thickened, 40 to 45 minutes; set aside.

Punch down dough; divide in half. Let rest 10 minutes. On lightly floured surface roll one half of dough to 20×9-inch rectangle; cut into 3 (3-inch-wide) strips. Spread *each* strip with ¼ cup apricot mixture to within ½ inch of edges. Bring 20-inch sides up together; pinch sides and ends tightly to seal well. Gently braid filled strips together. Place on greased large cookie sheet; form into wreath or leave as a braid. Pinch ends to seal well. Repeat with remaining dough and apricot mixture. Cover; let rise in warm place 30 minutes.

Heat oven to 350°. Bake for 25 to 30 minutes or until lightly browned. (Cover with aluminum foil if bread browns too quickly.) In small bowl stir together beaten egg and 2 tablespoons milk. Brush breads with egg mixture; sprinkle with large crystal sugar. Continue baking for 5 to 10 minutes or until golden brown. Remove from cookie sheets; cool on wire racks.

Makes 2 wreaths

Tip: For best results, bake 1 wreath at a time.

Blueberry Sour Cream Tea Ring

Streusel
    ¼ **cup firmly packed brown sugar**
    ¼ **cup chopped pecans**
    ½ **teaspoon ground cinnamon**
Cake
    1 **package DUNCAN HINES® Blueberry Muffin Mix**
    ½ **cup dairy sour cream**
    1 **egg**
    2 **tablespoons water**
Glaze
    ½ **cup confectioners sugar**
    1 **tablespoon milk**

1. Preheat oven to 350°F. Grease 7-cup tube pan.

2. **For streusel,** combine brown sugar, pecans and cinnamon in small bowl. Set aside.

3. Rinse blueberries from Mix with cold water and drain.

4. **For cake,** empty muffin mix into bowl. Break up any lumps. Add sour cream, egg and water. Stir until blended. Spread ⅔ cup batter in pan. Sprinkle ⅓ cup streusel over batter. Place one half of blueberries over streusel. Repeat layers ending with batter on top. Bake at 350°F for 28 to 32 minutes or until toothpick inserted in center comes out clean. Cool in pan 10 minutes. Invert onto cooling rack. Turn right-side up.

5. **For glaze,** combine confectioners sugar and milk in small bowl. Stir until smooth. Drizzle over warm cake.
                    12 Servings

Tip: This recipe may be baked in one 8½×4½-inch loaf pan at 350°F for 45 to 50 minutes or until toothpick inserted in center comes out clean.

Touch of Honey Bread

Touch of Honey Bread

    2½ **to 3 cups all-purpose flour**
    1 **cup QUAKER® Oat Bran™ hot cereal, uncooked**
    1 **package quick-rise yeast**
    ½ **teaspoon salt**
    1¼ **cups water**
    2 **tablespoons honey**
    2 **tablespoons margarine**

In large mixer bowl, combine 1 cup flour, oat bran, yeast and salt. Heat water, honey and margarine until very warm (120° to 130°F). Add to dry ingredients; beat at low speed of electric mixer until moistened. Increase speed to medium; continue beating 3 minutes. Stir in enough remaining flour to form a stiff dough.

Lightly spray bowl with no stick cooking spray or oil lightly. Turn dough out onto lightly floured surface. Knead 8 to 10 minutes or until dough is smooth and elastic. Place into prepared bowl, turning once to coat surface of dough. Cover; let rise in warm place 30 minutes or until doubled in size.

Lightly spray 8×4-inch loaf pan with no stick cooking spray or oil lightly. Punch down dough. Roll into 15×7-inch rectangle. Starting at narrow end, roll up dough tightly. Pinch ends and seam to seal; place seam side down in prepared pan. Cover; let rise in warm place 30 minutes or until doubled in size.

Heat oven to 375°F. Bake 35 to 40 minutes or until golden brown. Remove from pan; cool on wire rack at least 1 hour before slicing. Serve as sandwich bread, toasted or spread with jelly, jam or fruit preserves.
                    Makes 16 servings

Wholesome Wheat Bread

    5½ **to 6 cups whole wheat flour**
    2 **packages active dry yeast**
    1 **teaspoon salt**
    1 **teaspoon ground cinnamon**
    1 **cup KARO® Dark Corn Syrup**
    1 **cup water**
    ½ **cup HELLMANN'S® or BEST FOODS® Real Mayonnaise**
    2 **eggs**

In large mixer bowl, combine 2 cups of the flour, the yeast, salt and cinnamon. In medium saucepan, combine corn syrup, water and real mayonnaise; heat mixture over medium heat, stirring occasionally, until very warm (120° to 130°F). Pour hot mixture into flour mixture; beat at medium speed 2 minutes. Reduce speed to low; beat in 2 more cups of the flour and the eggs until well mixed. Beat at medium speed 2 minutes. By hand, stir in enough of the remaining flour to make dough easy to handle. Turn out onto lightly floured surface. Knead 10 minutes or until dough is smooth and elastic, adding as much remaining flour as needed to prevent sticking. Shape dough into a ball. Place in large, greased bowl; turn dough once to grease surface. Cover with towel; let rise in warm place (85°F) until doubled, about 1 hour.

Punch dough down; divide in half. Cover; let rest 10 minutes. Shape each half into 8×4-inch oval. Place on large, greased and floured baking sheet. Cut 3 slashes, ¼ inch deep, in top of each loaf. Cover; let rise in warm place until doubled, about 1½ hours. Bake in preheated 350°F oven 30 to 40 minutes or until loaves are browned and sound hollow when tapped. Immediately remove from baking sheet to wire racks to cool.
Makes 2 loaves

Bran Pita Bread

1 package active dry yeast
1¼ cups warm water
(110° to 115°F)
1½ cups KELLOGG'S®
ALL-BRAN® cereal
1½ cups all-purpose flour,
divided
½ teaspoon salt
¼ cup vegetable oil
1 cup whole wheat flour

1. In large bowl of electric mixer, dissolve yeast in warm water, about 5 minutes. Add

Kellogg's® All-Bran® cereal, mixing until combined. On low speed, beat in 1 cup of the all-purpose flour, the salt and oil. Beat on high speed 3 minutes, scraping sides of bowl.

2. Using dough hooks on mixer or by hand, stir in whole wheat flour. Continue kneading with mixer on low speed or by hand 5 minutes longer or until dough is smooth and elastic. Add the remaining ½ cup all-purpose flour, if needed, to make soft dough.

3. Divide dough into 12 portions. Roll each portion between floured hands into a smooth ball. Cover with plastic wrap or a damp cloth; let rest 10 minutes.

4. On a well-floured surface, lightly roll one piece of dough at a time into 6-inch rounds, turning dough over once. Do not stretch, puncture or crease dough. Keep unrolled dough covered while rolling each dough piece. Place 2 rounds of dough at a time on ungreased baking sheet.

5. Bake in 450°F oven about 4 minutes or until dough is puffed and slightly firm. Turn with a spatula; continue baking about 2 minutes or until lightly browned; cool. Repeat with remaining dough. Cut in half and fill with a vegetable or meat filling.
Makes 12 servings

Bran Pita Bread

60-Minute Oatmeal Nut Loaf

3¼ cups all-purpose flour,
divided
1 cup rolled oats
½ cup pecan pieces
2 teaspoons grated orange
peel
½ teaspoon salt
1 pkg. FLEISCHMANN'S®
RapidRise Yeast
1 cup milk
¼ cup water
2 tablespoons honey
1 tablespoon margarine or
butter
1 egg, beaten
½ cup powdered sugar
1 to 1½ teaspoons milk
Pecan halves

Set aside 1 cup flour. In large bowl, mix remaining 2¼ cups flour, oats, pecan pieces, orange peel, salt and yeast. In saucepan, over low heat, heat 1 cup milk, water, honey and margarine until very warm (125° to 130°F); stir into dry mixture. Mix in only enough reserved flour to make soft dough. On lightly floured surface, knead 4 minutes.

Roll dough into 13×9-inch rectangle. Roll up from short side, jelly-roll style; seal seam and ends. Place on greased baking sheet; flatten slightly. Cover; let rise in warm (80° to 85°F) draft-free place 20 minutes.

Preheat oven to 375°F. Make 3 diagonal slashes on top of loaf; brush with egg. Bake 20 to 25 minutes or until golden. Remove from baking sheet; cool on wire rack. In small bowl, mix powdered sugar and 1 teaspoon milk. Add additional milk, if necessary, to make desired consistency. Drizzle over loaf; garnish with pecan halves.
Makes 1 loaf

*Favorite recipe from **National Pecan Marketing Council***

COOKIES & CANDIES

Satisfy the cookie monster in your home in dozens of ways. Cookies of every description are filled with chocolate, oats, nuts, fruits and more. From peanut butter bar cookies to festive decorated cut-out cookies to rich, gooey brownies, you'll discover luscious ways to fill your cookie jar. Then tempt your friends and family with mouth-watering truffles, caramels, fudges and more. These candies are perfect for gift-giving and pleasing everyone's sweet tooth.

Chocolate-Dipped Crescents

1½ cups powdered sugar
1 cup LAND O LAKES® Butter, softened
1 egg
1½ teaspoons almond extract
2½ cups all-purpose flour
1 teaspoon cream of tartar
1 teaspoon baking soda
1 package (6 ounces) semi-sweet chocolate chips (1 cup), melted
Powdered sugar

Heat oven to 375°. In large mixer bowl combine 1½ cups powdered sugar and butter. Beat at medium speed, scraping bowl often, until creamy, 1 to 2 minutes. Add egg and almond extract; continue beating until well mixed, 1 to 2 minutes. Reduce speed to low. Add flour, cream of tartar and baking soda. Continue beating, scraping bowl often, until well mixed, 1 to 2 minutes. Shape into 1-inch balls. Roll balls into 2-inch ropes; shape into crescents. Place 2 inches apart on ungreased cookie sheets. Bake for 8 to 10 minutes or until set. Cookies do not brown. Cool completely. Dip half of *each* cookie into chocolate; sprinkle remaining half with powdered sugar. Refrigerate until set.

Makes about 4½ dozen cookies

Chocolate-Dipped Almond Horns

1 can SOLO® Almond Paste
3 egg whites
½ cup superfine sugar
½ teaspoon almond extract
¼ cup plus 2 tablespoons all-purpose flour
½ cup sliced almonds
5 squares (1 ounce each) semisweet chocolate, melted and cooled

Preheat oven to 350°F. Grease 2 cookie sheets; set aside. Break almond paste into small pieces and place in medium bowl or container of food processor. Add egg whites, sugar and almond extract. Beat with electric mixer or process until mixture is very smooth. Add flour and beat or process until blended.

Spoon almond mixture into pastry bag fitted with ½-inch (#8) plain tip. Pipe mixture into 5- or 6-inch crescent shapes on prepared cookie sheets about 1½ inches apart. Sprinkle with sliced almonds.

Bake 13 to 15 minutes or until edges are golden. Cool cookie sheets on wire racks 2 minutes. Remove from cookie sheets and cool completely on wire racks. Dip ends of cookies in melted chocolate and place on sheet of foil. Let stand until chocolate is set.

Makes about 16 cookies

Chocolate-Dipped Crescents

Double Chocolate Chunk Cookies

Chocolate Chip Lollipops

**1 package DUNCAN HINES®
Chocolate Chip
Cookie Mix
1 egg
2 teaspoons water
Flat ice cream sticks
Assorted decors**

1. Preheat oven to 375°F.

2. Combine cookie mix, contents of buttery flavor packet from Mix, egg and water in large bowl. Stir until thoroughly blended. Shape dough into 24 (1-inch) balls. Place balls 3 inches apart on ungreased baking sheets (see Tip). Push ice cream stick into center of each ball. Flatten dough ball with hand to form round lollipop. Decorate by pressing decors onto dough. Bake at 375°F for 8 to 9 minutes or until light golden brown. Cool 1 minute on baking sheets. Remove to cooling racks. Cool completely. Store in airtight container. *2 Dozen Cookies*

Tip: For best results, use shiny baking sheets for baking cookies. Dark baking sheets cause cookie bottoms to become too brown.

Double Chocolate Chunk Cookies

**4 squares BAKER'S®
Semi-Sweet Chocolate
½ cup (1 stick) margarine or
butter, slightly softened
½ cup granulated sugar
¼ cup firmly packed brown
sugar
1 egg
1 teaspoon vanilla
1 cup all-purpose flour
½ teaspoon CALUMET®
Baking Powder
¼ teaspoon salt
¾ cup chopped walnuts
(optional)
4 squares BAKER'S®
Semi-Sweet Chocolate**

MELT 1 square chocolate in small microwavable bowl on HIGH 1 to 2 minutes or until almost melted, stirring after each minute. **Stir until chocolate is completely melted.** Cut 3 squares chocolate into large chunks; set aside.

BEAT margarine, sugars, egg and vanilla until light and fluffy. Stir in 1 square melted chocolate.

Mix in flour, baking powder and salt. Stir in chocolate chunks and walnuts. Refrigerate 30 minutes.

HEAT oven to 375°F. Drop dough by heaping tablespoonfuls, about 2 inches apart, onto greased cookie sheets. Bake for 8 minutes or until lightly browned. Cool 5 minutes on cookie sheets. Remove and finish cooling on wire racks.

MELT 4 squares chocolate in small microwavable bowl on HIGH 1 to 2 minutes or until almost melted, stirring after each minute. **Stir until chocolate is completely melted.** Dip ½ of each cookie into melted chocolate. Let stand on waxed paper until chocolate is firm.

Makes about 2 dozen cookies

Prep time: 30 minutes
Chill time: 30 minutes
Baking time: 8 minutes

Double Chocolate Chunk Mocha Cookies: Prepare Double Chocolate Chunk Cookies as directed, adding 2 tablespoons instant coffee to the margarine mixture before beating.

Chocolate Chip Lollipops

Pecan Florentines

¾ **cup pecan halves,**
   pulverized*
½ **cup all-purpose flour**
⅓ **cup firmly packed brown**
   sugar
¼ **cup light corn syrup**
¼ **cup butter or margarine**
2 **tablespoons milk**
⅓ **cup semisweet chocolate**
   chips

Preheat oven to 350°F. Line cookie sheets with foil; lightly grease foil. Combine pecans and flour in small bowl. Combine brown sugar, syrup, butter and milk in medium saucepan. Stir over medium heat until mixture comes to a boil. Remove from heat; stir in flour mixture. Drop batter by teaspoonfuls about 3 inches apart onto prepared cookie sheets.

Bake 10 to 12 minutes or until lacy and golden brown. (Cookies are soft when hot, but become crispy as they cool.) Remove cookies by lifting foil from cookie sheet; set foil on flat, heat-proof surface. Cool cookies completely on foil.

Place chocolate chips in small heavy-duty plastic bag; close securely. Set bag in bowl of hot water until chips are melted, being careful not to let any water into bag. (Knead bag lightly to check that chips are completely melted.) Pat bag dry. With scissors, snip off a small corner from one side of bag. Squeeze melted chocolate over cookies to decorate. Let stand until chocolate is set. Peel foil off cookies.

Makes about 3 dozen cookies

*To pulverize pecans, place in food processor or blender. Process until thoroughly ground with a dry, not pasty, texture.

Original Toll House® Chocolate Chip Cookies

2¼ **cups all-purpose flour**
1 **teaspoon baking soda**
1 **teaspoon salt**
1 **cup (2 sticks) butter,**
   softened
¾ **cup granulated sugar**
¾ **cup firmly packed brown**
   sugar
1 **teaspoon vanilla extract**
2 **eggs**
One **12-oz.pkg. (2 cups)**
   NESTLÉ® Toll House®
   Semi-Sweet Chocolate
   Morsels
1 **cup nuts, chopped**

Preheat oven to 375°F. In small bowl, combine flour, baking soda and salt; set aside.

In large mixer bowl, beat butter, granulated sugar, brown sugar and vanilla extract until creamy. Beat in eggs. Gradually beat in flour mixture. Stir in semi-sweet chocolate morsels and nuts. Drop by rounded measuring tablespoonfuls onto ungreased cookie sheets.

Bake 9 to 11 minutes until edges are golden brown. Let stand on cookie sheets 2 minutes. Remove from cookie sheets; cool.

Makes about 5 dozen cookies

"M&M'S"® Chocolate Candies Party Cookies

1 **cup butter or margarine,**
   softened
1 **cup packed light brown**
   sugar
½ **cup granulated sugar**
2 **eggs**
2 **teaspoons vanilla**
2¼ **cups all-purpose flour**
1 **teaspoon salt**
1 **teaspoon baking soda**
1½ **cups "M&M'S"® Plain**
   Chocolate Candies,
   divided

Preheat oven to 375°F. Beat together butter, brown sugar and granulated sugar in large bowl until light and fluffy. Blend in eggs and vanilla. Combine flour, salt and baking soda in small bowl. Add to butter mixture; mix well. Stir in ½ cup of the candies. Drop dough by rounded teaspoonfuls 2 inches apart onto ungreased cookie sheets. Press additional candies into top of each cookie. Bake 10 to 12 minutes or until golden brown. Remove to wire racks to cool completely.

Makes about 6 dozen cookies

Double-Dipped Hazelnut Crisps (page 272) and Pecan Florentines

Choco-Caramel Delights

⅔ **cup sugar**
½ **cup butter or margarine, softened**
1 **egg, separated**
2 **tablespoons milk**
1 **teaspoon vanilla extract**
1 **cup all-purpose flour**
⅓ **cup HERSHEY'S Cocoa**
¼ **teaspoon salt**
1 **cup finely chopped pecans**
  Caramel Filling (recipe follows)
½ **cup HERSHEY'S Semi-Sweet Chocolate Chips or Premium Semi-Sweet Chocolate Chunks**
1 **teaspoon shortening**

In small mixer bowl, beat sugar, butter, egg yolk, milk and vanilla until blended. Stir together flour, cocoa and salt; blend into butter mixture. Chill dough at least 1 hour or until firm enough to handle.

Preheat oven to 350°F. Lightly grease cookie sheets. Beat egg white slightly. Shape dough into 1-inch balls. Dip each ball into egg white; roll in pecans to coat. Place 1 inch apart on prepared cookie sheet. Press thumb gently in center of each ball.

Bake 10 to 12 minutes or until set; cool slightly. While cookies bake, prepare Caramel Filling. Press center of each cookie again with thumb to make indentation. Immediately spoon about ½ teaspoon Caramel Filling in center of each cookie. Carefully remove to wire racks to cool completely.

In small microwave-safe bowl combine chocolate chips and shortening. Microwave at HIGH (100%) 1 minute or until softened; stir. Allow to stand several minutes to finish melting; stir until smooth. Place waxed paper under wire racks with cookies. Drizzle chocolate mixture over top of cookies.

Makes about 2 dozen cookies

CARAMEL FILLING: In small saucepan, combine 14 unwrapped light caramels and 3 tablespoons whipping cream. Cook over low heat, stirring frequently, until caramels are melted and mixture is smooth.

Double-Dipped Hazelnut Crisps

¾ **cup semisweet chocolate chips**
1¼ **cups all-purpose flour**
¾ **cup powdered sugar**
⅔ **cup whole hazelnuts, toasted, hulled and pulverized***
¼ **teaspoon instant espresso coffee powder**
  Dash salt
½ **cup butter or margarine, softened**
2 **teaspoons vanilla**
4 **squares (1 ounce each) bittersweet or semisweet chocolate**
4 **ounces white chocolate**
2 **teaspoons shortening, divided**

Preheat oven to 350°F. Lightly grease cookie sheets or line with parchment paper. Melt chocolate chips in top of double boiler over hot, not boiling, water. Remove from heat; cool. Blend flour, sugar, hazelnuts, coffee powder and salt in large bowl. Blend in butter, melted chocolate and vanilla until dough is stiff but smooth. (If dough is too soft to handle, cover and refrigerate until firm.)

Roll out dough, one fourth at a time, to ⅛-inch thickness on lightly floured surface. Cut out with 2-inch scalloped round cutter. Place 2 inches apart on prepared cookie sheets.

Bake 8 minutes or until not quite firm. (Cookies should not brown. They will puff up during baking and then fall again.) Remove to wire racks to cool.

Place bittersweet and white chocolates in separate small bowls. Add 1 teaspoon shortening to each bowl. Place

*To pulverize hazelnuts, place in food processor or blender. Process until thoroughly ground with a dry, not pasty, texture.

Choco-Caramel Delights

bowls over hot water; stir until chocolates are melted and smooth. Dip cookies, one at a time, halfway into bittersweet chocolate. Place on waxed paper; refrigerate until chocolate is set. Dip other halves of cookies into white chocolate; refrigerate until set. Store cookies in airtight container in cool place. (If cookies are frozen, chocolate may discolor.)

Makes about 4 dozen cookies

Chocolate Sugar Cookies

**3 squares BAKER'S®
    Unsweetened Chocolate
1 cup (2 sticks) margarine or
    butter
1 cup sugar
1 egg
1 teaspoon vanilla
2 cups all-purpose flour
1 teaspoon baking soda
¼ teaspoon salt
    Additional sugar**

MICROWAVE chocolate and margarine in large microwavable bowl on HIGH 2 minutes or until margarine is melted. **Stir until chocolate is completely melted.**

STIR 1 cup sugar into melted chocolate mixture until well blended. Stir in egg and vanilla until completely mixed. Mix in flour, soda and salt. Refrigerate 30 minutes.

HEAT oven to 375°F. Shape dough into 1-inch balls; roll in additional sugar. Place on ungreased cookie sheets. (If a flatter, crisper cookie is desired, flatten ball with bottom of drinking glass.)

BAKE for 8 to 10 minutes or until set. Remove from cookie sheets to cool on wire racks.

Makes about 3½ dozen cookies

Prep time: 15 minutes
Chill time: 30 minutes
Baking time: 8 to 10 minutes

Chocolate Sugar Cookies, Jam-Filled Chocolate Sugar Cookies and Chocolate-Caramel Sugar Cookies

Jam-Filled Chocolate Sugar Cookies: Prepare Chocolate Sugar Cookie dough as directed; roll in finely chopped nuts in place of sugar. Make indentation in each ball; fill center with your favorite jam. Bake as directed.

Chocolate-Caramel Sugar Cookies: Prepare Chocolate Sugar Cookie dough as directed; roll in finely chopped nuts in place of sugar. Make indentation in each ball; bake as directed. Microwave 1 package (14 ounces) KRAFT® Caramels with 2 tablespoons milk in microwavable bowl on HIGH 3 minutes or until melted, stirring after 2 minutes. Fill centers of cookies with caramel mixture. Place 1 square BAKER'S® Semi-Sweet Chocolate in a zipper-style sandwich bag. Close bag tightly. Microwave on HIGH about 1 minute or until chocolate is melted. Fold down top of bag tightly and snip a tiny piece off 1 corner (about ⅛ inch). Holding top of bag tightly, drizzle chocolate through opening over cookies.

Chocolate Pudding Cookies

**1 package (4-serving size)
    JELL-O® Instant
    Pudding, Chocolate
    Flavor
1 cup buttermilk baking mix
¼ cup oil
1 egg
    Peanut butter chips or
        other assorted candies**

PREHEAT oven to 350°. Put pudding mix and baking mix in bowl. Mix together with wooden spoon. Add oil and egg. Mix together until dough forms a ball.

SHAPE dough into ½-inch balls. Place balls about 2 inches apart on ungreased cookie sheet.

PRESS your thumb into middle of each ball to make a thumbprint. Put peanut butter chips or candies in thumbprint. Bake at 350° for 5 to 8 minutes or until lightly browned. Remove cookies to wire racks; cool.

Makes 36 cookies

Triple Chocolate Pretzels

- **2 squares (1 ounce each) unsweetened chocolate**
- **½ cup butter or margarine, softened**
- **½ cup granulated sugar**
- **1 egg**
- **2 cups cake flour**
- **1 teaspoon vanilla**
- **¼ teaspoon salt**
  Mocha Glaze (recipe follows)
- **2 ounces white chocolate, chopped**

Melt unsweetened chocolate in top of double boiler over hot, not boiling, water. Remove from heat; cool. Cream butter and granulated sugar in large bowl until light. Add egg and melted chocolate; beat until fluffy. Stir in flour, vanilla and salt until well blended. Cover; chill until firm, about 1 hour.

Preheat oven to 400°F. Lightly grease cookie sheets or line with parchment paper. Divide dough into 4 equal parts. Divide each part into 12 pieces. To form pretzels, knead each piece briefly to soften dough. Roll into a rope about 6 inches long. Form each rope on prepared cookie sheets into a pretzel shape. Repeat with all pieces of dough, spacing cookies 2 inches apart.

Bake 7 to 9 minutes or until firm. Remove to wire racks to cool. Prepare Mocha Glaze. Dip pretzel cookies, one at a time, into glaze to coat completely. Place on waxed paper, right side up. Let stand until glaze is set. Melt white chocolate in small bowl over hot water. Squeeze melted chocolate through pastry bag or drizzle over pretzels to decorate. Let stand until chocolate is completely set.

Makes 4 dozen cookies

Mocha Glaze

- **1 cup (6 ounces) semisweet chocolate chips**
- **1 teaspoon light corn syrup**
- **1 teaspoon shortening**
- **1 cup powdered sugar**
- **3 to 5 tablespoons hot coffee or water**

Combine chocolate chips, corn syrup and shortening in small heavy saucepan. Stir over low heat until chocolate is melted. Stir in powdered sugar and enough coffee to make a smooth glaze.

Chocolate No-Bake Cookies

- **1½ cups quick-cooking oats**
- **½ cup flaked coconut**
- **¼ cup chopped walnuts**
- **¾ cup sugar**
- **¼ cup milk**
- **¼ cup LAND O LAKES® Butter**
- **3 tablespoons unsweetened cocoa**

In medium bowl combine oats, coconut and walnuts; set aside. In 2-quart saucepan combine sugar, milk, butter and cocoa. Cook over medium heat, stirring occasionally, until mixture comes to a full boil, 3 to 4 minutes. Remove from heat. Stir in oats mixture. Quickly drop mixture by rounded teaspoonfuls onto waxed paper. Cool completely. Store in refrigerator.

Makes about 2 dozen cookies

Microwave Directions: In medium bowl combine oats, coconut and walnuts; set aside. In medium microwave-safe bowl melt butter on HIGH 50 to 60 seconds. Stir in sugar, milk and cocoa. Microwave on HIGH 1 minute; stir. Microwave on HIGH until mixture comes to a full boil, 1 to 2 minutes. Continue as directed.

Chocolate Cherry Cookies

- **2 squares (1 ounce each) unsweetened chocolate**
- **½ cup butter or margarine, softened**
- **½ cup sugar**
- **1 egg**
- **2 cups cake flour**
- **1 teaspoon vanilla**
- **¼ teaspoon salt**
  Maraschino cherries, well drained (about 48)
- **1 cup (6 ounces) semisweet or milk chocolate chips**

Melt unsweetened chocolate in top of double boiler over hot, not boiling, water. Remove from heat; cool. Cream butter and sugar in large bowl until light. Add egg and melted chocolate; beat until fluffy. Stir in flour, vanilla and salt until well blended. Cover; refrigerate until firm, about 1 hour.

Preheat oven to 400°F. Lightly grease cookie sheets or line with parchment paper. Shape dough into 1-inch balls. Place 2 inches apart on prepared cookie sheets. With knuckle of finger, make a deep indentation in center of each ball. Place a cherry into each indentation.

Bake 8 minutes or just until set. Meanwhile, melt chocolate chips in small bowl over hot water. Stir until melted. Remove cookies to wire racks to cool. Drizzle melted chocolate over tops while still warm. Refrigerate until chocolate is set.

Makes about 4 dozen cookies

Chocolate Cherry Cookies, Chocolate Spritz (page 280) and Triple Chocolate Pretzels

Double Mint Chocolate Cookies

Double Mint Chocolate Cookies

Cookies
2 cups granulated sugar
1 cup unsweetened cocoa
1 cup LAND O LAKES®
    Butter, softened
1 cup buttermilk or sour milk
1 cup water
2 eggs
2 teaspoons baking soda
1 teaspoon baking powder
½ teaspoon salt
1 teaspoon vanilla
4 cups all-purpose flour

Frosting
4 cups powdered sugar
1 cup LAND O LAKES®
    Butter, softened
1 teaspoon salt
2 tablespoons milk
2 teaspoons vanilla
½ teaspoon mint extract
½ cup crushed starlight
    peppermint candy

Preheat oven to 400°F. Grease cookie sheets. For cookies, in large bowl, combine granulated sugar, cocoa, 1 cup butter, buttermilk, water, eggs, baking soda, baking powder, ½ teaspoon salt and 1 teaspoon vanilla. Beat at low speed, scraping bowl often, until well mixed, 1 to 2 minutes. Stir in flour until well mixed, 3 to 4 minutes. Drop rounded teaspoonfuls of dough 2 inches apart onto prepared cookie sheets.

Bake 7 to 9 minutes or until top of cookie springs back when touched lightly in center. Remove to wire rack to cool.

For frosting, in small bowl, combine powdered sugar, 1 cup butter, 1 teaspoon salt, milk, 2 teaspoons vanilla and mint extract. Beat at medium speed, scraping bowl often, until light and fluffy, 2 to 3 minutes. Spread ½ tablespoonful of frosting on the top of each cookie. Sprinkle with candy.
Makes about 8 dozen cookies

Apricot-Pecan Tassies

Base
1 cup all-purpose flour
½ cup butter, cut into pieces
6 tablespoons reduced-
    calorie cream cheese

Filling
¾ cup firmly packed light
    brown sugar
1 egg, lightly beaten
1 tablespoon butter, softened
½ teaspoon vanilla
¼ teaspoon salt
⅔ cup California dried apricot
    halves, diced
    (about 4 ounces)
⅓ cup chopped pecans

For base, in food processor, combine flour, ½ cup butter and cream cheese; process until mixture forms large ball. Wrap dough in plastic wrap and chill 15 minutes.

For filling, combine brown sugar, egg, 1 tablespoon butter, vanilla and salt in bowl until smooth. Stir in apricots and nuts.

Preheat oven to 325°F. Shape dough into 2 dozen 1-inch balls and place in paper-lined or greased miniature muffin cups.

Apricot-Pecan Tassies

Brandy Lace Cookies

Chocolate Madeleines

- 1¼ **cups all-purpose flour**
- 1 **cup sugar**
- ⅛ **teaspoon salt**
- ¾ **cup butter**
- ⅓ **cup HERSHEY'S Cocoa**
- 3 **eggs**
- 2 **egg yolks**
- ½ **teaspoon vanilla extract**
  Chocolate Frosting
  (recipe follows)

Preheat oven to 350°F. Lightly grease indentations of madeleine mold pan (each shell is 3×2 inches). In small bowl, stir together flour, sugar and salt; set aside. In medium saucepan, melt butter; add cocoa. Gradually stir in dry ingredients. In small bowl, lightly beat eggs, egg yolks and vanilla with fork until well blended; stir into chocolate mixture, blending well. Cook over very low heat, stirring constantly, until mixture is warm; *do not simmer or boil.* Remove from heat. Fill each mold half full with batter (do not overfill).

Bake 8 to 10 minutes or until wooden pick inserted in center comes out clean. Invert onto wire rack; cool completely. Prepare Chocolate Frosting; frost flat sides of cookies. Press frosted sides together.
Makes about 1½ dozen filled cookies

CHOCOLATE FROSTING: In small bowl, stir together 1¼ cups powdered sugar and 2 tablespoons Hershey's Cocoa. In small bowl, beat 2 tablespoons softened butter and ¼ cup of the cocoa mixture until light and fluffy. Gradually add remaining cocoa mixture and 2 to 2½ tablespoons milk, beating to spreading consistency. Stir in ½ teaspoon vanilla extract.

Press dough on bottom and up side of each cup; fill each with 1 teaspoon apricot-pecan filling. Bake 25 minutes or until golden and filling sets. Cool and remove from cups. Cookies can be wrapped tightly in plastic wrap and frozen up to six weeks.
Makes 2 dozen cookies

Favorite recipe from **California Apricot Advisory Board**

Brandy Lace Cookies

- ¼ **cup sugar**
- ¼ **cup MAZOLA® Margarine**
- ¼ **cup KARO® Light or Dark Corn Syrup**
- ½ **cup all-purpose flour**
- ¼ **cup very finely chopped pecans or walnuts**
- 2 **tablespoons brandy**
  Melted white and/or semisweet chocolate (optional)

Preheat oven to 350°F. Lightly grease and flour cookie sheets. In small saucepan combine sugar, margarine and corn syrup. Bring to boil over medium heat, stirring constantly. Remove from heat. Stir in flour, pecans and brandy. Drop 12 evenly spaced half teaspoonfuls of batter onto prepared cookie sheets.

Bake 6 minutes or until golden. Cool 1 to 2 minutes or until cookies can be lifted but are still warm and pliable; remove with spatula. Curl around handle of wooden spoon; slide off when crisp. If cookies harden before curling, return to oven to soften. Drizzle with melted chocolate, if desired.
Makes 4 to 5 dozen cookies

Almond Rice Madeleines

Vegetable cooking spray
1 cup whole blanched almonds, lightly toasted
1½ cups sugar
¾ cup flaked coconut
3 cups cooked rice, chilled
3 egg whites
Fresh raspberries (optional)
Frozen nondairy whipped topping, thawed (optional)
Powdered sugar (optional)

Preheat oven to 350°F. Coat madeleine pans* with cooking spray. Place almonds in food processor fitted with knife blade; process until finely ground. Add sugar and coconut to processor; process until coconut is finely minced. Add rice; pulse to blend. Add egg whites; pulse to blend. Spoon mixture evenly into madeleine pans, filling to tops.

Bake 25 to 30 minutes or until lightly browned. Cool completely in pans on wire rack. Cover and refrigerate 2 hours or until serving time. Run a sharp knife around each madeleine shell and gently remove from pan. Invert onto serving plates; serve with raspberries and whipped topping, if desired. Sprinkle with powdered sugar, if desired.

Makes about 3 dozen madeleines

*You may substitute miniature muffin pans for madeleine pans, if desired.

Favorite recipe from **USA Rice Council**

Cherry Surprises

Cherry Surprises

1 package DUNCAN HINES®
Golden Sugar Cookie Mix
36 to 40 candied cherries
½ cup semi-sweet chocolate chips
1 teaspoon CRISCO® Shortening

1. Preheat oven to 375°F. Grease baking sheets.

2. Prepare cookie mix following package directions for original recipe. Shape thin layer of dough around each candied cherry. Place 2 inches apart on baking sheets. Bake at 375°F for 8 minutes or until set but not browned. Cool 1 minute on baking sheets. Remove to cooling racks. Cool completely.

3. Combine chocolate chips and shortening in small resealable plastic bag. Place bag in bowl of hot water for several minutes. Dry with paper towel. Knead until blended and chocolate is smooth. Snip pinpoint hole in corner of bag. Drizzle chocolate over cookies. Allow drizzle to set before storing between layers of waxed paper in airtight container.

3 to 3½ Dozen Cookies

Tip: Well-drained maraschino cherries may be substituted for candied cherries.

Almond Rice Madeleines

Linzer Hearts

**1 package DUNCAN HINES®
   Golden Sugar Cookie Mix**
½ cup all-purpose flour
½ cup finely ground almonds
1 egg
1 tablespoon water
**3 tablespoons confectioners
   sugar**
**½ cup *plus* 1 tablespoon
   seedless red raspberry
   jam, warmed**

1. Preheat oven to 375°F.

2. Combine cookie mix, contents of buttery flavor packet from Mix, flour, almonds, egg and water in large bowl. Stir with spoon until blended. Roll dough ⅛ inch thick on lightly floured board. Cut out 3-inch hearts with floured cookie cutter. Cut out centers of half the hearts with smaller heart cookie cutter. Reroll dough as needed. Place 2 inches apart on ungreased baking sheets. Bake whole hearts at 375°F for 8 to 9 minutes and cut-out hearts for 6 to 7 minutes or until edges are lightly browned. Cool 1 minute on baking sheets. Remove to cooling racks. Cool completely.

3. To assemble, dust cut-out hearts with sifted confectioners sugar. Spread warm jam over whole hearts almost to edges; top with cut-out hearts. Press together to make sandwiches. Fill center with ¼ teaspoon jam. Store between layers of waxed paper in airtight container.

22 (3-inch) Sandwich Cookies

Tip: If you like a softer cookie, make these a day ahead.

Bavarian Cookie Wreaths

3½ cups all-purpose flour
1 cup sugar, divided
**3 teaspoons grated orange
   peel, divided**
¼ teaspoon salt
1⅓ cups butter or margarine
¼ cup Florida orange juice
**⅓ cup finely chopped
   blanched almonds**
**1 egg white *beaten with*
   1 teaspoon water**
**Tinted Frosting
   (recipe follows)**

Preheat oven to 400°F. Lightly grease cookie sheets. In large bowl, mix flour, ¾ cup sugar, 2 teaspoons orange peel and salt. Using pastry blender, cut in butter until mixture resembles coarse crumbs; add orange juice, stirring until mixture holds together. Knead a few times and press into a ball.

Shape dough into ¾-inch balls; lightly roll each on floured surface into 6-inch-long strip. Using two strips, twist together to make a rope. Pinch ends of rope together to make wreath; place on prepared cookie sheet.

In shallow dish, mix almonds, remaining ¼ cup sugar and 1 teaspoon orange peel. Brush top of wreaths with egg white mixture and sprinkle with almond-sugar mixture. Bake 8 to 10 minutes or until lightly browned. Remove to wire racks to cool completely. Frost with Tinted Frosting, if desired.

Makes about 5 dozen cookies

Tinted Frosting

1 cup confectioners' sugar
**2 tablespoons butter or
   margarine, softened**
**1 to 2 teaspoons milk
   Few drops green food color
   Red cinnamon candies**

In small bowl, mix sugar, butter, 1 teaspoon milk and few drops green food color. Add more milk if necessary to make frosting spreadable. Fill pastry bag fitted with small leaf tip (#67). Decorate each wreath with 3 or 4 leaves and red cinnamon candies for berries.

Tip: Use various decorations for special holidays—or serve plain.

*Favorite recipe from **Florida Department of Citrus***

Linzer Hearts

Brandied Buttery Wreaths

Cookies
2¼ cups all-purpose flour
⅓ cup granulated sugar
⅔ cup LAND O LAKES®
 Butter, softened
1 egg
1 teaspoon ground nutmeg
¼ teaspoon salt
2 tablespoons grated orange
 peel
2 tablespoons brandy*
⅓ cup chopped maraschino
 cherries, drained

Glaze
1¼ cups powdered sugar
1 to 2 tablespoons milk
1 tablespoon brandy**
⅛ teaspoon ground nutmeg
 Red and green maraschino
 cherries, drained, halved

Heat oven to 350°. For cookies, in large mixer bowl combine flour, granulated sugar, butter, egg, 1 teaspoon nutmeg, salt, orange peel and 2 tablespoons brandy. Beat at low speed, scraping bowl often, until well mixed, 1 to 2 minutes. By hand, stir in ⅓ cup chopped cherries. Shape rounded teaspoonfuls of dough into 1-inch balls; form into 5-inch long strips. Shape strips into circles (wreaths), candy canes *or* leave as strips. Place 2 inches apart on greased cookie sheets. Bake for 8 to 12 minutes or until edges are lightly browned.

For glaze, in small bowl stir together all glaze ingredients *except* halved maraschino cherries. Dip or frost warm cookies with glaze. If desired, decorate with maraschino cherries.

Makes about 2 dozen cookies

*You may substitute 1 teaspoon brandy extract *plus* 2 tablespoons water for the 2 tablespoons brandy.

**You may substitute ¼ teaspoon brandy extract *plus* 1 tablespoon water for the 1 tablespoon brandy.

Best Ever Spritz

⅔ cup sugar
1 cup LAND O LAKES®
 Butter, softened
1 egg
½ teaspoon salt
2 teaspoons vanilla
2¼ cups all-purpose flour

Heat oven to 400°. In large mixer bowl combine sugar, butter, egg, salt and vanilla. Beat at medium speed, scraping bowl often, until mixture is light and fluffy, 2 to 3 minutes. Add flour. Beat at low speed, scraping bowl often, until well mixed, 2 to 3 minutes. If desired, add the ingredients from one of the following variations. If dough is too soft, cover; refrigerate until firm enough to form cookies, 30 to 45 minutes. Place dough into cookie press; form desired shapes 1 inch apart on cookie sheets. Bake for 6 to 8 minutes or until edges are lightly browned.

Makes about 5 dozen cookies

Variations:

Lebkuchen Spice Spritz: To Best Ever Spritz dough add *1 teaspoon each ground cinnamon* and *ground nutmeg, ½ teaspoon ground allspice* and *¼ teaspoon ground cloves.* Glaze: In small bowl stir together *1 cup powdered sugar, 2 tablespoons milk* and *½ teaspoon vanilla* until smooth. Drizzle or pipe over warm cookies.

Eggnog Glazed Spritz: To Best Ever Spritz dough add *1 teaspoon ground nutmeg.* Glaze: In small bowl stir together *1 cup powdered sugar; ¼ cup LAND O LAKES® Butter, softened; 2 tablespoons water* and *¼ teaspoon rum extract* until smooth. Drizzle over warm cookies.

Mint Kisses: To Best Ever Spritz dough add *¼ teaspoon mint extract.* Immediately after removing cookies from oven place *1 chocolate candy kiss* on *each* cookie.

Piña Colada Spritz: Omit vanilla in Best Ever Spritz recipe and add *1 tablespoon pineapple juice* and *¼ teaspoon rum extract;* stir in *½ cup finely chopped coconut.* Frosting: In small mixer bowl combine *1 cup powdered sugar; 2 tablespoons LAND O LAKES® Butter, softened; 2 tablespoons pineapple preserves* and *1 tablespoon pineapple juice.* Beat at medium speed, scraping bowl often, until light and fluffy, 2 to 3 minutes. Spread on cooled cookies. If desired, sprinkle with *toasted coconut.*

Chocolate Chip Spritz: To Best Ever Spritz dough add *¼ cup coarsely grated semi-sweet chocolate.*

Chocolate Spritz

2 squares (1 ounce each)
 unsweetened chocolate
1 cup butter, softened
½ cup granulated sugar
1 egg
1 teaspoon vanilla
¼ teaspoon salt
2¼ cups all-purpose flour
 Powdered sugar

Preheat oven to 400°F. Line cookie sheets with parchment paper or leave ungreased. Melt chocolate in top of double boiler over hot, not boiling, water. Remove from heat; cool. Cream butter, granulated sugar, egg, vanilla and salt in large bowl until light and fluffy. Blend in melted chocolate and flour until stiff. Fit cookie press with your choice of plate. Load press with dough. Press cookies out 2 inches apart onto prepared cookie sheets.

Bake 5 to 7 minutes or just until very slightly browned around edges. Remove to wire rack to cool. Dust with powdered sugar.

Makes about 5 dozen cookies

Lebkuchen Spice Spritz and Brandied Buttery Wreaths

Snowballs

½ cup DOMINO®
    Confectioners 10-X Sugar
¼ teaspoon salt
1 cup butter or margarine,
    softened
1 teaspoon vanilla extract
2¼ cups all-purpose flour
½ cup chopped pecans
    Additional DOMINO®
    Confectioners 10-X Sugar

In large bowl, combine ½ cup sugar, salt and butter; mix well. Add vanilla. Gradually stir in flour. Work nuts into dough. Cover and chill until firm.

Preheat oven to 400°F. Form dough into 1-inch balls. Place 1 inch apart on ungreased cookie sheets.

Bake 8 to 10 minutes or until set but not brown. Roll in additional sugar immediately. Cool on wire racks. Roll in sugar again. Store in airtight container.

Makes about 5 dozen cookies

Jingle Jumbles

¾ cup butter or margarine,
    softened
1 cup packed brown sugar
¼ cup molasses
1 egg
2¼ cups unsifted all-purpose
    flour
2 teaspoons baking soda
1 teaspoon ground ginger
1 teaspoon ground cinnamon
½ teaspoon salt
½ teaspoon ground cloves
1¼ cups SUN-MAID® Raisins
    Granulated sugar

In large bowl, cream butter and sugar. Add molasses and egg; beat until fluffy. In medium bowl, sift together flour, baking soda, ginger, cinnamon, salt and cloves. Stir into molasses mixture. Stir in raisins. Cover and chill about 30 minutes.

Preheat oven to 375°F. Grease cookie sheets. Form dough into 1½-inch balls; roll in granulated

Peanut Butter Cutout Cookies

sugar, coating generously. Place 2 inches apart on prepared cookie sheets.

Bake 12 to 14 minutes or until edges are firm and centers are still slightly soft. Remove to wire rack to cool.

Makes about 2 dozen cookies

Peanut Butter Cutout Cookies

1 cup REESE'S™ Peanut
    Butter Chips
½ cup butter or margarine
⅔ cup packed light brown
    sugar
1 egg
¾ teaspoon vanilla extract
1⅓ cups all-purpose flour
¾ teaspoon baking soda
½ cup finely chopped pecans
    Chocolate Chip Glaze
    (recipe follows)

Melt peanut butter chips and butter in medium saucepan over low heat, stirring constantly. Pour into large mixer bowl; add brown sugar, egg and vanilla, beating until well blended. Stir in flour, baking soda and pecans, blend well. Cover and chill 15 to 20 minutes or until firm enough to roll.

Preheat oven to 350°F. Roll out dough, a small portion at a time, to ¼-inch thickness on lightly floured surface. (Keep remaining dough in refrigerator.) With cookie cutters, cut into desired shapes. Place 2 inches apart on ungreased cookie sheets.

Bake 7 to 8 minutes or until almost set (do not overbake). Cool 1 minute. Remove to wire racks to cool completely. Drizzle Chocolate Chip Glaze onto each cookie; allow to set.

Makes about 3 dozen cookies

CHOCOLATE CHIP GLAZE: Melt 1 cup HERSHEY'S Semi-Sweet Chocolate Chips with 1 tablespoon shortening in top of double boiler over hot, not boiling, water; stir until smooth. Remove from heat; cool slightly, stirring occasionally.

Microwave directions: In small microwave-safe bowl, place 1 cup HERSHEY'S Semi-Sweet Chocolate Chips and 1 tablespoon shortening. Microwave at HIGH (100%) 1 minute; stir. If necessary, microwave at HIGH an additional 15 seconds at a time, stirring after each heating, just until chips are melted when stirred.

Philly® Cream Cheese Cookie Dough

**1 package (8 ounces)
    PHILADELPHIA BRAND®
    Cream Cheese, softened
¾ cup butter, softened
1 cup powdered sugar
2¼ cups all-purpose flour
½ teaspoon baking soda**

• Beat cream cheese, butter and sugar in large mixing bowl at medium speed with electric mixer until well blended.

• Add flour and soda; mix well.

Makes 3 cups dough

Chocolate Mint Cutouts

• Heat oven to 325°F.

• Add ¼ teaspoon mint extract and few drops green food coloring to 1½ cups Cookie Dough; mix well. Refrigerate 30 minutes.

• On lightly floured surface, roll dough to ⅛-inch thickness; cut with assorted 3-inch cookie cutters. Place on ungreased cookie sheet.

• Bake 10 to 12 minutes or until edges begin to brown. Cool on wire rack.

• Melt ¼ cup mint flavored semi-sweet chocolate chips in small saucepan over low heat, stirring until smooth. Drizzle over cookies.

Makes about 3 dozen cookies

Snowmen

• Heat oven to 325°F.

• Add ¼ teaspoon vanilla to 1½ cups Cookie Dough; mix well. Refrigerate 30 minutes.

• For each snowman, shape dough into two small balls, one slightly larger than the other. Place balls, slightly overlapping, on ungreased cookie sheet; flatten with bottom of glass. Repeat with remaining dough.

• Bake 18 to 20 minutes or until light golden brown. Cool on wire rack.

• Sprinkle each snowman with sifted powdered sugar. Decorate with icing as desired. Cut miniature peanut butter cups in half for hats.

Makes about 2 dozen cookies

Choco-Orange Slices

• Heat oven to 325°F.

• Add 1½ teaspoons grated orange peel to 1½ cups Cookie Dough; mix well. Shape into 8×1½-inch log. Refrigerate 30 minutes.

• Cut log into ¼-inch slices. Place on ungreased cookie sheet.

• Bake 15 to 18 minutes or until edges begin to brown. Cool on wire rack.

• Melt ⅓ cup BAKER'S® Semi-Sweet Real Chocolate Chips with 1 tablespoon orange juice and 1 tablespoon orange flavored liqueur in small saucepan over low heat, stirring until smooth. Dip cookies into chocolate mixture.

Makes about 2½ dozen cookies

Preserve Thumbprints

• Heat oven to 325°F.

• Add ½ cup chopped pecans and ½ teaspoon vanilla to 1½ cups Cookie Dough; mix well. Refrigerate 30 minutes.

• Shape dough into 1-inch balls. Place on ungreased cookie sheet. Indent centers; fill each with 1 teaspoon KRAFT® Preserves.

• Bake 14 to 16 minutes or until light golden brown. Cool on wire rack.

Makes about 3⅓ dozen cookies

Clockwise from top left: Preserve Thumbprints, Snowmen, Choco-Orange Slices and Chocolate Mint Cutouts

Peanut Butter Bears

- 1 cup SKIPPY® Creamy Peanut Butter
- 1 cup MAZOLA® Margarine, softened
- 1 cup packed brown sugar
- ⅔ cup KARO® Light or Dark Corn Syrup
- 2 eggs
- 4 cups flour, divided
- 1 tablespoon baking powder
- 1 teaspoon cinnamon
- ¼ teaspoon salt

In large bowl with mixer at medium speed, beat peanut butter, margarine, brown sugar, corn syrup and eggs until smooth. Reduce speed; beat in 2 cups of the flour, the baking powder, cinnamon and salt. With spoon stir in remaining 2 cups flour. Wrap dough in plastic wrap; refrigerate 2 hours. Preheat oven to 325°F. Divide dough in half; set aside half. On floured surface roll out dough to ⅛-inch thickness. Cut with floured bear cookie cutter. Repeat with remaining dough. Bake on ungreased cookie sheets 10 minutes or until lightly browned. Remove from cookie sheets; cool completely on wire racks. Decorate as desired.

Makes about 3 dozen bears

Prep Time: 35 minutes, plus chilling
Bake Time: 10 minutes, plus cooling

Note: Use dough scraps to make bear faces. Make one small ball of dough for muzzle. Form 3 smaller balls of dough and press gently to create eyes and nose; bake as directed. If desired, use frosting to create paws, ears and bow ties.

Old-Fashioned Molasses Cookies

- 4 cups sifted all-purpose flour
- 2 teaspoons ARM & HAMMER® Pure Baking Soda
- 1½ teaspoons ground ginger
- ½ teaspoon ground cinnamon
- ⅛ teaspoon salt
- 1½ cups molasses
- ½ cup lard or shortening, melted
- ¼ cup butter or margarine, melted
- ⅓ cup boiling water

Sift together flour, baking soda, spices and salt. Combine molasses, lard, butter and water in large bowl. Add dry ingredients to liquid and blend well. Cover and chill several hours or overnight.

Turn onto well-floured board. Using floured rolling pin, roll to ¼-inch thickness. Cut with 3½-inch floured cookie cutter. Sprinkle with sugar and place on ungreased baking sheets. Bake in 375°F oven 12 minutes. Cool on racks.

Makes about 3 dozen cookies

Favorite Butter Cookies

Cookies
- 2½ cups all-purpose flour
- 1 cup granulated sugar
- 1 cup LAND O LAKES® Butter, softened
- 1 egg
- 1 teaspoon baking powder
- 2 tablespoons orange juice
- 1 tablespoon vanilla

Frosting
- 4 cups powdered sugar
- ½ cup LAND O LAKES® Butter, softened
- 3 to 4 tablespoons milk
- 2 teaspoons vanilla
  Food coloring, colored sugars, flaked coconut and cinnamon candies for decorations

For cookies, in large mixer bowl combine all cookie ingredients. Beat at low speed, scraping bowl often, until well mixed, 1 to 2 minutes. If desired, divide dough into 3 equal portions; color ⅔ of dough with desired food colorings. Mix until dough is evenly colored. Wrap in plastic food wrap; refrigerate until firm, 2 to 3 hours.

Heat oven to 400°. On lightly floured surface, roll out dough, ⅓ at a time, to ¼-inch thickness. Cut out with cookie cutters. Place 1 inch apart on ungreased cookie sheets. If desired, sprinkle colored sugars on some of the cookies or bake and decorate later. Bake for 6 to 10 minutes or until edges are lightly browned. Remove immediately. Cool completely.

For frosting, in small mixer bowl combine powdered sugar, ½ cup butter, 3 to 4 tablespoons milk and 2 teaspoons vanilla. Beat at low speed, scraping bowl often, until fluffy, 1 to 2 minutes. Frost or decorate cookies.

Makes about 3 dozen (3-inch) cookies

Decorating Ideas:

Wreaths: Cut cookies with 2-inch round cookie cutter; bake as directed. Frost with green colored frosting. Color coconut green; sprinkle frosted cookies with coconut. Place 3 cinnamon candies together to resemble holly.

Christmas Trees: Color dough green; cut with Christmas tree cutter. Sprinkle with colored sugars; bake as directed.

Angels: Cut cookies with angel cookie cutter; bake as directed. Use blue frosting for dress, yellow frosting for hair and white frosting for wings, face and lace on dress.

Peanut Butter Bears

Peanut Butter Bars

- **1 package DUNCAN HINES® Peanut Butter Cookie Mix**
- **2 egg whites**
- **½ cup chopped peanuts**
- **1 cup confectioners sugar**
- **2 tablespoons water**
- **½ teaspoon vanilla extract**

1. Preheat oven to 350°F.

2. Combine cookie mix, contents of peanut butter packet from Mix and egg whites in large bowl. Stir until thoroughly blended. Press in ungreased 13×9×2-inch pan. Sprinkle peanuts over dough. Press lightly. Bake at 350°F for 16 to 18 minutes or until golden brown. Cool completely.

3. Combine confectioners sugar, water and vanilla extract in small bowl. Stir until blended. Drizzle glaze over top. Cut into bars.   *24 Bars*

Tip: Bar cookies look best when cut neatly into uniform sizes. Measure with ruler using knife to mark surface. Cut with sharp knife.

Linzer Bars

- **¾ cup butter or margarine, softened**
- **½ cup sugar**
- **1 egg**
- **½ teaspoon grated lemon peel**
- **½ teaspoon ground cinnamon**
- **¼ teaspoon salt**
- **⅛ teaspoon ground cloves**
- **2 cups all-purpose flour**
- **1 cup DIAMOND® Walnuts, finely chopped or ground**
- **1 cup raspberry or apricot jam**

Preheat oven to 325°F. Grease 9-inch square pan. In large bowl, cream butter, sugar, egg, lemon peel, cinnamon, salt and cloves. Blend in flour and walnuts. Set aside about ¼ of the dough for lattice top. Pat remaining dough into bottom and about ½ inch up sides of pan. Spread with jam. Make pencil-shaped strips of remaining dough, rolling against floured board with palms of hands. Arrange in lattice pattern over top, pressing ends against dough on sides.

Bake 45 minutes or until lightly browned. Cool in pan on wire rack. Cut into bars.
Makes 2 dozen small bars

Caramel Chocolate Pecan Bars

Caramel Chocolate Pecan Bars

Crust
- **2 cups all-purpose flour**
- **1 cup firmly packed brown sugar**
- **½ cup LAND O LAKES® Butter, softened**
- **1 cup pecan halves**

Filling
- **⅔ cup LAND O LAKES® Butter**
- **½ cup firmly packed brown sugar**
- **½ cup butterscotch chips**
- **½ cup semi-sweet chocolate chips**

Heat oven to 350°. For crust, in large mixer bowl combine flour, 1 cup brown sugar and ½ cup butter. Beat at medium speed, scraping bowl often, until well mixed and particles are fine, 2 to 3 minutes. Press on bottom of ungreased 13×9-inch baking pan. Sprinkle pecans evenly over unbaked crust.

For filling, in 1-quart saucepan combine ⅔ cup butter and ½ cup brown sugar. Cook over medium heat, stirring constantly, until mixture comes to a full boil, 4 to 5 minutes. Boil, stirring constantly, until candy thermometer reaches 242°F or small amount of mixture dropped

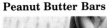

Peanut Butter Bars

into ice water forms a firm ball, 1 minute. Pour over pecans and crust. Bake for 18 to 20 minutes or until entire caramel layer is bubbly. Immediately sprinkle with butterscotch and chocolate chips. Allow to melt slightly, 3 to 5 minutes. Swirl chips leaving some whole for a marbled effect. Cool completely; cut into bars.

Makes 3 dozen bars

Blueberry Cheesecake Bars

1 package DUNCAN HINES® Bakery Style Blueberry Muffin Mix
¼ cup butter or margarine, softened
⅓ cup finely chopped pecans
1 package (8 ounces) cream cheese, softened
½ cup sugar
1 egg
3 tablespoons lemon juice
1 teaspoon grated lemon peel

1. Preheat oven to 350°F. Grease 9-inch square pan.

2. Rinse blueberries from Mix with cold water and drain.

3. Place muffin mix in medium bowl. Cut in butter with pastry blender or two knives. Stir in pecans. Press into bottom of pan. Bake at 350°F for 15 minutes or until set.

4. Combine cream cheese and sugar in medium bowl. Beat until smooth. Add egg, lemon juice and lemon peel. Beat well. Spread over baked crust. Sprinkle with blueberries. Sprinkle contents of topping packet from Mix over blueberries. Return to oven. Bake at 350°F for 35 to 40 minutes or until filling is set. Cool completely. Refrigerate until ready to serve. Cut into bars. *16 Bars*

Tip: Lower oven temperature by 25°F when using glass baking dishes. Glass heats more quickly and retains heat longer.

Apricot Oatmeal Bars

Crumb Mixture
1¼ cups all-purpose flour
1¼ cups quick-cooking oats
½ cup sugar
¾ cup LAND O LAKES® Butter, melted
½ teaspoon baking soda
¼ teaspoon salt
2 teaspoons vanilla

Filling
1 jar (10 ounces) apricot preserves
½ cup flaked coconut

Heat oven to 350°. For crumb mixture, in large mixer bowl combine all crumb mixture ingredients. Beat at low speed, scraping bowl often, until mixture is crumbly, 1 to 2 minutes. *Reserve 1 cup crumb mixture;* press remaining crumb mixture into greased 13×9-inch baking pan.

For filling, spread apricot preserves to within ½ inch from edge of crumb mixture; sprinkle with reserved crumb mixture and coconut. Bake for 22 to 27 minutes or until edges are lightly browned. Cool completely. Cut into bars.

Makes 3 dozen bars

Old-World Raspberry Bars

Crumb Mixture
2¼ cups all-purpose flour
1 cup sugar
1 cup chopped pecans
1 cup LAND O LAKES® Butter, softened
1 egg

Filling
1 jar (10 ounces) raspberry preserves

Heat oven to 350°. For crumb mixture, in large mixer bowl combine all crumb mixture ingredients. Beat at low speed, scraping bowl often, until mixture is crumbly, 2 to 3 minutes. *Reserve 1½ cups crumb mixture;* press remaining crumb mixture on bottom of greased 8-inch square baking pan. Spread preserves to within ½ inch from edge of unbaked crumb mixture. Crumble remaining crumb mixture over preserves. Bake for 42 to 50 minutes or until lightly browned. Cool completely. Cut into bars.

Makes 2 dozen bars

Top to bottom: Apricot Oatmeal Bars and Old-World Raspberry Bars

Walnut Crunch Brownies

Brownie Layer:
  4 squares BAKER'S®
    Unsweetened Chocolate
  ¾ cup (1½ sticks) margarine
    or butter
  2 cups granulated sugar
  4 eggs
  1 teaspoon vanilla
  1 cup all-purpose flour

Walnut Topping:
  ¼ cup (½ stick) margarine or
    butter
  ¾ cup firmly packed brown
    sugar
  2 eggs
  2 tablespoons all-purpose
    flour
  1 teaspoon vanilla
  4 cups chopped walnuts

HEAT oven to 350°F.

MICROWAVE chocolate and
¾ cup margarine in large
microwavable bowl on HIGH 2
minutes or until margarine is
melted. **Stir until chocolate is
completely melted.**

STIR granulated sugar into
melted chocolate mixture. Mix in
4 eggs and 1 teaspoon vanilla
until well blended. Stir in 1 cup
flour. Spread in greased
13×9-inch pan.

MICROWAVE ¼ cup margarine
and brown sugar in same bowl
on HIGH 1 minute or until
margarine is melted. Stir in 2
eggs, 2 tablespoons flour and 1
teaspoon vanilla until completely
mixed. Stir in walnuts. Spread
mixture evenly over brownie
batter.

BAKE for 45 minutes or until
toothpick inserted into center
comes out with fudgy crumbs. **Do
not overbake.** Cool in pan; cut
into squares.

Makes about 24 brownies

Prep time: 20 minutes
Baking time: 45 minutes

Almond Macaroon Brownies

Brownie Layer:
  6 squares BAKER'S®
    Semi-Sweet Chocolate
  ½ cup (1 stick) margarine or
    butter
  ⅔ cup sugar
  2 eggs
  1 teaspoon vanilla
  1 cup all-purpose flour
  ⅔ cup toasted chopped
    almonds

Cream Cheese Topping:
  4 ounces PHILADELPHIA
    BRAND® Cream Cheese,
    softened
  ⅓ cup sugar
  1 egg
  1 tablespoon all-purpose
    flour
  1 cup BAKER'S® ANGEL
    FLAKE® Coconut
  Whole almonds (optional)
  1 square BAKER'S®
    Semi-Sweet Chocolate,
    melted (optional)

HEAT oven to 350°F.

MICROWAVE 6 squares
chocolate and margarine in large
microwavable bowl on HIGH 2
minutes or until margarine is
melted. **Stir until chocolate is
completely melted.**

STIR ⅔ cup sugar into melted
chocolate mixture. Mix in 2 eggs
and vanilla until well blended.
Stir in 1 cup flour and ⅓ cup of
the almonds. Spread in greased
8-inch square pan.

MIX cream cheese, ⅓ cup sugar,
1 egg and 1 tablespoon flour in
same bowl until smooth. Stir in
the remaining ⅓ cup almonds
and the coconut. Spread over
brownie batter. Garnish with
whole almonds, if desired.

BAKE for 35 minutes or until
toothpick inserted into center
comes out with fudgy crumbs. **Do
not overbake.** Cool in pan.
Drizzle with 1 square melted
chocolate, if desired.

Makes about 16 brownies

Prep time: 20 minutes
Baking time: 35 minutes

Peanut-Layered Brownies

Brownie Layer:
  4 squares BAKER'S®
    Unsweetened Chocolate
  ¾ cup (1½ sticks) margarine
    or butter
  2 cups granulated sugar
  3 eggs
  1 teaspoon vanilla
  1 cup all-purpose flour
  1 cup chopped peanuts

Peanut Butter Layer:
  1 cup peanut butter
  ½ cup powdered sugar
  1 teaspoon vanilla

Glaze:
  4 squares BAKER'S®
    Semi-Sweet Chocolate
  ¼ cup (½ stick) margarine or
    butter

HEAT oven to 350°F.

MICROWAVE unsweetened
chocolate and ¾ cup margarine
in large microwavable bowl on
HIGH 2 minutes or until
margarine is melted. **Stir until
chocolate is completely
melted.**

STIR granulated sugar into
chocolate mixture. Mix in eggs
and 1 teaspoon vanilla until well
blended. Stir in flour and
peanuts. Spread in greased
13×9-inch pan.

BAKE for 30 to 35 minutes or
until toothpick inserted into
center comes out with fudgy
crumbs. **Do not overbake.** Cool
in pan.

MIX peanut butter, powdered
sugar and 1 teaspoon vanilla in
separate bowl until blended and
smooth. Spread over brownies.

MICROWAVE semi-sweet
chocolate and ¼ cup margarine
in small microwavable bowl on
HIGH 2 minutes or until
margarine is melted. **Stir until
chocolate is completely
melted.** Spread over peanut
butter layer. Cool until set. Cut
into squares.

Makes about 24 brownies

Prep time: 20 minutes
Baking time: 30 to 35 minutes

**Clockwise from top right: Peanut-Layered Brownies, Almond Macaroon Brownies
and Walnut Crunch Brownies**

Rich 'n' Creamy Brownie Bars

Brownies
  1 package DUNCAN HINES®
    Brownies Plus Double
    Fudge Mix
  2 eggs
  ⅓ cup water
  ¼ cup CRISCO® Oil or
    CRISCO® PURITAN® Oil
  ½ cup chopped pecans

Topping
  1 package (8 ounces) cream
    cheese, softened
  2 eggs
  1 pound (3½ cups)
    confectioners sugar
  1 teaspoon vanilla extract

1. Preheat oven to 350°F. Grease bottom of 13×9×2-inch pan.

2. **For brownies,** combine brownie mix, contents of fudge packet from Mix, eggs, water and oil in large bowl. Stir with spoon until well blended, about 50 strokes. Stir in pecans. Spread evenly in pan.

3. **For topping,** beat cream cheese in large bowl at medium speed with electric mixer until smooth. Beat in eggs, confectioners sugar and vanilla extract until smooth. Spread evenly over brownie mixture. Bake at 350°F for 45 to 50 minutes or until edges and top are golden brown and shiny. Cool completely. Refrigerate until well chilled. Cut into bars.

48 Bars

Tip: Always use the pan size called for in Duncan Hines® recipes. Using a different size pan can give brownies an altogether different texture.

Fudgy Rocky Road Brownies

Heath® Blond Brickle Brownies

  1⅓ cups all-purpose flour
  ½ teaspoon baking powder
  ¼ teaspoon salt
  2 eggs, room temperature
  ½ cup granulated sugar
  ½ cup packed brown sugar
  ⅓ cup butter or margarine,
    melted
  1 teaspoon vanilla
  ¼ teaspoon almond extract
  1 package (6 ounces)
    HEATH® BITS 'O
    BRICKLE®, divided
  ½ cup chopped pecans
    (optional)

Preheat oven to 350°F. Grease 8-inch square baking pan. Combine flour, baking powder and salt; set aside. Beat eggs well. Gradually add granulated and brown sugars; beat until thick and creamy. Add melted butter, vanilla and almond extract. Gently stir in flour mixture until moistened. Fold in ⅔ cup of the Heath® Bits 'O Brickle® and nuts. Pour into prepared pan.

Bake 30 minutes. Remove from oven and immediately sprinkle remaining Heath® Bits 'O Brickle® over top. Cool completely in pan on wire rack before cutting.

Makes 16 generous bars

Rich 'n' Creamy Brownie Bars

Fudgy Rocky Road Brownies

Brownies
  1 cup LAND O LAKES®
    Butter
  4 squares (1 ounce *each*)
    unsweetened chocolate
  2 cups granulated sugar
  1½ cups all-purpose flour
  4 eggs
  2 teaspoons vanilla
  ½ cup chopped salted
    peanuts

Frosting
  ¼ cup LAND O LAKES®
    Butter
  1 package (3 ounces) cream
    cheese
  1 square (1 ounce)
    unsweetened chocolate
  ¼ cup milk
  2¾ cups powdered sugar
  1 teaspoon vanilla
  2 cups miniature
    marshmallows
  1 cup salted peanuts

Heat oven to 350°. For brownies, in 3-quart saucepan combine 1 cup butter and 4 squares chocolate. Cook over medium heat, stirring constantly, until melted, 5 to 7 minutes. Stir in granulated sugar, flour, eggs and 2 teaspoons vanilla until well mixed. Stir in ½ cup chopped peanuts. Spread into greased 13×9-inch baking pan. Bake for 20 to 25 minutes or until brownies start to pull away from sides of pan.

For frosting, in 2-quart saucepan combine ¼ cup butter, cream cheese, 1 square chocolate and milk. Cook over medium heat, stirring occasionally, until melted, 6 to 8 minutes. Remove from heat; stir in powdered sugar and 1 teaspoon vanilla until smooth. Stir in marshmallows and 1 cup peanuts. Immediately spread over hot brownies. Cool completely; cut into bars. Store refrigerated.

Makes 4 dozen bars

One Bowl Brownies

One Bowl Brownies

  4 squares BAKER'S®
    Unsweetened Chocolate
  ¾ cup (1½ sticks) margarine
    or butter
  2 cups sugar
  3 eggs
  1 teaspoon vanilla
  1 cup all-purpose flour
  1 cup chopped nuts
    (optional)

HEAT oven to 350°F.

MICROWAVE chocolate and margarine in large microwavable bowl on HIGH 2 minutes or until margarine is melted. **Stir until chocolate is completely melted.**

STIR sugar into melted chocolate mixture. Mix in eggs and vanilla until well blended. Stir in flour and nuts. Spread in greased 13×9-inch pan.

BAKE for 30 to 35 minutes or until toothpick inserted into center comes out with fudgy crumbs. **Do not overbake.** Cool in pan; cut into squares.

Makes about 24 brownies

Prep time: 10 minutes
Baking time: 30 to 35 minutes

Tips:

• For cakelike brownies, stir in ½ cup milk with eggs and vanilla. Increase flour to 1½ cups.

• When using a glass baking dish, reduce oven temperature to 325°F.

Chocolate Cherry Brownies

- **1 jar (16 ounces) maraschino cherries**
- **⅔ cup (1 stick plus 3 tablespoons) margarine**
- **1 package (6 ounces) semi-sweet chocolate pieces (1 cup), divided**
- **1 cup sugar**
- **1 teaspoon vanilla**
- **2 eggs**
- **1¼ cups all-purpose flour**
- **¾ cup QUAKER® Oats (quick or old fashioned, uncooked)**
- **1 teaspoon baking powder**
- **¼ teaspoon salt (optional)**
- **½ cup chopped nuts (optional)**
- **2 teaspoons vegetable shortening**

Heat oven to 350°F. Lightly grease 13×9-inch baking pan. Drain cherries; reserve 12 and chop remainder. In large saucepan over low heat, melt margarine and ½ cup chocolate pieces, stirring until smooth. Remove from heat; cool slightly. Add sugar and vanilla. Beat in eggs, one at a time. Add combined flour, oats, baking powder and salt. Stir in chopped cherries and nuts. Spread into prepared pan. Bake about 25 minutes or until brownies pull away from sides of pan. Cool completely in pan on wire rack.

Cut reserved cherries in half; place evenly on top of brownies. In saucepan over low heat, melt remaining ½ cup chocolate pieces and vegetable shortening, stirring constantly until smooth.* Drizzle over brownies; cut into about 2½-inch squares. Store tightly covered.

Makes about 2 dozen bars

Microwave Directions: Place chocolate pieces and shortening in microwavable bowl. Microwave at HIGH 1 to 1½ minutes, stirring after 1 minute.

Cappucino Bon Bons

White Chocolate Brownies

- **1 package DUNCAN HINES® Brownies Plus Milk Chocolate Chunks Mix**
- **2 eggs**
- **⅓ cup water**
- **⅓ cup CRISCO® Oil or CRISCO® PURITAN® Oil**
- **¾ cup coarsely chopped white chocolate**
- **¼ cup sliced natural almonds**

1. Preheat oven to 350°F. Grease bottom of 13×9×2-inch pan.

2. Combine brownie mix, eggs, water and oil in large bowl. Stir with spoon until well blended, about 50 strokes. Fold in white chocolate. Spread in pan. Sprinkle top with almonds. Bake at 350°F for 25 to 28 minutes or until set. Cool completely. Cut into bars.

48 Small or 24 Large Brownies

Tip: For Decadent Brownies, combine 3 ounces coarsely chopped white chocolate and 2 tablespoons CRISCO® Shortening in small heavy saucepan. Melt over low heat, stirring constantly. Drizzle over cooled brownies.

Cappucino Bon Bons

- **1 package DUNCAN HINES® Fudge Brownie Mix, Family Size**
- **2 eggs**
- **⅓ cup water**
- **⅓ cup CRISCO® Oil or CRISCO® PURITAN® Oil**
- **1½ tablespoons FOLGERS® Coffee Crystals**
- **1 teaspoon ground cinnamon Whipped topping, for garnish Ground cinnamon, for garnish**

1. Preheat oven to 350°F. Place 40 (2-inch) foil liners on baking sheets.

2. Combine brownie mix, eggs, water, oil, coffee and 1 teaspoon cinnamon in large bowl. Stir with spoon until well blended, about 50 strokes. Fill each liner with 1 measuring tablespoonful batter. Bake at 350°F for 12 to 15 minutes or until toothpick inserted in center comes out clean. Cool completely. Garnish with whipped topping and a dash of cinnamon. Refrigerate until ready to serve. *40 Bon Bons*

Tip: To make larger Bon Bons, use twelve 2½-inch foil liners and fill with ¼ cup batter. Bake for 28 to 30 minutes.

Brownie Bon Bons

**2 jars (10 ounces each)
    maraschino cherries with
    stems
Cherry liqueur (optional)***
**4 squares BAKER'S®
    Unsweetened Chocolate**
**¾ cup (1½ sticks) margarine
    or butter**
2 cups granulated sugar
4 eggs
1 teaspoon vanilla
**1 cup all-purpose flour
    Chocolate Fudge Filling
    (recipe follows)**
½ cup powdered sugar

HEAT oven to 350°F.

MICROWAVE chocolate and margarine in large microwavable bowl on HIGH 2 minutes or until margarine is melted. **Stir until chocolate is completely melted.**

STIR granulated sugar into melted chocolate mixture. Mix in eggs and vanilla until well blended. Stir in flour. Fill greased 1¾×1-inch miniature muffin cups ⅔ full with batter.

BAKE for 20 minutes or until toothpick inserted into center comes out with fudgy crumbs. **Do not overbake.** Cool slightly in muffin pans; loosen edges with tip of knife. Remove from pans. Turn each brownie onto wax paper-lined tray while warm. Make ½-inch indentation into top of each brownie with end of wooden spoon. Cool completely.

PREPARE Chocolate Fudge Filling. Drain cherries, reserving liquid or liqueur. Let cherries stand on paper towels to dry. Combine powdered sugar with enough reserved liquid to form a thin glaze.

*For liqueur-flavored cherries, drain liquid from cherries. Do not remove cherries from jars. Refill jars with liqueur to completely cover cherries; cover tightly. Let stand at least 24 hours for best flavor.

SPOON or pipe about 1 teaspoon Chocolate Fudge Filling into indentation of each brownie. Gently press cherry into filling. Drizzle with powdered sugar glaze.

Makes about 48 bon bons

Prep time: 1 hour
Baking time: 20 minutes

Chocolate Fudge Filling

**3 squares BAKER'S®
    Unsweetened Chocolate**
**1 package (3 ounces)
    PHILADELPHIA BRAND®
    Cream Cheese, softened**
1 teaspoon vanilla
¼ cup corn syrup
1 cup powdered sugar

MELT chocolate in small microwavable bowl on HIGH 1 to 2 minutes or until almost melted, stirring after each minute. **Stir until chocolate is completely melted.** Set aside.

BEAT cream cheese and vanilla in small bowl until smooth. Slowly pour in corn syrup, beating until well blended. Add chocolate; beat until smooth. Gradually add powdered sugar, beating until well blended and smooth.   *Makes about 1 cup*

Brownie Candy Cups

**1 package DUNCAN HINES®
    Brownies Plus Double
    Fudge Mix**
2 eggs
⅓ cup water
**¼ cup CRISCO® Oil or
    CRISCO® PURITAN® Oil**
**30 miniature peanut butter cup
    candies, wrappers
    removed**

1. Preheat oven to 350°F. Place 30 (2-inch) foil liners in muffin pans or on baking sheets.

2. Combine brownie mix, contents of fudge packet from Mix, eggs, water and oil in large bowl. Stir with spoon until well blended, about 50 strokes. Fill each liner with 2 measuring tablespoonfuls batter. Bake at 350°F for 10 minutes. Remove from oven. Push 1 peanut butter cup candy in center of each cupcake until even with surface of brownie. Bake 5 to 7 minutes longer. Cool 5 to 10 minutes in pans. Remove to cooling racks. Cool completely.

30 Brownie Cups

Tip: Pack these brownies in your child's lunch bag for a special treat.

Brownie Bon Bons

Holiday Almond Treats

**2½ cups crushed vanilla
    wafers**
**1¾ cups toasted ground
    almonds, divided**
½ cup sifted powdered sugar
½ teaspoon ground cinnamon
**1 cup LIBBY'S® Pumpkin Pie
    Mix**
**⅓ cup almond liqueur or
    apple juice**

In medium bowl, blend vanilla
wafer crumbs, *1 cup* ground
almonds, powdered sugar and
cinnamon. Stir in pumpkin pie
mix and almond liqueur. Form
into 1-inch balls. Roll in
remaining ¾ cup ground
almonds. Refrigerate.

Makes 4 dozen

Rich Chocolate Pumpkin Truffles

**2½ cups crushed vanilla
    wafers**
**1 cup toasted ground
    almonds**
**¾ cup sifted powdered sugar,
    divided**
**2 teaspoons ground
    cinnamon**
**1 cup (6 ounces) chocolate
    pieces, melted**
**½ cup LIBBY'S® Solid Pack
    Pumpkin**
**⅓ cup coffee liqueur or apple
    juice**

In medium bowl, combine vanilla
wafer crumbs, ground almonds,
½ cup powdered sugar and
cinnamon. Blend in melted
chocolate, pumpkin and coffee
liqueur. Form into 1-inch balls.
Refrigerate. Dust with
remaining ¼ cup powdered sugar
just before serving.

Makes 4 dozen candies

Easy Chocolate Truffles

**1½ packages (12 ounces)
    BAKER'S® Semi-Sweet
    Chocolate**
**1 package (8 ounces)
    PHILADELPHIA BRAND®
    Cream Cheese, softened**
3 cups powdered sugar
1½ teaspoons vanilla
**Ground nuts, unsweetened
    cocoa or BAKER'S®
    ANGEL FLAKE®
    Coconut, toasted**

MELT chocolate in large
microwavable bowl on HIGH 2 to
3 minutes or until almost
melted, stirring after each
minute. **Stir until chocolate is
completely melted.** Set aside.

BEAT cream cheese until
smooth. Gradually add sugar,
beating until well blended. Add
melted chocolate and vanilla;
mix well. Refrigerate about 1
hour. Shape into 1-inch balls.
Roll in nuts, cocoa or coconut.
Store in refrigerator.

Makes about 5 dozen candies

Prep time: 15 minutes
Chill time: 1 hour

Variation: To flavor truffles with
liqueurs, omit vanilla. Divide
truffle mixture into thirds. Add 1
tablespoon liqueur (almond,
coffee or orange) to each third
mixture; mix well.

Milk Chocolate Orange Truffles

**One 11½-oz. pkg. (2 cups)
    NESTLÉ® Toll House®
    Milk Chocolate Morsels**
**One 6-oz. pkg. (1 cup) NESTLÉ®
    Toll House® Semi-Sweet
    Chocolate Morsels**
**¾ cup heavy or whipping
    cream**
**1 teaspoon grated orange
    rind**
**2 tablespoons orange
    flavored liqueur**
**1½ cups toasted walnuts,
    finely chopped**

Line three large cookie sheets
with wax paper. Place milk
chocolate morsels and semi-
sweet chocolate morsels in large
bowl; set aside. In small
saucepan over low heat, bring
heavy cream and orange rind
just to boil; pour over morsels.
Let stand 1 minute; whisk until
smooth. Whisk in liqueur.
Transfer to small mixer bowl;
press plastic wrap directly on
surface. Refrigerate 35 to 45
minutes, *just* until mixture
begins to thicken. Beat 10 to 15
seconds, *just* until chocolate
mixture has lightened in color.
(*Do not overbeat or truffles will
be grainy.*) Shape rounded
teaspoonfuls of chocolate mixture
into balls; place on prepared
cookie sheets. Refrigerate 10 to
15 minutes. Roll in walnuts.
Refrigerate in airtight
containers.

Makes about 6 dozen

Chocolate-Coated Truffles: Omit
walnuts. Line three large cookie
sheets with foil. Prepare
chocolate mixture and shape into
balls as directed. Freeze 30 to 40
minutes until firm. Melt one
11½-oz. pkg. (2 cups) Nestlé®
Toll House® Milk Chocolate
Morsels with 3 tablespoons
vegetable shortening. Drop
frozen truffles, one at a time,
into chocolate mixture. Stir
quickly and gently to coat;
remove with fork, shaking off
excess coating. Return to cookie
sheets. Refrigerate 10 to 15
minutes until firm. Refrigerate
in airtight containers.

Easy Chocolate Truffles and Chocolate-Coated Almond Toffee (page 297)

Creamy Nut Dipped Candies

- **5 cups powdered sugar**
- **¾ cup flaked coconut**
- **⅓ cup LAND O LAKES® Butter, softened**
- **¼ teaspoon salt**
- **3 tablespoons milk**
- **2 teaspoons vanilla**
- **1 cup mixed nuts**
- **1 package (10 ounces) almond bark, vanilla *or* chocolate candy coating**

In large mixer bowl combine *4 cups* powdered sugar, coconut, butter, salt, milk and vanilla. Beat at medium speed, scraping bowl often, until light and fluffy, 4 to 5 minutes. By hand, knead in remaining 1 cup powdered sugar. (Dough may be soft.) Form 1 teaspoon of dough around *each* nut; roll into ball. Refrigerate until firm, 2 hours. In 2-quart saucepan over low heat, melt almond bark. Dip chilled balls into melted coating; place on waxed paper. Drizzle with remaining almond bark. Store refrigerated.

Makes about 5½ dozen candies

Buttery Pecan Caramels

- **2 cups sugar**
- **2 cups half-and-half (1 pint)**
- **¾ cup light corn syrup**
- **½ cup LAND O LAKES® Butter**
- **½ cup semi-sweet real chocolate chips, melted**
- **64 pecan halves**

In 4-quart saucepan combine sugar, *1 cup* half-and-half, corn syrup and butter. Cook over medium heat, stirring occasionally, until mixture comes to a full boil, 7 to 8 minutes. Add remaining 1 cup half-and-half; continue cooking, stirring often, until candy thermometer reaches 245°F or small amount of mixture dropped into ice water forms a firm ball, 35 to 40 minutes. Pour into buttered 8-inch square pan. Cover; refrigerate 1 to 1½ hours to cool. Cut into 64 pieces. Drop ¼ teaspoon melted chocolate on top of *each* caramel; press pecan half into chocolate. Cover; store refrigerated.

Makes 64 caramels

Buttery Peanut Brittle (top) and Buttery Pecan Caramels (bottom)

Creamy Nut Dipped Candies

Buttery Peanut Brittle

- **2 cups sugar**
- **1 cup light corn syrup**
- **½ cup water**
- **1 cup LAND O LAKES® Butter, cut into pieces**
- **2 cups raw Spanish peanuts**
- **1 teaspoon baking soda**

In 3-quart saucepan combine sugar, corn syrup and water. Cook over low heat, stirring occasionally, until sugar is dissolved and mixture comes to a full boil, 20 to 30 minutes. Add butter; continue cooking, stirring occasionally, until candy thermometer reaches 280°F or small amount of mixture dropped into ice water forms a pliable strand, 80 to 90 minutes. Stir in peanuts; continue cooking, stirring constantly, until candy thermometer reaches 305°F or small amount of mixture dropped into ice water forms a brittle strand, 12 to 14 minutes. Remove from heat; stir in baking soda. Pour mixture onto 2 buttered cookie sheets; spread about ¼ inch thick. Cool completely; break into pieces.

Makes 2 pounds

Chocolate-Coated Almond Toffee

- 1 cup (2 sticks) butter or margarine
- 1 cup sugar
- 3 tablespoons water
- 1 tablespoon corn syrup
- ½ cup toasted chopped almonds
- 6 squares BAKER'S® Semi-Sweet Chocolate
- ⅓ cup toasted finely chopped almonds

COOK butter, sugar, water and corn syrup in heavy 2-quart saucepan over medium heat until mixture boils, stirring constantly. Boil gently, stirring frequently, 10 to 12 minutes or until golden brown and very thick. (Or until ½ teaspoon of mixture will form a hard, brittle thread when dropped in 1 cup cold water.)

REMOVE from heat. Stir in ½ cup almonds. Spread evenly onto well-buttered 15½×10½×1-inch baking pan. Let stand until almost cool to the touch.

MELT chocolate in small microwavable bowl on HIGH 2 minutes or until almost melted, stirring after each minute. **Stir until chocolate is completely melted.**

SPREAD melted chocolate over toffee; sprinkle with ⅓ cup almonds. Let stand until chocolate is firm. Break into pieces.

Makes about 1½ pounds candy

Prep time: 30 minutes

Butter Almond Crunch

- 1½ cups HERSHEY'S Semi-Sweet Chocolate Chips, divided
- 1¾ cups chopped almonds, divided
- 1½ cups butter or margarine
- 1¾ cups sugar
- 3 tablespoons light corn syrup
- 3 tablespoons water

Heat oven to 350°F. Line 13×9×2-inch pan with foil; butter foil. Sprinkle 1 cup chocolate chips into pan; set aside.

In shallow baking pan spread chopped almonds. Bake about 7 minutes or until golden brown; set aside.

In heavy 3-quart saucepan melt butter; blend in sugar, corn syrup and water. Cook over medium heat, stirring constantly, to 300°F on a candy thermometer (hard-crack stage) or until mixture, when dropped into very cold water, separates into threads that are hard and brittle. Bulb of candy thermometer should not rest on bottom of saucepan. Remove from heat; stir in 1½ cups toasted almonds. Immediately pour mixture evenly over chocolate chips in prepared pan; *do not disturb chips.* Sprinkle with remaining ¼ cup toasted almonds and remaining ½ cup chocolate chips; cool slightly.

With sharp knife score into 1½-inch squares, wiping knife blade after drawing through candy. Cool completely; remove from pan. Remove foil; break into pieces. Store in airtight container in cool, dry place.

Makes about 2 pounds candy

Butter Almond Crunch

Chocolate Caramel Drops

- 24 KRAFT® Caramels (about 7 ounces)
- 2 tablespoons heavy cream
- 1 cup (about) pecan halves
- 4 squares BAKER'S® Semi-Sweet Chocolate

MICROWAVE caramels and cream in large microwavable bowl on HIGH 1½ minutes; stir. Microwave 1½ minutes longer; stir until caramels are completely melted. Cool.

PLACE pecan halves on lightly greased cookie sheets in clusters of 3. Spoon caramel mixture over nuts, leaving ends showing. Let stand until set, about 30 minutes.

MELT chocolate in small microwavable bowl on HIGH 1 to 2 minutes or until almost melted, stirring after each minute. **Stir until chocolate is completely melted.** Spread melted chocolate over caramel mixture. Let stand until chocolate is set.

Makes about 2 dozen candies

Prep time: 20 minutes
Standing time: 30 minutes

Napoleon Crèmes

Crumb Mixture
 ¾ cup LAND O LAKES®
   Butter
 ¼ cup granulated sugar
 ¼ cup unsweetened cocoa
 1 teaspoon vanilla
 2 cups graham cracker
   crumbs

Filling
 2 cups powdered sugar
 ½ cup LAND O LAKES®
   Butter, softened
 1 package (3½ ounces)
   instant vanilla
   pudding mix
 3 tablespoons milk

Frosting
 1 package (6 ounces) semi-
   sweet real chocolate
   chips (1 cup)
 2 tablespoons
   LAND O LAKES® Butter

For crumb mixture, in 2-quart saucepan combine ¾ cup butter, granulated sugar, cocoa and vanilla. Cook over medium heat, stirring occasionally, until butter melts, 5 to 6 minutes. Remove from heat. Stir in crumbs. Press on bottom of buttered 9-inch square pan; cool.

Napoleon Crèmes

For filling, in small mixer bowl combine all filling ingredients. Beat at medium speed, scraping bowl often, until smooth, 1 to 2 minutes. Spread over crust; refrigerate until firm, about 30 minutes.

For frosting, in 1-quart saucepan melt frosting ingredients over low heat; spread over bars. Cover; refrigerate until firm, about 1 hour. Cut into squares; store refrigerated.
Makes 64 candies

Malted Milk Chocolate Balls

One 11½-oz. pkg. (2 cups)
   NESTLÉ® Toll House®
   Milk Chocolate Morsels,
   divided
 1 tablespoon vegetable oil
 1 cup CARNATION® Original
   Malted Milk Powder
 1 tablespoon vegetable
   shortening

Line two large cookie sheets with foil. In small saucepan over low heat, melt 1 cup milk chocolate morsels with oil, stirring until smooth. Remove from heat. Stir in malted milk powder. Transfer to small bowl. Refrigerate about 30 minutes until firm. Shape rounded measuring teaspoonfuls of dough mixture into balls; place on prepared cookie sheets. Freeze 20 minutes.

Melt remaining 1 cup milk chocolate morsels and shortening, stirring until smooth. Drop frozen milk balls, one at a time, into chocolate mixture. Stir quickly and gently to coat; remove with fork, shaking off excess coating. Return to cookie sheets. Refrigerate 10 to 15 minutes until firm. Gently loosen from foil with metal spatula. Refrigerate in airtight containers.
Makes about 2 dozen

Left to right: Rocky Road Fudge, Apricot Fudge and Macadamia Nut Fudge

Rich Chocolate Fudge

Fudge
 4 cups sugar
 ½ cup LAND O LAKES®
   Butter
 1 can (12 ounces) evaporated
   milk
 1 package (12 ounces) semi-
   sweet real chocolate
   chips (2 cups)
 3 bars (4 ounces *each*) sweet
   baking chocolate
 1 jar (7 ounces) marshmallow
   cream
 2 teaspoons vanilla

Variations

Macadamia Nut
 1¼ cups coarsely chopped
   macadamia nuts

Rocky Road
 1¼ cups coarsely chopped
   walnuts, toasted
 30 marshmallows (3 cups), cut
   into quarters

Apricot
 1¼ cups coarsely chopped
   dried apricots

In 4-quart saucepan combine sugar, butter and evaporated milk. Cook over medium-high heat, stirring occasionally, until mixture comes to a full boil, 10 to 14 minutes. Reduce heat to medium; boil, stirring constantly, until candy thermometer reaches 228°F or small amount of mixture dropped into ice water forms a 2-inch soft thread, 6 to 7 minutes. Remove from heat; gradually stir in chocolate chips and chocolate until melted. Stir in marshmallow cream and vanilla until well blended.

For Macadamia Nut Fudge, stir in *1 cup* nuts. Spread into buttered 13×9-inch pan. Sprinkle with remaining ¼ cup nuts.

For Rocky Road Fudge, stir in *1 cup* nuts, then stir in marshmallows, leaving marbled effect. Spread into buttered 13×9-inch pan. Sprinkle with remaining ¼ cup nuts.

For Apricot Fudge, stir in apricots. Spread into buttered 13×9-inch pan.

Cool completely at room temperature. Cut into 1-inch squares. Store covered in cool place.
Makes about 9 to 10 dozen pieces

Fantasy Fudge

¾ cup (1½ sticks) **margarine or butter**
3 cups **sugar**
⅔ cup **evaporated milk**
1 package (8 ounces) **BAKER'S® Semi-Sweet Chocolate, broken into pieces**
1 jar (7 ounces) **KRAFT® Marshmallow Creme**
1 teaspoon **vanilla**
1 cup **chopped nuts**

MICROWAVE margarine in 4-quart microwavable bowl on HIGH 1 minute or until melted. Add sugar and milk; mix well.

MICROWAVE on HIGH 3 minutes; stir. Microwave 2 minutes longer or until mixture begins to boil; mix well. Microwave 3 minutes; stir. Microwave 2½ minutes longer. Let stand 2 minutes.

STIR in chocolate until melted. Add marshmallow creme and vanilla; mix well. Stir in nuts. Pour into greased 13×9-inch pan. Cool at room temperature; cut into squares.
Makes about 4 dozen candies

Prep time: 20 minutes

White Peanut Butter Fudge

Two 6-oz. pkgs. (6 foil-wrapped **bars) NESTLÉ® Premier White baking bars, divided**
½ cup **creamy peanut butter**
One 7-oz. jar **marshmallow cream**
1½ cups **sugar**
⅔ cup **CARNATION® Evaporated Milk**
¼ teaspoon **salt**

Grease 8- or 9-inch square baking pan. Break up 1 foil-wrapped bar (2 oz.) Premier White baking bar; place in small saucepan with peanut butter. Stir over low heat until smooth; set aside. Break up remaining 5 foil-wrapped bars (10 oz.) Premier White baking bars; set aside.

In heavy-gauge medium saucepan, combine marshmallow cream, sugar, evaporated milk and salt. Bring to *full rolling boil* over medium-high heat, stirring constantly. *Boil 5 minutes,* stirring constantly. Remove from heat. Stir in broken Premier White baking bars until smooth; pour into prepared pan. Top with tablespoonfuls peanut butter mixture; swirl with metal spatula to marbleize. Refrigerate until firm. Cut into 1-inch squares.

Makes about 2 pounds or 64 squares

Top to bottom: Fantasy Fudge and Chocolate Caramel Drops (page 297)

PIES & PASTRIES

Picture-perfect pies filled with the season's bounty—who can resist them? Choose from an abounding assortment of America's favorites— unbeatable berry, crunchy pecan, light-as-air meringue, scrumptious cherry, luscious chocolate, creamy ice cream, traditional apple plus much more. And for extra-special occasions, try flaky Mini Almond Pastries, homemade Apple Turnovers and fancy Almond Heart Napoleons.

Georgia Peach Pie

Crust
   **10-inch Classic Crisco®
   Double Crust
   (see page 303)**

Filling
   **1 can (29 ounces) yellow
      cling peaches in heavy
      syrup**
   **3 tablespoons reserved
      peach syrup**
   3 tablespoons cornstarch
   1 cup sugar, divided
   3 eggs
   ⅓ cup buttermilk
   **½ cup butter or margarine,
      melted**
   1 teaspoon vanilla

Glaze
   **2 tablespoons butter or
      margarine, melted
      Sugar**

1. **For crust,** prepare recipe and press bottom crust into 10-inch pie plate. Do not bake. Heat oven to 400°F.

2. **For filling,** drain peaches, reserving 3 tablespoons syrup. Set aside. Cut peaches into small pieces. Place in large bowl. Combine cornstarch and 2 to 3 tablespoons sugar. Add 3 tablespoons reserved peach syrup. Add remaining sugar, eggs and buttermilk. Mix well. Stir in ½ cup melted butter and vanilla. Pour over peaches. Stir until peaches are coated. Pour filling into unbaked pie crust. Moisten pastry edge with water.

3. Cover pie with top crust. Cut slits or designs in top crust to allow steam to escape.

4. **For glaze,** brush with 2 tablespoons melted butter. Sprinkle with sugar. Bake at 400°F for 45 minutes or until filling in center is bubbly and crust is golden brown. Cool to room temperature before serving. Refrigerate leftover pie.

One 10-inch Pie

Peach Amaretto Cheese Pie

   **1 (9-inch) unbaked pastry
      shell**
   **1 (8-ounce) package cream
      cheese, softened**
   **1 (14-ounce) can EAGLE®
      Brand Sweetened
      Condensed Milk
      (NOT evaporated milk)**
   2 eggs
   **3 tablespoons amaretto
      liqueur**
   1½ teaspoons almond extract
   **3 fresh medium peaches,
      peeled and sliced**
   **2 tablespoons BAMA® Peach
      Preserves**

Preheat oven to 375°. Bake pastry shell 15 minutes. In large mixer bowl, beat cheese until fluffy. Gradually beat in sweetened condensed milk until smooth. Add eggs, *2 tablespoons* amaretto and *1 teaspoon* extract; mix well. Pour into pastry shell. Bake 25 minutes or until set. Cool. Arrange peach slices on top. In small saucepan, combine preserves, remaining *1 tablespoon* amaretto and *½ teaspoon* extract. Over low heat, cook and stir until hot. Spoon over top of pie. Chill. Refrigerate leftovers.

Makes one 9-inch pie

Georgia Peach Pie

Fruit and Cream Cookie Tart

Mom's Summer Fruit Lattice Pie

1 unbaked double 9-inch pie crust
10 fresh California nectarines or peaches, sliced
½ cup sugar
⅓ cup all-purpose flour
1 teaspoon finely grated lemon peel
Milk and sugar (optional)

Preheat oven to 425°F. Line 9-inch pie pan with one crust. Cut remaining crust into ½-inch strips. In large bowl, gently toss nectarines with sugar, flour and lemon peel. Spoon into crust. Weave dough strips over top to form lattice crust. Seal and crimp edges. Brush lattice top with milk and sprinkle with sugar, if desired. Place on baking sheet. Bake 10 minutes. Reduce heat to 350°F and bake 45 to 50 minutes or until lattice top is golden brown and fruit is tender. Cool.   *Makes 8 servings*

Favorite recipe from **California Tree Fruit Agreement**

Fruit and Cream Cookie Tart

Crust
1 package DUNCAN HINES® Golden Sugar Cookie Mix

Filling
1 package (8 ounces) cream cheese, softened
⅓ cup sugar
½ teaspoon vanilla extract

Topping
Peach slices
Banana slices
Fresh blueberries
Grape halves
Kiwifruit slices
Fresh strawberry slices
½ cup apricot preserves, heated and strained

1. Preheat oven to 350°F.

2. **For crust,** prepare cookie mix following package directions for original recipe. Spread evenly on ungreased 12-inch pizza pan. Bake at 350°F for 14 to 16 minutes or until edges are light brown. Cool completely.

3. **For filling,** combine cream cheese, sugar and vanilla extract in small bowl. Beat at low speed with electric mixer until smooth. Spread on cooled crust. Refrigerate until chilled.

4. **For topping,** dry fruits thoroughly on paper towels. Arrange fruit in circles on chilled crust working from outside edge toward center. Brush fruit with warmed preserves to glaze. Refrigerate until ready to serve.

12 Servings

Tip: To keep bananas and peaches from turning brown, dip slices in lemon juice.

Pastry Chef Tarts

1 package (10 ounces) pie crust mix
1 egg, beaten
1 to 2 tablespoons cold water
1½ cups cold half and half or milk
1 package (4-serving size) JELL-O® Instant Pudding and Pie Filling, French Vanilla or Vanilla Flavor
Assorted berries or fruit*
Mint leaves (optional)

PREHEAT oven to 425°. Combine pie crust mix with egg. Add just enough water to form dough. Form 2 to 3 tablespoons dough into a round. Press each round onto bottom and up sides of each 3- to 4-inch tart pan. (Use tart pans with removable bottoms, if possible.) Pierce pastry several times with fork. Place on baking sheet. Bake for 10 minutes or until golden. Cool slightly. Remove tart shells from pans; cool completely on racks.

POUR half and half into small bowl. Add pudding mix. Beat with wire whisk until well blended, 1 to 2 minutes. Spoon into tart shells. Chill until ready to serve.

ARRANGE fruit on pudding. Garnish with mint leaves, if desired.   *Makes 10 servings*

*We suggest any variety of berries, mandarin orange sections, melon balls, halved seedless grapes, sliced peaches, kiwifruit or plums.

Note: Individual graham cracker crumb tart shells may be substituted for baked tart shells.

Prep time: 20 minutes
Baking time: 10 minutes

Pastry Chef Tarts

Mixed Berry Pie

Crust
9-inch Classic Crisco®
Double Crust
(recipe follows)

Filling
2 cups canned or frozen
blackberries, thawed and
well drained
1½ cups canned or frozen
blueberries, thawed and
well drained
½ cup canned or frozen
gooseberries, thawed
and well drained
⅛ teaspoon almond extract
¼ cup sugar
3 tablespoons cornstarch

1. **For crust,** prepare recipe and press bottom crust into 9-inch pie plate. Do not bake. Heat oven to 425°F.

2. **For filling,** combine blackberries, blueberries, gooseberries and almond extract in large bowl. Combine sugar and cornstarch. Add to berries. Toss well to mix. Spoon into unbaked pie crust.

3. Cut top crust into leaf shapes and arrange on top of pie *or* cover pie with top crust. Flute edge. Cut slits in top crust, if using, to allow steam to escape.

4. Bake at 425°F for 40 minutes or until filling in center is bubbly and crust is golden brown. Cool until barely warm or to room temperature before serving. *One 9-inch Pie*

Classic Crisco® Crust

8-, 9- or 10-inch Single Crust
1⅓ cups all-purpose flour
½ teaspoon salt
½ cup CRISCO® Shortening
3 tablespoons cold water

8- or 9-inch Double Crust
2 cups all-purpose flour
1 teaspoon salt
¾ cup CRISCO® Shortening
5 tablespoons cold water

10-inch Double Crust
2⅔ cups all-purpose flour
1 teaspoon salt
1 cup CRISCO® Shortening
7 to 8 tablespoons cold water

1. **For pie dough,** spoon flour into measuring cup and level. Combine flour and salt in medium bowl. Cut in Crisco® using pastry blender (or 2 knives) until all flour is blended to form pea-size chunks. Sprinkle with water, 1 tablespoon at a time. Toss lightly with fork until dough will form a ball.

2. **For single crust,** press dough between hands to form 5- to 6-inch "pancake." Flour lightly on both sides. Roll between sheets of waxed paper on dampened countertop until 1 inch larger than upside-down pie plate. Peel off top sheet. Flip into pie plate. Remove other sheet. Fold dough edge under and flute.

3. For recipes using a **baked** pie crust, heat oven to 425°F. Prick bottom and sides thoroughly with fork (50 times) to prevent shrinkage. Bake 10 to 15 minutes or until lightly browned. (For recipes using an **unbaked** pie crust, follow baking directions given in that recipe.)

4. **For double crust,** divide dough in half. Roll each half separately as described in step 2. Transfer bottom crust to pie plate. Trim edge even with pie plate. Add desired filling to unbaked pie crust. Moisten pastry edge with water. Lift top crust onto filled pie. Trim ½-inch beyond edge of pie plate. Fold top edge under bottom crust. Flute. Cut slits in top crust to allow steam to escape. Bake according to specific recipe directions.

Mixed Berry Pie

Blackberry Ice Cream Pie

Crust
>   9-inch Classic Crisco®
>   Single Crust
>   (see page 303)

Filling
>   1 package (3 ounces) peach
>   or berry flavor gelatin
>   (not sugar free)
>   1 cup boiling water
>   1 pint vanilla ice cream,
>   softened
>   1¾ cups fresh or frozen dry
>   pack blackberries,
>   partially thawed

1. **For crust,** prepare recipe and bake. Cool.

2. **For filling,** combine gelatin and water in large bowl. Stir until dissolved. Cut ice cream into small chunks. Add to gelatin mixture, a spoonful at a time. Blend with wire whisk after each addition.

3. Dry blackberries between paper towels. Fold into gelatin mixture. Spoon into cooled baked pie crust. Refrigerate or freeze several hours before serving. Refrigerate or freeze leftover pie.
One 9-inch Pie

It's the Berries Pie

>   1 quart fresh strawberries,
>   washed and hulled,
>   reserving 8 for garnish
>   1 KEEBLER® Ready-Crust
>   Butter Flavored Pie Crust
>   1½ cups fresh or frozen
>   raspberries (without
>   sugar)
>   2 tablespoons sugar
>   1 package (3 ounces) triple
>   berry or raspberry
>   flavored sugar-free
>   gelatin
>   1 cup boiling water
>   Reduced-calorie whipped
>   topping (optional)

Place whole strawberries, hull side down, in the pie crust. Purée raspberries and sugar in blender or food processor. Press through a sieve to remove seeds. Set raspberry purée aside. Prepare gelatin according to package directions using 1 cup boiling water. Chill until slightly thickened. Stir raspberry purée into gelatin and pour over strawberries. Chill until firm. Garnish with a dollop of whipped topping and a fresh berry, if desired.   *Makes 8 servings*

Minnesota Blueberry Pie

Crust
>   8-inch Classic Crisco®
>   Double Crust
>   (see page 303)

Filling
>   ⅔ to 1 cup sugar, to taste
>   ¼ cup all-purpose flour
>   ½ teaspoon cinnamon
>   3 cups fresh blueberries
>   1 to 2 tablespoons butter or
>   margarine

1. **For crust,** prepare recipe and press bottom crust into 8-inch pie plate. Do not bake. Heat oven to 375°F.

2. **For filling,** combine sugar, flour and cinnamon. Sprinkle over blueberries in large bowl. Toss lightly to coat well. Spoon into unbaked pie crust. Dot with butter. Moisten pastry edge with water.

3. Cover pie with top crust. Cut slits in top crust to allow steam to escape.

4. Sprinkle lightly with sugar, if desired. Bake at 375°F for 45 to 60 minutes or until filling in center is bubbly and crust is golden brown. Cool until barely warm or to room temperature before serving.
One 8-inch Pie

Patriotic Pie

Crust
>   1 package DUNCAN HINES®
>   Blueberry Muffin Mix,
>   separated
>   ¼ cup butter or margarine,
>   softened

Filling
>   1 quart vanilla ice cream,
>   softened (see Tip)
>   ½ cup crumb mixture,
>   reserved from Crust

Topping
>   Can of blueberries from
>   Mix
>   1 pint fresh strawberries,
>   rinsed, drained and
>   sliced
>   2 tablespoons sugar
>   (optional)

1. Preheat oven to 400°F. Grease 9-inch pie plate.

2. **For crust,** place muffin mix in medium bowl. Cut in butter with pastry blender or 2 knives. Spread evenly in ungreased 9-inch square baking pan. *Do not press.* Bake at 400°F for 10 to 12 minutes. Stir. Reserve ½ cup crumb mixture for filling. Press remaining crumb mixture against bottom and sides of pie plate to form crust. Cool completely.

3. **For filling,** spread ice cream over crust. Sprinkle with reserved crumb mixture. Freeze several hours or until firm.

4. **For topping,** rinse blueberries from Mix with cold water and drain. Combine strawberries and sugar, if desired.

5. To serve, let pie stand 5 minutes at room temperature. Top with blueberries and strawberries. Cut into 8 wedges using sharp knife.
8 Servings

Tip: Ice cream can be softened by allowing to stand at room temperature for 15 minutes or placed in the refrigerator for 30 minutes.

Patriotic Pie

Strawberry Cheese Pie

1 (9-inch) baked pastry shell
  or graham cracker crumb
  crust
1 (8-ounce) package cream
  cheese, softened
1 (14-ounce) can EAGLE®
  Brand Sweetened
  Condensed Milk
  (NOT evaporated milk)
⅓ cup REALEMON® Lemon
  Juice from Concentrate
1 teaspoon vanilla extract
1 quart fresh strawberries,
  cleaned and hulled
  (about 1½ pounds)
1 (16-ounce) package
  prepared strawberry
  glaze, chilled

In large mixer bowl, beat cheese until fluffy. Gradually beat in sweetened condensed milk until smooth. Stir in ReaLemon® brand and vanilla. Pour into prepared pastry shell. Chill 3 hours or until set. Top with strawberries and desired amount of glaze. Refrigerate leftovers.

Makes one 9-inch pie

Cherry Cheese Pie: Omit strawberries and glaze. Top with 1 (21-ounce) can cherry pie filling, chilled.

Raspberry Crumble Tart

2 cups all-purpose flour
¾ cup granulated sugar
¾ cup LAND O LAKES®
  Butter, softened
3 egg yolks
1 teaspoon vanilla
½ cup coarsely chopped
  blanched almonds *or*
  pine nuts
½ cup raspberry *or* favorite
  flavor preserves
1 teaspoon grated lemon
  peel
  Powdered sugar
  Fresh raspberries
  Sweetened whipped cream

Heat oven to 350°. In large mixer bowl combine flour, granulated sugar, butter, egg yolks and vanilla. Beat at low speed, scraping bowl often, until well mixed, 2 to 3 minutes. By hand, stir in almonds. *Reserve 1½ cups mixture;* set aside. Press remaining mixture onto bottom of ungreased 9-inch removable bottom tart pan. Bake 10 minutes. Spread preserves to within ½ inch from edge; sprinkle with lemon peel. Crumble reserved mixture over preserves. Continue baking for 30 to 35 minutes or until lightly browned. Cool completely; remove from tart pan. Sprinkle with powdered sugar. Serve with fresh raspberries and sweetened whipped cream.

Makes 10 to 12 servings

Cinnamony Apple Pie

Crust
  9-inch Classic Crisco®
  Double Crust
  (see page 303)

Filling
1 tablespoon lemon juice
1 tablespoon cinnamon
  candies, crushed
⅓ cup honey
1 teaspoon cinnamon
3 to 4 cups thinly sliced,
  peeled Gravenstein or
  other baking apples
  (about 1½ pounds or
  3 to 4 medium)
1 tablespoon butter or
  margarine

Glaze
1 teaspoon half-and-half or
  milk

1. **For crust,** prepare recipe and press bottom crust into 9-inch pie plate. Do not bake. Heat oven to 450°F. Reserve dough scraps for cutouts, if desired.

2. **For filling,** heat lemon juice in small saucepan. Add crushed candies. Stir until dissolved. Stir in honey and cinnamon. Arrange apples in unbaked pie crust. Drizzle with honey mixture. Dot with butter. Moisten pastry edge with water.

3. Cover pie with top crust. Cut slits in top crust to allow steam to escape. Decorate with pastry cutouts, if desired.

4. **For glaze,** brush with half-and-half. Place pie in oven. *Reduce oven temperature to 350°F.* Bake for 1 hour or until filling in center is bubbly and crust is golden brown. Cool until barely warm or to room temperature before serving.

One 9-inch Pie

Cinnamony Apple Pie

Apple Gingerbread Pie

Crust
- ½ cup CRISCO® Shortening
- ¼ cup sugar
- 1¼ cups all-purpose flour
- ½ cup ground pecans
- ½ teaspoon ginger

Filling
- 4½ cups thinly sliced, peeled McIntosh or Granny Smith apples (about 1¾ pounds or 4 to 5 medium)
- 3 tablespoons honey
- 2 tablespoons water
- ⅓ cup golden raisins
- ⅓ cup currants
- ½ to 1 teaspoon apple pie spice, to taste

Topping
- 1 cup whipping cream, whipped
- 2 tablespoons finely chopped pecans

1. **For crust,** heat oven to 375°F. Cream Crisco® and sugar until light, using spoon. Stir in flour, ground pecans and ginger. Blend until mixture is uniform. Press into 9-inch pie plate. Bake at 375°F for 10 to 12 minutes or until lightly browned. Cool.

2. **For filling,** combine apples, honey and water in large saucepan. Simmer, covered, 20 minutes or until apples are tender. Stir in raisins, currants and apple pie spice. Cool. Spoon into cooled baked pie crust.

3. **For topping,** spread whipped cream over filling. Sprinkle with chopped pecans. Refrigerate until ready to serve. Refrigerate leftover pie.   *One 9-inch Pie*

Sour Cherry Pie

Sour Cherry Pie

Filling
- 2 cans (16 ounces each) pitted red tart cherries
- 1 cup reserved cherry liquid
- 1½ cups sugar, divided
- ⅓ cup cornstarch
- ⅛ teaspoon salt
- 1 tablespoon butter or margarine
- ¼ teaspoon almond extract
- 3 to 4 drops red food color

Crust and Glaze
- 9-inch Classic Crisco® Double Crust (see page 303)
- Milk
- Sugar

1. **For filling,** drain cherries in large strainer over bowl, reserving 1 cup liquid. Combine ¾ cup sugar, cornstarch and salt in medium saucepan. Stir in reserved 1 cup cherry liquid. Cook and stir on medium heat 3 to 4 minutes or until mixture thickens. Remove from heat. Stir in cherries, remaining ¾ cup sugar, butter, almond extract and food color. Refrigerate 1 hour.

2. **For crust,** heat oven to 400°F. Prepare recipe and press bottom crust into 9-inch pie plate. Spoon in filling. Cover pie with top crust. Cut slits in top crust to allow steam to escape.

3. **For glaze,** brush with milk. Sprinkle with sugar. Bake at 400°F for 10 minutes. *Reduce oven temperature to 350°F.* Bake for 40 to 45 minutes or until filling in center is bubbly and crust is golden brown. Cool until barely warm or to room temperature before serving.
          One 9-inch Pie

"Door County" Cherry Pie

Crust
> 9-inch Classic Crisco®
> Single Crust
> (see page 303)

Filling
> 1 package (8 ounces) cream
> cheese, softened
> ¾ cup confectioners sugar
> ½ to 1 teaspoon vanilla, to
> taste
> ½ teaspoon almond extract
> 1 cup whipping cream,
> whipped
> ⅛ to ¼ cup chopped, slivered
> almonds, to taste

Topping
> 2½ cups pitted "Door County"
> (or other variety) cherries
> (fresh or frozen)
> ½ cup cherry juice*
> 2 tablespoons granulated
> sugar (tart cherries will
> require more sugar)
> 1½ tablespoons cornstarch
> 1 tablespoon quick-cooking
> tapioca
> ½ teaspoon vanilla
> ½ teaspoon almond extract
> 3 or 4 drops red food color
> Whipped cream (optional)

1. **For crust,** prepare recipe and bake. Cool.

2. **For filling,** combine cream cheese and confectioners sugar in large bowl. Beat at medium speed of electric mixer until smooth. Beat in ½ to 1 teaspoon vanilla and ½ teaspoon almond extract. Fold in whipped cream and nuts. Spoon into cooled baked pie crust. Refrigerate until firm.

3. **For topping,** combine cherries, cherry juice, granulated sugar, cornstarch, tapioca, ½ teaspoon vanilla, ½ teaspoon almond extract and food color in medium saucepan. Cook and stir on medium heat until mixture comes to a boil. Boil 6 minutes. Remove from heat. Cool until

Key Lime Pie (left) and Banana Cream Pie (right)

thickened. Spread over filling. Garnish with whipped cream, if desired. Refrigerate leftover pie.
One 9-inch Pie

*Thaw cherries, if frozen. Mash and press additional cherries through large strainer over bowl to obtain ½ cup juice.

Classic Rhubarb Pie

Crust
> 9-inch Classic Crisco®
> Double Crust
> (see page 303)

Filling
> 4 cups fresh or thawed
> frozen rhubarb, cut into
> ½- to ¾-inch pieces
> 1⅓ to 1½ cups sugar, to taste
> ⅓ cup all-purpose flour
> 2 tablespoons butter or
> margarine

Glaze
> 1 tablespoon milk
> Sugar

1. **For crust,** prepare recipe and press bottom crust into 9-inch pie plate leaving overhang. Do not bake. Heat oven to 400°F.

2. **For filling,** combine rhubarb and sugar in large bowl. Mix well. Stir in flour. Spoon into unbaked pie crust. Dot with butter. Moisten pastry edge with water.

3. Cover pie with woven lattice top or top crust. Flute edge. Cut slits in top crust, if using, to allow steam to escape.

4. **For glaze,** brush with milk. Sprinkle with sugar. Cover edge with foil to prevent overbrowning. Bake at 400°F for 20 minutes. *Reduce oven temperature to 325°F.* Remove foil. Bake 30 minutes or until filling in center is bubbly and crust is golden brown (if using frozen rhubarb bake 60 to 70 minutes). Cool until barely warm or to room temperature before serving.
One 9-inch Pie

Banana Cream Pie

1 (9-inch) baked pastry shell
3 tablespoons cornstarch
1⅔ cups water
1 (14-ounce) can EAGLE®
   Brand Sweetened
   Condensed Milk
   (NOT evaporated milk)
3 egg *yolks,* beaten
2 tablespoons margarine or
   butter
1 teaspoon vanilla extract
3 medium bananas
   REALEMON® Lemon Juice
   from Concentrate
1 cup (½ pint) BORDEN® or
   MEADOW GOLD®
   Whipping Cream, stiffly
   whipped

In heavy saucepan, dissolve cornstarch in water; stir in sweetened condensed milk and egg *yolks.* Cook and stir until thickened and bubbly. Remove from heat; add margarine and vanilla. Cool slightly. Slice *2 bananas;* dip in ReaLemon® brand and drain. Arrange on bottom of prepared pastry shell. Pour filling over bananas; cover. Chill until set. Spread top with whipped cream. Slice remaining banana; dip in ReaLemon® brand, drain and garnish top of pie. Refrigerate leftovers.

Makes one 9-inch pie

Key Lime Pie

1 (9- or 10-inch) baked pastry
   shell *or* graham cracker
   crumb crust*
6 egg *yolks*
2 (14-ounce) cans EAGLE®
   Brand Sweetened
   Condensed Milk
   (NOT evaporated milk)
1 (8-ounce) bottle REALIME®
   Lime Juice from
   Concentrate
Yellow or green food
   coloring, optional
BORDEN® or MEADOW
   GOLD® Whipping Cream,
   stiffly whipped *or*
   whipped topping

Preheat oven to 325°. In large mixer bowl, beat egg *yolks* with sweetened condensed milk. Stir in ReaLime® brand and food coloring if desired. Pour into prepared pastry shell; bake 40 minutes. Cool. Chill. Top with whipped cream. Garnish as desired. Refrigerate leftovers.

Makes one 9- or 10-inch pie

*If using frozen packaged pie shell or 6-ounce packaged graham cracker crumb pie crust, use 1 can Eagle® Brand Sweetened Condensed Milk, 3 egg *yolks* and ½ cup ReaLime® brand. Bake 30 minutes. Proceed as above.

Classic Lemon Meringue Pie

Crust
   9-inch Classic Crisco®
      Single Crust
      (see page 303)

Filling
1½ cups sugar
   3 tablespoons plus
      1½ teaspoons cornstarch
1½ cups water
   4 egg yolks, lightly beaten
   ½ cup lemon juice
   3 tablespoons butter or
      margarine
   2 tablespoons grated lemon
      peel

Meringue
   4 egg whites
   ¼ teaspoon cream of tartar
   ½ cup sugar
   ½ teaspoon vanilla

1. **For crust,** prepare recipe and bake. Cool. Heat oven to 375°F.

2. **For filling,** combine 1½ cups sugar and cornstarch in medium saucepan. Stir in water gradually. Cook and stir on medium heat until mixture thickens and boils. Add about one-third of hot mixture to egg yolks. Mix well. Return to saucepan. Cook and stir 2 minutes. Stir in lemon juice, butter and lemon peel. Spoon into cooled baked crust.

3. **For meringue,** beat egg whites and cream of tartar at high speed of electric mixer until soft peaks form. Beat in ½ cup sugar, 1 tablespoon at a time, until sugar is dissolved and stiff peaks form. Beat in vanilla. Spread over filling, covering completely and sealing to edge of pie.

4. Bake at 375°F for 10 to 15 minutes or until meringue is lightly browned. Cool to room temperature before serving. Refrigerate leftover pie.

One 9-inch Pie

Classic Lemon Meringue Pie

Maple Walnut Cream Pie

Crust

> **9-inch Classic Crisco®
> Single Crust
> (see page 303)**

Filling

> 1 cup pure maple syrup or
>   maple-flavored pancake
>   syrup
> ½ cup milk
> 2 egg yolks, lightly beaten
> 1 envelope (1 tablespoon)
>   unflavored gelatin
> ¼ cup water
> 1 teaspoon maple flavor or
>   extract
> 1 cup whipping cream,
>   whipped
> ¾ cup chopped walnuts
>
> Sweetened whipped cream
> Baked pastry cutouts*
>   (optional)

1. **For crust,** prepare recipe and bake. Reserve dough scraps for pastry cutouts, if desired. Cool.

2. **For filling,** combine syrup and milk in small saucepan. Cook on low heat just until hot. *Do not boil.* Stir small amount of hot mixture gradually into egg yolks. Return egg mixture to saucepan. Bring to a boil on medium heat. Simmer 1 minute. Soften gelatin in water. Remove saucepan from heat. Add softened gelatin and maple flavor. Stir until gelatin dissolves. Refrigerate until mixture begins to thicken.

3. Fold whipped cream into maple mixture. Fold in nuts. Spoon into cooled baked pie crust. Refrigerate 2 hours or until firm. Garnish with whipped cream and baked pastry cutouts, if desired. Refrigerate leftover pie.   *One 9-inch Pie*

For baked pastry cutouts, roll dough scraps together. Cut into desired shapes. Brush with beaten egg white, if desired. Bake at 425°F for 5 minutes or until golden brown. Cool.

Deep-Dish Almond Pumpkin Pie

Crust

> **9-inch Classic Crisco®
> Single Crust
> (see page 303)**

Almond Layer

> 1 cup finely chopped
>   almonds
> ½ cup firmly packed brown
>   sugar
> 3 tablespoons butter or
>   margarine, softened
> 2 teaspoons all-purpose flour
> ¼ teaspoon almond extract

Pumpkin Filling

> 1¼ cups *granulated* brown
>   sugar
> 1 package (3 ounces) cream
>   cheese, softened
> 2 eggs
> 1¼ cups cooked or canned
>   solid pack pumpkin
>   (not pumpkin pie filling)
> ½ cup evaporated milk
> ⅓ cup dairy sour cream
> 1 tablespoon molasses
> 1 teaspoon cinnamon
> ½ teaspoon nutmeg
> ½ teaspoon salt
> ¼ teaspoon ginger
> ⅛ teaspoon ground cloves
> ½ teaspoon almond extract
>
> Baked pastry cutouts
>   (optional)

1. **For crust,** prepare recipe and press into 9-inch deep-dish pie plate. Do not bake. Reserve dough scraps for pastry cutouts (see previous recipe), if desired. Heat oven to 425°F.

2. **For almond layer,** combine nuts, brown sugar, butter, flour and ¼ teaspoon almond extract. Toss with fork until well blended. Spoon into unbaked pie crust. Press firmly on bottom and part way up sides. Refrigerate.

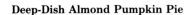

Deep-Dish Almond Pumpkin Pie

3. **For pumpkin filling,** combine *granulated* brown sugar and cream cheese in large bowl. Beat at medium speed of electric mixer until well blended. Beat in eggs, pumpkin, evaporated milk, sour cream and molasses at low speed. Add cinnamon, nutmeg, salt, ginger, cloves and ½ teaspoon almond extract. Beat 1 minute. Spoon over almond layer.

4. Bake at 425°F for 15 minutes. *Reduce oven temperature to 350°F.* Bake for 50 to 60 minutes. Cover edge of pie with foil, if necessary, to prevent overbrowning. Cool to room temperature. Decorate with baked pastry cutouts, if desired. Refrigerate leftover pie.

One 9-inch Pie

Honey Crunch Pecan Pie

Honey Crunch Pecan Pie

Crust
> 9-inch Classic Crisco®
> Single Crust
> (see page 303)

Filling
> 4 eggs, lightly beaten
> 1 cup light corn syrup
> ¼ cup firmly packed brown
>   sugar
> ¼ cup granulated sugar
> 2 tablespoons butter or
>   margarine, melted
> 1 tablespoon bourbon
> 1 teaspoon vanilla
> ½ teaspoon salt
> 1 cup chopped pecans

Topping
> ⅓ cup firmly packed brown
>   sugar
> 3 tablespoons butter or
>   margarine
> 3 tablespoons honey
> 1½ cups pecan halves

1. **For crust,** prepare recipe and press into 9-inch pie plate. Do not bake. Heat oven to 350°F.

2. **For filling,** combine eggs, corn syrup, sugars, melted butter, bourbon, vanilla and salt in large bowl. Stir in chopped pecans. Mix well. Spoon into unbaked pie crust. Bake at 350°F for 15 minutes. Cover edge with foil to prevent overbrowning. Bake for 20 minutes. Remove from oven. Remove foil and save.

3. **For topping,** combine brown sugar, butter and honey in medium saucepan. Cook about 2 minutes or until sugar dissolves. Add pecan halves. Stir until coated. Spoon over pie. Recover edge with foil. Bake 10 to 20 minutes or until topping is bubbly and crust is golden brown. Cool to room temperature before serving. Refrigerate leftover pie.   *One 9-inch Pie*

Chocolate Pecan Pie

> 1 package (4 ounces)
>   BAKER'S® GERMAN'S®
>   Sweet Chocolate
> 2 tablespoons margarine or
>   butter
> 1 cup corn syrup
> ⅓ cup sugar
> 3 eggs
> 1 teaspoon vanilla
> 1½ cups pecan halves
> 1 unbaked 9-inch pie shell
>   COOL WHIP® Whipped
>   Topping, thawed
>   (optional)

HEAT oven to 350°F.

MICROWAVE chocolate and margarine in large microwavable bowl on HIGH 2 minutes or until margarine is melted. **Stir until chocolate is completely melted.**

STIR in corn syrup, sugar, eggs and vanilla until well blended. Stir in pecans, reserving 8 halves for garnish, if desired. Pour filling into pie shell.

BAKE for 55 minutes or until knife inserted 1 inch from center comes out clean. Cool on wire rack. Garnish with whipped topping and chocolate-dipped pecan halves, if desired.

Makes 8 servings

Prep time: 20 minutes
Baking time: 55 minutes

Chocolate Truffle Tart

Chocolate Truffle Tart

Crust:
⅔ cup all-purpose flour
½ cup sugar
½ cup walnuts, ground
6 tablespoons (¾ stick) butter or margarine, softened
⅓ cup NESTLÉ® Cocoa

Filling:
1 cup heavy or whipping cream
¼ cup sugar
One 8-oz. pkg. (4 foil-wrapped bars) NESTLÉ® Semi-Sweet Chocolate baking bars, broken up
2 tablespoons seedless raspberry jam

Additional whipped cream for garnish
Fresh raspberries for garnish

Crust: Preheat oven to 350°F. In small mixer bowl, beat flour, ½ cup sugar, walnuts, butter and cocoa until soft dough forms. Press dough into 9-inch fluted tart pan with removable bottom.

Bake 12 to 14 minutes until puffed. Cool completely.

Filling: In medium saucepan, bring heavy cream and ¼ cup sugar just to a boil, stirring occasionally. Remove from heat. Stir in semi-sweet chocolate baking bars and jam; cool 5 minutes. Whisk until chocolate is melted and mixture is smooth. Transfer to small mixer bowl. Cover; refrigerate 45 to 60 minutes until mixture is cool and slightly thickened.

Beat Filling just until color lightens slightly. Pour into Crust. Refrigerate. Garnish with whipped cream and raspberries.
Makes 10 to 12 servings

Chocolate Turtle Pie

¼ cup caramel or butterscotch flavor dessert topping
1 baked 8- or 9-inch pie shell, cooled
¾ cup pecan halves
1 package (4-serving size) JELL-O® Pudding and Pie Filling, Chocolate Flavor*
1¾ cups milk*
1¾ cups (4 ounces) COOL WHIP® Whipped Topping, thawed

BRING caramel topping to boil in small saucepan, stirring constantly. Pour into pie shell. Arrange pecans on top; chill.

COMBINE pie filling mix and milk in medium saucepan. Cook and stir over medium heat until mixture comes to full boil. Cool 5 minutes, stirring twice. Pour into pie shell; place plastic wrap on surface of filling. Chill 3 hours. Remove plastic wrap. Cover with whipped topping. Drizzle with additional caramel topping and garnish with additional pecans, if desired.
Makes 8 servings

*1 package (4-serving size) instant pudding may be substituted for 1 package (4-serving size) cooked pudding mix. Prepare as directed on package, using 1½ cups *cold* milk.

Prep time: 15 minutes
Chill time: 3 hours

Chocolate Mudslide Pie

Chocolate Mudslide Pie

One 8-oz. pkg. (4 foil-wrapped
bars) NESTLÉ® Semi-
Sweet Chocolate baking
bars, broken up
1 teaspoon TASTER'S
CHOICE® Freeze-Dried
Instant Coffee
1 teaspoon water
¾ cup sour cream
½ cup granulated sugar
1 teaspoon vanilla extract
One 9-inch prepared chocolate
crumb crust
1 cup confectioners' sugar
¼ cup NESTLÉ® Cocoa
1½ cups heavy or whipping
cream
2 tablespoons NESTLÉ® Toll
House® Semi-Sweet
Chocolate Mini Morsels

In small saucepan over low heat,
melt semi-sweet chocolate baking
bars; cool 10 minutes. In small
bowl, dissolve instant coffee in
water. Add sour cream,
granulated sugar and vanilla
extract; stir until sugar is
dissolved. Blend in melted
chocolate. Spread in crust; set
aside.

In small mixer bowl, beat
confectioners' sugar, cocoa and
heavy cream until stiff peaks
form. Spoon cream mixture into
pastry bag fitted with star tip;
pipe onto pie. Sprinkle with mini
morsels. Cover; refrigerate at
least 4 hours until firm.
Makes 8 servings

German Sweet Chocolate Pie

1 package (4 ounces)
BAKER'S® GERMAN'S®
Sweet Chocolate
⅓ cup milk
1 package (3 ounces)
PHILADELPHIA BRAND®
Cream Cheese, softened
2 tablespoons sugar
(optional)
3½ cups (8 ounces) COOL
WHIP® Whipped Topping,
thawed
1 (9-inch) prepared crumb
crust
Chocolate shavings or
curls (optional)

MICROWAVE chocolate and 2
tablespoons of the milk in large
microwavable bowl on HIGH 1½
to 2 minutes or until chocolate is
almost melted, stirring halfway
through heating time. **Stir until
chocolate is completely
melted.**

BEAT in cream cheese, sugar
and the remaining milk until
well blended. Refrigerate to cool,
about 10 minutes.

STIR in whipped topping gently
until smooth. Spoon into crust.
Freeze until firm, about 4 hours.
Garnish with chocolate shavings
or curls, if desired.
Makes 8 servings

Prep time: 20 minutes
Freezing time: 4 hours

Saucepan preparation: Heat
chocolate and 2 tablespoons of
the milk in saucepan over very
low heat until chocolate is
melted, stirring constantly.
Remove from heat. Continue as
above.

German Sweet Chocolate Pie

Ice Cream Shop Pie

1½ cups cold half and half or milk
1 package (4-serving size) JELL-O® Instant Pudding and Pie Filling, any flavor
3½ cups (8 ounces) COOL WHIP® Whipped Topping, thawed
Ice Cream Shop Ingredients*
1 packaged chocolate, graham cracker or vanilla crumb crust

POUR half and half into large bowl. Add pudding mix. Beat with wire whisk until well blended, 1 to 2 minutes. Let stand 5 minutes or until slightly thickened.

FOLD whipped topping and Ice Cream Shop ingredients into pudding mixture. Spoon into crust.

FREEZE pie until firm, about 6 hours or overnight. Remove from freezer. Let stand at room temperature about 10 minutes before serving to soften. Store any leftover pie in freezer.

Makes 8 servings

Rocky Road Pie: Use any chocolate flavor pudding mix and chocolate crumb crust. Fold in ½ cup *each* BAKER'S® Semi-Sweet Real Chocolate Chips, KRAFT® Miniature Marshmallows and chopped nuts with whipped topping. Serve with chocolate sauce, if desired.

Toffee Bar Crunch Pie: Use French vanilla or vanilla flavor pudding mix and graham cracker crumb crust, spreading ⅓ cup butterscotch sauce onto bottom of crust before filling. Fold in 1 cup chopped chocolate-covered English toffee bars (about 6 bars) with whipped topping. Garnish with additional chopped toffee bars, if desired.

Strawberry Banana Split Pie: Use French vanilla or vanilla flavor pudding mix, reducing half and half to ¾ cup and adding ¾ cup pureed BIRDS EYE® Quick Thaw Strawberries with the half and half. Use vanilla crumb crust and line bottom with banana slices. Garnish with whipped topping, maraschino cherries and chopped nuts. Serve with remaining strawberries, pureed, if desired.

Chocolate Cookie Pie: Use French vanilla or vanilla flavor pudding mix and chocolate crumb crust. Fold in 1 cup chopped chocolate sandwich cookies with whipped topping.

Nutcracker Pie: Use butter pecan flavor pudding mix and graham cracker crumb crust. Fold in 1 cup chopped mixed nuts with whipped topping.

Peppermint Stick Pie: Use French vanilla or vanilla flavor pudding mix and chocolate crumb crust. Fold in ½ cup crushed hard peppermint candies, ½ cup BAKER'S® Semi-Sweet Real Chocolate Chips and 2 teaspoons peppermint extract with whipped topping.

Prep time: 15 minutes
Freezing time: 6 hours

Peppermint Parfait Pie

1 (9-inch) baked pastry shell
1 (1-ounce) square unsweetened chocolate
1 (14-ounce) can EAGLE® Brand Sweetened Condensed Milk (NOT evaporated milk)
½ teaspoon vanilla extract
1 (8-ounce) package cream cheese, softened
3 tablespoons white creme de menthe liqueur
Red food coloring, optional
1 (8-ounce) container frozen non-dairy whipped topping, thawed (3½ cups)

In small saucepan, melt chocolate with ½ cup sweetened condensed milk; stir in vanilla. Spread on bottom of prepared pastry shell. In large mixer bowl, beat cheese until fluffy. Gradually beat in remaining sweetened condensed milk. Stir in liqueur and food coloring if desired. Fold in whipped topping. Pour into prepared pastry shell. Chill 4 hours or until set. Garnish as desired. Refrigerate leftovers.

Makes one 9-inch pie

Fluffy Grasshopper Pie

2 cups finely crushed creme-filled chocolate sandwich cookies (about 24 cookies)
¼ cup margarine or butter, melted
1 (8-ounce) package cream cheese, softened
1 (14-ounce) can EAGLE® Brand Sweetened Condensed Milk (NOT evaporated milk)
3 tablespoons REALEMON® Lemon Juice from Concentrate
¼ cup green creme de menthe liqueur
¼ cup white creme de cacao liqueur
1 (4-ounce) container frozen non-dairy whipped topping, thawed (1¾ cups)

Combine crumbs and margarine; press firmly on bottom and up side to rim of buttered 9-inch pie plate. Chill. Meanwhile, in large mixer bowl, beat cheese until fluffy. Gradually beat in sweetened condensed milk until smooth. Stir in ReaLemon® brand and liqueurs. Fold in whipped topping. Chill 20 minutes; pour into crust. Chill or freeze 4 hours or until set. Garnish as desired. Refrigerate or freeze leftovers.

Makes one 9-inch pie

**Top to bottom: Rocky Road Pie, Toffee Bar Crunch Pie and
Strawberry Banana Split Pie**

Almond Heart Napoleons

- **1 package (17¼ ounces) frozen puff pastry sheets**
- **1¼ cups cold half and half or milk**
- **2 tablespoons almond liqueur***
- **1 package (4-serving size) JELL-O® Instant Pudding and Pie Filling, French Vanilla or Vanilla Flavor**
- **½ cup confectioners sugar**
- **2 teaspoons (about) hot water**
- **1 square BAKER'S® Semi-Sweet Chocolate, melted**

THAW puff pastry as directed on package. Preheat oven to 350°. Unfold pastry. Using 2-inch heart-shaped cookie cutter, cut each sheet into 12 hearts. Bake on ungreased baking sheets for 20 minutes or until golden. Remove from baking sheets. Cool on racks. When pastry is completely cooled, split each heart horizontally in half.

POUR half and half and liqueur into small bowl. Add pudding mix. Beat with wire whisk until well blended, 1 to 2 minutes. Chill 10 minutes.

SPREAD about 1 tablespoon of the pudding mixture onto bottom half of each pastry; top with remaining pastry half.

STIR together confectioners sugar and hot water in small bowl to make thin glaze. Spread over hearts. (If glaze becomes too thick, add more hot water until glaze is of desired consistency.) Before glaze dries, drizzle chocolate on top to form thin lines. Draw wooden pick through chocolate to make design. Chill until ready to serve.

Makes 2 dozen pastries

Prep time: 30 minutes
Baking time: 20 minutes

*½ teaspoon almond extract may be substituted for 2 tablespoons almond liqueur.

Slovakian Kolacky

- **2 packages (¼ ounce *each*) active dry yeast**
- **¼ cup warm water (105° to 115°F)**
- **7 cups all-purpose flour**
- **1 teaspoon salt**
- **2 cups LAND O LAKES® Butter, softened**
- **4 eggs, slightly beaten**
- **2 cups whipping cream (1 pint)**
- **Fruit preserves**

In small bowl dissolve yeast in warm water. In large bowl combine flour and salt; cut in butter until crumbly. Stir in yeast, eggs and whipping cream. Turn dough onto lightly floured surface; knead until smooth, 2 to 3 minutes. Place in greased bowl; turn greased side up. Cover; refrigerate until firm, 6 hours or overnight.

Heat oven to 375°. Roll out dough, ½ at a time, on sugared surface to ⅛-inch thickness. Cut into 3-inch squares. Spoon 1 teaspoon preserves in center of *each* square. Bring up two opposite corners to center; pinch together to seal. Fold sealed tip to one side; pinch to seal. Place 1-inch apart on ungreased cookie sheets. Bake for 10 to 15 minutes or until lightly browned.

Makes 5 dozen kolacky

Apple Turnovers

Filling
- **1¾ cups chopped, peeled tart cooking apples (about ⅔ pound or 2 medium)**
- **⅓ cup water**
- **⅓ cup firmly packed brown sugar**
- **¼ teaspoon cinnamon**
- **⅛ teaspoon nutmeg**
- **1 tablespoon all-purpose flour**
- **1 teaspoon granulated sugar**
- **1 tablespoon butter or margarine**

Pastry
- **9-inch Classic Crisco® Double Crust (see page 303)**

Glaze
- **½ cup confectioners sugar**
- **1 tablespoon milk**
- **¼ teaspoon vanilla**

Slovakian Kolacky

1. **For filling,** combine apples and water in small saucepan. Cook and stir on high heat until mixture comes to a boil. Reduce heat to low. Simmer 5 minutes. Stir in brown sugar, cinnamon and nutmeg. Simmer 5 minutes. Stir frequently. Combine flour and granulated sugar. Stir into apple mixture. Bring to a boil. Boil 1 minute. Stir in butter.

2. **For pastry,** heat oven to 425°F. Prepare dough and divide in half. Roll each half to 1/16-inch thickness. Use lid from 3-pound Crisco can as pattern. Cut six 5¼-inch circles from each half. (Reroll as necessary.)

3. Place about 1 tablespoon apple filling on each dough circle. Moisten edges with water. Fold in half over filling. Press with fork to seal. Place on ungreased baking sheet. Prick tops with fork. Bake at 425°F for 20 minutes or until golden brown. Cool 10 minutes on wire rack.

4. **For glaze,** combine confectioners sugar, milk and vanilla in small bowl. Stir well. Drizzle over turnovers. Serve warm or cool.   *12 Turnovers*

Note: Any canned fruit pie filling can be substituted for fresh apple filling.

Mini Almond Pastries

Mini Almond Pastries

  ¼ **cup powdered sugar**
  ¼ **cup LAND O LAKES®**
    Butter, softened
  1 **tube (3½ ounces) almond**
    paste (⅓ cup)
  2 **egg yolks**
  2 **teaspoons grated lemon**
    peel
  ½ **teaspoon almond extract**
  ¼ **cup granulated sugar**
  1 **package (17¼ ounces)**
    frozen prerolled sheets
    puff pastry, thawed
    (2 sheets)

In small mixer bowl combine powdered sugar, butter, almond paste, egg yolks, lemon peel and almond extract. Beat at low speed, scraping bowl often, until well mixed, 1 to 2 minutes; set aside. Sprinkle about *1 tablespoon* granulated sugar on surface or pastry cloth. Unfold 1 sheet puff pastry on sugared surface; sprinkle with about

1 tablespoon granulated sugar. Roll out puff pastry sheet into 12-inch square. Cut square into 2 (12×6-inch) rectangles. Spread ¼ of (*about 3 tablespoons*) almond paste mixture on *each* rectangle. Working with 1 (12×6-inch) rectangle at a time, fold ½ inch of both 12-inch sides in toward center of pastry. Continue folding both 12-inch sides, ½ inch at a time, until 12-inch sides meet in center. Fold one 12-inch side on top of other 12-inch side; firmly press layers together. Repeat with remaining 12×6-inch rectangle. Repeat with remaining ingredients. Wrap *each* pastry roll in plastic wrap; refrigerate at least 2 hours.

Heat oven to 400°. Cut pastry rolls into ½-inch slices. Place slices 2 inches apart on greased or parchment-lined cookie sheets. Bake for 7 to 11 minutes or until lightly browned. Remove from pan immediately.

Makes 7 to 8 dozen pastries

CAKES & CHEESECAKES

What better way to top off any celebration than with a moist, delectable cake! Create a special grand finale with an extravagant multi-tiered torte, cream-filled cake roll or dreamy chocolate layer cake. Delight children—young and old—with colorful shaped cakes for a birthday party or holiday gathering. Or treat your family to a simple shortcake to spruce up a weeknight meal. And when you desire the smooth and creamy decadence of fabulous cheesecake, select from a wide assortment including velvety chocolate, caramel apple, heavenly orange and rocky road.

Ice Cream Cone Cakes

1 package DUNCAN HINES® Moist Deluxe Cake Mix (any flavor)

Frosting
1 cup semi-sweet chocolate chips
5 cups confectioners sugar
¾ cup CRISCO® Shortening
½ cup water
⅓ cup non-dairy powdered creamer
2 teaspoons vanilla extract
½ teaspoon salt
Chocolate jimmies or sprinkles
Assorted decors
Candy gumdrops
2 maraschino cherries, for garnish

1. Preheat oven to 350°F. Grease and flour one 8-inch round cake pan and one 8-inch square pan.

2. Prepare cake following package directions for basic recipe. Pour about 2 cups batter into round pan. Pour about 3 cups batter into square pan. Bake at 350°F for 30 to 35 minutes or until toothpick inserted in center comes out clean. Cool following package directions.

3. **For frosting,** melt chocolate chips in small saucepan over low heat. Set aside. Combine confectioners sugar, shortening, water, non-dairy powdered creamer, vanilla extract and salt in large bowl. Beat at medium speed with electric mixer for 3 minutes. Beat at high speed for 5 minutes. Add confectioners sugar to thicken or water to thin frosting as needed. Divide frosting in half. Blend melted chocolate chips into one half.

4. To assemble, cut cooled cake and arrange as shown (see Tip). Frost cone with chocolate frosting, reserving ½ cup. Place writing tip in pastry bag. Fill with remaining ½ cup chocolate frosting. Pipe waffle pattern onto cones; sprinkle with chocolate jimmies. Spread white frosting on ice cream parts; decorate with assorted decors and gumdrops. Top each with maraschino cherry.   *12 to 16 Servings*

Tip: For ease in handling, freeze cake before cutting into ice cream and cone shapes.

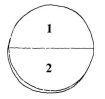
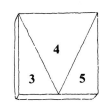
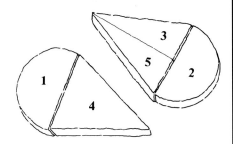

Ice Cream Cone Cakes

Dream Castle Cake

Dream Castle Cake

Cakes & Frostings
    3 (8-inch) square cakes
    5¼ cups Buttercream Frosting
        (page 337)*
    2 cups Base Frosting
        (page 337), if desired

Decorations & Equipment
    Assorted colored sugar
    4 sugar ice cream cones
    Small purple and white
        gumdrops
    Pastel candy-coated
        chocolate pieces
    2 pink sugar wafer cookies
    1 (19×13-inch) cake board,
        cut in half crosswise and
        covered

*Color ½ cup frosting blue and
½ cup yellow; reserve 4¼ cups
white frosting.

1. Trim tops and edges of cakes. Place one square cake on prepared cake board. Frost top with some of the white frosting.

2. Cut remaining cakes as shown in diagrams 1 and 2.

3. Place piece A over bottom layer. Frost top of piece A with some of the white frosting.

4. Position remaining pieces as shown in diagram 3, connecting with some of the white frosting.

5. Frost entire cake with Base Frosting to seal in crumbs.

6. Frost again with white frosting. Cover piece D (bridge) with colored sugar.

7. Frost cones with blue and yellow frostings. Place as shown in photo.

8. Decorate castle and towers as shown, using frosting to attach candies, if needed.

9. Arrange wafer cookies on front of castle for gate.

Makes 24 to 28 servings

Tip: For easier frosting of cones, hold cone over fingers of one hand while frosting with other hand. Place in position, touching up frosting, if needed.

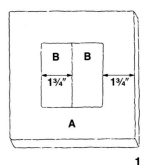

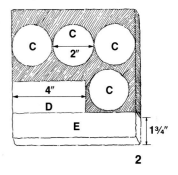

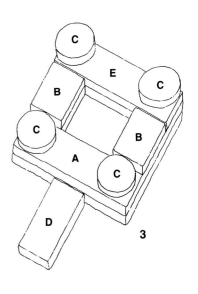

Speedy Racetrack Cake

Cakes & Frostings
   1 (9-inch) round cake
   1 (13×9-inch) cake
   3½ cups Buttercream Frosting
      (page 337)*
   1½ cups Base Frosting
      (page 337), if desired

Decorations & Equipment
   Green colored sugar
   2 to 3 rolls white donut-
      shaped hard candies, cut
      in half
   ½ (16-ounce) box cinnamon
      graham crackers
   2- to 3-inch race cars
   Flags, if desired
   1 (19×13-inch) cake board,
      cut to fit cake, if desired,
      and covered

*Mix 2 cups frosting with 2 tablespoons unsweetened cocoa powder. Color 1½ cups green.

1. Trim tops and edges of cakes. Cut round cake in half crosswise. Cut 13×9-inch cake as shown in diagram 1.

2. Position pieces on prepared cake board as shown in diagram 2, connecting with some of the green frosting.

3. Frost entire cake with Base Frosting to seal in crumbs.

4. Using wooden pick, draw area for track, about 2 inches wide, as shown in photo. Frost center of cake with green frosting. Sprinkle with colored sugar. Frost track and sides of cake with chocolate frosting.

5. Arrange hard candies, cut-side down, around inside of track. Cut graham crackers about ¼ inch higher than cake. Arrange around edge of cake, attaching with more chocolate frosting, if needed.

6. Let frosting harden before placing cars and flags on track.
Makes 20 to 24 servings

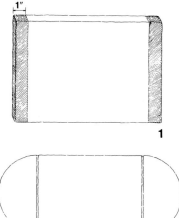

Drum Layer Cake

   1 package DUNCAN HINES®
      Moist Deluxe Cake Mix
      (any flavor)
   2 containers (16 ounces
      each) DUNCAN HINES®
      Vanilla Layer Cake
      Frosting, divided
   Green food coloring
   Candy-coated chocolate
      pieces
   Thin pretzel sticks
   2 Lollipops

1. Preheat oven to 350°F. Grease and flour two 8-inch round cake pans.

2. Prepare, bake and cool cake following package directions for basic recipe.

3. To assemble, place one cake layer on serving plate. Spread with ¾ cup Vanilla frosting. Top with second cake layer. Tint 1¼ cups frosting with green food coloring. Spread green frosting on sides of cake. Spread ¾ cup Vanilla frosting on top of cake. To decorate drum, place candy pieces around bottom and top edges of cake on green frosting. Arrange pretzel sticks in zig-zag design between candies. Place lollipops on top of cake with sticks crisscrossing for drumsticks.

12 to 16 Servings

Tip: Spread leftover frosting between graham crackers for a delicious snack.

Speedy Racetrack Cake

Candy Cane Cake

1 package DUNCAN HINES®
Moist Deluxe Cake Mix
(any flavor)

Frosting
5 cups confectioners sugar
¾ cup CRISCO® Shortening
½ cup water
⅓ cup non-dairy powdered
creamer
2 teaspoons vanilla extract
½ teaspoon salt
Red food coloring
Maraschino cherry halves,
well drained

1. Preheat oven to 350°F. Grease and flour 13×9×2-inch pan.

2. Prepare, bake and cool cake following package directions for basic recipe. Remove from pan. Freeze cake for ease in handling.

3. **For frosting,** combine confectioners sugar, shortening, water, non-dairy powdered creamer, vanilla extract and salt in large bowl. Beat at medium speed with electric mixer for 3 minutes. Beat at high speed for 5 minutes. Add confectioners sugar to thicken or water to thin

frosting as needed. Reserve 2 cups frosting. Tint remaining frosting with red food coloring.

4. Cut frozen cake and arrange as shown. Spread white frosting on cake. Mark candy cane stripes in frosting with tip of knife. Place star tip in decorating bag and fill with red frosting. To make stripes, arrange maraschino cherry halves and pipe red frosting following lines.
12 to 16 Servings

Tip: For a quick dessert, serve leftover cake pieces with sugared strawberries or dollops of whipped cream.

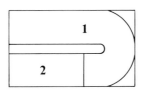

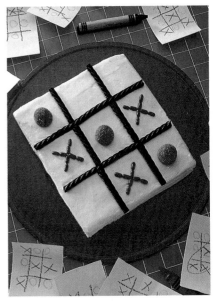

Tic-Tac-Toe Cake

Tic-Tac-Toe Cake

Cake & Frostings
1 (8-inch) square cake
2½ cups Buttercream Frosting
(page 337), divided
2 tablespoons milk

Decorations & Equipment
4 black licorice twists
3 large red gumdrops
24 small red candies
1 (19×13-inch) cake board,
cut in half crosswise and
covered, or large plate

1. Trim top and edges of cake. Place on prepared cake board.

2. Stir milk into 1 cup Buttercream Frosting until well blended. Frost entire cake with thinned frosting to seal in crumbs.

3. Frost again with remaining 1½ cups Buttercream Frosting.

4. Using wooden pick, mark cake into thirds, both horizontally and vertically. Arrange 2 licorice twists over horizontal lines; cut and place remaining licorice twists as shown in photo.

5. Decorate with gumdrops and candies as shown.
Makes 9 to 12 servings

Candy Cane Cake

Jet Plane Cake

Cake & Frostings
1 (13×9-inch) cake
3½ cups Buttercream Frosting
(page 337)*
1 cup Base Frosting
(page 337), if desired

Decorations & Equipment
4 pastel miniature
marshmallows
1 small red gumdrop
1 (19×13-inch) cake board,
cut to fit cake, if desired,
and covered
Pastry bag and medium
writing tip

Jet Plane Cake

1. Trim top and edges of cake. Cut as shown in diagram 1.

2. Place piece A in center of prepared cake board. Frost top with some of the white frosting, then place piece B over frosting. Starting 3 inches from 1 side make an angled cut in piece B toward the front as shown in diagram 2.

3. Position remaining pieces on prepared cake board as shown in diagram 3, connecting with some of the white frosting. Trim sides to make nose about 1 inch wide. Trim top side edges of piece B to give a rounded appearance as shown in photo.

4. Frost entire cake with Base Frosting to seal in crumbs.

5. Using wooden pick, draw areas for windows as shown. Frost with light gray frosting.

6. Frost remaining cake with white frosting.

7. Using writing tip and blue frosting, pipe outlines for windows and design on wings as shown. Attach flattened marshmallows and gumdrop as shown.

Makes 14 to 16 servings

*Color ½ cup frosting blue and ½ cup light gray; reserve 2½ cups white frosting.

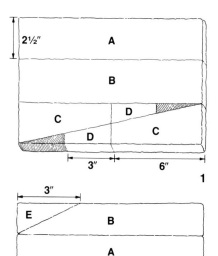

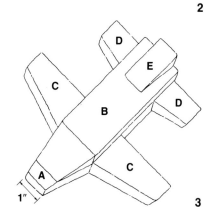

Baseball Cake

1 package DUNCAN HINES®
Moist Deluxe Yellow
Cake Mix
1 container (16 ounces)
DUNCAN HINES® Vanilla
Layer Cake Frosting
Red licorice laces
Green tinted shredded
coconut, optional

1. Preheat oven to 350°F. Grease and flour 2½-quart ovenproof glass bowl with rounded bottom.

2. Prepare cake following package directions for basic recipe; pour into bowl. Bake 55 to 65 minutes or until toothpick inserted in center comes out clean. Cool in bowl on cooling rack 15 minutes. Invert onto cooling rack. Cool completely.

3. To assemble, place cake on serving plate. Frost with Vanilla frosting. Cut 1 licorice lace into 1-inch pieces. Apply licorice laces and pieces on cake to resemble baseball seams. Arrange tinted coconut around base of cake, if desired.

12 to 16 Servings

Blueberry Angel Food Cake Roll

Blueberry Angel Food Cake Rolls

**1 package DUNCAN HINES®
Angel Food Cake Mix
Confectioners sugar
1 can (21 ounces) blueberry
pie filling
Mint leaves, for garnish
(optional)**

1. Preheat oven to 350°F. Line two 15½×10½×1-inch jelly-roll pans with aluminum foil.

2. Prepare cake following package directions. Divide into pans. Spread evenly. Cut through batter with knife or spatula to remove large air bubbles. Bake at 350°F for 15 minutes or until set. Invert cakes at once onto clean, lint-free dishtowels dusted with confectioners sugar. Remove foil carefully. Starting at short end, roll up each cake with towel jelly-roll fashion. Cool completely.

3. Unroll cakes. Spread about 1 cup blueberry pie filling to within 1 inch of edges on each cake. Reroll and place seam-side down on serving plate. Dust with confectioners sugar. Garnish with mint leaves, if desired.

16 to 20 Servings

Tip: For a variation in flavor, substitute cherry pie filling for blueberry pie filling.

Cherry Cream Nut Roll

**5 eggs, separated
½ cup granulated sugar
1 teaspoon brandy extract or
    rum extract
1 can SOLO® or 1 jar
    BAKER® Nut Filling
½ cup all-purpose flour
½ teaspoon baking powder
¼ teaspoon salt
Confectioners sugar**

Filling
**2 cups heavy cream
3 to 4 tablespoons
    confectioners sugar
1½ teaspoons brandy extract
    or rum extract
1 can SOLO® or 1 jar
    BAKER® Cherry Filling**

Preheat oven to 350°F. Grease 15×10-inch jelly-roll pan. Line pan with waxed paper. Grease paper and set aside.

Beat egg yolks and granulated sugar about 5 minutes in large bowl with electric mixer until thick and pale yellow. Beat in brandy extract and nut filling until well blended.

Beat egg whites in separate bowl with electric mixer until stiff peaks form. Stir 3 heaping tablespoons egg whites into nut mixture to lighten. Fold in remaining egg whites. Sift flour, baking powder and salt over nut mixture and fold in. Spread batter evenly in prepared pan.

Bake 20 to 22 minutes or until center springs back when lightly pressed.

Sprinkle towel with confectioners sugar. Invert cake onto sugared towel and remove pan. Peel off waxed paper and trim off any crusty edges. Roll up cake and towel, jelly-roll style, starting from short side. Place on wire rack and cool completely.

To fill cake, unroll cooled cake on flat surface. Whip cream in large bowl with electric mixer until soft peaks form. Add 3 to 4 tablespoons confectioners sugar and brandy extract and whip until firm. Fold whipped cream into cherry filling. Spread half of cherry cream over cake. Reroll cake without towel and place, seam-side down, on serving plate. Spread remaining cherry cream over side and top of cake. Refrigerate until ready to serve.

Makes 8 to 10 servings

Fresh Peach Mousse Cake

**¾ cup whipping cream
¼ cup sugar, divided
½ teaspoon vanilla extract
¼ teaspoon almond extract
3 egg whites
1 package (10¾ ounces)
    frozen pound cake,
    thawed
3 fresh California peaches,
    sliced
Mint sprigs
    (optional garnish)**

In large chilled bowl, whip cream until stiff, gradually beating in 2 tablespoons sugar and the extracts; set aside. In medium bowl, beat egg whites with remaining 2 tablespoons sugar until stiff. Carefully fold egg whites into whipped cream mixture so as not to reduce volume; refrigerate mousse mixture until chilled. Cut cake horizontally into 3 layers.

Reserve 5 peach slices for garnish. Place one cake layer on serving plate. Spread with ⅓ of mousse and ½ of remaining peach slices. Repeat layering, ending with mousse. Refrigerate until chilled. Garnish with reserved peach slices and mint sprigs, if desired.

Makes 8 servings

Favorite recipe from **California Tree Fruit Agreement**

Mini Morsel Pound Cake

    3 cups all-purpose flour
    2 teaspoons baking powder
    ½ teaspoon salt
    1½ cups (3 sticks) butter or
      margarine, softened
    1½ cups granulated sugar
    4 eggs
    1 teaspoon vanilla extract
    ¼ cup milk
One 12-oz. pkg. (2 cups)
      NESTLÉ® Toll House®
      Semi-Sweet Chocolate
      Mini Morsels
      Confectioners' sugar for
      garnish

Preheat oven to 350°F. Grease and flour 10-inch fluted tube pan or two 9×5-inch loaf pans. In small bowl, combine flour, baking powder and salt; set aside.

In large mixer bowl, beat butter and granulated sugar until creamy. Add eggs, one at a time, beating well after each addition. Blend in vanilla extract. Add flour mixture alternately with milk. Stir in mini morsels. Pour into prepared pan.

Bake 60 to 70 minutes until cake tester inserted into center comes out clean. Cool 15 minutes; remove from pan. Cool completely. Sprinkle with confectioners' sugar.

Makes 16 to 20 servings

Della Robbia Cake

Cake
    1 package DUNCAN HINES®
      Angel Food Cake Mix
    1½ teaspoons grated lemon
      peel

Glaze
    6 tablespoons sugar
    1½ tablespoons cornstarch
    1 cup water
    1 tablespoon lemon juice
    ½ teaspoon vanilla extract
      Few drops red food
      coloring
    6 cling peach slices
    6 medium strawberries,
      sliced

Della Robbia Cake

1. Preheat oven to 375°F.

2. **For cake,** prepare following package directions adding lemon peel with Cake Flour Mixture (red "B" packet). Bake and cool following package directions.

3. **For glaze,** combine sugar, cornstarch and water in small saucepan. Cook on medium-high heat until mixture thickens and clears. Remove from heat. Stir in lemon juice, vanilla extract and red food coloring.

4. Alternate peach slices with strawberry slices around top of cooled cake. Pour glaze over fruit and top of cake. Refrigerate leftovers.   *12 to 16 Servings*

Tip: Use only metal or glass mixing bowls when preparing angel food cake mixes. Plastic or ceramic bowls can retain traces of grease which will prevent the egg whites from reaching full volume.

Holiday Fruitcake

- 1 cup chopped candied fruit
- ⅔ cup pitted dates, chopped
- ½ cup chopped walnuts
- ¼ cup brandy or orange juice
- 1 package (6-serving size) JELL-O® Instant Pudding and Pie Filling, Vanilla Flavor
- 1 package (2-layer size) yellow cake mix
- 4 eggs
- 1 cup (½ pint) sour cream
- ⅓ cup vegetable oil
- 1 tablespoon grated orange rind
- ⅔ cup cold milk
  Marzipan Fruits (recipe follows) (optional)

MIX together candied fruit, dates, walnuts and brandy.

RESERVE ⅓ cup pudding mix; set aside. Combine cake mix, remaining pudding mix, eggs, sour cream, oil and orange rind in large bowl. Beat at low speed of electric mixer just to moisten, scraping sides of bowl often. Beat at medium speed 4 minutes. Stir in fruit mixture.

POUR batter into well-greased and floured 10-inch fluted tube pan. Bake at 350° for 45 minutes or until cake tester inserted in center comes out clean. Cool in pan 15 minutes. Remove from pan; finish cooling on wire rack.

BEAT reserved pudding mix and milk in small bowl until smooth. Spoon over top of cake to glaze. Garnish with Marzipan Fruits, if desired.   *Makes 12 servings*

Prep time: 30 minutes
Baking time: 45 minutes

Marzipan Fruits

- 1¾ cups BAKER'S® ANGEL FLAKE® Coconut, finely chopped
- 1 package (4-serving size) JELL-O® Brand Gelatin, any flavor
- 1 cup ground blanched almonds
- ⅔ cup sweetened condensed milk
- 1½ teaspoons sugar
- 1 teaspoon almond extract
  Food coloring (optional)
  Whole cloves (optional)
  Citron or angelica (optional)

MIX together coconut, gelatin, almonds, milk, sugar and extract. Shape by hand into small fruits, or use small candy molds. If desired, use food coloring to paint details on fruit; add whole cloves and citron for stems and blossom ends. Chill until dry. Store in covered container at room temperature up to 1 week.

Makes 2 to 3 dozen confections

Prep time: 30 minutes

Top to bottom: Eggnog Cheesecake (page 346), Holiday Fruitcake and Raspberry Gift Box (page 359)

Fudge Ribbon Cake

1 (18¼- or 18½-ounce)
  package chocolate cake
  mix
1 (8-ounce) package cream
  cheese, softened
2 tablespoons margarine or
  butter, softened
1 tablespoon cornstarch
1 (14-ounce) can EAGLE®
  Brand Sweetened
  Condensed Milk
  (NOT evaporated milk)
1 egg
1 teaspoon vanilla extract
  Confectioners' sugar or
  Chocolate Drizzle
  (recipe follows)

Preheat oven to 350°. Prepare cake mix as package directs. Pour batter into *well-greased* and floured 10-inch fluted tube pan. In small mixer bowl, beat cheese, margarine and cornstarch until fluffy. Gradually beat in sweetened condensed milk, then egg and vanilla until smooth. Pour evenly over cake batter. Bake 50 to 55 minutes or until wooden pick inserted near center comes out clean. Cool 15 minutes; remove from pan. Cool. Sprinkle with confectioners' sugar or drizzle with Chocolate Drizzle.

Makes one 10-inch cake

CHOCOLATE DRIZZLE: In small saucepan, over low heat, melt 1 (1-ounce) square unsweetened or semi-sweet chocolate and 1 tablespoon margarine or butter with 2 tablespoons water. Remove from heat. Stir in ¾ cup confectioners' sugar and ½ teaspoon vanilla extract. Stir until smooth. *Makes ⅓ cup*

Fudge Ribbon Sheet Cake:
Prepare cake mix as package directs. Pour batter into *well-greased* and floured 15×10-inch jellyroll pan. Prepare cream cheese topping as above; spoon evenly over batter. Bake 20 minutes or until wooden pick inserted near center comes out clean. Cool. Frost with 1 (16-ounce) can ready-to-spread chocolate frosting.

Left to right: Lemon Cheesecake with Raspberry Sauce (page 345) and Triple Chocolate Fantasy

Triple Chocolate Fantasy

Cake
  1 package DUNCAN HINES®
    Moist Deluxe Devil's
    Food Cake Mix
  3 eggs
  1⅓ cups water
  ½ cup CRISCO® Oil or
    CRISCO® PURITAN® Oil
  ½ cup ground walnuts
    (see Tip)

Chocolate Glaze
  1 package (12 ounces) semi-
    sweet chocolate chips
  ¼ cup *plus* 2 tablespoons
    butter or margarine
  ¼ cup coarsely chopped
    walnuts, for garnish

White Chocolate Glaze
  3 ounces white chocolate,
    coarsely chopped
  1 tablespoon CRISCO®
    Shortening

1. Preheat oven to 350°F. Grease and flour 10-inch Bundt® pan.

2. **For cake,** combine cake mix, eggs, water, oil and ground walnuts in large bowl. Beat at medium speed with electric mixer for 2 minutes. Pour into pan. Bake at 350°F for 45 to 55 minutes or until toothpick inserted in center comes out clean. Cool in pan 25 minutes. Invert onto serving plate. Cool completely.

3. **For chocolate glaze,** combine chocolate chips and butter in small heavy saucepan. Heat over low heat until chips are melted. Stir constantly until shiny and smooth. (Glaze will be very thick.) Spread hot glaze over cooled cake. Garnish with coarsely chopped walnuts.

4. **For white chocolate glaze,** combine white chocolate and shortening in small heavy saucepan. Heat on low heat until melted, stirring constantly. Drizzle hot glaze over top of cake. *12 to 16 Servings*

Tip: To grind walnuts, use a food processor fitted with steel blade. Process until fine.

Hot Fudge Sundae Cake

(use all the ice cream). Place top cake layer over ice cream. Cover and freeze.

4. **For fudge sauce,** combine evaporated milk and sugar in medium saucepan. Stir constantly on medium heat until mixture comes to a rolling boil. Boil and stir for 1 minute. Add unsweetened chocolate and stir until melted. Beat over heat until smooth. Remove from heat. Stir in butter, vanilla extract and salt.

5. To serve, cut cake into serving squares. Spoon hot fudge sauce on top of each cake square. Garnish with whipped cream, maraschino cherries and mint leaves, if desired.

12 to 16 Servings

Tip: Fudge sauce may be prepared ahead and refrigerated in tightly sealed jar. Reheat when ready to serve.

Caramel Fudge Cake

- **1 (18¼- or 18½-ounce) package chocolate cake mix**
- **1 (14-ounce) package EAGLE™ Brand Caramels, unwrapped**
- **½ cup margarine or butter**
- **1 (14-ounce) can EAGLE® Brand Sweetened Condensed Milk (NOT evaporated milk)**
- **1 cup coarsely chopped pecans**

Preheat oven to 350°. Prepare cake mix as package directs. Pour *2 cups* batter into greased 13×9-inch baking pan; bake 15 minutes. Meanwhile, in heavy saucepan, over low heat, melt caramels and margarine. Remove from heat; add sweetened condensed milk. *Mix well.* Spread caramel mixture evenly over cake; spread remaining cake batter over caramel mixture. Top with pecans. Return to oven; bake 30 to 35 minutes longer or until cake springs back when lightly touched. Cool. Garnish as desired.

Makes 10 to 12 servings

Hot Fudge Sundae Cake

- **1 package DUNCAN HINES® Moist Deluxe Dark Dutch Fudge Cake Mix**
- **½ gallon brick vanilla ice cream**

Fudge Sauce
- **1 can (12 ounces) evaporated milk**
- **1¾ cups sugar**
- **4 squares (1 ounce each) unsweetened chocolate**
- **¼ cup butter or margarine**
- **1½ teaspoons vanilla extract**
- **¼ teaspoon salt**
  Whipped cream, for garnish
  Maraschino cherries, for garnish
  Mint leaves, for garnish (optional)

1. Preheat oven to 350°F. Grease and flour 13×9×2-inch pan.

2. Prepare, bake and cool cake following package directions for basic recipe.

3. Remove cake from pan. Split cake in half horizontally. Place bottom layer back in pan. Cut ice cream into even slices and place evenly over bottom cake layer

Easy Carrot Cake

- **1¼ cups MIRACLE WHIP® Salad Dressing**
- **1 package (2-layer size) yellow cake mix**
- **4 eggs**
- **¼ cup cold water**
- **2 teaspoons ground cinnamon**
- **2 cups finely shredded carrots**
- **½ cup chopped walnuts**
- **1 container (16 ounces) ready-to-spread cream cheese frosting**

• Heat oven to 350°F.

• Beat salad dressing, cake mix, eggs, water and cinnamon at medium speed with electric mixer until well blended. Stir in carrots and walnuts. Pour into greased 13×9-inch baking pan.

• Bake 30 to 35 minutes or until wooden pick inserted in center comes out clean. Cool completely. Spread cake with frosting.

Makes 12 servings

Prep time: 15 minutes
Cooking time: 35 minutes

Light and Luscious Lemon Cake

**1 package DUNCAN HINES®
Moist Deluxe Lemon
Supreme Cake Mix**

Frosting
**1 can (6 ounces) frozen
lemonade concentrate,
thawed**
**1 can (14 ounces) sweetened
condensed milk**
**1 container (8 ounces) frozen
whipped topping, thawed**
**3 drops yellow food coloring
(optional)
Lemon slices, for garnish
Mint leaves, for garnish**

1. Preheat oven to 350°F. Grease
and flour 13×9×2-inch pan.

2. Prepare and bake cake
following package directions for
basic recipe. Cool in pan 15
minutes. Invert onto cooling
rack. Cool completely. Split cake
in half horizontally (see Tip).

Light and Luscious Lemon Cake

3. **For frosting,** combine
lemonade concentrate and
sweetened condensed milk in
medium bowl. Fold in whipped
topping. Add food coloring, if
desired. Blend well. Place bottom
cake layer on serving plate.
Spread one-third frosting on top.
Place top cake layer on frosting.
Frost sides and top with
remaining frosting. Garnish with
lemon slices and mint leaves.
Refrigerate until ready to serve.

12 to 16 Servings

Tip: To cut cake evenly, measure
cake with ruler. Divide into 2
equal layers. Mark with
toothpicks. Cut through layer
with large serrated knife using
toothpicks as guide.

Dainty Pineapple Upside Down Cakes

**1¼ cups firmly packed brown
sugar**
**⅔ cup butter or margarine,
melted**
**1 can (20 ounces) pineapple
slices, drained**
**15 maraschino cherries,
halved and drained**
**1 package DUNCAN HINES®
Moist Deluxe Pineapple
Supreme Cake Mix**

1. Preheat oven to 350°F.

2. Combine brown sugar and
butter in small bowl. Press about
2 teaspoons mixture in each
2½-inch diameter muffin cup.
Cut pineapple slices into thirds.
Place 1 pineapple section and 1
cherry half in each cup.

3. Prepare cake mix following
package directions for basic
recipe. Fill muffin cups ¾ full.
Bake at 350°F for 15 to 20
minutes or until toothpick
inserted in center comes out
clean. Loosen cupcakes from
sides of pan. Invert onto cooling
rack. Cool.   *30 Cupcakes*

Tip: For ease in removing
cupcakes, bake one muffin pan at
a time. If any topping remains in
pan, re-melt in warm oven for
several minutes and spread on
cupcakes.

Chocolate Surprise Cupcakes

Filling:
- **1 package (8 ounces) PHILADELPHIA BRAND® Cream Cheese, softened**
- **⅓ cup granulated sugar**
- **1 egg**
- **½ cup BAKER'S® Semi-Sweet Real Chocolate Chips**

Cupcakes:
- **2 squares BAKER'S® Unsweetened Chocolate**
- **⅓ cup vegetable oil**
- **1¼ cups all-purpose flour**
- **1 cup granulated sugar**
- **¾ cup water**
- **1 egg**
- **1 teaspoon vanilla**
- **½ teaspoon baking soda**
- **¼ teaspoon salt**
- **Powdered sugar (optional)**

HEAT oven to 350°F.

BEAT cream cheese, ⅓ cup granulated sugar and 1 egg until smooth. Stir in chips; set aside.

MELT chocolate in small microwavable bowl on HIGH 1 to 2 minutes or until almost melted, stirring after each minute. **Stir until chocolate is completely melted.**

BEAT melted chocolate, oil, flour, 1 cup granulated sugar, water, 1 egg, vanilla, baking soda and salt in large bowl with wire whisk or fork until blended and smooth. Spoon ½ the batter evenly into 18 greased or paper-lined muffin cups. Top each with 1 tablespoon of the cream cheese mixture. Spoon the remaining batter evenly over cream cheese mixture.

BAKE for 30 to 35 minutes or until toothpick inserted in center comes out clean. Remove from pans to cool on wire racks. Sprinkle with powdered sugar, if desired.   *Makes 18 cupcakes*

Prep time: 15 minutes
Baking time: 30 to 35 minutes

Glazed Cranberry Mini-Cakes

- **¼ cup butter or margarine, softened**
- **¼ cup packed light brown sugar**
- **¼ cup granulated sugar**
- **1 egg**
- **1 teaspoon vanilla extract**
- **1 cup all-purpose flour**
- **½ teaspoon baking powder**
- **¼ teaspoon baking soda**
- **¼ teaspoon salt**
- **1 cup coarsely chopped fresh cranberries**
- **½ cup coarsely chopped walnuts**
- **⅓ cup HERSHEY'S Vanilla Milk Chips**
- **Vanilla Glaze (recipe follows)**
- **Additional cranberries (optional)**

Heat oven to 350°F. Lightly grease or paper-line 36 small muffin cups (1¾ inches in diameter). In small mixer bowl beat butter, brown sugar, granulated sugar, egg and vanilla extract until light and fluffy. Stir together flour, baking powder, baking soda and salt; gradually blend into butter mixture. Stir in cranberries, walnuts and vanilla milk chips. Fill muffin cups ¾ full with batter. Bake 12 to 14 minutes or until wooden pick inserted in center comes out clean. Cool in pans on wire rack 5 minutes; invert onto rack. Cool completely. Prepare Vanilla Glaze; dip rounded portion of each mini-cake into glaze (or spread glaze over tops). Place on wax paper-covered tray; refrigerate 10 minutes to set glaze. Garnish with additional cranberries, if desired.
Makes about 3 dozen mini-cakes

VANILLA GLAZE: In small microwave-safe bowl stir together 1 cup Hershey's Vanilla Milk Chips and 2 tablespoons vegetable oil. Microwave at HIGH (100%) 30 seconds; stir until smooth. If

necessary, microwave at HIGH additional 30 seconds or just until chips are melted and smooth when stirred.

Strawberry Shortcake

Cake
- **1 package DUNCAN HINES® Moist Deluxe French Vanilla Cake Mix**
- **3 eggs**
- **1¼ cups water**
- **½ cup butter or margarine, softened**

Filling and Topping
- **2 cups whipping cream, chilled**
- **⅓ cup sugar**
- **½ teaspoon vanilla extract**
- **1 quart fresh strawberries, rinsed, drained and sliced**
- **Mint leaves, for garnish**

1. Preheat oven to 350°F. Grease two 9-inch round cake pans with butter or margarine. Sprinkle bottom and sides with granulated sugar.

2. **For cake,** combine cake mix, eggs, water and butter in large bowl. Beat at medium speed with electric mixer for 2 minutes. Pour into pans. Bake at 350°F for 30 to 35 minutes or until toothpick inserted in center comes out clean. Cool in pans 10 minutes. Invert onto cooling rack. Cool completely.

3. **For filling and topping,** beat whipping cream, sugar and vanilla extract until stiff in large bowl. Reserve ⅓ cup for garnish. Place one cake layer on serving plate. Spread with half the remaining whipped cream and sliced strawberries. Repeat with remaining layer and whipped cream. Garnish with reserved whipped cream and mint leaves. Refrigerate until ready to serve.
12 Servings

Tip: Whipping cream doubles in volume when whipped. For best results, chill bowl and beaters.

Strawberry Shortcake

Chocolate Strawberry Shortcake

2 pints strawberries, cut in half
2 tablespoons sugar
1 teaspoon vanilla
2 (9-inch) layers One Bowl Chocolate Cake
Semi-Sweet Chocolate Glaze (page 337)
3½ cups (8 ounces) COOL WHIP® Whipped Topping, thawed
Chocolate-dipped strawberries (optional)

MIX strawberries, sugar and vanilla. Spoon ½ of the strawberries on 1 cake layer. Drizzle with ½ the chocolate glaze; top with ½ the whipped topping. Repeat layers. Garnish with chocolate-dipped strawberries, if desired. Refrigerate.

Makes 12 servings

Prep time: 15 minutes

Chocolate Strawberry Shortcake

One Bowl Chocolate Cake

6 squares BAKER'S® Semi-Sweet Chocolate
¾ cup (1½ sticks) margarine or butter
1½ cups sugar
3 eggs
2 teaspoons vanilla
2½ cups all-purpose flour
1 teaspoon baking soda
¼ teaspoon salt
1½ cups water

HEAT oven to 350°F.

MICROWAVE chocolate and margarine in large microwavable bowl on HIGH 2 minutes or until margarine is melted. **Stir until chocolate is completely melted.**

STIR sugar into melted chocolate mixture until well blended. Beat in eggs, one at a time, with electric mixer until completely mixed. Add vanilla. Add ½ cup of the flour, the

baking soda and salt; mix well. Beat in the remaining 2 cups flour alternately with water until smooth. Pour into 2 greased and floured 9-inch layer pans.

BAKE for 35 minutes or until toothpick inserted into center comes out clean. Cool in pans 10 minutes. Remove from pans to cool on wire racks. Fill and frost as desired.

Makes 12 servings

Prep time: 15 minutes
Baking time: 35 minutes

Chocolate Toffee Crunch Fantasy

1 package DUNCAN HINES® Moist Deluxe Devil's Food Cake Mix
12 bars (1.4 ounces each) chocolate covered toffee bars, divided
2 cups whipping cream, chilled

1. Preheat oven to 350°F. Grease and flour 10-inch tube pan.

2. Prepare, bake and cool cake following package directions for basic recipe. Split cake horizontally into three layers. Chop 11 candy bars into pea-size pieces (see Tip). Whip cream until stiff peaks form. Fold candy pieces into whipped cream.

3. To assemble, place one split cake layer on serving plate. Spread 1½ cups whipped cream mixture on top. Repeat with remaining layers and whipped cream mixture. Frost sides and top with remaining whipped cream mixture. Chop remaining candy bar coarsely. Sprinkle over top. Refrigerate until ready to serve. *12 Servings*

Tip: To quickly chop toffee candy bars, place a few bars in food processor fitted with steel blade. Pulse several times until pea-size pieces form. Repeat with remaining candy bars.

German Sweet Chocolate Cake

- 1 package (4 ounces) BAKER'S® GERMAN'S® Sweet Chocolate
- ½ cup water
- 2 cups all-purpose flour
- 1 teaspoon baking soda
- ¼ teaspoon salt
- 1 cup (2 sticks) margarine or butter, softened
- 2 cups sugar
- 4 egg yolks
- 1 teaspoon vanilla
- 1 cup buttermilk
- 4 egg whites
  Classic Coconut-Pecan Filling and Frosting (page 337)

HEAT oven to 350°F. Line bottoms of three 9-inch layer pans with waxed paper.

MICROWAVE chocolate and water in large microwavable bowl on HIGH 1½ to 2 minutes until chocolate is almost melted. **Stir until chocolate is completely melted.**

MIX flour, baking soda and salt; set aside. Beat margarine and sugar until light and fluffy. Add egg yolks, one at a time, beating well after each addition. Stir in melted chocolate and vanilla. Add flour mixture alternately with buttermilk, beating after each addition until smooth.

BEAT egg whites until they form stiff peaks. Gently stir into batter; pour into prepared pans.

BAKE for 30 minutes or until cake springs back when lightly touched.

REMOVE from oven; immediately run spatula between cake and sides of pans. Cool in pans 15 minutes. Remove from pans; peel off waxed paper. Cool on wire racks.

SPREAD Classic Coconut-Pecan Filling and Frosting between layers and over top of cake.
Makes 12 servings

Prep time: 35 to 40 minutes
Baking time: 30 minutes

Top to bottom: German Sweet Chocolate Cake and Wellesley Fudge Cake with Easy Fudge Frosting (page 337)

Wellesley Fudge Cake

- 4 squares BAKER'S® Unsweetened Chocolate
- 1¾ cups sugar
- ½ cup water
- 1⅔ cups all-purpose flour
- 1 teaspoon baking soda
- ¼ teaspoon salt
- ½ cup (1 stick) margarine or butter, softened
- 3 eggs
- ¾ cup milk
- 1 teaspoon vanilla

HEAT oven to 350°F.

MICROWAVE chocolate, ½ cup of the sugar and the water in large microwavable bowl on HIGH 1 to 2 minutes or until chocolate is almost melted, stirring once. **Stir until chocolate is completely melted.** Cool to lukewarm.

MIX flour, baking soda and salt; set aside. Beat margarine and the remaining 1¼ cups sugar until light and fluffy. Add eggs, one at a time, beating well after each addition. Add flour mixture alternately with milk, beating after each addition until smooth. Stir in chocolate mixture and vanilla. Pour into 2 greased and floured 9-inch layer pans.

BAKE for 30 to 35 minutes or until cake springs back when lightly pressed. Cool in pans 10 minutes. Remove from pans to cool on wire racks. Frost as desired.   *Makes 12 servings*

Prep time: 30 minutes
Baking time: 30 to 35 minutes

Banana Fudge Marble Cake

Cake
   1 package DUNCAN HINES®
      DeLights Fudge Marble
      Cake Mix
   2 eggs
   1 cup ripe mashed banana
   ½ cup water

Frosting
   1 package (4-serving size)
      banana instant pudding
      and pie filling mix
   2 envelopes whipped topping
      mix
   1¼ cups milk
   1 banana, sliced
      Lemon juice
   ½ cup frozen whipped
      topping, thawed

1. Preheat oven to 350°F. Grease and flour two 9-inch round cake pans.

2. **For cake,** combine cake mix, eggs, mashed banana and water in large bowl. Beat at medium speed with electric mixer for 2 minutes. Pour into pans. Bake and cool following package directions.

3. **For frosting,** combine pudding mix, whipped topping mix and milk in large bowl. Beat at high speed with electric mixer for 2 to 3 minutes or until light and fluffy. Fill and frost cake. Refrigerate for several hours before serving. Dip banana slices in lemon juice. Blot dry. Garnish with whipped topping and banana slices.   *12 Servings*

Tip: Serve cake slices with 2 tablespoons Fudge Sauce (page 328).

Pecan Pumpkin Torte

Cake
   2 cups crushed vanilla
      wafers
   1 cup chopped pecans
   ¾ cup LAND O LAKES®
      Butter, softened
   1 package (18 ounces) spice
      cake mix
   1 can (16 ounces) solid-
      packed pumpkin
   ¼ cup LAND O LAKES®
      Butter, softened
   4 eggs

Filling
   3 cups powdered sugar
   ⅔ cup LAND O LAKES®
      Butter, softened
   4 ounces cream cheese,
      softened
   2 teaspoons vanilla
   ¼ cup caramel topping
      Pecan halves

Heat oven to 350°. For cake, in large mixer bowl combine wafer crumbs, 1 cup chopped pecans and ¾ cup butter. Beat at medium speed, scraping bowl often, until crumbly, 1 to 2 minutes. Press mixture evenly on bottom of 3 greased and floured 9-inch round cake pans. In same bowl combine cake mix, pumpkin, ¼ cup butter and eggs. Beat at medium speed, scraping bowl often, until well mixed, 2 to 3 minutes. Spread 1¾ cups batter over crumbs in *each* pan. Bake for 20 to 25 minutes or until wooden pick inserted in center comes out clean. Cool 5 minutes; remove from pans. Cool completely.

For filling, in small mixer bowl combine powdered sugar, ⅔ cup butter, cream cheese and vanilla. Beat at medium speed, scraping bowl often, until light and fluffy, 2 to 3 minutes. On serving plate layer 3 cakes, nut side down, with ½ cup filling spread between *each* layer. With remaining filling, frost sides only of cake. Spread caramel topping over top of cake, drizzling some

over the frosted sides. Arrange pecan halves in rings on top of cake. Store refrigerated.
                    Makes 16 servings

Tip: To remove cake easily from pan, place wire rack on top of cake and invert; repeat with remaining layers.

Coconut Lemon Torte

   1 (14-ounce) can EAGLE®
      Brand Sweetened
      Condensed Milk
      (NOT evaporated milk)
   2 egg *yolks*
   ½ cup REALEMON® Lemon
      Juice from Concentrate
   1 teaspoon grated lemon
      rind, optional
      Yellow food coloring,
      optional
   1 (18¼- or 18½-ounce)
      package white cake mix
   1 (4-ounce) container frozen
      non-dairy whipped
      topping, thawed
      (1¾ cups)
      Flaked coconut

Preheat oven to 350°. In medium saucepan, combine sweetened condensed milk, egg *yolks*, ReaLemon® brand, rind and food coloring if desired. Over medium heat, cook and stir until thickened, about 10 minutes. Chill. Meanwhile, prepare cake mix as package directs. Pour batter into two well-greased and floured 8- or 9-inch round layer cake pans. Bake 30 minutes or until lightly browned. Remove from pans; cool thoroughly. With sharp knife, remove crust from top of each cake layer. Split layers in half horizontally. Spread equal portions of lemon mixture between layers and on top to within 1 inch of edge. Frost side and 1-inch rim on top of cake with whipped topping. Coat side of cake with coconut; garnish as desired. Store covered in refrigerator.
                    Makes one 8- or 9-inch cake

Pecan Pumpkin Torte

Chocolate Raspberry Torte

- **3 eggs, separated**
- **⅛ teaspoon cream of tartar**
- **⅛ teaspoon salt**
- **1½ cups sugar**
- **1 cup LAND O LAKES® Butter, melted**
- **1½ teaspoons vanilla**
- **½ cup all-purpose flour**
- **½ cup unsweetened cocoa**
- **3 tablespoons water**
- **¾ cup finely chopped almonds**
- **⅓ cup raspberry preserves**
- **1 cup whipping cream, whipped, sweetened Fresh raspberries**

Heat oven to 350°. Grease 9-inch round cake pan. Line with aluminum foil leaving excess foil over edges; grease foil. Set aside. In small mixer bowl combine egg whites, cream of tartar and salt. Beat at high speed, scraping bowl often, until soft peaks form, 1 to 2 minutes; set aside. In large mixer bowl combine egg yolks, sugar, butter and vanilla. Beat at medium speed, scraping bowl often, until well mixed, 1 to 2 minutes. Add flour, cocoa and water. Continue beating, scraping bowl often, until well mixed, 1 to 2 minutes. By hand, stir in chopped almonds. Fold beaten egg whites into chocolate mixture. Spread into prepared pan. Bake for 40 to 55 minutes or until wooden pick inserted in center comes out clean. Cool on wire rack 1 hour; remove from pan by lifting foil. Cover; refrigerate until completely cooled, 2 to 3 hours.

To serve, remove foil; place on serving plate. Spread raspberry preserves on top. Pipe sweetened whipped cream to form a lattice top; garnish with raspberries.

Makes 12 servings

Chocolate Intensity

Chocolate Intensity

Cake:
- **One 8-oz. pkg. (4 foil-wrapped bars) NESTLÉ® Unsweetened Chocolate baking bars**
- **½ cup (1 stick) butter or margarine, softened**
- **1½ cups granulated sugar**
- **3 whole eggs**
- **2 teaspoons vanilla extract**
- **⅔ cup all-purpose flour**

Coffee Crème Anglaise:
- **⅓ cup granulated sugar**
- **2 teaspoons cornstarch**
- **1 tablespoon TASTER'S CHOICE® Freeze-Dried Instant Coffee**
- **1½ cups milk**
- **4 egg yolks, beaten**
- **1 teaspoon vanilla extract**

- **Confectioners' sugar for garnish**
- **Heavy or whipping cream for garnish**

Cake: Preheat oven to 350°F. Grease 9-inch springform pan. In small saucepan over low heat, melt unsweetened chocolate baking bars; set aside. In small mixer bowl, beat butter, 1½ cups granulated sugar, whole eggs

Chocolate Raspberry Torte

and 2 teaspoons vanilla extract until thick and pale yellow. Blend in melted chocolate. Gradually beat in flour. Spread in prepared pan.

Bake 25 to 28 minutes until cake tester inserted in center comes out clean. Cool 15 minutes; loosen and remove side of pan. Cool completely.

Coffee Crème Anglaise: In medium saucepan, combine ⅓ cup granulated sugar, cornstarch and instant coffee; stir in milk. Cook over medium heat, stirring constantly, until mixture comes to a boil; boil 1 minute. Remove from heat. Whisk small amount of hot milk mixture into yolks; return to saucepan. Cook over low heat, stirring constantly, until mixture thickens and coats back of spoon. Strain through a fine mesh sieve into small bowl. Stir in 1 teaspoon vanilla extract. Press plastic wrap directly on surface; refrigerate.

Sprinkle cake with confectioners' sugar; cut into wedges. Spoon 3 to 4 tablespoons Coffee Crème Anglaise onto each dessert plate. Dot with heavy cream. Pull toothpick through heavy cream to make decorative design. Top with cake.

Makes 10 to 12 servings

Base Frosting

3 cups powdered sugar, sifted
½ cup butter or margarine, softened
¼ cup milk
½ teaspoon vanilla

Combine powdered sugar, butter, milk and vanilla in large bowl. Beat with electric mixer until smooth. Add more milk, 1 teaspoon at a time, if necessary. Frosting should be fairly thin.

Makes about 2 cups

Buttercream Frosting

6 cups powdered sugar, sifted and divided
¾ cup butter or margarine, softened
¼ cup vegetable shortening
6 to 8 tablespoons milk, divided
1 teaspoon vanilla

Combine 3 cups powdered sugar, butter, shortening, 4 tablespoons milk and vanilla in large bowl. Beat with electric mixer until smooth. Add remaining powdered sugar; beat until light and fluffy, adding more milk, 1 tablespoon at a time, as needed for good spreading consistency.

Makes about 3½ cups

Easy Fudge Frosting

4 squares BAKER'S® Unsweetened Chocolate
2 tablespoons margarine or butter
4 cups powdered sugar
½ cup milk
1 teaspoon vanilla

MICROWAVE chocolate and margarine in large microwavable bowl on HIGH 1 minute or until margarine is melted. **Stir until chocolate is completely melted.**

STIR in sugar, milk and vanilla until smooth. Let stand, if necessary, until of spreading consistency, stirring occasionally. Spread quickly. (Add 2 to 3 tablespoons additional milk if frosting becomes too thick.)

Makes about 2½ cups or enough to frost tops and sides of 2 (8- to 9-inch) layer cakes.

Prep time: 10 minutes

Classic Coconut-Pecan Filling and Frosting

1½ cups (12 ounce can) evaporated milk
1½ cups sugar
4 egg yolks
¾ cup (1½ sticks) margarine or butter
1½ teaspoons vanilla
2 cups BAKER'S® ANGEL FLAKE® Coconut
1½ cups chopped pecans

COMBINE milk, sugar, egg yolks, margarine and vanilla in saucepan. Cook over medium heat until mixture thickens and is golden brown, about 12 minutes, stirring constantly. Remove from heat.

STIR in coconut and pecans. Beat until cool and of spreading consistency.

Makes about 4¼ cups or enough to fill and frost top of 1 (3-layer) cake, frost tops of 2 (13×9-inch) cakes or frost 24 cupcakes

Prep time: 20 minutes

Semi-Sweet Chocolate Glaze

3 squares BAKER'S® Semi-Sweet Chocolate
3 tablespoons water
1 tablespoon margarine or butter
1 cup powdered sugar
½ teaspoon vanilla

MICROWAVE chocolate, water and margarine in large microwavable bowl on HIGH 1 to 2 minutes until chocolate is almost melted, stirring once. **Stir until chocolate is completely melted.**

STIR in sugar and vanilla until smooth. For thinner glaze, add ½ to 1 teaspoon additional water.

Makes about ¾ cup

Prep time: 10 minutes

Kahlúa® Marbled Pumpkin Cheesecake

¾ **cup gingersnap crumbs**
¾ **cup graham cracker crumbs**
¼ **cup powdered sugar**
¼ **cup (4 tablespoons) melted unsalted butter**
2 **(8-ounce) packages cream cheese, softened**
1 **cup granulated sugar**
4 **eggs**
1 **(1-pound) can pumpkin**
½ **teaspoon ground cinnamon**
¼ **teaspoon ground ginger**
¼ **teaspoon ground nutmeg**
½ **cup KAHLÚA®**

Heat oven to 350°F. In bowl, combine gingersnap and graham cracker crumbs with powdered sugar and butter. Toss to combine. Press evenly onto bottom of 8-inch springform pan. Bake 5 minutes. Cool.

In mixer bowl, beat cream cheese until smooth. Gradually add granulated sugar and beat until light. Add eggs, one at a time, beating well after each addition. Transfer 1 cup mixture to separate bowl and blend in pumpkin, cinnamon, ginger, nutmeg and Kahlúa®. Pour half of pumpkin mixture into prepared crust. Top with half of cream cheese mixture. Repeat layers using remaining pumpkin and cream cheese mixtures. Using table knife, cut through layers with uplifting motion in four to five places to create marbled effect. Place on baking sheet and bake at 350°F for 45 minutes. Without opening oven door, let cake stand in turned-off oven 1 hour. Remove from oven and cool, then chill. Remove from pan.

Makes about 12 servings

Marble Cheesecake

Crust
1 **cup graham cracker crumbs**
3 **tablespoons sugar**
3 **tablespoons PARKAY® Margarine, melted**
Filling
3 **packages (8 ounces each) PHILADELPHIA BRAND® Cream Cheese, softened**
¾ **cup sugar**
1 **teaspoon vanilla**
3 **eggs**
1 **square BAKER'S® Unsweetened Chocolate, melted**

• *Crust:* Heat oven to 350°F.

• Mix crumbs, sugar and margarine; press onto bottom of 9-inch springform pan. Bake 10 minutes.

• *Filling:* Increase oven temperature to 450°F.

• Beat cream cheese, sugar and vanilla at medium speed with electric mixer until well blended. Add eggs, 1 at a time, mixing well after each addition.

• Blend chocolate into 1 cup batter. Spoon plain and chocolate batters alternately over crust; cut through batters with knife several times for marble effect.

• Bake 10 minutes. Reduce oven temperature to 250°F; continue baking 30 minutes. Loosen cake from rim of pan; cool before removing rim of pan. Refrigerate.

Makes 10 to 12 servings

Prep time: 20 minutes plus refrigerating
Cooking time: 40 minutes

Triple Chocolate & Vanilla Cheesecake

1½ **cups finely crushed creme-filled chocolate sandwich cookies (about 18 cookies)**
3 **tablespoons margarine or butter, melted**
4 **(8-ounce) packages cream cheese, softened**
1 **(14-ounce) can EAGLE® Brand Sweetened Condensed Milk (NOT evaporated milk)**
4 **eggs**
⅓ **cup unsifted flour**
1 **tablespoon vanilla extract**
2 **(1-ounce) squares semi-sweet chocolate, melted**
Chocolate Glaze

Preheat oven to 350°. Combine crumbs and margarine; press firmly on bottom of 9-inch springform pan. In large mixer bowl, beat cheese until fluffy. Gradually beat in sweetened condensed milk until smooth. Add eggs, flour and vanilla; mix well. Divide batter in half. Add chocolate to one half of batter; mix well. Pour into prepared pan. Top evenly with vanilla batter. Bake 50 to 55 minutes or until center springs back when lightly touched. Cool. Remove side of pan. Top with Chocolate Glaze. Chill. Refrigerate leftovers.

Makes one 9-inch cheesecake

CHOCOLATE GLAZE: In small saucepan, over low heat, melt 2 (1-ounce) squares semi-sweet chocolate with ¼ cup BORDEN® or MEADOW GOLD® Whipping Cream. Cook and stir until thickened and smooth. Remove from heat; spread over cheesecake.

Makes about ⅓ cup

Marble Cheesecake

Chocolate Velvet Cheesecake

Chocolate Velvet Cheesecake

Crust
- 1 cup vanilla wafer crumbs
- ½ cup chopped pecans
- 3 tablespoons granulated sugar
- ¼ cup (½ stick) PARKAY® Margarine, melted

Filling
- 2 packages (8 ounces each) PHILADELPHIA BRAND® Cream Cheese, softened
- ½ cup packed brown sugar
- 2 eggs
- 1 package (6 ounces) BAKER'S® Semi-Sweet Real Chocolate Chips, melted
- 3 tablespoons almond-flavored liqueur

Topping
- 2 cups BREAKSTONE'S® Sour Cream
- 2 tablespoons granulated sugar

• *Crust:* Heat oven to 325°F.

• Mix crumbs, pecans, granulated sugar and margarine; press onto bottom of 9-inch springform pan. Bake 10 minutes.

• *Filling:* Beat cream cheese and brown sugar at medium speed with electric mixer until well blended. Add eggs, 1 at a time, mixing well after each addition. Blend in chocolate and liqueur; pour over crust.

• Bake 35 minutes. Increase oven temperature to 425°F.

• *Topping:* Mix sour cream and granulated sugar; carefully spread over cheesecake. Bake 10 minutes. Loosen cake from rim of pan; cool before removing rim of pan. Refrigerate. Garnish with chocolate leaves, if desired.

Makes 10 to 12 servings

Prep time: 20 minutes plus refrigerating
Cooking time: 45 minutes

TO MAKE CHOCOLATE LEAVES: Wash and dry lemon leaves. Brush leaves with melted semi-sweet chocolate chips; refrigerate. Carefully peel back leaves from chocolate.

Boston Cream Cheesecake

Crust
- 1 package (one-layer size) yellow cake mix

Filling
- 2 packages (8 ounces each) PHILADELPHIA BRAND® Cream Cheese, softened
- ½ cup granulated sugar
- 1 teaspoon vanilla
- 2 eggs
- ⅓ cup BREAKSTONE'S® Sour Cream

Topping
- 2 squares BAKER'S® Unsweetened Chocolate
- 3 tablespoons PARKAY® Margarine
- 2 tablespoons boiling water
- 1 cup powdered sugar
- 1 teaspoon vanilla

• *Crust:* Heat oven to 350°F.

• Grease bottom of 9-inch springform pan. Prepare cake mix as directed on package; pour batter evenly into springform pan. Bake 20 minutes.

• *Filling:* Beat cream cheese, granulated sugar and vanilla at medium speed with electric mixer until well blended. Add eggs, 1 at a time, mixing well after each addition. Blend in sour cream; pour over cake layer.

• Bake 35 minutes. Loosen cake from rim of pan; cool before removing rim of pan.

• *Topping:* Melt chocolate and margarine over low heat, stirring until smooth. Remove from heat. Add water and remaining ingredients; mix well. Spread over cheesecake. Refrigerate. Garnish with strawberries and fresh mint, if desired.

Makes 10 to 12 servings

Prep time: 20 minutes plus refrigerating
Cooking time: 55 minutes

Chocolate Chip Cheesecake

Chocolate Chip Cheesecake

Crust
>   1 package DUNCAN HINES®
>   Moist Deluxe Devil's
>   Food Cake Mix
>   ½ cup CRISCO® Oil or
>   CRISCO® PURITAN® Oil

Filling
>   3 packages (8 ounces each)
>   cream cheese, softened
>   1½ cups sugar
>   1 cup dairy sour cream
>   1½ teaspoons vanilla extract
>   4 eggs, lightly beaten
>   ¾ cup mini semi-sweet
>   chocolate chips, divided
>   1 teaspoon all-purpose flour

1. Preheat oven to 350°F. Grease 10-inch springform pan.

2. **For crust,** combine cake mix and oil in large bowl. Mix well. Press into bottom of pan. Bake at 350°F for 22 to 25 minutes. Remove from oven. *Increase oven temperature to 450°F.*

3. **For filling,** place cream cheese in large bowl. Beat at low speed with electric mixer adding sugar gradually. Add sour cream and vanilla extract, mixing until blended. Add eggs, mixing only until incorporated. Toss ½ cup chocolate chips with flour. Fold into cream cheese mixture. Pour filling onto crust. Sprinkle with remaining ¼ cup chocolate chips. Bake at 450°F for 5 to 7 minutes. *Reduce oven temperature to 250°F.* Bake for 60 to 65 minutes longer or until set. Loosen cake from sides of pan with knife or spatula. Cool completely on cooling rack. Refrigerate until ready to serve. Remove sides of pan.   *12 to 16 Servings*

Tip: Place pan of water on bottom shelf of oven during baking to prevent cheesecake from cracking.

Premier White Lemon Cheesecake

Crust:
>   6 tablespoons (¾ stick)
>   butter or margarine,
>   softened
>   ¼ cup sugar
>   1 egg yolk
>   1¼ cups all-purpose flour
>   ⅛ teaspoon salt

Cheesecake:
> Two 6-oz. pkgs. (6 foil-wrapped
>   bars) NESTLÉ® Premier
>   White baking bars
>   ½ cup heavy or whipping
>   cream
> Two 8-oz. pkgs. cream cheese,
>   softened
>   1 tablespoon lemon juice
>   ¼ teaspoon salt
>   3 egg whites
>   1 whole egg

>   Lemon twist for garnish
>   Fresh mint leaves for
>   garnish
>   Premier White Curls for
>   garnish
>   (directions follow)

Crust: Preheat oven to 350°F. Grease 9-inch springform pan. In small mixer bowl, beat butter and sugar until creamy. Blend in egg yolk. Beat in flour and ⅛ teaspoon salt. Press mixture onto bottom and 1 inch up side of prepared pan. Bake 14 to 16 minutes until crust is set; set aside.

Cheesecake: In small saucepan over low heat, melt Premier White baking bars with heavy cream, stirring constantly until smooth. Set aside.

In large mixer bowl, beat cream cheese, lemon juice and ¼ teaspoon salt until smooth. Blend in Premier White mixture. Beat in egg whites and whole egg. Pour into Crust.

Bake 35 minutes or until edge is lightly browned. Loosen and remove side of pan. Cool completely. Refrigerate. Garnish with lemon, mint and Premier White Curls.

Makes 10 to 12 servings

PREMIER WHITE CURLS: Shave a few "curls" from edge of Nestlé® Premier White baking bar with a vegetable peeler.

Premier White Lemon Cheesecake

Cherry Heart Cheesecake

Crust
- 1⅓ cups crushed chocolate wafer cookies
- ¼ cup LAND O LAKES® Butter, melted
- 2 tablespoons sugar

Filling
- 4 eggs, separated
- ½ cup LAND O LAKES® Butter, softened
- 2 packages (8 ounces each) cream cheese, softened
- 1 cup sugar
- 1 tablespoon cornstarch
- 1 teaspoon baking powder
- 1 tablespoon lemon juice

Topping
- 1 carton (8 ounces) dairy sour cream (1 cup)
- 2 tablespoons sugar
- 1 teaspoon vanilla
- 1 can (21 ounces) cherry pie filling
- 3 tablespoons cherry flavored liqueur

Heat oven to 325°. For crust, in small bowl stir together all crust ingredients; press mixture on bottom of 9-inch springform pan. Bake 10 minutes; cool.

For filling, in small mixer bowl beat egg whites at high speed, scraping bowl often, until soft peaks form, 1 to 2 minutes; set aside. In large mixer bowl combine ½ cup butter, cream cheese and egg yolks. Beat at medium speed, scraping bowl often, until smooth and creamy, 2 to 3 minutes. Add 1 cup sugar, cornstarch, baking powder and lemon juice. Continue beating, scraping bowl often, until well mixed, 1 to 2 minutes. By hand, fold in beaten egg whites. Spoon filling into prepared pan. Bake for 60 to 80 minutes or until center is set and firm to the touch. (Cheesecake surface will be slightly cracked.) Cool 15 minutes; loosen sides of cheesecake from pan by running knife around inside of pan. Cool completely. (Cheesecake center will dip slightly upon cooling.)

For topping, in small bowl stir together sour cream, 2 tablespoons sugar and vanilla. Spread evenly over top of cheesecake. Spoon out 2 to 3 tablespoons of cherry sauce from pie filling; drop by teaspoonfuls onto sour cream topping. Carefully pull knife or spatula through cherry sauce forming hearts. Cover; refrigerate 4 hours or overnight. In medium bowl stir together remaining pie filling and liqueur. Serve over slices of cheesecake. Store refrigerated.

Makes 10 servings

Creamy Baked Cheesecake

- 1¼ cups graham cracker crumbs
- ¼ cup sugar
- ⅓ cup margarine or butter, melted
- 2 (8-ounce) packages cream cheese, softened
- 1 (14-ounce) can EAGLE® Brand Sweetened Condensed Milk (NOT evaporated milk)
- 3 eggs
- ¼ cup REALEMON® Lemon Juice from Concentrate
- 1 (8-ounce) container BORDEN® or MEADOW GOLD® Sour Cream, at room temperature
- Fresh strawberries, hulled and sliced

Preheat oven to 300°. Combine crumbs, sugar and margarine; press firmly on bottom of 9-inch springform pan. In large mixer bowl, beat cheese until fluffy. Gradually beat in sweetened condensed milk until smooth. Add eggs and ReaLemon® brand; mix well. Pour into prepared pan. Bake 50 to 55 minutes or until center is set; top with sour cream. Bake 5 minutes longer. Cool. Chill. Just before serving, remove side of springform pan. Top with strawberries. Refrigerate leftovers.

Makes one 9-inch cheesecake

Caramel-Apple Sundae Cheesecake

Crust
- ⅓ cup PARKAY® Margarine
- ⅓ cup sugar
- 1 egg
- 1¼ cups flour

Filling
- 2 packages (8 ounces each) PHILADELPHIA BRAND® Cream Cheese, softened
- ⅔ cup sugar, divided
- 2 tablespoons flour
- 3 eggs
- ½ cup BREAKSTONE'S® Sour Cream
- 1 cup chopped peeled apple
- ¾ teaspoon ground cinnamon
- ½ cup KRAFT® Caramel Topping, divided
- ¼ cup chopped pecans

- *Crust:* Heat oven to 450°F.
- Beat margarine and sugar at medium speed with electric mixer until light and fluffy. Blend in egg. Add flour; mix well. Spread dough onto bottom and sides of 9-inch springform pan. Bake 10 minutes.
- *Filling:* Reduce oven temperature to 350°F.
- Beat cream cheese, ⅓ cup sugar and flour at medium speed with electric mixer until well blended. Add eggs, 1 at a time, mixing well after each addition. Blend in sour cream.
- Toss apples in remaining sugar and cinnamon. Stir into cream cheese mixture. Pour over crust. Swirl ¼ cup caramel topping into cream cheese mixture.
- Bake 1 hour. Loosen cake from rim of pan; cool before removing rim of pan. Refrigerate. Top with remaining caramel topping and pecans.

Makes 10 to 12 servings

Prep time: 25 minutes plus refrigerating
Cooking time: 1 hour

Cherry Heart Cheesecake

Orange-Butterscotch Cheesecake

Crust
1¼ cups old fashioned or
  quick-cooking oats,
  uncooked
¼ cup packed brown sugar
2 tablespoons flour
¼ cup PARKAY® Squeeze
  Spread

Filling
3 packages (8 ounces each)
  PHILADELPHIA BRAND®
  Cream Cheese, softened
¾ cup granulated sugar
2 teaspoons grated orange
  peel
1 teaspoon vanilla
4 eggs

Topping
½ cup packed brown sugar
⅓ cup light corn syrup
¼ cup PARKAY® Squeeze
  Spread
1 teaspoon vanilla

• *Crust:* Heat oven to 350°F.

• Mix oats, brown sugar, flour and spread; press onto bottom of 9-inch springform pan. Bake 15 minutes.

• *Filling:* Reduce oven temperature to 325°F.

• Beat cream cheese, granulated sugar, peel and vanilla at medium speed with electric mixer until well blended. Add eggs, 1 at a time, mixing well after each addition; pour over crust.

• Bake 1 hour and 5 minutes. Loosen cake from rim of pan; cool before removing rim of pan.

• *Topping:* Mix brown sugar, corn syrup and spread in saucepan; bring to boil, stirring constantly. Remove from heat; stir in vanilla. Refrigerate until slightly thickened. Spoon over cheesecake. Garnish with orange slice and fresh mint, if desired.

Makes 10 to 12 servings

Prep time: 35 minutes plus
  refrigerating
Cooking time: 1 hour 5 minutes

Mini Cheesecakes

Mini Cheesecakes

1½ cups graham cracker or
  chocolate wafer crumbs
¼ cup sugar
¼ cup margarine or butter,
  melted
3 (8-ounce) packages cream
  cheese, softened
1 (14-ounce) can EAGLE®
  Brand Sweetened
  Condensed Milk
  (NOT evaporated milk)
3 eggs
2 teaspoons vanilla extract

Preheat oven to 300°. Combine crumbs, sugar and margarine; press equal portions onto bottoms of 24 lightly greased* or paper-lined muffin cups. In large mixer bowl, beat cheese until fluffy. Gradually beat in sweetened condensed milk until smooth. Add eggs and vanilla; mix well. Spoon equal amounts of mixture (about 3 tablespoons) into prepared cups. Bake 20 minutes or until cakes spring back when lightly touched. Cool. Chill. Garnish as desired. Refrigerate leftovers.

Makes about 2 dozen

*If greased muffin cups are used, cool baked cheesecakes. Freeze 15 minutes; remove from pans. Proceed as above.

Orange-Butterscotch Cheesecake

Lemon Cheesecake with Raspberry Sauce

Crust
 1 package DUNCAN HINES®
    Moist Deluxe Lemon
    Supreme Cake Mix
 ½ cup CRISCO® Oil or
    CRISCO® PURITAN® Oil
 ⅓ cup finely chopped pecans

Filling
 3 packages (8 ounces each)
    cream cheese, softened
 ¾ cup sugar
 2 tablespoons lemon juice
 1 teaspoon grated lemon
    peel
 3 eggs, lightly beaten

Raspberry Sauce
 1 package (12 ounces) frozen
    dry pack red raspberries,
    thawed
 ⅓ cup sugar
    Fresh raspberries, for
    garnish
    Lemon slices, for garnish
    Mint leaves, for garnish

1. Preheat oven to 350°F. Grease 10-inch springform pan.

2. **For crust,** combine cake mix and oil in large bowl. Mix well. Stir in pecans. Press mixture into bottom of pan. Bake at 350°F for about 20 minutes or until light golden brown. Remove from oven. *Increase oven temperature to 450°F.*

3. **For filling,** place cream cheese in large bowl. Beat at low speed with electric mixer, adding ¾ cup sugar gradually. Add lemon juice and lemon peel. Add eggs, mixing only until incorporated. Pour filling onto crust. Bake at 450°F for 5 to 7 minutes. *Reduce oven temperature to 250°F.* Bake 30 minutes longer or until set. Loosen cake from sides of pan with knife or spatula. Cool completely on cooling rack. Refrigerate 2 hours or until ready to serve. Remove sides of pan.

4. **For raspberry sauce,** combine thawed raspberries and ⅓ cup sugar in small saucepan. Bring to a boil. Simmer until

Heavenly Delight Cheesecake

berries are soft. Strain through sieve into small bowl to remove seeds. Cool completely.

5. To serve, garnish cheesecake with raspberries, lemon slices and mint leaves. Cut into slices and serve with raspberry sauce.
12 to 16 Servings

Tip: Overbeating cheesecake batter can incorporate too much air, which may cause the cheesecake to crack during baking.

Heavenly Delight Cheesecake

 1 tablespoon graham cracker
    crumbs
 1 cup lowfat (1% to 2%)
    cottage cheese
 2 packages (8 ounces each)
    Light PHILADELPHIA
    BRAND® Neufchatel
    Cheese, softened
 ⅔ cup sugar
 2 tablespoons flour
 3 eggs
 2 tablespoons skim milk
 ¼ teaspoon almond extract or
    vanilla

• Heat oven to 325°F.

• Lightly grease bottom of 9-inch springform pan. Sprinkle with crumbs. Dust bottom; remove excess crumbs.

• Place cottage cheese in blender container; cover. Blend at medium speed until smooth.

• Beat cottage cheese, neufchatel cheese, sugar and flour at medium speed with electric mixer until well blended. Add eggs, 1 at a time, mixing well after each addition. Blend in milk and extract; pour into pan.

• Bake 45 to 50 minutes or until center is almost set. (Center of cheesecake appears soft but firms upon cooling.) Loosen cake from rim of pan; cool before removing rim of pan. Refrigerate. Garnish with raspberries, strawberries or blueberries and fresh mint, if desired.
Makes 10 to 12 servings

Prep time: 15 minutes plus refrigerating
Cooking time: 50 minutes

Variations

Prepare as directed; omit blender method. Place cottage cheese in large bowl of electric mixer; beat at high speed until smooth. Add neufchatel cheese, sugar and flour, mixing at medium speed until well blended. Continue as directed.

Substitute 1 cup vanilla wafer crumbs and ¼ cup (½ stick) PARKAY® Margarine, melted, for graham cracker crumbs; press onto bottom of ungreased pan.

Heavenly Orange Cheesecake

Heavenly Orange Cheesecake

Crust
> 1 cup chocolate wafer
>   crumbs
> 3 tablespoons PARKAY®
>   Margarine, melted

Filling
> 1 envelope unflavored gelatin
> ½ cup orange juice
> 3 packages (8 ounces each)
>   PHILADELPHIA BRAND®
>   Cream Cheese, softened
> ¾ cup sugar
> 1 cup whipping cream,
>   whipped
> 2 teaspoons grated orange
>   peel

• *Crust:* Heat oven to 350°F.

• Mix crumbs and margarine; press onto bottom of 9-inch springform pan. Bake 10 minutes. Cool.

• *Filling:* Soften gelatin in juice; stir over low heat until dissolved. Beat cream cheese and sugar at medium speed with electric mixer until well blended. Gradually add gelatin; refrigerate until slightly thickened.

• Fold in whipped cream and peel; pour over crust. Refrigerate until firm. Garnish with orange slices and fresh mint, if desired.
Makes 10 to 12 servings

Prep time: 25 minutes plus refrigerating

Very Blueberry Cheesecake

Crust
> 1½ cups vanilla wafer crumbs
> ¼ cup (½ stick) PARKAY®
>   Margarine, melted

Filling
> 1 envelope unflavored gelatin
> ¼ cup cold water
> 2 packages (8 ounces each)
>   PHILADELPHIA BRAND®
>   Cream Cheese, softened
> 1 tablespoon lemon juice
> 1 teaspoon grated lemon
>   peel
> 1 jar (7 ounces) KRAFT®
>   Marshmallow Creme
> 3½ cups (8 ounces) COOL
>   WHIP® Non-Dairy
>   Whipped Topping,
>   thawed
> 2 cups blueberries, puréed

• *Crust:* Mix crumbs and margarine; press onto bottom of 9-inch springform pan. Refrigerate.

• *Filling:* Soften gelatin in water; stir over low heat until dissolved. Gradually add gelatin to cream cheese, mixing at medium speed with electric mixer until well blended. Blend in juice and peel. Beat in marshmallow creme. Fold in whipped topping and blueberries; pour over crust.

• Refrigerate until firm. Garnish with additional whipped topping and lemon peel, if desired.
Makes 10 to 12 servings

Prep time: 25 minutes plus refrigerating

Eggnog Cheesecake

> 2 packages (5½ ounces
>   each) chocolate-laced
>   pirouette cookies
> ⅓ cup graham cracker
>   crumbs
> 3 tablespoons PARKAY®
>   Margarine, melted
> 2 packages (8 ounces each)
>   PHILADELPHIA BRAND®
>   Cream Cheese, softened
> 2 cups cold prepared eggnog
> 2 cups cold milk
> 2 packages (4-serving size
>   each) JELL-O® Instant
>   Pudding and Pie Filling,
>   French Vanilla or Vanilla
>   Flavor
> 1 tablespoon rum
> ⅛ teaspoon ground nutmeg
>   COOL WHIP® Whipped
>   Topping, thawed
>   (optional)
>   Ribbon (optional)

RESERVE 1 cookie for garnish, if desired. Cut 1-inch piece off one end of each of the remaining cookies. Crush 1-inch pieces into crumbs; set aside remaining cookies for sides of cake. Combine cookie crumbs, graham cracker crumbs and margarine until well mixed. Press crumb mixture firmly onto bottom of 9-inch springform pan.

BEAT cream cheese at low speed of electric mixer until smooth. Gradually add 1 cup of the eggnog, blending until mixture is very smooth. Add remaining eggnog, milk, pudding mix, rum and nutmeg. Beat until well blended, about 1 minute. Pour cream cheese mixture carefully into pan. Chill until firm, about 3 hours. Run hot metal spatula or knife around edges of pan before removing sides of pan.

PRESS remaining cookies, cut sides down, into sides of cake. Garnish with whipped topping and reserved cookie, if desired. Tie ribbon around cake, if desired. *Makes 12 servings*

Prep time: 45 minutes
Chill time: 3 hours

Rocky Road Cheesecake

Crust
- 1 cup chocolate wafer crumbs
- 3 tablespoons PARKAY® Margarine, melted

Filling
- 1 envelope unflavored gelatin
- ¼ cup cold water
- 2 containers (8 ounces each) PHILADELPHIA BRAND® Soft Cream Cheese
- ¾ cup sugar
- ⅓ cup cocoa
- ½ teaspoon vanilla
- 2 cups KRAFT® Miniature Marshmallows
- 1 cup whipping cream, whipped
- ½ cup chopped nuts

• *Crust:* Heat oven to 350°F.

• Mix crumbs and margarine; press onto bottom of 9-inch springform pan. Bake 10 minutes. Cool.

• *Filling:* Soften gelatin in water; stir over low heat until dissolved. Beat cream cheese, sugar, cocoa and vanilla at medium speed with electric mixer until well blended. Gradually add gelatin.

• Fold in remaining ingredients; pour over crust. Refrigerate until firm. Garnish with additional miniature marshmallows, if desired.
Makes 10 to 12 servings

Prep time: 25 minutes plus refrigerating

Chilled Raspberry Cheesecake

- 1½ cups vanilla wafer crumbs (about 45 wafers, crushed)
- ⅓ cup HERSHEY'S Cocoa
- ⅓ cup powdered sugar
- ⅓ cup butter or margarine, melted
- 1 package (10 ounces) frozen raspberries, thawed
- 1 envelope unflavored gelatin
- ½ cup cold water
- ½ cup boiling water
- 2 packages (8 ounces *each*) cream cheese, softened
- ½ cup granulated sugar
- 1 teaspoon vanilla extract
- 3 tablespoons seedless red raspberry preserves
  Chocolate Whipped Cream (recipe follows)

Heat oven to 350°F. In medium bowl stir together crumbs, cocoa and powdered sugar; stir in melted butter. Press mixture onto bottom and 1½ inches up side of 9-inch springform pan. Bake 10 minutes; cool completely. Puree and strain raspberries; set aside. In small bowl sprinkle gelatin over cold water; let stand several minutes to soften. Add boiling water; stir until gelatin dissolves completely and mixture is clear. In large mixer bowl beat cream cheese, granulated sugar and vanilla, blending well. Gradually add raspberry puree and gelatin, mixing thoroughly; pour into prepared crust. Refrigerate several hours or overnight; remove rim of pan. Spread raspberry preserves over top. Garnish with Chocolate Whipped Cream. Cover; refrigerate leftovers.
Makes 10 to 12 servings

CHOCOLATE WHIPPED CREAM: In small mixer bowl stir together ½ cup powdered sugar and ¼ cup Hershey's Cocoa. Add 1 cup chilled whipping cream and 1 teaspoon vanilla extract; beat until stiff.

Chilled Raspberry Cheesecake

DESSERTS

Great meals demand a memorable dessert to conclude the perfect evening. Indulge in exquisite truffle loaves and bavarians, fluffy parfaits and mousses, fruit-filled cobblers and crêpes and inviting ice creams and sauces sure to satisfy every craving. Show off your culinary creativity with these divine desserts and win rave reviews!

Chocolate Hazelnut Truffle Dessert

Truffle Dessert
- **1 cup whipping cream**
- **¼ cup LAND O LAKES® Butter**
- **2 bars (8 ounces each) semi-sweet chocolate**
- **4 egg yolks**
- **¾ cup powdered sugar**
- **3 tablespoons rum or orange juice**
- **1 cup coarsely chopped hazelnuts or filberts, toasted**

Custard
- **1 cup whipping cream**
- **¼ cup granulated sugar**
- **1 teaspoon cornstarch**
- **3 egg yolks**
- **1 teaspoon vanilla**

For truffle dessert, in 2-quart saucepan combine 1 cup whipping cream, butter and chocolate. Cook over medium heat, stirring occasionally, until chocolate is melted, 5 to 7 minutes. Whisk in 4 egg yolks, one at a time. Continue cooking, stirring constantly, until mixture reaches 160°F and thickens slightly, 3 to 4 minutes. Remove from heat; whisk in powdered sugar and rum. Stir in hazelnuts. Line 8×4-inch loaf pan with aluminum foil leaving 1 inch of foil over each edge. Pour chocolate mixture into prepared pan. Freeze 8 hours or overnight.

For custard, in 2-quart saucepan cook 1 cup whipping cream over medium heat until it just comes to a boil, 4 to 6 minutes. Remove from heat. Meanwhile, in medium bowl combine granulated sugar and cornstarch. Whisk in 3 egg yolks until mixture is light and creamy, 3 to 4 minutes. Gradually whisk hot cream into beaten egg yolks. Return mixture to saucepan; stir in vanilla. Cook over medium heat, stirring constantly, until custard reaches 160°F and is thick enough to coat back of metal spoon, 4 to 5 minutes. (Do not boil because egg yolks will curdle.) Refrigerate 8 hours or overnight.

To serve, remove truffle dessert from pan using foil to lift out. Remove foil. Slice truffle dessert with hot knife into 16 slices. Spoon about 1 tablespoon custard onto individual dessert plates; place slice of truffle dessert over custard.   *Makes 16 servings*

Chocolate Hazelnut Truffle Dessert

Chocolate Truffle Loaf with Sweet Raspberry Sauce

Chocolate Truffle Loaf with Sweet Raspberry Sauce

    2 cups heavy cream, divided
    3 egg yolks
    16 squares (1 ounce *each*)
        semisweet chocolate
    ½ cup KARO® Light or Dark
        corn syrup
    ½ cup MAZOLA® Margarine
    ¼ cup confectioners sugar
    1 teaspoon vanilla
        Sweet Raspberry Sauce
        (recipe follows)

Line 9¼×5¼×2¾-inch loaf pan with plastic wrap. In small bowl mix ½ cup of the cream with the egg yolks. In large saucepan combine chocolate, corn syrup and margarine; stir over medium heat until melted. Add egg mixture. Cook 3 minutes over medium heat, stirring constantly. Cool to room temperature. In small bowl with mixer at medium speed, beat remaining 1½ cups cream, sugar and vanilla until soft peaks form. Gently fold into chocolate mixture just until combined. Pour into prepared pan; cover with plastic wrap.

Refrigerate overnight or chill in freezer 3 hours. Slice and serve with Sweet Raspberry Sauce.
Makes 12 servings

SWEET RASPBERRY SAUCE:
In blender or food processor puree 1 package (10 ounces) frozen raspberries, thawed; strain to remove seeds. Stir in ⅓ cup Karo® Light Corn Syrup.

Preparation Time: 30 minutes, plus chilling

Lemon Strawberry Stars

    1 pound cake loaf
        (about 12 ounces)
    1 package (4-serving size)
        JELL-O® Instant Pudding
        and Pie Filling, Lemon
        Flavor
    2 cups cold milk
        Sliced strawberries
        Strawberry Sauce (recipe
        follows) (optional)

SLICE pound cake horizontally into 5 layers. Cut each layer into 2 star shapes with large cookie cutter. (Reserve cake scraps for snacking or other use.)

PREPARE pudding mix with milk as directed on package.

TOP ½ of the pound cake stars with ½ of the sliced strawberries and ½ of the pudding. Cover with remaining stars, strawberries and pudding. Serve with Strawberry Sauce, if desired.　*Makes 5 servings*

Prep time: 15 minutes

Strawberry Sauce

    2 packages (10 ounces each)
        BIRDS EYE® Quick Thaw
        Strawberries, thawed
    2 teaspoons cornstarch

PLACE strawberries in food processor or blender; cover. Process until smooth. Combine cornstarch with small amount of the strawberries in medium saucepan; add remaining strawberries. Bring to boil over medium heat, stirring constantly; boil 1 minute. Chill.
Makes 2 cups

Prep time: 30 minutes
Chill time: 3 hours

Lemon Strawberry Stars

Strawberry-White Chocolate Tiramisu

**Two 6-oz. pkgs. (6 foil-wrapped
bars) NESTLÉ® Premier
White baking bars
1½ cups heavy or whipping
cream, divided
One 3-oz. pkg. cream cheese,
softened
36 ladyfingers, split
(three 3-oz. pkgs.)
1¼ cups cooled espresso or
strong coffee
2 tablespoons brandy,
optional
2 pints strawberries, divided**

Melt over hot (not boiling) water, Premier White baking bars with ¼ cup heavy cream, stirring until smooth; cool completely.

In large mixer bowl, beat cream cheese until fluffy. Stir in melted baking bar mixture. In small mixer bowl, beat remaining 1¼ cups cream until stiff peaks form; fold into cream cheese mixture.

Line side of 9×3-inch springform pan with ladyfinger halves, cut sides in. Arrange half of remaining ladyfingers on bottom of pan. In small bowl, combine espresso and brandy; brush half over ladyfingers in bottom of pan. Cover with half the cream cheese filling. Slice 1 pint strawberries; arrange over filling. Repeat ladyfinger, espresso mixture and filling layers. Halve remaining 1 pint strawberries; arrange decoratively on top. Cover; refrigerate until set, 4 hours or overnight. Remove side of pan before serving.

Makes 10 to 12 servings

Bittersweet Chocolate Delight

Bittersweet Chocolate Delight

**3 egg yolks
½ cup granulated sugar
1 cup milk
2 tablespoons cornstarch
3 foil-wrapped bars (6 oz.)
NESTLÉ® Unsweetened
Chocolate baking bars,
broken up
3 tablespoons almond-
flavored liqueur
Two 3-oz. pkgs. ladyfingers
(about 48), split
1½ cups heavy or whipping
cream
1 cup confectioners' sugar
Whipped cream for garnish
Chocolate Curls for garnish
(directions follow)**

In medium saucepan, whisk together egg yolks and granulated sugar. Whisk in milk and cornstarch until smooth. Cook over medium heat, stirring constantly with wire whisk, until mixture comes to a boil. Boil 1 minute, whisking constantly; remove from heat. Whisk in chocolate until smooth. Blend in liqueur. Transfer to large bowl; press plastic wrap directly on surface. Cool to room temperature.

Line side of 9-inch springform pan with ladyfinger halves, cut sides in. Arrange half of remaining ladyfingers on bottom of pan; set aside the remaining half.

Stir cooled chocolate mixture until smooth. In small mixer bowl, beat heavy cream with confectioners' sugar until soft peaks form; fold into chocolate mixture. Spoon half of the chocolate mixture into prepared pan; top with remaining ladyfingers and chocolate mixture. Cover; refrigerate overnight. Loosen and remove side of pan. Garnish with whipped cream and Chocolate Curls.

Makes 10 to 12 servings

CHOCOLATE CURLS: Shave a few "curls" from edge of 1 foil-wrapped bar (2 oz.) Nestlé® Semi-Sweet baking bar with vegetable peeler.

Angel Strawberry Bavarian

**1 package DUNCAN HINES®
   Angel Food Cake Mix**
**1 package (10 ounces)
   sweetened, frozen sliced
   strawberries, thawed**
**1 package (4-serving size)
   strawberry flavored
   gelatin**
1 cup boiling water
**2½ cups whipping cream,
   chilled and divided**
**2½ tablespoons confectioners
   sugar**
¾ teaspoon vanilla extract
**4 fresh strawberries, sliced
   and fanned, for garnish
   Mint leaves, for garnish**

1. Preheat oven to 375°F.

2. Prepare, bake and cool cake following package directions. Cut cooled cake into 1-inch cubes.

3. Drain thawed strawberries, reserving juice.

4. Combine gelatin and boiling water in small bowl. Stir until gelatin is dissolved. Add enough water to strawberry juice to measure 1 cup; stir into gelatin. Refrigerate until gelatin is slightly thickened. Beat gelatin until foamy.

5. Beat 1 cup whipping cream until stiff peaks form in large bowl. Fold into gelatin along with strawberries.

6. Alternate layers of cake cubes and strawberry mixture in 10-inch tube pan. Press lightly. Cover. Refrigerate overnight.

7. Unmold cake onto serving plate. Beat remaining 1½ cups whipping cream, confectioners sugar and vanilla extract until stiff peaks form. Frost sides and top of cake. Refrigerate until ready to serve. Garnish with fresh strawberries and mint leaves.   *12 to 16 Servings*

Tip: For easiest cutting, use a knife with a thin sharp blade.

Old-Fashioned Bread Pudding with Vanilla Sauce

Pudding
4 cups cubed white bread
½ cup raisins
2 cups milk
**¼ cup LAND O LAKES®
   Butter**
½ cup granulated sugar
2 eggs, slightly beaten
½ teaspoon ground nutmeg
1 teaspoon vanilla

Vanilla Sauce
½ cup granulated sugar
**½ cup firmly packed brown
   sugar**
½ cup whipping cream
**½ cup LAND O LAKES®
   Butter**
1 teaspoon vanilla

Heat oven to 350°. For pudding, in large bowl combine bread and raisins. In 1-quart saucepan combine milk and ¼ cup butter. Cook over medium heat until butter is melted, 4 to 7 minutes. Pour milk mixture over bread; let stand 10 minutes. Stir in remaining pudding ingredients. Pour into greased 1½-quart casserole. Bake for 40 to 50 minutes or until set in center.

For Vanilla Sauce, in 1-quart saucepan combine ½ cup granulated sugar, brown sugar, whipping cream and ½ cup butter. Cook over medium heat, stirring occasionally, until mixture thickens and comes to a full boil, 5 to 8 minutes. Stir in 1 teaspoon vanilla. Serve sauce over warm pudding. Store refrigerated.

Makes 6 servings

Angel Strawberry Bavarian

Apple Pumpkin Desserts

1 (21-ounce) can COMSTOCK® Brand Apple Filling or Topping
1 (16-ounce) can COMSTOCK® Brand Pumpkin (about 2 cups)
1 (14-ounce) can EAGLE® Brand Sweetened Condensed Milk (NOT evaporated milk)
2 eggs
1 teaspoon ground cinnamon
½ teaspoon ground nutmeg
½ teaspoon salt
1 cup gingersnap crumbs (about 18 cookies)
2 tablespoons margarine or butter, melted

Heat oven to 400°F. Spoon apple filling into 8 to 10 custard cups. In large mixer bowl, beat pumpkin, sweetened condensed milk, eggs, cinnamon, nutmeg and salt; spoon over apple filling. Combine crumbs and margarine. Sprinkle over pumpkin mixture. Place cups on 15×10-inch baking pan. Bake 10 minutes. *Reduce heat to 350°F;* bake 15 minutes or until set. Cool. Refrigerate leftovers.

Makes 8 to 10 servings

Bavarian Rice Cloud with Bittersweet Chocolate Sauce

1 envelope unflavored gelatin
1½ cups skim milk
3 tablespoons sugar
2 cups cooked rice
2 cups frozen light whipped topping, thawed
1 tablespoon almond-flavored liqueur
½ teaspoon vanilla extract
Vegetable cooking spray
Bittersweet Chocolate Sauce (recipe follows)
2 tablespoons sliced almonds, toasted

Bavarian Rice Cloud with Bittersweet Chocolate Sauce

Sprinkle gelatin over milk in small saucepan; let stand 1 minute or until gelatin is softened. Cook over low heat, stirring constantly until gelatin dissolves. Add sugar and stir until dissolved. Add rice; stir until well blended. Cover and chill until the consistency of unbeaten egg whites. Fold in whipped topping, liqueur, and vanilla. Spoon into 4-cup mold coated with cooking spray. Cover and chill until firm. To serve, unmold onto serving platter. Spoon chocolate sauce over rice dessert. Sprinkle with toasted almonds.   *Makes 10 servings*

Bittersweet Chocolate Sauce

3 tablespoons unsweetened cocoa
3 tablespoons sugar
½ cup low-fat buttermilk
1 tablespoon almond-flavored liqueur

Combine cocoa and sugar in small saucepan. Add buttermilk, mixing well. Place over medium heat and cook until sugar dissolves. Stir in liqueur; remove from heat.

Tip: Unmold gelatin desserts onto slightly dampened plate. This will allow you to move the mold and position it where you want it on the plate.

*Favorite recipe from **USA Rice Council***

Buried Treasures

"Treasures," such as:
   broken cookies,
   miniature marshmallows,
   peanut butter, fruit,
   chocolate chips, nuts
2 cups cold milk
1 package (4-serving size)
   JELL-O® Instant Pudding,
   any flavor

CHOOSE 4 different "treasures" to "bury." You will need about 2 tablespoons of each treasure. Put a treasure on the bottom of each dessert dish. You may put more than one treasure in each dish, if desired.

POUR 2 cups of cold milk into shaker. Add pudding mix. Put lid on shaker very tightly. Shake very hard for at least 45 seconds, holding top and bottom of shaker tightly.

OPEN shaker. Gently spoon or pour pudding from shaker over the treasures. Pudding will thicken quickly and be ready to eat in 5 minutes or put dishes into refrigerator to chill until serving time.

Makes 4 servings

Quick and Easy Raspberry Mousse

One 3-oz. pkg. raspberry-
   flavored gelatin
½ cup boiling water
One 6-oz. pkg. (1 cup) NESTLÉ®
   Toll House® Semi-Sweet
   Chocolate Morsels
1 cup ice cubes (about 8)
½ cup heavy or whipping
   cream
1 tablespoon sugar, optional
   Fresh raspberries for
   garnish

In blender container, combine gelatin and boiling water. Cover; remove center of cover. With blender running, gradually add semi-sweet chocolate morsels; blend until chocolate is melted and mixture is smooth. With blender running, add ice, one cube at a time, blending until ice is completely melted and mixture is creamy. Pour into six individual dessert dishes. Refrigerate 2 to 3 hours until set.

In small mixer bowl, beat heavy cream with sugar until soft peaks form. Spoon over desserts. Garnish with raspberries.

Makes 6 servings

Banana Chocolate Chip Parfaits

Chocolate Mousse

1½ cups cold lowfat milk
1 package (4-serving size)
   JELL-O® Sugar Free
   Instant Pudding and Pie
   Filling, Chocolate Flavor
1 cup thawed COOL WHIP®
   Whipped Topping
   Raspberries (optional)
   Mint leaves (optional)

POUR milk into small bowl. Add pudding mix. Beat with wire whisk until well blended, 1 to 2 minutes. Fold in whipped topping. Spoon into serving bowl or individual dessert dishes. Chill until ready to serve. Garnish with additional whipped topping, raspberries and mint leaves, if desired.

Makes 5 (½-cup) servings

Prep time: 5 minutes

Buried Treasures

Banana Chocolate Chip Parfaits

**1 package DUNCAN HINES®
    Chocolate Chip
    Cookie Mix**
Pudding
    3 tablespoons cornstarch
    ¼ teaspoon salt
 1⅔ cups water
    **1 can (14 ounces) sweetened
        condensed milk**
    3 egg yolks, beaten
    **2 tablespoons butter or
        margarine**
 1½ teaspoons vanilla extract
    **3 ripe bananas, sliced
        Whipped topping, for
        garnish
        Mint leaves, for garnish**

1. Preheat oven to 375°F. Grease
13×9×2-inch pan.

2. Prepare cookie mix following
package directions for original
recipe. Spread in pan. Bake at
375°F for 15 to 18 minutes or
until edges are light golden
brown. Cool.

3. **For pudding**, combine
cornstarch, salt and water in
medium saucepan. Add
sweetened condensed milk and
egg yolks. Cook over medium
heat, stirring constantly, until
thickened. Remove from heat.
Stir in butter and vanilla
extract. Cool.

4. To assemble, cut outer edges
from cookie bars. Crumble to
make about 1¾ cups crumbs.
Layer pudding, banana slices
and crumbs in parfait dishes.
Repeat layers 1 or 2 more times
ending with pudding. Garnish
with whipped topping and mint
leaves. Refrigerate until ready to
serve.   *6 Parfaits*

Tip: Cut remaining cookie bars
into 1×2-inch pieces. Serve with
parfaits.

Black Forest Parfaits

    **1 package (8 ounces)
        PHILADELPHIA BRAND®
        Cream Cheese, softened**
    2 cups cold milk
    **1 package (4-serving size)
        JELL-O® Instant Pudding
        and Pie Filling, Chocolate
        Flavor**
    **1 can (21 ounces) cherry pie
        filling**
    1 tablespoon cherry liqueur
    **½ cup chocolate wafer
        crumbs**

BEAT cream cheese with ½ cup
of the milk at low speed of
electric mixer until smooth. Add
pudding mix and remaining
milk. Beat until smooth, 1 to 2
minutes.

MIX together cherry pie filling
and liqueur. Reserve a few
cherries for garnish, if desired.
Spoon ½ of the pudding mixture
evenly into individual dessert
dishes; sprinkle with wafer
crumbs. Cover with pie filling;
top with remaining pudding
mixture. Chill until ready to
serve. Garnish with reserved
cherries and additional wafer
crumbs, if desired.
        Makes 4 to 6 servings

Prep time: 15 minutes

Two Great Tastes Pudding Parfaits

    **1 package (4¾ ounces)
        vanilla pudding and pie
        filling**
 3½ cups milk
    **1 cup REESE'S™ Peanut
        Butter Chips**
    **1 cup HERSHEY'S Semi-
        Sweet Chocolate Chips
        Whipped topping (optional)**

In large, heavy saucepan
combine pudding mix and 3½
cups milk (rather than amount
listed in package directions).
Cook over medium heat, stirring
constantly, until mixture comes
to full boil. Remove from heat;
divide hot mixture between 2
heatproof medium bowls.
Immediately stir peanut butter
chips into mixture in one bowl
and chocolate chips into mixture
in second bowl. Stir both
mixtures until chips are melted
and smooth. Cool slightly,
stirring occasionally. Alternately
spoon peanut butter and
chocolate mixtures into parfait
glasses, champagne glasses or
dessert dishes. Place plastic wrap
directly onto surface of each
dessert; refrigerate several hours
or overnight. Top with whipped
topping and garnish as desired.
    Makes about 4 to 6 servings

Two Great Tastes Pudding Parfaits

Double Fudge Brownie Baked Alaska

Brownies
- ¾ cup firmly packed brown sugar
- ½ cup LAND O LAKES® Butter, softened
- ¾ cup all-purpose flour
- 1½ cups semi-sweet miniature real chocolate chips, melted
- 3 eggs

Filling
- ½ gallon chocolate-flavored ice cream, softened

Meringue
- 6 egg whites
- ¼ teaspoon salt
- 1 teaspoon vanilla
- ¾ cup granulated sugar
- ½ cup semi-sweet miniature real chocolate chips

Heat oven to 350°. Grease 9-inch round cake pan. Line with aluminum foil leaving excess foil over edges; grease foil. Set aside.

For brownies, in large mixer bowl combine brown sugar and butter. Beat at medium speed, scraping bowl often, until smooth, 2 to 3 minutes. Add flour, melted chocolate and eggs. Continue beating, scraping bowl often, until well mixed, 2 to 3 minutes. Pour into prepared pan. Bake for 40 to 50 minutes or until wooden pick inserted halfway between edge and center comes out clean. Cool completely; remove from pan by lifting foil.

For filling, line 2½-quart bowl with foil; pack ice cream into bowl. Cover; freeze until firm, 3 to 4 hours.

Heat oven to 450°. For meringue, in large mixer bowl beat egg whites at high speed, scraping bowl often, until soft peaks form, 1 to 2 minutes. Add salt and vanilla. Continue beating, gradually adding granulated sugar, until stiff peaks form, 2 to 3 minutes. Fold in ½ cup chocolate chips.

To assemble, place brownies on ovenproof plate. Invert ice cream onto brownies; remove bowl and foil. Spread meringue evenly over entire surface, covering any holes. Bake for 3 to 5 minutes or until lightly browned. Serve immediately.

Makes 12 servings

Easy Chocolate Berry Charlotte

Cake:
- ½ cup all-purpose flour
- ¼ teaspoon baking powder
- ¼ teaspoon salt
- 3 eggs
- ½ cup granulated sugar
- 1 teaspoon vanilla extract
- 2 tablespoons vegetable oil Confectioners' sugar
- 1 cup strawberry jam

Filling:
- 3 foil-wrapped bars (6 oz.) NESTLÉ® Semi-Sweet Chocolate baking bars
- 1 cup heavy or whipping cream
- 4 to 6 cups strawberry ice cream, softened Whipped cream for garnish Strawberries for garnish

Cake: Preheat oven to 350°F. Grease 15½×10½×1-inch baking pan. Line bottom with wax paper. In small bowl, combine flour, baking powder and salt; set aside. In large mixer bowl, beat eggs, granulated sugar and vanilla extract until thick and pale yellow. Beat in oil and flour mixture. Spread in prepared pan.

Bake 13 to 16 minutes until golden brown. Sprinkle cloth towel with confectioners' sugar. Immediately invert cake onto towel. Gently peel off wax paper. Starting at long side, roll warm cake jelly-roll style with towel inside. Place seam-side down on wire rack; cool. Unroll cake. Spread jam over cake to within ½ inch of edges; roll up cake. Wrap tightly in foil; freeze 2 hours.

Filling: In small saucepan over low heat, melt semi-sweet chocolate baking bars with heavy cream, stirring until smooth. Remove from heat; cool completely.

Slice jelly roll into ½-inch slices. Tightly line bottom and sides of 2½-quart bowl or 6-cup charlotte mold with cake slices. Spoon one third of ice cream into lined mold. Spread half of Filling over ice cream. Repeat layers; top with remaining ice cream. Cover with plastic wrap; freeze until firm or up to 1 week.

To serve, remove plastic wrap; dip mold into bowl of warm water for 15 to 20 seconds. Invert mold onto serving platter; remove mold. Let stand at room temperature 15 minutes until slightly softened. Garnish with whipped cream and strawberries.

Makes 8 to 10 servings

Strawberry Ice

- 1 quart fresh strawberries, cleaned and hulled (about 1½ pounds)
- 1 cup sugar
- ½ cup water
- 3 tablespoons REALEMON® Lemon Juice from Concentrate Red food coloring, optional

In blender container, combine sugar, water and ReaLemon® brand; mix well. Gradually add strawberries; blend until smooth, adding food coloring if desired. Pour into 8-inch square pan; freeze about 1½ hours. In small mixer bowl, beat until slushy. Return to freezer. To soften, place in refrigerator 1 hour before serving. Return leftovers to freezer.   *Makes 6 servings*

Easy Chocolate Berry Charlotte

Fruit Sparkles

DISSOLVE raspberry flavor gelatin in remaining 1 cup boiling water. Spoon in ice cream, stirring until melted and smooth. Pour into serving bowl. Chill until set but not firm.

ARRANGE peach slices and raspberries on ice cream mixture in bowl. Add mint leaves, if desired. Spoon peach gelatin over fruit. Chill until firm, about 3 hours.   *Makes 10 servings*

Prep time: 20 minutes
Chill time: 4 hours

Fudgy Chocolate Ice Cream

>   **5 (1-ounce) squares unsweetened chocolate, melted**
>   **1 (14-ounce) can EAGLE® Brand Sweetened Condensed Milk (NOT evaporated milk)**
>   **2 teaspoons vanilla extract**
>   **2 cups (1 pint) BORDEN® or MEADOW GOLD® Half-and-Half**
>   **2 cups (1 pint) BORDEN® or MEADOW GOLD® Whipping Cream, unwhipped**
>   **½ cup chopped nuts, optional**

In large mixer bowl, beat chocolate, sweetened condensed milk and vanilla. Stir in half-and-half, whipping cream and nuts if desired. Pour into ice cream freezer container. Freeze according to manufacturer's instructions. Freeze leftovers.
         Makes about 1½ quarts

Refrigerator-Freezer Method: Omit half-and-half. Reduce chocolate to 3 (1-ounce) squares. Whip whipping cream. In large mixer bowl, beat chocolate, sweetened condensed milk and vanilla; fold in whipped cream and nuts if desired. Pour into 9×5-inch loaf pan or other 2-quart container; cover. Freeze 6 hours or until firm. Return leftovers to freezer.

Fruit Sparkles

>   **1 package (4-serving size) JELL-O® Brand Sugar Free Gelatin, any flavor**
>   **1 cup boiling water**
>   **1 cup chilled fruit flavor seltzer, sparkling water, club soda or other sugar free carbonated beverage**
>   **1 cup sliced banana and strawberries***
>   **Mint leaves (optional)**

DISSOLVE gelatin in boiling water. Add beverage. Chill until slightly thickened. Add fruit. Pour into individual dessert dishes. Chill until firm, about 1 hour. Garnish with additional fruit and mint leaves, if desired.
     Makes 6 (½-cup) servings

*1 cup drained mandarin orange sections or crushed pineapple may be substituted for bananas and strawberries.

Prep time: 15 minutes
Chill time: 1½ hours

Peach Melba Dessert

>   **1 package (4-serving size) JELL-O® Brand Gelatin, Peach Flavor**
>   **2 cups boiling water**
>   **¾ cup cold water**
>   **1 package (4-serving size) JELL-O® Brand Gelatin, Raspberry Flavor**
>   **1 pint vanilla ice cream, softened**
>   **1 can (8¾ ounces) sliced peaches, drained***
>   **½ cup fresh raspberries**
>   **Mint leaves (optional)**

DISSOLVE peach flavor gelatin in 1 cup of the boiling water. Add cold water. Chill until slightly thickened.

*1 fresh peach, peeled and sliced, may be substituted for canned peaches.

Fudgy Chocolate Ice Cream

Fresh Fruit Ice Cream

**3 cups (1½ pints) BORDEN®
or MEADOW GOLD®
Half-and-Half
1 (14-ounce) can EAGLE®
Brand Sweetened
Condensed Milk
(NOT evaporated milk)
1 cup puréed or mashed
fresh fruit (bananas,
peaches, raspberries or
strawberries)
1 tablespoon vanilla extract
Food coloring, optional**

In ice cream freezer container,
combine all ingredients; mix
well. Freeze according to
manufacturer's instructions.
Freeze leftovers.

Makes about 1½ quarts

Vanilla Ice Cream: Omit fruit
and food coloring. Increase half-
and-half to 4 cups. Proceed as
above.

Refrigerator-Freezer Method:
Omit half-and-half. In large
bowl, combine sweetened
condensed milk and vanilla; stir
in 1 cup puréed or mashed fruit
and food coloring if desired. Fold
in 2 cups Borden® or Meadow
Gold® Whipping Cream, whipped
(*do not use non-dairy whipped
topping*). Pour into 9×5-inch loaf
pan or other 2-quart container;
cover. Freeze 6 hours or until
firm. Return leftovers to freezer.

Raspberry Gift Box

**2 packages (4-serving size
each) or 1 package
(8-serving size) JELL-O®
Brand Gelatin, Raspberry
Flavor
1½ cups boiling water
¾ cup cran-raspberry juice
Ice cubes
3½ cups (8 ounces) COOL
WHIP® Whipped Topping,
thawed
Raspberry Sauce
(recipe follows)
Gumdrop Ribbon*
(optional)
Frosted Cranberries**
(optional)**

Dissolve gelatin in boiling water.
Combine cran-raspberry juice
and ice cubes to make 1¾ cups.
Add to gelatin, stirring until ice
is melted. Chill until slightly
thickened. Fold in whipped
topping. Pour into 9×5-inch loaf
pan. Chill until firm, about 4
hours.

Prepare Raspberry Sauce,
Gumdrop Ribbon and Frosted
Cranberries, if desired.

Unmold gelatin mixture onto
serving plate. Cut Gumdrop
Ribbon into 2 (10×1-inch) strips
and 1 (5×1-inch) strip. Place
strips on raspberry loaf, piecing
strips together as necessary, to
resemble ribbon. Cut 7 (3×1-
inch) strips; form into bow. Place
on gumdrop ribbon. Decorate
with Frosted Cranberries. Serve
with Raspberry Sauce.

Makes 8 servings

Raspberry Sauce

**2 packages (10 ounces each)
BIRDS EYE® Quick Thaw
Red Raspberries, thawed
2 teaspoons cornstarch**

Place raspberries in food
processor or blender; cover.
Process until smooth; strain to
remove seeds. Combine
cornstarch with small amount of
the raspberries in medium
saucepan; add remaining
raspberries. Bring to boil over
medium heat, stirring
constantly; boil 1 minute. Chill.

Makes 2 cups

Prep time: 30 minutes
Chill time: 4 hours

*To make ribbon, place
gumdrops on surface sprinkled
with sugar. Flatten into strips
with rolling pin. Cut with sharp
knife into 1-inch-wide strips. Use
to decorate as shown on
page 326.

**To frost cranberries, dip into
beaten egg white. Roll in sugar;
let stand until dry.

Fresh Fruit Ice Cream

Lace Cookie Ice Cream Cups

½ cup light corn syrup
½ cup LAND O LAKES®
Butter
1 cup all-purpose flour
½ cup firmly packed brown
sugar
1 package (2½ ounces)
slivered almonds, finely
chopped (½ cup)
Semi-sweet real chocolate
chips,* melted
Your favorite ice cream

Heat oven to 300°. In 2-quart saucepan over medium heat bring corn syrup to a full boil, 2 to 3 minutes. Add butter; reduce heat to low. Continue cooking, stirring occasionally, until butter melts, 3 to 5 minutes. Remove from heat. Stir in flour, brown sugar and almonds. Drop tablespoonfuls of dough 4 inches apart onto greased cookie sheets. Bake for 11 to 13 minutes or until cookies bubble and are golden brown. *Cool 1 minute on cookie sheets.* Working quickly, remove and shape cookies over inverted small custard cups to form cups. Cool completely; remove from custard cups.

For *each* cup, spread 1 tablespoon melted chocolate on outside bottom and 1 inch up outside edge of *each* cooled cookie cup. Refrigerate, chocolate side up, until hardened, about 30 minutes. Just before serving, fill *each* cup with large scoop of ice cream. If desired, drizzle with additional melted chocolate.

Makes 2 dozen cookie cups

*A 6-ounce (1 cup) package chocolate chips will coat 8 to 9 cookie cups, using 1 tablespoon chocolate per cup.

Tip: Make desired number of cups. With remaining dough, bake as directed above *except* shape into cones or leave flat. Serve as cookies.

Chocolate Covered Banana Pops

3 firm, large DOLE® Bananas,
peeled
9 wooden popsicle sticks
2 cups semisweet chocolate
chips or milk chocolate
chips
2 tablespoons vegetable
shortening
1½ cups DOLE® Chopped
Almonds

• Cut each banana into thirds. Insert wooden stick into each banana piece; place on tray covered with waxed paper. Freeze until firm, about 1 hour.

• In top of double boiler over hot, not boiling water, melt chocolate chips and shortening.

• Remove bananas from freezer just before dipping. Dip each banana into warm chocolate; allow excess to drip off. Immediately roll in almonds. Cover; return to freezer. Serve frozen. *Makes 9 pops*

Preparation Time: 15 minutes
Freezer Time: 60 minutes

Chocolate Peanut Butter Ice Cream Sauce

One 11½-oz. pkg. (2 cups)
NESTLÉ® Toll House®
Milk Chocolate Morsels
¼ cup peanut butter
⅓ cup milk

In small saucepan, combine all ingredients. Cook over very low heat, stirring constantly, until chocolate melts and mixture is smooth. Serve warm over ice cream or other desserts. Refrigerate leftover sauce. Reheat before serving.

Makes about 1½ cups

Quick Butterscotch Sauce

One 12-oz.pkg. (2 cups)
NESTLÉ® Toll House®
Butterscotch Flavored
Morsels
⅔ cup heavy or whipping
cream
Chopped nuts, optional

In small heavy-gauge saucepan, combine butterscotch morsels and heavy cream. Cook over low heat, stirring constantly, until morsels are melted and mixture is smooth; cool slightly. Serve warm over ice cream or other desserts; top with nuts. Refrigerate leftover sauce. Reheat before serving.

Makes about 1½ cups sauce

Luscious Chocolate Almond Sauce

1 cup (half of 12-oz. pkg.)
NESTLÉ® Toll House®
Semi-Sweet Chocolate
Mini Morsels
¼ cup heavy or whipping
cream
2 tablespoons (¼ stick)
butter
⅛ teaspoon salt
¼ cup almonds, chopped
2 tablespoons almond-
flavored liqueur

In small heavy-gauge saucepan over low heat, combine mini morsels, heavy cream, butter and salt, stirring constantly until smooth; remove from heat. Stir in almonds and liqueur; cool slightly. Serve warm over ice cream or other desserts. Refrigerate leftover sauce. Reheat before serving.

Makes about 1 cup sauce

Top to bottom: Chocolate Peanut Butter Ice Cream Sauce, Quick Butterscotch Sauce and Luscious Chocolate Almond Sauce

Chocolate Plunge

⅔ cup corn syrup
½ cup heavy cream
1 package (8 ounces)
 BAKER'S® Semi-Sweet
 Chocolate *or* 2 packages
 (4 ounces each)
 BAKER'S® GERMAN'S®
 Sweet Chocolate
Assorted fresh fruit
 (strawberries, sliced
 kiwifruit, pineapple,
 apples or bananas) or
 cake cubes

MICROWAVE corn syrup and cream in large microwavable bowl on HIGH 1½ minutes or until mixture boils. Add chocolate; stir until melted. Serve warm as a dip with fresh fruit or cake cubes.

Makes 1½ cups

Prep time: 10 minutes

 Saucepan preparation: Heat corn syrup and cream in 2-quart saucepan until boiling, stirring constantly. Remove from heat. Continue as above.

Chocolate Plunge

"All Grown Up" Mint Chocolate Sauce

One 10-oz. pkg. (1½ cups)
 NESTLÉ® Toll House®
 Mint Flavored Semi-
 Sweet Chocolate Morsels
1 cup half and half
1 tablespoon corn syrup
3 tablespoons butter or
 margarine, softened
3 tablespoons mint flavored
 liqueur
1 teaspoon vanilla extract

In medium saucepan, melt mint chocolate morsels with half and half and corn syrup, stirring until smooth. Remove from heat; stir in butter, liqueur and vanilla extract. Transfer to small bowl or decorative glass container; cover with plastic wrap. Cool. Refrigerate up to 1 week. Reheat before serving.

Makes about 2 cups

Lemon Ginger Sauce

Lemon Ginger Sauce

½ cup MIRACLE WHIP®
 FREE® Dressing
2 tablespoons lemon juice
1½ tablespoons packed brown
 sugar
1 teaspoon each: grated
 lemon peel, ground
 ginger

• Mix ingredients until well blended; refrigerate. Serve over fresh fruit. *Makes ½ cup*

Prep time: 5 minutes plus refrigerating

Mint Chocolate Chip Brownie Squares

1 (21.5- or 23.6-ounce)
 package fudge
 brownie mix
¾ cup coarsely chopped
 walnuts
1 (14-ounce) can EAGLE®
 Brand Sweetened
 Condensed Milk
 (NOT evaporated milk)
2 teaspoons peppermint
 extract
 Green food coloring,
 optional
2 cups (1 pint) BORDEN®
 or MEADOW GOLD®
 Whipping Cream,
 whipped
½ cup mini chocolate chips

Line 13×9-inch baking pan with aluminum foil; grease foil. Prepare brownie mix as package directs; stir in walnuts. Pour into prepared pan. Bake as directed. Cool thoroughly. In large bowl, combine sweetened condensed milk, peppermint extract and food coloring if desired. Fold in whipped cream and chips. Pour over brownie layer. Cover; freeze 6 hours or until firm. To serve, lift brownies from pan using foil; cut into squares. Garnish as desired. Freeze leftovers.

Makes 10 to 12 servings

Strawberry Sundae Dessert (left) and Frozen Lemon Squares (right)

Frozen Lemon Squares

1¼ cups graham cracker crumbs
¼ cup sugar
¼ cup margarine or butter, melted
3 egg *yolks*
1 (14-ounce) can EAGLE® Brand Sweetened Condensed Milk (NOT evaporated milk)
½ cup REALEMON® Lemon Juice from Concentrate
Yellow food coloring, optional
Whipped topping *or* BORDEN® or MEADOW GOLD® Whipping Cream, whipped

Preheat oven to 325°. Combine crumbs, sugar and margarine; press firmly on bottom of 8- or 9-inch square pan. In small mixer bowl, beat egg *yolks*, sweetened condensed milk, ReaLemon® brand and food coloring if desired. Pour into prepared pan. Bake 30 minutes. Cool. Top with whipped topping. Freeze 4 hours or until firm. Let stand 10 minutes before serving. Garnish as desired. Freeze leftovers.

Makes 6 to 9 servings

Tip: Dessert can be chilled instead of frozen.

Strawberry Sundae Dessert

1 (8½-ounce) package chocolate wafers, finely crushed (2½ cups crumbs)
½ cup margarine or butter, melted
1 (14-ounce) can EAGLE® Brand Sweetened Condensed Milk (NOT evaporated milk)
1 tablespoon vanilla extract
2 cups (1 pint) BORDEN® or MEADOW GOLD® Whipping Cream, whipped
2 (10-ounce) packages frozen strawberries in syrup, thawed
¼ cup sugar
1 tablespoon REALEMON® Lemon Juice from Concentrate
2 teaspoons cornstarch

Combine crumbs and margarine. Press half the crumb mixture on bottom of 9-inch square baking pan. In large bowl, combine sweetened condensed milk and vanilla. Fold in whipped cream. Pour into prepared pan. In blender or food processor, combine strawberries, sugar and ReaLemon® brand; blend until smooth. Spoon *¾ cup* strawberry mixture evenly over cream mixture. Top with remaining crumb mixture. Cover; freeze 6 hours or until firm. For sauce, in small saucepan, combine remaining strawberry mixture and cornstarch. Over medium heat, cook and stir until thickened. Cool. Chill. Cut dessert into squares; serve with sauce. Freeze leftover dessert; refrigerate leftover sauce.

Makes 9 to 12 servings

Apple Lasagna

Apple Lasagna

    2 cups (8 ounces) shredded
        Cheddar cheese
    1 cup ricotta cheese
    1 egg, lightly beaten
    ¼ cup granulated sugar
    1 teaspoon almond extract
    2 cans (20 ounces each)
        apple pie filling
    8 uncooked lasagna noodles,
        cooked, rinsed and
        drained
    6 tablespoons all-purpose
        flour
    6 tablespoons packed brown
        sugar
    ¼ cup quick-cooking oats
    ½ teaspoon ground cinnamon
        Dash ground nutmeg
    3 tablespoons margarine
    1 cup dairy sour cream
    ⅓ cup packed brown sugar

Combine Cheddar cheese, ricotta cheese, egg, granulated sugar and almond extract in medium bowl; blend well. Spread 1 can apple pie filling over bottom of greased 13×9-inch pan. Layer ½ of the noodles over filling, then spread cheese mixture over noodles. Top with remaining noodles, then remaining can of apple pie filling.

Combine flour, 6 tablespoons brown sugar, oats, cinnamon and nutmeg in small bowl. Cut in margarine until crumbly. Sprinkle over apple pie filling. Bake in preheated 350°F. oven 45 minutes. Cool 15 minutes.

Meanwhile, prepare garnish by blending sour cream and ⅓ cup brown sugar in small bowl until smooth. Cover; refrigerate.

To serve, cut lasagna into squares and garnish with sour cream mixture.

Makes 12 to 15 servings

Favorite recipe from **North Dakota Wheat Commission**

Seasonal Fruit Cobbler

Apple
    5 cups sliced, peeled
        cooking apples (about
        1⅔ pounds or 5 medium)
    1 cup sugar
    ⅓ cup water or apple juice
    2 tablespoons butter or
        margarine
    2 tablespoons all-purpose
        flour
    ½ teaspoon cinnamon
    ¼ teaspoon nutmeg

Blueberry
    4 cups blueberries
    ½ cup sugar
    1 tablespoon cornstarch
    1 teaspoon lemon juice
    1 teaspoon grated lemon
        peel

Cherry
    4 cups pitted fresh or thawed
        frozen dry pack red tart
        cherries
    1¼ cups sugar
    3 tablespoons cornstarch
    ¼ teaspoon cinnamon
    ¼ teaspoon almond extract

Peach
    4 cups sliced peaches or
        1 bag (20 ounces) thawed
        frozen dry pack peach
        slices
    ½ cup sugar
    ⅓ cup water
    1 tablespoon cornstarch
    ¼ teaspoon cinnamon
        Dash of nutmeg

Biscuit Topping
    1 cup all-purpose flour
    2 tablespoons sugar
    1½ teaspoons baking powder
    ¼ teaspoon salt
    ¼ cup CRISCO® Shortening
    1 egg, slightly beaten
    ¼ cup milk
    ½ teaspoon vanilla

1. **Select fruit recipe.** Heat oven to 400°F. Combine all ingredients in large saucepan. Cook and stir on medium heat until mixture comes to a boil and thickens. Stir and simmer 1 minute. Pour into 8-inch square glass baking dish or 2-quart baking dish. Place in oven.

2. **For biscuit topping,** combine flour, sugar, baking powder and salt. Cut in Crisco® until coarse crumbs form. Combine egg, milk and vanilla. Add all at once to flour mixture. Stir just until moistened. Remove baking dish from oven.

3. Drop biscuit mixture in 8 mounds on top of hot fruit. Bake at 400°F for 20 minutes or until golden brown. Serve warm with cream or ice cream, if desired.

8 Servings

Blueberry Crisp

Rice Crêpes

1 carton (8 ounces) egg substitute*
⅔ cup evaporated skim milk
1 tablespoon margarine, melted
½ cup all-purpose flour
1 tablespoon granulated sugar
1 cup cooked rice
Vegetable cooking spray
2½ cups fresh fruit (strawberries, raspberries, blueberries, or other favorite fruit)
Low-sugar fruit spread (optional)
Light sour cream (optional)
1 tablespoon confectioner's sugar for garnish (optional)

Rice Crêpe

Combine egg substitute, milk, and margarine in small bowl. Stir in flour and granulated sugar until smooth and well blended. Stir in rice; let stand 5 minutes. Heat 8-inch nonstick skillet or crêpe pan; coat with cooking spray. Spoon ¼ cup batter into pan. Lift pan off heat; quickly tilt pan in rotating motion so that bottom of pan is completely covered with batter. Place pan back on heat and continue cooking until surface is dry, about 45 seconds. Turn crêpe over and cook 15 to 20 seconds; set aside. Continue with remaining crêpe batter. Place waxed paper between crêpes. Spread each crêpe with your favorite filling: strawberries, raspberries, blueberries, fruit spread, or sour cream. Roll up and sprinkle with confectioner's sugar for garnish.

Makes 10 crêpes

*Substitute 8 egg whites or 4 eggs for 1 carton (8 ounces) egg substitute, if desired.

*Favorite recipe from **USA Rice Council***

Blueberry Crisp

3 cups cooked brown rice
3 cups fresh blueberries
¼ cup plus 3 tablespoons firmly packed brown sugar, divided
Vegetable cooking spray
⅓ cup rice bran
¼ cup whole-wheat flour
¼ cup chopped walnuts
1 teaspoon ground cinnamon
3 tablespoons margarine

Combine rice, blueberries, and 3 tablespoons sugar. Coat 8 individual custard cups or 2-quart baking dish with cooking spray. Place rice mixture in cups or baking dish; set aside. Combine bran, flour, walnuts, remaining ¼ cup sugar, and cinnamon in bowl. Cut in margarine with pastry blender until mixture resembles coarse meal. Sprinkle over rice mixture. Bake at 375°F. for 15 to 20 minutes or until thoroughly heated. Serve warm.

Makes 8 servings

*Favorite recipe from **USA Rice Council***

ACKNOWLEDGMENTS

The publishers would like to thank the companies and organizations listed below for the use of their recipes in this book.

Arm & Hammer Division, Church & Dwight Co., Inc.
Armour Swift-Eckrich
Best Foods, a Division of CPC International Inc.
Black-Eyed Pea Jamboree—Athens, Texas
Blue Diamond Growers
Borden Kitchens, Borden, Inc.
California Apricot Advisory Board
California Tree Fruit Agreement
Campbell Soup Company
Canned Food Information Council
Carnation, Nestlé Food Company
Castroville Artichoke Festival
Checkerboard Kitchens, Ralston Purina Company
Chef Paul Prudhomme's Magic Seasoning Blends™
Clear Springs Trout Company
Contadina Foods, Inc., Nestlé Food Company
Curtice Burns, Inc.
Delmarva Poultry Industry, Inc.
Del Monte Corporation
Diamond Walnut Growers, Inc.
Dole Food Company, Inc.
Domino Sugar Corporation

Durkee-French Foods, A Division of Reckitt & Colman Inc.
Florida Department of Citrus
The Fresh Garlic Association
Heinz U.S.A.
Hershey Chocolate U.S.A.
The HVR Company
Kahlúa Liqueur
Kansas Poultry Association
Keebler Company
Kellogg Company
Kraft General Foods, Inc.
Land O'Lakes, Inc.
Lawry's® Foods, Inc.
Leaf, Inc.
Libby's, Nestlé Food Company
Thomas J. Lipton Co.
M&M/Mars
McIlhenny Company
Nabisco Foods Group
National Broiler Council
National Fisheries Institute
National Live Stock & Meat Board
National Pasta Association
National Pecan Marketing Council
National Pork Producers Council
National Sunflower Association
National Turkey Federation

Nestlé Chocolate and Confection Company
New Jersey Department of Agriculture
Norseland Foods, Inc.
North Dakota Beef Commission
North Dakota Dairy Promotion Commission
North Dakota Wheat Commission
Ocean Spray Cranberries, Inc.
Oklahoma Peanut Commission
Pace Foods, Inc.
Perdue Farms
Pet Incorporated
Pollio Dairy Products
The Procter & Gamble Company, Inc.
The Quaker Oats Company
Sargento Cheese Company, Inc.
Sokol and Company
Southeast United Dairy Industry Association, Inc.
StarKist Seafood Company
Stella Cheese Company, Inc.
Sun-Maid Growers of California
Uncle Ben's Rice
USA Rice Council
Walnut Marketing Board
Western New York Apple Growers Association, Inc.
Wisconsin Milk Marketing Board

PHOTO CREDITS

The publishers would like to thank the companies and organizations listed below for the use of their photographs in this book.

Armour Swift-Eckrich
Best Foods, a Division of CPC International Inc.
Borden Kitchens, Borden, Inc.
California Apricot Advisory Board
California Tree Fruit Agreement
Campbell Soup Company
Canned Food Information Council
Checkerboard Kitchens, Ralston Purina Company
Chef Paul Prudhomme's Magic Seasoning Blends™

Contadina Foods, Inc., Nestlé Food Company
Dole Food Company, Inc.
Heinz U.S.A.
Hershey Chocolate U.S.A.
The HVR Company
Kellogg Company
Kraft General Foods, Inc.
Lawry's® Foods, Inc.
Thomas J. Lipton Co.
M&M/Mars
Nabisco Foods Group
National Live Stock & Meat Board

National Pork Producers Council
National Turkey Federation
Nestlé Chocolate and Confection Company
Perdue Farms
Pollio Dairy Products
The Procter & Gamble Company, Inc.
The Quaker Oats Company
Sargento Cheese Company, Inc.
StarKist Seafood Company
USA Rice Council
Wisconsin Milk Marketing Board

INDEX

METRIC CONVERSION CHART

VOLUME MEASUREMENT (dry)

⅛ teaspoon = .5 mL
¼ teaspoon = 1 mL
½ teaspoon = 2 mL
¾ teaspoon = 4 mL
1 teaspoon = 5 mL
1 tablespoon = 15 mL
2 tablespoons = 25 mL
¼ cup = 50 mL
⅓ cup = 75 mL
⅔ cup = 150 mL
¾ cup = 175 mL
1 cup = 250 mL
2 cups = 1 pint = 500 mL
3 cups = 750 mL
4 cups = 1 quart = 1 L

VOLUME MEASUREMENT (fluid)

1 fluid ounce (2 tablespoons) = 30 mL
4 fluid ounces (½ cup) = 125 mL
8 fluid ounces (1 cup) = 250 mL
12 fluid ounces (1½ cups) = 375 mL
16 fluid ounces (2 cups) = 500 mL

WEIGHT (MASS)

½ ounce = 15 g
1 ounce = 30 g
3 ounces = 85 g
3.75 ounces = 100 g
4 ounces = 115 g
8 ounces = 225 g
12 ounces = 340 g
16 ounces = 1 pound = 450 g

DIMENSION

1/16 inch = 2 mm
⅛ inch = 3 mm
¼ inch = 6 mm
½ inch = 1.5 cm
¾ inch = 2 cm
1 inch = 2.5 cm

OVEN TEMPERATURES

250°F = 120°C
275°F = 140°C
300°F = 150°C
325°F = 160°C
350°F = 180°C
375°F = 190°C
400°F = 200°C
425°F = 220°C
450°F = 230°C

BAKING PAN SIZES

Utensil	Size in Inches/Quarts	Metric Volume	Size in Centimeters
Baking or	8 × 8 × 2	2 L	20 × 20 × 5
Cake pan	9 × 9 × 2	2.5 L	22 × 22 × 5
(square or	12 × 8 × 2	3 L	30 × 20 × 5
rectangular)	13 × 9 × 2	3.5 L	33 × 23 × 5
Loaf Pan	8 × 4 × 3	1.5 L	20 × 10 × 7
	9 × 5 × 3	2 L	23 × 13 × 7
Round Layer	8 × 1½	1.2 L	20 × 4
Cake Pan	9 × 1½	1.5 L	23 × 4
Pie Plate	8 × 1¼	750 mL	20 × 3
	9 × 1¼	1 L	23 × 3
Baking Dish	1 quart	1 L	
or Casserole	1½ quart	1.5 L	
	2 quart	2 L	